Android Rec

A Problem-Solution Ap

Dave
Jeff F

Apress®

Android Recipes: A Problem-Solution Approach

ISBN-13 (pbk): 978-1-4302-4614-5

ISBN-13 (electronic): 978-1-4302-4615-2

President and Publisher: Paul Manning
Lead Editor: Steve Anglin
Developmental Editor: Tom Welsh
Technical Reviewer: Chád Darby

Coordinating Editor: Jill Balzano
Copy Editor: Christine Dahlin
Compositor: Bytheway Publishing Services
Indexer: SPi Global
Artist: SPi Global
Cover Designer: Anna Ishchenko

Distributed to the book trade worldwide by Springer Science+Business Media New York, 233 Spring Street, 6th Floor, New York, NY 10013. Phone 1-800-SPRINGER, fax (201) 348-4505, e-mail orders-ny@springer-sbm.com, or visit www.springeronline.com.

For information on translations, please e-mail rights@apress.com, or visit www.apress.com.

Apress and friends of ED books may be purchased in bulk for academic, corporate, or promotional use. eBook versions and licenses are also available for most titles. For more information, reference our Special Bulk Sales–eBook Licensing web page at www.apress.com/bulk-sales.

Any source code or other supplementary materials referenced by the author in this text is available to readers at www.apress.com. For detailed information about how to locate your book's source code, go to www.apress.com/source-code.

Contents at a Glance

Contents

Foreword

Dave Smith and Jeff Friesen have taken on a daunting task in writing this book. Knowing Dave for a long time in the mobile development community, I know he labored over every chapter, debating the best advice to give. How do I know this? Because I have the pleasure to work with Dave on a daily basis, and he brings a methodical, measured, deliberative approach to the problems we solve shipping Android software.

With the explosion of Android-powered devices in a very short period of time, a unique opportunity to shape the future of mobile computing has arisen. Android powers phones, tablets, industrial appliances, and in the future devices we have not yet imagined. This broad range of devices running on a common platform allows software developers to write once and run everywhere. Within this book, Dave and Jeff present examples that they have learned while writing real-world Android applications to start you on your journey. Now, take this information and build quality mobile experiences. When your app is launched, these devices become your application. With the flood of mobile devices will come a flood of software, much of which will be crap. Put yourself in the users' shoes, solve a problem they have, and create something to be proud of. Obsess on the details; your users will appreciate it–and, remember, "Real Artists Ship."

—Ben Reubenstein (@benr75)
benr@xcellentcreations.com
Xcellent Creations, Inc.

About the Authors

Dave Smith has been developing hardware and software for embedded platforms since graduating from Colorado School of Mines in 2006 with degrees in Electrical Engineering and Computer Science. Dave now focuses his engineering efforts full-time in the mobile space, working as a consultant in Denver, CO. Since 2009, Dave has worked on developing at all levels of the Android platform, from writing user applications using the SDK to building and customizing the Android source code. His favorite Android projects are those that integrate custom hardware with consumer devices or include building Android for custom embedded platforms. In addition, Dave regularly communicates via his development blog (`blog.wiresareobsolete.com`) and Twitter stream (`@devunwired`).

Jeff Friesen is a freelance tutor and software developer with an emphasis on Java (and now Android). In addition to writing this book, Jeff has written numerous articles on Java and other technologies for *JavaWorld* (`www.javaworld.com`), *informIT* (`www.informit.com`), *java.net*, *DevSource* (`www.devsource.com`), *SitePoint* (`www.sitepoint.com`), and *BuildMobile* (`www.buildmobile.com`). Jeff can be contacted via his website at `tutortutor.ca`.

About the Technical Reviewer

Chád Darby is an author, instructor, and speaker in the Java development world. As a recognized authority on Java applications and architectures, he has presented technical sessions at software development conferences worldwide. In his 15 years as a professional software architect, he's had the opportunity to work for Blue Cross/Blue Shield, Merck, Boeing, Northrop Grumman, and a handful of startup companies.

Chád is a contributing author to several Java books, including *Professional Java E-Commerce* (Wrox Press), *Beginning Java Networking* (Wrox Press), and *XML and Web Services Unleashed* (Sams Publishing). Chád has Java certifications from Sun Microsystems and IBM. He holds a B.S. in Computer Science from Carnegie Mellon University.

You can read Chád's blog at www.luv2code.com and follow him on Twitter @darbyluvs2code.

Acknowledgments

First and foremost, I would like to thank my wife, Lorie, for her eternal patience and support during the long hours I spent compiling and constructing the materials for this book. Next, many thanks to my coauthor, Jeff Friesen, whose willingness to explore new options and paths to Android development have given this book a diverse flavor that makes it great. To my friend and colleague Ben Reubenstein, thank you for taking time to provide the foreword for the book and for making the initial introductions between myself and the team here at Apress. Finally, I send a huge thank you to the team that Apress brought together to work with Jeff and me and make the book the best it could possibly be: Steve Anglin, Jill Balzano, Tom Welsh, Chád Darby, and everyone else. Without your time and effort, this project would not even exist.

—Dave Smith

I thank Steve Anglin for contacting me to write this book, Jill Balzano for guiding me through the various aspects of this project, Tom Welsh for helping me with the development of my chapters, and Chád Darby for his diligence in catching various flaws that would otherwise have made it into this book. I also thank my coauthor Dave Smith for making a fantastic contribution. I appreciate your efforts very much.

—Jeff Friesen

Preface

Welcome to the second edition of *Android Recipes*!

If you are reading this book, you probably don't need to be told of the immense opportunity that mobile devices represent for software developers and users. In recent years, Android has become one of the top mobile platforms for device users. This means that you, as a developer, must know how to harness Android so you can stay connected to this market and the potential that it offers. But any new platform brings with it uncertainty about best practices and solutions to common needs and problems.

What we aim to do with *Android Recipes* is give you the tools to write applications for the Android platform through direct examples targeted at the specific problems you are trying to solve. This book is not a deep dive into the Android SDK, NDK, or any of the other tools. We don't weigh you down with all the details and theory behind the curtain. That's not to say that those details aren't interesting or important. You should take the time to learn them, as they may save you from making future mistakes. However, more often than not, they are simply a distraction when you are just looking for a solution to an immediate problem.

This book is not meant to teach you Java programming or even the building blocks of an Android application. You won't find many basic recipes in this book (such as how to display text with `TextView`, for instance), as we feel these are tasks easily remembered once learned. Instead, we set out to address tasks that developers, once comfortable with Android, need to do often but find too complex to accomplish with a few lines of code.

Treat *Android Recipes* as a reference to consult, a resource-filled cookbook that you can always open to find the pragmatic advice you need to get the job done quickly and well.

What Will You Find in the Book?

Although this book is not a beginner's guide to Android, Chapter 1 offers an overview of those Android fundamentals that are necessary for understanding the rest of the book's content. This overview has been updated to include an introduction to fragments and coverage of resources. Chapter 1 also introduces you to a significant application named *Univerter*, and shows you how to prepare your environment so that you can develop Univerter and other Android applications. Specifically, it shows you how to install the Android SDK and Eclipse with the ADT Plugin and how to build Univerter in these contexts.

As you become a seasoned Android application developer, you're going to want to save time by not reinventing the wheel. Instead, you'll want to create and use your own libraries of reusable code, or use the libraries that others have created. Chapter 7 shows you how to create and use your own library code in the form of JAR-based libraries and Android library projects. In addition to creating your own libraries, we'll introduce a couple of Java libraries outside the

Android SDK that your applications can use. Also, you'll learn about Google's support package and how to use its `GridLayout` class.

Performance matters if you want your applications to succeed. Most of the time, this isn't a problem because (as of version 2.2) Android's Dalvik virtual machine features a Just-In-Time compiler that compiles Dalvik bytecode to the device's native code. However, if this isn't enough, you'll need to leverage the Android NDK to boost performance. Chapter 8 offers you an introduction to the NDK and demonstrates its usefulness in the context of an OpenGL example.

The NDK is a complex technology that requires use of the tedious Java Native Interface (JNI), which can impact performance when your application must make many JNI calls (not to mention that the native parts of your application are not portable). Also, you have a lot of work to do when you want to leverage multiple CPU cores. Fortunately, Google has eliminated this tedium and simplified the execute-on-multiple-cores task while achieving portability by introducing Renderscript. Chapter 8 introduces you to Renderscript and shows you how to use its compute engine (and automatically leverage CPU cores) to process images.

In the intervening chapters, we dive into using the Android SDK to solve real problems. You will learn tricks for effectively creating a user interface that runs well across device boundaries. You will become a master at incorporating the collection of hardware (radios, sensors, and cameras) that makes mobile devices unique platforms. We'll even discuss how to make the system work for you by integrating with the services and applications provided by Google and various device manufacturers. Along the way, you'll be introduced to some tools developed by Google and the community to help make the development and testing of your applications easier.

Are you interested in scripting languages (such as Python or Ruby)? If so, you'll want to check out Appendix A, which introduces you to Scripting Layer for Android. This special application lets you install scripting language interpreters and scripts on a device, and you can then run these scripts, which can speed up development.

To save you the bother of looking up the details on Android's many tools, Appendix B provides an overview of each supported tool. Among other items, you learn why Android 4.1's `systrace` tool does not run on the Android emulator.

When creating applications, you need to ensure that they perform well and are responsive, seamless, and secure. Applications that perform well drain less power from the battery, responsive apps avoid the dreaded *Application Not Responding* dialog box, seamless applications interact properly with other applications so as not to annoy or confuse the user, and secure applications help you avoid sleepless nights. Additionally, when you publish your application to Google Play, you don't want it to be visible to incompatible devices. Instead, you want Google Play to filter your application so that users of these incompatible devices cannot download (or even see) the application. Appendix C offers you guidelines for creating performant, responsive, and seamless apps, and for taking advantage of filtering so that an application can be downloaded (from Google Play) only by those users whose devices are compatible with your application.

Chapter 1 introduced you to the Univerter app. Appendix D rounds out this book by taking you on a detailed tour of Univerter's architecture.

Keep a Level Eye on the Target

Throughout the book, you will see that we have marked most recipes with the minimum API level that is required to support them. Most of the recipes in this book are marked API Level 1, meaning that the code used can be run in applications targeting any version of Android since 1.0. However, where necessary we make use of APIs introduced in later versions. Pay close attention to the API level marking of each recipe to ensure that you are not using code that doesn't match up with the version of Android your application is targeted to support.

Chapter 1

Getting Started with Android

Android is hot, and many people are developing Android applications (apps for short). Perhaps you too would like to develop apps but are unsure about how to get started. Although you could study Google's online *Android Developer's Guide* (`http://developer.android.com/index.html`) to acquire the needed knowledge, you might be overwhelmed by the guide's vast amount of information. In contrast, this chapter presents just enough theory to help you grasp the basics. Following this theory are recipes that teach you how to develop apps and prepare them for publication on Google Play (`https://play.google.com/store`).

What Is Android?

The *Android Developer's Guide* formerly defined *Android* as a *software stack*—a set of software subsystems needed to deliver a fully functional solution— for mobile devices. This stack includes an operating system (a modified version of the Linux kernel), *middleware* (software that connects the low-level operating system to high-level apps) that's partly based on Java, and key apps (written in Java) such as a web browser (known as Browser) and a contact manager (known as Contacts).

Android offers the following features:

- Application framework enabling reuse and replacement of app components (discussed later in this chapter)

- Bluetooth, EDGE, 3G, and WiFi support (hardware dependent)
- Camera, GPS, compass, and accelerometer support (hardware dependent)
- Dalvik virtual machine optimized for mobile devices
- GSM Telephony support (hardware dependent)
- Integrated browser based on the open source WebKit engine
- Media support for common audio, video, and still image formats (MPEG4, H.264, MP3, AAC, AMR, JPG, PNG, GIF)
- Optimized graphics powered by a custom 2D graphics library; 3D graphics based on the OpenGL ES 1.0, 1.1, or 2.0 specification (hardware acceleration optional)
- SQLite for structured data storage

Although not part of an Android device's software stack, Android's rich development environment (including a device emulator and a plug-in for the Eclipse integrated development environment [IDE]) could also be considered an Android feature.

History of Android

Contrary to what you might expect, Android did not originate with Google. Instead, Android was initially developed by Android, Inc., a small Palo Alto, California-based startup company. Google bought this company in the summer of 2005 and released a beta version of the Android SDK in November 2007.

On September 23, 2008, Google released Android 1.0, whose core features included a web browser, camera support, Google Search, and more. Table 1-1 outlines subsequent releases. (Starting with version 1.5, each major release comes under a code name that's based on a dessert item.)

Table 1-1. *Android Releases*

Version	Release Date and Changes
1.1	Google released SDK 1.1 on February 9, 2009. Changes included showing/hiding the speakerphone dialpad and saving attachments in messages.
1.5 (Cupcake) Based on Linux Kernel 2.6.27	Google released SDK 1.5 on April 30, 2009. Changes included recording and watching videos in MPEG-4 and 3GP formats, populating the *home screen* (a special app that is a starting point for using an

	Android device) with *widgets* (miniature app views), and animated screen transitions.
1.6 (Donut) Based on Linux Kernel 2.6.29	Google released SDK 1.6 on September 15, 2009. Changes included an expanded Gesture framework and the new GestureBuilder development tool, an integrated camera/camcorder/gallery interface, support for WVGA screen resolutions, and an updated search experience.
2.0/2.1 (Éclair) Based on Linux Kernel 2.6.29	Google released SDK 2.0 on October 26, 2009. Changes included live wallpapers, numerous new camera features (including flash support, digital zoom, scene mode, white balance, color effect, and macro focus), improved typing speed on virtual keyboard, a smarter dictionary that learns from word usage and includes contact names as suggestions, improved Google Maps 3.1.2, and Bluetooth 2.1 support. Google subsequently released SDK update 2.0.1 on December 3, 2009, and SDK update 2.1 on January 12, 2010. Version 2.0.1 focused on minor API changes, bug fixes, and framework behavioral changes. Version 2.1 presented minor amendments to the API and bug fixes.
2.2 (Froyo) Based on Linux Kernel 2.6.32	Google released SDK 2.2 on May 20, 2009. Changes included the integration of Chrome's V8 JavaScript engine into the Browser app, voice dialing and contact sharing over Bluetooth, Adobe Flash support, additional app speed improvements through JIT compilation, and USB tethering and WiFi hotspot functionality. Google subsequently released SDK update 2.2.1 on January 18, 2011, to offer bug fixes, security updates, and performance improvements. It then released SDK update 2.2.2 on January 22, 2011, to provide minor bug fixes, including SMS routing issues that affected the Nexus One. Finally, Google released SDK update 2.2.3 on November 21, 2011, and this contained two security patches.
2.3 (Gingerbread) Based on Linux Kernel 2.6.35	Google released SDK 2.3 on December 6, 2010. Changes included a new concurrent garbage collector that improves an app's responsiveness, support for gyroscope and barometer sensing, support for WebM/VP8 video playback and AAC audio encoding, support for near field communication, and enhanced copy/paste functionality that lets users select a word by press-hold, copy, and paste. Google subsequently released SDK update 2.3.3 on February 9, 2011, offering improvements and API fixes. SDK update 2.3.4 on April 28, 2011, added support for voice or video chat via Google Talk. SDK update 2.3.5 on July 25, 2011, offered system enhancements, shadow animations for list scrolling, improved battery efficiency, and more. SDK update 2.3.6 on September 2, 2011, fixed a voice search bug. SDK update 2.3.7 on September 21, 2011, brought support for Google Wallet to the Nexus S 4G.

3.0 (Honeycomb) Based on Linux 2.6.36	Google released SDK 3.0 on February 22, 2011. Unlike previous releases, version 3.0 focuses exclusively on tablets, such as Motorola Xoom, the first tablet to be released (on February 24, 2011). In addition to an improved user interface, version 3.0 improves multitasking, supports multicore processors, supports hardware acceleration, and provides a 3D desktop with redesigned widgets. Google subsequently released SDK updates 3.1, 3.2, 3.2.1, 3.2.2, 3.2.4, and 3.2.6 throughout 2011 and in February 2012.
4.0 (Ice Cream Sandwich) Based on Linux Kernel 3.0.1	Google released SDK 4.0.1 on October 19, 2011. SDK 4.0.1 and 4.x successors unify the 2.3.x smartphone and 3.x tablet SDKs. Features include 1080p video recording and a customizable launcher. Google subsequently released SDK updates 4.0.2, 4.0.3, and 4.0.4 in late 2011 and in March 2012.
4.1 (Jelly Bean)	Google released SDK 4.1 on June 27, 2012. Features include vsync timing, triple buffering, automatically resizable app widgets, improved voice search, multichannel audio, and expandable notifications. An over-the-air update (version 4.1.1) was released later in July. In early October, Google released SDK 4.1.2, which offers lock/home screen rotation support for the Nexus 7, one-finger gestures to expand/collapse notifications, and bug fixes/performance enhancements. Then, in late October, Google released SDK 4.2, which offers Photo Sphere panorama photos, multiple user accounts (tablets only), a "Daydream" screensaver that activates when the device is idle or docked, notification power controls, support for a wireless display (Miracast), and more.

Android Architecture

The Android software stack consists of apps at the top, middleware (consisting of an application framework, libraries, and the Android runtime) in the middle, and a Linux kernel with various drivers at the bottom. Figure 1-1 shows this layered architecture.

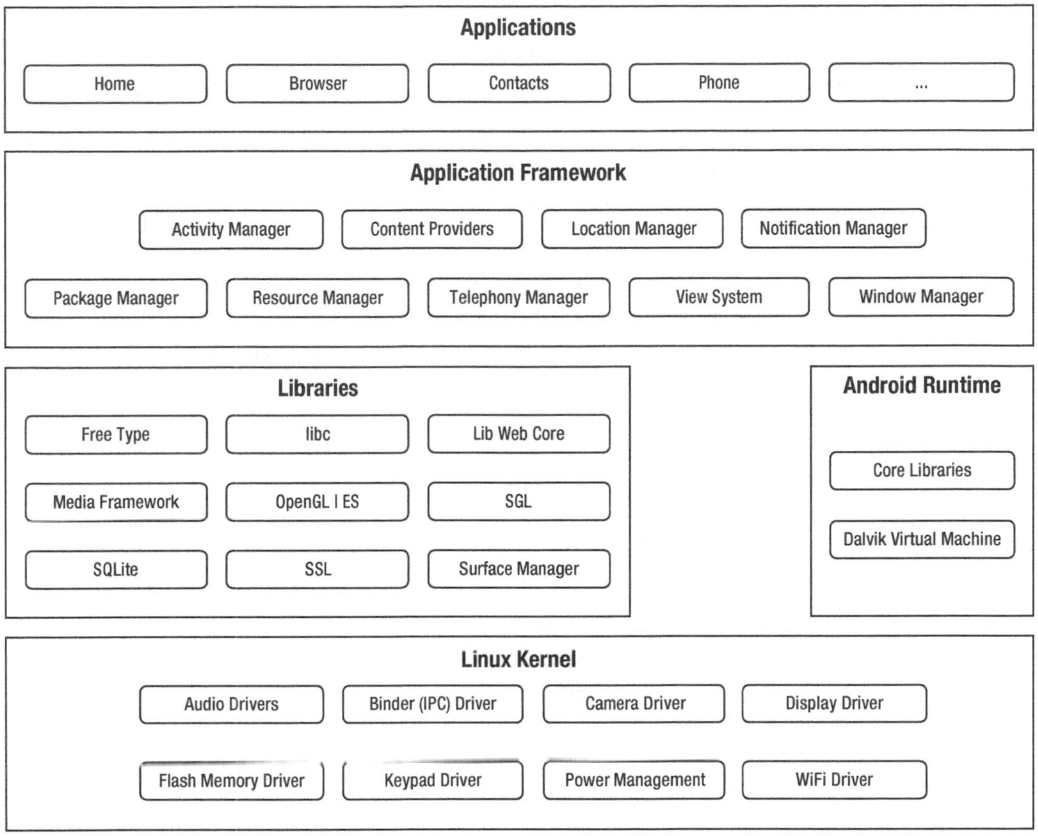

Applications

Home | Browser | Contacts | Phone | ...

Application Framework

Activity Manager | Content Providers | Location Manager | Notification Manager

Package Manager | Resource Manager | Telephony Manager | View System | Window Manager

Libraries

Free Type | libc | Lib Web Core

Media Framework | OpenGL | ES | SGL

SQLite | SSL | Surface Manager

Android Runtime

Core Libraries

Dalvik Virtual Machine

Linux Kernel

Audio Drivers | Binder (IPC) Driver | Camera Driver | Display Driver

Flash Memory Driver | Keypad Driver | Power Management | WiFi Driver

Figure 1-1. *Android's layered architecture consists of several major parts.*

Users care about apps, and Android ships with a variety of useful core apps, which include Browser, Contacts, and Phone. All apps are written in the Java programming language. Apps form the top layer of Android's architecture.

> **NOTE:** Apps are written in a nonstandard Java implementation that combines Android-specific APIs with Java 5 APIs and a small amount of Java 6 (such as the `java.io.File` class's `boolean setExecutable(boolean executable, boolean ownerOnly)` method). Because Android does not support most Java 6 and all Java 7 APIs, you cannot leverage newer Java APIs and dependent features. For example, you cannot use Java 7's try-with-resources statement, which depends upon Java 7's `java.lang.AutoCloseable` interface.

> Each Android version (including updates) is assigned an *API level*, an integer value uniquely identifying the framework API revision offered by that version of the Android platform. For example, Android 4.1 is assigned API Level 16 and Android 2.3.4 is assigned API Level 10. APIs with higher API levels typically cannot be used on devices with lower API levels. (Google's support library, which is discussed in Chapter 7, makes certain newer APIs available to older platform versions.) For example, you typically cannot use an API at Level 16 on a device that supports only API Level 10 (and lower). API-level constants are available in the `android.os.Build.VERSION_CODES` class. Consult "Android API Levels" (`http://developer.android.com/guide/topics/manifest/uses-sdk-element.html#ApiLevels`) in the *Android Developer's Guide* to learn more about API levels.

Directly beneath the app layer is the *application framework*, a set of high-level building blocks for creating apps. The application framework is preinstalled on Android devices and consists of the following components:

- *Activity Manager*: This component provides an app's *life cycle* and maintains a shared activity stack for navigating within and among apps. Both topics are discussed later in this chapter.
- *Content Providers*: These components encapsulate data (such as the Browser app's bookmarks) that can be shared among apps.
- *Location Manager*: This component makes it possible for an Android device to be aware of its physical location.
- *Notification Manager*: This component lets an app notify the user of a significant event (such as a message's arrival) without interrupting what the user is currently doing.
- *Package Manager*: This component lets an app learn about other app packages that are currently installed on the device. (App packages are discussed later in this chapter.)
- *Resource Manager*: This component lets an app access its resources, a topic that's discussed later in this chapter.
- *Telephony Manager*: This component lets an app learn about a device's telephony services. It also handles making and receiving phone calls.

- *View System*: This component manages user interface elements and user interface-oriented event generation. (These topics are briefly discussed later in this chapter.)
- *Window Manager*: This component organizes the screen's real estate into windows, allocates drawing surfaces, and performs other window-related jobs.

The components of the application framework rely on a set of C/C++ libraries to perform their functions. Developers interact with the following libraries by way of framework APIs:

- *FreeType*: This library supports bitmap and vector font rendering.
- *libc*: This library is a BSD-derived implementation of the standard C system library, tuned for embedded Linux-based devices.
- *LibWebCore*: This library offers a modern and fast web browser engine that powers the Android browser and an embeddable web view. It's based on WebKit (`http://en.wikipedia.org/wiki/WebKit`) and is also used by the Google Chrome and Apple Safari browsers.
- *Media Framework*: These libraries, which are based on PacketVideo's OpenCORE, support the playback and recording of many popular audio and video formats, as well as working with static image files. Supported formats include MPEG4, H.264, MP3, AAC, AMR, JPEG, and PNG.
- *OpenGL / ES*: These 3D graphics libraries provide an OpenGL implementation based on OpenGL ES 1.0/1.1/2.0 APIs. They use hardware 3D acceleration (where available) or the included (and highly optimized) 3D software rasterizer.
- *SGL*: This library provides the underlying 2D graphics engine.
- *SQLite*: This library provides a powerful and lightweight relational database engine that's available to all apps and that's also used by Mozilla Firefox and Apple's iPhone for persistent storage.
- *SSL*: This library provides secure sockets layer–based security for network communication.

- *Surface Manager*: This library manages access to the display subsystem, and it seamlessly composites 2D and 3D graphic layers from multiple apps.

Android provides a runtime environment that consists of core libraries (implementing a subset of the Apache Harmony Java version 5 implementation) and the *Dalvik virtual machine* (a non-Java virtual machine that's based on processor registers instead of being stack-based).

> **NOTE:** Google's Dan Bornstein created Dalvik and named this virtual machine after an Icelandic fishing village where some of his ancestors lived.

Each Android app defaults to running in its own Linux process, which hosts an instance of Dalvik. This virtual machine has been designed so that devices can run multiple virtual machines efficiently. This efficiency is largely due to Dalvik executing Dalvik Executable (DEX)-based files. DEX is a format that's optimized for a minimal memory footprint.

> **NOTE:** Android starts a process when any part of the app needs to execute, and it shuts down the process when it's no longer needed and system resources are required by other apps.

Perhaps you're wondering how it's possible to have a non-Java virtual machine run Java code. The answer is that Dalvik doesn't run Java code. Instead, Android transforms compiled Java classfiles into the DEX format via its dx tool, and it's this resulting code that gets executed by Dalvik.

Finally, the libraries and Android runtime rely on the Linux kernel (version 2.6.x or 3.0.x) for underlying core services, such as threading, low-level memory management, a network stack, process management, and a driver model. Furthermore, the kernel acts as an abstraction layer between the hardware and the rest of the software stack.

ANDROID SECURITY MODEL

Android's architecture includes a security model that prevents apps from performing operations considered harmful to other apps, Linux, or users. This security model, which is mostly based on process level enforcement via standard Linux features (such as user and group IDs), places processes in a security sandbox.

By default, the sandbox prevents apps from reading or writing the user's private data (such as contacts or e-mails), reading or writing another app's files, performing network access, keeping the device awake, accessing the camera, and so on. Apps that need to access the network or perform other sensitive operations must first obtain permission to do so.

Android handles permission requests in various ways, typically by automatically allowing or disallowing the request based upon a certificate or by prompting the user to grant or revoke the permission. Permissions required by an app are declared in the app's manifest file (discussed later in this chapter) so that they are known to Android when the app is installed. These permissions won't subsequently change.

App Architecture

Android app architecture differs from desktop application architecture. App architecture is largely based upon components that communicate via intents, resources that are often used in user interface contexts, a manifest that describes the app's components (and more), and an app package that stores components, resources, and the manifest.

Components

An app consists of *components* (activities, services, broadcast receivers, and content providers) that run in a Linux process and that are managed by Android:

- Activities present user interface screens.
- Services perform lengthy jobs (such as playing music) in the background and don't provide user interfaces.
- Broadcast receivers receive and react to broadcasts from Android or other components.
- Content providers encapsulate data and make them available to apps.

Each component is implemented as a class that's stored in the same Java package, which is known as the *app package*. From the Android SDK perspective, each class's source file is stored under a package directory hierarchy that is situated underneath an `src` directory. (You will learn about the Android SDK later in this chapter.)

Not all of these components need to be present in an app. For example, one app might consist of activities only, whereas another app might consist of activities and a service.

> **NOTE:** An app's activities, services, broadcast receivers, and/or content providers share a set of system resources, such as databases, preferences, a filesystem, and the Linux process.

Android communicates with activities, services, and broadcast receivers via *intents*, which are messages that describe operations to perform (such as launch an activity) or (in the case of broadcasts) that provide descriptions of external events that have occurred (a device's camera being activated, for example) and are being announced. Activities, services, and broadcast receivers can also use intents to communicate among themselves.

Intents are implemented as instances of the `android.content.Intent` class. An `Intent` object describes a message in terms of some combination of the following items:

- *Action*: A string naming the action to be performed or, in the case of broadcast intents, the action that took place and is being reported. Actions are described by `Intent` constants such as `ACTION_CALL` (initiate a phone call), `ACTION_EDIT` (display data for the user to edit), and `ACTION_MAIN` (start up as the initial activity). You can also define your own action strings for activating the components in your app. These strings should include the app package as a prefix (`"com.example.project.GET_NEWSFEEDS"`, for example).
- *Category*: A string that provides additional information about the kind of component that should handle the intent. For example, `CATEGORY_LAUNCHER` means that the calling activity should appear in the device's app launcher as a top-level app. (The app launcher is briefly discussed in Recipe 1-4.)
- *Component name*: A string that specifies the fully qualified name (package plus name) of a component class to use for the intent. The component name is optional. If set, the `Intent` object is delivered to an instance of the designated class. If not set, Android uses other information in the `Intent` object to locate a suitable target.
- *Data*: The uniform resource identifier of the data on which to operate (such as a person record in a contacts database).

- *Extras*: A set of key-value pairs providing additional information that should be delivered to the component handling the intent. For example, given an action for sending an e-mail message, this information could include the message's subject, body, and so on.
- *Flags:* Bit values that instruct Android on how to launch an activity (for example, which task the activity should belong to—tasks are discussed later in this chapter) and how to treat the activity after launch (for example, whether the activity can be considered a recent activity). Flags are represented by constants in the `Intent` class; for example, `FLAG_ACTIVITY_NEW_TASK` specifies that this activity will become the start of a new task on this activity stack—the activity stack is discussed later in this chapter.
- *Type*: The MIME type of the intent data. Normally, Android infers a type from the data. By specifying a type, you disable that inference.

Intents can be classified as explicit or implicit. An *explicit intent* designates the target component by its name (the previously mentioned component name item is assigned a value). Because component names are usually unknown to the developers of other apps, explicit intents are typically used for app-internal messages (such as an activity that launches another activity located within the same app). Android delivers an explicit intent to an instance of the designated target class. Only the `Intent` object's component name matters for determining which component should get the intent.

An *implicit intent* doesn't name a target (the component name is not assigned a value). Implicit intents are often used to start components in other apps. Android searches for the best component (a single activity or service to perform the requested action) or components (a set of broadcast receivers to respond to the broadcast announcement) to handle the implicit intent. During the search, Android compares the contents of the `Intent` object to *intent filters*, manifest information associated with components that can potentially receive intents.

Filters advertise a component's capabilities and identify only those intents that the component can handle. They open up the component to the possibility of receiving implicit intents of the advertised type. If a component has no intent filters, it can receive only explicit intents. In contrast, a component with filters can receive explicit and implicit intents. Android consults an `Intent` object's action, category, data, and type when comparing the intent against an intent filter. It doesn't take extras and flags into consideration.

> **NOTE:** Android widely uses intents, which offers many opportunities to replace existing components with your own components. For example, Android provides the intent for sending an e-mail. Your app can send this intent to activate the standard mail app, or it can register an activity that responds to the intent, replacing the standard mail app with its own activity.

This component-oriented architecture lets an app reuse the components of other apps, provided that those other apps permit reuse of their components. Component reuse reduces the overall memory footprint, which is very important for devices with limited memory.

For example, you're creating a drawing app that lets users choose a color from a palette, and another app contains a suitable color chooser and permits this component to be reused. In this scenario, the drawing app can call upon that other app's color chooser to have the user select a color rather than provide its own color chooser. The drawing app doesn't contain the other app's color chooser or even link to this other app. Instead, it starts up the other app's color chooser component when needed.

> **NOTE:** Android starts a process when any part of the app (such as the aforementioned color chooser) is needed, and it instantiates the Java objects for that part. This is why Android's apps don't have a single entry point (no C-style `main()` function, for example). Instead, apps use components that are instantiated and run as needed.

Activities in Depth

An *activity* is a component that presents a user interface screen with which the user interacts. For example, Android's Contacts app includes an activity for entering a new contact, its Phone app includes an activity for dialing a phone number, and its Calculator app includes an activity for performing basic calculations (see Figure 1-2).

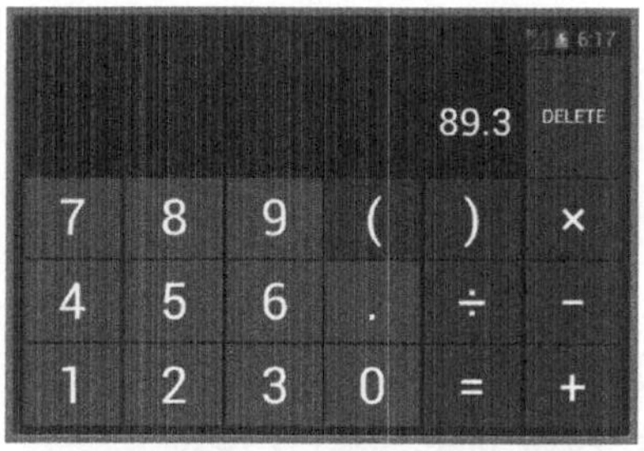

Figure 1-2. *The main activity of Android's Calculator app lets the user perform basic calculations.*

Although an app can include a single activity, it's more typical for apps to include multiple activities. For example, the Calculator app also includes an "advanced panel" activity that lets the user calculate square roots, perform trigonometry, and carry out other advanced mathematical operations.

Activities are described by subclasses of the `android.app.Activity` class, which is an indirect subclass of the `android.content.Context` class.

> **NOTE:** `Context` is an abstract class whose methods let apps access global information about their environments (such as their resources and filesystems), and let apps perform contextual operations, such as launching activities and services, broadcasting intents, and opening private files.

`Activity` subclasses override various `Activity` *life cycle callback methods* that Android calls during the life of an activity. For example, the `SimpleActivity` class in Listing 1-1 extends `Activity` and also overrides the `void onCreate(Bundle bundle)` and `void onDestroy()` life cycle callback methods.

Listing 1-1. *A Skeletal Activity*

```
import android.app.Activity;
import android.os.Bundle;

public class SimpleActivity extends Activity
{
   @Override
   public void onCreate(Bundle savedInstanceState)
   {
      super.onCreate(savedInstanceState); // Always call superclass method
first.
      System.out.println("onCreate(Bundle) called");
   }
   @Override
```

```
   public void onDestroy()
   {
      super.onDestroy(); // Always call superclass method first.
      System.out.println("onDestroy() called");
   }
}
```

The overriding onCreate(Bundle) and onDestroy() methods in Listing 1-1 first invoke their superclass counterparts, a pattern that must be followed when overriding the void onStart(), void onRestart(), void onResume(), void onPause(), and void onStop() life cycle callback methods.

- onCreate(Bundle) is called when the activity is first created. This method is used to create the activity's user interface, create background threads as needed, and perform other global initialization. onCreate() is passed an android.os.Bundle object containing the activity's previous state, if that state was captured (via void onSaveInstanceState(Bundle outState)); otherwise, the null reference is passed. Android always calls the onStart() method after calling onCreate(Bundle). All meaningful activities override onCreate(Bundle).
- onStart() is called just before the activity becomes visible to the user. Android calls the onResume() method after calling onStart() when the activity comes to the foreground, and calls the onStop() method after onStart() when the activity becomes hidden.
- onRestart() is called after the activity has been stopped, just prior to it being started again. Android always calls onStart() after calling onRestart().
- onResume() is called just before the activity starts interacting with the user. At this point the activity has the focus and user input is directed to the activity. Android always calls the onPause() method after calling onResume(), but only when the activity must be paused.

- `onPause()` is called when Android is about to resume another activity. This method is typically used to persist unsaved changes, stop animations that might be consuming processor cycles, and so on. It should perform its job quickly, because the next activity won't be resumed until it returns. Android calls `onResume()` after calling `onPause()` when the activity starts interacting with the user, and it calls `onStop()` when the activity becomes invisible to the user. Many activities implement `onPause()` to commit data changes and otherwise prepare to stop interacting with the user.
- `onStop()` is called when the activity is no longer visible to the user. This may happen because the activity is being destroyed or because another activity (either an existing one or a new one) has been resumed and is covering the activity. Android calls `onRestart()` after calling `onStop()`, when the activity is coming back to interact with the user, and it calls the `onDestroy()` method when the activity is going away.
- `onDestroy()` is called before the activity is destroyed, unless memory is tight and Android is forced to kill the activity's process. In this scenario, `onDestroy()` is never called. If `onDestroy()` is called, it will be the final call that the activity ever receives. Android can kill the process hosting the activity at any time after `onPause()`, `onStop()`, or `onDestroy()` returns. An activity is in a killable state from the time `onPause()` returns until the time `onResume()` is called. The activity won't again be killable until `onPause()` returns.

Figure 1-3 illustrates an activity's life cycle in terms of these seven methods.

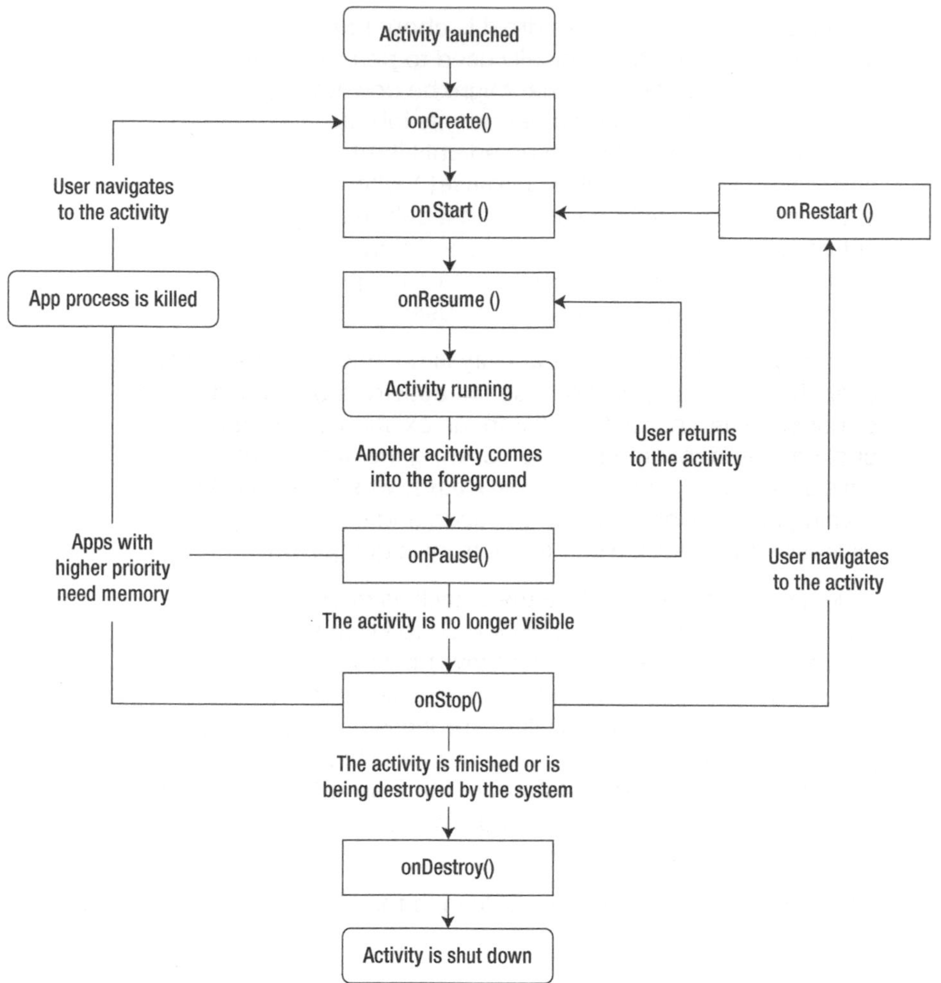

Figure 1-3. *The life cycle of an activity reveals that there's no guarantee of* `onDestroy()` *being called.*

Figure 1-3 reveals that an activity is started by calling `startActivity()`. More specifically, the activity is started by creating an `Intent` object describing an explicit or implicit intent and by passing this object to `Context`'s `void startActivity(Intent intent)` method (launch a new activity; no result is returned when it finishes).

Alternatively, the activity could be started by calling `Activity`'s `void startActivityForResult(Intent intent, int requestCode)` method. The specified int result is returned to Activity's void onActivityResult(int requestCode, int resultCode, Intent data) callback method as an argument.

NOTE: The responding activity can look at the intent that caused it to be launched by calling Activity's Intent getIntent() method. Android calls the activity's void onNewIntent(Intent intent) method (also located in the Activity class) to pass any subsequent intents to the activity.

Suppose that you've created an app named SimpleActivity, and that this app consists of SimpleActivity (described in Listing 1-1) and SimpleActivity2 classes. Now suppose that you want to launch SimpleActivity2 from SimpleActivity's onCreate(Bundle) method. The following example shows you how to start SimpleActivity2:

```
Intent intent = new Intent(SimpleActivity.this, SimpleActivity2.class);
SimpleActivity.this.startActivity(intent);
```

The first line creates an Intent object that describes an explicit intent. It initializes this object by passing the current SimpleActivity instance's reference and SimpleActivity2's Class instance to the Intent(Context packageContext, Class<?> cls) constructor.

The second line passes this Intent object to startActivity(Intent), which is responsible for launching the activity described by SimpleActivity2.class. If startActivity(Intent) was unable to find the specified activity (which shouldn't happen), it would throw an android.content.ActivityNotFoundException instance.

Figure 1-3 also reveals that onDestroy() might not be called before the app is terminated. As a result, you should not count on using this method as a place for saving data. For example, if an activity is editing a content provider's data, those edits should typically be committed in onPause().

NOTE: onDestroy() is usually implemented to free system resources (such as threads) that were acquired in onCreate(Bundle).

The seven life cycle callback methods define an activity's entire life cycle and describe the following three nested loops:

- The *entire lifetime* of an activity is defined as everything from the first call to `onCreate(Bundle)` through to a single final call to `onDestroy()`. An activity performs all of its initial setup of "global" state in `onCreate(Bundle)`, and it releases all remaining resources in `onDestroy()`. For example, if the activity has a thread running in the background to download data from the network, it might create that thread in `onCreate(Bundle)` and stop the thread in `onDestroy()`.
- The *visible lifetime* of an activity is defined as everything from a call to `onStart()` through to a corresponding call to `onStop()`. During this time, the user can see the activity onscreen, although it might not be in the foreground and interacting with the user. Between these two methods, the activity can maintain system resources that are needed to show itself to the user. For example, it can register a broadcast receiver in `onStart()` to monitor for changes that impact its user interface, and it can unregister this object in `onStop()` when the user can no longer see what the activity is displaying. The `onStart()` and `onStop()` methods can be called multiple times, as the activity alternates between being visible to and being hidden from the user.
- The *foreground lifetime* of an activity is defined as everything from a call to `onResume()` through to a corresponding call to `onPause()`. During this time, the activity is in front of all other activities onscreen and is interacting with the user. An activity can frequently transition between the resumed and paused states; for example, `onPause()` is called when the device goes to sleep or when a new activity is started, and `onResume()` is called when an activity result or a new intent is delivered. The code in these two methods should be fairly lightweight.

ACTIVITIES, TASKS, AND THE ACTIVITY STACK

Android refers to a sequence of related activities as a *task* and provides an *activity stack* (also known as *history stack* or *back stack*) to remember this sequence. The activity starting the task is the initial activity pushed onto the stack and is known as the *root activity*. This activity is typically the activity selected by the user via the device's app launcher. The activity that's currently running is located at the top of the stack.

When the current activity starts another, the new activity is pushed onto the stack and takes focus (becomes the running activity). The previous activity remains on the stack but is stopped. When an activity stops, the system retains the current state of its user interface.

When the user presses the device's BACK key, the current activity is popped from the stack (the activity is destroyed), and the previous activity resumes operation as the running activity (the previous state of its user interface is restored).

Activities in the stack are never rearranged, only pushed and popped from the stack. Activities are pushed onto the stack when started by the current activity, and they are popped off the stack when the user leaves them by pressing the BACK key. As such, the stack operates as a "last in, first out" object structure.

Each time the user presses BACK, an activity in the stack is popped off to reveal the previous activity. This continues until the user returns to the home screen or to whichever activity was running when the task began. When all activities are removed from the stack, the task no longer exists.

Check out the "Tasks and Back Stack" section in Google's online Android documentation to learn more about activities and tasks. You'll find this documentation located at `http://developer.android.com/guide/components/tasks-and-back-stack.html`.

Views, View Groups, and Event Listeners

An activity's user interface is based on *views* (user interface components), *view groups* (views that group together related views), and *event listeners* (objects that listen for events originating from views or view groups).

> **NOTE:** Android refers to views as widgets. Don't confuse widget in this context with the widgets that are shown on the Android home screen. Although the same term is used, user interface widgets and home screen widgets are different. User interface widgets are components; home screen widgets are miniature views of running apps.

Views are described by subclasses of the concrete `android.view.View` class and are analogous to Java Swing components. The `android.widget` package contains various `View` subclasses, such as `Button`, `EditText`, and `TextView` (the parent of `EditText`).

View groups are described by subclasses of the abstract `android.view.ViewGroup` class (which subclasses `View`) and are analogous to Java Swing containers. The `android.widget` package contains various subclasses, such as `LinearLayout`.

> **NOTE:** Because ViewGroup is a subclass of View, view groups are a kind of view. This arrangement lets you nest view groups within view groups to achieve screens of arbitrary complexity. Don't overdo it, however, because users typically don't want to navigate screens that are overly complex.

Event listeners are described by nested interface members of View and ViewGroup (and various subclasses). For example, View.OnClickListener declares a void onClick(View v) method that's invoked when a clickable view (such as a button) is clicked.

The following onCreate(Bundle) method uses Button, EditText, and LinearLayout to create a screen where the user enters text and subsequently clicks the button to display this text via a pop-up message:

```
@Override
public void onCreate(Bundle savedInstanceState)
{
    super.onCreate(savedInstanceState);
    LinearLayout layout = new LinearLayout(this);
    final EditText et = new EditText(this);
    et.setEms(10);
    layout.addView(et);
    Button btnOK = new Button(this);
    btnOK.setText("OK");
    layout.addView(btnOK);
    View.OnClickListener ocl;
    ocl = new View.OnClickListener()
    {
       @Override
       public void onClick(View v)
       {
          Toast.makeText(class.this, et.getText(),
                         Toast.LENGTH_SHORT).show();
       }
    };
    btnOK.setOnClickListener(ocl);
    setContentView(layout);
}
```

After calling its superclass counterpart, onCreate(Bundle) instantiates LinearLayout. This container arranges its children in a single column or row. Its default behavior is to arrange the children in a row.

The keyword this is passed to LinearLayout's constructor, a practice followed by other widget constructors. The current context object referenced by this lets a widget load and access resources (discussed later in this chapter) when necessary.

Next, EditText is instantiated and its inherited (from TextView) void setEms(int ems) method is called to set the widget's width to 10 *ems* (a relative measurement unit; one em equals the height of the capital letter "M" in the default font size).

At this point, LinearLayout's inherited (from its ViewGroup parent) void addView(View child) method is called to add the EditText widget instance to the LinearLayout widget container instance.

Having finished with EditText, onCreate(Bundle) instantiates Button, invokes its inherited (from TextView) void setText(CharSequence text) method to set the button label to OK, and adds the Button instance to the LinearLayout instance.

onCreate(Bundle) now instantiates an anonymous class that implements the View.OnClickListener interface, overriding onClick(View) to display a *toast* (a message that pops up on the surface of the window for a short period of time).

CAUTION: The code fragment demonstrates a problem where efficiency is concerned. Consider the approach to creating the click listener that is subsequently attached to the button. This approach is inefficient because it requires that a new object (an instance of an anonymous class that implements the View.OnClickListener interface) be created each time onCreate(Bundle) is called. (This method is called each time the device orientation changes.) A more efficient approach makes ocl an instance field and instantiates the anonymous class only when ocl does not contain the null reference. However, an even better solution exists. This solution is presented later in this chapter where resources are discussed.

The toast is created by invoking the android.widget.Toast class's Toast makeText(Context context, CharSequence text, int duration) factory method, where the value passed to duration is one of Toast.LENGTH_SHORT or Toast.LENGTH_LONG. After the Toast instance has been created, Toast's void show() method is called to display the toast for the specified period of time. (The message fades in when this method is called and fades out after the duration expires.)

Following listener creation, onCreate(Bundle) invokes Button's inherited (from View) void setOnClickListener(View.OnClickListener l) method to register the previously created listener object with the button.

Finally, `onCreate(Bundle)` invokes `Activity`'s `void setContentView(View view)` method. This method is used to install the `LinearLayout` instance into the activity's *view hierarchy* so that the edittext and button widgets can be displayed in a single row.

> **NOTE:** Although you can create user interfaces by instantiating widget classes, there are advantages to using resources for this task. This topic is discussed later in this chapter.

Fragments

Android 3.0 introduced the concept of *fragments*, which are objects that represent parts of an activity's user interface. A fragment serves as a modular section of an activity with its own life cycle and the ability to receive its own input events, and which you can add or remove while the activity is running. You can combine multiple fragments into a single activity to build a multipane user interface (typically in a tablet context) and reuse the fragment in multiple activities.

> **NOTE:** You must always embed a fragment in an activity.

Google introduced fragments in Honeycomb mainly to support more dynamic and flexible user interfaces on tablets and other large screens. Because a tablet's screen is much larger than that of a handset, there's more room to combine and interchange widgets. Fragments allow such designs without forcing you to manage complex changes to the view hierarchy. By organizing an activity's layout into fragments, you can modify its appearance at runtime and preserve changes in the activity-managed back stack.

> **TIP:** You should design each fragment as a modular and reusable activity component. Because each fragment defines its own layout and its own behavior with its own life cycle callbacks, you can include one fragment in multiple activities, so you should strive to design for reuse and avoid directly manipulating one fragment from another fragment. This is especially important because a modular fragment lets you change fragment combinations for different screen sizes.

For example, a news app presents a list of article titles and the content of the currently selected article. A tablet can display the titles list and the content on the same screen. However, a handset would display the titles list on one screen and the content on another. You would design the user interface such that one fragment manages the titles list and the other fragment manages the content. You can then reuse these fragments in different layout configurations to optimize the user experience based on the available screen space, as demonstrated in Figure 1-4.

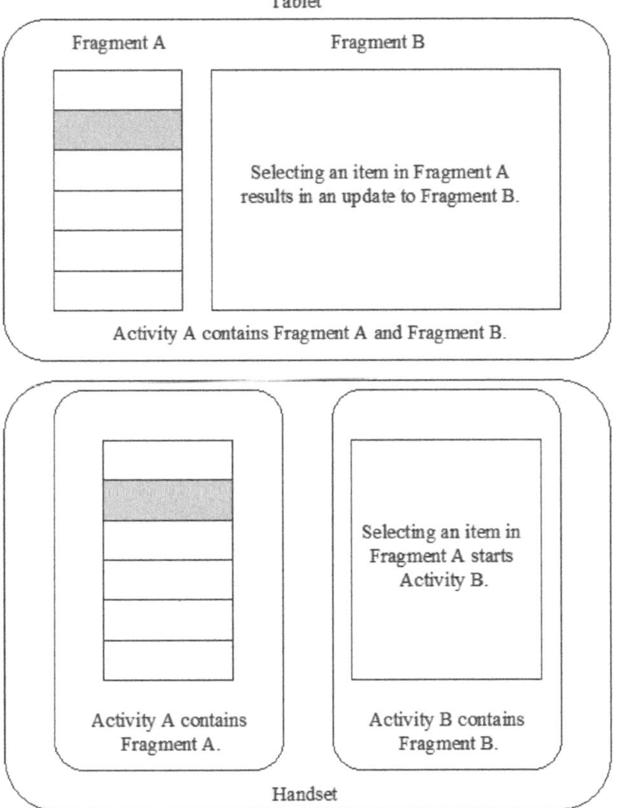

Figure 1-4. *Two user interfaces defined by fragments are combined into one activity for a tablet design, but they are separated into two activities for a handset design.*

According to Figure 1-4, the app embeds two fragments in Activity A when running on a tablet-sized device. However, on a handset-sized screen, where there is not enough room for both fragments, Activity A includes only the fragment for the list of articles. When the user selects an article, this activity starts Activity B, which includes the second fragment to read the article. Thus, the app supports tablets and handsets by reusing fragments in different combinations.

> **NOTE:** To learn more about fragments, check out Google's "Fragments" documentation at `http://developer.android.com/guide/components/fragments.html`

Services in Depth

A *service* is a component that runs in the background for an indefinite period of time and that doesn't provide a user interface. As with an activity, a service runs on the process's main thread; it must spawn another thread to perform a time-consuming operation. Services are classified as local or remote:

- A *local service* runs in the same process as the rest of the app. Such services make it easy to implement background tasks.
- A *remote service* runs in a separate process. Such services let you perform interprocess communications.

> **NOTE:** A service is not a separate process, although it can be specified to run in a separate process. Also, a service is not a thread. Instead, a service lets the app tell Android about something it wants to be doing in the background (even when the user is not directly interacting with the app), and lets the app expose some of its functionality to other apps.

Consider a service that plays music in response to a user's music choice via an activity. The user selects the song to play via this activity, and a service is started in response to the selection. The service plays the music on another thread to prevent the *Application Not Responding* dialog box (discussed in Appendix C) from appearing.

> **NOTE:** The rationale for using a service to play the music is that the user expects the music to keep playing even after the activity that initiated the music leaves the screen.

Services are described by subclasses of the abstract `android.app.Service` class, which is an indirect subclass of `Context`.

Service subclasses override various Service life cycle callback methods that Android calls during the life of a service. For example, the SimpleService class in Listing 1-2 extends Service and also overrides the void onCreate() and void onDestroy() life cycle callback methods.

Listing 1-2. *A Skeletal Service, Version 1*

```
import android.app.Service;

public class SimpleService extends Service
{
   @Override
   public void onCreate()
   {
      System.out.println("onCreate() called");
   }
   @Override
   public void onDestroy()
   {
      System.out.println("onDestroy() called");
   }
   @Override
   public IBinder onBind(Intent intent)
   {
      System.out.println("onBind(Intent) never called");
      return null;
   }
}
```

onCreate() is called when the service is initially created, and onDestroy() is called when the service is being removed. Because it is abstract, the IBinder onBind(Intent intent) life cycle callback method (described later in this section) must always be overridden, even if only to return null, which indicates that this method is ignored.

> **NOTE:** Service subclasses typically override onCreate() and onDestroy() to perform initialization and cleanup. Unlike Activity's onCreate(Bundle) and onDestroy() methods, Service's onCreate() method isn't repeatedly called and its onDestroy() method is always called.
>
> A service's lifetime happens between the time onCreate() is called and the time onDestroy() returns. As with an activity, a service initializes in onCreate() and cleans up in onDestroy(). For example, a music playback service could create the thread that plays music in onCreate() and stop the thread in onDestroy().

Local Services

Local services are typically started via Context's ComponentName startService(Intent intent) method, which returns an android.content.ComponentName instance that identifies the started service component, or the null reference when the service doesn't exist. Furthermore, startService(Intent) results in the life cycle shown in Figure 1-5.

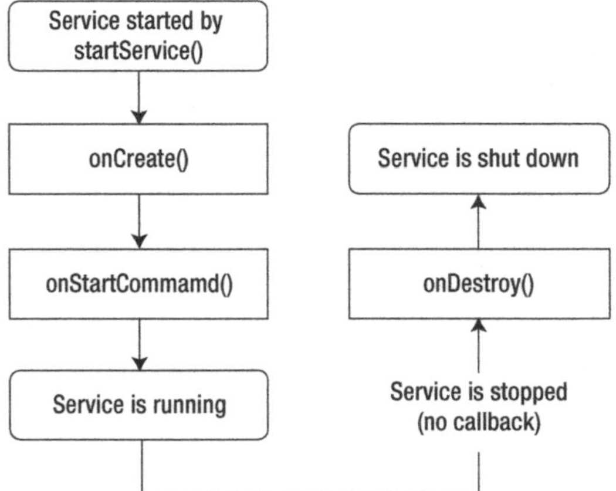

Figure 1-5. *The life cycle of a service that's started by* `startService(Intent)` *features a call to* `onStartCommand(Intent, int, int)`.

The call to startService(Intent) results in a call to onCreate(), followed by a call to int onStartCommand(Intent intent, int flags, int startId). This latter life cycle callback method, which replaces the deprecated void onStart(Intent intent, int startId) method, is called with the following arguments:

- intent is the Intent object passed to startService(Intent).
- flags can provide additional data about the start request but is often set to 0.
- startID is a unique integer that describes this start request. A service can pass this value to Service's boolean stopSelfResult(int startId) method to stop itself.

onStartCommand(Intent, int, int) processes the Intent object, and typically it returns the constant Service.START_STICKY to indicate that the service is to continue running until explicitly stopped. At this point, the service is running and will continue to run until one of the following events occurs:

- Another component stops the service by calling Context's boolean stopService(Intent intent) method. Only one stopService(Intent) call is needed no matter how often startService(Intent) was called.
- The service stops itself by calling one of Service's overloaded stopSelf() methods or by calling Service's stopSelfResult(int) method.

After stopService(Intent), stopSelf(), or stopSelfResult(int) has been called, Android calls onDestroy() to let the service perform cleanup tasks.

> **NOTE:** When a service is started by calling startService(Intent), onBind(Intent) is not called.

Listing 1-3 presents a skeletal service class that could be used in the context of the startService(Intent) method.

Listing 1-3. *A Skeletal Service, Version 2*

```
import android.app.Service;

public class SimpleService extends Service
{
   @Override
   public void onCreate()
   {
      System.out.println("onCreate() called");
   }
   @Override
   public int onStartCommand(Intent intent, int flags, int startId)
   {
      System.out.println("onStartCommand(Intent, int, int) called");
      return START_STICKY;
   }
   @Override
   public void onDestroy()
   {
      System.out.println("onDestroy() called");
   }
   @Override
   public IBinder onBind(Intent intent)
   {
      System.out.println("onBind(Intent) never called");
      return null;
   }
```

```
}
```

The following example, which is assumed to be located in the `onCreate()` method of Listing 1-1's `SimpleActivity` class, employs `startService(Intent)` to start an instance of Listing 1-3's `SimpleService` class via an explicit intent:

```
Intent intent = new Intent(SimpleActivity.this, SimpleService.class);
SimpleActivity.this.startService(intent);
```

Remote Services

Remote services are started via `Context`'s `boolean bindService(Intent service, ServiceConnection conn, int flags)` method, which connects to a running service (creating the service if necessary) and which returns "true" when successfully connected. `bindService(Intent, ServiceConnection, int)` results in Figure 1-6's life cycle.

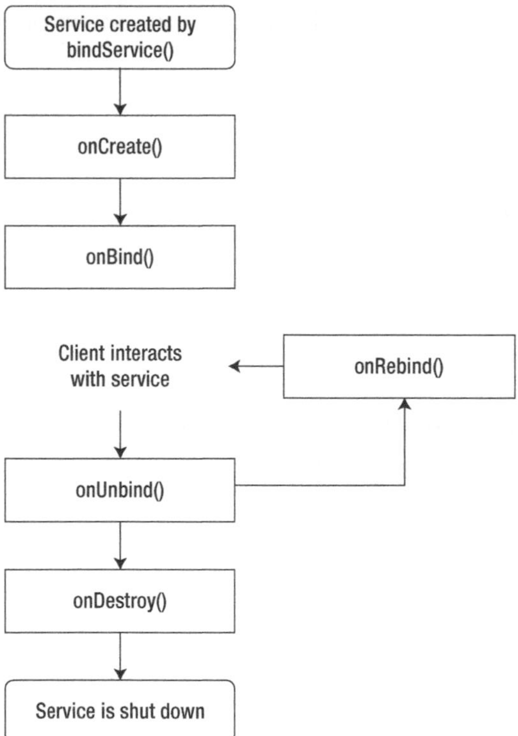

Figure 1-6. *The life cycle of a service started by `bindService(Intent, ServiceConnection, int)` doesn't include a call to `onStartCommand(Intent, int, int)`.*

The call to bindService(Intent, ServiceConnection, int) results in a call to onCreate() followed by a call to onBind(Intent), which returns the *communications channel* (an instance of a class that implements the android.os.IBinder interface) that clients use to interact with the service.

The client interacts with the service as follows:

1. The client subclasses android.content.ServiceConnection and overrides this class's abstract void onServiceConnected(ComponentName className, IBinder service) and void onServiceDisconnected(ComponentName name) methods in order to receive information about the service as the service is started and stopped. When bindService(Intent, ServiceConnection, int) returns true, the former method is called when a connection to the service has been established; the IBinder argument passed to this method is the same value returned from onBind(Intent). The latter method is called when a connection to the service has been lost.

   Lost connections typically occur when the process hosting the service has crashed or has been killed. The ServiceConnection instance itself is not removed—the binding to the service will remain active, and the client will receive a call to onServiceConnected(ComponentName, IBinder) when the service is next running.

2. The client passes the ServiceConnection subclass object to bindService(Intent, ServiceConnection, int).

A client disconnects from a service by calling Context's void unbindService(ServiceConnection conn) method. This component no longer receives calls as the service is restarted. When no other components are bound to the service, the service is allowed to stop at any time.

Before the service can stop, Android calls the service's boolean onUnbind(Intent intent) life cycle callback method with the Intent object that was passed to unbindService(ServiceConnection). Assuming that onUnbind(Intent) doesn't return true, which tells Android to call the service's void onRebind(Intent intent) life cycle callback method each time a client subsequently binds to the service, Android calls onDestroy() to destroy the service.

Listing 1-4 presents a skeletal service class that could be used in the context of the bindService(Intent, ServiceConnection, int) method.

Listing 1-4. *A Skeletal Service, Version 3*

```
import android.app.Service;

public class SimpleService extends Service
{
   public class SimpleBinder extends Binder
   {
      SimpleService getService()
      {
         return SimpleService.this;
      }
   }
   private final IBinder binder = new SimpleBinder();
   @Override
   public IBinder onBind(Intent intent)
   {
      return binder;
   }
   @Override
   public void onCreate()
   {
      System.out.println("onCreate() called");
   }
   @Override
   public void onDestroy()
   {
      System.out.println("onDestroy() called");
   }
}
```

Listing 1-4 first declares a SimpleBinder inner class that extends the android.os.Binder class. SimpleBinder declares a single SimpleService getService() method that returns an instance of the SimpleService subclass.

> **NOTE:** Binder works with the IBinder interface to support a remote procedure call mechanism for communicating between processes. Although this example assumes that the service is running in the same process as the rest of the app, Binder and IBinder are still required.

Listing 1-4 next instantiates SimpleBinder and assigns the instance's reference to the private binder field. This field's value is returned from the subsequently overriding onBind(Intent) method.

Let's assume that the SimpleActivity class in Listing 1-1 declares a private SimpleService field named ss (private SimpleService ss;). Continuing, let's assume that the following example is contained in SimpleActivity's onCreate(Bundle) method:

```
ServiceConnection sc = new ServiceConnection()
{
   @Override
   public void onServiceConnected(ComponentName className, IBinder service)
   {
      ss = ((SimpleService.SimpleBinder) service).getService();
      System.out.println("Service connected");
   }
   @Override
   public void onServiceDisconnected(ComponentName className)
   {
      ss = null; System.out.println("Service disconnected");
   }
};
bindService(new Intent(SimpleActivity.this, SimpleService.class), sc,
            Context.BIND_AUTO_CREATE);
```

The example first instantiates an anonymous subclass of ServiceConnection. The overriding onServiceConnected(ComponentName, IBinder) method uses the service argument to call SimpleBinder's getService() method and save the result.

Although it must be present, the overriding onServiceDisconnected(ComponentName) method should never be called because SimpleService runs in the same process as SimpleActivity.

The example next passes the ServiceConnection subclass object, along with an intent that identifies SimpleService as the intent's target and Context.BIND_AUTO_CREATE (create a persistent connection) to bindService(Intent, ServiceConnection, int).

> **NOTE:** This example used bindService(Intent, ServiceConnection, int) to start a local service, but it's more typical to use this method to start a remote service.
>
> A service can be started with startService(Intent) and have components bound to it with bindService(Intent, ServiceConnection, int). Android keeps the service running until all components have unbound and/or the service

stops itself or is stopped by another component (or Android when memory is low and it must recover system resources).

Broadcast Receivers in Depth

A *broadcast receiver* is a component that receives and reacts to broadcasts. Many broadcasts originate in system code; for example, an announcement is made to indicate that the timezone has been changed or the battery power is low.

Apps can also initiate broadcasts. For example, an app may want to let other apps know that some data has finished downloading from the network to the device and is now available for them to use.

Broadcast receivers are described by classes that subclass the abstract `android.content.BroadcastReceiver` class and override `BroadcastReceiver`'s abstract `void onReceive(Context context, Intent intent)` method. For example, Listing 1-5's `SimpleBroadcastReceiver` class extends `BroadcastReceiver` and overrides this method.

Listing 1-5. *A Skeletal Broadcast Receiver*

```
public class SimpleBroadcastReceiver extends BroadcastReceiver
{
   @Override
   public void onReceive(Context context, Intent intent)
   {
      System.out.println("onReceive(Context, Intent) called");
   }
}
```

You start a broadcast receiver by creating an `Intent` object and passing this object to any of `Context`'s broadcast methods (such as `Context`'s overloaded `sendBroadcast()` methods), which broadcast the message to all interested broadcast receivers.

The following example, which is assumed to be located in the `onCreate()` method of Listing 1-1's `SimpleActivity` class, starts an instance of Listing 1-5's `SimpleBroadcastReceiver` class:

```
Intent intent = new Intent(SimpleActivity.this, SimpleBroadcastReceiver.class);
intent.putExtra("message", "Hello, broadcast receiver!");
SimpleActivity.this.sendBroadcast(intent);
```

Intent's Intent putExtra(String name, String value) method is called to store the message as a key/value pair. As with Intent's other putExtra() methods, this method returns a reference to the Intent object so that method calls can be chained together.

Content Providers in Depth

A *content provider* is a component that makes a specific set of an app's data available to other apps. The data can be stored in the Android filesystem, in an SQLite database, or in any other manner that makes sense.

Content providers are preferable to directly accessing raw data because they decouple component code from raw data formats. This decoupling prevents code breakage when formats change.

Content providers are described by classes that subclass the abstract android.content.ContentProvider class and override ContentProvider's abstract methods (such as String getType(Uri uri)). For example, the SimpleContentProvider class in Listing 1-6 extends ContentProvider and overrides these methods.

Listing 1-6. *A Skeletal Content Provider*

```
public class SimpleContentProvider extends ContentProvider
{
   @Override
   public int delete(Uri uri, String selection, String[] selectionArgs)
   {
      System.out.println("delete(Uri, String, String[]) called");
      return 0;
   }
   @Override
   public String getType(Uri uri)
   {
      System.out.println("getType(Uri) called");
      return null;
   }
   @Override
   public Uri insert(Uri uri, ContentValues values)
   {
      System.out.println("insert(Uri, ContentValues) called");
      return null;
   }
   @Override
   public boolean onCreate()
   {
      System.out.println("onCreate() called");
```

```
      return false;
   }
   @Override
   public Cursor query(Uri uri, String[] projection, String selection,
                       String[] selectionArgs, String sortOrder)
   {
      System.out.println("query(Uri, String[], String, String[], String)
called");
      return null;
   }
   @Override
   public int update(Uri uri, ContentValues values, String selection,
                     String[] selectionArgs)
   {
      System.out.println("update(Uri, ContentValues, String, String[]) called");
      return 0;
   }
}
```

Clients don't instantiate `SimpleContentProvider` and call these methods directly. Rather, they instantiate a subclass of the abstract `android.content.ContentResolver` class and call its methods (such as `Cursor query(Uri uri, String[] projection, String selection, String[] selectionArgs, String sortOrder)`).

> **NOTE:** A `ContentResolver` instance can talk to any content provider; it cooperates with the provider to manage any interprocess communication that's involved.

Resources

Resources are images, strings, and other entities that support apps. Developers store them in external files to maintain them independently of code. Also, separating resources from the code that relies upon them makes it easier to adapt an app to run on multiple devices and support multiple *locales* (geographical, political, or cultural regions).

Android supports the following resource types:

- *Animation*: A simulation of movement specified as a *property animation* (an animation in which an object's property value(s) [for example, background color or alpha value] is/are modified over a period of time) or a *view animation* (an animation in which a series of transformations [for example, rotation or fading] are performed on a single image—a *tween animation*—or an animation in which images are successively shown—a *frame animation*)
- *Color State List*: A list of colors mapped to widget states (such as a button's pressed, focused, and neither pressed nor focused states)
- *Drawable*: A graphic to be drawn on the screen and retrieved via an appropriate API (a bitmap, for example)
- *Layout*: An arrangement for a screen's widgets (such as in a linear fashion)
- *Menu*: An app menu, such as *options menu* (an activity's primary collection of menu items) or *context menu* (a floating menu)
- *String*: A text item, an array of text items, or a pluralistic text item with optional styling and formatting
- *Style*: The format and look for a user interface, ranging from a single widget (such as a button) to an activity or app
- *Additional*: Boolean value, color value, dimension value, unique identifier, integer value, integer array, typed array, and raw/asset

> **NOTE:** A *style* is a collection of properties that specify the look and format for a view or a window. A *theme* is a style applied to an entire app or activity rather than an individual view.

Classifying Resources

Android classifies resources as default, alternative, or platform. Resources in the first two categories are supplied by the developer and organized as files in subdirectories of the app project's res directory. These files must not be placed directly in res. Doing so will result in an error when the app is being built.

Default Resources

Default resources are used when no alternative resources exist that match the current device configuration. For example, the same layout resource is used to arrange widgets on a device with a small screen and on a device with a large screen. A second example is strings of English text that are used regardless of the device's locale setting.

Default resources are stored in the following subdirectories of the res directory:

- anim stores XML files that define tween animations.
- animator stores XML files that define property animations. Property animation XML files can be saved in the anim directory as well. However, animator is preferred for property animations to distinguish between both types.
- color stores XML files that define state lists of colors.
- drawable stores either bitmap files (.png, .9.png, .jpg, .gif) or XML files that are compiled into bitmap files, *nine-patches* (resizable bitmaps), state lists, shapes, frame animation drawables, or other drawables.
- layout stores XML files that define user interface layouts.
- menu stores XML files that define different kinds of app menus (such as a context menu).
- raw stores arbitrary files in their raw form where the original file names no longer exist. To preserve their file names (and file hierarchy), save these files in the assets directory, which is at the same level as res.

- `values` stores XML files that define simple values such as strings, integers, or colors. Each file in this directory can define multiple resources, whereas XML files in other directories define single resources. Because each resource is defined with its own XML element, you can name these files whatever you want and place different resource types in the same file. However, it's clearer to place unique resource types in different files and adopt the following file name conventions: `arrays.xml` for resource arrays (that is, typed arrays), `colors.xml` for color values, `dimens.xml` for dimension values, `strings.xml` for string values, and `styles.xml` for styles.
- `xml` stores arbitrary XML files, including various configuration files, such as a *searchable configuration* (an XML-based configuration file that supports search with assistance from Android, in which search queries are delivered to an activity and search suggestions are provided).

Resources stored in these subdirectories define an app's default design and content. They are used by the current Android device unless overridden by alternative resources.

Alternative Resources

Alternative resources are resources that are used with a specific device configuration. For example, a layout resource that's optimal for landscape mode replaces the default portrait-oriented layout resource when the device is switched to landscape mode. A second example is strings of French text replacing default English-oriented strings when the device's locale setting is changed to French.

As with default resources, alternative resources are stored in specific subdirectories of the `res` directory. The name of each alternative subdirectory begins with the name of a default resource subdirectory, then continues with a hyphen followed by a configuration qualifier name. For example, `layout-land` identifies the subdirectory for storing landscape-oriented layout files.

The following list identifies a few of the configuration qualifier names that can be appended to default resource subdirectory names:

- *Language and region*: The language is defined by a two-letter "ISO 639-1" (`http://en.wikipedia.org/wiki/ISO_639-1`) language code and is optionally followed by a two-letter "ISO 3166-1-alpha-2" (`http://en.wikipedia.org/wiki/ISO_3166-1_alpha-2`) region code preceded by a lowercase letter `r`. These codes are not case-sensitive. The prefix `r` is used to distinguish the region portion; you cannot specify a region without a language. Examples include `en`, `fr`, `en-rUS`, `en-rGB`, `fr_rFR`, and `fr_rCA`.
- *Platform version*: The API level supported by the device is indicated by a numeric code beginning with a lowercase letter v. Examples include `v1` for API Level 1 (devices with Android 1.0 or higher), and `v4` for API Level 4 (devices with Android 1.6 or higher).
- *Screen orientation*: Either `port` for portrait (vertical) orientation or `land` for landscape (horizontal) orientation is specified.
- *Screen pixel density*: Specify `ldpi` for low-density screens (approximately 120 dpi [dots per inch]), `mdpi` for medium-density (on traditional HVGA) screens (approximately 160 dpi), `hdpi` for high-density screens (approximately 240 dpi), `xhdpi` for extra high-density screens (approximately 320 dpi), `nodpi` for bitmap resources that are not to be scaled to match the device's screen pixel density, or `tvdpi` for screens somewhere between `mdpi` and `hdpi` (approximately 213 dpi). The `xhdpi` qualifier was added in API Level 8 and the `tvdpi` qualifier was added in API Level 13.
- *Screen size*: Specify `small` for screens whose sizes are similar to the low-density QVGA screen (minimum layout size is 320x426 dp [density-independent pixel] units), `normal` for screens whose sizes are similar to the medium-density HVGA screen (minimum layout size is approximately 320x476 dp units), `large` for screens whose sizes are similar to the medium-density VGA screen (minimum layout size is approximately 480x640 dp units), and `xlarge` for screens whose sizes are much larger than the traditional medium-density HVGA screen (minimum layout size is approximately 720x960 dp units). Extra-large screen devices are most likely tablet-oriented devices. Support for screen-size configuration qualifiers was added in API Level 4. Support for the `xlarge` qualifier was not added until API Level 9.

SUPPORTING A WIDE VARIETY OF SCREENS

Android has been designed to support screens of various orientations, sizes, and densities, as is explained in Google's "Supporting Multiple Screens" document at `http://developer.android.com/guide/practices/screens_support.html`. Also, Google discusses Android's various units of measurement in its document on the dimension resource at `http://developer.android.com/guide/topics/resources/more-resources.html#Dimension`. Because this chapter and Appendix D refer to density-independent pixels and scale-independent pixels, these two units of measurement are defined below.

A *density-independent pixel (dip* or *dp)* is an abstract unit (that is, a virtual pixel) that is based on the physical density of the screen. This unit is relative to a 160 dpi screen, so one dp is one pixel on a 160 dpi screen. The ratio of dp-to-pixel will change with the screen density but not necessarily in direct proportion. Use this unit when defining layout to express layout dimensions or position in a density-independent way. For example, specify `android:padding="5dip"` (or `android:padding="5dp"`) instead of `android:padding="5px"` in your XML file to state that you want five density-independent pixels (instead of five density-dependent pixels) of padding around a view.

A *scale-independent pixel* (*sip* or *sp*) is similar to a dp but is scaled by the user's font size preference. Use this unit when specifying font sizes in your resources, so they will be adjusted for both the screen density and the user's preference. For example, you would specify `android:textSize="15sp"` instead of `android:textSize="15px"` in your XML file to set the size of a `<TextView>` element based on the user's font size.

You can often append multiple qualifiers to a default resource subdirectory name, provided that you place a hyphen between each qualifier and its predecessor. For example, `drawable-fr-port` refers to an alternative drawable resource to be used only when the device is set to the French locale and portrait orientation.

Android requires you to adhere to the following rules when using configuration qualifier names:

- When specifying multiple configuration qualifier names, they must be specified in the order shown in Table 2 of Google's "Providing Resources" (`http://developer.android.com/guide/topics/resources/providing-resources.html`) document; otherwise, the associated resources will be ignored. For example, `drawable-land-mdpi` is correct, whereas `drawable-mdpi-land` is incorrect.

- You cannot nest alternative resources. For example, you cannot specify `res/drawable/drawable-fr`. Instead, you would specify `res/drawable-fr`.
- You cannot specify multiple values for a qualifier type. For example, you cannot specify a `drawable-rCA-rFR` directory to store the same drawable files for Canada and France. Instead, you must create separate `drawable-rCA` and `drawable-rFR` directories so that each contains the appropriate files or aliases (which are discussed later in this chapter).

You must supply your app's default and alternative resources. You can also leverage the various platform resources that Google provides for use in your apps.

Platform Resources

Google has standardized several resources (for example, styles, themes, and layouts) that it makes available for your own use. These *platform resources* are accessible via the `android` package's `R` class and its various subclasses (e.g., `R.anim` and `R.layout`). I'll have more to say about platform resources later in this chapter.

Accessing Resources

After creating your app's default and alternative resources (whose file names follow the aforementioned conventions and which are stored in appropriately named subdirectories of `res`), you will want to access them from code and/or other XML files. You might also want to access platform resources.

Code-Based Access

The Android Asset Packager Tool (`aapt`) generates a file named `R.java` under the app project's package hierarchy within the project's `gen` directory. This Java source file stores resource IDs (as names and integer values) for all resources organized under the `res` directory. It reveals that resource ID names consist of the following two parts:

- *Resource type*: Each resource belongs to a type such as drawable, string, and layout. The type is id for XML-based resources that are defined via elements whose android:id attributes identify them via the @+id/*resource name* syntax. For example, <TextView android:id="@+id/msg" /> defines the XML <TextView> element msg.
- *Resource name*: Each resource has a name, which is a file name (excluding the extension), the value of an XML file's android:name attribute when the resource is a simple value (such as a string), or the resource name when the resource is defined according to the @+id/*resource name* syntax.

Given this information, you can access a resource from your code by typically adhering to the following syntax:

```
R.resource type.resource name
```

R identifies the class described by R.java, and *resource type* and *resource name* provide the resource's type and name. A period character separates each component. For example, R.string.cancel refers to the cancel resource name member of the string resource type in class R.

Various Android API methods require a resource ID argument. For example, the android.content.res.Resources class (whose instance is returned by invoking the Context class's Resources getResources() method) provides methods for returning an app's resources. These methods require specific resource IDs as arguments, as demonstrated below:

```
Resources res = getContext();
Drawable flag = res.getDrawable(R.drawable.canada);
String country = res.getString(R.string.canada);
```

The Drawable getDrawable(int id) method returns an android.graphics.drawable.Drawable object for the drawable resource identified by R.drawable.canada (probably a bitmap file stored in the res/drawable directory). Method String getString(int id) returns the string resource identified by R.string.canada, which is usually an entry in a strings.xml file located in the res/values directory.

Suppose you've created English and French strings.xml files with canada entries in res/values and res/values-fr. When the device's language is set to English, Android obtains R.string.canada's value from res/values/strings.xml. When the language is set to French, Android obtains the value from res/values-fr/strings.xml. If Android can't find canada in res/values-fr/strings.xml, it defaults to res/values/strings.xml.

> **NOTE:** You can access a raw resource by invoking one of the `Resources` class's `openRawResource()` methods with a resource ID specified as `R.raw.`*`file name`*, where *`file name`* corresponds to the original file name. Each of these methods returns a `java.io.InputStream` object from which you can read the resource. For any resource files saved in the `assets` directory, you need to use `android.content.res.AssetManager` to access them. Files stored in `assets` are not given resource IDs.

XML-Based Access

You can refer to existing resources from various XML element attributes. For example, you will often refer to string and image (that is, drawable) resources to supply the text and images for various widgets that you specify in your layout files. When referring to another resource from an XML context, you typically adhere to the following syntax:

```
@resource type/resource name
```

`@` signifies a reference to an existing resource. The forward slash-separated *`resource type`* and *`resource name`* have the same meaning as previously specified. For example, `@string/cancel` refers to the `cancel` resource name member of the `string` resource type, which is often located in a `strings.xml` file stored in the `res/values` directory.

You might want to use the same resource for multiple device configurations and you don't want to provide that resource as a default resource. Instead of storing the resource in multiple alternative resource directories, you can (in certain cases) create an alternative resource as an *alias* for the resource saved in your default resource directory.

For example, you need a unique version of your app icon (stored in `icon.png`) for different locales, but the English-Canadian and French-Canadian locales need to use the same version. Instead of copying the same image file into `res/drawable-en-rCA` and `res/drawable-fr-rCA` directories, you could do the following:

1. Store the image used for both locales in `icon_ca.png` (don't use `icon.png`) and place this file in the `res/drawable` directory.

2. Create an icon.xml file whose <bitmap> element refers to icon_ca.png (such as <bitmap xmlns:android="http://schemas.android.com/apk/res/android" android:src="@drawable/icon_ca" />) and store it in res/drawable-en-rCA and in res/drawable-fr-rCA. When icon.xml is saved in an alternative resource directory such as res/drawable-en-rCA, Android compiles it into a resource that can be referenced from code via R.drawable.icon and from XML via @drawable/icon. However, it is actually an alias for R.drawable.icon_ca (saved in res/drawable) or @drawable/icon_ca.

Platform-Based Access

A platform resource is accessed in code via its fully qualified package name, as in android.R.layout.simple_list_item_1 (a layout resource for items presented via an android.widget.ListView instance's list). It's accessed in XML via package name android, as in @android:color/white (the XML equivalent of android.R.color.white).

Resources and the User Interface

You previously learned how to create an activity's user interface by instantiating widgets. However, it's often better to create the user interface by declaring it in one or more XML files, to simplify maintenance and to more easily adapt the user interface to multiple devices and locales.

The following onCreate(Bundle) method uses the resource approach to create a user interface involving edittext and button widgets:

```
@Override
public void onCreate(Bundle savedInstanceState)
{
    super.onCreate(savedInstanceState);
    setContentView(R.layout.main);
}
```

After calling its superclass counterpart, onCreate(Bundle) executes setContentView(R.layout.main), passing resource ID R.layout.main to Activity's void setContentView(int layoutResID) method.

setContentView(int) *inflates* (converts from XML to a view hierarchy) the layout resource identified by R.layout.main into a hierarchy of view objects that describe the activity's user interface. This resource is stored in a file named main.xml that is located in the res/layout directory for portrait orientation or the res/layout-land directory for landscape orientation.

main.xml declaratively describes the edittext and button widgets, as well as their linear layout container. The following code fragment reveals the contents of this file (without the <?xml version="1.0" encoding="utf-8"?> XML prolog):

```
<LinearLayout xmlns:android="http://schemas.android.com/apk/res/android"
              android:layout_width="fill_parent"
              android:layout_height="fill_parent">
  <EditText android:id="@+id/et"
            android:ems="10"
            android:layout_width="wrap_content"
            android:layout_height="wrap_content"/>
  <Button android:id="@+id/btnOK"
          android:onClick="doClickOk"
          android:layout_width="wrap_content"
          android:layout_height="wrap_content"
          android:text="@string/ok"/>
</LinearLayout>
```

The <LinearLayout> element sandwiches <EditText> and <Button> elements, which are child elements of <LinearLayout>. They will be inflated along with <LinearLayout>.

Each of <LinearLayout>'s android:layout_width and android:layout_height attributes are assigned fill_parent so that this container will occupy the activity's entire screen.

> **NOTE:** The fill_parent attribute value means that the view wants to be as big as its parent (minus padding). Essentially, the view expands to take up as much space as is available within the container where the view has been placed. Starting, with API Level 8, fill_parent has been deprecated in favor of match_parent, which means the same thing.

The <EditText> element provides an android:ems element that corresponds to the setEms(int) method described earlier in the chapter. This element is assigned 10 ems. <EditText> also provides android:layout_width and android:layout_height attributes that are assigned wrap_content to ensure that this widget is shown at its preferred size.

> **NOTE:** The wrap_content attribute means that the view expands only as far as necessary to contain its content. This is analogous to stating that the view wants to be displayed at its *preferred (natural) size*. The preferred size is just large enough to display the view according to its preferences (such as 10 ems for the edittext widget).

The <Button> element offers similar android:layout_width and android:layout_height attributes that ensure this widget appears at its preferred size. Its android:text attribute refers to a string resource that supplies the button's label text (<string name="ok">OK</string>). This resource is most likely declared in a strings.xml file.

> **TIP:** Avoid hard-coding literal strings in your code and layout resources, and store them instead as separate resource entries in strings.xml. Doing so makes it easier to localize the app.

<Button> also provides an onClick attribute that identifies doClickOk, a void method with a solitary parameter of type View. This method is invoked when the button is clicked. (You don't have to instantiate a listener class and register the instance with the button.) The following code fragment presents void doClickOk(View view):

```
public void doClickOk(View view)
{
   EditText et = (EditText) findViewById(R.id.et);
   Toast.makeText(Test.this, et.getText(),
                  Toast.LENGTH_SHORT).show();
}
```

doClickOk(View) executes findViewById(R.id.et), passing edittext resource ID R.id.et to Activity's View findViewById(int id) method. findViewById(int) inflates the resource to an EditText object, which is assigned to variable et. (The (EditText) cast is required.)

> **NOTE:** findViewById(int) returns null when it cannot find the resource.

Lastly, doClickOk(View) displays the edittext content via a toast.

> **CAUTION:** The `setContentView(int)` method must be called at some point before `findViewById(int)`. If not, Android presents a message that the app has stopped. The reason for this message is that no layout resource has been installed, and therefore Android has no way to locate the XML-encoded edittext and button widgets.

Manifest

Android learns about an app's various components (and more) by examining the app's XML-structured manifest file, `AndroidManifest.xml`. For example, Listing 1-7 shows how this file might declare an activity component.

Listing 1-7. *A Manifest File Declaring an Activity*

```
<?xml version="1.0" encoding="utf-8"?>
<manifest xmlns:android="http://schemas.android.com/apk/res/android"
          package="com.example.project" android:versionCode="1"
          android:versionName="1.0">
   <application android:label="@string/app_name" android:icon="@drawable/icon">
      <activity android:name=".MyActivity" android:label="@string/app_name">
         <intent-filter>
            <action android:name="android.intent.action.MAIN" />
            <category android:name="android.intent.category.LAUNCHER" />
         </intent-filter>
      </activity>
   </application>
</manifest>
```

Listing 1-7 begins with the necessary `<?xml version="1.0" encoding="utf-8"?>` prolog, which identifies this file as an XML version 1.0 file, whose content is encoded according to the UTF-8 encoding standard.

Listing 1-7 next presents a `<manifest>` tag, which is this XML document's root element: `android` identifies the Android namespace, `package` identifies the app's Java package, and `versionCode`/`versionName` identify the version information.

Nested within `<manifest>` is `<application>`, which is the parent of app component tags. Its `android:icon` and `android:label` attributes refer to icon and label resources that Android devices display to represent the app.

> **NOTE:** The `android:label` attribute specifies the label shown in the list of apps when you select "Manage apps" from the app launcher screen's options menu (click

> the MENU button in the phone controls to access this menu, discussed later). This attribute also provides the default label for an `<activity>` element that doesn't provide an `android:label` attribute.

Nested within `<application>` is `<activity>`, which describes an activity component. This tag's `name` attribute identifies a class (`MyActivity`) that implements the activity. This name begins with a period character to imply that it's relative to `com.example.project`.

> **NOTE:** The period is not present when `AndroidManifest.xml` is created at the command line. However, this character is present when this file is created from within Eclipse (discussed in Recipe 1-10). Regardless, `MyActivity` is relative to `<manifest>`'s `package` value (`com.example.project`).

Nested within `<activity>` is `<intent-filter>`. This tag declares the capabilities of the component described by the enclosing tag. For example, it declares the capabilities of the activity component via its nested `<action>` and `<category>` tags:

- `<action>` identifies the action to perform via the string assigned to its `android:name` attribute. The `"android.intent.action.MAIN"` value signifies that the activity is to be started as the initial activity with no data input to the activity and no output returned from the activity. To launch an app, Android looks for an `<activity>` element with an `<intent-filter>` element whose `<action>` element's `android:name` attribute is set to `"android.intent.action.MAIN"`.
- `<category>` provides additional information about the kind of component that should handle the intent via the string assigned to its `android:name` attribute. The `"android.intent.category.LAUNCHER"` value signifies that the activity can serve as the app's initial activity and that it will appear on the app launcher screen in sorted order by its label.

Other components are similarly declared: services via `<service>` tags, broadcast receivers via `<receiver>` tags, and content providers via `<provider>` tags. Android doesn't create components not declared in the manifest.

> **NOTE:** You do not need to declare in the manifest broadcast receivers that are created at runtime.

The manifest may also contain `<uses-permission>` tags to identify permissions that the app needs. For example, an app that needs to use the camera would specify the following tag: `<uses-permission android:name="android.permission.CAMERA" />`.

> **NOTE:** `<uses-permission>` tags are nested within `<manifest>` tags— they appear at the same level as the `<application>` tag.

At app install time, permissions requested by the app (via `<uses-permission>`) are granted to it by Android's package installer, based upon checks against the digital signatures of the apps declaring those permissions and/or interaction with the user.

No checks with the user are done while an app is running. It was granted a specific permission when installed and can use that feature as desired, or the permission was not granted and any attempt to use the feature will fail without prompting the user.

> **NOTE:** `AndroidManifest.xml` provides additional information, such as naming any libraries that the app needs to be linked against (besides the default Android library), and identifying all app-enforced permissions (via `<permission>` tags) to other apps, such as controlling who can start the app's activities.

Additional Manifest Examples

Listing 1-8 presents an `AndroidManifest.xml` file that identifies Listing 1-1's `SimpleActivity` class and the subsequently mentioned `SimpleActivity2` class as the `SimpleActivity` app's two components—the ellipsis refers to content not relevant to this discussion.

Listing 1-8. *`SimpleActivity`'s Manifest File*

```
<?xml version="1.0" encoding="utf-8"?>
<manifest xmlns:android="http://schemas.android.com/apk/res/android"
          package="com.example.project" ...>
```

```
   <application ...>
      <activity android:name=".SimpleActivity" ...>
         <intent-filter ...>
            <action android:name="android.intent.action.MAIN" />
            <category android:name="android.intent.category.LAUNCHER" />
         </intent-filter>
      </activity>
      <activity android:name=".SimpleActivity2" ...>
          <intent-filter ...>
              <action android:name="android.intent.action.VIEW" />
              <data android:mimeType="image/jpeg" />
              <category android:name="android.intent.category.DEFAULT" />
          </intent-filter>
      </activity>
      ...
   </application>
</manifest>
```

Listing 1-8 reveals that each of `SimpleActivity` and `SimpleActivity2` is associated with an intent filter via an `<intent-filter>` tag that's nested within `<activity>`. `SimpleActivity2`'s `<intent-filter>` tag helps Android determine that this activity is to be launched when the `Intent` object's values match the following tag values:

- `<action>`'s `android:name` attribute is assigned `"android.intent.action.VIEW"`
- `<data>`'s `android:mimeType` attribute is assigned the `"image/jpeg"` MIME type—additional attributes (such as `android:path`) would typically be present to locate the data to be viewed.
- `<category>`'s `android:name` attribute is assigned `"android.intent.category.DEFAULT"` to allow the activity to be launched without explicitly specifying its component.

Given this information, the following example shows you how to start `SimpleActivity2` implicitly:

```
Intent intent = new Intent();
intent.setAction("android.intent.action.VIEW");
intent.setType("image/jpeg");
intent.addCategory("android.intent.category.DEFAULT");
SimpleActivity.this.startActivity(intent);
```

The first four lines create an `Intent` object describing an implicit intent. Values passed to `Intent`'s `Intent setAction(String action)`, `Intent setType(String type)`, and `Intent addCategory(String category)` methods specify the intent's action, MIME type, and category. They help Android identify SimpleActivity2 as the activity to be launched.

Listing 1-2 presented a SimpleService class. You would expand Listing 1-8 with the following entry so that you could access this class from your app:

```
<service android:name=".SimpleService">
</service>
```

Listing 1-5 presented a SimpleBroadcastReceiver class. You would expand Listing 1-8 with the following entry unless you will create the broadcast receiver at runtime:

```
<receiver android:name=".SimpleBroadcastReceiver">
</receiver>
```

Finally, Listing 1-6 presented a SimpleContentProvider class. You would expand Listing 1-8 with the following entry so that you could access this class from your app:

```
<provider android:name=".SimpleContentProvider">
</provider>
```

App Package

Android apps are written in Java. The compiled Java code for an app's components is further transformed into Dalvik's DEX format. The resulting code files along with any other required data and resources are subsequently bundled into an *App PacKage (APK)*, a zip file identified by the .apk suffix.

An APK is not an app but is used to distribute the app and install it on a mobile device. It's not an app because its components may reuse another APK's components, and (in this situation) not all of the app would reside in a single APK. However, it's common to refer to an APK as representing a single app.

An APK must be signed with a certificate (which identifies the app's author) whose private key is held by its developer. The certificate doesn't need to be signed by a certificate authority. Instead, Android allows APKs to be signed with self-signed certificates, which is typical. (APK signing is discussed in Recipe 1-8.)

APK FILES, USER IDS, AND SECURITY

Each APK installed on an Android device is given its own unique Linux user ID, and this user ID remains unchanged for as long as the APK resides on that device. Because security enforcement occurs at the process level, the code contained in any two APKs cannot normally run in the same process, because each APK's code needs to run as a different Linux user. However, you can have the code in both APKs run in the same process by assigning the same name of a user ID to the `<manifest>` tag's `sharedUserId` attribute in each APK's `AndroidManifest.xml` file. When you make these assignments, you tell Android that the two packages are to be treated as being the same app, with the same user ID and file permissions. In order to retain security, only two APKs signed with the same signature (and requesting the same `sharedUserId` value in their manifests) will be given the same user ID.

Installing the Android SDK

Problem

You've read the previous introduction to Android and are eager to develop your first Android app. However, you must install the Android SDK before you can develop apps.

Solution

Google provides the latest release of an Android SDK distribution file for each of the Windows, Intel-based Mac OS X, and i386-based Linux operating systems. Download and unarchive the appropriate file for your platform and move its unarchived home directory to a convenient location. You might also want to update your PATH environment variable so that you can access the SDK's command-line tools from anywhere in your filesystem.

Before downloading and installing this file, you must be aware of SDK requirements. You cannot use the SDK when your development platform doesn't meet these requirements.

The Android SDK supports the following operating systems:

- Windows XP (32-bit), Vista (32- or 64-bit), or Windows 7 (32- or 64-bit)
- Mac OS X 10.5.8 or later (x86 only)
- Linux (tested on Ubuntu Linux, Lucid Lynx). GNU C Library (`glibc`) 2.7 or later is required. On Ubuntu Linux, version 8.04 or later is required. 64-bit distributions must be able to run 32-bit applications. To learn how to add support for 32-bit applications, see the Ubuntu Linux installation notes at `http://developer.android.com/sdk/installing/index.html#Troubleshooting`.

You'll quickly discover that the Android SDK is organized into various separately downloadable components, which are known as *packages*. You will need to ensure that you have enough disk storage space to accommodate the various packages that you want to install. Plan for around 2 gigabytes of free storage. This figure takes into account the Android API documentation and multiple *Android platforms* (also known as Android software stacks).

Finally, you should ensure that the following additional software is installed:

- *JDK 6 or JDK 7*: You need to install one of these Java Development Kits (JDKs) to compile Java code. It's not sufficient to have only a Java Runtime Environment (JRE) installed. (JDK 7 is somewhat problematic when creating an app in release mode. Recipe 1-8 presents this problem and its solution.)
- *Apache Ant*: You need to install Ant version 1.8 or later so that you can build Android projects.

> **NOTE:** If a JDK is already installed on your development platform, take a moment to ensure that it meets the previously listed version requirement (6 or 7). Some Linux distributions may include JDK 1.4, which is not supported for Android development. Also, GNU Compiler for Java is not supported.

How It Works

Point your browser to `http://developer.android.com/sdk/index.html` and download one of the `android-sdk_r20-windows.zip` (Windows), `android-sdk_r20-macosx.zip` (Mac OS X), or `android-sdk_r20-linux.tgz` (Linux) distribution archives for Release 20 of the Android SDK. (Release 20 is the latest release at the time of writing.)

> **NOTE:** Windows developers have the option of downloading and running `installer_r20-windows.exe`. This tool automates most of the installation process.

For example, if you run Windows (the assumed platform in this chapter), you might choose to download `android-sdk_r20-windows.zip`. After unarchiving this file, move the unarchived `android-sdk-windows` home directory to a convenient location in your filesystem; for example, you might move the unarchived `C:\unzipped\android-sdk_r20-windows\android-sdk-windows` home directory to the root directory on your C: drive, resulting in `C:\android-sdk-windows`.

> **NOTE:** It is recommended that you rename `android-sdk-windows` to `android` to avoid a potential emulator crash when attempting to run an app from within Eclipse. Although this problem may no longer exist, it has been encountered in the past, and it most likely results from the hyphen (-) between `android` and `sdk`, and between `sdk` and `windows`.
>
> To complete the installation, add the `tools` subdirectory to your PATH environment variable so that you can access the SDK's command-line tools from anywhere in your filesystem.

A subsequent examination of `android-sdk-windows` (or `android`) shows that this home directory contains the following subdirectories and files:

- *add-ons*: This initially empty directory stores *add-ons* (additional SDKs beyond the core platform that apps can target) from Google and other vendors; for example, the Google APIs add-on is stored here.
- *platforms*: This initially empty directory stores Android platforms in separate subdirectories. For example, Android 4.1 would be stored in one `platforms` subdirectory, whereas Android 2.3.4 would be stored in another `platforms` subdirectory.
- *tools*: This directory contains a set of platform-independent development tools, such as the emulator. The tools in this directory, known as *basic tools*, may be updated at any time and are independent of Android platform releases.
- *AVD Manager.exe*: This tool is used to manage *Android Virtual Devices (AVDs)* (device configurations that are run with the Android emulator).
- *SDK Manager.exe*: This tool is used to manage SDK packages and runs `AVD Manager` in response to a menu selection.
- *SDK Readme.txt*: This text file welcomes you to the Android SDK and tells you that, in order to start developing apps, you need to use `SDK Manager` to install platform tools and at least one Android platform.

The `tools` directory contains various useful basic tools, including the following:

- *android*: Creates and updates Android projects; updates the Android SDK with new Android platforms and more; and creates, deletes, and views AVDs.
- *emulator*: Runs a full Android software stack down to the kernel level; includes a set of preinstalled apps (such as Browser) that you can access.
- *hierarchyviewer*: Provides a visual representation of a layout's view hierarchy (the Layout View) and a magnified inspector of the display (the Pixel Perfect View) so that you can debug and optimize your activity screens.
- *sqlite3*: Manages SQLite databases created by Android apps.
- *zipalign*: Performs archive alignment optimization on APK files.

Appendix B describes all of the SDK's basic tools.

Installing an Android Platform

Problem

Installing the Android SDK is insufficient for developing Android apps; you must also install at least one Android platform.

Solution

Use the SDK Manager tool to install an Android platform. If SDK Manager doesn't display its *Android SDK Manager* dialog box, you probably need to create a JAVA_HOME environment variable that points to your JDK's home directory (for example, set JAVA_HOME=C:\Program Files\Java\jdk1.7.0_04) and try again.

Alternatively, you can use the android tool to install an Android platform. If android shows "Failed to convert path to a short DOS path: C:\Windows\system32\java.exe", locate a file named find_java.bat (see C:\android\tools\lib\find_java.bat) and remove -s from each of the following lines:

```
for /f %%a in ('%~dps0\find_java.exe -s') do set java_exe=%%a
for /f %%a in ('%~dps0\find_java.exe -s -w') do set javaw_exe=%%a
```

How It Works

Run SDK Manager or android. Either tool presents the *Android SDK Manager* dialog box that is shown in Figure 1-7.

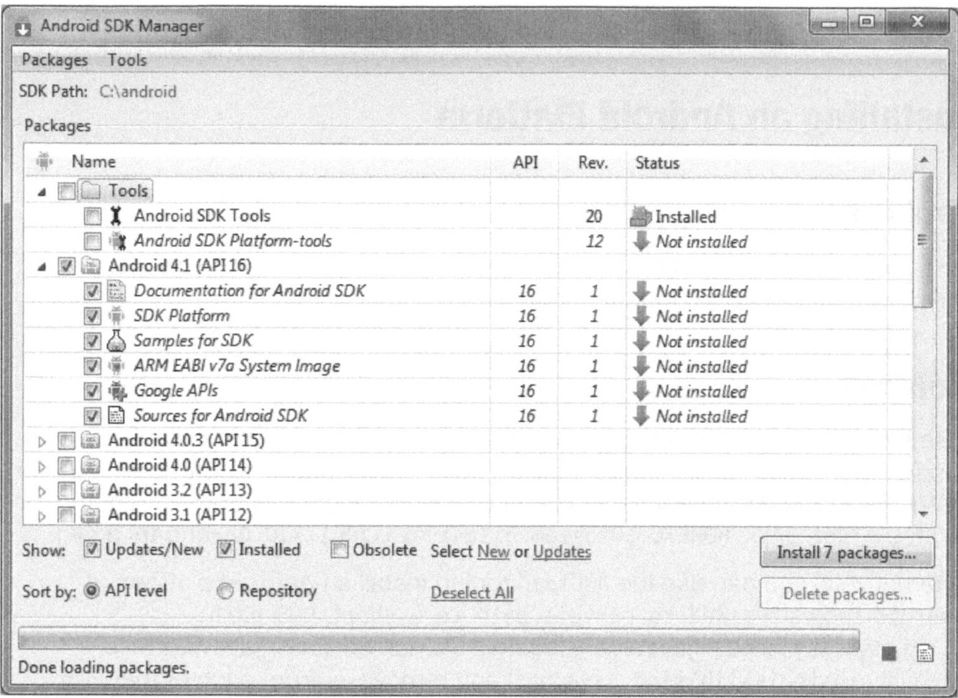

Figure 1-7. *Use this dialog box to install, update, and remove Android packages and to access the AVD Manager.*

Android SDK Manager presents a menubar and a content area. The menubar presents Packages and Tools menus:

- *Packages*: Use this menu to display a combination of updates/new packages, installed packages, and obsolete packages; to show archive details (or not); to sort packages by API level or repository; and to reload the list of packages shown in the content area.
- *Tools*: Use this menu to manage AVDs and add-on sites, to specify the proxy server and other options, and to display an *About* dialog box.

The content area shows you the path to the SDK, a table of information on packages, check boxes for choosing which packages to display, radio buttons for sorting packages by API level or repository, buttons for installing and deleting packages, and a progress bar that shows the progress of a scan of repositories for package information.

The Packages table classifies packages as tools, specific Android platforms, and extras. Each of these categories is associated with a check box that, when checked, selects all of the items in the category. Individual items can be deselected by unchecking their corresponding check boxes.

Tools are classified as SDK tools and SDK platform tools:

- *SDK tools* are the basic tools that are included in the SDK distribution file and that are stored in the `tools` directory. This fact is borne out by the Installed message in the status column for the Android SDK Tools item.
- *SDK platform tools* are platform-dependent tools for developing apps. These tools support the latest features of the Android platform and are typically updated only when a new platform becomes available. They are always backward-compatible with older platforms, but you must make sure that you have the latest version of these tools when you install a new platform. If you don't check the Android SDK Platform tools item (which is not checked by default), the platform tools will be installed automatically.

The only platform that you need to install for this book is Android 4.1 (Level 16). This category and all of its items are checked, so leave them as is. As well as this platform, you will install the documentation, samples, ARM *system image* (processor architecture emulation; x86 is another example, but is not supported for Android 4.1 at the time of writing), Google APIs, and source code.

Finally, you can install *extras*, which are external libraries or tools that can be included or used when building an app. For example, the Google USB Driver item is already checked in the Extras section. However, you only need to install this component when developing on a Windows platform and testing your apps on an actual Android device.

Click the Install 7 packages button (the number will differ should you choose to install more or fewer packages). You'll encounter the *Choose Packages to Install* dialog box shown in Figure 1-8.

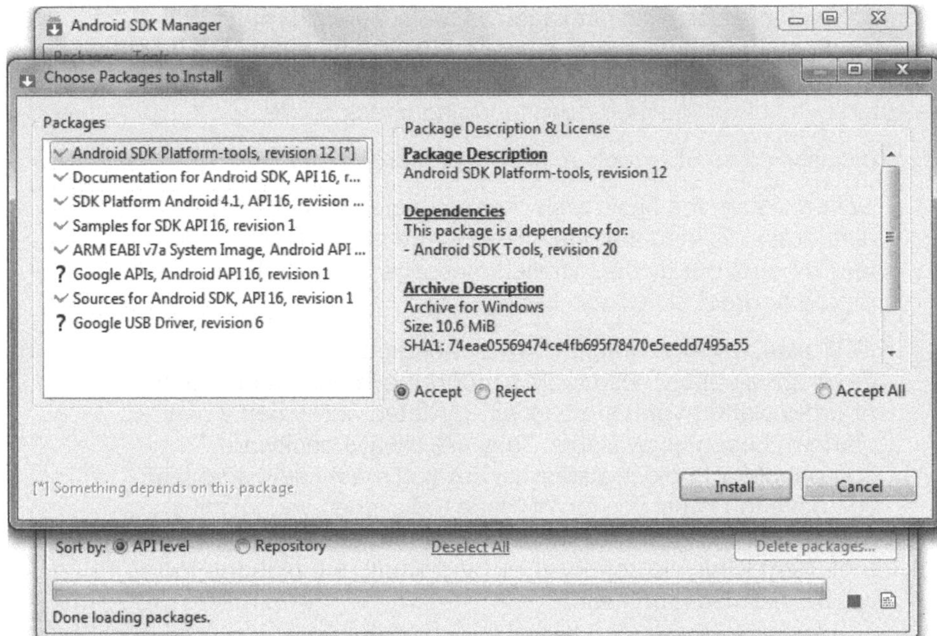

Figure 1-8. *The Packages list identifies those packages that can be installed.*

The *Choose Packages to Install* dialog box shows a Packages list that identifies those packages that can be installed. It displays green checkmarks beside packages that have been accepted for installation, and it displays question marks beside those packages that have not yet been selected.

> **NOTE:** Although Google APIs and Google USB Driver were initially selected, they are indicated as not having been selected. (Perhaps this is an example of a bug where information is not being carried forward.) You will need to highlight and accept these packages if you still want them.

For the highlighted package, Package Description & License presents a package description, a list of other packages that are dependent on this package being installed, information on the archive that houses the package, and additional information. Click the Accept or Reject radio button to accept or reject the package.

NOTE: A red X appears beside the package name in the Packages list when you reject the package. Click the Accept All radio button to accept all packages.

In some cases, an SDK component may require a specific minimum revision of another component or SDK tool. In addition to Package Description & License documenting these dependencies, the development tools will notify you with debug warnings when there is a dependency that you need to address.

Click the Install button to begin installation. Android proceeds to download and install the chosen packages, and you will also see the *Android SDK Manager Log* dialog box, which presents messages that show the state of the installation. This dialog box appears in Figure 1-9.

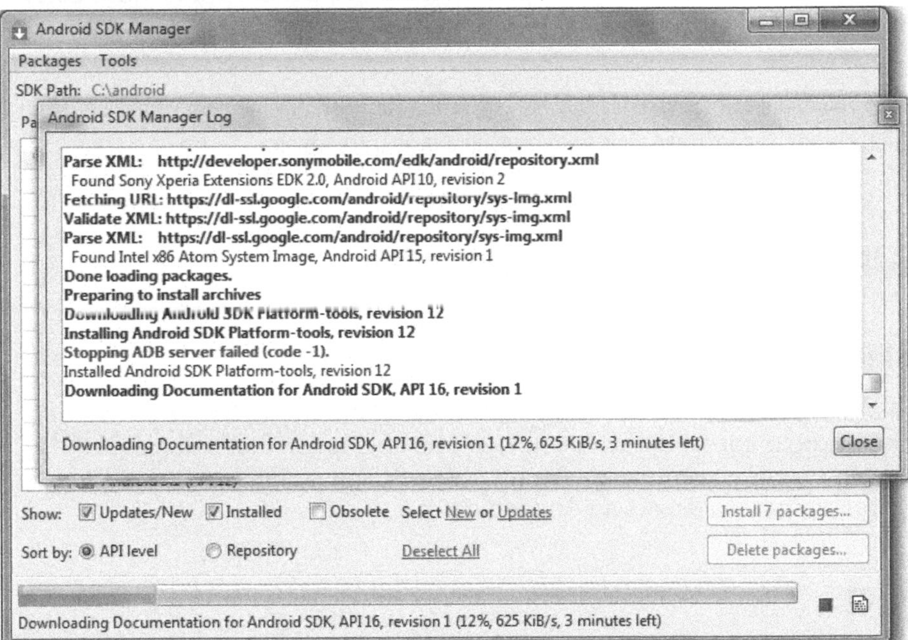

Figure 1-9. *The log window reveals the progress of downloading and installing each selected package archive.*

Consider Figure 1-9's "Stopping ADB server failed (code -1)." message. ADB stands for *Android Debug Bridge*, which is a tool consisting of client and server programs that let you control and interface with your Android device. This message appears because the ADB server isn't presently running (and it doesn't need to run at this point).

Upon completion, you should observe a "Done loading packages" message at the bottom of the *Android SDK Manager Log* and *Android SDK Manager* dialog boxes. Click the Close button on the former dialog box; the Status column in the Packages table on the latter dialog box will tell you which packages have been installed.

You should also observe several new subdirectories of the home directory, including the following:

- `platform-tools` (in `android`)
- `android-16` (in `android/platforms`)

`platform-tools` contains the latest platform tools—Appendix B describes all of these tools. `android-16` contains Android 4.1 specific files.

> **TIP:** You might want to add `platform-tools` to your PATH environment variable so that you can access these tools from anywhere in your filesystem.

Creating an Android Virtual Device

Problem

After installing the Android SDK and an Android platform, you're ready to start creating Android apps. However, you won't be able to run those apps via the `emulator` tool until you create an *Android Virtual Device (AVD)*, a device configuration that represents an Android device.

Solution

Use the `AVD Manager` or `android` tool to create an AVD.

How It Works

Run `AVD Manager` (or select Manage AVDs from the *Android SDK Manager* dialog box's Tools menu). Figure 1-10 shows the *Android Virtual Device Manager* dialog box.

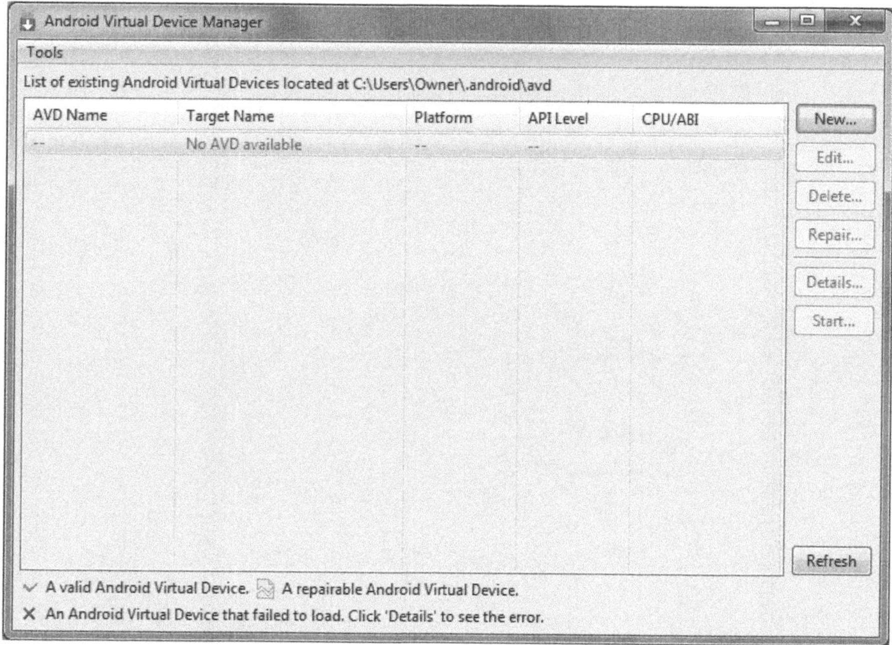

Figure 1-10. *No AVDs are initially installed.*

Click the New button. Figure 1-11 shows you the resulting *Create new Android Virtual Device (AVD)* dialog box.

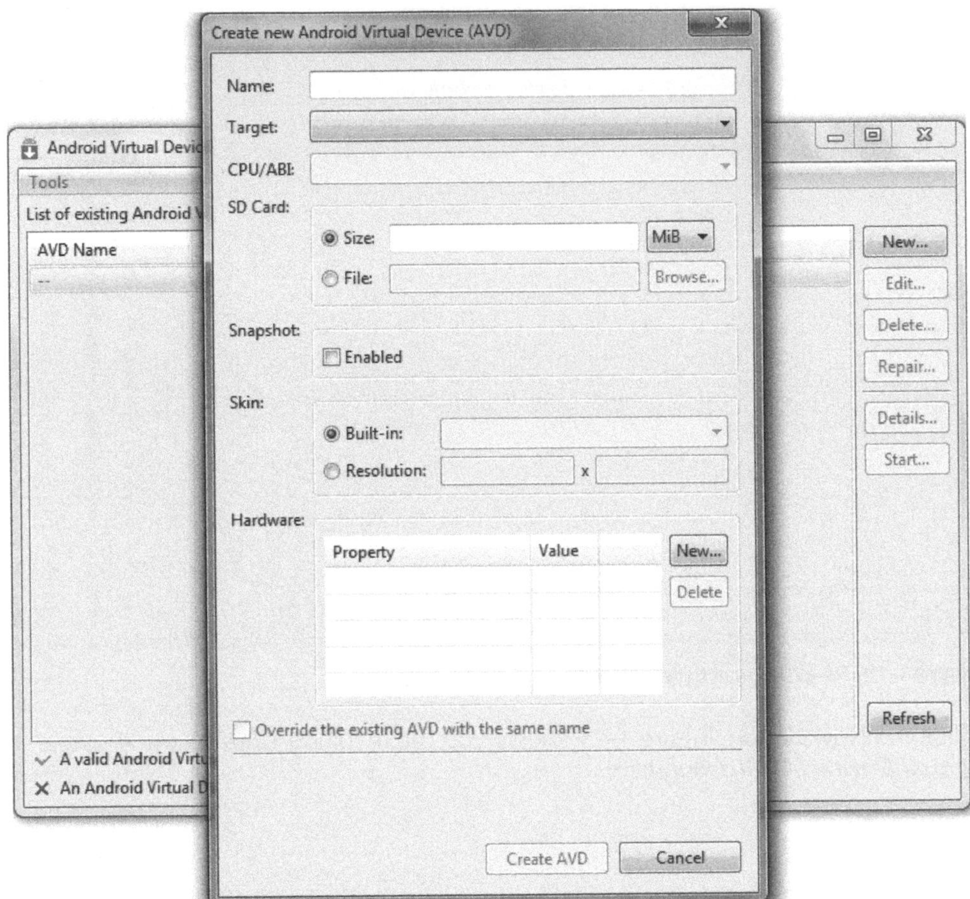

Figure 1-11. *An AVD consists of a name, a target Android platform, and more.*

Figure 1-11 reveals that an AVD has a name, targets a specific Android platform, targets a specific CPU/Application Binary Interface (such as ARM/armeabi-v7a), can emulate an SD card, provides a skin with a certain screen resolution, and has various hardware properties.

Enter `AVD1` for the name, select `Android 4.1 - API Level 16` for the target platform (this should be the only choice), and enter `100` into the Size field for the SD card.

> **NOTE:** You can check the Enabled check box in the Snapshot section to persist emulator state between emulator executions, to quickly start the emulator after the first startup.

Selecting `Android 4.1 - API Level 16` results in `Default (WVGA800)` being selected for the skin. Furthermore, the Hardware section's properties table presents an `Abstracted LCD density` property set to `240` dots per inch, a `Max VM application heap size` property set to `48` megabytes, and a `Device ram size` property set to `512` megabytes.

> **NOTE:** To emulate a tablet, choose `WXGA720`, `WXGA800`, or `WXGA800-7in` for the skin. The other values let you emulate a handset device, which is the focus of this chapter.

The New button to the right of the properties table lets you introduce additional hardware properties. For example, when using Android 4.0 or higher, you can choose to emulate a graphics processing unit (GPU), which results in an increased color depth and the absence of artifacts. Accomplish this task as follows:

1. Click New.
2. Select `GPU emulation` from the resulting dialog box and click Ok to close the dialog box.
3. Change the `GPU emulation` default value from no to yes.

After entering `AVD1`, selecting `Android 4.1 - API Level 16`, keeping the `WVGA800` handset skin default (or choosing another handset skin such as `HVGA`, which results in a smaller emulator window that fits nicely on the screen when the screen resolution is 1024x768, and which changes `Abstracted LCD density` to `160`), and introducing a `GPU emulation` property with a yes value, finish the AVD creation by clicking Create AVD. Figure 1-10's AVD pane now includes an `AVD1` entry.

> **CAUTION:** When creating an AVD that you plan to use to test compiled apps, make sure that the target platform has an API level greater than or equal to the API level required by your app. In other words, if you plan to test your app on the AVD, your

> app typically cannot access platform APIs that are more recent than those APIs supported by the AVD's API level.

Although it's easier to use `AVD Manager` to create an AVD, you can also accomplish this task via the `android` tool by specifying `android create avd -n` *`name`* `-t` *`targetID`* `[-option` *`value`*`]....` Given this syntax, *name* identifies the device configuration (such as `target_AVD`), *`targetID`* is an integer ID that identifies the targeted Android platform (you can obtain this integer ID by executing `android list targets`), and `[-option` *`value`*`]...` identifies a series of options (such as SD card size).

If you don't specify sufficient options, `android` prompts to create a custom hardware profile. Press the Enter key when you don't want a custom hardware profile and prefer to use the default hardware emulation options. For example, the `android create avd -n AVD1 -t 1` command line causes an AVD named `AVD1` to be created. This command line assumes that 1 corresponds to the Android 4.1 platform and prompts to create a custom hardware profile.

> **NOTE:** Each AVD functions as an independent device with its own private storage for user data, its own SD card, and so on. When you launch the `emulator` tool with an AVD, this tool loads user data and SD card data from the AVD's directory. By default, `emulator` stores user data, SD card data, and a cache in the directory assigned to the AVD.

Starting the AVD

Problem

You must start the emulator with the AVD so that you can install and run apps. You want to know how to accomplish this task.

Solution

Use the `AVD Manager` tool to start the AVD. Or start the AVD by using the `emulator` tool.

How It Works

Refer to Figure 1-10 and you'll notice a disabled Start button. This button is no longer disabled after an AVD entry is created (and highlighted). Click Start to run the `emulator` tool with the highlighted AVD entry as the emulator's device configuration.

A *Launch Options* dialog box appears. This dialog box identifies the AVD's skin and screen density. It also provides unchecked check boxes for scaling the resolution of the emulator's display to match the physical device's screen size, for wiping user data, for launching from a previously saved snapshot, and for saving device state to a snapshot upon device exit.

> **NOTE:** As you update your apps, you'll periodically package and install them on the emulator, which preserves the apps and their state data across AVD restarts in a user-data disk partition. To ensure that an app runs properly as you update it, you might need to delete the emulator's user-data partition, which is accomplished by checking Wipe user data.

Click the Launch button to launch the emulator with AVD1. `AVD Manager` responds by briefly displaying a *Starting Android Emulator* dialog box followed by the emulator window. See Figure 1-12.

Figure 1-12. *The emulator window (with an HVGA handset skin) presents the home screen on its left, and it presents phone controls and a keyboard on its right.*

Figure 1-12 shows that the emulator window is divided into a left pane, which displays the Android logo on a black background followed by the home screen, and a right pane, which displays phone controls and a keyboard.

A status bar appears above the home screen (and every app screen). The *status bar* presents the current time, amount of battery power remaining, and other information; it also provides access to notifications.

The home screen initially appears in locked mode. To unlock this screen, drag the lock icon to its right until it touches an unlock icon (or press the MENU button). You should end up with the unlocked home screen shown in Figure 1-13.

Figure 1-13. *The home screen now reveals the app launcher and more.*

The home screen presents the following items:

- *Wallpaper background*: Wallpaper appears behind everything else and can be dragged to the left or right. To change this background, press and hold down the left mouse button over the wallpaper, which causes a wallpaper-oriented pop-up menu to appear.

- *Widgets*: The Google Search widget appears near the top, the Clock widget appears upper-centered, and the Camera widget appears near the bottom left. A widget is a miniature app view that can be embedded in the home screen and other apps, and receives periodic updates.
- *App launcher*: The app launcher (along the bottom) presents icons for launching the commonly used Browser, Contacts, Messaging, and Phone apps; it also displays a rectangular grid of all installed apps, which are subsequently launched by single-clicking their icons. Figure 1-14 shows some of these icons.

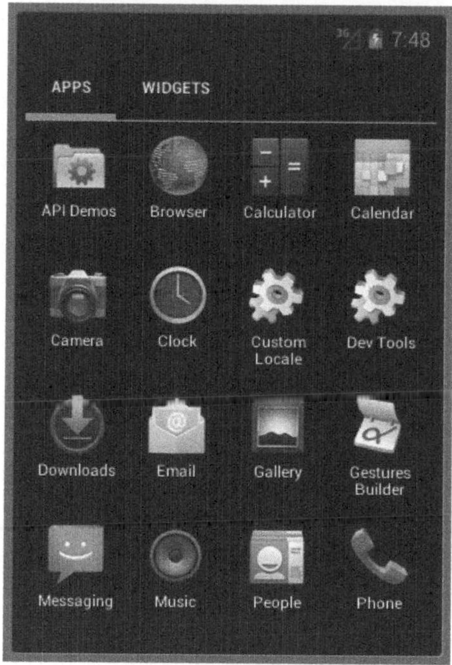

Figure 1-14. *Drag this screen to the left to reveal more icons.*

The app launcher organizes apps and widgets according to the tabs near the top left of the screen. You can run apps from the APPS tab, and select additional widgets to display on the home screen from the WIDGETS tab. (If you need more room for widgets on the home screen, drag its wallpaper in either direction.)

> **TIP:** The API Demos app demonstrates a wide variety of Android APIs. If you are new to Android app development, you should run the individual demos to acquaint yourself with what Android has to offer. You can view each demo's source code by accessing the source files that are located in the `android/samples/android-16/ApiDemos` folder.

The phone controls include the following commonly used buttons:

- The house icon phone control button takes you from wherever you are to the home screen.
- The MENU phone control button presents a menu of app-specific choices for the currently running app.
- The curved arrow icon phone control button takes you back to the previous activity in the activity stack.

While the AVD is running, you can interact with it by using your mouse to "touch" the touchscreen and your keyboard to "press" the AVD keys. Table 1-2 shows you the mappings between AVD keys and keyboard keys.

Table 1-2. *Mappings Between AVD Keys and Keyboard Keys*

AVD Key	Keyboard Key
Home	HOME
Menu (left softkey)	F2 or Page Up
Star (right softkey)	Shift-F2 or Page Down
Back	ESC
Call/dial button	F3
Hangup/end call button	F4
Search	F5
Power button	F7
Audio volume up button	KEYPAD_PLUS, Ctrl-5

Audio volume down button	KEYPAD_MINUS, Ctrl-F6
Camera button	Ctrl-KEYPAD_5, Ctrl-F3
Switch to previous layout orientation (for example, portrait or landscape)	KEYPAD_7, Ctrl-F11
Switch to next layout orientation	KEYPAD_9, Ctrl-F12
Toggle cell networking on/off	F8
Toggle code profiling	F9 (only with `-trace` startup option)
Toggle fullscreen mode	Alt-Enter
Toggle trackball mode	F6
Enter trackball mode temporarily (while key is pressed)	Delete
DPad left/up/right/down	KEYPAD_4/8/6/2
DPad center click	KEYPAD_5
Onion alpha increase/decrease	KEYPAD_MULTIPLY(*) / KEYPAD_DIVIDE(/)

> **TIP:** You must first disable NumLock on your development computer before you can use keypad keys.

Table 1-2 refers to the `-trace` startup option in the context of toggle code profiling. This option lets you store profiling results in a file when starting the AVD via the `emulator` tool.

For example, `emulator -avd AVD1 -trace results.txt` starts the emulator for device configuration `AVD1`, and it also stores profiling results in `results.txt` when you press F9—press F9 again to stop code profiling.

Figure 1-12 displays 5554:AVD1 on the title bar. The 5554 value identifies a console port that you can use to dynamically query and otherwise control the environment of the AVD.

> **NOTE:** Android supports up to 16 concurrently executing AVDs. Each AVD is assigned an even-numbered console port number starting with 5554.

You can connect to the AVD's console by specifying `telnet localhost` *`console-port`*. For example, specify `telnet localhost 5554` to connect to AVD1's console. Figure 1-15 shows you the resulting command window on Windows 7.

```
Telnet localhost
Android Console: type 'help' for a list of commands
OK
help
Android console command help:

    help|h|?          print a list of commands
    event             simulate hardware events
    geo               Geo-location commands
    gsm               GSM related commands
    cdma              CDMA related commands
    kill              kill the emulator instance
    network           manage network settings
    power             power related commands
    quit|exit         quit control session
    redir             manage port redirections
    sms               SMS related commands
    avd               control virtual device execution
    window            manage emulator window
    qemu              QEMU-specific commands
    sensor            manage emulator sensors

try 'help <command>' for command-specific help
OK
_
```

Figure 1-15. *Type a command name by itself for command-specific help.*

> **TIP:** The `telnet` command is disabled on Windows 7 by default (to help make the OS more secure). To enable `telnet` on Windows 7, start the control panel, select Programs and Features, select Turn Windows features on or off, and (from the *Windows Features* dialog box), check the Telnet Client check box.

Introducing Univerter

Problem

Now that you've installed the Android SDK, installed an Android platform, and created and started an AVD, you're ready to create an app and then to install and run this app on the AVD. You could create an app based on Listing 1-1's `SimpleActivity` class, but you'll probably find this recipe's `Univerter` app to be more interesting (and useful).

Solution

`Univerter` (an acronym for Units Converter) is an app (supporting Android 2.3.3 and higher) that lets you convert between types of units. For example, you can convert a specific number of degrees Celsius to its equivalent number of degrees Fahrenheit, a specific number of pounds to its equivalent number of kilograms, and so on.

> **NOTE:** Univerter supports 200 conversions in 13 categories.

`Univerter` is implemented as a single activity whose user interface consists of a display and a 16-button grid consisting of 10 digits, a decimal point, and the following:

- +/-: Click this button to enter a negative value. This button is enabled only for conversions where entering a negative value makes sense (such as converting from degrees Celsius or Fahrenheit).
- CLR (Clear): Click this button to clear the display.
- CAT (Category): Click this button to choose a new conversion category. The first conversion in the new category becomes the default conversion. ANGLE is the default category.
- CON (Conversion): Click this button to choose a new conversion for the current category.
- CVT (Convert): Click this button to convert the value presented on the display to a new value according to the current conversion. Click this button again to convert the conversion result to a new value according to the current conversion.

When CAT or CON is clicked, a dialog box appears with a list of selections. Make a selection and click the dialog box's Close button to confirm your choice.

> **NOTE:** Univerter presents an overflow toast when a conversion generates an absolute value larger than 1.0e+18, and an underflow toast is created when the absolute value is less than 0.00000001 but is not equal to 0.

Additionally, you can click the device's MENU button (when present; use an Android 3.0 or higher device's action bar when MENU is absent) to activate an options menu, from where you can obtain information about `Univerter` as well as help on using this app.

How It Works

`Univerter`'s implementation consists of the following four source files:

- `Category.java`: This source file declares a `Category` class that describes a single conversion category.
- `Conversion.java`: This source file declares a `Conversion` class that describes a single conversion.
- `Converter.java`: This source file declares a `Converter` interface whose solitary method is called to perform a conversion.
- `Univerter.java`: This source file declares a `Univerter` class that describes an activity.

`Univerter`'s implementation also consists of the following resource files:

- `res/drawable/gradientbg.xml`: This XML file describes the activity's gradient background.
- `res/drawable-hdpi/ic_launcher.png`: This PNG image file describes the launcher icon for high-density screens.
- `res/drawable-ldpi/ic_launcher.png`: This PNG image file describes the launcher icon for low-density screens.
- `res/drawable-mdpi/ic_launcher.png`: This PNG image file describes the launcher icon for medium-density screens.
- `res/drawable-xhdpi/ic_launcher.png`: This PNG image file describes the launcher icon for extra-high-density screens.

- res/layout/help.xml: This XML file describes the layout for the help dialog box in portrait or landscape orientation.
- res/layout/info.xml: This XML file describes the layout for the info dialog box in portrait or landscape orientation.
- res/layout/list_row.xml: This XML file describes the layout for a list row in the conversions dialog box in portrait or landscape orientation.
- res/layout/main.xml: This XML file describes the activity's layout for portrait orientation.
- res/layout-land/main.xml: This XML file describes the activity's layout for landscape orientation.
- res/menu/univerter.xml: This XML file describes the layout for the activity's options menu.
- res/values/colors.xml: This XML file stores the various colors used by Univerter.
- res/values/strings.xml: This XML file stores the various strings used by Univerter.
- res/values/styles.xml: This XML file stores a custom theme that shrinks the size of the title bar text at the top of the activity screen.

Additionally, Univerter's implementation consists of an AndroidManifest.xml file that describes this app to Android.

> **NOTE:** Appendix D explores these files. You can obtain them from the code archive that accompanies this book (see www.apress.com/9781430246145).

Creating Univerter

Problem

You want to use the Android SDK to create Univerter, but you don't know how to perform this task. (Recipe 1-10 shows how to create Univerter with Eclipse.)

Solution

Use the android tool to create Univerter and then use ant to build this project.

How It Works

Your first step in creating Univerter is to use the android tool to create a project. When used in this way, android requires you to adhere to the following syntax (which is spread across multiple lines for readability):

```
android create project --target target_ID
                       --name your_project_name
                       --path /path/to/your/project/project_name
                       --activity your_activity_name
                       --package your_package_namespace
```

Except for --name (or -n), which specifies the project's name (if provided, this name will be used for the resulting .apk file name when you build your app), all of the following options are required:

- The --target (or -t) option specifies the app's build target. The *target_ID* value is an integer value that identifies an Android platform. You can obtain this value by invoking android list targets. If you've only installed the Android 4.1 platform, this command should output a single Android 4.1 platform target identified as integer ID 1.
- The --path (or -p) option specifies the project directory's location. The directory is created when it doesn't exist.
- The --activity (or -a) option specifies the name for the default activity class. The resulting classfile is created inside */path/to/your/project/project_name/src/your_package_namespace/* and is used as the .apk file name when --name (or -n) isn't specified.
- The --package (or -k) option specifies the project's package namespace, which must follow the rules for packages that are specified in the Java language.

Assuming a Windows 7 platform, and assuming a C:\prj\dev hierarchy where the Univerter project is to be stored in C:\prj\dev\Univerter, invoke the following command (spread across two lines for readability) from anywhere in the filesystem (except the root directory) to create Univerter:

```
android create project -t 1 -p C:\prj\dev\Univerter -a Univerter
                       -k ca.tutortutor.univerter
```

This command creates various directories and adds files to some of these directories. It specifically creates the following file and directory structure in `C:\prj\dev\Univerter`:

- `AndroidManifest.xml` is the manifest file for the app being built. This file is synchronized to the `Activity` subclass previously specified via the `--activity` or `-a` option.
- `ant.properties` is a customizable properties file for the Ant build system. You can edit this file to override Ant's default build settings, and you can provide a pointer to your keystore and key alias so that the build tools can sign your app when it's built in release mode (discussed later in this recipe).
- `bin` is the output directory for the Apache Ant build script.
- `build.xml` is the Apache Ant build script for this project.
- `libs` contains private libraries (when required).
- `local.properties` is a generated file that contains the Android SDK home directory location.
- `proguard-project.txt` contains information on enabling *ProGuard*, an SDK tool that lets developers obfuscate their code (making it very difficult to reverse engineer the code) as an integrated part of a release build.
- `project.properties` is a generated file that identifies the project's target Android platform.
- `res` contains project resources.
- `src` contains the project's source code.

You will need to replace `AndroidManifest.xml` with the `AndroidManifest.xml` file included in this book's code archive.

`res` initially contains the following directories:

- `layout` contains layout files. A skeletal `main.xml` file is stored in this directory.
- `values` contains value files. A skeletal `strings.xml` file is stored in this directory.

You will need to replace this directory structure with the resource directory structure shown in Recipe 1-5.

src contains the ca\tutortutor\univerter directory structure, and the final univerter subdirectory contains a skeletal Univerter.java source file. You will need to copy the four source files mentioned in Recipe 1-5 to univerter.

Assuming that C:\prj\dev\Univerter is current, build this app with the help of Apache's ant tool, which defaults to processing this directory's build.xml file. At the command line, specify ant followed by debug or release to indicate the build mode:

- *Debug mode*: Build the app for testing and debugging. The build tools sign the resulting APK with a debug key and optimize the APK with zipalign. Specify ant debug.
- *Release mode*: Build the app for release to users. You must sign the resulting APK with your private key, and then optimize the APK with zipalign. (I discuss these tasks in Recipe 1-8.) Specify ant release.

Build Univerter in debug mode by invoking ant debug from the C:\prj\dev\Univerter directory. This command creates a gen subdirectory containing the ant-generated R.java file (in a ca\tutortutor\univerter directory hierarchy), and it stores the created Univerter-debug.apk file in the bin subdirectory.

Installing and Running Univerter

Problem

You want to learn how to install the Univerter-debug.apk package file that you created in the previous recipe on the previously started AVD1 and run this app.

Solution

Use the adb tool to install Univerter-debug.apk. Navigate to the app launcher screen to run Univerter.

How It Works

Assuming that AVD1 is still running, execute the following command to install Univerter-debug.apk on AVD1:

```
adb install C:\prj\dev\Univerter\bin\Univerter-debug.apk
```

After a few moments, you should see messages similar to those shown below:

```
* daemon not running. starting it now on port 5037 *
* daemon started successfully *
269 KB/s (75946 bytes in 0.275s)
        pkg: /data/local/tmp/Univerter-debug.apk
Success
```

The first two "daemon" messages signify that the ADB daemon is not running and that it has been started. Check out `http://developer.android.com/tools/help/adb.html` to learn more about the ADB daemon.

> **NOTE:** If you ever see a failure message while trying to install this app, the cause of this message is probably that the app is already installed.

From the home screen, click the app launcher icon (the rectangular grid icon centered at the bottom of the home screen), and swipe the contents of the APPS tab to the left. Figure 1-16 shows you the Univerter app entry.

Figure 1-16. *The Univerter app entry presents a golden balance-scale icon.*

Click the Univerter icon and you should see the screen shown in Figure 1-17.

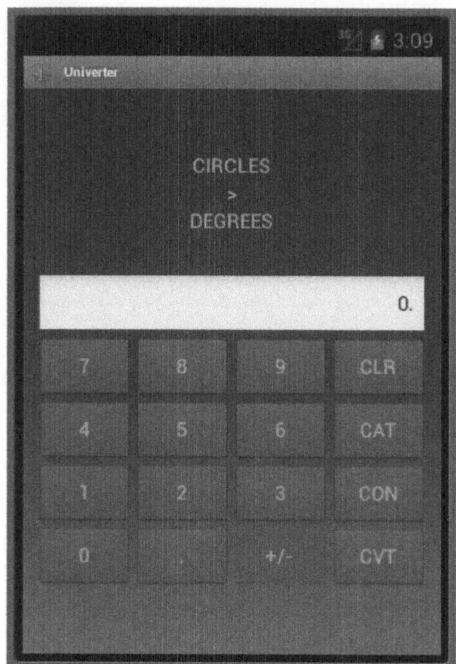

Figure 1-17. *The default category is ANGLE and the default conversion is CIRCLES > DEGREES.*

Switch AVD1's orientation to landscape and you should see Figure 1-18's screen.

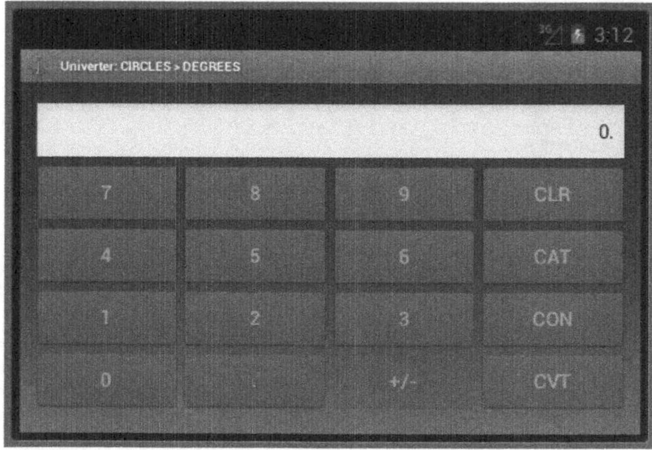

Figure 1-18. *The conversion title now appears on the title bar.*

Clicking the CAT button presents the list of categories shown in Figure 1-19.

Figure 1-19. *Click the Close button after selecting a category.*

Figure 1-20 shows that clicking the CON button presents the list of conversions for the current (ANGLE) category.

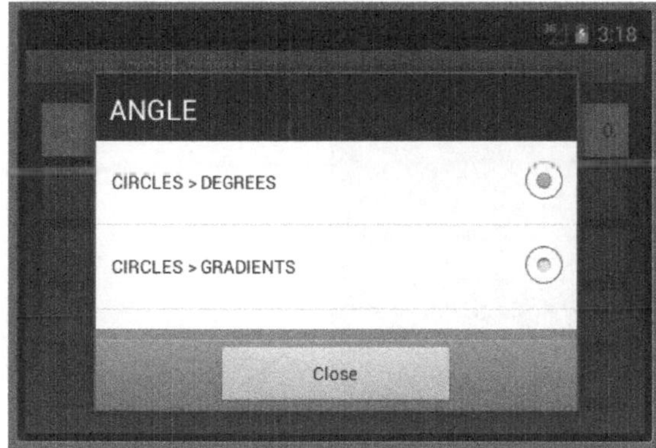

Figure 1-20. *Click the Close button after selecting a conversion.*

Clicking the MENU button (or its action bar overflow icon equivalent, which is three vertical dots) reveals the options menu. Click the help menu item to display the help dialog box shown in Figure 1-21.

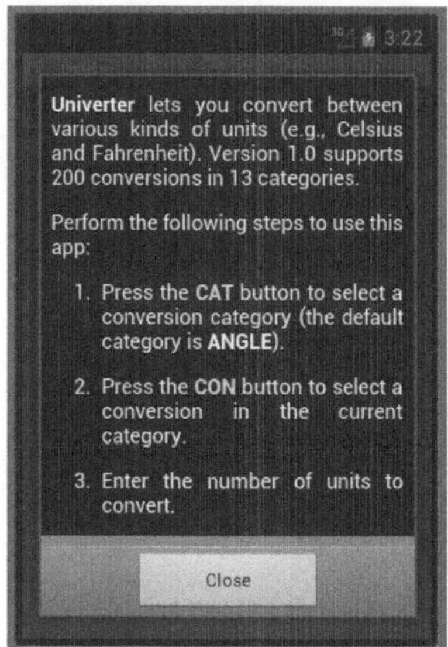

Figure 1-21. *Scroll through the help text to learn about* `Univerter`.

Finally, click the info menu item to display the info dialog box shown in Figure 1-22.

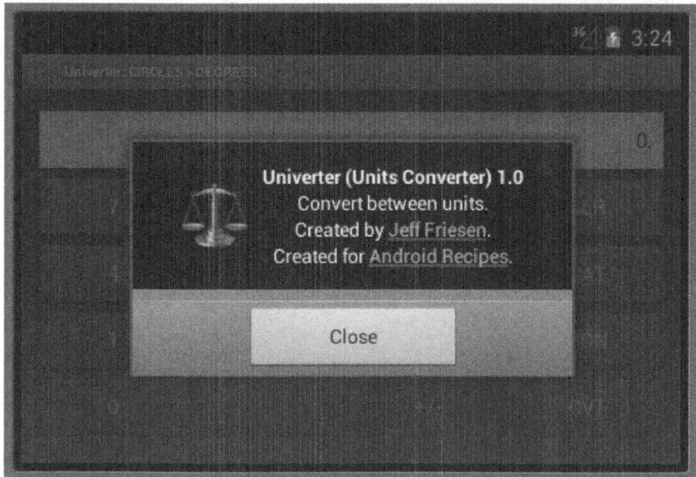

Figure 1-22. *Click the Android Recipes link in the info dialog box to visit this book's web page.*

Continue to play with `Univerter`. When you finish, return to the app launcher screen to try out other apps.

> **TIP:** You can uninstall `Univerter` in one of two ways. You can select "Manage apps" from the app launcher screen's options menu, scroll down to the Univerter entry, select this entry, and click the Uninstall button. Or you can specify `adb uninstall ca.tutortutor.univerter` at the command line. The second option is faster and more convenient during development.

Preparing Univerter for Publication on Google Play

Problem

You've enhanced `Univerter` with more conversions and other features, and now you want to publish this app on Google Play (`https://play.google.com/store`), which was previously known as Android Market. However, you don't know what is required to get this app ready for publication.

Solution

Before publishing `Univerter` or another app, you will need to follow six preparation steps:

1. Test the app thoroughly.
2. Version the app in the manifest.
3. Request all necessary permissions in the manifest.
4. Build the app in release mode.
5. Sign the app package.
6. Align the app package.

After completing these steps, register to upload apps on Google Play (if you have not done so already), and then upload the app's APK file.

How It Works

The following six sections elaborate on the six preparation steps.

Test Your App Thoroughly

Android supports various versions, device categories (handsets and tablets), and device characteristics (such as screen densities and the presence or absence of a camera), which collectively offer a challenging environment for developing apps. It is important to test your app thoroughly for all desired version/category/characteristic combinations.

Android provides tools and resources to help you with this testing. For example, Android includes JUnit-based unit testing via the packages `junit.framework` and `junit.runner`. Check out the "Testing" (`http://developer.android.com/tools/testing/index.html`) section in Google's Android documentation for more information.

Version Your App in the Manifest

Android lets you add version information to your app by specifying this information in `AndroidManifest.xml`'s `<manifest>` tag via its `versionCode` and `versionName` attributes.

`versionCode` is assigned an integer value that represents the version of the app's code. The value is an integer so that other apps can programmatically evaluate it to check an upgrade or downgrade relationship, for example. Although you can set the value to any desired integer, you should ensure that each successive release of your app uses a greater value. Android doesn't enforce this behavior, but increasing the value in successive releases is normative.

`versionName` is assigned a string value that represents the release version of the app's code, and it should be shown to users (by the app). This value is a string so that you can describe the app version as a *<major>.<minor>.<point>* string or as any other type of absolute or relative version identifier. As with `android:versionCode`, Android doesn't use this value for any internal purpose. Publishing services may extract the `versionName` value for display to users.

The `<manifest>` tag in `Univerter`'s `AndroidManifest.xml` file includes a `versionCode` attribute initialized to `"1"` and a `versionName` attribute initialized to `"1.0"`.

While on the subject of versioning, you should also specify the minimum SDK version that your app supports. You can accomplish this task by introducing, into `AndroidManifest.xml`, a `<uses-sdk>` element whose `minSdkVersion` attribute is set to the desired minimum API level. For example, the following `<uses-sdk>` element sets this level to 10 (Gingerbread/2.3.3), which is the minimum SDK that `Univerter` supports:

```
<uses-sdk android:minSdkVersion="10"/>
```

Request All Necessary Permissions in the Manifest

Your app may need to obtain permission before performing some task. For example, if your app uses the android.webkit.WebView class to view web pages over the Internet, you must add the following <uses-permission> element to AndroidManifest.xml:

```
<uses-permission android:name="android.permission.INTERNET"/>
```

You do not always have to provide this element when working with WebView. For example, Univerter works with WebView and doesn't provide this element. Permission is not required because Univerter obtains its HTML content from a string resource.

Build Your App in Release Mode

You cannot publish an app built in debug mode; you must rebuild the app in release mode. Accomplish this task by executing the following command:

```
ant release
```

Assuming that Univerter is being built in release mode, the bin directory should contain a Univerter-release-unsigned.apk file.

Sign the App Package

Android requires that all installed apps be digitally signed with a certificate whose private key is held by the app's developer. It uses the certificate as a means of identifying the app's author and establishing trust relationships between apps; it doesn't use the certificate to control which apps can be installed by the user.

> **NOTE:** Certificates don't need to be signed by certificate authorities: it's perfectly allowable, and typical, for Android apps to use self-signed certificates.
>
> Android tests a signer certificate's expiration date only at install time. If an app's signer certificate expires after the app is installed, the app will continue to function normally.

Before you can sign your app package, you must obtain a suitable private key. A private key is suitable when it meets the following criteria:

- The key represents the personal, corporate, or organizational entity to be identified with the app.
- The key has a validity period that exceeds the expected life span of the app. Google recommends a validity period of more than 25 years. If you plan to publish the app on Google Play, keep in mind that a validity period ending after October 22, 2033, is a requirement. You cannot upload an app when it's signed with a key whose validity expires before (and possibly even on) that date.
- The key is not the debug key generated by the Android SDK tools.

The JDK's `keytool` tool is used to create a suitable private key. The following command line (split over two lines for readability), which assumes that `C:\prj\dev\Univerter` is the current directory, uses `keytool` to generate this key:

```
keytool -genkey -v -keystore univerter-release-key.keystore -alias univerter_key
        -keyalg RSA -keysize 2048 -validity 10000
```

The following command-line arguments are specified:

- `-genkey` causes `keytool` to generate a public and a private key (a key pair).
- `-v` enables verbose output.
- `-keystore` identifies the *keystore* (a database of private keys and their associated X.509 certificate chains authenticating the corresponding public keys) that stores the private key; the keystore is named `univerter-release-key.keystore` in the command line.
- `-alias` identifies an alias for the keystore entry (only the first eight characters are used when the alias is specified during the actual signing operation); the alias is named `univerter_key` in the command line.
- `-keyalg` specifies the encryption algorithm to use when generating the key; although `DSA` and `RSA` are supported, `RSA` is specified in the command line.
- `-keysize` specifies the size of each generated key (in bits); `2048` is specified in the command line because Google recommends using a key size of 2048 bits or higher (the default size is 1024 bits).

- -validity specifies the period (in days) in which the key remains valid (Google recommends a value of 10000 or greater); 10000 is specified in the command line.

keytool prompts you for a password (to protect access to the keystore) and will then prompt you to reenter the same password. It then prompts for your first and last name, your organizational unit name, the name of your organization, the name of your city or locality, the name of your state or province, and a two-letter country code for your organizational unit.

keytool subsequently prompts you to indicate whether or not this information is correct (by typing yes and pressing Enter, or by pressing Enter for no). Assuming you entered yes, keytool lets you choose a different password for the key, or you can use the same password as that of the keystore.

> **CAUTION:** Keep your private key secure. Fail to do so and your app authoring identity and user trust could be compromised. Here are some tips for keeping your private key secure:
>
> * Select strong passwords for the keystore and key.
>
> * When you generate your key with keytool, don't supply the -storepass and -keypass options at the command line. If you do so, your passwords will be available in your shell history, which any user on your computer can access.
>
> * When signing your apps with jarsigner, don't supply the -storepass and -keypass options at the command line (for the same reason as mentioned in the previous tip).
>
> * Don't give or lend anyone your private key, and don't let unauthorized persons know your keystore and key passwords.

keytool creates univerter-release-key.keystore in the current directory. You can view this keystore's information by executing the following command line:

```
keytool -list -v -keystore univerter-release-key.keystore
```

After requesting the keystore password, keytool outputs the number of entries in the keystore (which should be one) and certificate information.

The JDK's jarsigner tool is used to sign Univerter-release-unsigned.apk. Assuming that C:\prj\dev\Univerter is the current directory, this directory contains the keytool-created univerter-release-key.keystore file, and this directory contains a bin subdirectory that contains Univerter-release-unsigned.apk, execute the following command line (split over two lines for readability) to sign this file:

```
jarsigner -verbose -keystore univerter-release-key.keystore
          bin/Univerter-release-unsigned.apk univerter_key
```

The following command-line arguments are specified:

- -verbose enables verbose output.
- -keystore identifies the keystore that stores the private key; univerter-release-key.keystore is specified in the command line.
- bin/Univerter-release-unsigned.apk identifies the location and name of the APK being signed.
- univerter-key identifies the previously created alias for the private key.

jarsigner prompts you to enter the keystore password that you previously specified via keytool. This tool then outputs messages similar to the following:

```
   adding: META-INF/MANIFEST.MF
   adding: META-INF/UNIVERTE.SF
   adding: META-INF/UNIVERTE.RSA
  signing: res/drawable/gradientbg.xml
  signing: res/layout/help.xml
  signing: res/layout/info.xml
  signing: res/layout/list_row.xml
  signing: res/layout/main.xml
  signing: res/menu/univerter.xml
  signing: AndroidManifest.xml
  signing: resources.arsc
  signing: res/drawable-hdpi/ic_launcher.png
  signing: res/drawable-ldpi/ic_launcher.png
  signing: res/drawable-mdpi/ic_launcher.png
  signing: res/drawable-xhdpi/ic_launcher.png
  signing: res/layout-land/main.xml
  signing: classes.dex
```

NOTE: The previous jarsigner command is problematic with JDK 7. After signing the release version of the APK file (and aligning the APK, which is discussed shortly), the APK cannot be installed on the device. This problem and its solution, which consists of adding -digestalg SHA1 -sigalg MD5withRSA to the command line, is documented at http://code.google.com/p/android/issues/detail?id=19567. For JDK 7 users, the following command line (split over three lines for readability) should be used instead:

```
jarsigner -verbose -keystore univerter-release-key.keystore
          bin/Univerter-release-unsigned.apk -digestalg SHA1
          -sigalg MD5withRSA univerter_key
```

Execute the following command line (split over two lines for readability) to verify that `Univerter-release-unsigned.apk` has been signed:

```
jarsigner -verify -keystore univerter-release-key.keystore
          bin/Univerter-release-unsigned.apk
```

Assuming success, you should notice a single "`jar verified.`" message.

Align the App Package

As a performance optimization, Android requires that a signed APK's uncompressed content be aligned relative to the start of the file, and it supplies the `zipalign` SDK tool for this task. According to Google's documentation, all uncompressed data within the APK, such as images or raw files, are aligned on 4-byte boundaries.

`zipalign` requires the following syntax to align an input APK to an output APK:

```
zipalign [-f] [-v] alignment infile.apk outfile.apk
```

The following command-line arguments are specified:

- `-f` forces *`outfile`*`.apk` to be overwritten if it exists.
- `-v` enables verbose output.
- *`alignment`* specifies that the APK content is to be aligned on this number of bytes boundary; it appears that `zipalign` ignores any value other than `4`.
- *`infile`*`.apk` identifies the signed APK file to be aligned.
- *`outfile`*`.apk` identifies the resulting signed and aligned APK file.

Assuming that `C:\prj\dev\Univerter\bin` is the current directory, execute the following command line to align `Univerter-release-unsigned.apk` to `Univerter.apk`:

```
zipalign -f -v 4 Univerter-release-unsigned.apk Univerter.apk
```

zipalign requires the following syntax to verify that an existing APK is aligned:

```
zipalign -c -v alignment existing.apk
```

The following command-line arguments are specified:

- -c confirms the alignment of *existing*.apk.
- -v enables verbose output.
- *alignment* specifies that the APK content is aligned on this number of bytes boundary; it appears that zipalign ignores any value other than 4.
- *existing*.apk identifies the signed APK file to be aligned.

Execute the following command line to verify that Univerter.apk is aligned:

```
zipalign -c -v 4 Univerter.apk
```

zipalign presents a list of APK entries, indicating which are compressed and which are not, followed by a verification successful or a verification failed message.

Univerter.apk is now ready for publication.

Migrating to Eclipse

Problem

You prefer to develop apps by using the Eclipse IDE.

Solution

To develop apps with Eclipse, you need to install an IDE such as Eclipse Classic 4.2. Furthermore, you need to install the Android Development Tools (ADT) Plugin.

How It Works

Before you can develop Android apps with Eclipse, you must complete at least the first two of the following three tasks:

1. Install the Android SDK and at least one Android platform (see Recipes 1-1 and 1-2). JDK 6 or JDK 7 must also be installed.

2. Install a version of Eclipse that's compatible with the Android SDK and the ADT Plugin for the Eclipse IDE.
3. Install the ADT Plugin.

You should complete these tasks in the order presented. You cannot install the ADT Plugin before installing Eclipse, and you cannot configure or use the ADT Plugin before installing the Android SDK and at least one Android platform.

THE BENEFICIAL ADT PLUGIN

Although you can develop Android apps in Eclipse without using the ADT Plugin, it's much faster and easier to create, debug, and otherwise develop these apps with this plug-in.

The ADT Plugin offers the following features:

- It gives you access to other Android development tools from inside the Eclipse IDE. For example, ADT lets you access the many capabilities of the Dalvik Debug Monitor Server (DDMS) tool, allowing you to take screenshots, manage port-forwarding, set breakpoints, and view thread and process information directly from Eclipse.
- It provides a New Project Wizard, which helps you quickly create and set up all of the basic files you'll need for a new Android app.
- It automates and simplifies the process of building your Android app.
- It provides an Android code editor that helps you write valid XML for your Android manifest and resource files.
- It lets you export your project into a signed APK, which can be distributed to users.

You'll learn how to install the ADT Plugin after learning how to install Eclipse.

The Eclipse.org website makes available for download several IDE packages that meet different requirements. Google places the following stipulations on which IDE package you should download and install:

- Install an Eclipse 3.6.2 (Helios) or greater IDE package.
- Make sure that the Eclipse package being downloaded includes the Eclipse JDT (Java Development Tools) Plugin. Most packages include this plug-in.

Complete the following steps to install Eclipse Classic 4.2, which is the latest version of this IDE at the time of writing:

1. Point your browser to the Eclipse Classic 4.2 page at `http://eclipse.org/downloads/packages/eclipse-classic-42/junor`.
2. Select the appropriate distribution file by clicking one of the links in the Download Links box on the right side of this page. For example, you might click Windows 64-bit platform.
3. Click a download link and save the distribution file to your hard drive. For example, you might save `eclipse-SDK-4.2-win32-x86_64.zip` to your hard drive.
4. Unarchive the distribution file and move the `eclipse` home directory to a convenient location. For example, on 64-bit Windows 7, you would move `eclipse` to your `C:\Program Files` directory, which organizes 64-bit programs.
5. You might also want to create a desktop shortcut to the `eclipse` application located in the `eclipse` home directory.

Complete the following steps to install the latest revision of the ADT Plugin:

1. Start Eclipse.
2. The first time you start Eclipse, you will discover a *Workspace Launcher* dialog box following the splash screen. You can use this dialog box to select a workspace folder in which to store your projects. You can also tell Eclipse to not display this dialog box on subsequent startups. Change or keep the default folder setting and click OK.
3. Once Eclipse displays its main window, select Install New Software from the Help menu.
4. Click the Add button on the resulting *Install* dialog box's Available Software pane.
5. On the resulting *Add Repository* dialog box, enter a name for the remote site (for example, `Android Plugin`) in the Name field, and enter `https://dl-ssl.google.com/android/eclipse/` into the Location field. Click OK.
6. You should now see Developer Tools and NDK Plugins in the list that appears in the middle of the *Install* dialog box.

7. Check the check box next to these categories, which will automatically check the nested items underneath. Click Next.
8. The resulting Install Details pane lists Android DDMS, Android Development Tools, Android Hierarchy Viewer, Android Native Development Tools, Android Traceview, and Tracer for OpenGL ES. Click Next to read and accept the various license agreements, and then click Finish.
9. An *Installing Software* dialog box appears and takes care of installation. If you encounter a *Security Warning* dialog box, click OK.
10. Finally, Eclipse presents a *Software Updates* dialog box that prompts you to restart this IDE. Click Yes to restart.

> **TIP:** If you have trouble acquiring the plug-in in Step 5, try specifying `http` instead of `https` (`https` is preferred for security reasons) in the Location field.

To complete the installation of the ADT Plugin, you may have to configure this plug-in by modifying the ADT preferences in Eclipse to point to the Android SDK home directory. Accomplish this task by completing the following steps:

1. Select Preferences from the Window menu to open the *Preferences* dialog box. For Mac OS X, select Preferences from the Eclipse menu.
2. Select Android from the left panel.
3. If the SDK Location textfield presents the SDK's home directory (such as `C:\android`), close the Preferences dialog box. You have nothing further to do.
4. If the SDK Location textfield does not present the SDK's home directory, click the Browse button beside this textfield and locate your downloaded SDK's home directory on the resulting *Browse For Folder* dialog box. Select this location, click OK to close this dialog box, and click Apply on the *Preferences* dialog box to confirm this location, which should result in a list of SDK Targets (such as Android 4.1) appearing below the textfield.

> **NOTE:** For more information on installing the ADT Plugin, which includes helpful information in case of difficulty, check out the "Installing the Eclipse Plugin" page (`http://developer.android.com/sdk/installing/installing-adt.html`) in Google's online Android documentation.

Creating and Running Univerter with Eclipse

Problem

Now that you've installed Eclipse Classic 4.2 and the ADT Plugin, you want to learn how to use this IDE and plug-in to create and run `Univerter`.

Solution

You first need to create an Android Eclipse project named `Univerter`. You then copy `Univerter`'s source files and resources into this project. Finally, you execute `Univerter` by selecting Run from the menubar.

How It Works

The first task in creating and running `Univerter` with Eclipse is to create a new Android project. Complete the following steps to create this project:

1. Start Eclipse if not running.
2. Select New from the File menu, and select Project from the resulting pop-up menu.
3. On the *New Project* dialog box, expand the Android node in the wizard tree (if necessary), select the Android Application Project branch below this node (if necessary), and click the Next button.

4. On the resulting *New Android App* dialog box, enter `Univerter` into the Application name textfield (this entered name also appears in the Project name textfield, and it identifies the directory in which the `Univerter` project is stored) and `ca.tutortutor.univerter` into the Package Name textfield. Also, select `API 10: Android 2.3.3 (Gingerbread)` in the Minimum Required SDK list, and uncheck the Create custom launcher icon. Leave the other settings as is and click Next.
5. On the resulting Create Activity pane, uncheck Create Activity and click Finish.

Eclipse responds by creating a `Univerter` directory with the following subdirectories and files within your Eclipse workspace directory:

- *.settings*: This directory contains an `org.eclipse.jdt.core.prefs` file that records project-specific settings.
- *assets*: This directory is used to store an unstructured hierarchy of files. Anything stored in this directory can later be retrieved by an app via a raw byte stream.
- *bin*: Your APK file is stored here.
- *gen*: The generated `R.java` file is stored in a subdirectory structure that reflects the package hierarchy (such as `ca\tutortutor\univerter`).
- *res*: App resources are stored in various subdirectories.
- *src*: App source code is stored according to a package hierarchy.
- *.classpath*: This file stores the project's classpath information so that external libraries on which the project depends can be located.
- *.project*: This file contains important project information, such as the name of the project and the build specification.
- *AndroidManifest.xml*: This file contains `Univerter`'s manifest.
- `proguard-project.txt`: This file contains information on enabling ProGuard.

- `project.properties`: This file identifies the project's target Android platform.

Close the Welcome tab (if showing). Eclipse then presents the user interface that's shown in Figure 1-23.

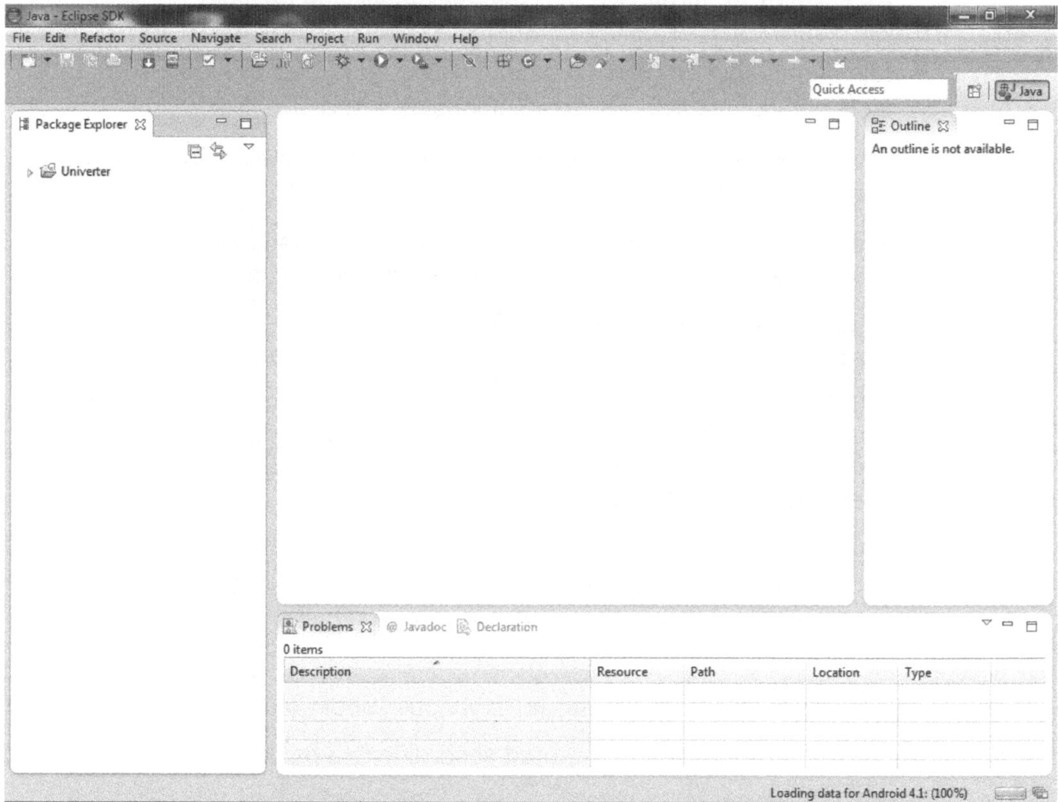

Figure 1-23. *Eclipse's user interface is organized around a menubar, a toolbar, several windows such as Package Explorer and Outline, a statusbar, and a blank area that's reserved for editor windows.*

This user interface is known as the *workbench*. The Package Explorer window appears on the left and presents an expandable list of nodes that identify the various projects in the current workspace and their components. Figure 1-23 reveals that `Univerter` is the only project in the workspace.

To learn how Eclipse organizes the `Univerter` project, click the triangle icon to the left of the Univerter node. Figure 1-24 reveals an expanded project hierarchy.

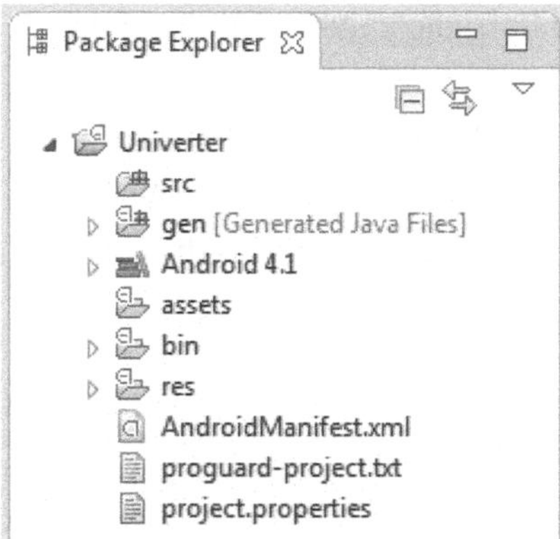

Figure 1-24. *This hierarchy reveals the important `src` and `res` directories along with `AndroidManifest.xml`.*

The src node is empty. Complete the following steps to create a `ca\tutortutor\univerter` directory structure under the equivalent `src` directory:

1. Right-click the src node, and select New followed by Folder from the pop-up menus.
2. On the resulting *New Folder* dialog box, enter `ca/tutortutor/univerter` into the Folder name textfield, and click Finish.

Next, place the `Category.java`, `Conversion.java`, `Converter.java`, and `Univerter.java` source files into `ca\tutortutor\univerter` by completing the following steps:

1. Copy these files to the clipboard.
2. Right-click the ca.tutortutor.univerter node underneath src, and select Paste from the pop-up menu.

You should now observe Category.java, Conversion.java, Converter.java, and Univerter.java nodes under ca.tutortutor.univerter.

The res node contains various nodes that are not needed. Complete the following steps to populate this directory with `Univerter`'s resource structure:

1. Delete all of the nodes under res by highlighting these nodes, right-clicking, and selecting Delete from the pop-up menu.
2. Copy all of the directories under Univerter's `res` directory to the clipboard.

3. Right-click the res node, and select Paste from the pop-up menu.

You should now observe drawable, drawable-hdpi, drawable-ldpi, drawable-mdpi, drawable-xhdpi, layout, layout-land, menu, and values nodes under res.

Finally, you need to update the AndroidManifest.xml node to refer to the correct manifest. Accomplish this task as follows:

1. Copy Univerter's `AndroidManifest.xml` file to the clipboard.
2. Right-click the AndroidManifest.xml node and select Paste from the pop-up menu.

At this point, Eclipse will probably report nine errors on the Problems tab at the bottom of the workspace. These errors have to do with specifying the `@Override` annotation on overriding interface methods (such as `public void convert(Context ctx, double value)`). In Java 5 (1.5), you could not annotate such methods `@Override`, but this practice was allowed starting in Java 6.

You can easily correct this problem by completing the following steps:

1. Right-click the Univerter node and select Properties from the pop-up menu.
2. On the resulting *Properties for Univerter* dialog box, select Java Compiler.
3. On the resulting Java Compiler pane, change the Compiler compliance level setting from 1.5 to 1.6, and close the dialog box.

The errors report should be gone.

Now that the file structure and compliance level have been specified, select Run from the menubar, and select Run from the resulting drop-down menu. On the resulting *Run As* dialog box, select Android Application and click OK.

If all goes well, Eclipse launches the `emulator` tool with AVD1, installs the `Univerter-debug.apk` file, and causes this app to start running (see Figure 1-17). (You will probably have to bypass the introductory home and launcher screens to see the app when you start up AVD1 on the first run.)

ECLIPSE AND RELEASE MODE

At some point, you will want to build a release version of Univerter in Eclipse. Accomplish this task as follows:

1. Select Export from the File menu.
2. On the resulting *Export* dialog box, select Export Android Application under Android. Click Next.
3. On the resulting *Export Android Application* dialog box, enter Univerter into the Project textfield. Click Next.
4. On the resulting Keystore selection pane, enter the location of the keystore (such as C:\prj\dev\Univerter\univerter-release-key.keystore) into the Location textfield and enter the password (univerter) into the Password textfield. Click Next.
5. On the resulting Key alias selection pane, select the keystore alias (univerter_key) and enter the password (univerter). Click Next.
6. On the resulting Destination and key/certificate checks pane, enter the location for the destination APK file (such as C:\temp\Univerter.apk) and click Finish.

After a few moments, a signed Univerter.apk file should be created in the destination directory.

Summary

Android has excited many people who are developing (and even selling) apps for this platform. It's not too late to join in the fun, and this chapter showed you how by taking you on a rapid tour of key Android concepts and development tools.

You first learned that Android is a software stack for mobile devices and that this stack consists of apps, middleware, and the Linux operating system. You then learned about Android's history, including the various SDK updates that have been made available.

You next encountered Android's layered architecture, which includes apps at the top; an application framework, C/C++ libraries, and the Dalvik virtual machine as middleware; and a modified version of the Linux kernel at the bottom.

Continuing, you encountered app architecture, which is based upon components that communicate via intents, resources that are often used in user interface contexts, a manifest that describes the app's components (and more), and an app package that stores components, resources, and the manifest.

At this point, we moved away from this essential theory and focused on practical matters via a series of recipes. Initial recipes focused on installing the Android SDK and an Android platform, creating an AVD, and starting the emulator with this AVD.

The next batch of recipes introduced you to `Univerter`, a sample units converter app. They also showed you how to create this app, install it on the emulator, run it from the emulator, and how to prepare a release version for publication to Google Play.

Working with command-line tools in a command-line environment can be tedious. For this reason, the final two recipes focused on migrating to the Eclipse IDE, and showed you how to create and run `Univerter` in the context of this graphical environment.

While exploring `Univerter`, you were introduced to various user interface concepts. Chapter 2 builds upon these concepts by presenting recipes that show you how to accomplish various user interface-oriented tasks.

Chapter 2

User Interface Recipes

The Android platform is designed to operate on a variety of different device types, screen sizes, and screen resolutions. To assist developers in meeting this challenge, Android provides a rich toolkit of user interface (UI) components to utilize and customize to the needs of their specific applications. Android also relies very heavily on an extensible XML framework and set resource qualifiers to create liquid layouts that can adapt to these environmental changes. In this chapter, we take a look at some practical ways to shape this framework to fit your specific development needs.

2-1. Customizing the Window

Problem

You want to create a consistent look and feel for your application across all the different versions of Android your users may be running. Your application may also need to toggle the system elements to obtain more screen real estate.

Solution

(API Level 1)

Customize the window attributes and features by using themes and the `WindowManager`. Without any customization, an Activity in an Android application will load with the default system theme. Depending on the version of Android you have targeted, this may be the standard flat-black theme common in

Android 2.x, the Holo theme prominent in Android 3.x and 4.x, or a manufacturer-defined skin that has replaced the Android device's default theme.

In order to guarantee that your application looks the way you want across all devices, you need to declare use of a system or custom theme.

How It Works

Customize Window Attributes with a Theme

A theme in Android is a type of appearance style that is applicable to an entire application or Activity. There are two choices when applying a theme: use a system theme or create a custom one. In either case, a theme is applied in the AndroidManifest.xml file as shown in Listing 2-1.

Listing 2-1. *AndroidManifest.xml*

```
<?xml version="1.0" encoding="utf-8"?>
<manifest xmlns:android="http://schemas.android.com/apk/res/android"
    ...>
    <!—Apply to the application tag for a global theme -->
    <application android:theme="THEME_NAME"
        ...>
        <!—Apply to the activity tag for an individual theme -->
        <activity android:name=".Activity" android:theme="THEME_NAME"
            ...>
            <intent-filter>
                ...
            </intent-filter>
        </activity>
    </application>
</manifest>
```

System Themes

The styles.xml file packaged with the Android framework includes a few options for themes with some useful custom properties. Referencing R.style in the SDK documentation will provide the full list, but here are a few useful examples:

- Theme.Light: Variation on the standard theme that uses an inverse color scheme for the background and user elements. This is the default recommended base theme for applications prior to Android 3.0.

- Theme.NoTitleBar.Fullscreen: Remove the title bar and status bar, filling the entire screen (minus any onscreen controls that may be present).
- Theme.Dialog: A useful theme to make an Activity look like a dialog.
- Theme.Holo.Light: (API Level 11) Theme that uses an inverse color scheme and that has an `ActionBar` by default. This is the default recommended base theme for applications on Android 3.0.
- Theme.Holo.Light.DarkActionBar: (API Level 14) Theme with an inverse color scheme but with a dark solid `ActionBar`. This is the default recommended base theme for applications on Android 4.0.

Listing 2-2 is an example of a system theme applied to the entire application by setting the `android:theme` attribute in the `AndroidManifest.xml` file:

Listing 2-2. *Manifest with Theme Set on Application*

```
<?xml version="1.0" encoding="utf-8"?>
<manifest xmlns:android="http://schemas.android.com/apk/res/android"
    ...>
    <!–Apply to the application tag for a global theme -->
    <application android:theme="Theme.NoTitleBar"
        ...>
        ...
    </application>
</manifest>
```

Custom Themes

Sometimes the provided system choices aren't enough. After all, some of the customizable elements in the window are not even addressed in the system options. Defining a custom theme to do the job is simple.

If there is not one already, create a `styles.xml` file in the res/values path of the project. Remember, themes are just styles applied on a wider scale, so they are defined in the same place. Theme aspects related to window customization can be found in the R.attr reference of the SDK, but here are the most common items:

- `android:windowNoTitle`
    - Governs whether to remove the default title bar.

    - Set to `true` to remove the title bar.
- `android:windowFullscreen`
    - Governs whether to remove the system status bar.
    - Set to `true` to remove the status bar and fill the entire screen.
- `android:windowBackground`
    - Color or Drawable resource to apply as a background
    - Set to color or Drawable value or resource
- `android:windowContentOverlay`
    - Drawable placed over the window content foreground. By default, this is a shadow below the status bar.
    - Set to any resource to use in place of the default status bar shadow, or null (`@null` in XML) to remove it.
- `android:windowTitleBackgroundStyle`
    - Style to apply to the window's title view
    - Set to any style resource.
- `android:windowTitleSize`
    - Height of the window's title view
    - Set to any dimension or dimension resource
- `android:windowTitleStyle`
    - Style to apply to the window's title text
    - Set to any style resource
- `android:actionBarStyle` attribute
    - Style to apply to the window's `ActionBar`
    - Set to any style resource

Listing 2-3 is an example of a styles.xml file that creates two custom themes:

- `MyTheme.One: No title bar and the default status bar shadow removed`
- `MyTheme.Two: Fullscreen with a custom background image`

Listing 2-3. *res/values/styles.xml with Two Custom Themes*

```
<?xml version="1.0" encoding="utf-8"?>
<resources>
    <style name="MyTheme.One" parent="@android:style/Theme">
        <item name="android:windowNoTitle">true</item>
        <item name="android:windowContentOverlay">@null</item>
    </style>
    <style name="MyTheme.Two" parent="@android:style/Theme">
        <item name="android:windowBackground">@drawable/window_bg</item>
        <item name="android:windowFullscreen">true</item>
    </style>
</resources>
```

Notice that a theme (or style) may also indicate a parent from which to inherit properties, so the entire theme need not be created from scratch. In the example, we chose to inherit from Android's default system theme, customizing only the properties that we needed to differentiate. All platform themes are defined in `res/values/themes.xml` of the Android package. Refer to the SDK documentation on styles and themes for more details.

Listing 2-4 shows how to apply these themes to individual Activity instances in the AndroidManifest.xml:

Listing 2-4. *Manifest with Themes Set on Each Activity*

```
<?xml version="1.0" encoding="utf-8"?>
<manifest xmlns:android="http://schemas.android.com/apk/res/android"
    …>
    <!–Apply to the application tag for a global theme -->
    <application
        …>
        <!–Apply to the activity tag for an individual theme -->
        <activity android:name=".ActivityOne" android:theme="MyTheme.One"
            …>
            <intent-filter>
                …
            </intent-filter>
        </activity>
        <activity android:name=".ActivityTwo" android:theme="MyTheme.Two"
            …>
            <intent-filter>
                …
            </intent-filter>
        </activity>

    </application>
</manifest>
```

Customizing Window Features in Code

In addition to using XML styles, window properties may also be customized from the Java code in an Activity. This method opens up a slightly different feature set to the developer for customization, although there is some overlap with the XML styling.

Customizing the window through coding involves making requests of the system using the `Activity.requestWindowFeature()` method for each feature change prior to setting the content view for the Activity.

> **NOTE:** All requests for extended window features with `Activity.requestWindowFeature()` must be made PRIOR to calling `Activity.setContentView()`. Any changes made after this point will not take place.

The features you can request from the window, and their meanings, are defined in the following:

- `FEATURE_CUSTOM_TITLE`: Set a custom layout resource as the Activity title view.
- `FEATURE_NO_TITLE`: Remove the title view from Activity.
- `FEATURE_PROGRESS`: Utilize a determinate (0–100%) progress bar in the title.
- `FEATURE_INDETERMINATE_PROGRESS`: Utilize a small indeterminate (circular) progress indicator in the title view.
- `FEATURE_LEFT_ICON`: Include a small title icon on the left side of the title view.
- `FEATURE_RIGHT_ICON`: Include a small title icon on the right side of the title view.

FEATURE_CUSTOM_TITLE

Use this window feature to replace the standard title with a completely custom layout resource (see Listing 2-5).

Listing 2-5. *Activity Setting a Custom TitleLayout*

```
protected void onCreate(Bundle savedInstanceState) {
    super.onCreate(savedInstanceState);
    //Request window features before setContentView
    requestWindowFeature(Window.FEATURE_CUSTOM_TITLE);
    setContentView(R.layout.main);

    //Set the layout resource to use for the custom title
    getWindow().setFeatureInt(Window.FEATURE_CUSTOM_TITLE, R.layout.custom_title);

}
```

> **NOTE:** Because this feature completely replaces the default title view, it cannot be combined with any of the other window feature flags.

FEATURE_NO_TITLE

Use this window feature to remove the standard title view (see Listing 2-6).

Listing 2-6. *Activity Removing the Standard Title View*

```
protected void onCreate(Bundle savedInstanceState) {
    super.onCreate(savedInstanceState);
    //Request window features before setContentView
    requestWindowFeature(Window.FEATURE_NO_TITLE);
    setContentView(R.layout.main);

}
```

> **NOTE:** Because this feature completely removes the default title view, it cannot be combined with any of the other window feature flags.

FEATURE_PROGRESS

Use this window feature to access a determinate progress bar in the window title. This is an indicator that shows finite progress. The progress can be set to any value from 0 (0%) to 10000 (100%). (See Listing 2-7.)

Listing 2-7. *Activity Using Window's Progress Bar*

```
protected void onCreate(Bundle savedInstanceState) {
    super.onCreate(savedInstanceState);
    //Request window features before setContentView
    requestWindowFeature(Window.FEATURE_PROGRESS);
    setContentView(R.layout.main);

    //Set the progress bar visibility
    setProgressBarVisibility(true);
    //Control progress value with setProgress
    setProgress(0);
    //Setting progress to 100% will cause it to disappear
    setProgress(10000);

}
```

FEATURE_INDETERMINATE_PROGRESS

Use this window feature to access an indeterminate progress indicator, also known as a spinning progress indicator, to show background activity. Because this indicator is indeterminate, it can only be shown or hidden (see Listing 2-8).

Listing 2-8. *Activity Using Window's Indeterminate Progress Bar*

```
protected void onCreate(Bundle savedInstanceState) {
    super.onCreate(savedInstanceState);
    //Request window features before setContentView
    requestWindowFeature(Window.FEATURE_INDETERMINATE_PROGRESS);
    setContentView(R.layout.main);

    //Show the progress indicator
    setProgressBarIndeterminateVisibility(true);

    //Hide the progress indicator
    setProgressBarIndeterminateVisibility(false);
}
```

FEATURE ICONS

(API Level 8)

Use this window feature to place a small Drawable icon on the left or right side of the title view (see Listing 2-9).

Listing 2-9. *Activity Using Feature Icons*

```
protected void onCreate(Bundle savedInstanceState) {
    super.onCreate(savedInstanceState);
    //Request window features before setContentView
    requestWindowFeature(Window.FEATURE_LEFT_ICON);
    requestWindowFeature(Window.FEATURE_RIGHT_ICON);

    setContentView(R.layout.main);

    //Set the layout resource to use for the custom icons
    setFeatureDrawableResource(Window.FEATURE_LEFT_ICON, R.drawable.icon);
    setFeatureDrawableResource(Window.FEATURE_RIGHT_ICON, R.drawable.icon);

}
```

> **NOTE:** These features were available prior to API Level 8, but there was a bug that kept FEATURE_RIGHT_ICON from actually being placed on the right side of the title text.

FEATURE_ACTION_BAR

(API Level 11)

This window feature is enabled by default if your application is targeting an SDK version of 11 or higher as part of the default style. However, it can also be requested in code if you are using an older style theme but want to enable the ActionBar in certain specific cases. See Listing 2-10.

Listing 2-10. *Activity Using ActionBar Overlay*

```
protected void onCreate(Bundle savedInstanceState) {
    super.onCreate(savedInstanceState);
    //Request window features before setContentView
    requestWindowFeature(Window.FEATURE_ACTION_BAR);
    setContentView(R.layout.main);

    //Access the ActionBar to modify it
    ActionBar actionBar = getActionBar();
}
```

FEATURE_ACTION_BAR_OVERLAY

(API Level 11)

Use this window feature to request that the `ActionBar` element be laid out over the top of your view content, rather than above it. This can be advantageous in applications where you want to temporarily hide and show the `ActionBar` and when you don't want the overall layout to change each time you do so (more on this in the next section). See Listing 2-11.

Listing 2-11. *Activity Using ActionBar Overlay*

```
protected void onCreate(Bundle savedInstanceState) {
    super.onCreate(savedInstanceState);
    //Request window features before setContentView
    requestWindowFeature(Window.FEATURE_ACTION_BAR_OVERLAY);
    setContentView(R.layout.main);
}
```

Figure 2-1 shows an Activity with all the icon and progress features enabled simultaneously and another with the ActionBar feature enabled.

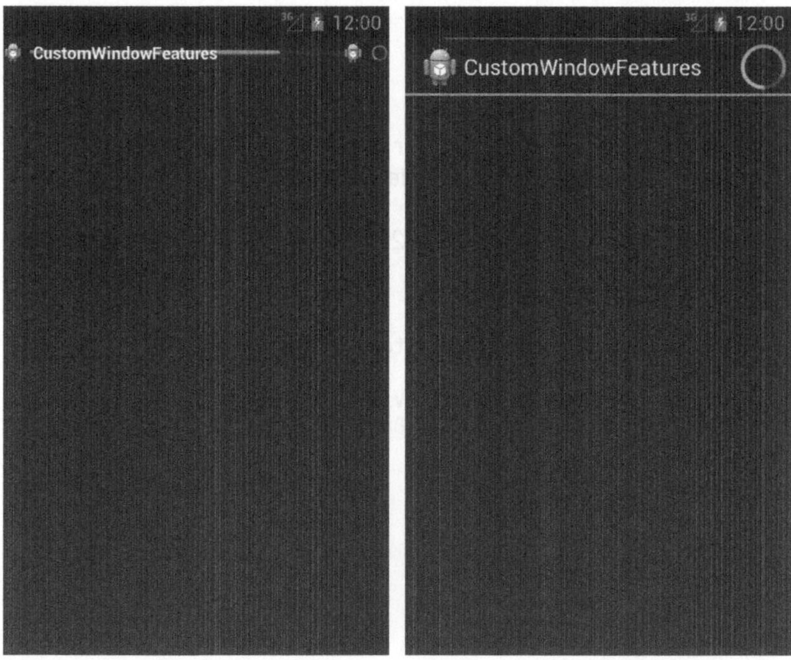

Figure 2-1. *This shows window features enabled in a title view (left) and in an ActionBar (right).*

Dynamically Toggling System UI Components

Many applications that target a more immersive content experience (such as readers or video players) can benefit from temporarily hiding the system's UI components to provide as much screen real estate as possible to the application when the content is visible. Beginning with Android 3.0, developers are able to adjust many of these properties at runtime without the need to statically request a window feature or declare values inside of a theme.

Dark Mode

(API Level 11)

This is also often called "lights out" mode. It refers to dimming the onscreen navigation controls (and the system status bar in later releases) without actually removing them to relieve any system elements onscreen that might distract the user from the current view in the application.

To enable this mode, we simply have to call `setSystemUiVisibility()` on any `View` in our hierarchy with the `SYSTEM_UI_FLAG_LOW_PROFILE` flag. To set the mode back to default, call the same method with `SYSTEM_UI_FLAG_VISIBLE` instead. We can determine which mode we are in by calling `getSystemUiVisibility()` and checking the current status of the flags (see Listings 2-12 and 2-13).

> **NOTE:** These flag names were introduced in API Level 14 (Android 4.0); prior to that they were named `STATUS_BAR_HIDDEN` and `STATUS_BAR_VISIBLE`. The values of each are the same, so the new flags will produce the same behavior on Android 3.x devices.

Listing 2-12. *res/layout/main.xml*

```
<?xml version="1.0" encoding="utf-8"?>
<RelativeLayout xmlns:android="http://schemas.android.com/apk/res/android"
    android:layout_width="match_parent"
    android:layout_height="match_parent" >
    <Button
        android:layout_width="match_parent"
        android:layout_height="wrap_content"
        android:layout_centerVertical="true"
        android:text="Toggle Mode"
        android:onClick="onToggleClick" />
</RelativeLayout>
```

Listing 2-13. *Activity Toggling Dark Mode*

```
public class DarkActivity extends Activity {

    @Override
    protected void onCreate(Bundle savedInstanceState) {
        super.onCreate(savedInstanceState);
        setContentView(R.layout.main);
    }

    public void onToggleClick(View v) {
        int currentVis = v.getSystemUiVisibility();
        int newVis;
        if ((currentVis & View.SYSTEM_UI_FLAG_LOW_PROFILE)
                == View.SYSTEM_UI_FLAG_LOW_PROFILE) {
            newVis = View.SYSTEM_UI_FLAG_VISIBLE;
        } else {
            newVis = View.SYSTEM_UI_FLAG_LOW_PROFILE;
        }
        v.setSystemUiVisibility(newVis);
    }
}
```

The methods `setSystemUiVisibility()` and `getSystemUiVisibility()` can be called on any `View` currently visible inside the `Window` where you want to adjust these parameters.

Hiding Navigation Controls

(API Level 14)

This view flag removes the onscreen HOME and BACK controls for devices that do not have physical buttons. While Android gives developers the ability to do this, it is with caution because these functions are extremely important to the user. If the navigation controls are manually hidden, any tap on the screen will bring them back. Listing 2-14 shows an example of this in practice.

Listing 2-14. *Activity Toggling Navigation Controls*

```
public class HideActivity extends Activity {

    @Override
    protected void onCreate(Bundle savedInstanceState) {
        super.onCreate(savedInstanceState);
        setContentView(R.layout.main);

    }
```

```
    public void onToggleClick(View v) {
        //Here we only need to hide the controls on a tap because
        // the system will make the controls reappear automatically
        // anytime the screen is tapped after they are hidden.
        v.setSystemUiVisibility(View.SYSTEM_UI_FLAG_HIDE_NAVIGATION);
    }
}
```

Notice also when running this example that the button will shift up and down to accommodate the changes in content space due to our centering requirement in the root layout. If you plan to use this flag, make note of the fact that any views being laid out relative to the bottom of the screen will move as the layout changes.

Fullscreen UI Mode

(API Level 11)

Prior to Android 4.1, there is no method of hiding the system status bar dynamically; it has to be done with a static theme. To hide and show the `ActionBar`, however, `ActionBar.show()` and `ActionBar.hide()` will animate the element in and out of view. If `FEATURE_ACTION_BAR_OVERLAY` is requested, this change will not affect the content of the Activity; otherwise, the view content will shift up and down to accommodate the change.

(API Level 16)

Listing 2-15 illustrates an example of how to hide all system UI temporarily.

Listing 2-15. *Activity Toggling All System UI*

```
public class FullActivity extends Activity {

    @Override
    protected void onCreate(Bundle savedInstanceState) {
        super.onCreate(savedInstanceState);
        //Request this feature so the ActionBar will hide
        requestWindowFeature(Window.FEATURE_ACTION_BAR_OVERLAY);
        setContentView(R.layout.main);
    }

    public void onToggleClick(View v) {
        //Here we only need to hide the UI on a tap because
        // the system will make the controls reappear automatically
        // anytime the screen is tapped after they are hidden.
        v.setSystemUiVisibility(
                /* This flag tells Android not to shift
                 * our layout when resizing the window to
```

```
                 * hide/show the system elements
                 */
                View.SYSTEM_UI_FLAG_LAYOUT_STABLE
                /* This flag hides the system status bar.  If
                 * ACTION_BAR_OVERLAY is requested, it will hide
                 * the ActionBar as well.
                 */
                | View.SYSTEM_UI_FLAG_FULLSCREEN
                /* This flag hides the onscreen controls
                 */
                | View.SYSTEM_UI_FLAG_HIDE_NAVIGATION);
    }
}
```

Similar to the example of hiding only the navigation controls, we do not need to show the controls again because any tap on the screen will bring them back. As a convenience beginning in Android 4.1, when the system clears the SYSTEM_UI_FLAG_HIDE_NAVIGATION in this way, it will also clear the SYSTEM_UI_FLAG_FULLSCREEN, so the top and bottom elements will become visible together. Android will only hide the ActionBar as part of the fullscreen flag if we request FEATURE_ACTION_BAR_OVERLAY; otherwise, only the status bar will be affected.

We have added one other flag of interest in this example: SYSTEM_UI_LAYOUT_STABLE. This flag tells Android not to shift our content view as a result of adding and removing the system UI. Because of this, our button will stay centered as the elements toggle.

2-2. Creating and Displaying Views

Problem

Your application needs view elements in order to display information and interact with the user.

Solution

(API Level 1)

Whether using one of the many views and widgets available in the Android SDK or creating a custom display, all applications need views to interact with the user. The preferred method for creating user interfaces in Android is to define them in XML and inflate them at runtime.

The view structure in Android is a tree, with the root typically being the Activity or Window's content view. ViewGroups are special views that manage the display of one or more child views, of which could be another ViewGroup, and the tree continues to grow. All the standard layout classes descend from ViewGroup, and they are the most common choices for the root node of the XML layout file.

How It Works

Let's define a layout with two Button instances and an EditText to accept user input. We can define a file in res/layout/ called main.xml with the following contents (see Listing 2-16).

Listing 2-16. *res/layout/main.xml*

```
<LinearLayout xmlns:android="http://schemas.android.com/apk/res/android"
    android:layout_width="fill_parent"
    android:layout_height="fill_parent"
    android:orientation="vertical">
    <EditText
        android:id="@+id/editText"
        android:layout_width="fill_parent"
        android:layout_height="wrap_content"
    />
    <LinearLayout
        android:layout_width="fill_parent"
        android:layout_height="wrap_content"
        android:orientation="horizontal">
        <Button
            android:id="@+id/save"
            android:layout_width="wrap_content"
            android:layout_height="wrap_content"
            android:text="Save"
        />
        <Button
            android:id="@+id/cancel"
            android:layout_width="wrap_content"
            android:layout_height="wrap_content"
            android:text="Cancel"
        />
    </LinearLayout>
</LinearLayout>
```

LinearLayout is a ViewGroup that lays out its elements one after the other in either a horizontal or vertical fashion. In main.xml, the EditText and inner LinearLayout are laid out vertically in order. The contents of the inner LinearLayout (the buttons) are laid out horizontally. The view elements with an android:id value are elements that will need to be referenced in the Java code for further customization or display.

To make this layout the display contents of an Activity, it must be inflated at runtime. The Activity.setContentView() method is overloaded with a convenience method to do this for you, only requiring the layout ID value. In this case, setting the layout in the Activity is as simple as this:

```
public void onCreate(Bundle savedInstanceState) {
    super.onCreate(savedInstanceState);
    setContentView(R.layout.main);
    //Continue Activity initialization
}
```

Nothing beyond supplying the ID value (main.xml automatically has an ID of R.layout.main) is required. If the layout needs a little more customization before it is attached to the window, you can inflate it manually and do some work before adding it as the content view. Listing 2-17 inflates the same layout and adds a third button before displaying it.

Listing 2-17. *Layout Modification Prior to Display*

```
public void onCreate(Bundle savedInstanceState) {
    super.onCreate(savedInstanceState);
    //Inflate the layout file
    LinearLayout layout = (LinearLayout)getLayoutInflater().inflate(R.layout.main,
        null);
    //Add a new button
    Button reset = new Button(this);
    reset.setText("Reset Form");
    layout.addView(reset,
        new LinearLayout.LayoutParams(LayoutParams.FILL_PARENT,
                LayoutParams.WRAP_CONTENT));

    //Attach the view to the window
    setContentView(layout);
}
```

In this instance the XML layout is inflated in the Activity code with a LayoutInflater, whose inflate() method returns a handle to the inflated View. Since LayoutInflater.inflate() returns a View, we must cast it to the specific subclass in the XML in order to do more than just attach it to the window.

> **NOTE:** The root element in the XML layout file is the View element returned from LayoutInflater.inflate().

The second parameter to inflate() is the parent ViewGroup, and this is extremely important because it defines how the LayoutParams from the inflated layout are interpreted. Whenever possible, if you know the parent of this inflated hierarchy it should be passed here; otherwise, the LayoutParams from the root view of the XML will be ignored. When passing a parent, also note that the third parameter of inflate() controls whether the inflated layout is automatically attached to the parent. We will see in future recipes how this can be useful for doing custom views. In this instance, however, we are inflating the top-level view of our Activity, so we pass null here.

2-3. Monitoring Click Actions

Problem

The application needs to do some work when the user taps on a view.

Solution

(API Level 1)

Attach a View.OnClickListener to handle user click events. By default, many widgets in the SDK are already clickable, such as Button, ImageButton, and CheckBox. However, any view can be made to receive click events by setting android:clickable="true" in XML, by calling View.setClickable(true) from code, or just by attaching a listener, which will enable the clickable flag on the View if it is not already set.

How It Works

To receive and handle the click events, create an OnClickListener and attach it to the view object. In this example, the view is a button defined in the root layout like so:

```
<Button
    android:id="@+id/myButton"
    android:layout_width="wrap_content"
    android:layout_height="wrap_content"
    android:text="My Button"
/>
```

In the Activity code, the button is retrieved by its `android:id` value and the listener is attached (see Listing 2-18).

Listing 2-18. *Setting Listener on a Button*

```
public void onCreate(Bundle savedInstanceState) {
    super.onCreate(savedInstanceState);
    //Retrieve the button object
    Button myButton = (Button)findViewById(R.id.myButton);
    //Attach the listener
    myButton.setOnClickListener(clickListener);
}

//Listener object to handle the click events
View.OnClickListener clickListener = new View.OnClickListener() {
    public void onClick(View v) {
        //Code to handle the click event
    }
};
```

> **REMINDER:** Any widget that is a `View` can be set as clickable. You don't need to use `Button` or `ImageButton` to have interactive widgets in your application. In fact, these widgets are just clickable and focusable versions of `TextView` and `ImageView`!

(API Level 4)

Starting with API Level 4, there is a more efficient way to attach basic click listeners to view widgets. View widgets can set the `android:onClick` attribute in XML, and the runtime will use Java Reflection to call the required method when events occur. If we modify the previous example to use this method, the button's XML will become the following:

```
<Button
    android:layout_width="wrap_content"
    android:layout_height="wrap_content"
    android:text="My Button"
    android:onClick="onMyButtonClick"
/>
```

The `android:id` attribute is no longer required in this example since the only reason we referenced it in code was to add the listener. This simplifies the Java code as well to look like Listing 2-19.

Listing 2-19. *Listener Attached in XML*

```
public void onCreate(Bundle savedInstanceState) {
    super.onCreate(savedInstanceState);
    //No code required here to attach the listener
}

public void onMyButtonClick(View v) {
    //Code to handle the click event
}
```

> **TIP:** The `android:onClick` mechanism works by creating a new `OnClickListener` under the hood and calling the method name passed in the attribute by reflection on the current `Context`. Therefore, these listeners can really only be set on an `Activity`. If you want click events to be handled by a `Fragment` or other component, you will need to manually attach those listeners using the previous method.

2-4. Resolution-Independent Assets

Problem

Your application uses graphic assets that do not scale well using Android's traditional mechanism for scaling images up on higher-resolution screens.

Solution

(API Level 4)

Use resource qualifiers and supply multiple sizes of each asset. The Android SDK has defined four types of screen resolutions, or densities, listed here:

- Low (ldpi): 120 dpi
- Medium (mdpi): 160 dpi
- High (hdpi): 240 dpi
- Extra High (xhdpi): 320 dpi (added in API Level 8)

- Extra-Extra High (xxhdpi): 480 dpi (added in API Level 16)
  - Used primarily for launcher icons on high-resolution, large screen devices

By default, an Android project may only have one `res/drawable/` directory where all graphic assets are stored. In this case, Android will take those images to be 1:1 in size on medium-resolution screens. When the application is run on a higher-resolution screen, Android will scale up the image to 150% (200% for xhdpi), which can result in loss of quality.

How It Works

To avoid this issue, you should provide multiple copies of each image resource at different resolutions and place them into resource-qualified directory paths.

- `res/drawable-ldpi/`
  - 75% of the size at mdpi
- `res/drawable-mdpi/`
  - Noted as the original image size
- `res/drawable-hdpi/`
  - 150% of the size at mdpi
- `res/drawable-xhdpi/`
  - 200% of the size at mdpi
  - Only if application supports API Level 8 as the minimum target
- res/drawable-xxhdpi/
  - 300% of the size at mdpi
  - Only if application supports API Level 16

The image must have the same file name in all directories. For example, if you had left the default launcher icon value in AndroidManifest.xml (i.e., `android:icon="@drawable/icon"`), then you would place the following resource files in the project:

```
res/drawable-ldpi/icon.png (36x36 pixels)
res/drawable-mdpi/icon.png (48x48 pixels)
```

```
res/drawable-hdpi/icon.png (72x72 pixels)
res/drawable-xhdpi/icon.png (96x96 pixels, if supported)
res/drawable-xxhdpi/icon.png (144x144 pixels, if supported)
```

Android will select the asset that fits the device resolution and display it as the application icon on the Launcher screen, resulting in no scaling and no loss of image quality. As of Android 3.0, the system will automatically select an image one density level higher than the screen configuration, so, for example, the xxhdpi asset will be used on an xhdpi device.

As another example, a logo image is to be displayed in several places throughout an application, and it is 200 by 200 pixels on a medium-resolution device. That image should be provided in all supported sizes using resource qualifiers:

```
res/drawable-ldpi/logo.png (150x150 pixels)
res/drawable-mdpi/logo.png (200x200 pixels)
res/drawable-hdpi/logo.png (300x300 pixels)
```

This application doesn't support extra-high-resolution displays, so we only provide three images. When the time comes to reference this resource, simply use `@drawable/logo` (from XML) or `R.drawable.logo` (from Java code), and Android will display the appropriate resource.

2-5. Locking Activity Orientation

Problem

A certain Activity in your application should not be allowed to rotate, or rotation requires more direct intervention from the application code.

Solution

(API Level 1)

Using static declarations in the AndroidManifest.xml file, each individual Activity can be modified to lock into either portrait or landscape orientation. This can only be applied to the `<activity>` tag, so it cannot be done once for the entire application scope. Simply add `android:screenOrientation="portrait"` or `android:screenOrientation="landscape"` to the `<activity>` element and they will always display in the specified orientation, regardless of how the device is positioned.

There is also an option you can pass in the XML entitled "behind." If an Activity element has `android:screenOrientation="behind"` set, it will take its settings from the previous Activity in the stack. This can be a useful way for an Activity to match the locked orientation of its originator for some slightly more dynamic behavior.

How It Works

The example AndroidManifest.xml depicted in Listing 2-20 has three Activities. Two of them are locked into portrait orientation (MainActivity and ResultActivity), while the UserEntryActivity is allowed to rotate, presumably because the user may want to rotate and use a physical keyboard.

Listing 2-20. *Manifest with Some Activities Locked in Portrait*

```
<?xml version="1.0" encoding="utf-8"?>
<manifest xmlns:android="http://schemas.android.com/apk/res/android"
      package="com.examples.rotation"
      android:versionCode="1"
      android:versionName="1.0">
    <application android:icon="@drawable/icon" android:label="@string/app_name">
        <activity android:name=".MainActivity"
            android:label="@string/app_name"
            android:screenOrientation="portrait">
            <intent-filter>
                <action android:name="android.intent.action.MAIN" />
                <category android:name="android.intent.category.LAUNCHER" />
            </intent-filter>
        </activity>
        <activity android:name=".ResultActivity"
            android:screenOrientation="portrait" />
        <activity android:name=".UserEntryActivity" />
    </application>
</manifest>
```

2-6. Dynamic Orientation Locking

Problem

Conditions exist during which the screen should not rotate, but the condition is temporary or dependent on user wishes.

Solution

(API Level 1)

Using the requested orientation mechanism in Android, an application can adjust the screen orientation used to display the Activity, fixing it to a specific orientation or releasing it to the device to decide. This is accomplished through the use of the `Activity.setRequestedOrientation()` method, which takes an integer constant from the `ActivityInfo.screenOrientation` attribute grouping.

By default, the requested orientation is set to `SCREEN_ORIENTATION_UNSPECIFIED`, which allows the device to decide for itself which orientation should be used. This is a decision typically based on the physical orientation of the device. The current requested orientation can be retrieved at any time as well by using `Activity.getRequestedOrientation()`.

How It Works

User Rotation Lock Button

As an example of this, let's create a ToggleButton instance that controls whether or not to lock the current orientation, allowing the user to control at any point whether or not the Activity should change orientation.

Somewhere in the main.xml layout, a ToggleButton instance is defined:

```
<ToggleButton
    android:id="@+id/toggleButton"
    android:layout_width="wrap_content"
    android:layout_height="wrap_content"
    android:textOff="Lock"
    android:textOn="LOCKED"
/>
```

In the Activity code, we will create a listener to the button's state that locks and releases the screen orientation based on its current value (see Listing 2-21).

Listing 2-21. *Activity to Dynamically Lock/Unlock Screen Orientation*

```
public class LockActivity extends Activity {

    protected void onCreate(Bundle savedInstanceState) {
        super.onCreate(savedInstanceState);
        setContentView(R.layout.main);
```

```
        //Get handle to the button resource
        ToggleButton toggle = (ToggleButton)findViewById(R.id.toggleButton);
        //Set the default state before adding the listener
        if( getRequestedOrientation() !=
                ActivityInfo.SCREEN_ORIENTATION_UNSPECIFIED ) {
            toggle.setChecked(true);
        } else {
            toggle.setChecked(false);
        }
        //Attach the listener to the button
        toggle.setOnCheckedChangeListener(listener);
    }

    OnCheckedChangeListener listener = new OnCheckedChangeListener() {
        public void onCheckedChanged(CompoundButton buttonView,
                boolean isChecked) {
            int current = getResources().getConfiguration().orientation;
            if(isChecked) {
                switch(current) {
                case Configuration.ORIENTATION_LANDSCAPE:
                    setRequestedOrientation(
                            ActivityInfo.SCREEN_ORIENTATION_LANDSCAPE);
                    break;
                case Configuration.ORIENTATION_PORTRAIT:
                    setRequestedOrientation(
                            ActivityInfo.SCREEN_ORIENTATION_PORTRAIT);
                    break;
                default:
                    setRequestedOrientation(
                            ActivityInfo.SCREEN_ORIENTATION_UNSPECIFIED);
                }
            } else {
                setRequestedOrientation(
                        ActivityInfo.SCREEN_ORIENTATION_UNSPECIFIED);
            }
        }
    }
}
```

The code in the listener is the key ingredient to this recipe. If the user presses the button and it toggles to the ON state, the current orientation is read by storing the `orientation` parameter from `Resources.getConfiguration()`. The Configuration object and the requested orientation use different constants to map the states, so we switch on the current orientation and call `setRequestedOrientation()` with the appropriate constant.

> **NOTE:** If an orientation is requested that is different from the current state, and your Activity is in the foreground, the Activity will change immediately to accommodate the request.

If the user presses the button and it toggles to the OFF state, we no longer want to lock the orientation, so `setRequestedOrientation()` is called with the `SCREEN_ORIENTATION_UNSPECIFIED` constant again to return control back to the device. This may also cause an immediate change to occur if the device orientation dictates that the Activity be different than where the application had it locked.

> **NOTE:** Setting a requested orientation does not keep the default Activity life cycle from occurring. If a device configuration change occurs (the keyboard slides out or the device orientation changes), the Activity will still be destroyed and recreated, so all rules about persisting Activity state still apply.

2-7. Manually Handling Rotation

Problem

The default behavior destroying and recreating an Activity during rotation causes an unacceptable performance penalty in the application.

Without customization, Android will respond to configuration changes by finishing the current Activity instance and creating a new one in its place, appropriate for the new configuration. This can cause undue performance penalties because the UI state must be saved, and then completely rebuilt.

Solution

(API Level 1)

Utilize the `android:configChanges` manifest parameter to instruct Android that a certain Activity will handle rotation events without assistance from the runtime. This not only reduces the amount of work required from Android, destroying and recreating the Activity instance, but also from your application. With the Activity instance intact, the application does not have to necessarily spend time to save and restore the current state in order to maintain consistency to the user.

An Activity that registers for one or more configuration changes will be notified via the `Activity.onConfigurationChanged()` callback method, where it can perform any necessary manual handling associated with the change.

There are two configuration change parameters the Activity should register for in order to handle rotation completely: `orientation` and `keyboardHidden`. The `orientation` parameter registers the Activity for any event when the device orientation changes. The `keyboardHidden` parameter registers the Activity for the event when the user slides a physical keyboard in or out. While the latter may not be directly of interest, if you do not register for these events Android will recreate your Activity when they occur, which may subvert your efforts in handling rotation in the first place.

How It Works

These parameters are added to any `<activity>` element in AndroidManifest.xml like so:

```
<activity android:name=".MyActivity"
    android:configChanges="orientation|keyboardHidden" />
```

Multiple changes can be registered in the same assignment statement, using a pipe "|" character between them. Because these parameters cannot be applied to an `<application>` element, each individual Activity must register in the AndroidManifest.xml.

With the Activity registered, a configuration change results in a call to the Activity's `onConfigurationChanged()` method. Listing 2-22 is a simple Activity definition that can be used to handle the callback received when the changes occur.

Listing 2-22. *Activity to Manage Rotation Manually*

```
public class MyActivity extends Activity {

    @Override
    protected void onCreate(Bundle savedInstanceState) {
        //Calling super is required
        super.onCreate(savedInstanceState);
        //Load view resources
        loadView();
    }
```

```
    @Override
    public void onConfigurationChanged(Configuration newConfig) {
        //Calling super is required
        super.onConfigurationChanged(newConfig);
        //Store important UI state
        saveState();
        //Reload the view resources
        loadView();
    }

    private void saveState() {
        //Implement any code to persist the UI state
    }

    private void loadView() {
        setContentView(R.layout.main);

        //Handle any other required UI changes upon a new configuration
        //Including restoring and stored state
    }
}
```

> **NOTE:** Google does not recommend handling rotation in this fashion unless it is necessary for the application's performance. All configuration-specific resources must be loaded manually in response to each change event.

Google recommends allowing the default recreation behavior on Activity rotation unless the performance of your application requires circumventing it. Primarily, this is because you lose all assistance Android provides for loading alternative resources if you have them stored in resource-qualified directories (such as `res/layout-land/` for landscape layouts).

In the example Activity, all code dealing with the view layout is abstracted to a private method, `loadView()`, called from both `onCreate()` and `onConfigurationChanged()`. In this method, code like `setContentView()` is placed to ensure that the appropriate layout is loaded to match the configuration.

Calling `setContentView()` will completely reload the view, so any UI state that is important still needs to be saved, without the assistance of life-cycle callbacks like `onSaveInstanceState()` and `onRestoreInstanceState()`. The example implements a method called `saveState()` for this purpose.

2-8. Creating Pop-Up Menu Actions

Problem

You want to provide the user with multiple actions to take as a result of them selecting some part of the UI.

Solution

Display a ContextMenu or ActionMode in response to the user action.

How It Works

ContextMenu

(API Level 1)

Using a ContextMenu is a useful solution, particularly when you want to provide a list of actions based on an item click in a ListView or other AdapterView. This is because the ContextMenu.ContextMenuInfo object provides useful information about the specific item that was selected, such as id and position, which may be helpful in constructing the menu.

First, create an XML file in res/menu/ to define the menu itself; we'll call this one contextmenu.xml (see Listing 2-23).

Listing 2-23. *res/menu/contextmenu.xml*

```
<?xml version="1.0" encoding="utf-8"?>
<menu xmlns:android="http://schemas.android.com/apk/res/android">
    <item
        android:id="@+id/menu_delete"
        android:icon="@android:drawable/ic_menu_delete"
        android:title="Delete Item"
    />
    <item
        android:id="@+id/menu_edit"
        android:icon="@android:drawable/ic_menu_edit"
        android:title="Edit Item"
    />
</menu>
```

Then utilize onCreateContextMenu() and onContextItemSelected() in the Activity to inflate the menu and handle user selection (see Listing 2-24).

Listing 2-24. *Activity Utilizing Custom Menu*

```
@Override
public void onCreateContextMenu(ContextMenu menu, View v,
        ContextMenu.ContextMenuInfo menuInfo) {
    super.onCreateContextMenu(menu, v, menuInfo);
    getMenuInflater().inflate(R.menu.contextmenu, menu);
    menu.setHeaderTitle("Choose an Option");
}

@Override
public boolean onContextItemSelected(MenuItem item) {
    //Switch on the item's ID to find the action the user selected
    switch(item.getItemId()) {
    case R.id.menu_delete:
        //Perform delete actions
        break;
    case R.id.menu_edit:
        //Perform edit actions
        break;
    default:
        return super.onContextItemSelected(item);
    }
    return true;
}
```

In order for these callback methods to fire, you must register the view that will trigger the menu. In effect, this sets the View.OnCreateContextMenuListener for the view to the current Activity:

```
protected void onCreate(Bundle savedInstanceState) {
        super.onCreate(savedInstanceState);
    //Register a button for context events
    ListView list = new ListView(this);
    ArrayAdapter<String> adapter = new ArrayAdapter<String>(this,
            android.R.layout.simple_list_item_1, ITEMS);
    list.setAdapter(adapter);
    registerForContextMenu(list);

    setContentView(list);
}
```

The default user behavior in Android is for many views to show a ContextMenu when a long-press occurs as an alternate to the main click action. Following suit, in our example long-pressing on the items in the ListView will display our options menu.

> **TIP:** You can also trigger a ContextMenu for any arbitrary view by calling the Activity.openContextMenu() method, passing it the view you had previously registered.

Tying all the pieces together, we have a simple Activity that registers a button to show our menu when tapped (see Listing 2-25).

Listing 2-25. *Activity Utilizing Context Action Menu*

```
public class ContextActivity extends Activity {

    private static final String[] ITEMS =
            {"Mom", "Dad", "Brother", "Sister", "Uncle", "Aunt"};

    protected void onCreate(Bundle savedInstanceState) {
        super.onCreate(savedInstanceState);
        //Register a button for context events
        ListView list = new ListView(this);
           ArrayAdapter<String> adapter = new ArrayAdapter<String>(this,
                   android.R.layout.simple_list_item_1, ITEMS);
           list.setAdapter(adapter);
           registerForContextMenu(list);

           setContentView(list);
    }

    @Override
    public void onCreateContextMenu(ContextMenu menu, View v,
            ContextMenu.ContextMenuInfo menuInfo) {
        super.onCreateContextMenu(menu, v, menuInfo);
        getMenuInflater().inflate(R.menu.contextmenu, menu);
        menu.setHeaderTitle("Choose an Option");
    }

    @Override
    public boolean onContextItemSelected(MenuItem item) {
        //You can obtain the item that was clicked from the bundled
        // ContextMenuInfo object, which is an instance of AdapterContextMenuInfo
        // in the case of a ListView
        AdapterContextMenuInfo info = (AdapterContextMenuInfo) item.getMenuInfo();
        int listPosition = info.position;

        //Switch on the item's ID to find the action the user selected
        switch(item.getItemId()) {
        case R.id.menu_delete:
            //Perform delete actions
            break;
```

```
        case R.id.menu_edit:
            //Perform edit actions
            break;
        default:
            return super.onContextItemSelected(item);
        }
        return true;
    }
}
```

When the user makes a selection, you can determine which action they took by checking the `MenuItem` passed in. In addition, this `MenuItem` has with it a `ContextMenuInfo` object, which contains data about the item in the original list that was selected. This can also be quite useful in order for you to actually perform the requested action on the data item. The resulting application is shown in Figure 2-2.

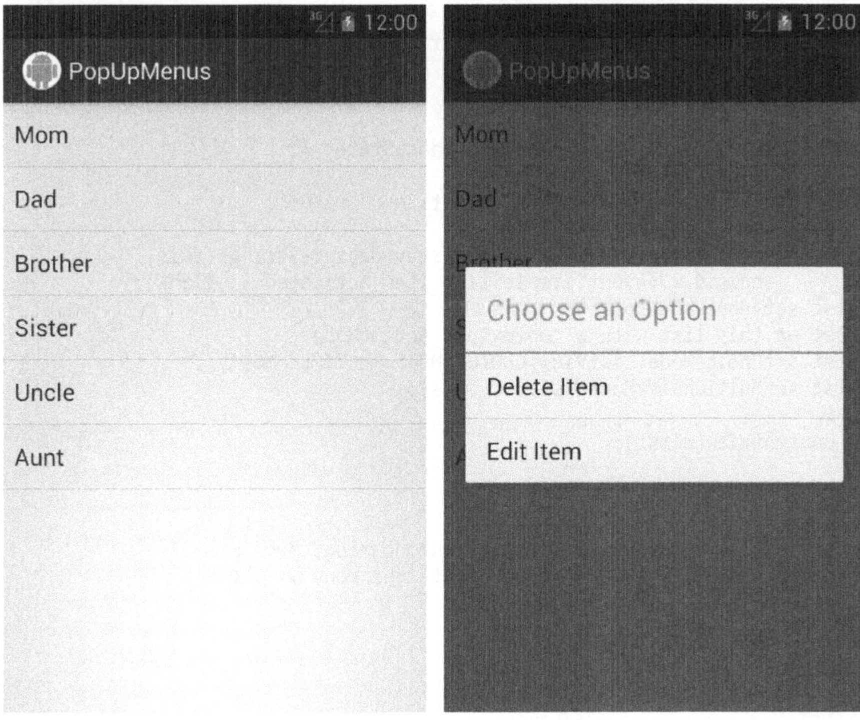

Figure 2–2. *Context action menu*

ActionMode

(API Level 11)

The ActionMode API solves a similar problem to ContextMenu, allowing the user to take actions on specific items in your user interface; however, it does so in a slightly different way. Activating an ActionMode overtakes the system ActionBar with an overlay that includes menu options you provide and an extra option to exit the ActionMode. It also allows you to select multiple items at once on which to apply a single action. Listing 2-26 illustrates this feature.

Listing 2-26. *Activity Utilizing Context ActionMode*

```
public class ActionActivity extends Activity implements
        AbsListView.MultiChoiceModeListener {

    private static final String[] ITEMS =
            {"Mom", "Dad", "Brother", "Sister", "Uncle", "Aunt"};

    private ListView mList;

    protected void onCreate(Bundle savedInstanceState) {
        super.onCreate(savedInstanceState);
        //Register a button for context events
        mList = new ListView(this);
        ArrayAdapter<String> adapter = new ArrayAdapter<String>(this,
                android.R.layout.simple_list_item_activated_1, ITEMS);
        mList.setAdapter(adapter);
        //Set up this list with a contextual ActionMode
        mList.setChoiceMode(ListView.CHOICE_MODE_MULTIPLE_MODAL);
        mList.setMultiChoiceModeListener(this);

        setContentView(mList);
    }

    @Override
    public boolean onPrepareActionMode(ActionMode mode, Menu menu) {
        //You can do extra work here to update the menu if the
        // ActionMode is ever invalidated
        return true;
    }

    @Override
    public void onDestroyActionMode(ActionMode mode) {
        //This is called when the ActionMode has been exited
    }
```

```
    @Override
    public boolean onCreateActionMode(ActionMode mode, Menu menu) {
        MenuInflater inflater = mode.getMenuInflater();
        inflater.inflate(R.menu.contextmenu, menu);
        return true;
    }

    @Override
    public boolean onActionItemClicked(ActionMode mode, MenuItem item) {
        //Obtain a list of checked item locations to do the operation
        SparseBooleanArray items = mList.getCheckedItemPositions();
        //Switch on the item's ID to find the action the user selected
        switch(item.getItemId()) {
        case R.id.menu_delete:
            //Perform delete actions
            break;
        case R.id.menu_edit:
            //Perform edit actions
            break;
        default:
            return false;
        }
        return true;
    }

    @Override
    public void onItemCheckedStateChanged(ActionMode mode, int position,
            long id, boolean checked) {
        int count = mList.getCheckedItemCount();
        mode.setTitle(String.format("%d Selected", count));
    }
}
```

To use our ListView to activate a multiple selection ActionMode, we set its choiceMode attribute to CHOICE_MODE_MULTIPLE_MODAL. This is different from the traditional CHOICE_MODE_MULTIPLE, which will provide selection widgets on each list item to make the selection. The modal flag only applies this selection mode while an ActionMode is active.

There are a series of callbacks required to implement an ActionMode that are not built directly into an Activity like the ContextMenu. We need to implement the ActionMode.Callback interface to respond to the events of creating the menu and selecting options. ListView has a special interface called MultiChoiceModeListener, which is a subinterface of ActionMode.Callback, which we implement in the example.

In onCreateActionMode() we respond similarly to onCreateContextMenu(), just inflating our menu options for the overlay to display. Your Menu does not need to contain icons; `ActionMode` can display the item names instead. The `onItemCheckedStateChanged()` method is where we will get feedback for each item selection. Here, we use that change to update the title of the ActionMode to display how many items are currently checked.

The `onActionItemClicked()` method will be called when the user has finished making selections and taps an option item. Because there are multiple items to work on, we go back to the list to get all the items checked with `getCheckedItemPositions()` so we can apply the selected operation. Figure 2-3 shows how the `ActionMode` looks with our previous list.

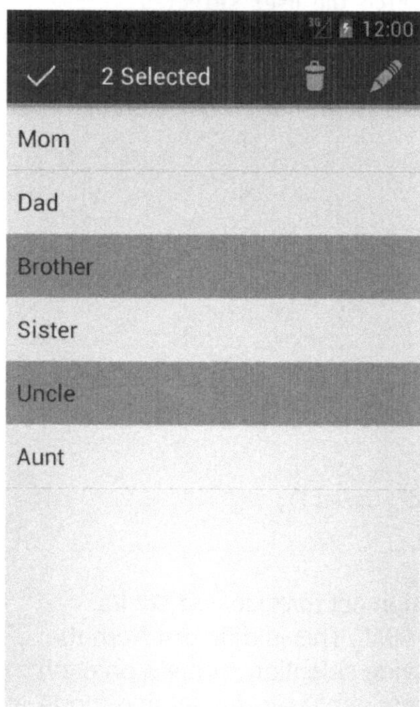

Figure 2-3. *ActionMode with two selections made*

2-9. Displaying A User Dialog

Problem

You need to display a simple pop-up dialog to the user to either notify of an event or to present a list of selections.

Solution

(API Level 1)

AlertDialog is the most efficient method of displaying important modal information to your user quickly. The content it displays is easy to customize, and the framework provides a convenient AlertDialog.Builder class to construct a pop-up quickly.

How It Works

When you use an AlertDialog.Builder, you can construct a similar AlertDialog but with some additional options. AlertDialog is a very versatile class for creating simple pop-ups to get feedback from the user. With AlertDialog.Builder, a single or multichoice list, buttons, and a message string can all be easily added into one compact widget.

To illustrate this, let's create the same pop-up selection as before using an AlertDialog. This time, we will add a Cancel button to the bottom of the options list (see Listing 2-27).

Listing 2-27. *Action Menu Using AlertDialog*

```
public class DialogActivity extends Activity
        implements DialogInterface.OnClickListener, View.OnClickListener {

    private static final String[] ZONES = {"Pacific Time", "Mountain Time",
            "Central Time", "Eastern Time", "Atlantic Time"};

    Button mButton;
    AlertDialog mActions;

    @Override
    protected void onCreate(Bundle savedInstanceState) {
        super.onCreate(savedInstanceState);
        setTitle("Activity");
        mButton = new Button(this);
        mButton.setText("Click for Time Zones");
        mButton.setOnClickListener(this);


        AlertDialog.Builder builder = new AlertDialog.Builder(this);
        builder.setTitle("Select Time Zone");
        builder.setItems(ZONES, this);
        //Cancel action does nothing but dismiss, we could add another listener
        // here to do something extra when the user hits the Cancel button
        builder.setNegativeButton("Cancel", null);
```

```
        mActions = builder.create();

        setContentView(mButton);
    }

    //List selection action handled here
    @Override
    public void onClick(DialogInterface dialog, int which) {
        String selected = ZONES[which];
        mButton.setText(selected);
    }

    //Button action handled here (pop up the dialog)
    @Override
    public void onClick(View v) {
        mActions.show();
    }
}
```

In this example, we create a new `AlertDialog.Builder` instance and use its convenience methods to add the following items:

- A title, using `setTitle()`
- The selectable list of options, using `setItems()` with an array of strings (also works with array resources)
- A Cancel button, using `setNegativeButton()`

The listener that we attach to the list items returns which list item was selected as a zero-based index into the array we supplied, so we use that information to update the text of the button with the user's selection. We pass in null for the Cancel button's listener, because in this instance we just want Cancel to dismiss the dialog. If there is some important work to be done upon pressing Cancel, another listener could be passed in to the `setNegativeButton()` method.

There are several other options that the builder provides you to set the content of the dialog to something other than a selectable list:

- `setMessage()` will apply a simple text message as the body content.
- `setSingleChoiceItems()` and `setMultiChoiceItems()` create a list similar to this example but with selection modes applied so that the items will appear as being checked.
- `setView()` will apply any arbitrary custom view as the dialog's content.

The resulting application now looks like Figure 2-4 when the button is pressed.

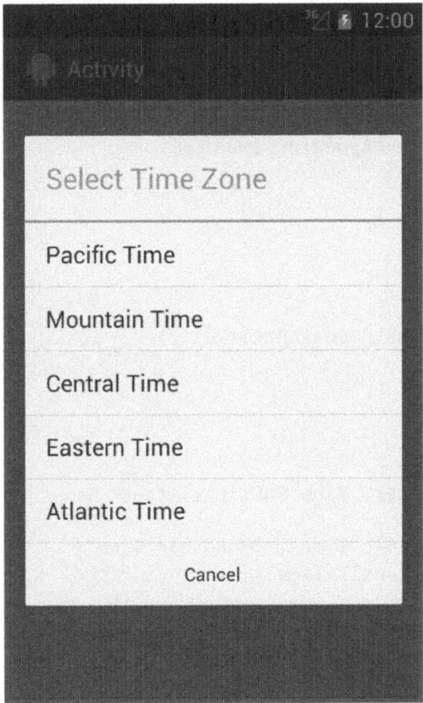

Figure 2-4. *AlertDialog with items list*

Custom List Items

`AlertDialog.Builder` allows for a custom `ListAdapter` to be passed in as the source of the list items the dialog should display. This means we can create custom row layouts to display more detailed information to the user. In Listings 2-28 and 2-29 we enhance the previous example by using a custom row layout to display extra data for each item.

Listing 2-28. *res/layout/list_item.xml*

```
<?xml version="1.0" encoding="utf-8"?>
<RelativeLayout xmlns:android="http://schemas.android.com/apk/res/android"
    android:layout_width="match_parent"
    android:layout_height="wrap_content"
    android:paddingLeft="10dp"
    android:paddingRight="10dp"
    android:minHeight="?android:attr/listPreferredItemHeight">
```

```
    <TextView
        android:id="@+id/text_name"
        android:layout_width="wrap_content"
        android:layout_height="wrap_content"
        android:layout_centerVertical="true"
        android:textAppearance="?android:attr/textAppearanceMedium"/>
    <TextView
        android:id="@+id/text_detail"
        android:layout_width="wrap_content"
        android:layout_height="wrap_content"
        android:layout_alignParentRight="true"
        android:layout_centerVertical="true"
        android:textAppearance="?android:attr/textAppearanceSmall"/>
</RelativeLayout>
```

Listing 2-29. *AlertDialog with Custom Layout*

```
public class CustomItemActivity extends Activity
        implements DialogInterface.OnClickListener, View.OnClickListener {

    private static final String[] ZONES = {"Pacific Time", "Mountain Time",
            "Central Time", "Eastern Time", "Atlantic Time"};
    private static final String[] OFFSETS =
            {"GMT-08:00", "GMT-07:00", "GMT-06:00", "GMT-05:00", "GMT-04:00"};

    Button mButton;
    AlertDialog mActions;

    @Override
    protected void onCreate(Bundle savedInstanceState) {
        super.onCreate(savedInstanceState);
        setTitle("Activity");
        mButton = new Button(this);
        mButton.setText("Click for Time Zones");
        mButton.setOnClickListener(this);

        ArrayAdapter<String> adapter = new ArrayAdapter<String>(this,
                R.layout.list_item) {
            @Override
            public View getView(int position, View convertView, ViewGroup parent) {
                View row = convertView;
                if (row == null) {
                    row = getLayoutInflater().inflate(R.layout.list_item,
                            parent, false);
                }

                TextView name = (TextView) row.findViewById(R.id.text_name);
                TextView detail = (TextView) row.findViewById(R.id.text_detail);
```

```
                name.setText(ZONES[position]);
                detail.setText(OFFSETS[position]);

                return row;
            }

            @Override
            public int getCount() {
                return ZONES.length;
            }
        };

        AlertDialog.Builder builder = new AlertDialog.Builder(this);
        builder.setTitle("Select Time Zone");
        builder.setAdapter(adapter, this);
        //Cancel action does nothing but dismiss, we could add another listener
        // here to do something extra when the user hits the Cancel button
        builder.setNegativeButton("Cancel", null);
        mActions = builder.create();

        setContentView(mButton);
    }

    //List selection action handled here
    @Override
    public void onClick(DialogInterface dialog, int which) {
        String selected = ZONES[which];
        mButton.setText(selected);
    }

    //Button action handled here (pop up the dialog)
    @Override
    public void onClick(View v) {
        mActions.show();
    }
}
```

Here we have provided an `ArrayAdapter` to the builder instead of simply passing the array of items. This adapter has a custom implementation of `getView()` that returns a custom layout we've defined in XML to display two text labels: one aligned left and the other aligned right. With this custom layout we can now display the GMT offset value alongside the time zone name. We'll talk more about the specifics of custom adapters later in this chapter. Figure 2-5 displays our new, more useful pop-up dialog.

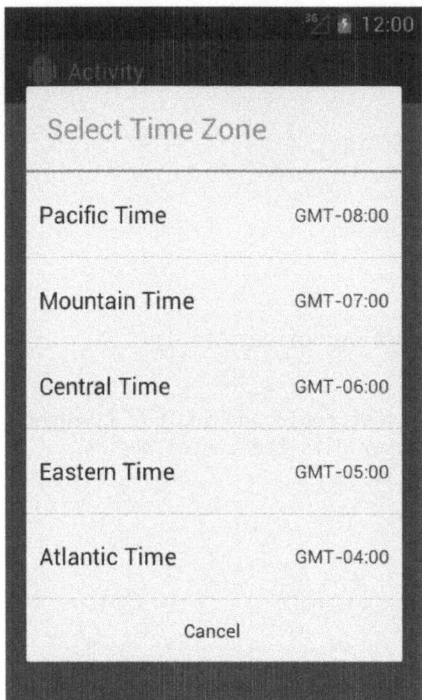

Figure 2-5. *AlertDialog with custom items*

2-10. Customizing Options Menu

Problem

Your application needs to provide a set of actions to the user that you don't want to have taking up screen real estate in your view hierarchy.

Solution

(API Level 1)

Use the options menu functionality in the framework to provide a pop-up menu of actions the user can choose from. The menu functionality in Android varies, depending on the platform version. In early releases, all Android devices had a physical MENU key that would trigger this functionality. Starting with Android

3.0, devices without physical buttons started to emerge and the menu functionality became part of the ActionBar.

Despite the variation, both versions use the same options menu API that is part of the Activity, so your application code will not have to branch based on Android versions.

How It Works

Listing 2-30 defines the options menu we will use in XML.

Listing 2-30. *res/menu/options.xml*

```
<menu xmlns:android="http://schemas.android.com/apk/res/android">
    <item android:id="@+id/menu_add"
        android:title="Add Item"
        android:icon="@android:drawable/ic_menu_add"
        android:showAsAction="always" />
    <item android:id="@+id/menu_remove"
        android:title="Remove Item"
        android:icon="@android:drawable/ic_menu_delete"
        android:showAsAction="always" />
    <item android:id="@+id/menu_edit"
        android:title="Edit Item"
        android:icon="@android:drawable/ic_menu_edit"
        android:showAsAction="ifRoom" />
    <item android:id="@+id/menu_settings"
        android:title="Settings"
        android:icon="@android:drawable/ic_menu_preferences"
        android:showAsAction="never" />
</menu>
```

The title and icon attributes define how each item will be displayed; older platforms will show both values while newer versions will show one or the other based on placement. Only Android 3.0 and later devices will recognize the showAsAction attribute, which defines whether the item should be promoted to an action on the ActionBar or placed into the overflow menu. The most common values for this attribute are as follows:

- always: Always display as an action by its icon
- never: Always display in the overflow menu by its name
- ifRoom: Display as an action if there is room on the ActionBar; otherwise, place in overflow

Listing 2-31 illustrates how to attach this menu to an Activity.

Listing 2-31. *Activity Overriding Menu Action*

```
public class OptionsActivity extends Activity {

    @Override
    public void onCreate(Bundle savedInstanceState) {
        super.onCreate(savedInstanceState);
    }

    @Override
    public boolean onCreateOptionsMenu(Menu menu) {
        //Use this callback to create the menu and do any
        // initial setup necessary
        getMenuInflater().inflate(R.menu.options, menu);
        return true;
    }

    @Override
    public boolean onPrepareOptionsMenu(Menu menu) {
        //Use this callback to do setup that needs to happen
        // each time the menu opens
        return super.onPrepareOptionsMenu(menu);
    }

    @Override
    public boolean onOptionsItemSelected(MenuItem item) {
        //Get the selected option by id
        switch (item.getItemId()) {
        case R.id.menu_add:
            //Do add action
            break;
        case R.id.menu_remove:
            //Do remove action
            break;
        case R.id.menu_edit:
            //Do edit action
            break;
        case R.id.menu_settings:
            //Do settings action
            break;
        default:
            break;
        }

        return true;
    }
}
```

When the user presses the MENU key on the device, or an Activity loads with an `ActionBar` present, the `onCreateOptionsMenu()` method is called to set up the menu. There is a special LayoutInflater object called MenuInflater that is used to create menus from XML. We use the instance already available to the Activity with `getMenuInflater()` to return our XML menu.

If there are any actions you need to take each time the user opens the menu, you can do so in `onPrepareOptionsMenu()`. Be advised that any actions promoted to the `ActionBar` will not trigger this callback when the user selects them; actions in the overflow menu, however, will still trigger it.

When the user makes a selection, the `onOptionsItemSelected()` callback will be triggered with the selected menu item. Since we defined a unique ID for each item in our XML menu, we can use a switch statement to check which item the user selected and take the appropriate action.

Figure 2-6 shows how this menu is displayed across different device versions and configurations. Devices prior to Android 3.0 will display the whole menu floating at the bottom of the screen. Newer devices that still have physical keys will display the promoted actions in the `ActionBar`, but the overflow menu is still triggered by the MENU key. Finally, devices with soft keys will display the overflow menu as a button next to the `ActionBar` actions.

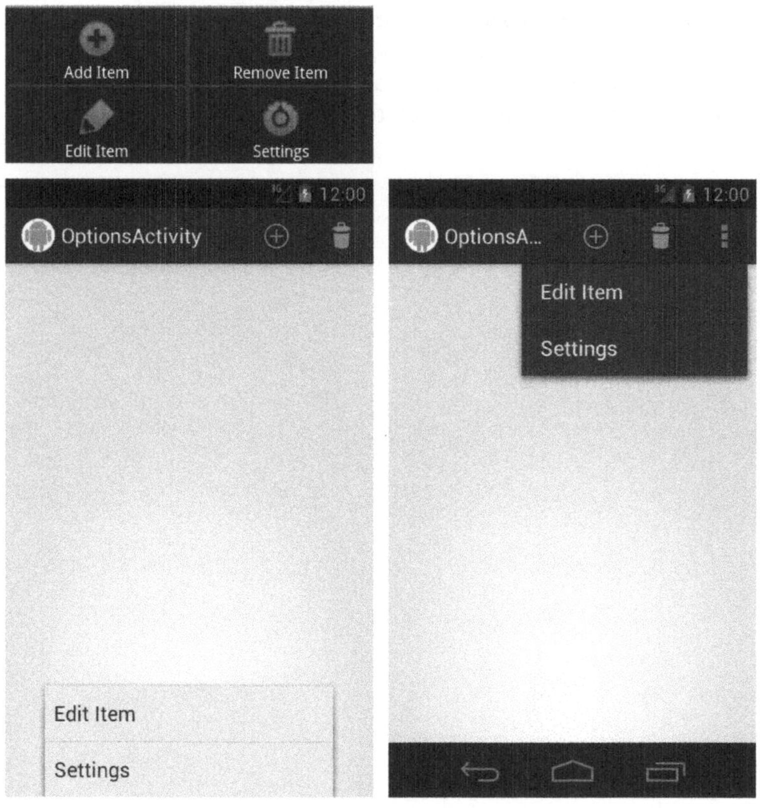

Figure 2-6. *Options menu in Android 2.3 (top), Android 4.1 with physical keys (left), and Android 4.0 with soft keys (right)*

2-11. Customizing Back Behavior

Problem

Your application needs to handle the user pressing the hardware BACK button in a custom manner.

Solution

(API Level 5)

Make use of the onBackPressed() callback inside an Activity, or manipulate the back stack inside a Fragment.

How It Works

If you need to be notified when the user presses BACK on your Activity, you can override onBackPressed() as follows:

```
@Override
public void onBackPressed() {
    //Custom back button processing

    //Call super to do normal processing (like finishing Activity)
    super.onBackPressed();
}
```

The default implementation of this method will pop any fragments currently on the back stack and then finish the Activity. If you are not intending to interrupt this workflow, you will want to make sure and call the super class implementation when you are done to ensure this processing still happens normally.

> **CAUTION:** Overriding hardware button events should be done with care. All hardware buttons have consistent functionality across the Android system, and adjusting the functionality to work outside these bounds will be confusing and upsetting to users.

BACK Behavior and Fragments

When working with fragments in your UI, there are further opportunities to customize the behavior of the devices' BACK button. By default, the action of adding or replacing fragments in your UI is not something added to the task's back stack, so when the user presses the BACK button they won't be able to step backward through those actions. However, any FragmentTransaction can be added as an entry in the back stack by simply calling addToBackStack() as before the transaction is committed.

By default, Activity will call FragmentManager.popBackStackImmediate() when the user presses BACK, so each FragmentTransaction added in this way will unravel with each tap until there are none left, then the Activity will finish. There are variations on this method, however, that allow you to jump directly to places in the stack as well. Let's take a look at Listings 2-32 and 2-33.

Listing 2-32. *res/layout/main.xml*

```
<?xml version="1.0" encoding="utf-8"?>
<LinearLayout xmlns:android="http://schemas.android.com/apk/res/android"
    android:layout_width="match_parent"
    android:layout_height="match_parent"
    android:orientation="vertical">
    <Button
        android:layout_width="match_parent"
        android:layout_height="wrap_content"
        android:text="Go Home"
        android:onClick="onHomeClick" />
    <FrameLayout
        android:id="@+id/container_fragment"
        android:layout_width="match_parent"
        android:layout_height="match_parent"/>
</LinearLayout>
```

Listing 2-33. *Activity Customizing Fragment Back Stack*

```
public class MyActivity extends FragmentActivity {

    @Override
    protected void onCreate(Bundle savedInstanceState) {
        super.onCreate(savedInstanceState);
        setContentView(R.layout.main);
        //Build a stack of UI fragments
        FragmentTransaction ft = getSupportFragmentManager().beginTransaction();
        ft.add(R.id.container_fragment, MyFragment.newInstance("First Fragment"));
        ft.commit();
```

```
        ft = getSupportFragmentManager().beginTransaction();
        ft.add(R.id.container_fragment, MyFragment.newInstance("Second Fragment"));
        ft.addToBackStack("second");
        ft.commit();

        ft = getSupportFragmentManager().beginTransaction();
        ft.add(R.id.container_fragment, MyFragment.newInstance("Third Fragment"));
        ft.addToBackStack("third");
        ft.commit();

        ft = getSupportFragmentManager().beginTransaction();
        ft.add(R.id.container_fragment, MyFragment.newInstance("Fourth Fragment"));
        ft.addToBackStack("fourth");
        ft.commit();
    }

    public void onHomeClick(View v) {
        getSupportFragmentManager().popBackStack("second",
                FragmentManager.POP_BACK_STACK_INCLUSIVE);
    }

    public static class MyFragment extends Fragment {
        private CharSequence mTitle;

        public static MyFragment newInstance(String title) {
            MyFragment fragment = new MyFragment();
            fragment.setTitle(title);

            return fragment;
        }

        @Override
        public View onCreateView(LayoutInflater inflater, ViewGroup container,
                Bundle savedInstanceState) {
            TextView text = new TextView(getActivity());
            text.setText(mTitle);
            text.setBackgroundColor(Color.WHITE);

            return text;
        }

        public void setTitle(CharSequence title) {
            mTitle = title;
        }
    }
}
```

> **NOTE:** We are using the support library in this example to allow the use of fragments prior to Android 3.0. If your application is targeting API Level 11 or higher, you can replace `FragmentActivity` with `Activity` and `getSupportFragmentManager()` with `getFragmentManager()`.

This example loads up four custom `Fragment` instances into a stack, so the last one added is displayed when the application runs. With each transaction, we call `addToBackStack()` with a tag name to identify this transaction. This is not required, and if you do not wish to jump to places in the stack, it is easier to just pass `null` here. With each press of the BACK button, a single `Fragment` is removed until only the first remains, at which point the Activity will finish normally.

Notice the first transaction was not added to the stack; this is because here we want the first fragment to act as the root view. Adding it to the back stack as well would cause it to pop off the stack before finishing the Activity, leaving the UI in a blank state.

This application also has a button marked "Go Home" which immediately takes the user back to the root `Fragment` no matter where they currently are. It does this by calling `popBackStack()` on `FragmentManager`, taking the tag of the transaction we want to jump back to. We also pass the flag `POP_BACK_STACK_INCLUSIVE` to instruct the manager to also remove the transaction we've indicated from the stack. Without this flag, the example would jump to the "second" fragment, rather than the root.

> **NOTE:** Android pops back to the first transaction that matches the given tag. If the same tag is used multiple times, it will pop to the first transaction added, not the most recent.

We cannot go directly to root with this method because we do not have a back stack tag associated with that transaction to reference. There is another version of this method that takes a unique transaction ID (the return value from `commit()` on `FragmentTransaction`). Using this method we could jump directly to root without requiring the inclusive flag.

2-12. Emulating the HOME Button

Problem

Your application needs to take the same action as if the user pressed the hardware HOME button.

Solution

(API Level 1)

When the user hits the HOME button, this sends an Intent to the system telling it to load the Home Activity. This is no different from starting any other Activity in your application; you just have to construct the proper Intent to get the effect.

How It Works

Add the following lines wherever you want this action to occur in your Activity:

```
Intent intent = new Intent(Intent.ACTION_MAIN);
intent.addCategory(Intent.CATEGORY_HOME);
startActivity(intent);
```

A common use of this function is to override the BACK button to go home instead of to the previous Activity. This is useful in cases where everything underneath the foreground Activity may be protected (a login screen, for instance), and letting the default BACK button behavior occur could allow unsecured access to the system. Here is an example of using the two in concert to make a certain Activity bring up the home screen when BACK is pressed:

```
@Override
public boolean onKeyDown(int keyCode, KeyEvent event) {
    if(keyCode == KeyEvent.KEYCODE_BACK) {
        Intent intent = new Intent(Intent.ACTION_MAIN);
        intent.addCategory(Intent.CATEGORY_HOME);
        startActivity(intent);
        return true;
    }
    return super.onKeyDown(keyCode, event);
}
```

2-13. Monitoring TextView Changes

Problem

Your application needs to continuously monitor for text changes in a TextView widget (like EditText).

Solution

(API Level 1)

Implement the `android.text.TextWatcher` interface. `TextWatcher` provides three callback methods during the process of updating text:

```
public void beforeTextChanged(CharSequence s, int start, int count, int after);
public void onTextChanged(CharSequence s, int start, int before, int count);
public void afterTextChanged(Editable s);
```

The `beforeTextChanged()` and `onTextChanged()` methods are provided mainly as notifications, as you cannot actually make changes to the CharSequence in either of these methods. If you are attempting to intercept the text entered into the view, changes may be made when `afterTextChanged()` is called.

How It Works

To register a `TextWatcher` instance with a `TextView`, call the `TextView.addTextChangedListener()` method. Notice from the syntax that more than one `TextWatcher` can be registered with a `TextView`.

Character Counter Example

A simple use of TextWatcher is to create a live character counter that follows an EditText as the user types or deletes information. Listing 2-34 is an example Activity that implements TextWatcher for this purpose, registers with an EditText widget, and prints the character count in the Activity title.

Listing 2-34. *Character Counter Activity*

```
public class MyActivity extends Activity implements TextWatcher {

    EditText text;
    int textCount;
```

```
    @Override
    protected void onCreate(Bundle savedInstanceState) {
        super.onCreate(savedInstanceState);
        //Create an EditText widget and add the watcher
        text = new EditText(this);
        text.addTextChangedListener(this);

        setContentView(text);
    }

    /* TextWatcher Implemention Methods */
    public void beforeTextChanged(CharSequence s, int start, int count,
            int after) { }

    public void onTextChanged(CharSequence s, int start, int before, int count) {
        textCount = text.getText().length();
        setTitle(String.valueOf(textCount));
    }

    public void afterTextChanged(Editable s) { }

}
```

Because our needs do not include modifying the text being inserted, we can read the count from `onTextChanged()`, which happens as soon as the text change occurs. The other methods are unused and left empty.

Currency Formatter Example

The SDK has a handful of predefined `TextWatcher` instances to format text input; `PhoneNumberFormattingTextWatcher` is one of these. Their job is to apply standard formatting for users while they type, reducing the number of keystrokes required to enter legible data.

In Listing 2-35, we create a CurrencyTextWatcher to insert the currency symbol and separator point into a TextView.

Listing 2-35. *Currency Formatter*

```
public class CurrencyTextWatcher implements TextWatcher {

    boolean mEditing;

    public CurrencyTextWatcher() {
        mEditing = false;
    }
```

```
    public synchronized void afterTextChanged(Editable s) {
        if(!mEditing) {
            mEditing = true;

            //Strip symbols
            String digits = s.toString().replaceAll("\\D", "");
            NumberFormat nf = NumberFormat.getCurrencyInstance();
            try{
                String formatted = nf.format(Double.parseDouble(digits)/100);
                s.replace(0, s.length(), formatted);
            } catch (NumberFormatException nfe) {
                s.clear();
            }

            mEditing = false;
        }
    }

    public void beforeTextChanged(CharSequence s, int start, int count,
            int after) { }

    public void onTextChanged(CharSequence s, int start, int before, int count) { }

}
```

> **NOTE:** Making changes to the `Editable` value in `afterTextChanged()` will cause the `TextWatcher` methods to be called again (after all, you just changed the text). For this reason, custom TextWatcher implementations that edit should use a boolean or some other tracking mechanism to track where the editing is coming from, or you may create an infinite loop.

We can apply this custom text formatter to an EditText in an Activity (see Listing 2-36).

Listing 2-36. *Activity Using Currency Formatter*

```
public class MyActivity extends Activity {

    EditText text;

    @Override
    protected void onCreate(Bundle savedInstanceState) {
        super.onCreate(savedInstanceState);
        text = new EditText(this);
        text.addTextChangedListener(new CurrencyTextWatcher());
```

```
        setContentView(text);
    }

}
```

It is very handy if you are formatting user input with this formatter to define the EditText in XML so you can apply the `android:inputType` and `android:digits` constraints to easily protect the field against entry errors. In particular, adding `android:digits="0123456789."` (notice the period at the end for a decimal point) to the EditText will protect this formatter as well as the user.

2-14. Scrolling TextView Ticker

Problem

You want to create a "ticker" view that continuously scrolls its contents across the screen.

Solution

(API Level 1)

Use the built-in marquee feature of `TextView`. When the content of a `TextView` is too large to fit within its bounds, the text is truncated by default. This truncation can be configured using the `android:ellipsize` attribute, which can be set to one of the following options:

- none
  - Default.
  - Truncate the end of the text with no visual indicator.
- start
  - Truncate the start of the text with an ellipsis at the beginning of the view.
- middle
  - Truncate the middle of the text with an ellipsis in the middle of the view.

- end
    - Truncate the end of the text with an ellipsis at the end of the view.
- marquee
    - Do not ellipsize; animate and scroll the text while selected.

> **NOTE:** The marquee feature is designed to only animate and scroll the text when the `TextView` is selected. Setting the `android:ellipsize` attribute to marquee alone will not animate the view.

How It Works

In order to create an automated ticker that repeats indefinitely, we add a TextView to an XML layout that looks like this:

```
<TextView
    android:id="@+id/ticker"
    android:layout_width="fill_parent"
    android:layout_height="wrap_content"
    android:singleLine="true"
    android:scrollHorizontally="true"
    android:ellipsize="marquee"
    android:marqueeRepeatLimit="marquee_forever"
/>
```

The key attributes to configuring this view are the last four. Without `android:singleLine` and `android:scrollHorizontally`, the TextView will not properly lay itself out to allow for the text to be longer than the view (a key requirement for ticker scrolling). Setting the `android:ellipsize` and `android:marqueeRepeatLimit` allow the scrolling to occur for an indefinite amount of time. The repeat limit can be set to any integer value as well, which will repeat the scrolling animation that many times and then stop.

With the TextView attributes properly set in XML, the Java code must set the selected state to true, which enables the scrolling animation:

```
TextView ticker = (TextView)findViewById(R.id.ticker);
ticker.setSelected(true);
```

If you need to have the animation start and stop based on certain events in the user interface, just call `setSelected()` each time with either true or false, respectively.

2-15. Animating a View

Problem

Your application needs to animate a view object, either as a transition or for effect.

Solution

(API Level 1)

An `Animation` object can be applied to any view and can be run using the `View.startAnimation()` method; this will run the animation immediately. You may also use `View.setAnimation()` to schedule an animation and attach the object to a view but not run it immediately. In this case, the `Animation` must have its start time parameter set. Modifications made through this API will modify where the view is temporarily drawn onscreen, but not the view itself.

(API Level 12)

An `ObjectAnimator` instance, such as `ViewPropertyAnimator`, can be used to manipulate the properties of a `View`, such as its position or rotation. `ViewPropertyAnimator` is obtained through `View.animate()`, and then modified with the specifics of the animation. Modifications made through this API will alter the actual properties of the `View` itself.

How It Works

System Animations

For convenience, the Android SDK provides a handful of transition animations that you can apply to views, which can be loaded at runtime using the `AnimationUtils` class:

- Slide and Fade In
  - `AnimationUtils.makeInAnimation()`
  - Use the boolean parameter to determine if the slide is left or right.
- Slide Up and Fade In
  - `AnimationUtils.makeInChildBottomAnimation()`
  - The view always slides up from the bottom.
- Slide and Fade Out
  - `AnimationUtils.makeOutAnimation()`
  - Use the boolean parameter to determine if the slide is left or right.
- Fade Out
  - `AnimationUtils.loadAnimation()`
  - Set the int parameter to `android.R.anim.fade_out`.
- Fade In
  - `AnimationUtils.loadAnimation()`
  - Set the int parameter to `android.R.anim.fade_in`.

> **NOTE:** These transition animations only temporarily change how the view is drawn. The visibility parameter of the view must also be set if you mean to permanently add or remove the object.

Listing 2-37 animates the appearance and disappearance of a view with each button click event.

Listing 2-37. *res/layout/main.xml*

```
<?xml version="1.0" encoding="utf-8"?>
<LinearLayout xmlns:android="http://schemas.android.com/apk/res/android"
    android:orientation="vertical"
    android:layout_width="fill_parent"
    android:layout_height="fill_parent">
    <Button
        android:id="@+id/toggleButton"
        android:layout_width="fill_parent"
        android:layout_height="wrap_content"
```

```
        android:text="Click to Toggle"
    />
    <View
        android:id="@+id/theView"
        android:layout_width="fill_parent"
        android:layout_height="wrap_content"
        android:background="#AAA"
    />
</LinearLayout>
```

In Listing 2-38 each user action on the button toggles the visibility of the gray view below it with an animation.

Listing 2-38. *Activity Animating View Transitions*

```
public class AnimateActivity extends Activity implements View.OnClickListener {

    View viewToAnimate;

    @Override
    public void onCreate(Bundle savedInstanceState) {
        super.onCreate(savedInstanceState);
        setContentView(R.layout.main);

        Button button = (Button)findViewById(R.id.toggleButton);
        button.setOnClickListener(this);

        viewToAnimate = findViewById(R.id.theView);
    }

    @Override
    public void onClick(View v) {
        if(viewToAnimate.getVisibility() == View.VISIBLE) {
            //If the view is visible already, slide it out to the right
            Animation out = AnimationUtils.makeOutAnimation(this, true);
            viewToAnimate.startAnimation(out);
            viewToAnimate.setVisibility(View.INVISIBLE);
        } else {
            //If the view is hidden, do a fade_in in-place
            Animation in = AnimationUtils.loadAnimation(this,
                    android.R.anim.fade_in);
            viewToAnimate.startAnimation(in);
            viewToAnimate.setVisibility(View.VISIBLE);
        }
    }
}
```

The view is hidden by sliding off to the right and fading out simultaneously, whereas the view simply fades into place when it is shown. We chose a simple

View as the target here to demonstrate that any UI element (since they are all subclasses of View) can be animated in this way.

Custom Animations

Creating custom animations to add an effect to views by scaling, rotation, and transforming them can provide invaluable additions to a UI as well. In Android, we can create the following animation elements:

- AlphaAnimation
    - Animate changes to a view's transparency.
- RotateAnimation
    - Animate changes to a view's rotation.
    - The point about which rotation occurs is configurable. The top left corner is chosen by default.
- ScaleAnimation
    - Animate changes to a view's scale (size).
    - The center point of the scale change is configurable. The top left corner is chosen by default.
- TranslateAnimation
    - Animate changes to a view's position.

Let's illustrate how to construct and add a custom animation object by creating a sample application that creates a "coin flip" effect on an image (see Listings 2-39 and 2-40).

Listing 2-39. *res/layout/main.xml*

```
<?xml version="1.0" encoding="utf-8"?>
<RelativeLayout xmlns:android="http://schemas.android.com/apk/res/android"
    android:layout_width="fill_parent"
    android:layout_height="fill_parent">
    <ImageView
        android:id="@+id/flip_image"
        android:layout_width="wrap_content"
        android:layout_height="wrap_content"
        android:layout_centerInParent="true"
    />
</RelativeLayout>
```

Listing 2-40. *Activity with Custom Animations*

```
public class Flipper extends Activity {

    boolean isHeads;
    ScaleAnimation shrink, grow;
    ImageView flipImage;

    @Override
    public void onCreate(Bundle savedInstanceState) {
        super.onCreate(savedInstanceState);
        setContentView(R.layout.main);

        flipImage = (ImageView)findViewById(R.id.flip_image);
        flipImage.setImageResource(R.drawable.heads);
        isHeads = true;

        shrink = new ScaleAnimation(1.0f, 0.0f, 1.0f, 1.0f,
                         ScaleAnimation.RELATIVE_TO_SELF, 0.5f,
                         ScaleAnimation.RELATIVE_TO_SELF, 0.5f);
        shrink.setDuration(150);
        shrink.setAnimationListener(new Animation.AnimationListener() {
            @Override
            public void onAnimationStart(Animation animation) {}

            @Override
            public void onAnimationRepeat(Animation animation) {}

            @Override
            public void onAnimationEnd(Animation animation) {
                if(isHeads) {
                    isHeads = false;
                    flipImage.setImageResource(R.drawable.tails);
                } else {
                    isHeads = true;
                    flipImage.setImageResource(R.drawable.heads);
                }
                flipImage.startAnimation(grow);
            }
        });
        grow = new ScaleAnimation(0.0f, 1.0f, 1.0f, 1.0f,
                        ScaleAnimation.RELATIVE_TO_SELF, 0.5f,
                        ScaleAnimation.RELATIVE_TO_SELF, 0.5f);
        grow.setDuration(150);
    }
```

```
    @Override
    public boolean onTouchEvent(MotionEvent event) {
        if(event.getAction() == MotionEvent.ACTION_DOWN) {
            flipImage.startAnimation(shrink);
            return true;
        }
        return super.onTouchEvent(event);
    }
}
```

This example includes the following pertinent components:

- Two image resources for the coin's head and tail (we named them heads.png and tails.png)
    - These images may be any two-image resources placed in res/drawable. The ImageView defaults to displaying the heads image.
- Two ScaleAnimation objects
    - Shrink: Reduce the image width from full to nothing about the center.
    - Grow: Increase the image width from nothing to full about the center.
- Anonymous AnimationListener to link the two animations in sequence

Custom animation objects can be defined either in XML or code. In the next section we will look at making the animations as XML resources. Here we created the two `ScaleAnimation` objects using the following constructor:

```
ScaleAnimation(
    float fromX,
    float toX,
    float fromY,
    float toY,
    int pivotXType,
    float pivotXValue,
    int pivotYType,
    float pibotYValue
)
```

The first four parameters are the horizontal and vertical scaling factors to apply. Notice in Listing 2-40 that X went from 100% to 0% to shrink and 0% to 100% to grow, while leaving Y alone at 100% always.

The remaining parameters define an anchor point for the view while the animation occurs. In this case, we tell the application to anchor the midpoint of the view, and we then bring both sides in toward the middle as the view shrinks. The reverse is true for expanding the image: the center stays in place and the image grows outward toward its original edges.

Android does not inherently have a way to link multiple animation objects together in a sequence, so we use an `Animation.AnimationListener` for this purpose. The listener has methods to notify when an animation begins, repeats, and completes. In this case, we are only interested in the latter so that when the shrink animation is done, we can automatically start the grow animation after it.

The final method used in the example is the `setDuration()` method to set the animation duration of time. The value supplied here is in milliseconds, so our entire coin flip would take 300 ms to complete, 150 ms a piece for each `ScaleAnimation`.

AnimationSet

Many times the custom animation you are searching to create requires a combination of the basic types described previously; this is where `AnimationSet` becomes useful. `AnimationSet` defines a group of animations that should be run simultaneously. By default, all animations will be started together and will complete at their respective durations.

In this section we will also expose how to define custom animations using Android's preferred method of XML resources. XML animations should be defined in the res/anim/ folder of a project. The following tags are supported, and all of them can be either the root or child node of an animation:

- `<alpha>`: An AlphaAnimation object
- `<rotate>`: A RotateAnimation object
- `<scale>`: A ScaleAnimation object
- `<translate>`: A TranslateAnimation object
- `<set>`: An AnimationSet

Only the `<set>` tag, however, can be a parent and contain other animation tags.

In this example, let's take our coin flip animations and add another dimension. We will pair each ScaleAnimation with a TranslateAnimation as a set. The desired effect will be for the image to slide up and down the screen as it "flips." To do this, in Listings 2-41 and 2-42 we will define our animations in two XML files and place them in res/anim/. The first will be grow.xml.

Listing 2-41. *res/anim/grow.xml*

```
<?xml version="1.0" encoding="utf-8"?>
<set xmlns:android="http://schemas.android.com/apk/res/android">
    <scale
        android:duration="150"
        android:fromXScale="0.0"
        android:toXScale="1.0"
        android:fromYScale="1.0"
        android:toYScale="1.0"
        android:pivotX="50%"
        android:pivotY="50%"
    />
    <translate
        android:duration="150"
        android:fromXDelta="0%"
        android:toXDelta="0%"
        android:fromYDelta="50%"
        android:toYDelta="0%"
    />
</set>
```

This is followed by shrink.xml:

Listing 2-42. *res/anim/shrink.xml*

```
<?xml version="1.0" encoding="utf-8"?>
<set xmlns:android="http://schemas.android.com/apk/res/android">
    <scale
        android:duration="150"
        android:fromXScale="1.0"
        android:toXScale="0.0"
        android:fromYScale="1.0"
        android:toYScale="1.0"
        android:pivotX="50%"
        android:pivotY="50%"
    />
    <translate
        android:duration="150"
        android:fromXDelta="0%"
        android:toXDelta="0%"
        android:fromYDelta="0%"
        android:toYDelta="50%"
    />
</set>
```

Defining the scale values isn't any different than previously when using the constructor in code. One thing to make note of, however, is the definition style of units for the pivot parameters. All animation dimensions that can be defined as ABSOULUTE, RELATIVE_TO_SELF, or RELATIVE_TO_PARENT use the following XML syntax:

- ABSOLUTE: Use a float value to represent an actual pixel value (e.g., "5.0").
- RELATIVE_TO_SELF: Use a percentage value from 0 to 100 (e.g., "50%").
- RELATIVE_TO_PARENT: Use a percentage value with a "p" suffix (e.g., "25%p").

With these animation files defined, we can modify the previous example to now load these sets (see Listings 2-43 and 2-44).

Listing 2-43. *res/layout/main.xml*

```
<?xml version="1.0" encoding="utf-8"?>
<RelativeLayout xmlns:android="http://schemas.android.com/apk/res/android"
    android:layout_width="fill_parent"
    android:layout_height="fill_parent">
    <ImageView
        android:id="@+id/flip_image"
        android:layout_width="wrap_content"
        android:layout_height="wrap_content"
        android:layout_centerInParent="true"
    />
</RelativeLayout>
```

Listing 2-44. *Activity Using Animation Sets*

```
public class Flipper extends Activity {

    boolean isHeads;
    Animation shrink, grow;
    ImageView flipImage;

    @Override
    public void onCreate(Bundle savedInstanceState) {
        super.onCreate(savedInstanceState);
        setContentView(R.layout.main);

        flipImage = (ImageView)findViewById(R.id.flip_image);
        flipImage.setImageResource(R.drawable.heads);
        isHeads = true;

        shrink = AnimationUtils.loadAnimation(this, R.anim.shrink);
        shrink.setAnimationListener(new Animation.AnimationListener() {
            @Override
            public void onAnimationStart(Animation animation) {}
```

```
            @Override
            public void onAnimationRepeat(Animation animation) {}

            @Override
            public void onAnimationEnd(Animation animation) {
                if(isHeads) {
                    isHeads = false;
                    flipImage.setImageResource(R.drawable.tails);
                } else {
                    isHeads = true;
                    flipImage.setImageResource(R.drawable.heads);
                }
                flipImage.startAnimation(grow);
            }
        });
        grow = AnimationUtils.loadAnimation(this, R.anim.grow);
    }

    @Override
    public boolean onTouchEvent(MotionEvent event) {
        if(event.getAction() == MotionEvent.ACTION_DOWN) {
            flipImage.startAnimation(shrink);
            return true;
        }
        return super.onTouchEvent(event);
    }
}
```

The result is a coin that flips, but it also slides down and up the y axis of the screen slightly with each flip.

ViewPropertyAnimator

(API Level 12)

Starting with Android 3.2, a much more convenient method of animating views was introduced with `ViewPropertyAnimator`. The API works similarly to a builder, where the calls to modify the different properties can be chained together to create a single animation. Any calls made to the same `ViewPropertyAnimator` during the same iteration of the current thread's `Looper` will be lumped into a single animation. Listing 2-45 illustrates our same view transition example, modified to use the new API.

Listing 2-45. *Activity Using ViewPropertyAnimator*

```
public class AnimateActivity extends Activity implements View.OnClickListener {

    View viewToAnimate;

    @Override
    public void onCreate(Bundle savedInstanceState) {
        super.onCreate(savedInstanceState);
        setContentView(R.layout.main);

        Button button = (Button)findViewById(R.id.toggleButton);
        button.setOnClickListener(this);

        viewToAnimate = findViewById(R.id.theView);
    }

    @Override
    public void onClick(View v) {
        if(viewToAnimate.getAlpha() > 0f) {
            //If the view is visible already, slide it out to the right
            viewToAnimate.animate().alpha(0f).translationX(1000f);
        } else {
            //If the view is hidden, do a fade-in in place
            //Property Animations actually modify the view, so
            // we have to reset the view's location first
            viewToAnimate.setTranslationX(0f);
            viewToAnimate.animate().alpha(1f);
        }
    }
}
```

In this example, the slide and fade-out transition is accomplished by chaining together a modification of the `alpha` and `translationX` properties, with a translation value sufficiently large to go offscreen. We do not have to chain these methods together for them to be considered a single animation. If we had called them on two separate lines they would still execute together because they were both set in the same iteration of the main thread's `Looper`.

Notice that we have to reset the translation property for our `View` to fade-in without a slide. This is because property animations manipulate the actual `View`, rather than where it is temporarily drawn (which is the case with the older animation APIs). If we did not reset this property, it would fade-in but would still be 1,000 pixels off to the right.

ObjectAnimator

(API Level 11)

While ViewPropertyAnimator is convenient for animating simple properties quickly, you may find it a bit limiting if you want to do more complex work like chaining animations together. For this purpose we can go to the parent class, ObjectAnimator. With ObjectAnimator we can set listeners to be notified when the animation begins and ends; also, they can be notified with incremental updates as to what point of the animation we are in. Listing 2-46 shows how we can use this to update our Flipper animation code.

Listing 2-46. *Flipper Animation with ObjectAnimator*

```
public class Flipper extends Activity {

    boolean isHeads;
    ObjectAnimator flipper;
    Bitmap headsImage, tailsImage;
    ImageView flipImage;

    @Override
    public void onCreate(Bundle savedInstanceState) {
        super.onCreate(savedInstanceState);
        setContentView(R.layout.main);

        headsImage = BitmapFactory.decodeResource(getResources(),
                R.drawable.heads);
        tailsImage = BitmapFactory.decodeResource(getResources(),
                R.drawable.tails);

        flipImage = (ImageView)findViewById(R.id.flip_image);
        flipImage.setImageBitmap(headsImage);
        isHeads = true;

        flipper = ObjectAnimator.ofFloat(flipImage, "rotationY", 0f, 360f);
        flipper.setDuration(500);
        flipper.addUpdateListener(new AnimatorUpdateListener() {
            @Override
            public void onAnimationUpdate(ValueAnimator animation) {
                if (animation.getAnimatedFraction() >= 0.25f && isHeads) {
                    flipImage.setImageBitmap(tailsImage);
                    isHeads = false;
                }
                if (animation.getAnimatedFraction() >= 0.75f && !isHeads) {
                    flipImage.setImageBitmap(headsImage);
                    isHeads = true;
                }
            }
```

```
        });
    }

    @Override
    public boolean onTouchEvent(MotionEvent event) {
        if(event.getAction() == MotionEvent.ACTION_DOWN) {
            flipper.start();
            return true;
        }
        return super.onTouchEvent(event);
    }
}
```

Property animations provide transformations that were not previously available with the older animation system, such as rotations about the x and y axes that create the effect of a three-dimensional transformation. In this example we don't have to fake the rotation by doing a calculated scale; we can just tell the view to rotate about the y axis. Because of this, we no longer need two animations to flip the coin; we can just animate the `rotationY` property of the view for one full rotation.

Another powerful addition is the `AnimationUpdateListener`, which provides regular callbacks while the animation is going on. The `getAnimatedFraction()` method returns the current percentage to completion of the animation. You can also use `getAnimatedValue()` to get the exact value of the property at the current point in time.

In the example, we use the first of these methods to swap the heads and tails images when the animation reaches the two points where the coin should change sides (90 degrees and 270 degrees, or 25% and 75% of the animation duration). Because there is no guarantee that we will get called for every degree, we just change the image as soon as we have crossed the threshold. We also set a boolean flag to avoid setting the image to the same value on each iteration afterward, which would slow down performance unnecessarily.

`ObjectAnimator` also supports a more traditional `AnimationListener` for major animation events such as start, end, and repeat, if chaining multiple animations together is still necessary for the application.

2-16. Animating Layout Changes

Problem

Your application dynamically adds or removes views from a layout, and you would like those changes to be animated.

Solution

(API Level 11)

Make use of the LayoutTransition object to customize how modifications to the view hierarchy in a given layout should be animated. In Android 3.0 and later, any ViewGroup can have changes to its layout animated by simply enabling the android:animateLayoutChanges flag in XML or by adding a LayoutTransition object in Java code.

There are five states during a layout transition that each View in the layout may incur. An application can set a custom animation for each one of the following states:

- APPEARING: An item that is appearing in the container.
- DISAPPEARING: An item that is disappearing from the container.
- CHANGING: An item that is changing due to a layout change, such as a resize, that doesn't involve views being added or removed.
- CHANGE_APPEARING: An item changing due to another view appearing.
- CHANGE_DISAPPEARING: An item changing due to another view disappearing.

How It Works

Listings 2-47 and 2-48 illustrate an application that animates changes on a basic LinearLayout.

Listing 2-47. *res/layout/main.xml*

```
<?xml version="1.0" encoding="utf-8"?>
<LinearLayout xmlns:android="http://schemas.android.com/apk/res/android"
    android:layout_width="match_parent"
    android:layout_height="match_parent"
    android:gravity="center_horizontal"
    android:orientation="vertical" >

    <Button
        android:id="@+id/button_add"
        android:layout_width="wrap_content"
        android:layout_height="wrap_content"
        android:onClick="onAddClick"
        android:text="Click To Add Item" />

    <LinearLayout
        android:id="@+id/verticalContainer"
        android:layout_width="match_parent"
        android:layout_height="match_parent"
        android:animateLayoutChanges="true"
        android:orientation="vertical" />

</LinearLayout>
```

Listing 2-48. *Activity Adding and Removing Views*

```
public class MainActivity extends Activity {

    LinearLayout mContainer;

    @Override
    public void onCreate(Bundle savedInstanceState) {
        super.onCreate(savedInstanceState);
        setContentView(R.layout.main);
        mContainer = (LinearLayout) findViewById(R.id.verticalContainer);
    }

    //Add a new button that can remove itself
    public void onAddClick(View v) {
        Button button = new Button(this);
        button.setText("Click To Remove");
        button.setOnClickListener(new View.OnClickListener() {
            @Override
            public void onClick(View v) {
                mContainer.removeView(v);
            }
        });
```

```
        mContainer.addView(button, new LinearLayout.LayoutParams(
                LayoutParams.MATCH_PARENT, LayoutParams.WRAP_CONTENT));
    }
}
```

This simple example adds `Button` instances to a `LinearLayout` when the Add Item button is tapped. Each new `Button` is outfitted with the ability to remove itself from the layout when it is tapped. In order to animate this process, all we need to do is set `android:animateLayoutChanges="true"` on the `LinearLayout`, and the framework does the rest. By default, a new `Button` will fade in to its new location without disturbing the other views, and a removed `Button` will fade out while the surrounding items slide in to fill the gap.

We can customize the transition animations individually to create custom effects. Take a look at Listing 2-49, where we add some custom transitions to the previous Activity.

Listing 2-49. *Activity Using Custom LayoutTransition*

```
public class MainActivity extends Activity {

    LinearLayout mContainer;

    @Override
    public void onCreate(Bundle savedInstanceState) {
        super.onCreate(savedInstanceState);
        setContentView(R.layout.main);

        // Layout Changes Animation
        mContainer = (LinearLayout) findViewById(R.id.verticalContainer);
        LayoutTransition transition = new LayoutTransition();
        mContainer.setLayoutTransition(transition);

        // Override the default appear animation with a flip in
        Animator appearAnim = ObjectAnimator.ofFloat(null, "rotationY", 90f, 0f)
            .setDuration(transition.getDuration(LayoutTransition.APPEARING));
        transition.setAnimator(LayoutTransition.APPEARING, appearAnim);

        // Override the default disappear animation with a flip out
        Animator disappearAnim = ObjectAnimator.ofFloat(null, "rotationX", 0f, 90f)
            .setDuration(transition.getDuration(LayoutTransition.DISAPPEARING));
        transition.setAnimator(LayoutTransition.DISAPPEARING, disappearAnim);

        // Override the default change animation with a more animated slide
        // We are animating several properties at once, so we create an animation
        // out of multiple PropertyValueHolder objects.  This animation slides the
        // views in and temporarily shrinks the view to half size.
        PropertyValuesHolder pvhSlide = PropertyValuesHolder.ofFloat("y", 0, 1);
        PropertyValuesHolder pvhScaleY =
```

```
            PropertyValuesHolder.ofFloat("scaleY", 1f, 0.5f, 1f);
        PropertyValuesHolder pvhScaleX =
            PropertyValuesHolder.ofFloat("scaleX", 1f, 0.5f, 1f);
        Animator changingAppearingAnim = ObjectAnimator.ofPropertyValuesHolder(
            this, pvhSlide, pvhScaleY, pvhScaleX);
        changingAppearingAnim.setDuration(
            transition.getDuration(LayoutTransition.CHANGE_DISAPPEARING));
        transition.setAnimator(LayoutTransition.CHANGE_DISAPPEARING,
                changingAppearingAnim);
    }

    public void onAddClick(View v) {
        Button button = new Button(this);
        button.setText("Click To Remove");
        button.setOnClickListener(new View.OnClickListener() {
            @Override
            public void onClick(View v) {
                mContainer.removeView(v);
            }
        });

        mContainer.addView(button, new LinearLayout.LayoutParams(
                LayoutParams.MATCH_PARENT, LayoutParams.WRAP_CONTENT));
    }
}
```

In this example we have modified the APPEARING, DISAPPEARING, and CHANGE_DISAPPEARING transition animations for our Button layout. The first two transitions affect the item being added or removed. When the Add Item button is clicked, the new item horizontally rotates into view. When any of the remove buttons are clicked, that item will vertically rotate out of view. Both of these transitions are created by making a new ObjectAnimator for the custom rotation property, setting its duration to the default duration for that transition type and attaching it to our LayoutTransition instance along with a key for the specific transition type. The final transition is a little more complicated; we need to create an animation that slides the surrounding views into their new location, but we also want to apply a scale animation during that time.

> **NOTE:** When customizing a change transition, it is important to add a component that moves the location of the view, or else you will likely see flickering as the view moves to create or fill the view gap.

In order to do this, we need to create an ObjectAnimator that operates on several properties, in the form of PropertyValuesHolder instances. Each property that will be part of the animation becomes a separate

PropertyValuesHolder, and all of them are added to the animator using the ofPropertyValuesHolder() factory method. This final transition will cause the remaining items below any removed button to slide up and shrink slightly as they move into place.

2-17. Creating Drawables as Backgrounds

Problem

Your application needs to create custom backgrounds with gradients and rounded corners, and you don't want to waste time scaling lots of image files.

Solution

(API Level 1)

Use Android's most powerful implementation of the XML resources system: creating shape Drawables. When you are able to do so, creating these views as an XML resource makes sense because they are inherently scalable, and they will fit themselves to the bounds of the view when set as a background.

When defining a Drawable in XML using the <shape> tag, the actual result is a GradientDrawable object. You may define objects in the shape of a rectangle, oval, line, or ring, although the rectangle is the most commonly used for backgrounds. In particular, when working with the rectangle the following parameters can be defined for the shape:

- Corner radius
    - Define the radius to use for rounding all four corners or individual radii to round each corner differently
- Gradient
    - Linear, radial, or sweep
    - Two or three color values
    - Orientation on any multiple of 45 degrees (0 is left to right, 90 bottom to top, and so on)
- Solid color
    - Single color to fill the shape

    - Doesn't play nice with the gradient also defined
- Stroke
    - Border around shape
    - Define width and color
- Size and padding

How It Works

Creating static background images for views can be tricky, given that the image must often be created in multiple sizes to display properly on all devices. This issue is compounded if it is expected that the size of the view may dynamically change based on its contents.

To avoid this problem, we create an XML file in res/drawable to describe a shape that we can apply as the `android:background` attribute of any view.

Gradient ListView Row

Our first example for this technique will be to create a gradient rectangle that is suitable to be applied as the background of individual rows inside of a `ListView`. The XML for this shape is defined in Listing 2-50.

Listing 2-50. *res/drawable/backgradient.xml*

```
<?xml version="1.0" encoding="utf-8"?>
<shape xmlns:android="http://schemas.android.com/apk/res/android"
    android:shape="rectangle">
    <gradient
        android:startColor="#EFEFEF"
        android:endColor="#989898"
        android:type="linear"
        android:angle="270"
    />
</shape>
```

Here we chose a linear gradient between two shades of gray, moving from top to bottom. If we wanted to add a third color to the gradient, we would add an `android:middleColor` attribute to the `<gradient>` tag.

Now this Drawable can be referenced by any view or layout used to create the custom items of your ListView (we will discuss more about creating these views in Recipe 2-23). The Drawable would be added as the background by including the attribute `android:background="@drawable/backgradient"` to the view's XML or by calling `View.setBackgroundResource(R.drawable.backgradient)` in Java code.

> **ADVANCED TIP:** The limit on colors in XML is three, but the constructor for `GradientDrawable` takes an `int[]` parameter for colors, and you may pass as many as you like.

When we apply this Drawable as the background to rows in a `ListView`, the result will be similar to Figure 2-7.

Figure 2-7. *Gradient Drawable as row background*

Rounded View Group

Another popular use of XML Drawables is to create a background for a layout that visually groups a handful of widgets together. For style, rounded corners and a thin border are often applied as well. This shape defined in XML would look like Listing 2-51.

Listing 2-51. *res/drawable/roundback.xml*

```
<?xml version="1.0" encoding="utf-8"?>
<shape xmlns:android="http://schemas.android.com/apk/res/android"
    android:shape="rectangle">
    <solid
        android:color="#FFF"
    />
    <corners
        android:radius="10dip"
    />
    <stroke
        android:width="5dip"
        android:color="#555"
    />
</shape>
```

In this case, we chose white for the fill color and gray for the border stroke. As mentioned in the previous example, this Drawable can be referenced by any view or layout as the background by including the attribute `android:background="@drawable/roundback"` to the view's XML or by calling `View.setBackgroundResource(R.drawable.roundback)` in Java code.

When applied as the background to a view, the result is shown in Figure 2-8.

Figure 2-8. *Rounded rectangle with border as view background*

Drawable Patterns

The next category of Drawables we are going to look at is patterns. Using XML, we can define some rules around which a smaller image should be stepped and repeated to make a pattern. This can be a great way to make full-screen background images that don't require a large `Bitmap` to be loaded in to memory.

Applications can create a pattern by setting the `tileMode` attribute on a `<bitmap>` element to one of the following values:

- `clamp`: The source bitmap will have the pixels along its edges replicated.
- `repeat`: The source bitmap will be stepped and repeated in both directions.
- `mirror`: The source bitmap will be stepped and repeated, alternating between normal and flipped images on each iteration.

Figure 2-9 illustrates two small square images that will become the source for our patterns.

Figure 2-9. *Pattern source bitmaps*

Listings 2-52 and 2-53 show examples of how to define an XML pattern as a background.

Listing 2-52. *res/drawable/pattern_checker.xml*

```
<?xml version="1.0" encoding="utf-8"?>
<bitmap xmlns:android="http://schemas.android.com/apk/res/android"
    android:src="@drawable/checkers"
    android:tileMode="repeat" />
```

Listing 2-53. *res/drawable/pattern_stripes.xml*

```
<?xml version="1.0" encoding="utf-8"?>
<bitmap xmlns:android="http://schemas.android.com/apk/res/android"
    android:src="@drawable/stripes"
    android:tileMode="mirror" />
```

> **TIP:** Patterns can be made only with a `bitmap` that has intrinsic bounds, such as external images. XML shapes cannot be used as the source for a pattern.

Figure 2-10 reveals the result of applying each of these patterns as view backgrounds.

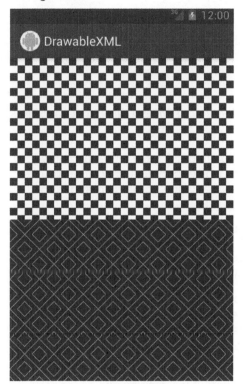

Figure 2-10. *Background patterns*

You can see that the checkerboard image is repeated unmodified, while the stripe pattern image is reflected both horizontally and vertically as it is repeated across the screen.

Nine-Patch Images

The `NinePatchDrawable` is one of Android's greatest strengths when it comes to designing user interfaces that are flexible across devices. The nine-patch is a special image that is designed to stretch in only certain areas by designating sections of the image that are stretchable and areas that are not. In fact, the image type gets its name from the nine stretch zones that get created when an image is mapped (more on this in a moment).

Let's take a look at an example to better understand how this works. Figure 2-11 shows two images; the image on the left is the original, and the image on the right has been converted into a nine-patch.

Figure 2-11. *Speech Bubble Source Image speech_background.png (left) and Nine-Patch Conversion speech_background.9.png (right)*

Notice the black markings on each side of the image. A valid nine-patch image file is simply a PNG image in which the outer 1 pixel contains only either black or transparent pixels. The black pixels on each side define something about how the image will stretch and wrap the content inside.

- Left side: Black pixels here define areas where the image should stretch vertically. The pixels in these areas will be stepped and repeated to accomplish the stretch. The example image in Figure 2-10 has one of these areas.
- Top side: Black pixels here define areas where the image should stretch horizontally. The pixels in these areas will be stepped and repeated to accomplish the stretch. The example image in Figure 2-10 has two of these areas.
- Right side: Black pixels here define the vertical content area, which is the area where the view's content will display. In effect, it is defining the top and bottom padding values, but inherent to the background image.
- Bottom side: Black pixels here define the horizontal content area, which is the area where the view's content will display. In effect, it is defining the left and right padding values, but inherent to the background image. This must contain a single line of solid pixels defining the area.

This image was created using the `draw9patch` tool that is part of the Android SDK. To better visualize how these markings affect the resulting image, let's take a look at the image when loaded into this tool. See Figure 2-12.

Figure 2-12. *Speech bubble inside draw9patch*

You can now start to see where the nine-patch gets its name. The areas of the image that are not highlighted will not be stretched. The highlighted areas of each image will stretch in a single direction (either horizontal or vertical, based on their orientation), and the areas where the highlights intersect will stretch in both directions. In an image with the minimum of one stretchable zone in each direction, this would create nine individual mapped zones in the image: four corners that aren't modified, four middle areas that stretch once, and the single center section that stretches twice.

There isn't any special code required to create a `NinePatchDrawable` and use it as a background; the image file just needs to be named with the special `.9.png` extension so Android can package it correctly. Listing 2-54 shows how you might set this image as a background, and Figure 2-13 reveals what this image looks like when set as the background for a `TextView`.

Listing 2-54. *res/layout/main.xml*

```
<?xml version="1.0" encoding="utf-8"?>
<RelativeLayout xmlns:android="http://schemas.android.com/apk/res/android"
    android:layout_width="match_parent"
    android:layout_height="match_parent" >
    <TextView
        android:layout_width="match_parent"
        android:layout_height="wrap_content"
        android:layout_centerVertical="true"
        android:gravity="center"
        android:text="This is a text speech bubble"
        android:background="@drawable/speech_background"/>
</RelativeLayout>
```

Figure 2-13. *Speech bubble as TextView background*

Note how the two three-pixel-wide horizontal stretch zones evenly distributed the excess space between them, centering the origin point of the speech bubble. If you would like to create an offset between two stretch points, this can be done by varying their distance from the image center or by varying their size. If one zone is three pixels wide and the other is only one pixel wide, the wider zone will take up three times as much space when stretched.

2-18. Creating Custom State Drawables

Problem

You want to customize an element such as a `Button` or `CheckBox` that has multiple states (default, pressed, selected, and so on).

Solution

(API Level 1)

Create a state-list Drawable to apply to the element. Whether you have defined your Drawable graphics yourself in XML, or you are using images, Android provides the means via another XML element, the `<selector>`, to create a single reference to multiple images and the conditions under which they should be visible.

How It Works

Let's take a look at an example state-list Drawable and then discuss its parts:

```
<?xml version="1.0" encoding="utf-8"?>
<selector xmlns:android="http://schemas.android.com/apk/res/android">
    <item android:state_enabled="false" android:drawable="@drawable/disabled" />
    <item android:state_pressed="true" android:drawable="@drawable/selected" />
    <item android:state_focused="true" android:drawable="@drawable/selected" />
    <item android:drawable="@drawable/default" />
</selector>
```

> **NOTE:** The `<selector>` is order specific. Android will return the Drawable of the first state it matches completely as it traverses the list. Bear this in mind when determining which state attributes to apply to each item.

Each item in the list identifies the state(s) that must be in effect for the referenced Drawable to be the one chosen. Multiple state parameters can be added for one item if multiple state values need to be matched. Android will traverse the list and pick the first state that matches all criteria of the current view the Drawable is attached to. For this reason, it is considered good practice to put your normal, or default, state at the bottom of the list with no criteria attached.

Here is a list of the most commonly useful state attributes. All of these are boolean values:

- `state_enabled`
  - Value the view would return from `isEnabled()`.
- `state_pressed`
  - View is pressed by the user on the touch screen.

- state_focused
    - View has focus.
- state_selected
    - View is selected by the user using keys or a D-pad.
- state_checked
    - Value a checkable view would return from isChecked().

Now let's look at how to apply these state-list Drawables to different views.

Button and other Clickable Widgets

Widgets like Button are designed to have their background Drawable change when the view moves through the above states. As such, the android:background attribute in XML or the View.setBackgroundDrawable() method are the proper methods for attaching the state-list. Listing 2-55 is an example with a file defined in res/drawable/ called button_states.xml:

Listing 2-55. *res/drawable/button_states.xml*

```
<?xml version="1.0" encoding="utf-8"?>
<selector xmlns:android="http://schemas.android.com/apk/res/android">
    <item android:state_enabled="false" android:drawable="@drawable/disabled" />
    <item android:state_pressed="true" android:drawable="@drawable/selected" />
    <item android:drawable="@drawable/default" />
</selector>
```

The three @drawable resources listed here are images in the project that the selector is meant to switch between. As we mentioned in the previous section, the last item will be returned as the default if no other items include matching states to the current view; therefore, we do not need to include a state to match on that item. Attaching this to a view defined in XML looks like the following:

```
<Button
    android:layout_width="wrap_content"
    android:layout_height="wrap_content"
    android:text="My Button"
    android:background="@drawable/button_states" />
```

CheckBox and other Checkable Widgets

Many of the widgets that implement the Checkable interface, like CheckBox and other subclasses of CompoundButton, have a slightly different mechanism for changing their state. In these cases, the background is not associated with the state, and customizing the Drawable to represent the "checked" states is done through another attribute called the button. In XML, this is the `android:button` attribute, and in code the `CompoundButton.setButtonDrawable()` method should do the trick.

Listing 2-56 is an example with a file defined in res/drawable/ called check_states.xml. Again, the `@drawable` resources listed are meant to reference images in the project to be switched.

Listing 2-56. *res/drawable/check_states.xml*

```
<?xml version="1.0" encoding="utf-8"?>
<selector xmlns:android="http://schemas.android.com/apk/res/android">
    <item android:state_enabled="false" android:drawable="@drawable/disabled" />
    <item android:state_checked="true" android:drawable="@drawable/checked" />
    <item android:drawable="@drawable/unchecked" />
</selector>
```

And here they are attached to a CheckBox in XML:

```
<CheckBox
    android:layout_width="wrap_content"
    android:layout_height="wrap_content"
    android:button="@drawable/check_states" />
```

2-19. Applying Masks to Images

Problem

You need to apply one image or shape as a clipping mask to define the visible boundaries of a second image in your application.

Solution

(API Level 1)

Using 2D Graphics and a `PorterDuffXferMode`, you can apply any arbitrary mask (in the form of another bitmap) to a bitmap image. The basic steps to this recipe are as follows:

Create a mutable `Bitmap` instance (blank), and a Canvas to draw into it.

1. Draw the mask pattern onto the Canvas first.
2. Apply a `PorterDuffXferMode` to the Paint.
3. Draw the source image on the Canvas using the transfer mode.

They key ingredient is the `PorterDuffXferMode`, which considers the current state of both the source and destination objects during a paint operation. The destination is the existing Canvas data, and the source is the graphic data being applied in the current operation.

There are many mode parameters that can be attached to this, which create varying effects on the result, but for masking we are interested in using the `PorterDuff.Mode.SRC_IN` mode. This mode will only draw at locations where the source and destination overlap, and the pixels drawn will be from the source; in other words, the source is clipped by the bounds of the destination.

How It Works

Rounded Corner Bitmap

One extremely common use of this technique is to apply rounded corners to a bitmap image before displaying it in an `ImageView`. For this example, Figure 2-14 is the original image we will be masking.

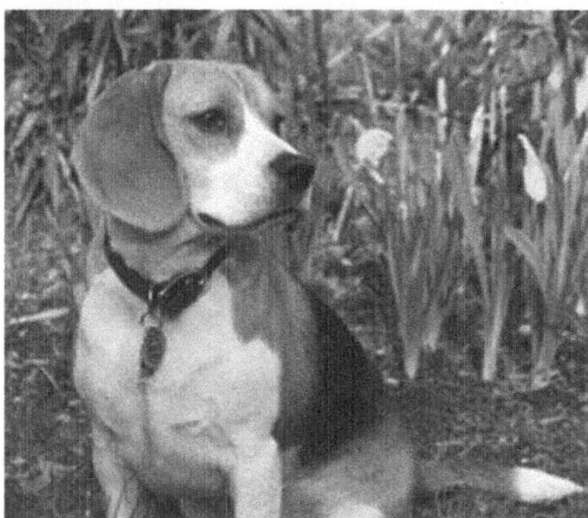

Figure 2-14. *Original source image*

We will first create a rounded rectangle on the `Canvas` with the required corner radius, and this will serve as our "mask" for the image. Then, applying the

PorterDuff.Mode.SRC_IN transform as we paint the source image into the same Canvas, the result will be the source image with rounded corners.

This is because the SRC_IN transfer mode tells the paint object to only paint pixels on the Canvas locations where there is overlap between the source and destination (the rounded rectangle we already drew), and the pixels that get drawn come from the source. Listing 2-57 is the code inside an Activity.

Listing 2-57. *Activity Applying a Rounded Rectangle Mask to a Bitmap*

```
public class MaskActivity extends Activity {

    @Override
    public void onCreate(Bundle savedInstanceState) {
        super.onCreate(savedInstanceState);
        ImageView iv = new ImageView(this);

        //Create and load images (immutable, typically)
        Bitmap source = BitmapFactory.decodeResource(getResources(),
            R.drawable.dog);

        //Create a *mutable* location, and a Canvas to draw into it
        Bitmap result = Bitmap.createBitmap(source.getWidth(), source.getHeight(),
            Config.ARGB_8888);
        Canvas canvas = new Canvas(result);
        Paint paint = new Paint(Paint.ANTI_ALIAS_FLAG);

        //Create and draw the rounded rectangle "mask" first
        RectF rect = new RectF(0,0,source.getWidth(),source.getHeight());
        float radius = 25.0f;
        paint.setColor(Color.BLACK);
        canvas.drawRoundRect(rect, radius, radius, paint);
        //Switch over and paint the source using the transfer mode
        paint.setXfermode(new PorterDuffXfermode(Mode.SRC_IN));
        canvas.drawBitmap(source, 0, 0, paint);
        paint.setXfermode(null);

        iv.setImageBitmap(result);
        setContentView(iv);
    }
}
```

The result of your efforts is shown in Figure 2-15.

Figure 2-15. *Image with a rounded rectangle mask applied*

Arbitrary Mask Image

Let's look at an example that's a little more interesting. Here we take two images: the source image and an image representing the mask we want to apply (in this case, an upside-down triangle; see Figure 2-16).

Figure 2-16. *Original source image (left) and arbitrary mask image to apply (right)*

The chosen mask image does not have to conform to the style chosen here, with black pixels for the mask and transparent everywhere else. However, it is the best choice to guarantee that the system draws the mask exactly as you expect it to be. Listing 2-58 is the simple Activity code to mask the image and display it in a view.

Listing 2-58. *Activity Applying an Arbitrary Mask to a Bitmap*

```
public class MaskActivity extends Activity {

    @Override
    public void onCreate(Bundle savedInstanceState) {
        super.onCreate(savedInstanceState);
        ImageView iv = new ImageView(this);

        //Create and load images (immutable, typically)
        Bitmap source = BitmapFactory.decodeResource(getResources(),
            R.drawable.dog);
        Bitmap mask = BitmapFactory.decodeResource(getResources(),
            R.drawable.triangle);

        //Create a *mutable* location, and a Canvas to draw into it
        Bitmap result = Bitmap.createBitmap(source.getWidth(), source.getHeight(),
            Config.ARGB_8888);
        Canvas canvas = new Canvas(result);
        Paint paint = new Paint(Paint.ANTI_ALIAS_FLAG);

        //Draw the mask image first, then paint the source using the transfer mode
        canvas.drawBitmap(mask, 0, 0, paint);
        paint.setXfermode(new PorterDuffXfermode(Mode.SRC_IN));
        canvas.drawBitmap(source, 0, 0, paint);
        paint.setXfermode(null);

        iv.setImageBitmap(result);
        setContentView(iv);
    }
}
```

As with before, we draw the mask onto the Canvas first and then draw the source image in using the PorterDuff.Mode.SRC_IN mode to only paint the source pixels where they overlap the existing mask pixels. The result looks something like Figure 2-17.

Figure 2-17. *Image with a mask applied*

Please Try This at Home

Applying the `PorterDuffXferMode` in this fashion to blend two images can create lots of interesting results. Try taking this same example code, but changing the `PorterDuff.Mode` parameter to one of the many other options. Each of the modes will blend the two bitmaps in a slightly different way. Have fun with it!

2-20. Creating Dialogs That Persist

Problem

You want to create a user dialog that has multiple input fields or some other set of information that needs to be persisted if the device is rotated.

Solution

(API Level 1)

Don't use a dialog at all; create an Activity with the Dialog theme. Dialogs are managed objects that must be handled properly when the device rotates while they are visible; otherwise, they will cause a leaked reference in the window manager. You can mitigate this issue by having your Activity manage the dialog for you using methods like `Activity.showDialog()` and `Activity.dismissDialog()` to present it, but that only solves one problem.

The dialog does not have any mechanism of its own to persist state through a rotation, and this job (by design) falls back to the Activity that presented it. This results in extra required effort to ensure that the dialog can pass back or persist any values entered into it before it is dismissed.

If you have an interface to present to the user that will need to persist state and stay front-facing through rotation, a better solution is to make it an Activity. This allows that object access to the full set of life-cycle callback methods for saving/restoring state. Plus, as an Activity, it does not have to be managed to dismiss and present again during rotation, which removes the worry of leaking references. You can still make the Activity behave like a dialog from the user's perspective by using the `Theme.Dialog` system theme.

How It Works

Listing 2-59 is an example of a simple Activity that has a title and some text in a TextView.

Listing 2-59. *Activity to Be Themed as a Dialog*

```
public class DialogActivity extends Activity {
    @Override
    public void onCreate(Bundle savedInstanceState) {
        super.onCreate(savedInstanceState);
        setTitle("Activity");
        TextView tv = new TextView(this);
        tv.setText("I'm Really An Activity!");
        //Add some padding to keep the dialog borders away
        tv.setPadding(15, 15, 15, 15);
        setContentView(tv);
    }
}
```

We can apply the Dialog theme to this Activity in the AndroidManifest.xml file for the application (see Listing 2-60).

Listing 2-60. *Manifest Setting the Above Activity with the Dialog Theme*

```
<?xml version="1.0" encoding="utf-8"?>
<manifest xmlns:android="http://schemas.android.com/apk/res/android"
      package="com.examples.dialogs"
      android:versionCode="1"
      android:versionName="1.0">
    <application android:icon="@drawable/icon" android:label="@string/app_name">
        <activity android:name=".DialogActivity"
                  android:label="@string/app_name"
                  android:theme="@android:style/Theme.Dialog">
            <intent-filter>
                <action android:name="android.intent.action.MAIN" />
                <category android:name="android.intent.category.LAUNCHER" />
            </intent-filter>
        </activity>
    </application>
</manifest>
```

Note the `android:theme="@android:style/Theme.Dialog"` parameter, which creates the look and feel of a dialog, with all the benefits of a full-blown Activity. When you run this application, you will see a screen like the one shown in Figure 2-18.

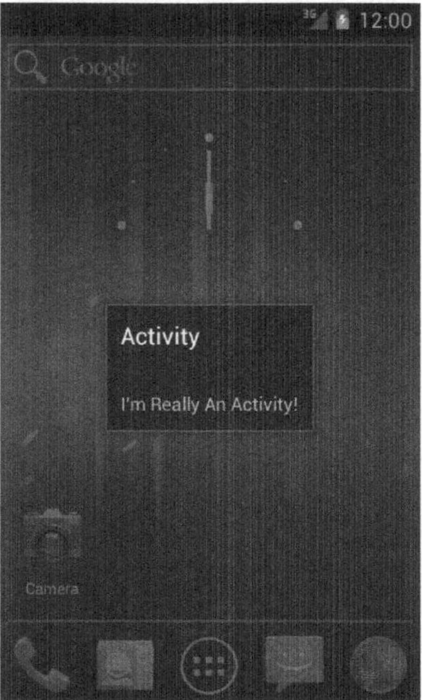

Figure 2-18. *Applying the Dialog theme to an Activity*

Even though this is an Activity for all intents and purposes, it can act as a dialog inside your UI, partially covering the Activity underneath it (in this case, the Home screen).

2-21. Implementing Situation-Specific Layouts

Problem

Your application must be universal, running on different screen sizes and orientations. You need to provide different layout resources for each of these instances.

Solution

(API Level 4)

Build multiple layout files, and use resource qualifiers to let Android pick what's appropriate. We will look at using resources to create layouts specific for different screen orientations and sizes. We will also explore using layout aliases to reduce duplication in cases where multiple configurations share the same layout.

How It Works

Orientation-Specific

In order to create different resources for an Activity to use in portrait versus landscape, use the following qualifiers:

- resource-land
- resource-port

This works for all resource types, but the most common in this case is to do this with layouts. Therefore, instead of a res/layout/ directory in the project, there would be a res/layout-port/ and a res/layout-land/ directory.

> **NOTE:** It is good practice to include a default resource directory without a qualifier. This gives Android something to fall back on if it is running on a device that doesn't match any of the specific criteria you list.

Size-Specific

There are also screen-size qualifiers (physical size, not to be confused with pixel density) that we can use to target large screen devices like tablets. In most cases, a single layout will suffice for all physical screen sizes of mobile phones. However, you may want to add more features to a tablet layout to assist in filling the noticeably larger screen real estate the user has to operate.

Prior to Android 3.2 (API Level 13), the following resource qualifiers were acceptable for physical screen sizes:

- resource-small
  - Screen measuring at least 426 dp x 320 dp
- resource-medium
  - Screen measuring at least 470 dp x 320 dp
- resource-large
  - Screen measuring at least 640 dp x 480 dp
- resource-xlarge
  - Screen measuring at least 960 dp x 720 dp

As larger screens became more common on both handset devices and tablets, it was apparent that the four generalized buckets weren't enough to avoid overlap in defining resources. In Android 3.2, a new system based on the screen's actual dimensions (in dp units) was introduced. With the new system, the following resource qualifiers are acceptable for physical screen sizes:

- Smallest Width: resource-sw___dp
  - Screen with at least the noted density-independent pixels in the shortest direction (meaning irrespective of orientation).
  - A 640 dp x 480 dp screen always has a smallest width of 480 dp

- Width: resource-w___dp
  - Screen with at least the noted density-independent pixels in the current horizontal direction.
  - A 640 dp x 480 dp screen has a width of 640 dp when in landscape and 480 dp when in portrait.
- Height: resource-h___dp
  - Screen with at least the noted density-independent pixels in the current vertical direction.
  - A 640 dp x 480 dp screen has a height of 640 dp when in portrait and 480 dp when in landscape.

So, to include a tablet-only layout to a universal application, we could add a res/layout-large/ directory for older tablets and a res/layout-sw720dp/ directory for newer tablets as well.

Layout Aliases

There is one final concept to discuss when creating universal application UIs, and that is layout aliases. Often it is the case that the same layout should be used for multiple different device configurations, but chaining multiple resource qualifiers together (such as a smallest width qualifier and a traditional size qualifier) on the same resource directory can be problematic. This can often lead developers to create multiple copies of the same layout in different directories, which is a maintenance nightmare.

We can solve this problem with aliasing. By creating a single layout file in the default resource directory, we can create multiple aliases to that single file in resource-qualified values directories for each configuration that uses the layout. The following snippet illustrates an alias to the `res/layout/main_tablet.xml` file.

```
<resources>
    <item name="main" type="layout">@layout/main_tablet</item>
</resources>
```

The name attribute represents the aliased name, which is the resource this alias is meant to represent in the selected configuration. This alias links the `main_tablet.xml` file to be used when `R.layout.main` is requested in code. This code could be placed into `res/values-xlarge/layout.xml` and `res/values-sw720dp/layout.xml`, and both configurations would link to the same layout.

Tying It Together

Let's look at a quick example that puts this into practice. We'll define a single Activity that loads a single layout resource in code. However, this layout will be defined differently in the resources to produce different results in portrait, in landscape, and on tablet devices. First, the Activity is shown in Listing 2-61.

Listing 2-61. *Simple Activity Loading One Layout*

```
public class UniversalActivity extends Activity {

    @Override
    public void onCreate(Bundle savedInstanceState) {
        super.onCreate(savedInstanceState);
        setContentView(R.layout.main);
    }
}
```

We'll now define three separate layouts to use for this Activity in different configurations. Listings 2-62 through 2-64 show layouts to be used for the default, landscape, and tablet configurations of the UI.

Listing 2-62. *res/layout/main.xml*

```
<?xml version="1.0" encoding="utf-8"?>
<!-- DEFAULT LAYOUT -->
<LinearLayout xmlns:android="http://schemas.android.com/apk/res/android"
    android:layout_width="match_parent"
    android:layout_height="match_parent"
    android:orientation="vertical" >
    <TextView
        android:layout_width="match_parent"
        android:layout_height="wrap_content"
        android:text="This is the default layout" />
    <Button
        android:layout_width="match_parent"
        android:layout_height="wrap_content"
        android:text="Button One" />
    <Button
        android:layout_width="match_parent"
        android:layout_height="wrap_content"
        android:text="Button Two" />
    <Button
        android:layout_width="match_parent"
        android:layout_height="wrap_content"
        android:text="Button Three" />
</LinearLayout>
```

Listing 2-63. *res/layout-land/main.xml*

```
<?xml version="1.0" encoding="utf-8"?>
<!-- LANDSCAPE LAYOUT -->
<LinearLayout xmlns:android="http://schemas.android.com/apk/res/android"
    android:layout_width="fill_parent"
    android:layout_height="fill_parent"
    android:orientation="vertical" >
    <TextView
        android:layout_width="wrap_content"
        android:layout_height="wrap_content"
        android:text="This is a horizontal layout for LANDSCAPE" />
    <!-- Three buttons to fill screen equally using weight -->
    <LinearLayout
        android:layout_width="match_parent"
        android:layout_height="wrap_content"
        android:orientation="horizontal" >
        <Button
            android:layout_width="0dp"
            android:layout_height="wrap_content"
            android:layout_weight="1"
            android:text="Button One" />
        <Button
            android:layout_width="0dp"
            android:layout_height="wrap_content"
            android:layout_weight="1"
            android:text="Button Two" />
        <Button
            android:layout_width="0dp"
            android:layout_height="wrap_content"
            android:layout_weight="1"
            android:text="Button Three" />
    </LinearLayout>
</LinearLayout>
```

Listing 2-64. *res/layout/main_tablet.xml*

```
<?xml version="1.0" encoding="utf-8"?>
<!-- TABLET LAYOUT -->
<LinearLayout xmlns:android="http://schemas.android.com/apk/res/android"
    android:layout_width="match_parent"
    android:layout_height="match_parent"
    android:orientation="horizontal" >
    <!-- Group of user buttons taking 25% of screen width -->
    <LinearLayout
        android:layout_width="0dp"
        android:layout_height="match_parent"
        android:layout_weight="1"
        android:orientation="vertical">
        <TextView
```

```
            android:layout_width="match_parent"
            android:layout_height="wrap_content"
            android:text="This is the layout for TABLETS" />
        <Button
            android:layout_width="match_parent"
            android:layout_height="wrap_content"
            android:text="Button One" />
        <Button
            android:layout_width="match_parent"
            android:layout_height="wrap_content"
            android:text="Button Two" />
        <Button
            android:layout_width="match_parent"
            android:layout_height="wrap_content"
            android:text="Button Three" />
        <Button
            android:layout_width="match_parent"
            android:layout_height="wrap_content"
            android:text="Button Four" />
    </LinearLayout>


    <!-- Extra view to show detail content -->
    <TextView
        android:layout_width="0dp"
        android:layout_height="match_parent"
        android:layout_weight="3"
        android:text="Detail View"
        android:background="#CCC" />
</LinearLayout>
```

One option would have been to create three files with the same name and to place them in qualified directories, such as res/layout-land for landscape and res/layout-large for tablet. That scheme works great if each layout file is used only once, but we will need to reuse each layout in multiple configurations, so in this example we will create qualified aliases to these three layouts. Listings 2-65 through 2-68 reveal how we link each layout to the correct configuration.

Listing 2-65. *res/values-large-land/layout.xml*

```
<?xml version="1.0" encoding="utf-8"?>
<resources xmlns:android="http://schemas.android.com/apk/res/android">
    <item name="main" type="layout">@layout/main_tablet</item>
</resources>
```

Listing 2-66. *res/value-sw600dp-land/layout.xml*

```
<?xml version="1.0" encoding="utf-8"?>
<resources xmlns:android="http://schemas.android.com/apk/res/android">
    <item name="main" type="layout">@layout/main_tablet</item>
```

```
</resources>
```

Listing 2-67. *res/values-xlarge/layout.xml*

```
<?xml version="1.0" encoding="utf-8"?>
<resources xmlns:android="http://schemas.android.com/apk/res/android">
    <item name="main" type="layout">@layout/main_tablet</item>
</resources>
```

Listing 2-68. *res/values-sw720dp/layout.xml*

```
<?xml version="1.0" encoding="utf-8"?>
<resources xmlns:android="http://schemas.android.com/apk/res/android">
    <item name="main" type="layout">@layout/main_tablet</item>
</resources>
```

We have defined configuration groups to accommodate three classes of devices: handsets, seven-inch tablet devices, and ten-inch tablet devices. Handset devices will load the default layout when in portrait mode and the landscape layout when the device is rotated. Because this is the only configuration using these files, they are placed directly into the `res/layout` and `res/layout-land` directories, respectively.

Seven-inch tablet devices in the previous size scheme were typically defined as large screens, and in the new scheme they have a smallest width of around 600 dp. In portrait mode, we have decided that our application should use the default layout, but in landscape mode we have significantly more real estate, so we load the tablet layout instead. To do this, we create qualified directories for the landscape orientation that match this device size class. Using both smallest width and bucket size qualifiers ensures we are compatible with older and newer tablets.

Ten-inch tablet devices in the previous size scheme were considered xlarge screens, and in the new scheme they have a smallest width of around 720 dp. For these devices, the screen is large enough to use the tablet layout in both orientations, so we create qualified directories that call out only the screen size. Again, as with the smaller tablets, using both smallest width and bucket size qualifiers ensures we are compatible with all tablet versions.

In all cases in which the tablet layout was referenced, we only had to create one layout file to manage, thanks to the power of using aliases. Now, when we run the application, you can see how Android selects the appropriate layout to match our configuration. Figure 2-19 shows default and landscape layouts on a handset device.

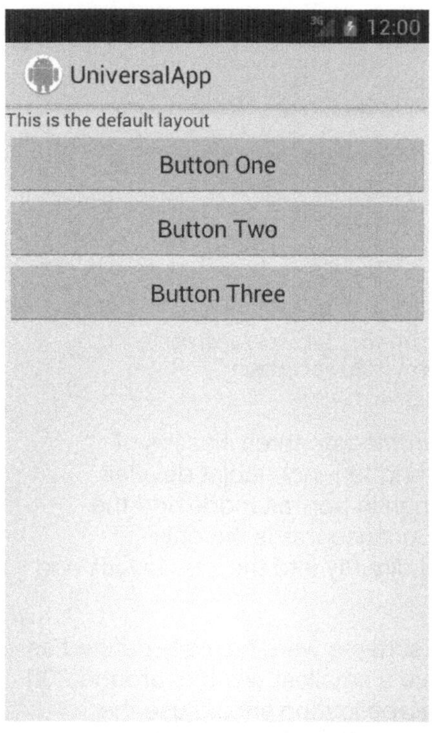

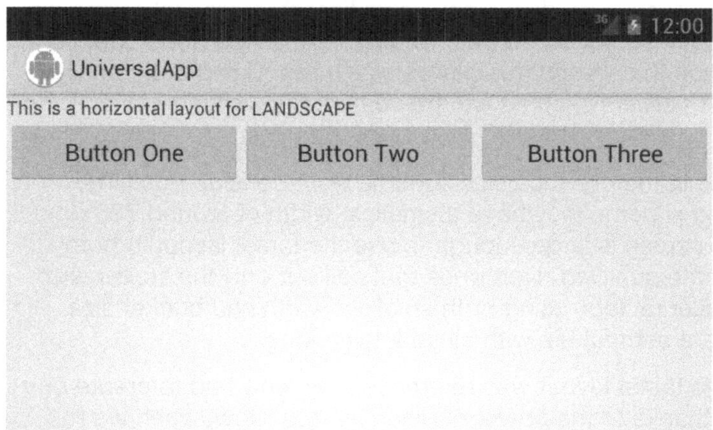

Figure 2-19. *Handset portrait and landscape layouts*

The same application on a seven-inch tablet device displays the default layout in portrait orientation, but we get the full tablet layout in landscape (see Figure 2-20).

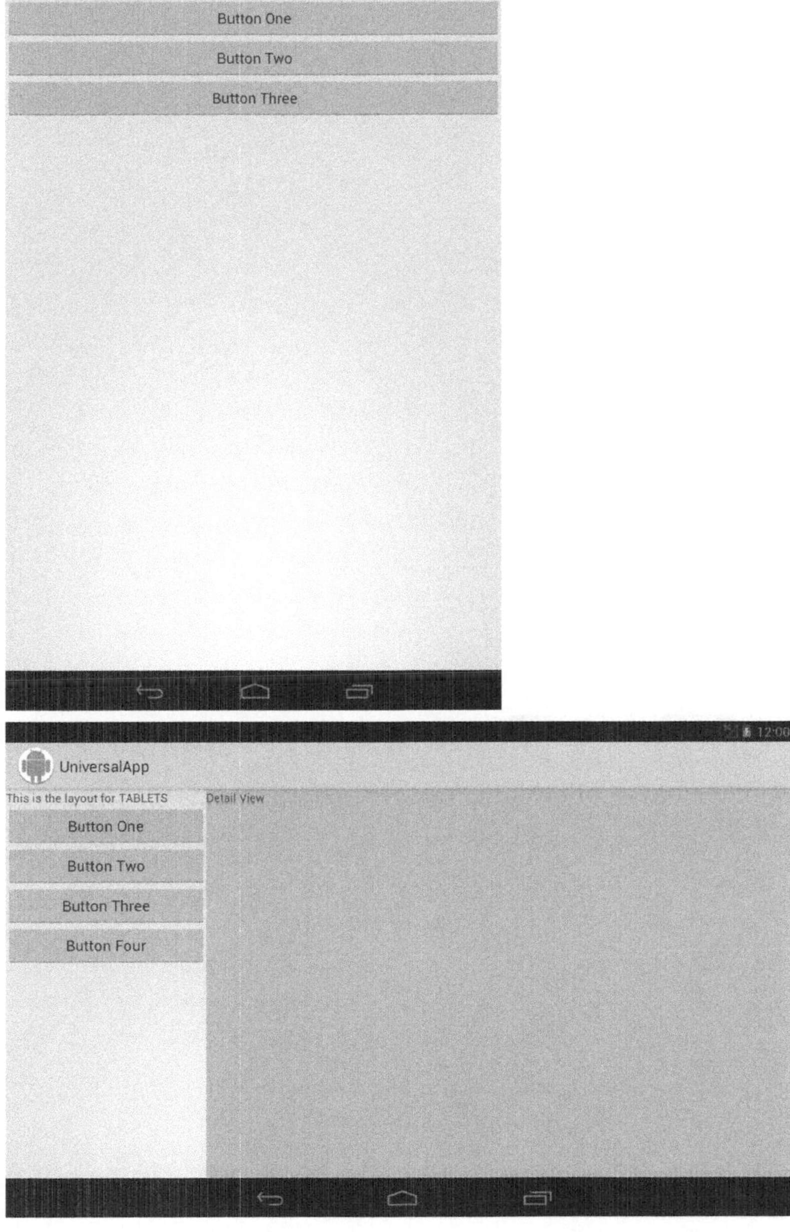

Figure 2-20. *Seven-inch tablet: Default portrait and tablet landscape layout*

Finally, in Figure 2-21 we can see the larger screen on the ten-inch tablet running the full tablet layout in both portrait and landscape orientations.

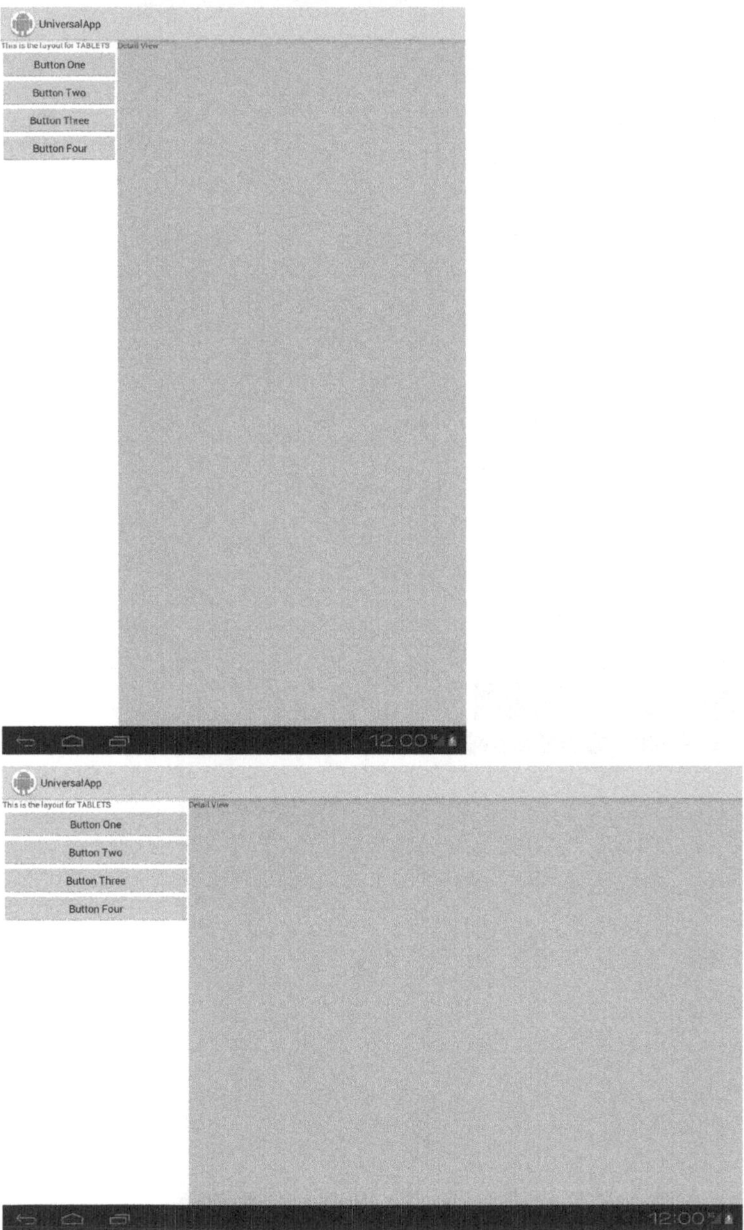

Figure 2-21. *Ten-inch tablet: Full tablet layout in both orientations*

With the extensive capabilities of the Android resource selection system, the difficulty of supporting different UI layouts optimized for each device type is greatly reduced.

2-22. Customizing Keyboard Actions

Problem

You want to customize the appearance of the soft keyboard's Enter key, the action that occurs when a user taps it, or both.

Solution

(API Level 3)

Customize the input method (IME) options for the widget in which the keyboard is entering data.

How It Works

Custom Enter Key

When the keyboard is visible onscreen, the text on the Enter key typically has an action based on the order of focusable items in the view. While unspecified, the keyboard will display a "next" action if there are more focusables in the view to move to or a "done" action if the last item is currently focused on. In the case of a multi-line field, this action is a line return. This value is customizable, however, for each input view by setting the `android:imeOptions` value in the view's XML. The values you may set to customize the Enter key are listed here:

- actionUnspecified: Default. Display action of the device's choice
    - Action event will be IME_NULL
- actionGo: Display "Go" as the Enter key
    - Action event will be IME_ACTION_GO
- actionSearch: Display a search glass as the Enter key
    - Action event will be IME_ACTION_SEARCH

- actionSend: Display “Send” as the Enter key
  - Action event will be IME_ACTION_SEND
- actionNext: Display “Next” as the Enter key
  - Action event will be IME_ACTION_NEXT
- actionDone: Display “Done” as the Enter key
  - Action event will be IME_ACTION_DONE

Let’s look at an example layout with two editable textfields, shown in Listing 2-69. The first will display the search glass on the Enter key, and the second will display “Go.”

Listing 2-69. *Layout with Custom Input Options on EditText Widgets*

```
<LinearLayout xmlns:android="http://schemas.android.com/apk/res/android"
  android:layout_width="fill_parent"
  android:layout_height="fill_parent"
  android:orientation="vertical">
  <EditText
    android:id="@+id/text1"
    android:layout_width="fill_parent"
    android:layout_height="wrap_content"
    android:singleLine="true"
    android:imeOptions="actionSearch"
  />
  <EditText
    android:id="@+id/text2"
    android:layout_width="fill_parent"
    android:layout_height="wrap_content"
    android:singleLine="true"
    android:imeOptions="actionGo"
  />
</LinearLayout>
```

The resulting display of the keyboard will vary somewhat as some manufacturer-specific UI kits include different keyboards, but the results on a pure Google UI will show up as in Figure 2-22.

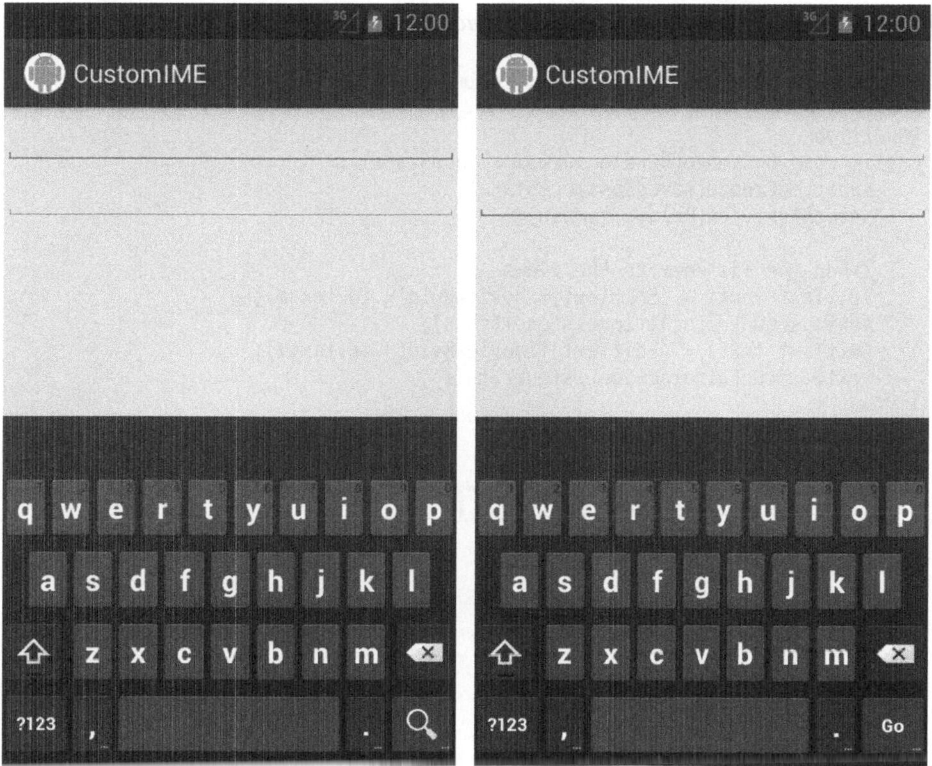

Figure 2-22. *Result of custom input options on Enter key*

> **NOTE:** Custom editor options apply only to the soft input methods. Changing this value will not affect the events that get generated when the user presses Enter on a physical hardware keyboard.

Custom Action

Customizing what happens when the user presses the Enter key can be just as important as adjusting its display. Overriding the default behavior of any action simply requires that a `TextView.OnEditorActionListener` be attached to the view of interest. Let's continue with the example layout above, and this time we'll add a custom action to both views (see Listing 2-70).

Listing 2-70. *Activity Implementing a Custom Keyboard Action*

```
public class MyActivity extends Activity implements OnEditorActionListener {

    @Override
    public void onCreate(Bundle savedInstanceState) {
        super.onCreate(savedInstanceState);
        setContentView(R.layout.main);

        //Add the listener to the views
        EditText text1 = (EditText)findViewById(R.id.text1);
        text1.setOnEditorActionListener(this);
        EditText text2 = (EditText)findViewById(R.id.text2);
        text2.setOnEditorActionListener(this);
    }

    @Override
    public boolean onEditorAction(TextView v, int actionId, KeyEvent event) {
        if(actionId == IME_ACTION_SEARCH) {
            //Handle search key click
            return true;
        }
        if(actionId == IME_ACTION_GO) {
            //Handle go key click
            return true;
        }
        return false;
    }
}
```

The boolean return value of `onEditorAction()` tells the system whether your implementation has consumed the event or whether it should be passed on to the next possible responder, if any. It is important for you to return `true` when your implementation handles the event so no other processing occurs. However, it is just as important for you to return `false` when you are not handling the event so your application does not steal key events from the rest of the system.

2-23. Dismissing Soft Keyboard

Problem

You need an event on the UI to hide or dismiss the soft keyboard from the screen.

Solution

(API Level 3)

Tell the Input Method Manager explicitly to hide any visible input methods by using the InputMethodManager.hideSoftInputFromWindow() method.

How It Works

Here is an example of how to call this method inside of a View.OnClickListener:

```
public void onClick(View view) {
    InputMethodManager imm = (InputMethodManager)getSystemService(
            Context.INPUT_METHOD_SERVICE);
    imm.hideSoftInputFromWindow(view.getWindowToken(), 0);
}
```

The hideSoftInputFromWindow() takes an IBinder window token as a parameter. This can be retrieved from any View object currently attached to the window via View.getWindowToken(). In most cases, the callback method for the specific event will either have a reference to the TextView where the editing is taking place or the view that was tapped to generate the event (like a button). These views are the most convenient objects to call on to get the window token and pass it to the InputMethodManager.

2-24. Customizing AdapterView Empty Views

Problem

You want to display a custom view when an AdapterView (ListView, GridView, and the like) has an empty data set.

Solution

(API Level 1)

Lay out the view you would like displayed in the same tree as the AdapterView and call AdapterView.setEmptyView() to have the AdapterView manage it. The AdapterView will switch the visibility parameters between itself and its empty view based on the result of the attached ListAdapter's isEmpty() method.

> **IMPORTANT:** Be sure to include both the AdapterView and the empty view in your layout. The AdapterView *only* changes the visibility parameters on the two objects; it does not insert or remove them in the layout tree.

How It Works

Here is how this would look with a simple TextView used as the empty view. First, a layout includes both views, shown in Listing 2-71.

Listing 2-71. *Layout Containing AdapterView and an Empty View*

```
<?xml version="1.0" encoding="utf-8"?>
<FrameLayout xmlns:android="http://schemas.android.com/apk/res/android"
    android:layout_width="fill_parent"
    android:layout_height="fill_parent">
    <TextView
        android:id="@+id/myempty"
        android:layout_width="fill_parent"
        android:layout_height="wrap_content"
        android:text="No Items to Display"
    />
    <ListView
        android:id="@+id/mylist"
        android:layout_width="fill_parent"
        android:layout_height="fill_parent"
    />
</FrameLayout>
```

Then, in the Activity, give the ListView a reference to the empty view so it can be managed (see Listing 2-72).

Listing 2-72. *Activity Connecting the Empty View to the List*

```
public void onCreate(Bundle savedInstanceState) {
    super.onCreate(savedInstanceState);
    ListView list = (ListView)findViewById(R.id.mylist);
    TextView empty = (TextView)findViewById(R.id.myempty);
    //Attach the reference
    list.setEmptyView(empty);

    //Continue adding adapters and data to the list

}
```

Make Empty Interesting

Empty views don't have to be simple and boring like the single TextView. Let's try to make things a little more useful for the user and add a Refresh button when the list is empty (see Listing 2-73).

Listing 2-73. *Interactive Empty Layout*

```
<?xml version="1.0" encoding="utf-8"?>
<FrameLayout xmlns:android="http://schemas.android.com/apk/res/android"
    android:layout_width="fill_parent"
    android:layout_height="fill_parent">
    <LinearLayout
        android:id="@+id/myempty"
        android:layout_width="fill_parent"
        android:layout_height="wrap_content"
        android:orientation="vertical">
        <TextView
            android:layout_width="fill_parent"
            android:layout_height="wrap_content"
            android:text="No Items to Display"
        />
        <Button
            android:layout_width="fill_parent"
            android:layout_height="wrap_content"
            android:text="Tap Here to Refresh"
        />
    </LinearLayout>
    <ListView
        android:id="@+id/mylist"
        android:layout_width="fill_parent"
        android:layout_height="fill_parent"
    />
</FrameLayout>
```

Now, with the same Activity code from before, we have set an entire layout as the empty view and have added the ability for users to do something about their lack of data.

2-25. Customizing ListView Rows

Problem

Your application needs to use a more customized look for each row in a ListView.

Solution

(API Level 1)

Create a custom XML layout and pass it to one of the common adapters, or extend your own. You can then apply custom state Drawables for overriding the background and selected states of each row.

How It Works

Simply Custom

If your needs are simple, create a layout that can connect to an existing ListAdapter for population; we'll use ArrayAdapter as an example. The ArrayAdapter can take parameters for a custom layout resource to inflate and the ID of one TextView in that layout to populate with data. Let's create some custom Drawables for the background and a layout that meets these requirements (see Listings 2-74 through 2-76).

Listing 2-74. *res/drawable/row_background_default.xml*

```
<?xml version="1.0" encoding="utf-8"?>
<shape xmlns:android="http://schemas.android.com/apk/res/android"
    android:shape="rectangle">
    <gradient
        android:startColor="#EFEFEF"
        android:endColor="#989898"
        android:type="linear"
        android:angle="270"
    />
</shape>
```

Listing 2-75. *res/drawable/row_background_pressed.xml*

```
<?xml version="1.0" encoding="utf-8"?>
<shape xmlns:android="http://schemas.android.com/apk/res/android"
    android:shape="rectangle">
    <gradient
        android:startColor="#0B8CF2"
        android:endColor="#0661E5"
        android:type="linear"
        android:angle="270"
    />
</shape>
```

Listing 2-76. *res/drawable/row_background.xml*

```
<?xml version="1.0" encoding="utf-8"?>
<selector xmlns:android="http://schemas.android.com/apk/res/android">
    <item android:state_pressed="true"
        android:drawable="@drawable/row_background_pressed"/>
  <item android:drawable="@drawable/row_background_default"/>
</selector>
```

Listing 2-77 shows a custom layout with the text fully centered in the row instead of aligned to the left.

Listing 2-77. *res/layout/custom_row.xml*

```
<?xml version="1.0" encoding="utf-8"?>
<LinearLayout xmlns:android="http://schemas.android.com/apk/res/android"
    android:layout_width="fill_parent"
    android:layout_height="wrap_content"
    android:padding="10dip"
    android:background="@drawable/row_background">
    <TextView
        android:id="@+id/line1"
        android:layout_width="wrap_content"
        android:layout_height="wrap_content"
        android:layout_gravity="center"
    />
</LinearLayout>
```

This layout has the custom gradient state-list set as its background, and this sets up the default and pressed states for each item in the list. Now, because we have defined a layout that matches up with what an ArrayAdapter expects, we can create one and set it on our list without any further customization (see Listing 2-78).

Listing 2-78. *Activity Using the Custom Row Layout*

```
public void onCreate(Bundle savedInstanceState) {
    super.onCreate(savedInstanceState);
    ListView list = new ListView(this);
    ArrayAdapter<String> adapter = new ArrayAdapter<String>(this,
                R.layout.custom_row,
                R.id.line1,
                new String[] {"Bill","Tom","Sally","Jenny"});
    list.setAdapter(adapter);

    setContentView(list);
}
```

Adapting to a More Complex Choice

Sometimes customizing the list rows means extending a ListAdapter as well. This is usually the case if you have multiple pieces of data in a single row or if any of them are not text. In this example, let's utilize the custom Drawables again for the background, but we'll make the layout a little more interesting (see Listing 2-79).

Listing 2-79. *res/layout/custom_row.xml Modified*

```
<?xml version="1.0" encoding="utf-8"?>
<RelativeLayout xmlns:android="http://schemas.android.com/apk/res/android"
    android:layout_width="fill_parent"
    android:layout_height="wrap_content"
    android:orientation="horizontal"
    android:padding="10dip">
    <ImageView
        android:id="@+id/leftimage"
        android:layout_width="32dip"
        android:layout_height="32dip"
    />
    <ImageView
        android:id="@+id/rightimage"
        android:layout_width="32dip"
        android:layout_height="32dip"
        android:layout_alignParentRight="true"
    />

    <TextView
        android:id="@+id/line1"
        android:layout_width="fill_parent"
        android:layout_height="wrap_content"
        android:layout_toLeftOf="@id/rightimage"
        android:layout_toRightOf="@id/leftimage"
        android:layout_centerVertical="true"
        android:gravity="center_horizontal"
    />
</RelativeLayout>
```

This layout contains the same centered TextView but bordered with an ImageView on each side. In order to apply this layout to the ListView, we will need to extend one of the ListAdapters in the SDK. Which one you extend depends on the data source you are presenting in the list. If the data is still just a simple array of strings, an extension of ArrayAdapter is sufficient. If the data is more complex, a full extension of the abstract BaseAdapter may be necessary. The only required method to extend is getView(), which governs how each row in the list is presented.

In our case, the data is a simple array of strings, so we will create a simple extension of ArrayAdapter (see Listing 2-80).

Listing 2-80. *Activity and Custom ListAdapter to Display the New Layout*

```
public class MyActivity extends Activity {

    public void onCreate(Bundle savedInstanceState) {
        super.onCreate(savedInstanceState);
        ListView list = new ListView(this);
        setContentView(list);

        CustomAdapter adapter = new CustomAdapter(this,
                    R.layout.custom_row,
                    R.id.line1,
                    new String[] {"Bill","Tom","Sally","Jenny"});
        list.setAdapter(adapter);

    }

    private static class CustomAdapter extends ArrayAdapter<String> {

        public CustomAdapter(Context context, int layout, int resId,
                String[] items) {
            //Call through to ArrayAdapter implementation
            super(context, layout, resId, items);
        }

        @Override
        public View getView(int position, View convertView, ViewGroup parent) {
            View row = convertView;
            //Inflate a new row if one isn't recycled
            if(row == null) {
                row = LayoutInflater.from(getContext())
                        .inflate(R.layout.custom_row, parent, false);
            }
            String item = getItem(position);
            ImageView left = (ImageView)row.findViewById(R.id.leftimage);
            ImageView right = (ImageView)row.findViewById(R.id.rightimage);
            TextView text = (TextView)row.findViewById(R.id.line1);

            left.setImageResource(R.drawable.icon);
            right.setImageResource(R.drawable.icon);
            text.setText(item);

            return row;
        }
    }
}
```

Notice that we use the same constructor to create an instance of the adapter as before, because it is inherited from `ArrayAdapter`. We have overridden the view display mechanism of the adapter, and the only reason the `R.layout.custom_row` and `R.id.line1` are now passed into the constructor is that they are required parameters of the constructor; they don't serve a useful purpose in this example anymore.

Now, when the ListView wants to display a row it will call `getView()` on its adapter, which we have customized so we can control how each row returns. The `getView()` method is passed a parameter called the convertView, which is very important for performance. Layout inflation from XML is an expensive process: to minimize its impact on the system, `ListView` recycles views as the list scrolls. If a recycled view is available to be reused, it is passed into `getView()` as the convertView. Whenever possible, reuse these views instead of inflating new ones to keep the scrolling performance of the list fast and responsive.

In this example, we use `getItem()` to get the current value at that position in the list (our array of strings), and then later on we set that value on the `TextView` for that row. We can also set the images in each row to something significant for the data, although here they are set to the app icon for simplicity.

2-26. Making ListView Section Headers

Problem

You want to create a list with multiple sections, each with a header at the top.

Solution

(API Level 1)

Use the SimplerExpandableListAdapter code defined here and an `ExpandableListView`. Android doesn't officially have an extensible way to create sections in a list, but it does offer the `ExpandableListView` widget and associated adapters designed to handle a two-dimensional data structure in a sectioned list. The drawback is that the adapters provided with the SDK to handle this data are cumbersome to work with for simple data structures.

How It Works

Enter the SimplerExpandableListAdapter (see Listing 2-81), an extension of the BaseExpandableListAdapter that, as an example, handles an `array` of string arrays, with a separate string array for the section titles.

Listing 2-81. *SimplerExpandableListAdapter*

```
public class SimplerExpandableListAdapter extends BaseExpandableListAdapter {
    private Context mContext;
    private String[][] mContents;
    private String[] mTitles;

    public SimplerExpandableListAdapter(Context context, String[] titles,
            String[][] contents) {
        super();
        //Check arguments
        if(titles.length != contents.length) {
            throw new IllegalArgumentException(
                    "Titles and Contents must be the same size.");
        }

        mContext = context;
        mContents = contents;
        mTitles = titles;
    }

    //Return a child item
    @Override
    public String getChild(int groupPosition, int childPosition) {
        return mContents[groupPosition][childPosition];
    }

    //Return an item's id
    @Override
    public long getChildId(int groupPosition, int childPosition) {
        return 0;
    }

    //Return view for each item row
    @Override
    public View getChildView(int groupPosition, int childPosition,
            boolean isLastChild, View convertView, ViewGroup parent) {
        TextView row = (TextView)convertView;
        if(row == null) {
            row = new TextView(mContext);
        }
        row.setText(mContents[groupPosition][childPosition]);
        return row;
```

```
    }

    //Return number of items in each section
    @Override
    public int getChildrenCount(int groupPosition) {
        return mContents[groupPosition].length;
    }

    //Return sections
    @Override
    public String[] getGroup(int groupPosition) {
        return mContents[groupPosition];
    }

    //Return the number of sections
    @Override
    public int getGroupCount() {
        return mContents.length;
    }

    //Return a section's id
    @Override
    public long getGroupId(int groupPosition) {
        return 0;
    }

    //Return a view for each section header
    @Override
    public View getGroupView(int groupPosition, boolean isExpanded,
            View convertView, ViewGroup parent) {
        TextView row = (TextView)convertView;
        if(row == null) {
            row = new TextView(mContext);
        }
        row.setTypeface(Typeface.DEFAULT_BOLD);
        row.setText(mTitles[groupPosition]);
        return row;
    }

    @Override
    public boolean hasStableIds() {
        return false;
    }


    @Override
    public boolean isChildSelectable(int groupPosition, int childPosition) {
        return true;
    }
```

```
}
```

Now we can create a simple data structure and use it to populate an ExpandableListView in an example Activity (see Listing 2-82).

Listing 2-82. *Activity Using the SimplerExpandableListAdapter*

```
public void onCreate(Bundle savedInstanceState) {
    super.onCreate(savedInstanceState);
    //Set up an expandable list
    ExpandableListView list = new ExpandableListView(this);
    list.setGroupIndicator(null);
    list.setChildIndicator(null);

    //Set up simple data and the new adapter
    String[] titles = {"Fruits","Vegetables","Meats"};
    String[] fruits = {"Apples","Oranges"};
    String[] veggies = {"Carrots","Peas","Broccoli"};
    String[] meats = {"Pork","Chicken"};
    String[][] contents = {fruits,veggies,meats};
    SimplerExpandableListAdapter adapter = new SimplerExpandableListAdapter(this,
        titles, contents);

    list.setAdapter(adapter);
    setContentView(list);
}
```

That Darn Expansion

There is one catch to utilizing ExpandableListView in this fashion: it expands. ExpandableListView is designed to expand and collapse the child data underneath the group heading when the heading it tapped. Also, by default all the groups are collapsed, so you can see only the header items.

In some cases this may be desirable behavior, but often it is not if you just want to add section headers. In that case, there are two additional steps to take:

1. In the Activity code, expand all the groups:

```
for(int i=0; i < adapter.getGroupCount(); i++) {
    list.expandGroup(i);
}
```

2. In the Adapter, override onGroupCollapsed() to force a re-expansion. This will require adding a reference to the list widget to the adapter.

```
@Override
public void onGroupCollapsed(int groupPosition) {
    list.expandGroup(groupPosition);
}
```

2-27. Creating Compound Controls

Problem

You need to create a custom widget that is a collection of existing elements.

Solution

(API Level 1)

Create a custom widget by extending a common ViewGroup and adding functionality. One of the simplest and most powerful ways to create custom or reusable UI elements is to create compound controls leveraging the existing widgets provided by the Android SDK.

How It Works

`ViewGroup`, and its subclasses `LinearLayout`, `RelativeLayout`, and so on, gives you the tools to make this simple by assisting you with component placement, so you can be more concerned with the added functionality.

TextImageButton

Let's create an example by making a widget that the Android SDK does not have natively: a button containing either an image or text as its content. To do this, we are going to create the TextImageButton class, which is an extension of `FrameLayout`. It will contain a `TextView` to handle text content as well as an `ImageView` for image content (see Listing 2-83).

Listing 2-83. *Custom TextImageButton Widget*

```
public class TextImageButton extends FrameLayout {

    private ImageView imageView;
    private TextView textView;
```

```
/* Constructors */
public TextImageButton(Context context) {
    this(context, null);
}

public TextImageButton(Context context, AttributeSet attrs) {
    this(context, attrs, 0);
}

public TextImageButton(Context context, AttributeSet attrs, int defaultStyle) {
    //Initialize the parent layout with the system's button style
    // This sets the clickable attributes and button background to match
    // the current theme.
    super(context, attrs, android.R.attr.buttonStyle);
    //Create the child views
    imageView = new ImageView(context, attrs, defaultStyle);
    textView = new TextView(context, attrs, defaultStyle);
    //Create LayoutParams for children to wrap content and center in the parent
    FrameLayout.LayoutParams params = new FrameLayout.LayoutParams(
            LayoutParams.WRAP_CONTENT,
            LayoutParams.WRAP_CONTENT,
            Gravity.CENTER);
    //Add the views
    this.addView(imageView, params);
    this.addView(textView, params);

    //If an image is present, switch to image mode
    if(imageView.getDrawable() != null) {
        textView.setVisibility(View.GONE);
        imageView.setVisibility(View.VISIBLE);
    } else {
        textView.setVisibility(View.VISIBLE);
        imageView.setVisibility(View.GONE);
    }
}

/* Accessors */
public void setText(CharSequence text) {
    //Switch to text
    textView.setVisibility(View.VISIBLE);
    imageView.setVisibility(View.GONE);
    //Apply text
    textView.setText(text);
}


public void setImageResource(int resId) {
    //Switch to image
    textView.setVisibility(View.GONE);
    imageView.setVisibility(View.VISIBLE);
```

```
            //Apply image
            imageView.setImageResource(resId);
        }

        public void setImageDrawable(Drawable drawable) {
            //Switch to image
            textView.setVisibility(View.GONE);
            imageView.setVisibility(View.VISIBLE);
            //Apply image
            imageView.setImageDrawable(drawable);
        }
    }
```

All of the widgets in the SDK have at least two, and often three, constructors. The first constructor takes only Context as a parameter and is generally used to create a new view in code. The remaining two are used when a view is inflated from XML, where the attributes defined in the XML file are passed in as the AttributeSet parameter. Here we use Java's `this()` notation to drill the first two constructors down to the one that really does all the work. Building the custom control in this fashion ensures that we can still define this view in XML layouts. Without implementing the attributed constructors, this would not be possible.

In order to make the `FrameLayout` look like a standard button, we pass the attribute `android.R.attr.buttonStyle` to the constructor. This defines the style value that should be pulled from the current theme and applied to the view. This sets up the background to match other `button` instances, but it also makes the view clickable and focusable, as those flags are also part of the system's style. Whenever possible you should load your custom widget's look and feel from the current theme to allow easy customization and consistency with the rest of your application.

The constructor also creates a `TextView` and `ImageView`, and it places them inside the layout. Each child constructor is passed the same set of attributes so that any XML attributes that were set specific to one or the other (such as text or image state) are properly read. The remaining code sets the default display mode (either text or image) based on the data that was passed in as attributes.

The accessor functions are added as a convenience to later switch the button contents. These functions are also tasked with switching between text and image mode if the content change warrants it.

Because this custom control is not in the `android.view` or `android.widget` packages, we must use the fully qualified name when it is used in an XML layout. Listings 2-84 and 2-85 show an example Activity displaying the custom widget.

Listing 2-84. *res/layout/main.xml*

```
<?xml version="1.0" encoding="utf-8"?>
<LinearLayout xmlns:android="http://schemas.android.com/apk/res/android"
    android:layout_width="fill_parent"
    android:layout_height="fill_parent"
    android:orientation="vertical" >
    <com.examples.customwidgets.TextImageButton
        android:layout_width="match_parent"
        android:layout_height="wrap_content"
        android:text="Click Me!"
        android:textColor="#000" />
    <com.examples.customwidgets.TextImageButton
        android:layout_width="match_parent"
        android:layout_height="wrap_content"
        android:src="@drawable/ic_launcher" />
</LinearLayout>
```

Listing 2-85. *Activity Using the New Custom Widget*

```
public class MyActivity extends Activity {

    @Override
    public void onCreate(Bundle savedInstanceState) {
        super.onCreate(savedInstanceState);
        setContentView(R.layout.main);
    }
}
```

Notice that we can still use traditional attributes to define properties like the text or image to display. This is due to the fact that we construct each item (the FrameLayout, TextView, and ImageView) with the attributed constructors, so each view sets the parameters it is interested in and ignores the rest.

If we define an Acitivity to use this layout, the result looks like Figure 2-23.

Figure 2-23. *TextImageButton displayed in both text and image modes*

2–28. Handling Complex Touch Events

Problem

Your application needs to implement customized single or multitouch interactions with the UI.

Solution

(API Level 3)

Make use of the `GestureDetector` and `ScaleGestureDetector` in the framework, or just manually handle all touch events passed to your views by overriding `onTouchEvent()` and `onInterceptTouchEvent()`. Working with the former is a very simple way to add complex gesture control to your application. The latter option is extremely powerful, but it has some pitfalls to be aware of.

Android handles touch events on the UI by using a top-down dispatch system, which is a common pattern in the framework for sending messages through a hierarchy. Touch events originate at the top-level window and are delivered to the Activity first. From there, they are dispatched to the root view of the loaded hierarchy and subsequently passed down from parent to child view until something consumes the event or the entire chain has been traversed.

It is the job of each parent view to validate which children a touch event should be sent to (usually by checking the view's bounds) and to dispatch the event in the correct order. If multiple children are valid candidates (such as when they overlap), the parent will deliver the event to each child in the reverse order that they were added, so as to guarantee that the child view with the highest z-order (visibly layered on top) gets a chance first. If no children consume the event, the parent itself will get a chance to consume it before the event is passed back up the hierarchy.

Any `view` can declare interest in a particular touch event by returning `true` from its `onTouchEvent()` method, which consumes the event and stops it from being delivered elsewhere. Any `ViewGroup` has the additional ability to intercept or steal touch events being delivered to its children via the `onInterceptTouchEvent()` callback. This is helpful in cases where the parent view needs to take over control for a particular use case, such as a `ScrollView` takes control of touches once it detects that the user is dragging their finger.

There are several different action identifiers that touch events will have during the course of a gesture.

- `ACTION_DOWN`: Initial event when the first finger hits the screen. This event is always the beginning of a new gesture.
- `ACTION_MOVE`: Event where one of the fingers on the screen has changed location.
- `ACTION_UP`: Final event when the last finger leaves the screen. This event is always the end of a gesture.
- `ACTION_CANCEL`: Received by child views when their parent has intercepted the gesture they were currently receiving. Like `ACTION_UP`, this should signal the view that the gesture is over from their perspective.
- `ACTION_POINTER_DOWN`: Event when an additional finger hits the screen. Useful for switching into a multitouch gesture.

- ACTION_POINTER_UP: Event when an additional finger leaves the screen. Useful for switching out of a multitouch gesture.

For efficiency, Android will not deliver subsequent events to any view that did not consume ACTION_DOWN. Therefore, if you are doing custom touch handling and want to do something interesting with later events, you must return true for ACTION_DOWN.

If you are implementing a custom touch handler inside a parent ViewGroup, you will probably also need to have some code in onInterceptTouchEvent(). This method works in a similar fashion to onTouchEvent() in that, if you return true your custom view will take over receiving all touch events for the remainder of that gesture (i.e., until ACTION_UP). This operation cannot be undone, so do not intercept these events until you are sure you want to take them all!

Finally, Android provides a number of useful threshold constants that are scaled for device screen density and should be used to build custom touch interaction. These constants are all housed in the ViewConfiguration class. In this example we will make use of the minimum and maximum fling velocity values and the touch slop constant, which denotes how far ACTION_MOVE events should be allowed to vary before considering them as an actual move of the user's finger.

How It Works

Listing 2-86 illustrates a custom ViewGroup that implements pan-style scrolling, meaning it allows the user to scroll in both horizontal and vertical directions, assuming the content is large enough to do so. This implementation uses GestureDetector to handle the touch events.

Listing 2-86. *Custom ViewGroup with GestureDetector*

```
public class PanGestureScrollView extends FrameLayout {

    private GestureDetector mDetector;
    private Scroller mScroller;

    /* Positions of the last motion event */
    private float mInitialX, mInitialY;
    /* Drag threshold */
    private int mTouchSlop;

    public PanGestureScrollView(Context context) {
        super(context);
        init(context);
    }
```

```
public PanGestureScrollView(Context context, AttributeSet attrs) {
    super(context, attrs);
    init(context);
}

public PanGestureScrollView(Context context, AttributeSet attrs,
        int defStyle) {
    super(context, attrs, defStyle);
    init(context);
}

private void init(Context context) {
    mDetector = new GestureDetector(context, mListener);
    mScroller = new Scroller(context);
    // Get system constants for touch thresholds
    mTouchSlop = ViewConfiguration.get(context).getScaledTouchSlop();
}

/*
 * Override the measureChild... implementations to guarantee that the child
 * view gets measured to be as large as it wants to be. The default
 * implementation will force some children to be only as large as this view.
 */
@Override
protected void measureChild(View child, int parentWidthMeasureSpec,
        int parentHeightMeasureSpec) {
    int childWidthMeasureSpec;
    int childHeightMeasureSpec;

    childWidthMeasureSpec = MeasureSpec.makeMeasureSpec(0,
            MeasureSpec.UNSPECIFIED);
    childHeightMeasureSpec = MeasureSpec.makeMeasureSpec(0,
            MeasureSpec.UNSPECIFIED);

    child.measure(childWidthMeasureSpec, childHeightMeasureSpec);
}

@Override
protected void measureChildWithMargins(View child,
        int parentWidthMeasureSpec, int widthUsed,
        int parentHeightMeasureSpec, int heightUsed) {
    final MarginLayoutParams lp = (MarginLayoutParams) child.getLayoutParams();

    final int childWidthMeasureSpec = MeasureSpec.makeMeasureSpec(
            lp.leftMargin + lp.rightMargin, MeasureSpec.UNSPECIFIED);
    final int childHeightMeasureSpec = MeasureSpec.makeMeasureSpec(
            lp.topMargin + lp.bottomMargin, MeasureSpec.UNSPECIFIED);

    child.measure(childWidthMeasureSpec, childHeightMeasureSpec);
}
```

```
// Listener to handle all the touch events
private SimpleOnGestureListener mListener = new SimpleOnGestureListener() {
    public boolean onDown(MotionEvent e) {
        // Cancel any current fling
        if (!mScroller.isFinished()) {
            mScroller.abortAnimation();
        }
        return true;
    }

    public boolean onFling(MotionEvent e1, MotionEvent e2, float velocityX,
            float velocityY) {
        // Call a helper method to start the scroller animation
        fling((int) -velocityX / 3, (int) -velocityY / 3);
        return true;
    }

    public boolean onScroll(MotionEvent e1, MotionEvent e2,
            float distanceX, float distanceY) {
        // Any view can be scrolled by simply calling its scrollBy() method
        scrollBy((int) distanceX, (int) distanceY);
        return true;
    }
};

@Override
public void computeScroll() {
    if (mScroller.computeScrollOffset()) {
        // This is called at drawing time by ViewGroup. We use
        // this method to keep the fling animation going through
        // to completion.
        int oldX = getScrollX();
        int oldY = getScrollY();
        int x = mScroller.getCurrX();
        int y = mScroller.getCurrY();

        if (getChildCount() > 0) {
            View child = getChildAt(0);
            x = clamp(x, getWidth() - getPaddingRight() - getPaddingLeft(),
                    child.getWidth());
            y = clamp(y,
                    getHeight() - getPaddingBottom() - getPaddingTop(),
                    child.getHeight());
            if (x != oldX || y != oldY) {
                scrollTo(x, y);
            }
        }
```

```
            // Keep on drawing until the animation has finished.
            postInvalidate();
        }
    }

    // Override scrollTo to do bounds checks on any scrolling request
    @Override
    public void scrollTo(int x, int y) {
        // we rely on the fact the View.scrollBy calls scrollTo.
        if (getChildCount() > 0) {
            View child = getChildAt(0);
            x = clamp(x, getWidth() - getPaddingRight() - getPaddingLeft(),
                    child.getWidth());
            y = clamp(y, getHeight() - getPaddingBottom() - getPaddingTop(),
                    child.getHeight());
            if (x != getScrollX() || y != getScrollY()) {
                super.scrollTo(x, y);
            }
        }
    }

    /*
     * Monitor touch events passed down to the children and intercept as soon as
     * it is determined we are dragging
     */
    @Override
    public boolean onInterceptTouchEvent(MotionEvent event) {
        switch (event.getAction()) {
        case MotionEvent.ACTION_DOWN:
            mInitialX = event.getX();
            mInitialY = event.getY();
            // Feed the down event to the detector so it has
            // context when/if dragging begins
            mDetector.onTouchEvent(event);
            break;
        case MotionEvent.ACTION_MOVE:
            final float x = event.getX();
            final float y = event.getY();
            final int yDiff = (int) Math.abs(y - mInitialY);
            final int xDiff = (int) Math.abs(x - mInitialX);
            // Verify that either difference is enough to be a drag
            if (yDiff > mTouchSlop || xDiff > mTouchSlop) {
                // Start capturing events
                return true;
            }
            break;
        }
```

```
        return super.onInterceptTouchEvent(event);
    }

    /*
     * Feed all touch events we receive to the detector for processing.
     */
    @Override
    public boolean onTouchEvent(MotionEvent event) {
        return mDetector.onTouchEvent(event);
    }

    /*
     * Utility method to initialize the Scroller and start redrawing
     */
    public void fling(int velocityX, int velocityY) {
        if (getChildCount() > 0) {
            int height = getHeight() - getPaddingBottom() - getPaddingTop();
            int width = getWidth() - getPaddingLeft() - getPaddingRight();
            int bottom = getChildAt(0).getHeight();
            int right = getChildAt(0).getWidth();

            mScroller.fling(getScrollX(), getScrollY(), velocityX, velocityY,
                    0, Math.max(0, right - width), 0,
                    Math.max(0, bottom - height));

            invalidate();
        }
    }

    /*
     * Utility method to assist in doing bounds checking
     */
    private int clamp(int n, int my, int child) {
        if (my >= child || n < 0) {
            // The child is beyond one of the parent bounds
            // or is smaller than the parent and can't scroll
            return 0;
        }
        if ((my + n) > child) {
            // Requested scroll is beyond right bound of child
            return child - my;
        }
        return n;
    }
}
```

Similar to `ScrollView` or `HorizontalScrollView`, this example takes a single child and scrolls its contents based on user input. Much of the code in this example is not directly related to touch handling; instead it scrolls and keeps the scroll position from going beyond the bounds of the child.

As a ViewGroup, the first place where we will see any touch event will be onInterceptTouchEvent(). This method is where we must analyze the user touches and see if they are actually dragging. The interaction between ACTION_DOWN and ACTION_MOVE in this method is designed to determine how far the user has moved their finger, and if it's greater than the system's touch slop constant, we call it a drag event and intercept subsequent touches. This implementation allows simple tap events to go on to the children, so buttons and other widgets can safely be children of this view and still get click events. If no interactive widgets were children of this view, the events would pass directly to our onTouchEvent() method, but since we want to allow that possibility we have to do this initial checking here.

The onTouchEvent() method here is straightforward because all events simply get forwarded to our GestureDetector, who does all the tracking and calculations to know when the user is doing specific actions. We then react to those events through the SimpleOnGestureListener, specifically the onScroll() and onFling() events. To ensure that the GestureDetector has the initial point of the gesture correctly set, we also forward the ACTION_DOWN event from onInterceptTouchEvent() to it.

The onScroll() method is called repeatedly as the user moves their finger with the distance traveled. Conveniently, we can pass these values directly to the view's scrollBy() method to move the content while the finger is dragging.

The onFling() method requires slightly more work. For those unaware, a fling is an operation where the user rapidly moves their finger on the screen and lifts it. The resulting expected behavior of this is an animated inertial scroll. Again, the work of calculating the velocity of the user's finger when it is lifted is done for us, but we must still do the scrolling animation. This is where the Scroller component comes in. Scroller is a component of the framework designed to take the user input values and provide the time-interpolated animation slices necessary to animate the view's scrolling. The animation is started by calling fling() on the Scroller and invalidating the view.

> **NOTE:** If you are targeting API Level 9 and higher, you can drop OverScroller in place of Scroller and it will provide more consistent performance on newer devices. It will also allow you to include the overscroll glow animations. You can spice up the fling animation by passing a custom Interpolator to either one.

This starts a looping process in which the framework will call computeScroll() regularly as it draws the view, and we use this opportunity to check the current state of the Scroller and to nudge the view forward if the animation is not complete. This is something many developers can find confusing about Scroller. It is a component designed to animate the view, but it doesn't actually do any animation. It simply provides the timing and calculations for how far the view should move on each draw frame. The application must both call computeScrollOffset() to get the new locations and then actually call a method to incrementally change the view, which in our example is scrollTo().

The final callback we make use of in the GestureDetector is onDown(), which gets called with any ACTION_DOWN the detector receives. We use this callback to abort any currently running fling animation if the user presses their finger back onto the screen. Listing 2-87 shows how we can use this custom view inside of an Activity.

Listing 2-87. *Activity Using PanGestureScrollView*

```
public class PanScrollActivity extends Activity {

    @Override
    protected void onCreate(Bundle savedInstanceState) {
        super.onCreate(savedInstanceState);

        PanGestureScrollView scrollView = new PanGestureScrollView(this);

        LinearLayout layout = new LinearLayout(this);
        layout.setOrientation(LinearLayout.VERTICAL);
        for(int i=0; i < 5; i++) {
            ImageView iv = new ImageButton(this);
            iv.setImageResource(R.drawable.ic_launcher);
            //Make each view large enough to require scrolling
            layout.addView(iv, new LinearLayout.LayoutParams(1000, 500));
        }

        scrollView.addView(layout);
        setContentView(scrollView);
    }
}
```

We use a handful of ImageButton instances to fill up the custom scroller view on purpose to illustrate that you can click on any one of these buttons and the event will still go through, but as soon as you drag or fling your finger, the scrolling will take over. To illustrate just how much work GestureDetector does for us, take a look at Listing 2-88, which implements the same functionality but by manually handling all touches in onTouchEvent().

Listing 2-88. *PanScrollView Using Custom Touch Handling*

```
public class PanScrollView extends FrameLayout {

    // Fling components
    private Scroller mScroller;
    private VelocityTracker mVelocityTracker;

    /* Positions of the last motion event */
    private float mLastTouchX, mLastTouchY;
    /* Drag threshold */
    private int mTouchSlop;
    /* Fling Velocity */
    private int mMaximumVelocity, mMinimumVelocity;
    /* Drag Lock */
    private boolean mDragging = false;

    public PanScrollView(Context context) {
        super(context);
        init(context);
    }

    public PanScrollView(Context context, AttributeSet attrs) {
        super(context, attrs);
        init(context);
    }

    public PanScrollView(Context context, AttributeSet attrs, int defStyle) {
        super(context, attrs, defStyle);
        init(context);
    }

    private void init(Context context) {
        mScroller = new Scroller(context);
        mVelocityTracker = VelocityTracker.obtain();
        // Get system constants for touch thresholds
        mTouchSlop = ViewConfiguration.get(context).getScaledTouchSlop();
        mMaximumVelocity = ViewConfiguration.get(context)
                .getScaledMaximumFlingVelocity();
        mMinimumVelocity = ViewConfiguration.get(context)
                .getScaledMinimumFlingVelocity();
    }

    /*
     * Override the measureChild... implementations to guarantee that the child
     * view gets measured to be as large as it wants to be. The default
     * implementation will force some children to be only as large as this view.
     */
    @Override
    protected void measureChild(View child, int parentWidthMeasureSpec,
```

```
            int parentHeightMeasureSpec) {
        int childWidthMeasureSpec;
        int childHeightMeasureSpec;

        childWidthMeasureSpec = MeasureSpec.makeMeasureSpec(0,
                MeasureSpec.UNSPECIFIED);
        childHeightMeasureSpec = MeasureSpec.makeMeasureSpec(0,
                MeasureSpec.UNSPECIFIED);

        child.measure(childWidthMeasureSpec, childHeightMeasureSpec);
    }

    @Override
    protected void measureChildWithMargins(View child,
            int parentWidthMeasureSpec, int widthUsed,
            int parentHeightMeasureSpec, int heightUsed) {
        final MarginLayoutParams lp = (MarginLayoutParams) child
                .getLayoutParams();

        final int childWidthMeasureSpec = MeasureSpec.makeMeasureSpec(
                lp.leftMargin + lp.rightMargin, MeasureSpec.UNSPECIFIED);
        final int childHeightMeasureSpec = MeasureSpec.makeMeasureSpec(
                lp.topMargin + lp.bottomMargin, MeasureSpec.UNSPECIFIED);

        child.measure(childWidthMeasureSpec, childHeightMeasureSpec);
    }

    @Override
    public void computeScroll() {
        if (mScroller.computeScrollOffset()) {
            // This is called at drawing time by ViewGroup. We use
            // this method to keep the fling animation going through
            // to completion.
            int oldX = getScrollX();
            int oldY = getScrollY();
            int x = mScroller.getCurrX();
            int y = mScroller.getCurrY();

            if (getChildCount() > 0) {
                View child = getChildAt(0);
                x = clamp(x, getWidth() - getPaddingRight() - getPaddingLeft(),
                        child.getWidth());
                y = clamp(y,
                        getHeight() - getPaddingBottom() - getPaddingTop(),
                        child.getHeight());
                if (x != oldX || y != oldY) {
                    scrollTo(x, y);
                }
            }
```

```
            // Keep on drawing until the animation has finished.
            postInvalidate();
        }
    }

    // Override scrollTo to do bounds checks on any scrolling request
    @Override
    public void scrollTo(int x, int y) {
        // we rely on the fact the View.scrollBy calls scrollTo.
        if (getChildCount() > 0) {
            View child = getChildAt(0);
            x = clamp(x, getWidth() - getPaddingRight() - getPaddingLeft(),
                    child.getWidth());
            y = clamp(y, getHeight() - getPaddingBottom() - getPaddingTop(),
                    child.getHeight());
            if (x != getScrollX() || y != getScrollY()) {
                super.scrollTo(x, y);
            }
        }
    }

    /*
     * Monitor touch events passed down to the children and intercept as soon as
     * it is determined we are dragging. This allows child views to still
     * receive touch events if they are interactive (i.e., Buttons)
     */
    @Override
    public boolean onInterceptTouchEvent(MotionEvent event) {
        switch (event.getAction()) {
        case MotionEvent.ACTION_DOWN:
            // Stop any flinging in progress
            if (!mScroller.isFinished()) {
                mScroller.abortAnimation();
            }
            // Reset the velocity tracker
            mVelocityTracker.clear();
            mVelocityTracker.addMovement(event);
            // Save the initial touch point
            mLastTouchX = event.getX();
            mLastTouchY = event.getY();
            break;
        case MotionEvent.ACTION_MOVE:
            final float x = event.getX();
            final float y = event.getY();
            final int yDiff = (int) Math.abs(y - mLastTouchY);
            final int xDiff = (int) Math.abs(x - mLastTouchX);
            // Verify that either difference is enough to be a drag
            if (yDiff > mTouchSlop || xDiff > mTouchSlop) {
                mDragging = true;
                mVelocityTracker.addMovement(event);
```

```
                // Start capturing events ourselves
                return true;
            }
            break;
        case MotionEvent.ACTION_CANCEL:
        case MotionEvent.ACTION_UP:
            mDragging = false;
            mVelocityTracker.clear();
            break;
        }

        return super.onInterceptTouchEvent(event);
    }


    /*
     * Feed all touch events we receive to the detector for processing.
     */
    @Override
    public boolean onTouchEvent(MotionEvent event) {
        mVelocityTracker.addMovement(event);

        switch (event.getAction()) {
        case MotionEvent.ACTION_DOWN:
            // We've already stored the initial point,
            // but if we got here a child view didn't capture
            // the event, so we need to.
            return true;
        case MotionEvent.ACTION_MOVE:
            final float x = event.getX();
            final float y = event.getY();
            float deltaY = mLastTouchY - y;
            float deltaX = mLastTouchX - x;
            // Check for slop on direct events
            if ((Math.abs(deltaY) > mTouchSlop || Math.abs(deltaX) > mTouchSlop)
                    && !mDragging) {
                mDragging = true;
            }
            if (mDragging) {
                // Scroll the view
                scrollBy((int) deltaX, (int) deltaY);
                // Update the last touch event
                mLastTouchX = x;
                mLastTouchY = y;
            }
            break;
        case MotionEvent.ACTION_CANCEL:
            mDragging = false;
            // Stop any flinging in progress
            if (!mScroller.isFinished()) {
```

```
                mScroller.abortAnimation();
            }
            break;
        case MotionEvent.ACTION_UP:
            mDragging = false;
            // Compute the current velocity and start a fling if it is above
            // the minimum threshold.
            mVelocityTracker.computeCurrentVelocity(1000, mMaximumVelocity);
            int velocityX = (int) mVelocityTracker.getXVelocity();
            int velocityY = (int) mVelocityTracker.getYVelocity();
            if (Math.abs(velocityX) > mMinimumVelocity
                    || Math.abs(velocityY) > mMinimumVelocity) {
                fling(-velocityX, -velocityY);
            }
            break;
        }
        return super.onTouchEvent(event);
    }

    /*
     * Utility method to initialize the Scroller and start redrawing
     */
    public void fling(int velocityX, int velocityY) {
        if (getChildCount() > 0) {
            int height = getHeight() - getPaddingBottom() - getPaddingTop();
            int width = getWidth() - getPaddingLeft() - getPaddingRight();
            int bottom = getChildAt(0).getHeight();
            int right = getChildAt(0).getWidth();

            mScroller.fling(getScrollX(), getScrollY(), velocityX, velocityY,
                    0, Math.max(0, right - width), 0,
                    Math.max(0, bottom - height));

            invalidate();
        }
    }

    /*
     * Utility method to assist in doing bounds checking
     */
    private int clamp(int n, int my, int child) {
        if (my >= child || n < 0) {
            // The child is beyond one of the parent bounds
            // or is smaller than the parent and can't scroll
            return 0;
        }
        if ((my + n) > child) {
            // Requested scroll is beyond right bound of child
            return child - my;
        }
```

```
        return n;
    }
}
```

In this example, both onInterceptTouchEvent() and onTouchEvent() have a bit more going on. If a child view is currently handling initial touches, ACTION_DOWN and the first few move events will be delivered through onInterceptTouchEvent() before we take control; however, if no interactive child exists, all those initial events will go directly to onTouchEvent(). Therefore, we must do the slop checking for the initial drag in both places and set a flag to indicate when a scroll event has truly started. Once we have flagged the user dragging, the code to scroll the view is the same as before, with a call to scrollBy().

> **TIP:** As soon as a ViewGroup returns "true" from onTouchEvent(), no more events will be delivered to onInterceptTouchEvent(), even if an intercept was not explicitly requested.

To implement the fling behavior, we must manually track the user's scroll velocity using a VelocityTracker object. This object collects touch events as they occur with the addMovement() method, and it then calculates the average velocity on demand with computeCurrentVelocity(). Our custom view calculates this value each time the user's finger is lifted and determines, based on the ViewConfiguration minimum velocity, whether or not to start a fling animation.

> **TIP:** In cases where you don't need to explicitly return true to consume an event, return the super implementation rather than false. Often there is a lot of hidden processing for View and ViewGroup that you don't want to override.

Listing 2-89 shows our example Activity again, this time with the new custom view in place.

Listing 2-89. *Activity Using PanScrollView*

```
public class PanScrollActivity extends Activity {

    @Override
    protected void onCreate(Bundle savedInstanceState) {
        super.onCreate(savedInstanceState);

        PanScrollView scrollView = new PanScrollView(this);
```

```
        LinearLayout layout = new LinearLayout(this);
        layout.setOrientation(LinearLayout.VERTICAL);
        for(int i=0; i < 5; i++) {
            ImageView iv = new ImageView(this);
            iv.setImageResource(R.drawable.ic_launcher);
            layout.addView(iv, new LinearLayout.LayoutParams(1000, 500));
        }

        scrollView.addView(layout);
        setContentView(scrollView);
    }
}
```

We have also changed the content to be `ImageView` instead of `ImageButton` to illustrate the contrast when the child views are not interactive.

Multitouch Handling

(API Level 8)

Now let's take a look at an example of handling multitouch events. Listing 2-90 contains a customized `ImageView` with some multitouch interactions added in.

Listing 2-90. *ImageView With Multitouch Handling*

```
public class RotateZoomImageView extends ImageView {

    private ScaleGestureDetector mScaleDetector;
    private Matrix mImageMatrix;
    /* Last Rotation Angle */
    private int mLastAngle = 0;
    /* Pivot Point for Transforms */
    private int mPivotX, mPivotY;

    public RotateZoomImageView(Context context) {
        super(context);
        init(context);
    }

    public RotateZoomImageView(Context context, AttributeSet attrs) {
        super(context, attrs);
        init(context);
    }

    public RotateZoomImageView(Context context, AttributeSet attrs, int defStyle) {
        super(context, attrs, defStyle);
        init(context);
    }
```

```
private void init(Context context) {
    mScaleDetector = new ScaleGestureDetector(context, mScaleListener);

    setScaleType(ScaleType.MATRIX);
    mImageMatrix = new Matrix();
}

/*
 * Use onSizeChanged() to calculate values based on the view's size.
 * The view has no size during init(), so we must wait for this
 * callback.
 */
@Override
protected void onSizeChanged(int w, int h, int oldw, int oldh) {
    if (w != oldw || h != oldh) {
        //Shift the image to the center of the view
        int translateX = Math.abs(w - getDrawable().getIntrinsicWidth()) / 2;
        int translateY = Math.abs(h - getDrawable().getIntrinsicHeight()) / 2;
        mImageMatrix.setTranslate(translateX, translateY);
        setImageMatrix(mImageMatrix);
        //Get the center point for future scale and rotate transforms
        mPivotX = w / 2;
        mPivotY = h / 2;
    }
}

private SimpleOnScaleGestureListener mScaleListener =
        new SimpleOnScaleGestureListener() {
    @Override
    public boolean onScale(ScaleGestureDetector detector) {
        // ScaleGestureDetector calculates a scale factor based on whether
        // the fingers are moving apart or together
        float scaleFactor = detector.getScaleFactor();
        //Pass that factor to a scale for the image
        mImageMatrix.postScale(scaleFactor, scaleFactor, mPivotX, mPivotY);
        setImageMatrix(mImageMatrix);

        return true;
    }
};

/*
 * Operate on two-finger events to rotate the image.
 * This method calculates the change in angle between the
 * pointers and rotates the image accordingly.  As the user
 * rotates their fingers, the image will follow.
 */
private boolean doRotationEvent(MotionEvent event) {
    //Calculate the angle between the two fingers
```

```
    float deltaX = event.getX(0) - event.getX(1);
    float deltaY = event.getY(0) - event.getY(1);
    double radians = Math.atan(deltaY / deltaX);
    //Convert to degrees
    int degrees = (int)(radians * 180 / Math.PI);

    switch (event.getAction()) {
    case MotionEvent.ACTION_DOWN:
        //Mark the initial angle
        mLastAngle = degrees;
        break;
    case MotionEvent.ACTION_MOVE:
        // ATAN returns a converted value between -90deg and +90deg
        // which creates a point when two fingers are vertical where the
        // angle flips sign.  We handle this case by rotating a small amount
        // (5 degrees) in the direction we were traveling

        if ((degrees - mLastAngle) > 45) {
            //Going CCW across the boundary
            mImageMatrix.postRotate(-5, mPivotX, mPivotY);
        } else if ((degrees - mLastAngle) < -45) {
            //Going CW across the boundary
            mImageMatrix.postRotate(5, mPivotX, mPivotY);
        } else {
            //Normal rotation, rotate the difference
            mImageMatrix.postRotate(degrees - mLastAngle, mPivotX, mPivotY);
        }
        //Post the rotation to the image
        setImageMatrix(mImageMatrix);
        //Save the current angle
        mLastAngle = degrees;
        break;
    }

    return true;
}

@Override
public boolean onTouchEvent(MotionEvent event) {
    if (event.getAction() == MotionEvent.ACTION_DOWN) {
        // We don't care about this event directly, but we declare
        // interest so we can get later multitouch events.
        return true;
    }

    switch (event.getPointerCount()) {
    case 3:
        // With three fingers down, zoom the image
        // using the ScaleGestureDetector
        return mScaleDetector.onTouchEvent(event);
```

```
        case 2:
            // With two fingers down, rotate the image
            // following the fingers
            return doRotationEvent(event);
        default:
            //Ignore this event
            return super.onTouchEvent(event);
        }
    }
}
```

This example creates a custom ImageView that listens for multitouch events and transforms the image content in response. The two events this view will detect are a two-finger rotate and a three-finger pinch. The rotate event is handled manually by processing each `MotionEvent`, while a `ScaleGestureDetector` handles the pinch events. The `ScaleType` of the view is set to `MATRIX`, which will allow us to modify the image's appearance by applying different `Matrix` transformations.

Once the view is measured and laid out, the `onSizeChanged()` callback will trigger. This method can get called more than once, so we make changes only if the values from one instance to the next have changed. We take this opportunity to set up some values based around the view's size that we will need to center the image content inside the view and later perform the correct transformations. We also perform the first transformation here, which centers the image inside the view.

We decide which event to process by analyzing the events we receive in `onTouchEvent()`. By checking the `getPointerCount()` method of each `MotionEvent`, we can determine how many fingers are down and deliver the event to the appropriate handler. As we've said before, we must also consume the initial `ACTION_DOWN` event here; otherwise, the subsequent event for the user's other fingers will never get delivered to this view. While we don't have anything interesting to do in this case, it is still necessary to explicitly return `true`.

`ScaleGestureDetector` operates by analyzing each touch event the application feeds to it and calling a series of `OnScaleGestureListener` callback methods when scale events occur. The most important callback is `onScale()`, which gets called regularly as the user's fingers move, but developers can also make use of `onScaleBegin()` and `onScaleEnd()` to do processing before and after the gesture.

`ScaleGestureDetector` provides a number of useful calculated values that the application can use in modifying the UI.

- `getCurrentSpan()`: Get the distance between the two pointers being used in this gesture.

- `getFocusX()`/`getFocusY()`: Get the coordinates of the focal point for the current gesture. This is the average location about which the pointers are expanding and contracting.
- `getScaleFactor()`: Get the ratio of span changes between this event and the previous event. As fingers move apart, this value will be slightly larger than 1, and as they move together it will be slightly less than 1.

This example takes the scale factor from the detector and uses it to scale up or down the image content of the view by using `postScale()` on the image's `Matrix`.

Our two-finger rotate event is handled manually. For each event that is passed in, we calculate the x and y distance between the two fingers with `getX()` and `getY()`. The parameter these methods take is the pointer index, where 0 would be the initial pointer and 1 would be the secondary pointer.

With these distances we can do a little trigonometry to figure out the angle of the invisible line that would be formed between the two fingers. This angle is the control value we will use for our transformation. During `ACTION_DOWN`, we take whatever that angle is to be the initial value and simply store it. On subsequent `ACTION_MOVE` events, we post a rotation to the image based on the difference in angle between each touch event.

There is one edge case this example has to handle, and it has to do with the `Math.atan()` trig function. This method will return an angle in the range of -90 degrees to +90 degrees, and this rollover happens when the two fingers are vertically one above the other. The issue this creates is that the touch angle is no longer a gradual change: it jumps from +90 to -90 immediately as the fingers rotate, making the image jump. To solve this issue, we check for the case where the previous and current angle values cross this boundary, and then apply a small 5-degree rotation in the same direction of travel to keep the animation moving smoothly.

Notice in all cases that we are transforming the image with `postScale()` and `postRotate()`, rather than the `setXXX` versions of these methods like we did with `setTranslation()`. The reason for this is because each transformation is meant to be additive, meaning it should augment the current state rather than replacing it. Calling `setScale()` or `setRotate()` would erase the existing state and leave that as the only transformation in the `Matrix`.

We also do each of these transformations around the pivot point that we calculated in `onSizeChanged()` as the midpoint of the view. We do this because, by default, the transformations would occur with a target point of (0,0), which is the top left corner of the view. Because we have centered the image, we need to make sure all transformations also occur at the same center.

2-29. Forwarding Touch Events

Problem

You have views or other touch targets in your application that are too small for the average finger to reliably activate.

Solution

(API Level 1)

Use TouchDelegate to designate an arbitrary rectangle to forward touch events to your small views. TouchDelegate is designed to attach to a parent ViewGroup for the purpose of forwarding touch events it detects within a specific space to one of its children. TouchDelegate modifies each event to look to the target view as if it had happened within its own bounds.

How It Works

Listings 2-91 and 2-92 illustrate the use of TouchDelegate within a custom parent ViewGroup.

Listing 2-91. *Custom Parent Implementing TouchDelegate*

```
public class TouchDelegateLayout extends FrameLayout {

    public TouchDelegateLayout(Context context) {
        super(context);
        init(context);
    }

    public TouchDelegateLayout(Context context, AttributeSet attrs) {
        super(context, attrs);
        init(context);
    }

    public TouchDelegateLayout(Context context, AttributeSet attrs, int defStyle) {
        super(context, attrs, defStyle);
        init(context);
```

```
    }

    private CheckBox mButton;
    private void init(Context context) {
        //Create a small child view we want to forward touches to.
        mButton = new CheckBox(context);
        mButton.setText("Tap Anywhere");

        LayoutParams lp = new FrameLayout.LayoutParams(LayoutParams.WRAP_CONTENT,
                LayoutParams.WRAP_CONTENT, Gravity.CENTER);
        addView(mButton, lp);
    }


    /*
     * TouchDelegate is applied to this view (parent) to delegate all touches
     * within the specified rectangle to the CheckBox (child).  Here, the rectangle
     * is the entire size of this parent view.
     *
     * This must be done after the view has a size so we know how big to make the
     * Rect, thus we've chosen to add the delegate in onSizeChanged()
     */
    @Override
    protected void onSizeChanged(int w, int h, int oldw, int oldh) {
        if (w != oldw || h != oldh) {
            //Apply the whole area of this view as the delegate area
            Rect bounds = new Rect(0, 0, w, h);
            TouchDelegate delegate = new TouchDelegate(bounds, mButton);
            setTouchDelegate(delegate);
        }
    }
}
```

Listing 2-92. *Example Activity*

```
public class DelegateActivity extends Activity {

    @Override
    protected void onCreate(Bundle savedInstanceState) {
        super.onCreate(savedInstanceState);
        TouchDelegateLayout layout = new TouchDelegateLayout(this);

        setContentView(layout);
    }
}
```

In this example, we create a parent view that contains a centered check box. This view also contains a `TouchDelegate` that will forward touches received anywhere inside the bounds of the parent to the check box. Because we want to pass the full size of the parent layout as the rectangle to forward events, we wait until onSizeChanged() is called on the view to construct and attach the TouchDelegate instance. Doing so in the constructor would not work because at that point the view has not been measured and will not have a size we can read.

The framework automatically dispatches unhandled touch events from the parent through TouchDelegate to its delegate view, so no additional code is needed to forward these events. You can see in Figure 2-24 that this application is receiving touch events far away from the check box, and the check box reacts as if it has been touched directly.

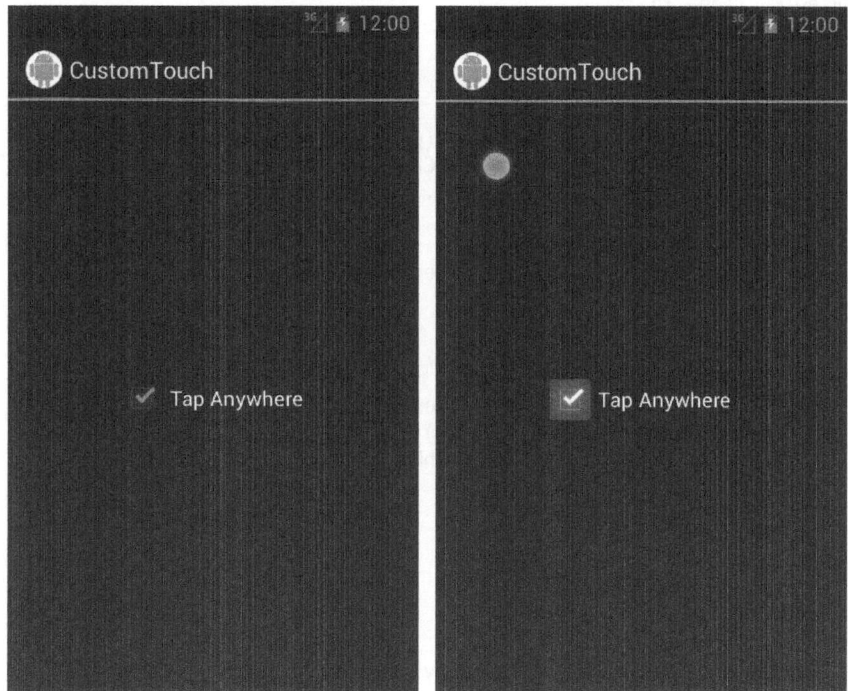

Figure 2-24. *Sample application with check box (left), and check box receiving a forwarded touch event (right)*

Custom Touch Forwarding (Remote Scroller)

TouchDelegate is great for forwarding tap events, but it has one drawback. Each event forwarded to the delegate first has its location reset to the exact midpoint of the delegate view. What this means is that if you attempt to forward a series of ACTION_MOVE events through TouchDelegate, the results won't be what you expect because they will look to the delegate view like the finger isn't really moving at all.

If you have a need to re-route touch events in a more pure form, you can do so by manually calling the dispatchTouchEvent() method of the target view. Have a look at Listings 2-93 and 2-94 to see how this works.

Listing 2-93. *res/layout/main.xml*

```
<LinearLayout xmlns:android="http://schemas.android.com/apk/res/android"
    android:layout_width="match_parent"
    android:layout_height="match_parent"
    android:orientation="vertical" >

    <TextView
        android:id="@+id/text_touch"
        android:layout_width="match_parent"
        android:layout_height="0dp"
        android:layout_weight="1"
        android:gravity="center"
        android:text="Scroll Anywhere Here" />

    <HorizontalScrollView
        android:id="@+id/scroll_view"
        android:layout_width="match_parent"
        android:layout_height="0dp"
        android:layout_weight="1"
        android:background="#CCC">
        <LinearLayout
            android:layout_width="wrap_content"
            android:layout_height="match_parent"
            android:orientation="horizontal" >
            <ImageView
                android:layout_width="250dp"
                android:layout_height="match_parent"
                android:scaleType="fitXY"
                android:src="@drawable/ic_launcher" />
            <ImageView
                android:layout_width="250dp"
                android:layout_height="match_parent"
                android:scaleType="fitXY"
                android:src="@drawable/ic_launcher" />
            <ImageView
                android:layout_width="250dp"
                android:layout_height="match_parent"
                android:scaleType="fitXY"
                android:src="@drawable/ic_launcher" />
            <ImageView
                android:layout_width="250dp"
                android:layout_height="match_parent"
                android:scaleType="fitXY"
                android:src="@drawable/ic_launcher" />
        </LinearLayout>
```

```
    </HorizontalScrollView>
</LinearLayout>
```

Listing 2-94. *Activity Forwarding Touches*

```
public class RemoteScrollActivity extends Activity implements
        View.OnTouchListener {

    private TextView mTouchText;
    private HorizontalScrollView mScrollView;

    @Override
    protected void onCreate(Bundle savedInstanceState) {
        super.onCreate(savedInstanceState);
        setContentView(R.layout.main);

        mTouchText = (TextView) findViewById(R.id.text_touch);
        mScrollView = (HorizontalScrollView) findViewById(R.id.scroll_view);
        //Attach a listener for touch events to the top view
        mTouchText.setOnTouchListener(this);
    }

    @Override
    public boolean onTouch(View v, MotionEvent event) {
        // You can massage the event location if necessary.
        // Here we set the vertical location for each event to
        // the middle of the HorizontalScrollView.

        // View's expect events to be relative to their own coordinates.
        event.setLocation(event.getX(), mScrollView.getHeight() / 2);

        // Forward each event from the TextView to the
        // HorizontalScrollView
        mScrollView.dispatchTouchEvent(event);
        return true;
    }
}
```

This example displays an Activity that is divided in half. The top half is a TextView that prompts you to touch and scroll around, and the bottom half is a HorizontalScrollView with a series of images contained inside. The Activity is set as the OnTouchListener for the TextView so that we can forward all touches it receives to the HorizontalScrollView.

We want the events that the HorizontalScrollView sees to look, from its perspective, like they were originally inside the view bounds. So before we forward the event, we call setLocation() to change the x/y coordinates. In this case, the x coordinate is fine as is, but we adjust the y coordinate to be in the center of the HorizontalScrollView. Now the events look as if the user's finger is moving back and forth along the middle of the view. We then call `dispatchTouchEvent()` with the modified event to have the `HorizontalScrollView` process it.

> **NOTE:** Avoid calling `onTouchEvent()` directly to forward touches. Calling `dispatchTouchEvent()` allows the event processing of the target view to take place the same way it does for normal touch events, including any intercepts that may be necessary.

2-30. Making Drag-and-Drop Views

Problem

Your application's UI needs to allow the user to drag views around on the screen and to possibly drop them on top of other views.

Solution

(API Level 11)

Use the drag-and-drop APIs available in the Android 3.0 framework. The `View` class includes all the enhancements necessary to manage a drag event on the screen, and the `OnDragListener` interface can be attached to any `View` that needs to be notified of drag events as they occur. To begin a drag event, simply call `startDrag()` on the view you would like the user to begin dragging. This method takes a DragShadowBuilder instance, which will be used to construct what the dragging portion of the view should look like, and two additional parameters that will be passed forward to the drop targets and listeners.

The first of these is a `ClipData` object to pass forward a set of text or a `Uri` instance. This can be useful for passing a file location or a query to be made on a `ContentProvider`. The second is an `Object` referred to as the "local state" of the drag event. This can be any `object` and is designed to be a lightweight instance describing something application-specific about the drag. The `ClipData` will only be available to the listener where the dragged view is dropped, but the local state will be accessible to any listener at any time by calling `getLocalState()` on the `DragEvent`.

The OnDragListener.onDrag() method will get called for each specific event that occurs during the drag-and-drop process, passing in a DragEvent to describe the specifics of each event. Each DragEvent will have one of the following actions:

- ACTION_DRAG_STARTED: Sent to all views when a new drag event begins with a call to startDrag().
  - The location can be obtained with getX() and getY().
- ACTION_DRAG_ENTERED: Sent to a view when the drag event enters its bounding box.
- ACTION_DRAG_EXITED: Sent to a view when the drag event leaves its bounding box.
- ACTION_DRAG_LOCATION: Sent to a view between ACTION_DRAG_ENTERED and ACTION_DRAG_EXITED with the current location of the drag inside of that view.
  - The location can be obtained with getX() and getY().
- ACTION_DROP: Sent to a view when the drag terminates and is still currently inside the bounds of that view.
  - The location can be obtained with getX() and getY().
  - ClipData passed with the event can be obtained with getClipData() for this action only.
- ACTION_DRAG_ENDED: Sent to all views when the current drag event is complete.
  - The result of the drag operation can be obtained here with getResult().
  - This return value is based on whether the target view of the drop had an active OnDragListener that returned true for the ACTION_DROP event.

This method works in a similar way to custom touch handling, in that the value you return from the listener will govern how future events are delivered. If a particular OnDragListener does not return true for ACTION_DRAG_STARTED, it will not receive any further events for the remainder of the drag except for ACTION_DRAG_ENDED.

How It Works

Let's look at an example of the drag-and-drop functionality, starting with Listing 2-95. Here we have created a custom `ImageView` that implements the `OnDragListener` interface.

Listing 2-95. *Custom View Implementing OnDragListener*

```
public class DropTargetView extends ImageView implements OnDragListener {

    private boolean mDropped;

    public DropTargetView(Context context) {
        super(context);
        init();
    }

    public DropTargetView(Context context, AttributeSet attrs) {
        super(context, attrs);
        init();
    }

    public DropTargetView(Context context, AttributeSet attrs, int defaultStyle) {
        super(context, attrs, defaultStyle);
        init();
    }

    private void init() {
        //We must set a valid listener to receive DragEvents
        setOnDragListener(this);
    }

    @Override
    public boolean onDrag(android.view.View v, DragEvent event) {
        PropertyValuesHolder pvhX, pvhY;
        switch (event.getAction()) {
        case DragEvent.ACTION_DRAG_STARTED:
            //React to a new drag by shrinking the view
            pvhX = PropertyValuesHolder.ofFloat("scaleX", 0.5f);
            pvhY = PropertyValuesHolder.ofFloat("scaleY", 0.5f);
            ObjectAnimator.ofPropertyValuesHolder(this, pvhX, pvhY).start();
            //Clear the current drop image on a new event
            setImageDrawable(null);
            mDropped = false;
            break;
        case DragEvent.ACTION_DRAG_ENDED:
            // React to a drag ending by resetting the view size
            // if we weren't the drop target.
            if (!mDropped) {
```

```
                pvhX = PropertyValuesHolder.ofFloat("scaleX", 1f);
                pvhY = PropertyValuesHolder.ofFloat("scaleY", 1f);
                ObjectAnimator.ofPropertyValuesHolder(this, pvhX, pvhY).start();
                mDropped = false;
            }
            break;
        case DragEvent.ACTION_DRAG_ENTERED:
            //React to a drag entering this view by growing slightly
            pvhX = PropertyValuesHolder.ofFloat("scaleX", 0.75f);
            pvhY = PropertyValuesHolder.ofFloat("scaleY", 0.75f);
            ObjectAnimator.ofPropertyValuesHolder(this, pvhX, pvhY).start();
            break;
        case DragEvent.ACTION_DRAG_EXITED:
            //React to a drag leaving this view by returning to previous size
            pvhX = PropertyValuesHolder.ofFloat("scaleX", 0.5f);
            pvhY = PropertyValuesHolder.ofFloat("scaleY", 0.5f);
            ObjectAnimator.ofPropertyValuesHolder(this, pvhX, pvhY).start();
            break;
        case DragEvent.ACTION_DROP:
            // React to a drop event with a short animation keyframe animation
            // and setting this view's image to the drawable passed along with
            // the drag event

            // This animation shrinks the view briefly down to nothing
            // and then back.
            Keyframe frame0 = Keyframe.ofFloat(0f, 0.75f);
            Keyframe frame1 = Keyframe.ofFloat(0.5f, 0f);
            Keyframe frame2 = Keyframe.ofFloat(1f, 0.75f);
            pvhX = PropertyValuesHolder.ofKeyframe("scaleX", frame0, frame1,
                    frame2);
            pvhY = PropertyValuesHolder.ofKeyframe("scaleY", frame0, frame1,
                    frame2);
            ObjectAnimator.ofPropertyValuesHolder(this, pvhX, pvhY).start();
            //Set our image from the Object passed with the DragEvent
            setImageDrawable((Drawable) event.getLocalState());
            //We set the dropped flag to the ENDED animation will not also run
            mDropped = true;
            break;
        default:
            //Ignore events we aren't interested in
            return false;
        }
        //Declare interest in all events we have noted
        return true;
    }

}
```

This ImageView is set up to monitor incoming drag events and animate itself accordingly. Whenever a new drag begins, the `ACTION_DRAG_STARTED` event will be sent here, and this view will scale itself down to 50% size. This is a good indication to the user where they can drag this view they've just picked up. We also make sure that this listener is structured to return `true` from this event so that it receives other events during the drag.

If the user drags their view onto this one, `ACTION_DRAG_ENTERED` will trigger the view to scale up slightly, indicating it as the active recipient if the view were to be dropped. `ACTION_DRAG_EXITED` will be received if the view is dragged away, and this view will respond by scaling back down to the same size as when we entered "drag mode". If the user releases the drag over the top of this view, `ACTION_DROP` will be triggered and a special animation is run to indicate the drop was received. We also read the local state variable of the event at this point, assume it is a `Drawable`, and set it as the image content for this view.

`ACTION_DRAG_ENDED` will notify this view to return to its original size because we are no longer in "drag mode". However, if this view was also the target of the drop, we want it to keep its size, so we ignore this event in that case.

Listings 2-96 and 2-97 show an example Activity that allows the user to long-press on an image and then drag that image to our custom drop target.

Listing 2-96. *res/layout/main.xml*

```
<?xml version="1.0" encoding="utf-8"?>
<RelativeLayout xmlns:android="http://schemas.android.com/apk/res/android"
    android:layout_width="match_parent"
    android:layout_height="match_parent" >

    <!-- Top Row of Draggable Items -->
    <LinearLayout
        android:layout_width="match_parent"
        android:layout_height="wrap_content"
        android:orientation="horizontal" >
        <ImageView
            android:id="@+id/image1"
            android:layout_width="0dp"
            android:layout_height="wrap_content"
            android:layout_weight="1"
            android:src="@drawable/ic_send" />
        <ImageView
            android:id="@+id/image2"
            android:layout_width="0dp"
            android:layout_height="wrap_content"
            android:layout_weight="1"
            android:src="@drawable/ic_share" />
        <ImageView
            android:id="@+id/image3"
            android:layout_width="0dp"
```

```
            android:layout_height="wrap_content"
            android:layout_weight="1"
            android:src="@drawable/ic_favorite" />
    </LinearLayout>

    <!-- Bottom Row of Drop Targets -->
    <LinearLayout
        android:layout_width="match_parent"
        android:layout_height="wrap_content"
        android:layout_alignParentBottom="true"
        android:orientation="horizontal" >
        <com.examples.dragtouch.DropTargetView
            android:id="@+id/drag_target1"
            android:layout_width="0dp"
            android:layout_height="100dp"
            android:layout_weight="1"
            android:background="#A00" />
        <com.examples.dragtouch.DropTargetView
            android:id="@+id/drag_target2"
            android:layout_width="0dp"
            android:layout_height="100dp"
            android:layout_weight="1"
            android:background="#0A0" />
        <com.examples.dragtouch.DropTargetView
            android:id="@+id/drag_target3"
            android:layout_width="0dp"
            android:layout_height="100dp"
            android:layout_weight="1"
            android:background="#00A" />
    </LinearLayout>

</RelativeLayout>
```

Listing 2-97. *Activity Forwarding Touches*

```
public class DragTouchActivity extends Activity implements OnLongClickListener {

    @Override
    public void onCreate(Bundle savedInstanceState) {
        super.onCreate(savedInstanceState);
        setContentView(R.layout.main);
        //Attach long-press listener to each ImageView
        findViewById(R.id.image1).setOnLongClickListener(this);
        findViewById(R.id.image2).setOnLongClickListener(this);
        findViewById(R.id.image3).setOnLongClickListener(this);
    }
```

```
    @Override
    public boolean onLongClick(View v) {
        DragShadowBuilder shadowBuilder = new DragShadowBuilder(v);
        // Start a drag, and pass the View's image along as the local state
        v.startDrag(null, shadowBuilder, ((ImageView) v).getDrawable(), 0);

        return true;
    }

}
```

This example displays a row of three images at the top of the screen, along with three of our custom drop target views at the bottom of the screen. Each image is set up with a listener for long-press events, and the long-press triggers a new drag via `startDrag()`. The `DragShadowBuilder` passed to the drag initializer is the default implementation provided by the framework. In the next section we'll look at how this can be customized, but this version just creates a slightly transparent copy of the view being dragged and places it centered underneath the touch point.

We also capture the image content of the view the user selected with `getDrawable()` and pass that along as the local state of the drag, which the custom drop target will use to set as its image. This will create the appearance that the view was dropped on the target. See Figure 2-25 to see how this example looks when it loads, during a drag operation, and after the image has been dropped on a target.

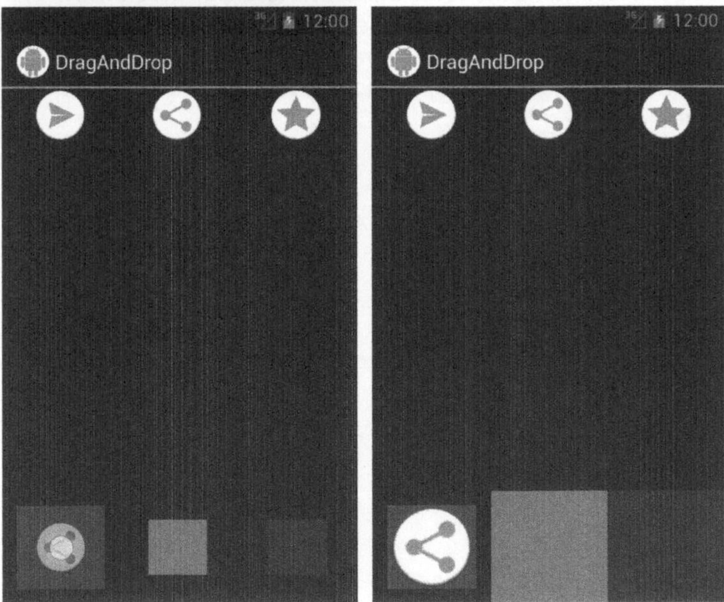

Figure 2-25. *Drag example before the drag (top), while the user is dragging and hovering over a target (left), and after the view has been dropped (right)*

Customizing DragShadowBuilder

The default implementation of DragShadowBuilder is extremely convenient, but it may not be what your application needs. Let's take a look at Listing 2-98, which is a customized builder implementation.

Listing 2-98. *Custom DragShadowBuilder*

```
public class DrawableDragShadowBuilder extends DragShadowBuilder {
    private Drawable mDrawable;

    public DrawableDragShadowBuilder(View view, Drawable drawable) {
        super(view);
        // Set the Drawable and apply a green filter to it
        mDrawable = drawable;
        mDrawable.setColorFilter(
                new PorterDuffColorFilter(Color.GREEN, PorterDuff.Mode.MULTIPLY));
    }

    @Override
    public void onProvideShadowMetrics(Point shadowSize, Point touchPoint) {
        // Fill in the size
        shadowSize.x = mDrawable.getIntrinsicWidth();
        shadowSize.y = mDrawable.getIntrinsicHeight();
        // Fill in the location of the shadow relative to the touch.
        // Here we center the shadow under the finger.
        touchPoint.x = mDrawable.getIntrinsicWidth() / 2;
        touchPoint.y = mDrawable.getIntrinsicHeight() / 2;

        mDrawable.setBounds(new Rect(0, 0, shadowSize.x, shadowSize.y));
    }

    @Override
    public void onDrawShadow(Canvas canvas) {
        //Draw the shadow view onto the provided canvas
        mDrawable.draw(canvas);
    }
}
```

This custom implementation takes the image that it will display as the shadow in as a separate Drawable parameter rather than making a visual copy of the source view. We also apply a green ColorFilter to it for added effect. It turns out that DragShadowBuilder is a fairly straightforward class to extend. There are two primary methods that are required to effectively override it.

The first is onProvideShadowMetrics(), which is called once initially with two Point objects for the builder to fill in. The first should be filled with the size of the image to be used for the shadow, where the desired width is set as the x value and the desired height is set as the y value. In our example we have set this to be the intrinsic width and height of the image. The second should be filled with the desired touch location for the shadow. This defines how the shadow image should be positioned in relation to the user's finger; for example, setting both x and y to zero would place it at the top left corner of the image. In our example, we have set it to the image's midpoint so the image will be centered under the user's finger.

The second method is `onDrawShadow()`, which is called repeatedly to render the shadow image. The `Canvas` passed into this method is created by the framework based on the information contained in `onProvideShadowMetrics()`. Here you can do all sorts of custom drawing as you might with any other custom view. Our example simply tells the `Drawable` to draw itself on the `Canvas`.

2-31. Customizing Transition Animations

Problem

Your application needs to customize the transition animations that happen when moving from one Activity to another or between fragments.

Solution

(API Level 5)

To modify an `Activity` transition, use the `overridePendingTransition()` API for a single occurrence, or declare custom animation values in your application's theme to make a more global change. To modify a `Fragment` transition, use the `onCreateAnimation()` or `onCreateAnimator()` API methods.

How It Works

Activity

When customizing the transitions from one `Activity` to another, there are four animations to consider: the enter and exit animation pair when a new `Activity` opens, and the entry and exit animation pair when the current `Activity` closes. Each animation is applied to one of the two `Activity` elements involved in the transition. For example, when starting a new Activity, the current Activity will run the "open exit" animation and the new Activity will run the "open enter" animation. Because these are run simultaneously, they should create somewhat of a complementary pair or they may look visually incorrect. Listings 2-99 through 2-102 illustrate four such animations.

Listing 2-99. *res/anim/activity_open_enter.xml*

```
<?xml version="1.0" encoding="utf-8"?>
<set xmlns:android="http://schemas.android.com/apk/res/android">
    <rotate
        android:fromDegrees="90" android:toDegrees="0"
        android:pivotX="0%" android:pivotY="0%"
        android:fillEnabled="true"
        android:fillBefore="true" android:fillAfter="true"
        android:duration="500"  />
    <alpha
        android:fromAlpha="0.0" android:toAlpha="1.0"
        android:fillEnabled="true"
        android:fillBefore="true" android:fillAfter="true"
        android:duration="500" />
</set>
```

Listing 2-100. *res/anim/activity_open_exit.xml*

```
<?xml version="1.0" encoding="utf-8"?>
<set xmlns:android="http://schemas.android.com/apk/res/android">
    <rotate
        android:fromDegrees="0" android:toDegrees="-90"
        android:pivotX="0%" android:pivotY="0%"
        android:fillEnabled="true"
        android:fillBefore="true" android:fillAfter="true"
        android:duration="500"  />
    <alpha
        android:fromAlpha="1.0" android:toAlpha="0.0"
        android:fillEnabled="true"
        android:fillBefore="true" android:fillAfter="true"
        android:duration="500" />
</set>
```

Listing 2-101. *res/anim/activity_close_enter.xml*

```
<?xml version="1.0" encoding="utf-8"?>
<set xmlns:android="http://schemas.android.com/apk/res/android">
    <rotate
        android:fromDegrees="-90" android:toDegrees="0"
        android:pivotX="0%p" android:pivotY="0%p"
        android:fillEnabled="true"
        android:fillBefore="true" android:fillAfter="true"
        android:duration="500"  />
    <alpha
```

```
        android:fromAlpha="0.0" android:toAlpha="1.0"
        android:fillEnabled="true"
        android:fillBefore="true" android:fillAfter="true"
        android:duration="500" />
</set>
```

Listing 2-102. *res/anim/activity_close_exit.xml*

```
<?xml version="1.0" encoding="utf-8"?>
<set xmlns:android="http://schemas.android.com/apk/res/android" >
    <rotate
        android:fromDegrees="0" android:toDegrees="90"
        android:pivotX="0%p" android:pivotY="0%p"
        android:fillEnabled="true"
        android:fillBefore="true" android:fillAfter="true"
        android:duration="500" />
    <alpha
        android:fromAlpha="1.0" android:toAlpha="0.0"
        android:fillEnabled="true"
        android:fillBefore="true" android:fillAfter="true"
        android:duration="500" />
</set>
```

What we have created are two "open" animations that rotate the old Activity out and the new Activity in clockwise. The complementary "close" animations rotate the current Activity out and the previous Activity in counterclockwise. Each animation also has with it a fade-out or fade-in effect to make the transition seem more smooth. To apply these custom animations at a specific moment, we can call the method overridePendingTransition() immediately after either startActivity() or finish() like so:

```
//Start a new Activity with custom transition
Intent intent = new Intent(...);
startActivity(intent);
overridePendingTransition(R.anim.activity_open_enter,
R.anim.activity_open_exit);

//Close the current Activity with custom transition
finish();
overridePendingTransition(R.anim.activity_close_enter,
R.anim.activity_close_exit);
```

This is useful if you only need to customize transitions in a few places. But suppose you need to customize every Activity transition in your application; calling this method everywhere would be quite a hassle. Instead it would make more sense to customize the animations in your application's theme. Listing 2-103 illustrates a custom theme that overrides these transitions globally.

Listing 2-103. *res/values/styles.xml*

```
<resources>
    <style name="AppTheme" parent="android:Theme.Holo.Light">
        <item name="android:windowAnimationStyle">@style/ActivityAnimation</item>
    </style>

    <style name="ActivityAnimation" parent="@android:style/Animation.Activity">
        <item
            name="android:activityOpenEnterAnimation">@anim/activity_open_enter
        </item>
        <item
            name="android:activityOpenExitAnimation">@anim/activity_open_exit
        </item>
        <item
            name="android:activityCloseEnterAnimation">@anim/activity_close_enter
        </item>
        <item
            name="android:activityCloseExitAnimation">@anim/activity_close_exit
        </item>
    </style>

</resources>
```

By supplying a custom attribute for the android:windowAnimationStyle value of the theme, we can customize these transition animations. It is important to also refer back to the parent style in the framework because these four animations are not the only ones defined in this style, and you don't want to erase the other existing window animations inadvertently.

Support Fragments

Customizing the animations for Fragment transitions is different, depending on whether you are using the support library or not. The variance exists because the native version uses the new Animator objects, which are not available in the support library version.

When using the support library, you can override the transition animations for a single FragmentTransaction by calling setCustomAnimations(). The version of this method that takes two parameters will set the animation for the add/replace/remove action, but it will not animate on popping the back stack. The version that takes four parameters will add custom animations for popping the back stack as well. Using the same Animation objects from our previous example, the following snippet shows how to add these animations to a FragmentTransaction.

```
FragmentTransaction ft = getSupportFragmentManager().beginTransaction();
    //Must be called first!
    ft.setCustomAnimations(R.anim.activity_open_enter, R.anim.activity_open_exit,
            R.anim.activity_close_enter, R.anim.activity_close_exit);
    ft.replace(R.id.container_fragment, fragment);
    ft.addToBackStack(null);
ft.commit();
```

> **IMPORTANT:** `setCustomAnimations()` *must* be called before `add()`, `replace()`, or any other action method or the animation will not run. It is good practice to simply call this method first in the transaction block.

If you would like the same animations to run for a certain `Fragment` all the time, you may want to override the `onCreateAnimation()` method inside the `Fragment` instead. Listing 2-104 reveals a `Fragment` with its animations defined in this way.

Listing 2-104. *Fragment with Custom Animations*

```
public class SupportFragment extends Fragment {

    @Override
    public View onCreateView(LayoutInflater inflater, ViewGroup container,
            Bundle savedInstanceState) {
        TextView tv = new TextView(getActivity());
        tv.setText("Fragment");
        tv.setBackgroundColor(Color.RED);
        return tv;
    }

    @Override
    public Animation onCreateAnimation(int transit, boolean enter, int nextAnim) {
        switch (transit) {
        case FragmentTransaction.TRANSIT_FRAGMENT_FADE:
            if (enter) {
                return AnimationUtils.loadAnimation(getActivity(),
                        android.R.anim.fade_in);
            } else {
                return AnimationUtils.loadAnimation(getActivity(),
                        android.R.anim.fade_out);
            }
        case FragmentTransaction.TRANSIT_FRAGMENT_CLOSE:
            if (enter) {
                return AnimationUtils.loadAnimation(getActivity(),
                        R.anim.activity_close_enter);
            } else {
                return AnimationUtils.loadAnimation(getActivity(),
                        R.anim.activity_close_exit);
```

```
            }
        case FragmentTransaction.TRANSIT_FRAGMENT_OPEN:
        default:
            if (enter) {
                return AnimationUtils.loadAnimation(getActivity(),
                        R.anim.activity_open_enter);
            } else {
                return AnimationUtils.loadAnimation(getActivity(),
                        R.anim.activity_open_exit);
            }
        }
    }
}
```

How the Fragment animations behave has a lot to do with how the FragmentTransaction is set up. There are a number of different transition values that can be attached to the transaction with setTransition(). If no call to set transition is made, the Fragment cannot determine the difference between an open or close animation set, and the only data we have to determine which animation to run is whether this is an entry or exit.

To obtain the same behavior as we implemented previously with setCustomAnimations(), the transaction should be run with the transition set to TRANSIT_FRAGMENT_OPEN. This will call the initial transaction with this transition value, but it will call the pop back stack action with TRANSIT_FRAGMENT_CLOSE, allowing the Fragment to provide a different animation in this case. The following snippet illustrates constructing a transaction in this way:

```
FragmentTransaction ft = getSupportFragmentManager().beginTransaction();
    //Set the transition value to trigger the correct animations
    ft.setTransition(FragmentTransaction.TRANSIT_FRAGMENT_OPEN);
    ft.replace(R.id.container_fragment, fragment);
    ft.addToBackStack(null);
ft.commit();
```

Fragments also have a third state that you won't find on Activity, and it is defined by the TRANSIT_FRAGMENT_FADE transition value. This animation should occur when the transition is not part of a change, such as add or replace, but rather the Fragment is just being hidden or shown. In our example, we use the standard system-fade animations for this case.

Native Fragments

If your application is targeting API Level 11 or later, you do not need to use fragments from the support library, and in this case the custom animation code works slightly differently. The native Fragment implementation uses the newer Animator object to create the transitions rather than the older Animation object.

This requires a few modifications to the code; first of all, we need to define all our XML animations with Animator instead. Listings 2-105 through 2-108 show this.

Listing 2-105. *res/animator/fragment_exit.xml*

```
<?xml version="1.0" encoding="utf-8"?>
<set xmlns:android="http://schemas.android.com/apk/res/android" >
    <objectAnimator
        android:valueFrom="0" android:valueTo="-90"
        android:valueType="floatType"
        android:propertyName="rotation"
        android:duration="500"/>
    <objectAnimator
        android:valueFrom="1.0" android:valueTo="0.0"
        android:valueType="floatType"
        android:propertyName="alpha"
        android:duration="500"/>
</set>
```

Listing 2-106. *res/animator/fragment_enter.xml*

```
<?xml version="1.0" encoding="utf-8"?>
<set xmlns:android="http://schemas.android.com/apk/res/android" >
    <objectAnimator
        android:valueFrom="90" android:valueTo="0"
        android:valueType="floatType"
        android:propertyName="rotation"
        android:duration="500"/>
    <objectAnimator
        android:valueFrom="0.0" android:valueTo="1.0"
        android:valueType="floatType"
        android:propertyName="alpha"
        android:duration="500"/>
</set>
```

Listing 2-107. *res/animator/fragment_pop_exit.xml*

```
<?xml version="1.0" encoding="utf-8"?>
<set xmlns:android="http://schemas.android.com/apk/res/android" >
    <objectAnimator
        android:valueFrom="0" android:valueTo="90"
        android:valueType="floatType"
        android:propertyName="rotation"
        android:duration="500"/>
    <objectAnimator
        android:valueFrom="1.0" android:valueTo="0.0"
```

```
        android:valueType="floatType"
        android:propertyName="alpha"
        android:duration="500"/>
</set>
```

Listing 2-108. *res/animator/fragment_pop_enter.xml*

```
<?xml version="1.0" encoding="utf-8"?>
<set xmlns:android="http://schemas.android.com/apk/res/android" >
    <objectAnimator
        android:valueFrom="-90" android:valueTo="0"
        android:valueType="floatType"
        android:propertyName="rotation"
        android:duration="500"/>
    <objectAnimator
        android:valueFrom="0.0" android:valueTo="1.0"
        android:valueType="floatType"
        android:propertyName="alpha"
        android:duration="500"/>
</set>
```

Apart from the slightly different syntax, these animations are almost identical to the versions we created previously. The only other difference is that these animations are set to pivot around the center of the view (the default behavior) rather than the top left corner.

As before, we can customize a single transition directly on a FragmentTransaction with setCustomAnimations(); however, the newer version takes our Animator instances. The following snippet shows this with the newer API:

```
FragmentTransaction ft = getFragmentManager().beginTransaction();
    //Must be called first!
    ft.setCustomAnimations(R.animator.fragment_enter, R.animator.fragment_exit,
            R.animator.fragment_pop_enter, R.animator.fragment_pop_exit);
    ft.replace(R.id.container_fragment, fragment);
    ft.addToBackStack(null);
ft.commit();
```

If you prefer to set the same transitions to always run for a given subclass, we can customize the Fragment as before. However, a native Fragment will not have onCreateAnimation(), but rather an onCreateAnimator() method instead. Have a look at Listing 2-109, which redefines the Fragment we created using the newer API.

Listing 2-109. *Native Fragment with Custom Transitions*

```
public class NativeFragment extends Fragment {
```

```
    @Override
    public View onCreateView(LayoutInflater inflater, ViewGroup container,
            Bundle savedInstanceState) {
        TextView tv = new TextView(getActivity());
        tv.setText("Fragment");
        tv.setBackgroundColor(Color.BLUE);
        return tv;
    }

    @Override
    public Animator onCreateAnimator(int transit, boolean enter, int nextAnim) {
        switch (transit) {
        case FragmentTransaction.TRANSIT_FRAGMENT_FADE:
            if (enter) {
                return AnimatorInflater.loadAnimator(getActivity(),
                        android.R.animator.fade_in);
            } else {
                return AnimatorInflater.loadAnimator(getActivity(),
                        android.R.animator.fade_out);
            }
        case FragmentTransaction.TRANSIT_FRAGMENT_CLOSE:
            if (enter) {
                return AnimatorInflater.loadAnimator(getActivity(),
                        R.animator.fragment_pop_enter);
            } else {
                return AnimatorInflater.loadAnimator(getActivity(),
                        R.animator.fragment_pop_exit);
            }
        case FragmentTransaction.TRANSIT_FRAGMENT_OPEN:
        default:
            if (enter) {
                return AnimatorInflater.loadAnimator(getActivity(),
                        R.animator.fragment_enter);
            } else {
                return AnimatorInflater.loadAnimator(getActivity(),
                        R.animator.fragment_exit);
            }
        }
    }
}
```

Again, we are checking for the same transition values as in the support example; we are just returning `Animator` instances instead. Here is the same snippet of code to properly begin a transaction with the transition value set:

```
FragmentTransaction ft = getFragmentManager().beginTransaction();
    //Set the transition value to trigger the correct animations
    ft.setTransition(FragmentTransaction.TRANSIT_FRAGMENT_OPEN);
    ft.replace(R.id.container_fragment, fragment);
    ft.addToBackStack(null);
ft.commit();
```

The final method you can use to set these custom transitions globally for the entire application is to attach them to your application's theme. Listing 2-110 shows a custom theme with our Fragment animations applied.

Listing 2-110. *res/values/styles.xml*

```
<resources>
    <style name="AppTheme" parent="android:Theme.Holo.Light">
        <item name="android:windowAnimationStyle">@style/FragmentAnimation</item>
    </style>

    <style name="FragmentAnimation" parent="@android:style/Animation.Activity">
        <item
          name="android:fragmentOpenEnterAnimation">@animator/fragment_enter
        </item>
        <item
          name="android:fragmentOpenExitAnimation">@animator/fragment_exit
        </item>
        <item
          name="android:fragmentCloseEnterAnimation">@animator/fragment_pop_enter
        </item>
        <item
          name="android:fragmentCloseExitAnimation">@animator/fragment_pop_exit
        </item>
        <item
          name="android:fragmentFadeEnterAnimation">@android:animator/fade_in
        </item>
        <item
          name="android:fragmentFadeExitAnimation">@android:animator/fade_out
        </item>
    </style>
</resources>
```

As you can see, the attributes for a theme's default Fragment animations are part of the same windowAnimationStyle attribute. Therefore, when we customize them we make sure to inherit from the same parent so as not to erase the other system defaults, such as Activity transitions. You must still properly request the correct transition type in your FragmentTransaction to trigger the animation.

If you wanted to customize both the Activity and Fragment transitions in the theme, you could do so by putting them all together in the same custom style (see Listing 2-111).

Listing 2-111. *res/values/styles.xml*

```
<resources>
    <style name="AppTheme" parent="android:Theme.Holo.Light">
        <item name="android:windowAnimationStyle">@style/TransitionAnimation</item>
    </style>

    <style name="TransitionAnimation" parent="@android:style/Animation.Activity">
        <item
          name="android:activityOpenEnterAnimation">@anim/activity_open_enter
        </item>
        <item
          name="android:activityOpenExitAnimation">@anim/activity_open_exit
        </item>
        <item
          name="android:activityCloseEnterAnimation">@anim/activity_close_enter
        </item>
        <item
          name="android:activityCloseExitAnimation">@anim/activity_close_exit
        </item>
        <item
          name="android:fragmentOpenEnterAnimation">@animator/fragment_enter
        </item>
        <item
          name="android:fragmentOpenExitAnimation">@animator/fragment_exit
        </item>
        <item
          name="android:fragmentCloseEnterAnimation">@animator/fragment_pop_enter
        </item>
        <item
          name="android:fragmentCloseExitAnimation">@animator/fragment_pop_exit
        </item>
        <item
          name="android:fragmentFadeEnterAnimation">@android:animator/fade_in
        </item>
        <item
          name="android:fragmentFadeExitAnimation">@android:animator/fade_out
        </item>
    </style>
</resources>
```

CAUTION: Adding `Fragment` transitions to the theme will work only for the native implementation. The support library cannot look for these attributes in a theme because they did not exist in earlier platform versions.

2-32. Creating View Transformations

Problem

Your application needs to dynamically transform how views look in order to add visual effects such as perspective.

Solution

(API Level 1)

The static transformations API available on `ViewGroup` provides a simple method of applying visual effects such as rotation, scale, or alpha changes without resorting to animations. It can also be a convenient place to apply transforms that are easier to apply from the context of a parent view, such as a scale that varies with position.

Static transformations can be enabled on any `ViewGroup` by calling `setStaticTranformationsEnabled(true)` during initialization. With this enabled, the framework will regularly call `getChildStaticTransformation()` for each child view to allow your application to apply the transform.

How It Works

Let's first take a look at an example where the transformations are applied once and don't change (see Listing 2-112).

Listing 2-112. *Custom Layout with Static Transformations*

```
public class PerspectiveLayout extends LinearLayout {

    public PerspectiveLayout(Context context) {
        super(context);
        init();
    }

    public PerspectiveLayout(Context context, AttributeSet attrs) {
        super(context, attrs);
        init();
    }

    public PerspectiveLayout(Context context, AttributeSet attrs, int defStyle) {
        super(context, attrs, defStyle);
```

```
        init();
    }

    private void init() {
        // Enable static transformations so getChildStaticTransformation()
        // will be called for each child.
        setStaticTransformationsEnabled(true);
    }

    @Override
    protected boolean getChildStaticTransformation(View child, Transformation t) {
        // Clear any existing transformation
        t.clear();

        if (getOrientation() == HORIZONTAL) {
            // Scale children based on distance from left edge
            float delta = 1.0f - ((float) child.getLeft() / getWidth());

            t.getMatrix().setScale(delta, delta, child.getWidth() / 2,
                    child.getHeight() / 2);
        } else {
            // Scale children based on distance from top edge
            float delta = 1.0f - ((float) child.getTop() / getHeight());

            t.getMatrix().setScale(delta, delta, child.getWidth() / 2,
                    child.getHeight() / 2);
            //Also apply a fade effect based on its location
            t.setAlpha(delta);
        }
        return true;
    }
}
```

This example illustrates a custom LinearLayout that applies a scale transformation to each of its children, based on that child's location from the beginning edge of the view. The code in getChildStaticTransformation() calculates the scale factor to apply by figuring out the distance from the left or top edge as a percentage of the full parent size. The return value from this method notifies the framework when a transformation has been set. In any case where your application sets a custom transform, you must also return "true" to ensure that it gets attached to the view.

Most of the visual effects such as rotation or scale are actually applied to the Matrix of the Transformation. In our example, we adjust the scale of each child by calling getMatrix().setScale() and passing in the scale factor and the pivot point. The pivot point is the location about which the scale will take place; we set this to the midpoint of the view so that the scaled result is centered.

If the layout orientation is vertical, we also apply an alpha fade to the child view based on the same distance value, which is set directly on the Transformation with setAlpha(). See Listing 2-113 for an example layout that uses this view.

Listing 2-113. *res/layout/main.xml*

```
<?xml version="1.0" encoding="utf-8"?>
<LinearLayout xmlns:android="http://schemas.android.com/apk/res/android"
    android:layout_width="match_parent"
    android:layout_height="match_parent"
    android:orientation="vertical">
    <!-- Horizontal Custom Layout -->
    <com.examples.statictransforms.PerspectiveLayout
        android:layout_width="match_parent"
        android:layout_height="wrap_content"
        android:orientation="horizontal" >
        <ImageView
            android:layout_width="wrap_content"
            android:layout_height="wrap_content"
            android:src="@drawable/ic_launcher" />
        <ImageView
            android:layout_width="wrap_content"
            android:layout_height="wrap_content"
            android:src="@drawable/ic_launcher" />
        <ImageView
            android:layout_width="wrap_content"
            android:layout_height="wrap_content"
            android:src="@drawable/ic_launcher" />
        <ImageView
            android:layout_width="wrap_content"
            android:layout_height="wrap_content"
            android:src="@drawable/ic_launcher" />
    </com.examples.statictransforms.PerspectiveLayout>
    <!-- Vertical Custom Layout -->
    <com.examples.statictransforms.PerspectiveLayout
        android:layout_width="wrap_content"
        android:layout_height="match_parent"
        android:orientation="vertical" >
        <ImageView
            android:layout_width="wrap_content"
            android:layout_height="wrap_content"
            android:src="@drawable/ic_launcher" />
        <ImageView
            android:layout_width="wrap_content"
            android:layout_height="wrap_content"
            android:src="@drawable/ic_launcher" />
        <ImageView
            android:layout_width="wrap_content"
            android:layout_height="wrap_content"
            android:src="@drawable/ic_launcher" />
```

```
        <ImageView
            android:layout_width="wrap_content"
            android:layout_height="wrap_content"
            android:src="@drawable/ic_launcher" />
    </com.examples.statictransforms.PerspectiveLayout>
</LinearLayout>
```

Figure 2-26 shows the results of the example transformation.

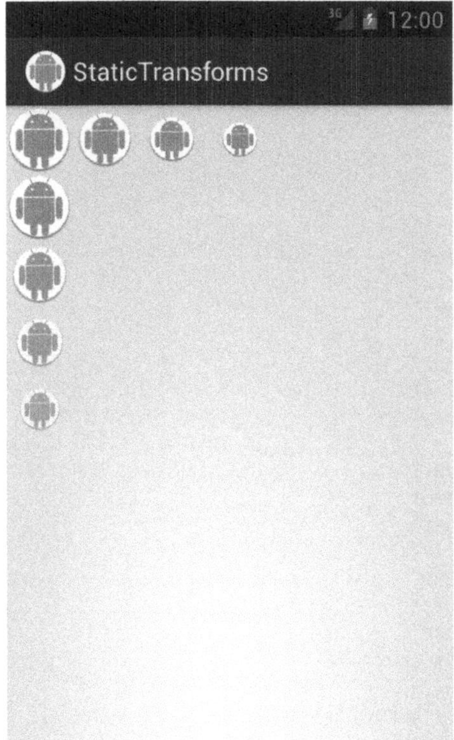

Figure 2-26. *Horizontal and vertical perspective layouts*

In the horizontal layout, as the views move to the right they have a smaller-scale factor applied to them. Similarly, the vertical views reduce in scale as they move down. Additionally, the vertical views also begin to fade out due to the additional alpha change.

Now let's look at an example that provides a more dynamic change. Listing 2-114 shows a custom layout that is meant to be housed within a HorizontalScrollView. This layout uses static transformations to scale the child views as they scroll. The view in the center of the screen is always normal size, and each view scales down as it approaches the edge. This provides the effect that the views are coming closer and moving away as they scroll.

Listing 2-114. *Custom Perspective Scroll Content*

```
public class PerspectiveScrollContentView extends LinearLayout {

    /* Adjustable scale factor for child views */
    private static final float SCALE_FACTOR = 0.7f;
    /* Anchor point for transformation.  (0,0) is top left,
     * (1,1) is bottom right.  This is currently set for
     * the bottom middle (0.5, 1)
     */
    private static final float ANCHOR_X = 0.5f;
    private static final float ANCHOR_Y = 1.0f;

    public PerspectiveScrollContentView(Context context) {
        super(context);
        init();
    }

    public PerspectiveScrollContentView(Context context, AttributeSet attrs) {
        super(context, attrs);
        init();
    }

    public PerspectiveScrollContentView(Context context, AttributeSet attrs,
            int defStyle) {
        super(context, attrs, defStyle);
        init();
    }

    private void init() {
        // Enable static transformations so getChildStaticTransformation()
        // will be called for each child.
        setStaticTransformationsEnabled(true);
    }

    /*
     * Utility method to calculate the current position of any
     * View in the screen's coordinates
     */
    private int getViewCenter(View view) {
        int[] childCoords = new int[2];
        view.getLocationOnScreen(childCoords);
        int childCenter = childCoords[0] + (view.getWidth() / 2);

        return childCenter;
    }
```

```
    @Override
    protected boolean getChildStaticTransformation(View child, Transformation t) {
        HorizontalScrollView scrollView = null;
        if (getParent() instanceof HorizontalScrollView) {
            scrollView = (HorizontalScrollView) getParent();
        }
        if (scrollView == null) {
            return false;
        }

        int childCenter = getViewCenter(child);
        int viewCenter = getViewCenter(scrollView);


        // Calculate the difference between this child and our parent's center.
        // That will determine the scale factor applied.
        float delta = Math.min(1.0f, Math.abs(childCenter - viewCenter)
                / (float) viewCenter);
        //Set the minimum scale factor to 0.4
        float scale = Math.max(0.4f, 1.0f - (SCALE_FACTOR * delta));
        float xTrans = child.getWidth() * ANCHOR_X;
        float yTrans = child.getHeight() * ANCHOR_Y;

        //Clear any existing transformation
        t.clear();
        //Set the transformation for the child view
        t.getMatrix().setScale(scale, scale, xTrans, yTrans);

        return true;
    }
}
```

In this example the custom layout calculates the transformation for each child based on its location with respect to the center of the parent `HorizontalScrollView`. As the user scrolls, each child's transformation will be recalculated so the views will grow and shrink dynamically as they move. The example sets the anchor point of the transformation at the bottom center of each child, which will create the effect of each view growing vertically by remaining centered horizontally. Listing 2-115 shows an example Activity that puts this custom layout into practice.

Listing 2-115. *Activity Using PerspectiveScrollContentView*

```
public class ScrollActivity extends Activity {

    @Override
    protected void onCreate(Bundle savedInstanceState) {
        super.onCreate(savedInstanceState);
```

```
        HorizontalScrollView parentView = new HorizontalScrollView(this);
        PerspectiveScrollContentView contentView =
                new PerspectiveScrollContentView(this);

        // Disable hardware acceleration for this view because dynamic adjustment
        // of child transformations does not currently work in hardware.
        // You can also disable for the entire Activity or Application with
        // android:hardwareAccelerated="false" in the manifest, but it is better to
        // disable acceleration in as few places as possible for best performance.
        if (Build.VERSION.SDK_INT >= Build.VERSION_CODES.HONEYCOMB) {
            contentView.setLayerType(View.LAYER_TYPE_SOFTWARE, null);
        }

        //Add a handful of images to scroll through
        for (int i = 0; i < 20; i++) {
            ImageView iv = new ImageView(this);
            iv.setImageResource(R.drawable.ic_launcher);
            contentView.addView(iv);
        }
        //Add the views to the display
        parentView.addView(contentView);
        setContentView(parentView);
    }
}
```

This example creates a scrolling view and attaches a custom `PerspectiveScrollContentView` with several images to scroll through. The code here isn't much to look at, but there is one very important piece worth mentioning. While static transformations in general are supported, dynamically updating the transform when the view is invalidated does not work with hardware acceleration in the current versions of the SDK. As a result, if your application has a target SDK of 11 or higher, or has enabled hardware acceleration in some other way, it will need to be disabled for this view.

This is done globally in the manifest via `android:hardwareAccelerated="false"` on any `<activity>` or the entire `<application>`, but we can also set it discretely in Java code for just this custom view by calling `setLayerType()` and setting it to `LAYER_TYPE_SOFTWARE`. If your application is targeting an SDK lower than this, hardware acceleration is disabled by default, even on newer devices, for compatibility reasons so this code may not be necessary.

2-33. Swiping Between Views

Problem

You need to implement paging with a swipe gesture in your application's UI in order to move between views or fragments.

Solution

(API Level 4)

Implement the ViewPager widget to provide paging with swipe scroll gestures. ViewPager is a widget currently available only in the support library; it is not part of the native SDK at any platform level. However, any application targeting API Level 4 or later can make use of the widget with the support library included.

ViewPager is a modified implementation of the AdapterView pattern that the framework uses for widgets like ListView and GridView. It requires its own adapter implementation as a subclass of PagerAdapter, but it is conceptually very similar to the patterns used in BaseAdapter and ListAdapter. It does not inherently implement recycling of the components being paged, but it does provide callbacks to create and destroy the items on the fly so that only a fixed number of the content views is in memory at a given time.

How It Works

Most of the heavy lifting in working with ViewPager is in the PagerAdapter implementation you provide. Let's start with a simple example, shown in Listing 2-116, that pages between a series of images.

Listing 2-116. *Custom PagerAdapter for Images*

```
public class ImagePagerAdapter extends PagerAdapter {
    private Context mContext;

    private static final int[] IMAGES = {
        android.R.drawable.ic_menu_camera,
        android.R.drawable.ic_menu_add,
        android.R.drawable.ic_menu_delete,
        android.R.drawable.ic_menu_share,
        android.R.drawable.ic_menu_edit
    };
```

```
private static final int[] COLORS = {
    Color.RED,
    Color.BLUE,
    Color.GREEN,
    Color.GRAY,
    Color.MAGENTA
};

public ImagePagerAdapter(Context context) {
    super();
    mContext = context;
}

/*
 * Provide the total number of pages
 */
@Override
public int getCount() {
    return IMAGES.length;
}

/*
 * Override this method if you want to show more than one page
 * at a time inside the ViewPager's content bounds.
 */
@Override
public float getPageWidth(int position) {
    return 1f;
}

@Override
public Object instantiateItem(ViewGroup container, int position) {
    // Create a new ImageView and add it to the supplied container
    ImageView iv = new ImageView(mContext);
    // Set the content for this position
    iv.setImageResource(IMAGES[position]);
    iv.setBackgroundColor(COLORS[position]);

    // You MUST add the view here, the framework will not do that for you
    container.addView(iv);
    //Return this view also as the key object for this position
    return iv;
}

@Override
public void destroyItem(ViewGroup container, int position, Object object) {
    //Remove the view from the container here
    container.removeView((View) object);
}
```

```
    @Override
    public boolean isViewFromObject(View view, Object object) {
        // Validate that the object returned from instantiateItem() is associated
        // with the view added to the container in that location.  Our example uses
        // the same object in both places.
        return (view == object);
    }

}
```

In this example, we have an implementation of PagerAdapter that serves up a series of ImageView instances for the user to page through. The first required override in the adapter is getCount(), which, just like its AdapterView counterpart, should return the total number of items available.

ViewPager works by keeping track of a "key" Object for each item alongside a View to display for that object; this keeps the separation between the adapter items and their views that developers are used to with AdapterView. However, the implementation is a bit different. With AdapterView, the adapter's getView() method is called to construct and return the view to display for that item. With ViewPager, the callbacks instantiateItem() and destroyItem() will be called when a new view needs to be created, or when one has scrolled outside the bounds of the pager's limit and should be removed; the number of items that any ViewPager will keep hold of is set by the setOffscreenPageLimit() method.

> **NOTE:** The default value for the offscreen page limit is 3. This means ViewPager will track the currently visible page, one to the left, and one to the right. The number of tracked pages is always centered around the currently visible page.

In our example, we use instantiateItem() to create a new ImageView and then apply the properties for that particular position. Unlike AdapterView, the PagerAdapter must attach the View to display to the supplied ViewGroup in addition to returning the unique key Object to represent this item. These two things don't have to be the same, but they can be in a simple example like this. The callback isViewFromObject(), is a required override on PagerAdapter so the application can provide the link between which key Object goes with which View. In our example, we attach the ImageView to the supplied parent and then also return the same instance as the key from instantiateItem(). The code for isViewFromObject() becomes simple, then, as we return true if both parameters are the same instance.

Complementary to instantiate, PagerAdapter must also remove the specified View from the parent container in destroyItem(). If the views displayed in the pager are heavyweight and you wanted to implement some basic view recycling in your adapter, you could hold on to the view after it was removed so it could be handed back to `instantiateItem()` to attach to another key `Object`. See Listing 2-117, which shows an example `Activity` using our custom adapter with a `ViewPager`, and the resulting application is shown in Figure 2-27.

Listing 2-117. *Activity Using ViewPager and ImagePagerAdapter*

```
public class PagerActivity extends Activity {

    @Override
    protected void onCreate(Bundle savedInstanceState) {
        super.onCreate(savedInstanceState);
        ViewPager pager = new ViewPager(this);
        pager.setAdapter(new ImagePagerAdapter(this));

        setContentView(pager);
    }
}
```

Figure 2-27. *ViewPager dragging between two pages*

Running this application, the user can horizontally swipe a finger to page between all the images provided by the custom adapter, and each page displays full-screen. There is one method defined in the example we did not mention: `getPageWidth()`. This method allows you to define for each position how large the page should be as a percentage of the ViewPager size. By default it is set to 1, and the previous example didn't change this. But let's say we wanted to display multiple pages at once, we can adjust the value this method returns.

If we modify the getPageWidth() like the following snippet, we can display three pages at once:

```
/*
 * Override this method if you want to show more than one page
 * at a time inside the ViewPager's content bounds.
 */
@Override
public float getPageWidth(int position) {
    //Page width should be 1/3 of the view
    return 0.333f;
}
```

You can see in Figure 2-28 how this modifies the resulting application.

Figure 2-28. *ViewPager showing three pages at once*

Adding and Removing Pages

Listing 2-118 illustrates a slightly more complex adapter for use with `ViewPager`. This example uses `FragmentPagerAdapter` as a base, which is another class in the framework where each page item is a `Fragment` instead of a simple `View`.

This example is designed to take a long list of data and break it up into smaller sections that display on each page. The `Fragment` this adapter displays is a custom inner implementation that receives a `List` of items and displays them in a `ListView`.

Listing 2-118. *FragmentPagerAdapter to Display a List*

```
public class ListPagerAdapter extends FragmentPagerAdapter {

    private static final int ITEMS_PER_PAGE = 3;

    private List<String> mItems;

    public ListPagerAdapter(FragmentManager manager, List<String> items) {
        super(manager);
        mItems = items;
    }

    /*
     * This method will only get called the first time a fragment is
     * needed for this position.
     */
    @Override
    public Fragment getItem(int position) {
        int start = position * ITEMS_PER_PAGE;
        return ArrayListFragment.newInstance(getPageList(position), start);
    }

    @Override
    public int getCount() {
        // Get whole number
        int pages = mItems.size() / ITEMS_PER_PAGE;
        // Add one more page for any remaining values if list size
        // is not divisible by page size
        int excess = mItems.size() % ITEMS_PER_PAGE;
        if (excess > 0) {
            pages++;
        }

        return pages;
    }
```

```
/*
 * This will get called after getItem() for new Fragments, but also when
 * Fragments beyond the offscreen page limit are added back; we need to make
 * sure to update the list for these elements.
 */
@Override
public Object instantiateItem(ViewGroup container, int position) {
    ArrayListFragment fragment =
            (ArrayListFragment) super.instantiateItem(container, position);
    fragment.updateListItems(getPageList(position));
    return fragment;
}

/*
 * Called by the framework when notifyDataSetChanged() is called, we must
 * decide how each Fragment has changed for the new data set.  We also return
 * POSITION_NONE if a Fragment at a particular position is no longer needed so
 * the adapter can remove it.
 */
@Override
public int getItemPosition(Object object) {
    ArrayListFragment fragment = (ArrayListFragment)object;
    int position = fragment.getBaseIndex() / ITEMS_PER_PAGE;
    if(position >= getCount()) {
        //This page no longer needed
        return POSITION_NONE;
    } else {
        //Refresh fragment data display
        fragment.updateListItems(getPageList(position));

        return position;
    }
}

/*
 * Helper method to obtain the piece of the overall list that should be
 * applied to a given Fragment
 */
private List<String> getPageList(int position) {
    int start = position * ITEMS_PER_PAGE;
    int end = Math.min(start + ITEMS_PER_PAGE, mItems.size());
    List<String> itemPage = mItems.subList(start, end);

    return itemPage;
}
```

```
/*
 * Internal custom Fragment that displays a list section inside
 * of a ListView, and provides external methods for updating the list
 */
public static class ArrayListFragment extends Fragment {
    private ArrayList<String> mItems;
    private ArrayAdapter<String> mAdapter;
    private int mBaseIndex;

    //Fragments are created by convention using a Factory pattern
    static ArrayListFragment newInstance(List<String> page, int baseIndex) {
        ArrayListFragment fragment = new ArrayListFragment();
        fragment.updateListItems(page);
        fragment.setBaseIndex(baseIndex);
        return fragment;
    }

    public ArrayListFragment() {
        super();
        mItems = new ArrayList<String>();
    }

    @Override
    public void onCreate(Bundle savedInstanceState) {
        super.onCreate(savedInstanceState);
        //Make a new adapter for the list items
        mAdapter = new ArrayAdapter<String>(getActivity(),
                android.R.layout.simple_list_item_1, mItems);
    }

    @Override
    public View onCreateView(LayoutInflater inflater, ViewGroup container,
            Bundle savedInstanceState) {
        //Construct and return a ListView with our adapter attached
        ListView list = new ListView(getActivity());
        list.setAdapter(mAdapter);
        return list;
    }

    //Save the index in the global list where this page starts
    public void setBaseIndex(int index) {
        mBaseIndex = index;
    }

    //Retrieve the index in the global list where this page starts
    public int getBaseIndex() {
        return mBaseIndex;
    }
```

```
        public void updateListItems(List<String> items) {
            mItems.clear();
            for (String piece : items) {
                mItems.add(piece);
            }

            if (mAdapter != null) {
                mAdapter.notifyDataSetChanged();
            }
        }
    }
}
```

FragmentPagerAdapter implements some of the underlying requirements of PagerAdapter for us. Instead of implementing instantiateItem(), destroyItem(), and isViewFromObject(), we only need to override getItem() to provide the Fragment for each page position. This example defines a constant for the number of list items that should display on each page. When we create the Fragment in getItem(), we pass in a subsection of the list based on the index offset and this constant. The number of pages required, returned by getCount(), is determined by the total size of the items list divided by the constant number of items per page.

This adapter also overrides one more method we did not see in the simple example, which is getItemPosition(). This method will get called when notifyDataSetChanged() gets called externally by the application. Its primary function is to sort out whether page items should be moved or removed as a result of the change. If the item's position has changed, the implementation should return the new position value. If the item should not be moved, the implementation should return the constant value PagerAdapter.POSITION_UNCHANGED. If the page should be removed, the application should return PagerAdapter.POSITION_NONE.

The example checks the current page position (which we have to re-create from the initial index data) against the current page count. If this page is greater than the count, we have removed enough items from the list so that this page is no longer needed, and we return POSITION_NONE. In any other case, we update the list of items that should now be displayed for the current Fragment and return the new calculated position.

The method getItemPosition() will get called for every page currently being tracked by the ViewPager, which will be the number of pages returned by getOffscreenPageLimit(). However, even though ViewPager doesn't track a Fragment that scrolls outside the limit, FragmentManager still does. So when a previous Fragment is scrolled back in, getItem() will not be called again because the Fragment exists. But, because of this, if a data set change occurs during this time the Fragment list data will not update. This is why we have overridden instantiateItem(). While it is not required to override instantiateItem() for this adapter, we do need to update fragments that are outside the offscreen page limit when modifications to the list take place. Because instantiateItem() will get called each time, a Fragment scrolls back inside the page limit, it is an opportune place to reset the display list.

Let's look at an example application that uses this adapter. See Listings 2-119 and 2-120.

Listing 2-119. *res/layout/main.xml*

```
<?xml version="1.0" encoding="utf-8"?>
<LinearLayout xmlns:android="http://schemas.android.com/apk/res/android"
    android:layout_width="match_parent"
    android:layout_height="match_parent"
    android:orientation="vertical" >
    <Button
        android:layout_width="match_parent"
        android:layout_height="wrap_content"
        android:text="Add Item"
        android:onClick="onAddClick" />
    <Button
        android:layout_width="match_parent"
        android:layout_height="wrap_content"
        android:text="Remove Item"
        android:onClick="onRemoveClick" />

    <!-- ViewPager is a support widget, it needs the full package name -->
    <android.support.v4.view.ViewPager
        android:id="@+id/view_pager"
        android:layout_width="match_parent"
        android:layout_height="match_parent" />
</LinearLayout>
```

Listing 2–120. *Activity With ListPagerAdapter*

```
public class FragmentPagerActivity extends FragmentActivity {

    private ArrayList<String> mListItems;
    private ListPagerAdapter mAdapter;

    @Override
    protected void onCreate(Bundle savedInstanceState) {
        super.onCreate(savedInstanceState);
        setContentView(R.layout.main);
        //Create the initial data set
        mListItems = new ArrayList<String>();
        mListItems.add("Mom");
```

```
        mListItems.add("Dad");
        mListItems.add("Sister");
        mListItems.add("Brother");
        mListItems.add("Cousin");
        mListItems.add("Niece");
        mListItems.add("Nephew");
        //Attach the data to the pager
        ViewPager pager = (ViewPager) findViewById(R.id.view_pager);
        mAdapter = new ListPagerAdapter(getSupportFragmentManager(), mListItems);

        pager.setAdapter(mAdapter);
    }

    public void onAddClick(View v) {
        //Add a new unique item to the end of the list
        mListItems.add("Crazy Uncle " + System.currentTimeMillis());
        mAdapter.notifyDataSetChanged();
    }

    public void onRemoveClick(View v) {
        //Remove an item from the head of the list
        if (!mListItems.isEmpty()) {
            mListItems.remove(0);
        }
        mAdapter.notifyDataSetChanged();
    }
}
```

This example consists of two buttons to add and remove items from the data set as well as a ViewPager. Notice that the ViewPager must be defined in XML using its fully qualified package name because it is only part of the support library and does not exist in the android.widget or android.view packages. The Activity constructs a default list of items, and it passes it to our custom adapter, which is then attached to the ViewPager.

Each Add Button click appends a new item to the end of the list and triggers ListPagerAdapter to update by calling notifyDataSetChanged(). Each Remove Button click removes an item from the front of the list and again notifies the adapter. With each change the adapter adjusts the number of pages available and updates the ViewPager. If all the items are removed from the currently visible page, that page is removed and the previous page will be displayed.

Other Helpful Methods

There are a few other methods on ViewPager that can be useful in your applications:

- setPageMargin() and setPageMarginDrawable() allow you to set some extra space in between pages and optionally supply a Drawable that will be used to fill the margin spaces.
- setCurrentItem() allows you to programmatically set the page that should be shown, with an option to disable the scrolling animation while it switches pages.
- OnPageChangeListener can be used to notify the application of scroll and change actions.
  - onPageSelected() will be called when a new page is displayed.
  - onPageScrolled() will be called continuously while a scroll operation is taking place.
  - onPageScrollStateChanged() will be called when the ViewPager toggles from being idle, to being actively scrolled by the user, to automatically scrolling to snap to the closest page.

2-34. Creating Modular Interfaces

Problem

You want to increase code reuse in your application's UI between multiple device configurations.

Solution

(API Level 4)

Use fragments to create reusable modules that can be inserted into your Activity code to tailor your UI to different device configurations or apply common interface elements to multiple Activities. Fragments were originally introduced to the Android SDK in 3.0 (API Level 11) but are a main part of the support library that allows them to be used in applications targeting any platform version after Android 1.6 (API Level 4).

When using fragments with the support library, you must use the FragmentActivity class instead of the default Activity implementation. This version has all the Fragment functionality built into it, such as a local

FragmentManager, that the newer platforms have natively. If your application is targeting Android 3.0 or later, you will not need the support library for this purpose, and you can use Activity instead.

Fragments have a life-cycle just like an Activity, so the same callback methods such as onCreate(), onResume(), onPause(), and onDestroy() exist for a Fragment. There are a few additional life-cycle callbacks as well, such as onAttach() and onDetach() when a Fragment is connected to its parent Activity. In place of a setContentView() method, the method onCreateView() is called by the framework to obtain the content to display.

A Fragment is not required to have a UI component like an Activity does. By not overriding onCreateView(), a Fragment can exist purely as a data source or other module in your application. This can be a great way to modularize the model portion of your application because FragmentManager provides simple ways for one Fragment to access another. A Fragment can also be retained by FragmentManager, which can allow fragments that may be housing your data or obtaining it from the network to avoid getting re-created on device configuration changes.

How It Works

This example illustrates a simple master-detail application that makes use of three fragments. The master Fragment displays a list of web sites the user can visit, while the detail Fragment contains a WebView to display the URL of the selected list item. The third Fragment does not have a UI component to it, and it exists purely to serve the model data to the other Fragments. Depending on the orientation configuration of the device, we will display these elements differently to best use the screen real estate.

Let's first look at the data Fragment in Listing 2-121.

Listing 2-121. *Data Fragment*

```
public class DataFragment extends Fragment {
    /*
     * This is an example of a fragment that does not have a UI.
     * It exists solely to encapsulate the data logic for the application
     * in a way that is friendly for other fragments to access.
     */

    public static final String TAG = "DataFragment";
```

```
    /*
     * Custom data model class to house our application's data
     */
    public static class DataItem {
        private String mName;
        private String mUrl;

        public DataItem(String name, String url) {
            mName = name;
            mUrl = url;
        }

        public String getName() {
            return mName;
        }

        public String getUrl() {
            return mUrl;
        }
    }

    /*
     * Factory method to create new instances
     */
    public static DataFragment newInstance() {
        return new DataFragment();
    }

    private ArrayList<DataItem> mDataSet;

    @Override
    public void onCreate(Bundle savedInstanceState) {
        super.onCreate(savedInstanceState);
        //Construct the initial data set
        mDataSet = new ArrayList<DataFragment.DataItem>();
        mDataSet.add(new DataItem("Google", "http://www.google.com"));
        mDataSet.add(new DataItem("Yahoo", "http://www.yahoo.com"));
        mDataSet.add(new DataItem("Bing", "http://www.bing.com"));
        mDataSet.add(new DataItem("Android", "http://www.android.com"));
    }

    //Accessor to serve the current data the application
    public ArrayList<DataItem> getLatestData() {
        return mDataSet;
    }
}
```

This `Fragment` defines a custom model class for our list data, and it constructs the data set for the application to use. This example is simplified and the data set is static, but you could place the logic to download feed data from a web service or obtain database information from a ContentProvider (both of which we will describe in great detail in the coming chapters). It has no view component to it, but we can still attach it to the FragmentManager for other modules of the application to access.

Next, see Listing 2-122 where we define the master Fragment.

Listing 2-122. *Master View Fragment*

```
public class MasterFragment extends DialogFragment implements
        AdapterView.OnItemClickListener {

    /*
     * Callback interface to feed data selections up to the parent Activity
     */
    public interface OnItemSelectedListener {
        public void onDataItemSelected(DataItem selected);
    }

    /*
     * Factory method to create new instances
     */
    public static MasterFragment newInstance() {
        return new MasterFragment();
    }

    private ArrayAdapter<DataItem> mAdapter;
    private OnItemSelectedListener mItemSelectedListener;

    /*
     * Using onAttach to connect the listener interface, and guarantee that the
     * Activity we attach to supports the interface.
     */
    @Override
    public void onAttach(Activity activity) {
        super.onAttach(activity);
        try {
            mItemSelectedListener = (OnItemSelectedListener) activity;
        } catch (ClassCastException e) {
            throw new IllegalArgumentException(
                    "Activity must implement OnItemSelectedListener");
        }
    }

    /*
     * Construct a custom adapter to display the name field from our data model.
     */
    @Override
    public void onCreate(Bundle savedInstanceState) {
        super.onCreate(savedInstanceState);
```

```
        mAdapter = new ArrayAdapter<DataFragment.DataItem>(getActivity(),
                android.R.layout.simple_list_item_1) {
            @Override
            public View getView(int position, View convertView, ViewGroup parent) {
                View row = convertView;
                if (row == null) {
                    row = LayoutInflater.from(getContext())
                            .inflate(android.R.layout.simple_list_item_1,
                                    parent, false);
                }

                DataItem item = getItem(position);
                TextView tv = (TextView) row.findViewById(android.R.id.text1);
                tv.setText(item.getName());

                return row;
            }
        };
    }

    @Override
    public View onCreateView(LayoutInflater inflater, ViewGroup container,
            Bundle savedInstanceState) {
        ListView list = new ListView(getActivity());
        list.setOnItemClickListener(this);
        list.setAdapter(mAdapter);
        return list;
    }

    /*
     * onCreateDialog is the opportunity to directly access the dialog that will
     * be shown.  We use this callback to set the title of the dialog
     */
    @Override
    public Dialog onCreateDialog(Bundle savedInstanceState) {
        Dialog dialog = super.onCreateDialog(savedInstanceState);
        dialog.setTitle("Select a Site");

        return dialog;
    }

    /*
     * When we resume, get the latest model information from our DataFragment
     */
    @Override
    public void onResume() {
        super.onResume();
        //Get the latest data list
        DataFragment fragment = (DataFragment) getFragmentManager()
```

```
                .findFragmentByTag(DataFragment.TAG);
        if (fragment != null) {
            mAdapter.clear();
            for (DataItem item : fragment.getLatestData()) {
                mAdapter.add(item);
            }
            mAdapter.notifyDataSetChanged();
        }
    }

    @Override
    public void onItemClick(AdapterView<?> parent, View v, int position, long id) {
        // Notify the Activity
        mItemSelectedListener.onDataItemSelected(mAdapter.getItem(position));

        // Hide the dialog, if shown.  This returns false when the fragment
        // is embedded in the view.
        if (getShowsDialog()) {
            dismiss();
        }
    }
}
```

This component inherits from DialogFragment, which is a special instance in the SDK that has a secret power. DialogFragment can display its contents embedded in an Activity or it can display them inside a Dialog. This will allow us to use the same code to display the list, but it will only embed itself in the UI when there is room to do so. In onCreate(), we implement a custom ArrayAdapter that can display the data out of our custom model class. In onCreateView(), we create a simple ListView that will display the model items.

In onResume(), we see how fragments can communicate with one another. This component asks the FragmentManager for an instance of the DataFragment we defined previously. If one exists, it obtains the latest data model list from that Fragment. The Fragment is found by referencing its tag value, which we will see shortly how that link is made.

This Fragment also defines a custom listener interface that we will use to communicate back to the parent Activity. In the onAttach() callback, we set the Activity we attach to as the listener for this Fragment. This is one of many patterns we could use to call back to the parent. If the Fragment will always be attached to the same Activity in your application, another common method is to simply call getActivity() and cast the result to access the methods you have written on your Activity directly. We could have asked the MasterFragment to talk directly to the DetailsFragment in a similar fashion in which the DataFragment was accessed.

Whenever an item is selected in the list, the listener is notified. DialogFragment provides the getShowsDialog() method to determine if the view is currently embedded in the Activity or being shown as a Dialog. If the Fragment is currently shown as a Dialog, we also call dismiss() after the selection.

> **TIP:** The dismiss() method technically does work even when the Fragment is not shown as a Dialog. It just removes the view from its container. This behavior can be a bit awkward, so it is best to always check the mode first.

Now let's look at our last item, the detail view, in Listing 2-123.

Listing 2-123. *Detail View Fragment*

```
public class DetailFragment extends Fragment {

    private WebView mWebView;

    /*
     * Custom client to enable progress visibility.  Adding a client also
     * sets the WebView to load all requests directly rather than handing them
     * off to the browser.
     */
    private WebViewClient mWebViewClient = new WebViewClient() {
        @Override
        public void onPageStarted(WebView view, String url, Bitmap favicon) {
            getActivity().setProgressBarIndeterminateVisibility(true);
        }

        public void onPageFinished(WebView view, String url) {
            getActivity().setProgressBarIndeterminateVisibility(false);
        }
    };
    /*
     * Create and set up a basic WebView for the display
     */
    @Override
    public View onCreateView(LayoutInflater inflater, ViewGroup container,
            Bundle savedInstanceState) {
        mWebView = new WebView(getActivity());
        mWebView.getSettings().setJavaScriptEnabled(true);
        mWebView.setWebViewClient(mWebViewClient);

        return mWebView;
    }
```

```
    /*
     * External method to load a new site into the view
     */
    public void loadUrl(String url) {
        mWebView.loadUrl(url);
    }

}
```

This component is the simplest of the bunch. Here we just create a `WebView` that will load the contents of the URL passed to it. We also attach a `WebViewClient` to monitor the loading progress so we can display a progress indicator to the user. For more detailed information about `WebView` and `WebViewClient`, check out the recipes in Chapter 3.

> **IMPORTANT:** Because this application uses a `WebView` to access remote sites, you will need to declare the `android.permission.INTERNET` permission in your manifest.

Finally, take a look at the Activity defined for the example in Listings 2-124 through 2-126.

Listing 2-124. *res/layout/main.xml*

```
<?xml version="1.0" encoding="utf-8"?>
<!-- Portrait Device Layout -->
<LinearLayout xmlns:android="http://schemas.android.com/apk/res/android"
    android:layout_width="match_parent"
    android:layout_height="match_parent"
    android:orientation="vertical" >
    <Button
        android:layout_width="match_parent"
        android:layout_height="wrap_content"
        android:text="Show List"
        android:onClick="onShowClick" />
    <fragment android:name="com.examples.fragmentsample.DetailFragment"
        android:id="@+id/fragment_detail"
        android:layout_width="match_parent"
        android:layout_height="match_parent" />
</LinearLayout>
```

Listing 2-125. *res/layout-land/main.xml*

```
<?xml version="1.0" encoding="utf-8"?>
<!-- Landscape Device Layout -->
<LinearLayout xmlns:android="http://schemas.android.com/apk/res/android"
    android:layout_width="match_parent"
```

```
    android:layout_height="match_parent"
    android:orientation="horizontal" >
    <FrameLayout
        android:id="@+id/fragment_master"
        android:layout_width="0dp"
        android:layout_height="match_parent"
        android:layout_weight="1" />
    <fragment
        android:name="com.examples.fragmentsample.DetailFragment"
        android:id="@+id/fragment_detail"
        android:layout_width="0dp"
        android:layout_height="match_parent"
        android:layout_weight="3" />
</LinearLayout>
```

Listing 2-126. *Master Detail Activity*

```
public class MainActivity extends FragmentActivity implements
        MasterFragment.OnItemSelectedListener {

    private MasterFragment mMaster;
    private DetailFragment mDetail;

    @Override
    protected void onCreate(Bundle savedInstanceState) {
        super.onCreate(savedInstanceState);

        // Enable a progress indicator on the window
        requestWindowFeature(Window.FEATURE_INDETERMINATE_PROGRESS);
        setContentView(R.layout.main);
        setProgressBarIndeterminateVisibility(false);

        // Load the data fragment.
        // If an instance does not exist in the FragmentManager attach a new one.
        DataFragment fragment = (DataFragment) getSupportFragmentManager()
                .findFragmentByTag(DataFragment.TAG);
        if (fragment == null) {
            fragment = DataFragment.newInstance();
            // We want to retain this instance so we get the same one back on
            // configuration changes.
            fragment.setRetainInstance(true);
            //Attach the fragment with a tag rather than a container id
            FragmentTransaction ft =
                    getSupportFragmentManager().beginTransaction();
            ft.add(fragment, DataFragment.TAG);
            ft.commit();
        }
```

```
        // Get the details fragment
        mDetail = (DetailFragment) getSupportFragmentManager()
                .findFragmentById(R.id.fragment_detail);

        // Either embed the master fragment or hold onto it to show as a dialog
        mMaster = MasterFragment.newInstance();
        // If the container view exists, embed the fragment
        View container = findViewById(R.id.fragment_master);
        if (container != null) {
            FragmentTransaction ft =
                    getSupportFragmentManager().beginTransaction();
            ft.add(R.id.fragment_master, mMaster);
            ft.commit();
        }
    }

    @Override
    public void onDataItemSelected(DataItem selected) {
        //Pass the selected item to show in the detail view
        mDetail.loadUrl(selected.getUrl());
    }

    public void onShowClick(View v) {
        //When this button exists and is clicked, show the DetailFragment
        //as a dialog
        mMaster.show(getSupportFragmentManager(), null);
    }
}
```

We have created two different layouts for portrait (default) orientation and landscape orientation. In the portrait layout, we embed the detail Fragment directly into the UI using the <fragment> tag. This will automatically create the Fragment and attach it when the layout is inflated. In this orientation the master list will not fit, so we add a button instead that will show the master list as a Dialog. In the landscape layout we have room to display both elements side-by-side. In this case we embed the detail view again and then place an empty container view where we will eventually attach the master view.

When the Activity is first created, the first thing we do is ensure that a DataFragment is attached to the FragmentManager; if not, we create a new instance and attach it. On this Fragment specifically we call setRetainInstance(), which tells FragmentManager to hold onto this even when a configuration change occurs. This allows the component responsible for the data model to only exist once and not be affected by changes to the user interface.

Fragments are added, removed, or replaced through a FragmentTransaction. This is because Fragment operations are asynchronous. All the data associated with a particular operation, such as what operation to perform and whether that operation should be part of the BACK button stack, is set on a particular FragmentTransaction and that transaction is committed.

We obtain the DetailsFragment using the findFragmentById() method on FragmentManager. Notice that this ID matches the value placed on the <fragment> tag in each layout. The MasterFragment is created in code, and then we decide what to do with it based on the state of the layout. If our empty container exists, then we attach the fragment to the FragmentManager, referencing the ID of the container where we want the content view to display. This effectively embeds the MasterFragment into the view hierarchy. If the container view is not there, we do nothing further because the Fragment will be shown later.

In a portrait layout, the user can press the Show List button, which will call show() on our MasterFragment, causing it to display inside of a Dialog. It is also at this point that the MasterFragment gets attached to the FragmentManager. Remember that, when a user clicks an option in the list, the listener interface method will be called. This Activity forwards that selection on to the DetailsFragment for the content to be displayed in the WebView.

You can see in Figures 2-29 and 2-30 how the application displays in portrait and landscape orientation.

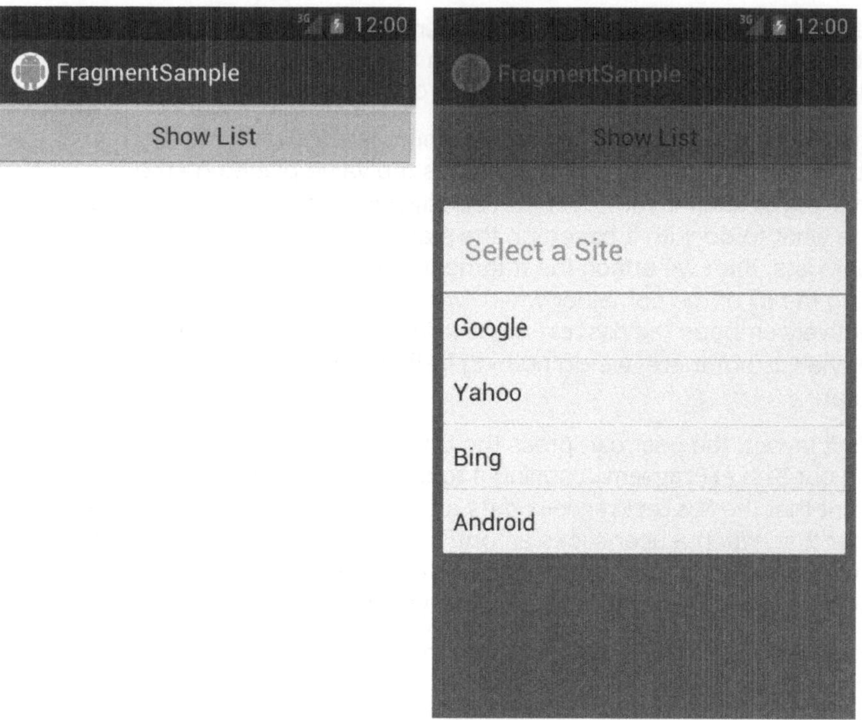

Figure 2-29. *Portrait layout (left) and dialog display (right)*

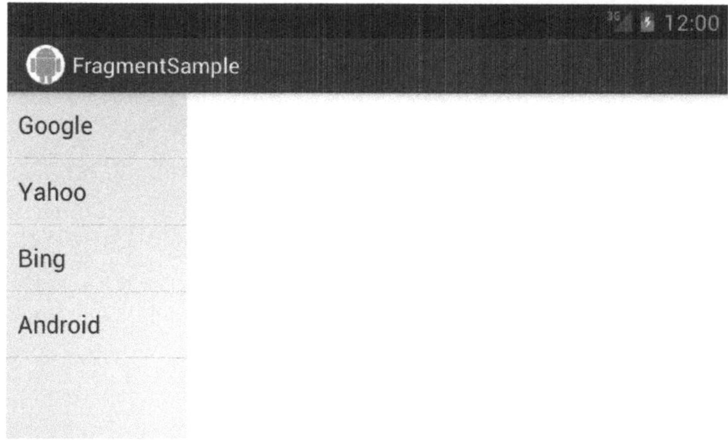

Figure 2-30. *Landscape layout with fragments side-by-side*

Fragments are a fantastic way to break up your code into modules that can be reorganized and reused in order to allow your application to scale easily to multiple device types while staying easy to maintain.

2-35. High-Performance Drawing

Problem

Your application needs to render and draw a complex scene or animation to the screen, often from a background thread.

Solution

(API Level 1)

Use `SurfaceView` or `TextureView` to render content from a background thread to the screen. The general rule in developing Android user interfaces is to never modify any properties associated with a `View` from any thread other than the main thread. These two classes are the exception to this rule, and they are designed specifically to take draw commands from a background thread and post them to the screen. You will also see in later chapters how these two classes are used by the framework to render camera preview data and video output. However, for now we are going to focus on doing our own drawing.

`SurfaceView` is rather unique in that it doesn't really behave like a traditional `View`. When one is instantiated, a secondary `Window` is actually created at the location of the `View` but underneath the current `Window`, and the `View` component simply "punches a hole" in the top-level `Window` by displaying transparently. The advantage to this approach is that it allows us to do this high-performance drawing without any assistance from hardware acceleration. However, it also means that `SurfaceView` is fairly static and does not respond well to being animated or transformed in any way.

`TextureView` is available in Android 4.0 and later and in most cases can be a drop-in replacement for `SurfaceView`. It behaves more like a traditional `View` in that it can be animated and transformed while content is being drawn to it. However, it requires the context it is running in to be hardware accelerated, which may cause compatibility issues in some applications.

How It Works

Let's take a look at an example application where a background thread continuously renders a series of objects to a SurfaceView. In this example, we create a display that animates the motion of several icons continuously on the screen. See Listings 2-127 and 2-128.

Listing 2-127. *res/layout/main.xml*

```
<FrameLayout xmlns:android="http://schemas.android.com/apk/res/android"
    android:layout_width="match_parent"
    android:layout_height="match_parent"
    android:orientation="vertical" >
    <Button
        android:id="@+id/button_erase"
        android:layout_width="match_parent"
        android:layout_height="wrap_content"
        android:text="Erase" />
    <SurfaceView
        android:id="@+id/surface"
        android:layout_width="300dp"
        android:layout_height="300dp"
        android:layout_gravity="center" />

</FrameLayout>
```

Listing 2-128. *Surface Drawing Activity*

```
public class SurfaceActivity extends Activity implements View.OnClickListener,
        View.OnTouchListener, SurfaceHolder.Callback {

    private SurfaceView mSurface;
    private DrawingThread mThread;

    @Override
    public void onCreate(Bundle savedInstanceState) {
        super.onCreate(savedInstanceState);
        setContentView(R.layout.main);
        //Attach listener to button
        findViewById(R.id.button_erase).setOnClickListener(this);

        //Set up the surface with a touch listener and callback
        mSurface = (SurfaceView) findViewById(R.id.surface);
        mSurface.setOnTouchListener(this);
        mSurface.getHolder().addCallback(this);
    }
```

```
@Override
public void onClick(View v) {
    mThread.clearItems();
}

public boolean onTouch(View v, MotionEvent event) {
    if (event.getAction() == MotionEvent.ACTION_DOWN) {
        mThread.addItem((int) event.getX(), (int) event.getY());
    }
    return true;
}

@Override
public void surfaceCreated(SurfaceHolder holder) {
    mThread = new DrawingThread(holder,
            BitmapFactory.decodeResource(getResources(),
                    R.drawable.ic_launcher));
    mThread.start();
}

@Override
public void surfaceChanged(SurfaceHolder holder, int format, int width,
        int height) {
    mThread.updateSize(width, height);
}

@Override
public void surfaceDestroyed(SurfaceHolder holder) {
    mThread.quit();
    mThread = null;
}

private static class DrawingThread extends HandlerThread implements
        Handler.Callback {
    private static final int MSG_ADD = 100;
    private static final int MSG_MOVE = 101;
    private static final int MSG_CLEAR = 102;

    private int mDrawingWidth, mDrawingHeight;

    private SurfaceHolder mDrawingSurface;
    private Paint mPaint;
    private Handler mReceiver;
    private Bitmap mIcon;
    private ArrayList<DrawingItem> mLocations;

    private class DrawingItem {
        //Current location marker
        int x, y;
        //Direction markers for motion
```

```
        boolean horizontal, vertical;

        public DrawingItem(int x, int y, boolean horizontal, boolean vertical) {
            this.x = x;
            this.y = y;
            this.horizontal = horizontal;
            this.vertical = vertical;
        }
    }

    public DrawingThread(SurfaceHolder holder, Bitmap icon) {
        super("DrawingThread");
        mDrawingSurface = holder;
        mLocations = new ArrayList<DrawingItem>();
        mPaint = new Paint(Paint.ANTI_ALIAS_FLAG);
        mIcon = icon;
    }

    @Override
    protected void onLooperPrepared() {
        mReceiver = new Handler(getLooper(), this);
        //Start the rendering
        mReceiver.sendEmptyMessage(MSG_MOVE);
    }

    @Override
    public boolean quit() {
        // Clear all messages before dying
        mReceiver.removeCallbacksAndMessages(null);
        return super.quit();
    }

    @Override
    public boolean handleMessage(Message msg) {
        switch (msg.what) {
        case MSG_ADD:
            //Create a new item at the touch location,
            //with a randomized start direction
            DrawingItem newItem = new DrawingItem(msg.arg1, msg.arg2,
                    Math.round(Math.random()) == 0,
                    Math.round(Math.random()) == 0);
            mLocations.add(newItem);
            break;
        case MSG_CLEAR:
            //Remove all objects
            mLocations.clear();
            break;
        case MSG_MOVE:
            //Render a frame
            Canvas c = mDrawingSurface.lockCanvas();
```

```
                if (c == null) {
                    break;
                }
                //Clear Canvas first
                c.drawColor(Color.BLACK);
                //Draw each item
                for (DrawingItem item : mLocations) {
                    //Update location
                    item.x += (item.horizontal ? 5 : -5);
                    if (item.x >= (mDrawingWidth - mIcon.getWidth()) ) {
                        item.horizontal = false;
                    } else if (item.x <= 0) {
                        item.horizontal = true;
                    }
                    item.y += (item.vertical ? 5 : -5);
                    if (item.y >= (mDrawingHeight - mIcon.getHeight()) ) {
                        item.vertical = false;
                    } else if (item.y <= 0) {
                        item.vertical = true;
                    }
                    //Draw to the Canvas
                    c.drawBitmap(mIcon, item.x, item.y, mPaint);
                }
                //Release to be rendered to the screen
                mDrawingSurface.unlockCanvasAndPost(c);
                break;
            }
            //Post the next frame
            mReceiver.sendEmptyMessage(MSG_MOVE);
            return true;
        }

        public void updateSize(int width, int height) {
            mDrawingWidth = width;
            mDrawingHeight = height;
        }

        public void addItem(int x, int y) {
            //Pass the location into the Handler using Message arguments
            Message msg = Message.obtain(mReceiver, MSG_ADD, x, y);
            mReceiver.sendMessage(msg);
        }

        public void clearItems() {
            mReceiver.sendEmptyMessage(MSG_CLEAR);
        }
    }
}
```

This example constructs a simple background DrawingThread to render and draw content to a SurfaceView. This thread is a subclass of HandlerThread, which is a convenient framework helper for generating background workers that process incoming messages. We talk in more detail about this pattern in Chapter 6, but for now suffice it to say that our background thread operates by responding to messages sent to the Handler it owns inside of handleMessage(). SurfaceView is really two components: a Surface underneath the Window and a clear View in the hierarchy. To do drawing, we really need access to the underlying Surface, which is wrapped in a SurfaceHolder.

The construction of the Surface doesn't actually happen until the view gets attached to the current window, so we can't just grab it right away. Instead, SurfaceHolder has a callback interface when the Surface is created, destroyed, or changed so that we can use it to manage the life cycle of the components that depend on it (in this case the DrawingThread). Here we wait for surfaceCreated() to construct a new DrawingThread and start rendering, and in surfaceDestroyed() we need to stop rendering to the Surface as it is no longer valid. The final callback, surfaceChanged(), is the only place where the dimensions of the Surface are supplied, so we make sure to update our drawing code with those values whenever they are available.

We have defined three different commands for the thread to react to: add, clear, and move. The add method will be triggered when the user taps on the SurfaceView by adding a drawing item to the display list with its initial location set to the location of the touch. The clear method will remove all items from the display list, which is triggered when the button is pressed.

The move method is effectively where the thread renders each frame to the SurfaceView. Every drawing operation should be prefaced with lockCanvas(), which provides a Canvas to apply drawing calls. Then the thread iterates through each item in its display list, updates it to a new position, and draws an icon to the Canvas at that location. It also checks if any item has hit a boundary of the Surface, so it can reverse direction in those cases. We must preface each frame with drawColor() to clear the previous frame's contents. Without this, as the icons move you would see a trail behind them of the icon's previous locations. In some applications this may be desirable (like a painting application where each event should be added to the others), but not for our example. After all the drawing calls are made, the application must call unlockCanvasAndPost() to actually render the data to the screen.

By continuously posting MSG_MOVE to itself, the DrawingThread runs through this process indefinitely until the thread is quit by the application. An advantage to doing this processing via HandlerThread is that the operations can be cancelled at any time with `quit()` and the thread can die cleanly, rather than trying to interrupt the thread execution.

You can see the results of this application running in Figure 2-31. The user can tap on the black box an indefinite number of times and watch the number of flying icons stack up. Because the drawing code only uses one bitmap for all the icons, the number of items the view can support is very high without running into any memory concerns.

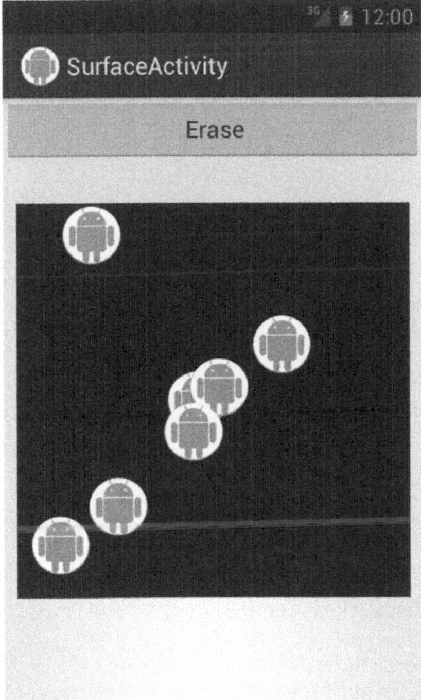

Figure 2-31. *SurfaceView drawing scene*

TextureView

(API Level 14)

If your application is targeting Android 4.0 and later, you can also make use of `TextureView`, which has a few additional properties that may make it ideal for your application; the most useful is that it can be transformed. Have a look at Listings 2-129 and 2-130, where we have modified the previous example to use `TextureView`.

Listing 2-129. *res/layout/main.xml*

```
<FrameLayout xmlns:android="http://schemas.android.com/apk/res/android"
    android:layout_width="match_parent"
    android:layout_height="match_parent">
    <Button
        android:id="@+id/button_transform"
        android:layout_width="match_parent"
        android:layout_height="wrap_content"
        android:text="Rotate" />
    <TextureView
        android:id="@+id/surface"
        android:layout_width="300dp"
        android:layout_height="300dp"
        android:layout_gravity="center" />

</FrameLayout>
```

Listing 2-130. *Texture Drawing Activity*

```
public class TextureActivity extends Activity implements View.OnClickListener,
        View.OnTouchListener, TextureView.SurfaceTextureListener {

    private TextureView mSurface;
    private DrawingThread mThread;

    @Override
    public void onCreate(Bundle savedInstanceState) {
        super.onCreate(savedInstanceState);
        setContentView(R.layout.texture);
        //Attach listener to button
        findViewById(R.id.button_transform).setOnClickListener(this);

        //Set up the surface with a touch listener and callback
        mSurface = (TextureView) findViewById(R.id.surface);
        mSurface.setOnTouchListener(this);
        mSurface.setSurfaceTextureListener(this);
    }

    @Override
    public void onClick(View v) {
        mSurface.animate()
            .rotationBy(180.0f)
            .setDuration(750);
    }
```

```
public boolean onTouch(View v, MotionEvent event) {
    if (event.getAction() == MotionEvent.ACTION_DOWN) {
        mThread.addItem((int) event.getX(), (int) event.getY());
    }
    return true;
}

@Override
public void onSurfaceTextureAvailable(SurfaceTexture surface, int width,
        int height) {
    mThread = new DrawingThread(new Surface(surface),
            BitmapFactory.decodeResource(getResources(),
                    R.drawable.ic_launcher));
    mThread.updateSize(width, height);
    mThread.start();
}

@Override
public void onSurfaceTextureSizeChanged(SurfaceTexture surface, int width,
        int height) {
    mThread.updateSize(width, height);
}

@Override
public void onSurfaceTextureUpdated(SurfaceTexture surface) {
    //Do any processing that needs to happen on each frame
}

@Override
public boolean onSurfaceTextureDestroyed(SurfaceTexture surface) {
    mThread.quit();
    mThread = null;

    //Return true to allow the framework to release the surface
    return true;
}

private static class DrawingThread extends HandlerThread implements
        Handler.Callback {
    private static final int MSG_ADD = 100;
    private static final int MSG_MOVE = 101;
    private static final int MSG_CLEAR = 102;

    private int mDrawingWidth, mDrawingHeight;

    private Surface mDrawingSurface;
    private Rect mSurfaceRect;
    private Paint mPaint;

    private Handler mReceiver;
```

```
    private Bitmap mIcon;
    private ArrayList<DrawingItem> mLocations;

    private class DrawingItem {
        //Current location marker
        int x, y;
        //Direction markers for motion
        boolean horizontal, vertical;

        public DrawingItem(int x, int y, boolean horizontal,
                boolean vertical) {
            this.x = x;
            this.y = y;
            this.horizontal = horizontal;
            this.vertical = vertical;
        }
    }

    public DrawingThread(Surface surface, Bitmap icon) {
        super("DrawingThread");
        mDrawingSurface = surface;
        mSurfaceRect = new Rect();
        mLocations = new ArrayList<DrawingItem>();
        mPaint = new Paint(Paint.ANTI_ALIAS_FLAG);
        mIcon = icon;
    }

    @Override
    protected void onLooperPrepared() {
        mReceiver = new Handler(getLooper(), this);
        //Start the rendering
        mReceiver.sendEmptyMessage(MSG_MOVE);
    }

    @Override
    public boolean quit() {
        // Clear all messages before dying
        mReceiver.removeCallbacksAndMessages(null);
        return super.quit();
    }

    @Override
    public boolean handleMessage(Message msg) {
        switch (msg.what) {
        case MSG_ADD:
            // Create a new item at the touch location,
            // with a randomized start direction
            DrawingItem newItem = new DrawingItem(msg.arg1, msg.arg2,
                    Math.round(Math.random()) == 0,
                    Math.round(Math.random()) == 0);
```

```
            mLocations.add(newItem);
            break;
        case MSG_CLEAR:
            //Remove all objects
            mLocations.clear();
            break;
        case MSG_MOVE:
            //Render a frame
            try {
                Canvas c = mDrawingSurface.lockCanvas(mSurfaceRect);
                if (c == null) {
                    break;
                }
                //Clear Canvas first
                c.drawColor(Color.BLACK);
                //Draw each item
                for (DrawingItem item : mLocations) {
                    //Update location
                    item.x += (item.horizontal ? 5 : -5);
                    if (item.x >= (mDrawingWidth - mIcon.getWidth()) ) {
                        item.horizontal = false;
                    } else if (item.x <= 0) {
                        item.horizontal = true;
                    }
                    item.y += (item.vertical ? 5 : -5);
                    if (item.y >= (mDrawingHeight - mIcon.getHeight()) ) {
                        item.vertical = false;
                    } else if (item.y <= 0) {
                        item.vertical = true;
                    }
                    //Draw to the Canvas
                    c.drawBitmap(mIcon, item.x, item.y, mPaint);
                }
                //Release the surface to be rendered
                mDrawingSurface.unlockCanvasAndPost(c);
            } catch (Exception e) {
                e.printStackTrace();
            }
            break;
        }
        //Post the next frame
        mReceiver.sendEmptyMessage(MSG_MOVE);
        return true;
    }

    public void updateSize(int width, int height) {
        mDrawingWidth = width;
        mDrawingHeight = height;
        mSurfaceRect.set(0, 0, mDrawingWidth, mDrawingHeight);
    }
```

```
        public void addItem(int x, int y) {
            //Pass the location into the Handler using Message arguments
            Message msg = Message.obtain(mReceiver, MSG_ADD, x, y);
            mReceiver.sendMessage(msg);
        }

        public void clearItems() {
            mReceiver.sendEmptyMessage(MSG_CLEAR);
        }
    }
}
```

In this modified example, our layout has a TextureView instance. Similar to SurfaceView, the underlying surface to draw on is not created until the view is attached to the Window, so we must rely on a callback before accessing it. For TextureView, this callback is a SurfaceTextureListener. For the most part, the functionality mirrors SurfaceHolder.Callback with onSurfaceTextureAvailable(), onSurfaceTextureChanged(), and onSurfaceTextureDestroyed(). However, there is one additional callback method we aren't currently using in this example called onSurfaceTextureUpdated(). This method will be called anytime the SurfaceTexture renders a new frame.

The drawing surface that TextureView provides is slightly different, in that there is no SurfaceHolder wrapping it to access. Instead, we can access a SurfaceTexture instance, which we can wrap in a new Surface to do our drawing. This, in turn, requires one small modification of our DrawingThread. SurfaceHolder has a convenience version of lockCanvas() that takes no parameters and marks the entire Surface as dirty. When working with Surface directly, this method does not exist, so we need to pass a Rect into lockCanvas() that tells it which section of the Surface to return as a Canvas for new rendering. Because we still want this to be the entire surface, we maintain the size of the Rect in updateSize(), which will get called by the listener whenever the surface changes.

To showcase the ability to transform the SurfaceTexture live while it is rendering, we have replaced the Erase button with a Rotate button. Clicking this button will cause the TextureView to do a half-circle rotation animation each time. Clicking the button while the current animation is running will cancel it and start a new rotation from the current point, so if you click the button rapidly you can get the view to rotate into some pretty odd angles. The entire time the SurfaceTexture will continue to animate without skipping a beat. You can see in Figure 2-32 the application with the TextureView rotated upside-down.

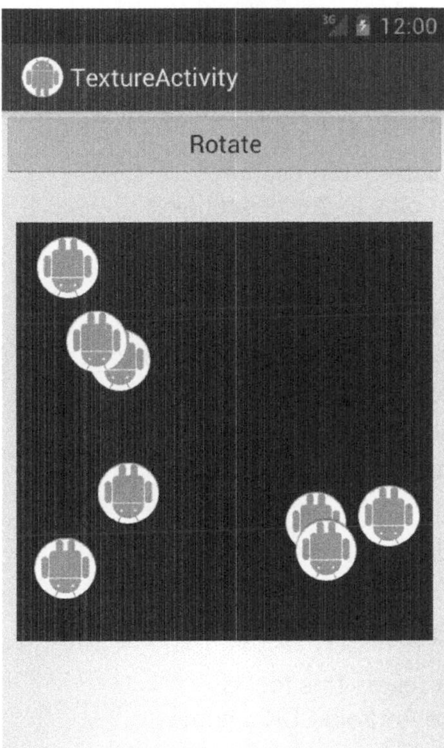

Figure 2-32. *TextureView drawing scene*

Useful Tools to Know: Hierarchy Viewer and Lint

Sometimes your app's layout can slow down the app. To help debug issues in your layout, the Android SDK provides the Hierarchy Viewer and Lint tools.

Hierarchy Viewer

Hierarchy Viewer is a GUI-based tool that lets you debug and optimize your UI. It provides a visual representation of the layout's View hierarchy (the Layout View) and a magnified inspector of the display (the Pixel Perfect View).

Running Hierarchy Viewer

Hierarchy Viewer can be run from the command line or from within Eclipse. Complete the following steps to run Hierarchy Viewer from the command line:

1. Connect your device or launch an emulator. To preserve security, Hierarchy Viewer can connect only to devices running a developer version of the Android system.

> **NOTE:** If you are testing on a device, you can grant Hierarchy Viewer discrete permission to access individual windows in your application using the open source ViewServer project developed by the UI Framework team at Google. For more information on including this in your project, visit `https://github.com/romainguy/ViewServer`

2. If you have not done so already, install the app you want to work with.
3. Run the app and ensure that its user interface is visible.
4. From your platform, launch `hierarchyviewer`. This tool is located in the `tools` subdirectory of the Android SDK's home directory.
5. The first window that you see displays a list of devices and emulators. To expand the list of activity objects for a specific device or emulator, click the arrow on the left. Doing so displays a list of the activity objects whose user interfaces are currently visible on the device or emulator. The objects are listed by their Android component names. The list includes both your app activity and system activity objects. A screenshot of this window appears in Figure 2-33.
6. Select the name of your activity from the list. You can now look at its view hierarchy via the View Hierarchy window, or you can look at a magnified image of the UI via the Pixel Perfect window.

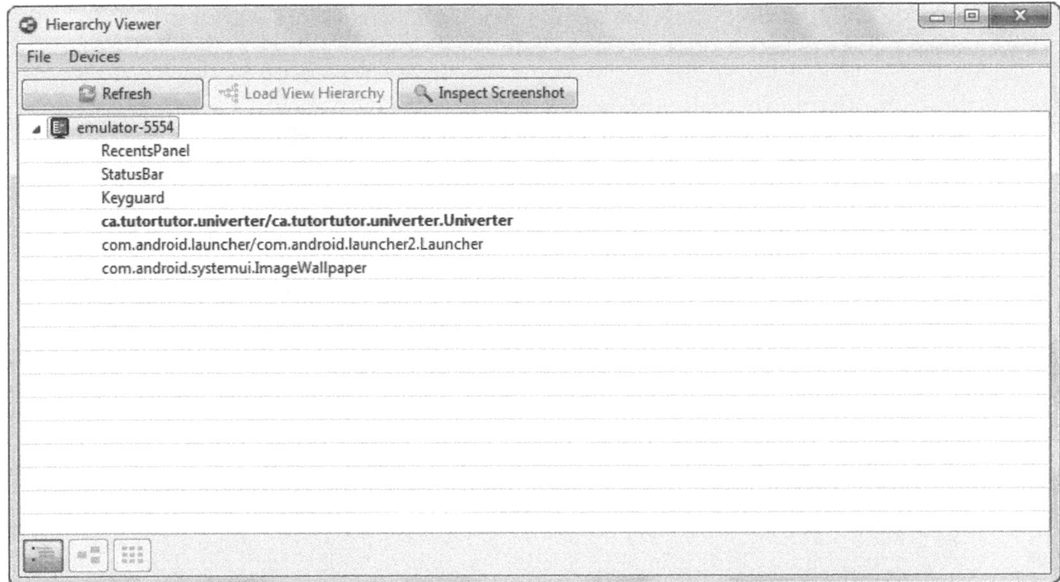

Figure 2-33. *The Hierarchy Viewer device window is your gateway to accessing the View Hierarchy and Pixel Perfect windows.*

Figure 2-33 presents Hierarchy Viewer's user interface. The menubar at the top offers File and Devices menus, with File offering About and Exit menu items, and Devices offering Refresh, Load View Hierarchy, and Inspect Screenshot menu items, which also appear on the toolbar underneath the menubar.

The device window sits beneath the toolbar and presents a hierarchy of all connected devices and emulators (only emulator-5554 is running) together with a list of all active windows on the emulator or device. The bolded entry identifies the window that is currently visible, which happens to be the `Univerter` app's activity window.

> **NOTE:** Chapter 1 introduces `Univerter`. Appendix D explores its source code, resources, and manifest.

Finally, a status bar is situated beneath the device window. The three buttons on the left let you switch between the device and the View Hierarchy and Pixel Perfect windows.

To access the View Hierarchy window for one of the active window items in the device window, select the item and click the Load View Hierarchy button.

(Alternatively, double-click the item.) Click the Inspect Screenshot button to access the bolded window's Pixel Perfect window.

Exploring the View Hierarchy Window

The View Hierarchy window displays the view objects that form the UI of the activity that is running on your device or emulator. Use this window to look at individual view objects within the context of the entire view hierarchy. For each view object, the View Hierarchy window also displays rendering performance data.

Figure 2-34 shows the View Hierarchy window for the ca.tutortutor.univerter/ca.tutortutor.univerter.Univerter entry. (The Tree View pane, which is discussed shortly, has been dragged around, and the LinearLayout node on the left of this pane has been selected.)

Figure 2-34. *The View Hierarchy window is divided into four panes.*

The View Hierarchy window is divided into four panes:

- Tree View: The left-hand pane displays the Tree View, which offers a diagram of the Activity object's hierarchy of views. Use the Tree View to examine individual view objects and see the relationships between view objects in your user interface.
  - To zoom in on the pane, use the slider at the bottom of the pane, or use your mouse scroll wheel. To move around in the pane or reveal view objects that are not currently visible, click and drag the pane.
  - To highlight the nodes in the tree whose class or ID matches a search string, enter the string in the "Filter by class or id:" textfield at the bottom of the window. The background of nodes that match the search string will change from gray to bright blue.
    To save a screenshot of the Tree View to a PNG file, click Save As PNG at the top of the View Hierarchy window. Doing so displays a dialog box in which you can choose a directory and file name.
  - To save a layered screenshot of your device or emulator to an Adobe Photoshop (PSD) file, click Capture Layers at the top of the View Hierarchy window. Doing so displays a dialog box in which you can choose a directory or file name. Each view in the user interface is saved as a separate Photoshop layer.
  - In Photoshop (or a similar program that accepts `.psd` files), you can hide, show, or edit a layer independently of others. When you save a layered screenshot, you can examine and modify the image of an individual view object, which helps you experiment with design changes.
- Tree Overview: The upper right-hand pane displays the Tree Overview, a smaller map representation of the entire Tree View window. Use Tree Overview to identify the part of the view tree that is being displayed in Tree View.
  - You can also use Tree Overview to move around in the Tree View pane. Click and drag the shaded rectangle over an area to reveal it in Tree View.

- Properties View: The middle right-hand pane displays the Properties View, a list of the properties for a selected view object. With Properties View, you can examine all properties without having to look at your app source.
  - The properties are organized by category. To find an individual property, expand a category name by clicking the arrow on its left. Doing so reveals all properties in that category.
- Layout View: The lower right-hand pane displays the Layout View, a block representation of the user interface. Layout View is another way to navigate through your user interface. When you click on a view object in Tree View, its position in the UI is highlighted. Conversely, when you click in an area of Layout View, the view object for that area is highlighted in Tree View.
  - The outline colors of blocks in Layout View provide additional information:
  - Bold red: The block represents the view that is currently selected in Tree View.
  - Light red: The block represents the parent of the block outlined in bold red.
  - White: The block represents a visible view that is not a parent or child of the view that is currently selected in Tree View.
  - Check the Show Extras check box or click the Load All Views button in the Properties View to see the actual contents of a viewgroup (such as a linear layout) in the Layout View.

When the UI of the current activity changes, the View Hierarchy window is not automatically updated. To update it, click Load View Hierarchy at the top of the window.

Also, the window is not updated when you switch to a new Activity. To update it, click the left-most (device window) icon in the bottom left-hand corner of the window, which navigates back to the device window. From this window, click the Android component name of the new activity, and then click Load View Hierarchy at the top of the window.

Working with an Individual View in Tree View

Each node in Tree View represents a single view. Some information is always visible. Starting with the selected node, you see (or do not see) the following:

- View class: The view object's class, which happens to be `LinearLayout` in Figure 2-34.
- View object address: A pointer to the view object, which happens to be @4103c250 in Figure 2-34.
- View object ID: The value of the `android:id` attribute. No ID appears in Figure 2-34 because the `<LinearLayout>` element in the `res/layout/main.xml` file (`Univerter` is running in portrait orientation) does not have an `android:id` attribute.
- Performance indicators: A set of three colored dots that indicate the rendering speed of this view relative to other view objects in the tree. The three dots represent (from left to right) the measure, layout, and draw times of the rendering.
- The colors indicate the following relative performance:
  - Green: For this part of the render time, this view is in the faster 50% of all the view objects in the tree. For example, a green dot for the measure time means that this view has a faster measure time than 50% of the view objects in the tree.
  - Yellow: For this part of the render time, this view is in the slower 50% of all the view objects in the tree. For example, a yellow dot for the layout time means that this view has a slower layout time than 50% of the view objects in the tree.
  - Red: For this part of the render time, this view is the slowest one in the tree. For example, a red dot for the draw time means that this view takes the most time to draw of all the view objects in the tree.
  - Although the selected LinearLayout node presents the performance indicators textually, it does not present any dots, which might be caused by a bug in Hierarchy Viewer.
- View index: The zero-based index of the view in its parent view. If the view is the only child, this index is 0.

When you select a node, additional information for the view appears in a small window above the node. When you click one of the nodes, you see the following:

- Image: The actual image of the view, as it would appear in the emulator. If the view has children, they are also displayed.
- View count: The number of view objects represented by this node, which includes the view itself and a count of its children. For example, this value is 4 for a view that has 3 children.
- Render times: The actual measure, layout, and draw times (in milliseconds) for the view rendering. These values correspond to the performance indicators mentioned earlier.

Debugging with View Hierarchy

The View Hierarchy window helps you debug an app by providing a static display of the user interface. The display starts with your app's opening screen. As you step through your app, the display remains unchanged until you redraw it by invalidating and then requesting layout for a view.

Complete the following steps to redraw a view:

1. Select a view in Tree View. As you move up toward the root of the tree (to the left in the Tree View), you see the highest-level view objects. Redrawing a high-level object usually forces the lower-level objects to redraw as well.
2. Click Invalidate at the top of the window. This marks the view as invalid and then schedules it for a redraw at the next point that a layout is requested.
3. Click Request Layout to request a layout. The view and its children are redrawn, as well as any other view objects that need to be redrawn.

Manually redrawing a view lets you watch the view object tree and examine the properties of individual view objects one step at a time as you go through breakpoints in your code.

Optimizing with View Hierarchy

The View Hierarchy helps you identify slow rendering performance. View nodes with red or yellow performance indicators (the three dots) to identify slower view objects in terms of the amount of time to measure, layout, and draw.

Remember that slow performance is not necessarily evidence of a problem, especially for ViewGroup objects. View objects that have more children, and more complex view objects, will render more slowly.

Exploring the Pixel Perfect Window

The Pixel Perfect window displays a magnified image of the screen that is currently visible on the emulator or device. You can examine the properties of individual pixels in the screen image. You can also use the Pixel Perfect window to help you lay out your app's UI based on a bitmap design.

Figure 2-35 shows the ca.tutortutor.univerter/ca.tutortutor.univerter.Univerter entry's Pixel Perfect window.

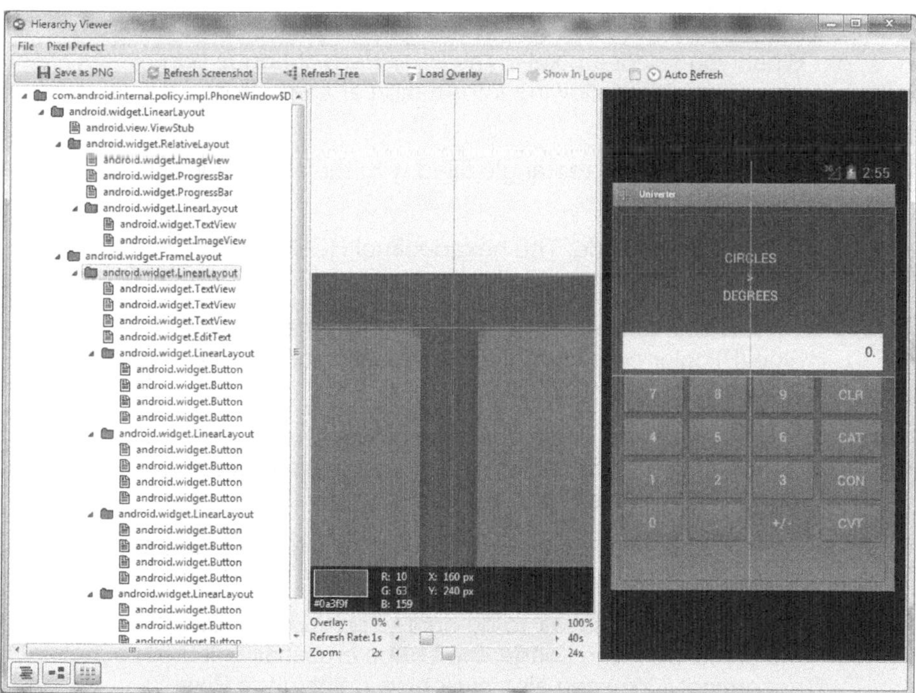

Figure 2-35. *The Pixel Perfect window is divided into three panes.*

The Pixel Perfect window is divided into three panes:

- View Object: This is a hierarchical list of the view objects that are currently visible on the device or emulator screen, including the ones in your app and the ones generated by the system. The objects are listed by their view class. To see the class names of a view object's children, expand the view by clicking the arrow to its left. When you click a view, its position is highlighted in the Pixel Perfect pane on the right.
- Pixel Perfect Loupe: This is the magnified screen image. It is overlaid by a grid in which each square represents one pixel. To look at the information for a pixel, click in its square. Its color and x/y coordinates appear at the bottom of the pane.
  - The magenta crosshair in this pane corresponds to the positioning crosshair in the next pane. It only moves when you move the crosshair in the next pane.
  - To zoom in or out on the image, use the Zoom slider at the bottom of this pane, or use your mouse's scroll wheel.
  - When you select a pixel in the Pixel Perfect Loupe pane, you will see the following information at the bottom of this pane:
  - Pixel swatch: A rectangle filled with the same color as the pixel.
  - HTML color code: The hexadecimal RGB code corresponding to the pixel color.
  - RGB color values: A list of the red (R), green (G), and blue (B) color components of the pixel color. Each value ranges from 0 through 255.
  - X and Y coordinates: The pixel's coordinates, in device-specific pixel units. The values are zero-based, with X = 0 at the left of the screen and Y = 0 at the top.
- Pixel Perfect: This pane displays the currently visible screen as it would appear in the emulator.
  - Use the cyan crosshair to do coarse positioning. Drag the crosshair in the image; the Loupe crosshair will move accordingly. You can also click on a point in the Pixel Perfect pane, and the crosshair will move to that point.

- The image corresponding to the view object selected in the View Object pane is outlined in a box that indicates the view object's position on the screen. For the selected object, the box is bold red. Sibling and parent view objects have a light red box. View objects that are neither parents nor siblings are colored white.
- The layout box may have other rectangles on the inside or outside; each rectangle indicates part of the view. A purple or green rectangle indicates the view bounding box. A white or black box inside the layout box represents the padding, the defined distance between the view object's content and its bounding box. An outer white or black rectangle represents the margins, the distance between the view bounding box and adjacent view objects. The padding and margin boxes are colored white when the layout background is black, and they are colored black when the layout background is white.
- You can save the screen image being displayed in the Pixel Perfect pane as a PNG file. Doing so creates a screenshot of the current screen. To accomplish this task, click Save as PNG at the top of the window. A dialog box appears in which you can choose a directory and file name.

The panes are not automatically refreshed when you change one of the view objects or go to another activity. To refresh the Pixel Perfect and Loupe panes, click Refresh Screenshot at the top of the window. Clicking this button changes the panes to reflect the current screen image. You still might need to refresh the View Object pane. Accomplish this task by clicking Refresh Tree at the top of the window.

To automatically refresh the panes while debugging, check the Auto Refresh check box at the top of the window and then set a refresh rate with the Refresh Rate slider at the bottom of the Loupe pane.

Working with Pixel Perfect Overlays

You often construct a UI based on a design done as a bitmap image. The Pixel Perfect window helps you match up your view layout to a bitmap image by allowing you to load the bitmap as an overlay on the screen image.

Complete the following steps to use a bitmap image as an overlay:

1. Start your app in a device or emulator, and navigate to the activity whose UI you want to work with.
2. Start Hierarchy Viewer and navigate to the Pixel Perfect window.
3. At the top of the window, click Load Overlay. A dialog box opens, prompting for the image file to load. Load the image file.
4. Pixel Perfect displays the overlay over the screen image in the Pixel Perfect pane. The lower-left corner of the bitmap image (X = 0, Y = max value) is anchored on the lower-leftmost pixel (X = 0, Y = max screen) of the screen.
5. By default, the overlay has a 50% transparency, which lets you see the screen image underneath. You can adjust this with the Overlay slider at the bottom of the Loupe pane.
6. Also by default, the overlay is not displayed in the Loupe pane. To display it, set Show In Loupe at the top of the window.

The overlay is not saved as part of the screenshot when you save the screen image as a PNG file.

Lint

Lint is a static code-scanning tool that helps you optimize the layouts and layout hierarchies of your apps, as well as to detect other common coding problems. You can run this tool against your layout files or resource directories to quickly check for inefficiencies or other types of problems that could be affecting the performance of your app.

> **NOTE:** Poorly structured code can impact the reliability and efficiency of your Android apps and make your code harder to maintain. For example, unused namespaces in your XML resource files take up space and incur unnecessary processing. Other structural issues, such as the use of deprecated elements or API calls that are not supported by the target API versions, might lead to code failing to run correctly.

Each problem detected by Lint is reported with a description message and a severity level so that you can quickly prioritize the critical improvements that need to be made. You can also configure a problem's severity level to ignore issues that are not relevant for your project or that raise the severity level. The tool has a command-line interface, so you can easily integrate it into your automated testing process.

Figure 2-36 shows how Lint processes app source files.

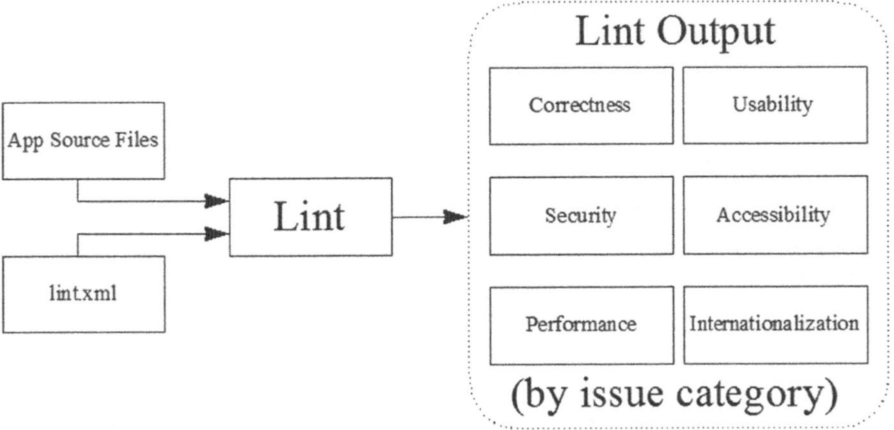

Figure 2-36. *Code scanning workflow with lint.*

Figure 2-36 presents the following components:

- App source files: Source files consisting of files that make up your Android project, including Java and XML files, icons, and ProGuard configuration files.
- lint.xml: A configuration file that you can use to specify any lint checks that you want to exclude and to customize problem severity levels.
- Lint: A static code-scanning tool that you can run on your Android project from the command line or from Eclipse. Lint checks for structural code problems that could affect the quality and performance of your Android app. It is strongly recommended that you correct any errors that Lint detects before publishing your app.
- Lint Output: You can view Lint's results at the console or in the Lint Warnings view in Eclipse. Each issue is identified by the location in the source file where it occurred and by a description.

Running Lint

Lint can be run from the command line or from within Eclipse. In the former case, specify `lint` (located in the `tools` subdirectory of the Android SDK's home directory) followed by a project directory. For example, assuming that the current directory contains the `Univerter` project directory, execute the following command:

```
lint Univerter
```

`Lint` generates output that starts with the following line:

```
Scanning Univerter: ................
```

If the project directory does not contain a `bin` subdirectory, you should then observe the following output (split across two lines for readability):

```
Univerter: Error: No .class files were found in project "Univerter", so none of
the classfile based checks could be run. Does the project need to be built
first?
```

You should then observe output similar to that shown below (split across multiple lines for readability):

```
res\layout-land\main.xml:9: Warning: This text field does not specify an
inputType or a hint [TextFields]
  <EditText android:id="@+id/display"
  ^
res\layout\main.xml:25: Warning: This text field does not specify an
inputType or a hint [TextFields]
  <EditText android:id="@+id/display"
  ^
res\layout\info.xml:7: Warning: [Accessibility] Missing contentDescription
attribute on image [ContentDescription]
  <ImageView android:id="@+id/image"
  ^
res\layout-land\main.xml:14: Warning: [I18N] Hardcoded string "0.", should
use @string resource [HardcodedText]
            android:text="0."
            ^
res\layout\main.xml:16: Warning: [I18N] Hardcoded string ">", should use
@string resource [HardcodedText]
            android:text=">"
            ^
res\layout\main.xml:30: Warning: [I18N] Hardcoded string "0.", should use
@string resource [HardcodedText]
            android:text="0."
            ^
0 errors, 6 warnings
```

This output reveals six warnings about the `Univerter` project. The first two warnings have to do with the `<EditText>` tag in each of the `res/layout/main.xml` and `res/layout-land/main.xml` files. This tag does not have an `android:inputType` or an `android:hint` attribute.

The `android:inputType` attribute identifies the type of data being entered into a textfield, whereas the `android:hint` attribute specifies hint text to display when this field is empty. The former attribute is not present because the user is not allowed to enter data from the keyboard into the textfield. The latter attribute is not present because the textfield is never empty.

Although the absence of these attributes does not cause a problem, good form would suggest including `android:inputType="text"` in the `<EditText>` tag of each `main.xml` file. Consider it an exercise to make this change.

The third warning addresses the absence of an `android:contentDescription` attribute on the `<ImageView>` tag in the `res/layout/info.xml` file. This attribute defines text that briefly describes the content of nontext views (such as image views). This property is used primarily for accessibility. Consider adding this attribute to `<ImageView>`, as in `android:contentDescription="@string/desc"`, where `strings.xml` contains a `<string>` element named `desc`.

The final three warnings address hard-coded text in the `res/layout/main.xml` and `res/layout-land/main.xml` files. The "`0.`" and "`>`" text is hardcoded here (and "`0.`", along with the "`%,.8f`" format string, is encoded in `Univerter.java`) to get you thinking about how far to localize an app.

Should "`0.`" be localized or not? That depends on how many locales you want to support. For example, if you plan to support the input of Arabic digits, you will have to localize this text.

Should "`%,.8f`" be localized? Again, the answer depends on how many locales you want to support. For example, Spanish uses a comma character for the decimal point and the decimal point character for the thousands separator. In this case, you will want to look into the `java.util.DateFormat` class to learn how to format a string for the current locale.

As an exercise, introduce string resources into `res/values/strings.xml` for the "`0.`" and "`>`" literal text, and add references to these resources in the `main.xml` files. Then, rerun Lint and discover whether or not you still get these warning messages.

By default, `Lint` searches for every possible kind of problem. However, you can narrow the search by specifying the `--check` option followed by a comma-separated list of issue categories and IDs. (Execute `lint --list` to obtain this list.)

For example, execute the following command to check for contentDescription omissions:

```
lint --check contentDescription Univerter
```

This command results in a single warning message:

```
Scanning Univerter: .....
res\layout\info.xml:7: Warning: [Accessibility] Missing contentDescription
attribute on image [ContentDescription]
  <ImageView android:id="@+id/image"
  ^
0 errors, 1 warnings
```

Now execute the following command to check for contentDescription omissions and hard-coded text:

```
lint --check contentDescription,HardcodedText Univerter
```

This command results in four warning messages:

```
Scanning Univerter: .....
res\layout\info.xml:7: Warning: [Accessibility] Missing contentDescription
attribute on image [ContentDescription]
  <ImageView android:id="@+id/image"
  ^
res\layout-land\main.xml:14: Warning: [I18N] Hardcoded string "0.", should use
@string resource [HardcodedText]
            android:text="0."
            ^
res\layout\main.xml:16: Warning: [I18N] Hardcoded string ">", should use
@string resource [HardcodedText]
            android:text=">"
            ^
res\layout\main.xml:30: Warning: [I18N] Hardcoded string "0.", should use
@string resource [HardcodedText]
            android:text="0."
            ^
0 errors, 4 warnings
```

> **NOTE:** For more information on Lint, check out Google's "Improving Your Code with lint" page (http://developer.android.com/tools/debugging/improving-w-lint.html). Also, you might want to check out the "Android Lint" page (http://tools.android.com/tips/lint/) at the Android Tools Project Site.

Summary

As you have seen, Android provides some very flexible and extensible UI tools in the provided SDK. Properly using these tools means you can be free of worrying whether or not your application will look and feel the same across the broad range of devices running Android today.

In this chapter, we explored how to use Android's resource framework to supply resources for multiple devices. You saw techniques for manipulating static images as well as creating Drawables of your own. We looked at overriding the default behavior of the window decorations as well as system input methods. We looked at ways to add user value through animating views. Finally we extended the default toolkit by creating new custom controls and customizing the AdapterViews used to display sets of data.

In the next chapter, we will look at using the SDK to communicate with the outside world by accessing network resources and talking to other devices.

Chapter 3

Communications and Networking

The key to many successful mobile applications is their ability to connect and interact with remote data sources. Web services and APIs are abundant in today's world, allowing an application to interact with just about any service, from weather forecasts to personal financial information. Bringing this data into the palm of a user's hand and making it accessible from anywhere is one of the greatest powers of the mobile platform. Android builds on the Web foundations that Google is known for and provides a rich toolset for communicating with the outside world.

3–1. Displaying Web Information

Problem

HTML or image data from the Web needs to be presented in the application without any modification or processing.

Solution

(API Level 1)

Display the information in a `WebView`. `WebView` is a view widget that can be embedded in any layout to display web content, both local and remote, in your application. WebView is based on the same open source WebKit technology that powers the Android Browser application, affording applications the same level of power and capability.

How It Works

WebView has some very desirable properties when displaying assets downloaded from the Web , not the least of which are two-dimensional scrolling (horizontal and vertical at the same time) and zoom controls. A WebView can be the perfect place to house a large image, such as a stadium map, in which the user may want to pan and zoom around. Here we will discuss how to do this with both local and remote assets.

Display a URL

The simplest case is displaying an HTML page or image by supplying the URL of the resource to the WebView. The following are a handful of practical uses for this technique in your applications:

- Provide access to your corporate site without leaving the application.
- Display a page of live content from a web server, such as an FAQ section, that can be changed without requiring an upgrade to the application.
- Display a large image resource that the user would want to interact with using pan/zoom.

Let's take a look at a simple example that loads a very popular web page inside the content view of an Activity instead of within the browser (see Listings 3-1 and 3-2).

Listing 3-1. *Activity Containing a WebView*

```
public class MyActivity extends Activity {
    @Override
    public void onCreate(Bundle savedInstanceState) {
        super.onCreate(savedInstanceState);

        WebView webview = new WebView(this);
        //Enable JavaScript support
        webview.getSettings().setJavaScriptEnabled(true);
        webview.loadUrl("http://www.google.com/");
```

```
        setContentView(webview);
    }
}
```

> **NOTE:** By default, WebView has JavaScript support disabled. Be sure to enable JavaScript in the WebView.WebSettings object if the content you are displaying requires it.

Listing 3-2. *AndroidManifest.xml Setting The Required Permissions*

```
<?xml version="1.0" encoding="utf-8"?>
<manifest xmlns:android="http://schemas.android.com/apk/res/android"
      package="com.examples.webview"
      android:versionCode="1"
      android:versionName="1.0">
    <application android:icon="@drawable/icon"
        android:label="@string/app_name">
        <activity android:name=".MyActivity">
            <intent-filter>
                <action android:name="android.intent.action.MAIN" />
                <category android:name="android.intent.category.LAUNCHER" />
            </intent-filter>
        </activity>
    </application>
    <uses-permission android:name="android.permission.INTERNET" />
</manifest>
```

> **IMPORTANT:** If the content you are loading into WebView is remote, AndroidManifest.xml must declare that it uses the android.permission.INTERNET permission.

The result displays the HTML page in your Activity (see Figure 3-1).

Figure 3-1. *HTML page in a WebView.*

Local Assets

`WebView` is also quite useful in displaying local content to take advantage of either HTML/CSS formatting or the pan/zoom behavior it provides to its contents. You may use the `assets` directory of your Android project to store resources you would like to display in a `WebView`, such as large images or HTML files. To better organize the assets, you may also create subdirectories under `assets` to store files in.

`WebView.loadUrl()` can display files stored under `assets` by using the *file:///android_asset/<resource path>* URL schema. For example, if the file `android.jpg` was placed into the `assets` directory, it could be loaded into a `WebView` using

```
file:///android_asset/android.jpg
```

If that same file were placed in a directory named `images` under `assets`, `WebView` could load it with the following URL:

```
file:///android_asset/images/android.jpg
```

In addition, WebView.loadData() will load raw HTML stored in a string resource or variable into the view. Using this technique, preformatted HTML text could be stored in res/values/strings.xml or downloaded from a remote API and displayed in the application.

Listings 3-3 and 3-4 show an example Activity with two WebView widgets stacked vertically on top of one another. The upper view is displaying a large image file stored in the assets directory, and the lower view is displaying an HTML string stored in the application's string resources.

Listing 3-3. *res/layout/main.xml*

```
<LinearLayout xmlns:android="http://schemas.android.com/apk/res/android"
  android:layout_width="fill_parent"
  android:layout_height="fill_parent"
  android:orientation="vertical">
  <WebView
    android:id="@+id/upperview"
    android:layout_width="fill_parent"
    android:layout_height="fill_parent"
    android:layout_weight="1"
  />
  <WebView
    android:id="@+id/lowerview"
    android:layout_width="fill_parent"
    android:layout_height="fill_parent"
    android:layout_weight="1"
  />
</LinearLayout>
```

Listing 3-4. *Activity to Display Local Web Content*

```
public class MyActivity extends Activity {
    @Override
    public void onCreate(Bundle savedInstanceState) {
        super.onCreate(savedInstanceState);
        setContentView(R.layout.main);

        WebView upperView = (WebView)findViewById(R.id.upperview);
        //Zoom feature must be enabled
        upperView.getSettings().setBuiltInZoomControls(true);
        upperView.loadUrl("file:///android_asset/android.jpg");

        WebView lowerView = (WebView)findViewById(R.id.lowerview);
        String htmlString = "<h1>Header</h1><p>This is HTML text<br />"
                + "<i>Formatted in italics</i></p>";
        lowerView.loadData(htmlString, "text/html", "utf-8");
    }
}
```

When the Activity is displayed, each `WebView` occupies half of the screen's vertical space. The HTML string is formatted as expected, while the large image can be scrolled both horizontally and vertically; the user may even zoom in or out (see Figure 3-2).

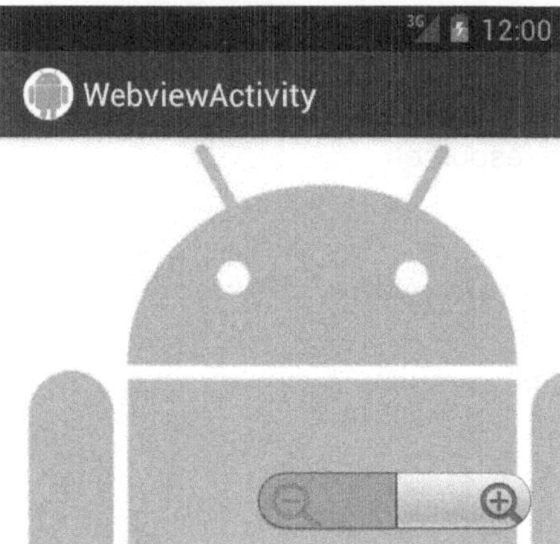

Figure 3-2. *Two WebViews displaying local resources.*

3–2. Intercepting WebView Events

Problem

Your application is using a `WebView` to display content, but it also needs to listen and respond to users clicking links on the page.

Solution

(API Level 1)

Implement a WebViewClient and attach it to the WebView. WebViewClient and WebChromeClient are two WebKit classes that allow an application to get event callbacks and customize the behavior of the WebView. By default, WebView will pass a URL to the ActivityManager to be handled if no WebViewClient is present, which usually results in any clicked link loading in the Browser application instead of the current WebView.

How It Works

In Listing 3-5, we create an Activity with a WebView that will handle its own URL loading.

Listing 3-5. *Activity with a WebView That Handles URLs*

```
public class MyActivity extends Activity {
    @Override
    public void onCreate(Bundle savedInstanceState) {
        super.onCreate(savedInstanceState);

        WebView webview = new WebView(this);
        webview.getSettings().setJavaScriptEnabled(true);
        //Add a client to the view
        webview.setWebViewClient(new WebViewClient());
        webview.loadUrl("http://www.google.com");
        setContentView(webview);
    }
}
```

In this example, simply providing a plain vanilla WebViewClient to WebView allows it to handle any URL requests itself, instead of passing them up to the ActivityManager, so clicking on a link will load the requested page inside the same view. This is because the default implementation simply returns false for shouldOverrideUrlLoading(), which tells the client to pass the URL to the WebView and not to the application.

In this next case, we will take advantage of the WebViewClient.shouldOverrideUrlLoading() callback to intercept and monitor user activity (see Listing 3-6).

Listing 3-6. *Activity That Intercepts WebView URLs*

```
public class MyActivity extends Activity {
    @Override
    public void onCreate(Bundle savedInstanceState) {
        super.onCreate(savedInstanceState);

        WebView webview = new WebView(this);
        webview.getSettings().setJavaScriptEnabled(true);
        //Add a client to the view
        webview.setWebViewClient(mClient);
        webview.loadUrl("http://www.google.com");
        setContentView(webview);
    }

    private WebViewClient mClient = new WebViewClient() {
        @Override
        public boolean shouldOverrideUrlLoading(WebView view, String url) {
            Uri request = Uri.parse(url);

            if(TextUtils.equals(request.getAuthority(), "www.google.com")) {
                //Allow the load
                return false;
            }

            Toast.makeText(MyActivity.this, "Sorry, buddy", Toast.LENGTH_SHORT)
                .show();
            return true;
        }
    };
}
```

In this example, `shouldOverrideUrlLoading()` determines whether to load the content back in this `WebView` based on the URL it was passed, keeping the user from leaving Google's site. `Uri.getAuthority()` returns the hostname portion of a URL, and we use that to check if the link the user clicked is on Google's domain (www.google.com). If we can verify the link is to another Google page, returning false allows the `WebView` to load the content. If not, we notify the user and, returning true, tell the `WebViewClient` that the application has taken care of this URL and not to allow the `WebView` to load it.

This technique can be more sophisticated, where the application actually handles the URL by doing something interesting. A custom schema could even be developed to create a full interface between your application and the `WebView` content.

3–3. Accessing WebView with JavaScript

Problem

Your application needs access to the raw HTML of the current contents displayed in a WebView, either to read or modify specific values.

Solution

(API Level 1)

Create a JavaScript interface to bridge between the WebView and application code.

How It Works

WebView.addJavascriptInterface() binds a Java object to JavaScript so that its methods can then be called within the WebView. Using this interface, JavaScript can be used to marshal data between your application code and the WebView's HTML.

> **CAUTION:** Allowing JavaScript to control your application can inherently present a security threat, allowing remote execution of application code. This interface should be utilized with that possibility in mind.

Let's look at an example of this in action. Listing 3-7 presents a simple HTML form to be loaded into the WebView from the local assets directory. Listing 3-8 is an Activity that uses two JavaScript functions to exchange data between the Activity preferences and content in the WebView.

Listing 3-7. *assets/form.html*

```
<!DOCTYPE HTML PUBLIC "-//W3C//DTD HTML 4.01//EN"
    "http://www.w3.org/TR/html4/strict.dtd">
<html>
<form name="input" action="form.html" method="get">
Enter Email: <input type="text" id="emailAddress" />
<input type="submit" value="Submit" />
</form>
</html>
```

Listing 3-8. *Activity with JavaScript Bridge Interface*

```
public class MyActivity extends Activity {
    @Override
    public void onCreate(Bundle savedInstanceState) {
        super.onCreate(savedInstanceState);

        WebView webview = new WebView(this);
        webview.getSettings().setJavaScriptEnabled(true);
        webview.setWebViewClient(mClient);
        //Attach the custom interface to the view
        webview.addJavascriptInterface(new MyJavaScriptInterface(), "BRIDGE");

        setContentView(webview);
        //Load the form
        webview.loadUrl("file:///android_asset/form.html");
    }

    private static final String JS_SETELEMENT =
        "javascript:document.getElementById('%s').value='%s'";
    private static final String JS_GETELEMENT =
  "javascript:window.BRIDGE.storeElement('%s',document.getElementById('%s').value)";
    private static final String ELEMENTID = "emailAddress";

    private WebViewClient mClient = new WebViewClient() {
        @Override
        public boolean shouldOverrideUrlLoading(WebView view, String url) {
            //Before leaving the page, attempt to get the email via JavaScript
            view.loadUrl(String.format(JS_GETELEMENT, ELEMENTID, ELEMENTID));
            return false;
        }

        @Override
        public void onPageFinished(WebView view, String url) {
            //When page loads, inject address into page using JavaScript
            SharedPreferences prefs = getPreferences(Activity.MODE_PRIVATE);
            view.loadUrl(String.format(JS_SETELEMENT, ELEMENTID,
                prefs.getString(ELEMENTID, "")));
        }
    };

    private class MyJavaScriptInterface {
        //Store an element in preferences
        @SuppressWarnings("unused")
        public void storeElement(String id, String element) {
            SharedPreferences.Editor edit =
                getPreferences(Activity.MODE_PRIVATE).edit();
            edit.putString(id, element);
            edit.commit();
            //If element is valid, raise a Toast
```

```
            if(!TextUtils.isEmpty(element)) {
                Toast.makeText(MyActivity.this, element, Toast.LENGTH_SHORT)
                    .show();
            }
        }
    }
}
```

In this somewhat contrived example, a single element form is created in HTML and displayed in a WebView. In the Activity code, we look for a form value in the WebView with the ID of "emailAddress," and its value is saved to SharedPreferences every time a link is clicked on the page (in this case, the submit button of the form) through the shouldOverrideUrlLoading() callback. Whenever the page finished loading (i.e., onPageFinished() is called), we attempt to inject the current value from SharedPreferences back into the web form.

A Java class is created called MyJavaScriptInterface, which defines the method storeElement(). When the view is created, we call the WebView.addJavascriptInterface() method to attach this object to the view and give it the name BRIDGE. When calling this method, the string parameter is a name used to reference the interface inside of JavaScript code.

We have defined two JavaScript methods as constant strings here: JS_GETELEMENT and JS_SETELEMENT. These methods are executed on the WebView by being passed to. loadUrl(). Notice that JS_GETELEMENT is a reference to calling our custom interface function (referenced as BRIDGE.storeElement), which will call that method on MyJavaScriptInterface and store the form element's value in preferences. If the value retrieved from the form is not blank, a Toast will also be raised.

Any JavaScript may be executed on the WebView in this manner, and it does not need to be a method included as part of the custom interface. JS_SETELEMENT, for example, uses pure JavaScript to set the value of the form element on the page.

One popular application of this technique is to remember form data that a user may need to enter in the application, but the form must be web-based, such as a reservation form or payment form for a web application that doesn't have a lower-level API to access.

3–4. Downloading an Image File

Problem

Your application needs to download and display an image from the Web or another remote server.

Solution

(API Level 3)

Use AsyncTask to download the data in a background thread. AsyncTask is a wrapper class that makes threading long-running operations into the background painless and simple; it also manages concurrency with an internal thread pool. In addition to handling the background threading, callback methods are also provided before, during, and after the operation executes, allowing you to make any updates required on the main UI thread.

How It Works

In the context of downloading an image, let's create a subclass of ImageView called WebImageView, which will lazily load an image from a remote source and display it as soon as it is available. The downloading will be performed inside of an AsyncTask operation (see Listing 3-9).

Listing 3-9. *WebImageView*

```
public class WebImageView extends ImageView {

    private Drawable mPlaceholder, mImage;

    public WebImageView(Context context) {
        this(context, null);
    }

    public WebImageView(Context context, AttributeSet attrs) {
        this(context, attrs, 0);
    }

    public WebImageView(Context context, AttributeSet attrs, int defStyle) {
        super(context, attrs, defaultStyle);
    }
```

```
    public void setPlaceholderImage(Drawable drawable) {
        mPlaceholder = drawable;
        if(mImage == null) {
            setImageDrawable(mPlaceholder);
        }
    }

    public void setPlaceholderImage(int resid) {
        mPlaceholder = getResources().getDrawable(resid);
        if(mImage == null) {
            setImageDrawable(mPlaceholder);
        }
    }

    public void setImageUrl(String url) {
        DownloadTask task = new DownloadTask();
        task.execute(url);
    }

    private class DownloadTask extends AsyncTask<String, Void, Bitmap> {
        @Override
        protected Bitmap doInBackground(String... params) {
            String url = params[0];
            try {
                URLConnection connection = (new URL(url)).openConnection();
                InputStream is = connection.getInputStream();
                BufferedInputStream bis = new BufferedInputStream(is);

                ByteArrayBuffer baf = new ByteArrayBuffer(50);
                int current = 0;
                while ((current = bis.read()) != -1) {
                    baf.append((byte)current);
                }
                byte[] imageData = baf.toByteArray();
                return BitmapFactory.decodeByteArray(imageData, 0,
                        imageData.length);
            } catch (Exception exc) {
                return null;
            }
        }

        @Override
        protected void onPostExecute(Bitmap result) {
            mImage = new BitmapDrawable(result);
            if(mImage != null) {
                setImageDrawable(mImage);
            }
        }
    };
}
```

As you can see, WebImageView is a simple extension of the Android ImageView widget. The setPlaceholderImage() methods allow a local drawable to be set as the display image until the remote content is finished downloading. The bulk of the interesting work begins once the view has been given a remote URL using setImageUrl(), at which point the custom AsyncTask begins work.

Notice that an AsyncTask is strongly typed with three values for the input parameter, progress value, and result. In this case, a string is passed to the task's execute method and the background operation should return a Bitmap. The middle value, the progress, we are not using in this example, so it is set as Void. When extending AsyncTask, the only required method to implement is doInBackground(), which defines the chunk of work to be run on a background thread. In the previous example, this is where a connection is made to the remote URL provided and the image is downloaded. Upon completion, we attempt to create a Bitmap from the downloaded data. If an error occurs at any point, the operation will abort and return null.

The other callback methods defined in AsyncTask, such as onPreExecute(), onPostExecute(), and onProgressUpdate(), are called on the main thread for the purposes of updating the user interface. In the previous example, onPostExecute() is used to update the view's image with the result data.

> **IMPORTANT:** Android UI classes are not thread-safe. Be sure to use one of the callback methods that occur on the main thread to make any updates to the UI. Do not update views from within doInBackground().

Listings 3-10 and 3-11 show simple examples of using this class in an Activity. Because this class is not part of the android.widget or android.view packages, we must write the fully qualified package name when using it in XML.

Listing 3-10. *res/layout/main.xml*

```
<?xml version="1.0" encoding="utf-8"?>
<LinearLayout xmlns:android="http://schemas.android.com/apk/res/android"
  android:layout_width="fill_parent"
  android:layout_height="fill_parent"
  android:orientation="vertical">
  <com.examples.WebImageView
    android:id="@+id/webImage"
    android:layout_width="wrap_content"
    android:layout_height="wrap_content"
  />
</LinearLayout>
```

Listing 3-11. *Example Activity*

```
public class WebImageActivity extends Activity {
    @Override
    public void onCreate(Bundle savedInstanceState) {
        super.onCreate(savedInstanceState);
        setContentView(R.layout.main);

        WebImageView imageView = (WebImageView)findViewById(R.id.webImage);
        imageView.setPlaceholderImage(R.drawable.icon);
        imageView.setImageUrl(
                "http://apress.com/resource/weblogo/Apress_120x90.gif");
    }
}
```

In this example we first set a local image (the application icon) as the `WebImageView` placeholder. This image is displayed immediately to the user. We then tell the view to fetch an image of the Apress logo from the Web. As noted previously, this downloads the image in the background and, when it is complete, replaces the placeholder image in the view. It is this simplicity in creating background operations that has led the Android team to refer to `AsyncTask` as "painless threading."

3–5. Downloading Completely in the Background

Problem

The application must download a large resource to the device, such as a movie file, that must not require the user to keep the application active.

Solution

(API Level 9)

Use the `DownloadManager` API. The `DownloadManager` is a service added to the SDK with API Level 9 that allows a long-running download to be handed off and managed completely by the system. The primary advantage of using this service is that `DownloadManager` will continue attempting to download the resource despite failures, connection changes, and even device reboots.

How It Works

Listing 3-12 is a sample Activity that makes use of DownloadManager to handle the download of a large image file. When complete, the image is displayed in an ImageView. Whenever you utilize DownloadManager to access content from the Web, be sure to declare you are using the android.permission.INTERNET in the application's manifest.

Listing 3-12. *DownloadManager Sample Activity*

```
public class DownloadActivity extends Activity {

    private static final String DL_ID = "downloadId";
    private SharedPreferences prefs;

    private DownloadManager dm;
    private ImageView imageView;

    @Override
    public void onCreate(Bundle savedInstanceState) {
        super.onCreate(savedInstanceState);
        imageView = new ImageView(this);
        setContentView(imageView);

        prefs = PreferenceManager.getDefaultSharedPreferences(this);
        dm = (DownloadManager)getSystemService(DOWNLOAD_SERVICE);
    }

    @Override
    public void onResume() {
        super.onResume();

        if(!prefs.contains(DL_ID)) {
            //Start the download
            Uri resource = Uri.parse("http://www.bigfoto.com/dog-animal.jpg");
            DownloadManager.Request request =
                    new DownloadManager.Request(resource);
            //Set allowed connections to process download
            request.setAllowedNetworkTypes(Request.NETWORK_MOBILE |
                Request.NETWORK_WIFI);
            request.setAllowedOverRoaming(false);
            //Display in the notification bar
            request.setTitle("Download Sample");
            long id = dm.enqueue(request);
            //Save the unique id
            prefs.edit().putLong(DL_ID, id).commit();
        } else {
            //Download already started, check status
            queryDownloadStatus();
```

```
        }

        registerReceiver(receiver,
            new IntentFilter(DownloadManager.ACTION_DOWNLOAD_COMPLETE));
    }

    @Override
    public void onPause() {
        super.onPause();
        unregisterReceiver(receiver);
    }

    private BroadcastReceiver receiver = new BroadcastReceiver() {
        @Override
        public void onReceive(Context context, Intent intent) {
            queryDownloadStatus();
        }
    };

    private void queryDownloadStatus() {
        DownloadManager.Query query = new DownloadManager.Query();
        query.setFilterById(prefs.getLong(DL_ID, 0));
        Cursor c = dm.query(query);
        if(c.moveToFirst()) {
            int status =
                c.getInt(c.getColumnIndex(DownloadManager.COLUMN_STATUS));
            switch(status) {
            case DownloadManager.STATUS_PAUSED:
            case DownloadManager.STATUS_PENDING:
            case DownloadManager.STATUS_RUNNING:
                //Do nothing, still in progress
                break;
            case DownloadManager.STATUS_SUCCESSFUL:
                //Done, display the image
                try {
                    ParcelFileDescriptor file =
                        dm.openDownloadedFile(prefs.getLong(DL_ID, 0));
                    FileInputStream fis =
                        new ParcelFileDescriptor.AutoCloseInputStream(file);
                    imageView.setImageBitmap(BitmapFactory.decodeStream(fis));
                } catch (Exception e) {
                    e.printStackTrace();
                }
                break;
            case DownloadManager.STATUS_FAILED:
                //Clear the download and try again later
                dm.remove(prefs.getLong(DL_ID, 0));
                prefs.edit().clear().commit();
                break;
            }
```

```
        }
    }
}
```

> **IMPORTANT:** As of this book's publishing date, there is a bug in the SDK that throws an `Exception` claiming `android.permission.ACCESS_ALL_DOWNLOADS` is required to use `DownloadManager`. This `Exception` is actually thrown when `android.permission.INTERNET` is not in your manifest.

This example does all of its useful work in the `Activity.onResume()` method so the application can determine the status of the download each time the user returns to the Activity. Downloads within the manager can be references using a long ID value that is returned when `DownloadManager.enqueue()` is called. In the example, we persist that value in the application's preferences in order to monitor and retrieve the downloaded content at any time.

Upon the first launch of the example application, a `DownloadManager.Request` object is created to represent the content to download. At a minimum, this request needs the `Uri` of the remote resource. However, there are many useful properties to set on the request as well to control its behavior. Some of the useful properties include the following:

- Request.setAllowedNetworkTypes(): Set specific network types over which the download may be retrieved.
- Request.setAllowedOverRoaming(): Set if the download is allowed to occur while the device is on a roaming connection.
- Request.setDescription(): Set a description to be displayed in the system notification for the download.
- Request.setTitle(): Set a title to be displayed in the system notification for the download.

Once an ID has been obtained, the application uses that value to check the status of the download. By registering a `BroadcastReceiver` to listen for the `ACTION_DOWNLOAD_COMPLETE` broadcast, the application will react to the download finishing by setting the image file on the Activity's `ImageView`. If the Activity is paused while the download completes, upon the next resume the status will be checked and the `ImageView` content will be set.

It is important to note that the `ACTION_DOWNLOAD_COMPLETE` is a broadcast sent by the `DownloadManager` for every download it may be managing. Because of this, we still must check that the download ID we are interested in is really ready.

Destinations

In Listing 3-12, we never told the `DownloadManager` where to place the file. Instead, when we wanted to access the file we used the `DownloadManager.openDownloadedFile()` method with the ID value stored in preferences to get a `ParcelFileDescriptor`, which can be turned into a stream the application can read from. This is a simple and straightforward way to gain access to the downloaded content, but it has some caveats to be aware of.

Without a specific destination, files are downloaded to the shared download cache, where the system retains the right to delete them at any time to reclaim space. Because of this, downloading in this fashion is a convenient way to get data quickly, but if your needs for the download are more long term, a permanent destination should be specific on external storage by using one of the `DownloadManager.Request` methods:

- Request.setDestinationInExternalFilesDir(): Set the destination to a hidden directory on external storage.
- Request.setDestinationInExternalPublicDir(): Set the destination to a public directory on external storage.
- Request.setDestinationUri(): Set the destination to a file Uri located on external storage.

> **NOTE:** All destination methods writing to external storage will require your application to declare use of `android.permission.WRITE_EXTERNAL_STORAGE` in the manifest.

Files without an explicit destination also often get removed when `DownloadManager.remove()` gets called to clear the entry from the manager list or the user clears the downloads list; files downloaded to external storage will not be removed by the system under these conditions.

3–6. Accessing a REST API

Problem

Your application needs to access a RESTful API over HTTP to interact with the web services of a remote host.

> **NOTE:** REST stands for Representational State Transfer. It is a common architectural style for web services today. RESTful APIs are typically built using standard HTTP verbs to create requests of the remote resource and the responses are typically returned in a structured document format, such as XML, JSON, or comma-separated values (CSV).

Solution

There are two recommended ways to use HTTP to send and receive data over a network connection in Android: the first is the Apache `HttpClient`, and the second is the Java `HttpURLConnection`. The decision about which to use in your application should be based primarily on what versions of Android you aim to support.

(API Level 3)

If you are targeting earlier Android versions, use the Apache HTTP classes inside of an `AsyncTask`. Android includes the Apache HTTP components library, which provides a robust method of creating connections to remote APIs. The Apache library includes classes to create GET, POST, PUT, and DELETE requests with ease, as well as providing support for Secure Sockets Layer (SSL), cookie storage, authentication, and other HTTP requirements that your specific API may have in its `HttpClient`.

The other primary advantage of this approach is the level of abstraction provided by the Apache library. Applications require very little code in most cases to do most network operations over HTTP. Much of the lower-level transaction code is hidden away from the developer.

One major disadvantage is that the version of the Apache components bundled with Android does not include `MultipartEntity`, a class that is necessary to do binary or multipart form data POST transactions. If you need this functionality and want to use `HttpClient`, you must pull in a newer version of the components library as an external JAR.

(API Level 9)

Use the Java `HttpURLConnection` class inside of an `AsyncTask`. This class has been part of the Android framework since API Level 1 but has only been the recommended method for network I/O since the release of Android 2.3. The primary reason for this is that there were a few bugs in its implementation prior to that which made `HttpClient` a more stable choice. However, moving forward,

HttpURLConnection is where the Android team will continue to make performance and stability enhancements, so it is the recommended implementation choice.

The biggest advantage to using HttpURLConnection is performance. The classes are lightweight and newer versions of Android have response compression and other enhancements built in. Its API is also lower level so it is more ubiquitous, and implementing any type of HTTP transaction is possible. The drawback to this is that it requires more coding by the developer (but isn't that why you bought this book?).

How It Works

HttpClient

Let's look first at using HTTP with the Apache HttpClient. Listing 3-13 is an AsyncTask that can process any HttpUriRequest and return the string response.

Listing 3-13. *AsyncTask Processing HttpRequest*

```
public class RestTask extends AsyncTask<HttpUriRequest, Void, Object> {
    private static final String TAG = "RestTask";

    public interface ResponseCallback {
        public void onRequestSuccess(String response);
        public void onRequestError(Exception error);
    }

    private AbstractHttpClient mClient;

    private WeakReference<ResponseCallback> mCallback;

    public RestTask() {
        this(new DefaultHttpClient());
    }

    public RestTask(AbstractHttpClient client) {
        mClient = client;
    }

    public void setResponseCallback(ResponseCallback callback) {
        mCallback = new WeakReference<ResponseCallback>(callback);
    }

    @Override
    protected Object doInBackground(HttpUriRequest... params) {
```

```
        try{
            HttpUriRequest request = params[0];
            HttpResponse serverResponse = mClient.execute(request);

            BasicResponseHandler handler = new BasicResponseHandler();
            String response = handler.handleResponse(serverResponse);
            return response;
        } catch (Exception e) {
            Log.w(TAG, e);
            return e;
        }
    }

    @Override
    protected void onPostExecute(Object result) {
        if (mCallback != null && mCallback.get() != null) {
            if (result instanceof String) {
                mCallback.get().onRequestSuccess((String) result);
            } else if (result instanceof Exception) {
                mCallback.get().onRequestError((Exception) result);
            } else {
                mCallback.get().onRequestError(
                        new IOException("Unknown Error Contacting Host"));
            }
        }
    }

}
```

The RestTask can be constructed with or without an HttpClient parameter. The reason for allowing this is so multiple requests can use the same client object. This is extremely useful if your API requires cookies to maintain a session or if there is a specific set of required parameters that are easier to set up once (like SSL stores). The task takes an HttpUriRequest parameter to process (of which HttpGet, HttpPost, HttpPut, and HttpDelete are all subclasses) and executes it.

A BasicResponseHandler processes the response, which is a convenience class that abstracts our task from needing to check the response for errors. BasicResponseHandler will return the HTTP response as a string if the response code is 1XX or 2XX, but it will throw an HttpResponseException if the response code was 300 or greater.

The final important piece of this class exists in onPostExecute(), after the interaction with the API is complete. RestTask has an optional callback interface that will be notified when the request is complete (with a string of the response data) or an error has occurred (with the exception that was triggered). This callback is stored in the form of a WeakReference so that we can safely use an Activity or other system component as the callback, without worrying about a running task keeping that component from being removed if it gets paused or stopped. Now let's use this powerful new tool to create some basic API requests.

GET Example

In the following example we utilize the Google Custom Search REST API. This API takes a few parameters for each request:

- key: Unique value to identify that application making the request
- cx: Identifier for the custom search engine you want to access
    - q: String representing the search query you want to execute

Visit https://developers.google.com/custom-search/ to receive more information about this API.

A GET request is the simplest and most common request in many public APIs. Parameters that must be sent with the request are encoded into the URL string itself, so no additional data must be provided. Let's create a GET request to search for "Android" (see Listing 3-14).

Listing 3-14. *Activity Executing API GET Request*

```
public class SearchActivity extends Activity implements ResponseCallback {

    private static final String SEARCH_URI =
            "https://www.googleapis.com/customsearch/v1?key=%s&cx=%s&q=%s";
    private static final String SEARCH_KEY =
            "AIzaSyBbW-W1SHCK4eWOkK74VGMLJj_b-byNzkI";
    private static final String SEARCH_CX =
            "008212991319514020231:1mkouq8yagw";
    private static final String SEARCH_QUERY = "Android";

    private TextView mResult;
    private ProgressDialog mProgress;

    @Override
    public void onCreate(Bundle savedInstanceState) {
        super.onCreate(savedInstanceState);
        ScrollView scrollView = new ScrollView(this);
        mResult = new TextView(this);
        scrollView.addView(mResult,
                new ViewGroup.LayoutParams(LayoutParams.MATCH_PARENT,
                        LayoutParams.WRAP_CONTENT));
        setContentView(scrollView);
```

```
        try{
            //Simple GET
            String url = String.format(SEARCH_URI, SEARCH_KEY,
                    SEARCH_CX, SEARCH_QUERY);
            HttpGet searchRequest = new HttpGet(url);

            RestTask task = new RestTask();
            task.setResponseCallback(this);
            task.execute(searchRequest);

            //Display progress to the user
            mProgress = ProgressDialog.show(this, "Searching",
                    "Waiting For Results...", true);
        } catch (Exception e) {
            mResult.setText(e.getMessage());
        }
    }

    @Override
    public void onRequestSuccess(String response) {
        //Clear progress indicator
        if(mProgress != null) {
            mProgress.dismiss();
        }

        //Process the response data (here we just display it)
        mResult.setText(response);
    }

    @Override
    public void onRequestError(Exception error) {
        //Clear progress indicator
        if(mProgress != null) {
            mProgress.dismiss();
        }

        //Process the response data (here we just display it)
        mResult.setText(error.getMessage());
    }
}
```

In the example, we create the type of HTTP request that we need with the URL that we want to connect to (in this case, a GET request to search.yahooapis.com). The URL is stored as a constant format string, and the required parameters for the Google API are added at runtime just before the request is created.

A RestTask is created with the Activity set as its callback, and the task is executed. When the task is complete, either onRequestSuccess() or onRequestError() will be called and, in the case of a success, the API response can be unpacked and processed. We will discuss parsing structured XML and JSON responses like this one in Recipes 3-7 and 3-8, so for now the example simply displays the raw response to the user interface.

POST Example

Many times, APIs require that you provide some data as part of the request, perhaps an authentication token or the contents of a search query. The API will require you to send the request over HTTP POST so these values may be encoded into the request body instead of the URL. To demonstrate a working POST, we will be sending a request to httpbin.org, which is a development site designed to read and validate the contents of a request and echo them back (see Listing 3-15).

Listing 3-15. *Activity Executing API POST Request*

```
public class SearchActivity extends Activity implements ResponseCallback {

    private static final String POST_URI = "http://httpbin.org/post";

    private TextView mResult;
    private ProgressDialog mProgress;

    @Override
    public void onCreate(Bundle savedInstanceState) {
        super.onCreate(savedInstanceState);
        ScrollView scrollView = new ScrollView(this);
        mResult = new TextView(this);
        scrollView.addView(mResult,
                new ViewGroup.LayoutParams(LayoutParams.MATCH_PARENT,
                        LayoutParams.WRAP_CONTENT));
        setContentView(scrollView);

        try{
            //Simple POST
            HttpPost postRequest = new HttpPost( new URI(POST_URI) );
            List<NameValuePair> parameters = new ArrayList<NameValuePair>();
            parameters.add(new BasicNameValuePair("title", "Android Recipes"));
            parameters.add(new BasicNameValuePair("summary",
                    "Learn Android Quickly"));
            parameters.add(new BasicNameValuePair("authors", "Smith/Friesen"));
            postRequest.setEntity(new UrlEncodedFormEntity(parameters));

            RestTask task = new RestTask();
            task.setResponseCallback(this);
            task.execute(postRequest);
```

```
            //Display progress to the user
            mProgress = ProgressDialog.show(this, "Searching",
                    "Waiting For Results...", true);
        } catch (Exception e) {
            mResult.setText(e.getMessage());
        }
    }

    @Override
    public void onRequestSuccess(String response) {
        //Clear progress indicator
        if(mProgress != null) {
            mProgress.dismiss();
        }

        //Process the response data (here we just display it)
        mResult.setText(response);
    }

    @Override
    public void onRequestError(Exception error) {
        //Clear progress indicator
        if(mProgress != null) {
            mProgress.dismiss();
        }

        //Process the response data (here we just display it)
        mResult.setText(error.getMessage());
    }
}
```

Notice in this example that the parameters passed to the API are encoded into an `HttpEntity` instead of passed directly in the request URL. The request created in this case was an `HttpPost` instance, which is still a subclass of `HttpUriRequest` (like `HttpGet`), so we can use the same `RestTask` to run the operation. As with the GET example, we will discuss parsing structured XML and JSON responses like this one in Recipes 3-7 and 3-8, so for now the example simply displays the raw response to the user interface.

> **REMINDER:** The Apache library bundled with the Android SDK does not include support for multipart HTTP POSTs. However, `MultipartEntity`, from the publicly available `org.apache.http.mime` library, is compatible and can be brought in to your project as an external source.

Basic Authorization

Another common requirement for working with an API is some form of authentication. Standards are emerging for REST API authentication such as OAuth 2.0, but a common authentication method is still a basic username and password authorization over HTTP. In Listing 3-16, we modify the RestTask to enable authentication in the HTTP header per request.

Listing 3-16. *RestTask with Basic Authorization*

```
public class RestAuthTask extends AsyncTask<HttpUriRequest, Void, Object> {
    private static final String TAG = "RestTask";

    private static final String AUTH_USER = "user@mydomain.com";
    private static final String AUTH_PASS = "password";

    public interface ResponseCallback {
        public void onRequestSuccess(String response);

        public void onRequestError(Exception error);
    }

    private AbstractHttpClient mClient;
    private WeakReference<ResponseCallback> mCallback;

    public RestAuthTask(boolean authenticate) {
        this(new DefaultHttpClient(), authenticate);

    }

    public RestAuthTask(AbstractHttpClient client, boolean authenticate) {
        mClient = client;
        if(authenticate) {
            UsernamePasswordCredentials creds =
                    new UsernamePasswordCredentials(AUTH_USER, AUTH_PASS);
            mClient.getCredentialsProvider()
                    .setCredentials(AuthScope.ANY, creds);
        }
    }

    @Override
    protected Object doInBackground(HttpUriRequest... params) {
        try{
            HttpUriRequest request = params[0];
            HttpResponse serverResponse = mClient.execute(request);

            BasicResponseHandler handler = new BasicResponseHandler();
            String response = handler.handleResponse(serverResponse);
            return response;
```

```
        } catch (Exception e) {
            Log.w(TAG, e);
            return e;
        }
    }

    @Override
    protected void onPostExecute(Object result) {
        if (mCallback != null && mCallback.get() != null) {
            if (result instanceof String) {
                mCallback.get().onRequestSuccess((String) result);
            } else if (result instanceof Exception) {
                mCallback.get().onRequestError((Exception) result);
            } else {
                mCallback.get().onRequestError(
                        new IOException("Unknown Error Contacting Host"));
            }
        }
    }

}
```

Basic authentication is added to the `HttpClient` in the Apache paradigm. Because our example task allows for a specific client object to be passed in for use, which may already have the necessary authentication credentials, we have only modified the case where a default client is created. In this case, a `UsernamePasswordCredentials` instance is created with the username and password strings, and then set on the client's `CredentialsProvider`.

HttpUrlConnection

Now let's take a look at making HTTP requests with the preferred method for newer applications, `HttpUrlConnection`. We'll start off by defining our same `RestTask` implementation in Listing 3-17, with a helper class in Listing 3-18.

Listing 3-17. *RestTask Using HttpUrlConnection*

```
public class RestTask extends AsyncTask<Void, Integer, Object> {
    private static final String TAG = "RestTask";

    public interface ResponseCallback {
        public void onRequestSuccess(String response);

        public void onRequestError(Exception error);
    }

    public interface ProgressCallback {
        public void onProgressUpdate(int progress);
```

```
    }

    private HttpURLConnection mConnection;
    private String mFormBody;
    private File mUploadFile;
    private String mUploadFileName;

    // Activity callbacks. Use WeakReferences to avoid
    // blocking operations causing linked objects to stay in memory
    private WeakReference<ResponseCallback> mResponseCallback;
    private WeakReference<ProgressCallback> mProgressCallback;

    public RestTask(HttpURLConnection connection) {
        mConnection = connection;
    }

    public void setFormBody(List<NameValuePair> formData) {
        if (formData == null) {
            mFormBody = null;
            return;
        }

        StringBuilder sb = new StringBuilder();
        for (int i = 0; i < formData.size(); i++) {
            NameValuePair item = formData.get(i);
            sb.append( URLEncoder.encode(item.getName()) );
            sb.append("=");
            sb.append( URLEncoder.encode(item.getValue()) );
            if (i != (formData.size() - 1)) {
                sb.append("&");
            }
        }

        mFormBody = sb.toString();
    }

    public void setUploadFile(File file, String fileName) {
        mUploadFile = file;
        mUploadFileName = fileName;
    }

    public void setResponseCallback(ResponseCallback callback) {
        mResponseCallback = new WeakReference<ResponseCallback>(callback);
    }

    public void setProgressCallback(ProgressCallback callback) {
        mProgressCallback = new WeakReference<ProgressCallback>(callback);
    }
```

```
private void writeMultipart(String boundary, String charset,
        OutputStream output, boolean writeContent) throws IOException {
    BufferedWriter writer = null;
    try {
        writer = new BufferedWriter(new OutputStreamWriter(output,
                Charset.forName(charset)), 8192);
        // Post Form Data Component
        if (mFormBody != null) {
            writer.write("--" + boundary);
            writer.write("\r\n");
            writer.write(
                    "Content-Disposition: form-data; name=\"parameters\"");
            writer.write("\r\n");
            writer.write("Content-Type: text/plain; charset=" + charset);
            writer.write("\r\n");
            writer.write("\r\n");
            if (writeContent) {
                writer.write(mFormBody);
            }
            writer.write("\r\n");
            writer.flush();
        }
        // Send binary file.
        writer.write("--" + boundary);
        writer.write("\r\n");
        writer.write("Content-Disposition: form-data; name=\""
                + mUploadFileName + "\"; filename=\""
                + mUploadFile.getName() + "\"");
        writer.write("\r\n");
        writer.write("Content-Type: "
                + URLConnection.guessContentTypeFromName(
                mUploadFile.getName()));
        writer.write("\r\n");
        writer.write("Content-Transfer-Encoding: binary");
        writer.write("\r\n");
        writer.write("\r\n");
        writer.flush();
        if (writeContent) {
            InputStream input = null;
            try {
                input = new FileInputStream(mUploadFile);
                byte[] buffer = new byte[1024];
                for (int length = 0; (length = input.read(buffer)) > 0;) {
                    output.write(buffer, 0, length);
                }
                // Don't close the OutputStream yet
                output.flush();
            } catch (IOException e) {
                Log.w(TAG, e);
            } finally {
```

```
                if (input != null) {
                    try {
                        input.close();
                    } catch (IOException e) {
                    }
                }
            }
        }
        // This CRLF signifies the end of the binary data chunk
        writer.write("\r\n");
        writer.flush();

        // End of multipart/form-data.
        writer.write("--" + boundary + "--");
        writer.write("\r\n");
        writer.flush();
    } finally {
        if (writer != null) {
            writer.close();
        }
    }
}

private void writeFormData(String charset, OutputStream output)
        throws IOException {
    try {
        output.write(mFormBody.getBytes(charset));
        output.flush();
    } finally {
        if (output != null) {
            output.close();
        }
    }
}

@Override
protected Object doInBackground(Void... params) {
    //Generate random string for boundary
    String boundary = Long.toHexString(System.currentTimeMillis());
    String charset = Charset.defaultCharset().displayName();

    try {
        // Set up output if applicable
        if (mUploadFile != null) {
            //We must do a multipart request
            mConnection.setRequestProperty("Content-Type",
                    "multipart/form-data; boundary=" + boundary);

            //Calculate the size of the extra metadata
            ByteArrayOutputStream bos = new ByteArrayOutputStream();
```

```
        writeMultipart(boundary, charset, bos, false);
        byte[] extra = bos.toByteArray();
        int contentLength = extra.length;
        //Add the file size to the length
        contentLength += mUploadFile.length();
        //Add the form body, if it exists
        if (mFormBody != null) {
            contentLength += mFormBody.length();
        }

        mConnection.setFixedLengthStreamingMode(contentLength);
    } else if (mFormBody != null) {
        //In this case, it is just form data to post
        mConnection.setRequestProperty("Content-Type",
                "application/x-www-form-urlencoded; charset="+charset);
        mConnection.setFixedLengthStreamingMode(mFormBody.length());
    }

    //This is the first call on URLConnection that actually
    // does Network IO.  Even openConnection() is still just
    // doing local operations.
    mConnection.connect();

    // Do output if applicable (for a POST)
    if (mUploadFile != null) {
        OutputStream out = mConnection.getOutputStream();
        writeMultipart(boundary, charset, out, true);
    } else if (mFormBody != null) {
        OutputStream out = mConnection.getOutputStream();
        writeFormData(charset, out);
    }

    // Get response data
    int status = mConnection.getResponseCode();
    if (status >= 300) {
        String message = mConnection.getResponseMessage();
        return new HttpResponseException(status, message);
    }

    InputStream in = mConnection.getInputStream();
    String encoding = mConnection.getContentEncoding();
    int contentLength = mConnection.getContentLength();
    if (encoding == null) {
        encoding = "UTF-8";
    }
    BufferedReader reader = new BufferedReader(new InputStreamReader(
            in, encoding));
    char[] buffer = new char[4096];

    StringBuilder sb = new StringBuilder();
```

```
            int downloadedBytes = 0;
            int len1 = 0;
            while ((len1 = reader.read(buffer)) > 0) {
                downloadedBytes += len1;
                publishProgress((downloadedBytes * 100) / contentLength);
                sb.append(buffer);
            }

            return sb.toString();
        } catch (Exception e) {
            Log.w(TAG, e);
            return e;
        } finally {
            if (mConnection != null) {
                mConnection.disconnect();
            }
        }
    }

    @Override
    protected void onProgressUpdate(Integer... values) {
        // Update progress UI
        if (mProgressCallback != null && mProgressCallback.get() != null) {
            mProgressCallback.get().onProgressUpdate(values[0]);
        }
    }

    @Override
    protected void onPostExecute(Object result) {
        if (mResponseCallback != null && mResponseCallback.get() != null) {
            if (result instanceof String) {
                mResponseCallback.get().onRequestSuccess((String) result);
            } else if (result instanceof Exception) {
                mResponseCallback.get().onRequestError((Exception) result);
            } else {
                mResponseCallback.get().onRequestError(
                        new IOException("Unknown Error Contacting Host"));
            }
        }
    }
}
```

Listing 3-18. *Util Class to Create Requests*

```
public class RestUtil {

    public static final RestTask obtainGetTask(String url)
            throws MalformedURLException, IOException {
        HttpURLConnection connection = (HttpURLConnection) (new URL(url))
                .openConnection();
```

```
            connection.setReadTimeout(10000);
            connection.setConnectTimeout(15000);
            connection.setDoInput(true);

            RestTask task = new RestTask(connection);
            return task;
        }

        public static final RestTask obtainFormPostTask(String url,
                List<NameValuePair> formData) throws MalformedURLException,
                IOException {
            HttpURLConnection connection = (HttpURLConnection) (new URL(url))
                    .openConnection();

            connection.setReadTimeout(10000);
            connection.setConnectTimeout(15000);
            connection.setDoOutput(true);

            RestTask task = new RestTask(connection);
            task.setFormBody(formData);

            return task;
        }

        public static final RestTask obtainMultipartPostTask(String url,
                List<NameValuePair> formPart, File file, String fileName)
                throws MalformedURLException, IOException {
            HttpURLConnection connection = (HttpURLConnection) (new URL(url))
                    .openConnection();

            connection.setReadTimeout(10000);
            connection.setConnectTimeout(15000);
            connection.setDoOutput(true);

            RestTask task = new RestTask(connection);
            task.setFormBody(formPart);
            task.setUploadFile(file, fileName);

            return task;
        }
    }
```

So the first thing you probably noticed is that this example requires a lot more code to implement certain requests, due to the low-level nature of the API. We have written a `RestTask` that is capable of handling GET, simple POST, and multipart POST requests, and we define the parameters of the request dynamically based on the components added to `RestTask`.

As before, we can attach an optional callback to be notified when the request has completed. However, in addition to that we have added a progress callback interface that the task will call to update any visible UI of the progress while downloading response content. This is simpler to use to implement using this API because we are interacting directly with the data streams.

In this example, an application would create an instance of `RestTask` through the `RestUtil` helper class. This subdivides the setup required on `HttpURLConnection`, which doesn't actually do any network I/O from the portions that connect and interact with the host. The helper class creates the connection instance and also sets up any timeout values and the HTTP request method.

> **NOTE:** By default, any `URLConnection` will have its request method set to GET. Calling `setDoOutput()` implicitly sets that method to POST. If you need to set that value to any other HTTP verb, use `setRequestMethod()`.

If there is any body content, in the case of a POST, those values are set directly on our custom task to be written when the task executes.

Once a `RestTask` is executed, it goes through and determines if there is any body data attached that it needs to write. If we have attached form data (as name-value pairs) or a file for upload, it takes that as a trigger to construct a POST body and send it. With `HttpURLConnection`, we are responsible for all aspects of the connection, including telling the server the amount of data that is coming. Therefore, `RestTask` takes the time to calculate how much data will be posted and calls `setFixedLengthStreamingMode()` to construct a header field telling the server how large our content is. In the case of a simple form post, this calculation is trivial, and we just pass the length of the body string.

A multipart POST that may include file data is more complex, however. Multipart has lots of extra data in the body to designate the boundaries between each part of the POST, and all those bytes must be accounted for in the length we set. In order to accomplish this, `writeMultipart()` is constructed in such a way that we can pass a local `OutputStream` (in this case, a `ByteArrayOutputStream`) to write all the extra data into it so we can measure it. When the method is called in this way, it skips over the actual content pieces, like the file and form data, as those can be added in later by calling their respective `length()` methods, and we don't want to waste time loading them into memory.

> **NOTE:** If you do not know how big the content is that you want to POST, `HttpURLConnection` also supports chunked uploads via `setChunkedStreamingMode()`. In this case, you need only to pass the size of the data chunks you will be sending.

Once the task has written any POST data to the host, it is time to read the response content. If the initial request was a GET request, the task skips directly to this step because there was no additional data to write. The task first checks the value of the response code to make sure there were no server-side errors, and it then downloads the contents of the response into a `StringBuilder`. The download reads in chunks of data roughly 4 KB at a time, notifying the progress callback handler with a percentage downloaded as a fraction of the total response content length. When all the content is downloaded, the task completes by handing back the resulting response as a string.

GET Example

Let's take a look at our same Google Custom Search example, but this time let's use the new and improved `RestTask` (see Listing 3-19).

Listing 3-19. *Activity Executing API GET Request*

```
public class SearchActivity extends Activity implements
        RestTask.ProgressCallback, RestTask.ResponseCallback {

    private static final String SEARCH_URI =
            "https://www.googleapis.com/customsearch/v1?key=%s&cx=%s&q=%s";
    private static final String SEARCH_KEY =
            "AIzaSyBbW-W1SHCK4eW0kK74VGMLJj_b-byNzkI";
    private static final String SEARCH_CX =
            "008212991319514020231:1mkouq8yagw";
    private static final String SEARCH_QUERY = "Android";

    private TextView mResult;
    private ProgressDialog mProgress;

    @Override
    public void onCreate(Bundle savedInstanceState) {
        super.onCreate(savedInstanceState);
        ScrollView scrollView = new ScrollView(this);
        mResult = new TextView(this);
        scrollView.addView(mResult,
                new ViewGroup.LayoutParams(LayoutParams.MATCH_PARENT,
                        LayoutParams.WRAP_CONTENT));
```

```
        setContentView(scrollView);

        //Create the request
        try{
            //Simple GET
            String url = String.format(SEARCH_URI, SEARCH_KEY,
                    SEARCH_CX, SEARCH_QUERY);
            RestTask getTask = RestUtil.obtainGetTask(url);
            getTask.setResponseCallback(this);
            getTask.setProgressCallback(this);

            getTask.execute();

            //Display progress to the user
            mProgress = ProgressDialog.show(this, "Searching",
                    "Waiting For Results...", true);
        } catch (Exception e) {
            mResult.setText(e.getMessage());
        }
    }

    @Override
    public void onProgressUpdate(int progress) {
        if (progress >= 0) {
            if (mProgress != null) {
                mProgress.dismiss();
                mProgress = null;
            }
            //Update user of progress
            mResult.setText(
                    String.format("Download Progress: %d%%", progress));
        }
    }

    @Override
    public void onRequestSuccess(String response) {
        //Clear progress indicator
        if(mProgress != null) {
            mProgress.dismiss();
        }
        //Process the response data (here we just display it)
        mResult.setText(response);
    }

    @Override
    public void onRequestError(Exception error) {
        //Clear progress indicator
        if(mProgress != null) {
            mProgress.dismiss();
        }
```

```
        //Process the response data (here we just display it)
        mResult.setText("An Error Occurred: "+error.getMessage());
    }
}
```

The example is almost identical to our previous iteration. We still construct the URL out of the necessary query parameters and obtain a `RestTask` instance. We then set this Activity as the callback for the request and execute.

You can see, however, that we have added `ProgressCallback` to the list of interfaces this Activity implements so it can be notified of how the download is going. Not all web servers return a valid content length for requests, instead returning -1, which makes progress based on the percentage difficult to do. In those cases, our callback simply leaves the indeterminate progress dialog visible until the download is complete. However, in cases where valid progress can be determined, the dialog is dismissed and the percentage of progress is displayed on the screen.

Once the download is complete, the Activity receives a callback with the resulting JSON string. We will discuss parsing structured XML and JSON responses like this one in Recipes 3-7 and 3-8, so for now the example simply displays the raw response to the user interface.

POST Example

Listing 3-20 illustrates doing a simple form data POST using the new `RestTask`. The endpoint will be httpbin.org once again, so the resulting data displayed on the screen will be an echo back to the form parameters we passed in.

Listing 3-20. *Activity Executing API POST Request*

```
public class SearchActivity extends Activity implements
        RestTask.ProgressCallback, RestTask.ResponseCallback {

    private static final String POST_URI = "http://httpbin.org/post";

    private TextView mResult;
    private ProgressDialog mProgress;

    @Override
    public void onCreate(Bundle savedInstanceState) {
        super.onCreate(savedInstanceState);
        ScrollView scrollView = new ScrollView(this);
        mResult = new TextView(this);
        scrollView.addView(mResult,
                new ViewGroup.LayoutParams(LayoutParams.MATCH_PARENT,
                        LayoutParams.WRAP_CONTENT));
```

```
        setContentView(scrollView);

        //Create the request
        try{
            //Simple POST
            List<NameValuePair> parameters = new ArrayList<NameValuePair>();
            parameters.add(new BasicNameValuePair("title", "Android Recipes"));
            parameters.add(new BasicNameValuePair("summary",
                    "Learn Android Quickly"));
            parameters.add(new BasicNameValuePair("authors", "Smith/Friesen"));
            RestTask postTask =
                    RestUtil.obtainFormPostTask(POST_URI, parameters);
            postTask.setResponseCallback(this);
            postTask.setProgressCallback(this);

            postTask.execute();

            //Display progress to the user
            mProgress = ProgressDialog.show(this, "Searching",
                    "Waiting For Results...", true);
        } catch (Exception e) {
            mResult.setText(e.getMessage());
        }
    }

    @Override
    public void onProgressUpdate(int progress) {
        if (progress >= 0) {
            if (mProgress != null) {
                mProgress.dismiss();
                mProgress = null;
            }
            //Update user of progress
            mResult.setText(
                    String.format("Download Progress: %d%%", progress));
        }
    }

    @Override
    public void onRequestSuccess(String response) {
        //Clear progress indicator
        if(mProgress != null) {
            mProgress.dismiss();
        }
        //Process the response data (here we just display it)
        mResult.setText(response);
    }

    @Override
    public void onRequestError(Exception error) {
```

```
            //Clear progress indicator
            if(mProgress != null) {
                mProgress.dismiss();
            }
            //Process the response data (here we just display it)
            mResult.setText("An Error Occurred: "+error.getMessage());
        }
    }
```

It should be noted here that the progress callbacks are only related to the download of the response, and not the upload of the POST data, though that is certainly possible for the developer to implement.

Upload Example

Listing 3-21 illustrates something we cannot do natively with the Apache components in the Android framework: multipart POST.

Listing 3-21. *Activity Executing API Multipart POST Request*

```
public class SearchActivity extends Activity implements
RestTask.ProgressCallback,
        RestTask.ResponseCallback {

    private static final String POST_URI = "http://httpbin.org/post";

    private TextView mResult;
    private ProgressDialog mProgress;

    @Override
    public void onCreate(Bundle savedInstanceState) {
        super.onCreate(savedInstanceState);
        ScrollView scrollView = new ScrollView(this);
        mResult = new TextView(this);
        scrollView.addView(mResult,
                new ViewGroup.LayoutParams(LayoutParams.MATCH_PARENT,
                        LayoutParams.WRAP_CONTENT));
        setContentView(scrollView);

        //Create the request
        try{
            //File POST
            Bitmap image = BitmapFactory.decodeResource(getResources(),
                    R.drawable.ic_launcher);
            File imageFile = new File(getExternalCacheDir(), "myImage.png");
            FileOutputStream out = new FileOutputStream(imageFile);
            image.compress(CompressFormat.PNG, 0, out);
            out.flush();
            out.close();
```

```
            List<NameValuePair> fileParameters =
                    new ArrayList<NameValuePair>();
            fileParameters.add(new BasicNameValuePair("title",
                    "Android Recipes"));
            fileParameters.add(new BasicNameValuePair("description",
                    "Image File Upload"));
            RestTask uploadTask = RestUtil.obtainMultipartPostTask(POST_URI,
                    fileParameters, imageFile, "avatarImage");
            uploadTask.setResponseCallback(this);
            uploadTask.setProgressCallback(this);

            uploadTask.execute();

            //Display progress to the user
            mProgress = ProgressDialog.show(this, "Searching",
                    "Waiting For Results...", true);
        } catch (Exception e) {
            mResult.setText(e.getMessage());
        }
    }

    @Override
    public void onProgressUpdate(int progress) {
        if (progress >= 0) {
            if (mProgress != null) {
                mProgress.dismiss();
                mProgress = null;
            }
            //Update user of progress
            mResult.setText(
                    String.format("Download Progress: %d%%", progress));
        }
    }

    @Override
    public void onRequestSuccess(String response) {
        //Clear progress indicator
        if(mProgress != null) {
            mProgress.dismiss();
        }
        //Process the response data (here we just display it)
        mResult.setText(response);
    }

    @Override
    public void onRequestError(Exception error) {
        //Clear progress indicator
        if(mProgress != null) {
            mProgress.dismiss();
        }
```

```
            //Process the response data (here we just display it)
            mResult.setText("An Error Occurred: "+error.getMessage());
        }
    }
```

In this example, we construct a POST request that has two distinct parts: a form data part (made up of name-value pairs) and a file part. For the purposes of the example, we take the application's icon and quickly write it out to external storage as a PNG file to use for the upload.

In this case, the JSON response from HttpBin will echo back both the form data elements as well as a Base64-encoded representation of the PNG image.

Basic Authorization

Adding basic authorization to the new RestTask is fairly straightforward. It can be done in one of two ways: either directly on each request or globally using a class called Authenticator. First let's take a look at attaching basic authorization to an individual request. Listing 3-22 modifies RestUtil to include methods that attach a username and password in the proper format.

Listing 3-22. *RestUtil with Basic Authorization*

```
public class RestUtil {

    public static final RestTask obtainGetTask(String url)
            throws MalformedURLException, IOException {
        HttpURLConnection connection = (HttpURLConnection) (new URL(url))
                .openConnection();

        connection.setReadTimeout(10000);
        connection.setConnectTimeout(15000);
        connection.setDoInput(true);

        RestTask task = new RestTask(connection);
        return task;
    }

    public static final RestTask obtainAuthenticatedGetTask(String url,
            String username, String password) throws
            MalformedURLException, IOException {
        HttpURLConnection connection = (HttpURLConnection) (new URL(url))
                .openConnection();

        connection.setReadTimeout(10000);
        connection.setConnectTimeout(15000);
        connection.setDoInput(true);
```

```
        attachBasicAuthentication(connection, username, password);

        RestTask task = new RestTask(connection);
        return task;
    }

    public static final RestTask obtainAuthenticatedFormPostTask(String url,
            List<NameValuePair> formData, String username, String password)
            throws MalformedURLException, IOException {
        HttpURLConnection connection = (HttpURLConnection) (new URL(url))
                .openConnection();

        connection.setReadTimeout(10000);
        connection.setConnectTimeout(15000);
        connection.setDoOutput(true);

        attachBasicAuthentication(connection, username, password);

        RestTask task = new RestTask(connection);
        task.setFormBody(formData);

        return task;
    }

    private static void attachBasicAuthentication(URLConnection connection,
            String username, String password) {
        //Add Basic Authentication Headers
        String userpassword = username + ":" + password;
        String encodedAuthorization =
                Base64.encodeToString(userpassword.getBytes(), Base64.NO_WRAP);
        connection.setRequestProperty("Authorization", "Basic "+
              encodedAuthorization);
    }

}
```

Basic Authorization is added to an HTTP request as a header field with the name "Authorization" and the value of "Basic" followed by a Base64-encoded string of your username and password. The helper method `attachBasicAuthentication()` applies this property to the `URLConnection` before it is given to `RestTask`. The `Base64.NO_WRAP` flag is added to ensure that the encoder doesn't add any extra new lines, which will create an invalid value.

This is a really nice way of applying authentication to requests if not all your requests need to be authenticated in the same way. However, sometimes it's easier to just set your credentials once and let all your requests use them. This is where `Authenticator` comes in. `Authenticator` allows you to globally set the username and password credentials for the requests in your application process. Let's take a look at Listing 3-23, which shows how this can be done.

Listing 3-23. *Activity Using Authenticator*

```
public class AuthActivity extends Activity implements ResponseCallback {

    private static final String URI =
            "http://httpbin.org/basic-auth/android/recipes";
    private static final String USERNAME = "android";
    private static final String PASSWORD = "recipes";

    private TextView mResult;
    private ProgressDialog mProgress;

    @Override
    protected void onCreate(Bundle savedInstanceState) {
        super.onCreate(savedInstanceState);
        mResult = new TextView(this);
        setContentView(mResult);

        Authenticator.setDefault(new Authenticator() {
            @Override
            protected PasswordAuthentication getPasswordAuthentication() {
                return new PasswordAuthentication(USERNAME,
                        PASSWORD.toCharArray());
            }
        });

        try {
            RestTask task = RestUtil.obtainGetTask(URI);
            task.setResponseCallback(this);
            task.execute();
        } catch (Exception e) {
            mResult.setText(e.getMessage());
        }
    }

    @Override
    public void onRequestSuccess(String response) {
        if (mProgress != null) {
            mProgress.dismiss();
            mProgress = null;
        }
        mResult.setText(response);
    }

    @Override
    public void onRequestError(Exception error) {
        if (mProgress != null) {
            mProgress.dismiss();
            mProgress = null;
        }
```

```
        mResult.setText(error.getMessage());
    }
}
```

This example connects to HttpBin again, this time to an endpoint used to validate credentials. The username and password the host will require are coded into the URL path, and if those credentials are not properly supplied the response from the host will be UNAUTHORIZED.

With a single call to `Authenticator.setDefault()`, passing in a new `Authenticator` instance, all subsequent requests will use the provided credentials for authentication challenges. So we pass the correct username and password to `Authenticator` by creating a new `PasswordAuthentication` instance whenever asked, and all `URLConnection` instances in our process will make use of that. Notice that in this example our request does not have credentials attached to it, but when the request is made we will get an authenticated response.

Caching Responses

(API Level 13)

One final platform enhancement you can take advantage of when you use `HttpURLConnection` is response caching with `HttpResponseCache`. A great way to speed up the response of your application is to cache responses coming back from the remote host so your application can load frequent requests from the cache rather than hitting the network each time. Installing and removing a cache in your application requires just a few simple lines of code.

```
//Installing a response cache
try {
    File httpCacheDir = new File(context.getCacheDir(), "http");
    long httpCacheSize = 10 * 1024 * 1024; // 10 MiB
    HttpResponseCache.install(httpCacheDir, httpCacheSize);
catch (IOException e) {
    Log.i(TAG, "HTTP response cache installation failed:" + e);
}

//Clearing a response cache
HttpResponseCache cache = HttpResponseCache.getInstalled();
if (cache != null) {
    cache.flush();
}
```

> **NOTE:** `HttpResponseCache` only works with `HttpURLConnection` variants. It will not work if you are using Apache `HttpClient`.

3–7. Parsing JSON

Problem

Your application needs to parse responses from an API or other source that is formatted in JavaScript Object Notation (JSON).

Solution

(API Level 1)

Use the org.json parser classes that are baked into Android. The SDK comes with a very efficient set of classes for parsing JSON-formatted strings in the org.json package. Simply create a new `JSONObject` or `JSONArray` from the formatted string data and you'll be armed with a set of accessor methods to get primitive data or nested `JSONObjects` and `JSONArrays` from within.

How It Works

This JSON parser is strict by default, meaning that it will halt with an exception when encountering invalid JSON data or an invalid key. Accessor methods that prefix with "get" will throw a `JSONException` if the requested value is not found. In some cases this behavior is not ideal, and for that there is a companion set of methods that are prefixed with "opt". These methods will return null instead of throwing an exception when a value for the requested key is not found. In addition, many of them have an overloaded version that also takes a fallback parameter to return instead of null.

Let's look at an example of how to parse a JSON string into useful pieces. Consider the JSON in Listing 3-24.

Listing 3-24. *Example JSON*

```
{
    "person": {
        "name": "John",
        "age": 30,
        "children": [
            {
                "name": "Billy"
                "age": 5
            },
            {
                "name": "Sarah"
                "age": 7
            },
            {
                "name": "Tommy"
                "age": 9
            }
        ]
    }
}
```

This defines a single object with three values: name (string), age (integer), and children. The parameter entitled "children" is an array of three more objects, each with its own name and age. If we were to use org.json to parse this data and display some elements in TextViews, it would look like the examples in Listings 3-25 and 3-26.

Listing 3-25. *res/layout/main.xml*

```
<?xml version="1.0" encoding="utf-8"?>
<LinearLayout xmlns:android="http://schemas.android.com/apk/res/android"
  android:layout_width="fill_parent"
  android:layout_height="fill_parent"
  android:orientation="vertical">
  <TextView
    android:id="@+id/line1"
    android:layout_width="fill_parent"
    android:layout_height="wrap_content"
  />
  <TextView
    android:id="@+id/line2"
    android:layout_width="fill_parent"
    android:layout_height="wrap_content"
  />
  <TextView
    android:id="@+id/line3"
    android:layout_width="fill_parent"
```

```
    android:layout_height="wrap_content"
  />
</LinearLayout>
```

Listing 3-26. *Sample JSON Parsing Activity*

```
public class MyActivity extends Activity {
    private static final String JSON_STRING =
            "{\"person\":{\"name\":\"John\",\"age\":30,\"children\":["
            + "{\"name\":\"Billy\",\"age\":5},"
            + "{\"name\":\"Sarah\",\"age\":7},"
            + "{\"name\":\"Tommy\",\"age\":9}"
            + "] } }";
    @Override
    public void onCreate(Bundle savedInstanceState) {
        super.onCreate(savedInstanceState);
        setContentView(R.layout.main);

        TextView line1 = (TextView)findViewById(R.id.line1);
        TextView line2 = (TextView)findViewById(R.id.line2);
        TextView line3 = (TextView)findViewById(R.id.line3);
        try {
            JSONObject person =
                    (new JSONObject(JSON_STRING)).getJSONObject("person");
            String name = person.getString("name");
            line1.setText("This person's name is " + name);
            line2.setText(name + " is " + person.getInt("age")
                    + " years old.");
            line3.setText(name + " has "
                    + person.getJSONArray("children").length()
                    + " children.");
        } catch (JSONException e) {
            e.printStackTrace();
        }
    }
}
```

For this example, the JSON string has been hard-coded as a constant. When the Activity is created, the string is turned into a JSONObject, at which point all its data can be accessed as key-value pairs, just as if it were stored in a map or dictionary. All the business logic is wrapped in a try/catch statement because we are using the strict methods for accessing data.

Functions like `JSONObject.getString()` and `JSONObject.getInt()` are used to read primitive data out and place it in the `TextView`; the `getJSONArray()` method pulls out the nested "children" array. `JSONArray` has the same set of accessor methods as `JSONObject` to read data, but they take an index into the array as a parameter instead of the name of the key. In addition, a `JSONArray` can return its length, which we used in the example to display how many children the person had.

The result of the sample application is shown in Figure 3-3.

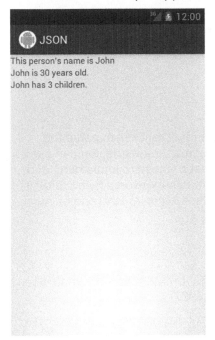

Figure 3-3. *Display of parsed JSON data in Activity.*

Debugging Trick

JSON is a very efficient notation; however, it can be difficult for humans to read a raw JSON string, which can make it hard to debug parsing issues. Quite often the JSON you are parsing is coming from a remote source or is not completely familiar to you, and you need to display it for debugging purposes. Both JSONObject and JSONArray have an overloaded `toString()` method that takes an integer parameter for pretty-printing the data in a returned and indented fashion, making it easier to decipher. Often adding something like `myJsonObject.toString(2)` to a troublesome section can save you time and a headache.

3–8. Parsing XML

Problem

Your application needs to parse responses, from an API or other source, that are formatted as XML.

Solution

(API Level 1)

Implement a subclass of `org.xml.sax.helpers.DefaultHandler` to parse the data using event-based SAX. Android has three primary methods you can use to parse XML data: DOM, SAX, and Pull. The simplest of these to implement, and the most memory-efficient, is the SAX parser. SAX parsing works by traversing the XML data and generating callback events at the beginning and end of each element.

How It Works

To describe this further, let's look at the format of the XML that is returned when requesting an RSS/ATOM news feed (see Listing 3-27).

Listing 3-27. *RSS Basic Structure*

```
<rss version="2.0">
  <channel>
    <item>
      <title></title>
      <link></link>
      <description></description>
    </item>
    <item>
      <title></title>
      <link></link>
      <description></description>
    </item>
    <item>
      <title></title>
      <link></link>
      <description></description>
    </item>
    …
  </channel>
</rss>
```

Between each set of <title>, <link>, and <description> tags is the value associated with each item. Using SAX, we can parse this data out into an array of items that the application could then display to the user in a list (see Listing 3-28).

Listing 3-28. *Custom Handler to Parse RSS*

```
public class RSSHandler extends DefaultHandler {

    public class NewsItem {
        public String title;
        public String link;
        public String description;

        @Override
        public String toString() {
            return title;
        }
    }

    private StringBuffer buf;
    private ArrayList<NewsItem> feedItems;
    private NewsItem item;

    private boolean inItem = false;

    public ArrayList<NewsItem> getParsedItems() {
        return feedItems;
    }

    //Called at the head of each new element
    @Override
    public void startElement(String uri, String name, String qName, Attributes atts) {
        if("channel".equals(name)) {
            feedItems = new ArrayList<NewsItem>();
        } else if("item".equals(name)) {
            item = new NewsItem();
            inItem = true;
        } else if("title".equals(name) && inItem) {
            buf = new StringBuffer();
        } else if("link".equals(name) && inItem) {
            buf = new StringBuffer();
        } else if("description".equals(name) && inItem) {
            buf = new StringBuffer();
        }
    }

    //Called at the tail of each element end
    @Override
```

```
    public void endElement(String uri, String name, String qName) {
        if("item".equals(name)) {
            feedItems.add(item);
            inItem = false;
        } else if("title".equals(name) && inItem) {
            item.title = buf.toString();
        } else if("link".equals(name) && inItem) {
            item.link = buf.toString();
        } else if("description".equals(name) && inItem) {
            item.description = buf.toString();
        }

        buf = null;
    }

    //Called with character data inside elements
    @Override
    public void characters(char ch[], int start, int length) {
        //Don't bother if buffer isn't initialized
        if(buf != null) {
            for (int i=start; i<start+length; i++) {
                buf.append(ch[i]);
            }
        }
    }
}
```

The `RSSHandler` is notified at the beginning and end of each element via `startElement()` and `endElement()`. In between, the characters that make up the element's value are passed into the `characters()` callback.

1. When the parser encounters the first element, the list of items is initialized.
2. When each item element is encountered, a new NewsItem model is initialized.
3. Inside of each item element, data elements are captured in a StringBuffer and inserted into the members of the NewsItem.
4. When the end of each item is reached, the NewsItem is added to the list.
5. When parsing is complete, feedItems is a complete list of all the items in the feed.

Let's look at this in action by using some of the tricks from the API example in Recipe 3-6 to download the latest Google News in RSS form (see Listing 3-29).

Listing 3-29. *Activity That Parses the XML and Displays the Items*

```
public class FeedActivity extends Activity implements ResponseCallback {
    private static final String TAG = "FeedReader";
    private static final String FEED_URI =
            "http://news.google.com/?output=rss";

    private ListView mList;
    private ArrayAdapter<NewsItem> mAdapter;
    private ProgressDialog mProgress;

    @Override
    public void onCreate(Bundle savedInstanceState) {
        super.onCreate(savedInstanceState);

        mList = new ListView(this);
        mAdapter = new ArrayAdapter<NewsItem>(this,
                android.R.layout.simple_list_item_1,
                android.R.id.text1);
        mList.setAdapter(mAdapter);
        mList.setOnItemClickListener(new AdapterView.OnItemClickListener() {
            @Override
            public void onItemClick(AdapterView<?> parent, View v,
                    int position, long id) {
                NewsItem item = mAdapter.getItem(position);
                Intent intent = new Intent(Intent.ACTION_VIEW);
                intent.setData(Uri.parse(item.link));
                startActivity(intent);
            }
        });

        setContentView(mList);
    }

    @Override
    public void onResume() {
        super.onResume();
        //Retrieve the RSS feed
        try{
            HttpGet feedRequest = new HttpGet( new URI(FEED_URI) );
            RestTask task = new RestTask();
            task.setResponseCallback(this);
            task.execute(feedRequest);
            mProgress = ProgressDialog.show(this, "Searching",
                    "Waiting For Results...", true);
        } catch (Exception e) {
            Log.w(TAG, e);
        }
    }
```

```
    @Override
    public void onRequestSuccess(String response) {
        if (mProgress != null) {
            mProgress.dismiss();
            mProgress = null;
        }
        //Process the response data
        try {
            SAXParserFactory factory = SAXParserFactory.newInstance();
            SAXParser p = factory.newSAXParser();
            RSSHandler parser = new RSSHandler();
            p.parse(new InputSource(new StringReader(response)), parser);

            mAdapter.clear();
            for(NewsItem item : parser.getParsedItems()) {
                mAdapter.add(item);
            }
            mAdapter.notifyDataSetChanged();
        } catch (Exception e) {
            Log.w(TAG, e);
        }
    }

    @Override
    public void onRequestError(Exception error) {
        if (mProgress != null) {
            mProgress.dismiss();
            mProgress = null;
        }
        //Display the error
        mAdapter.clear();
        mAdapter.notifyDataSetChanged();
        Toast.makeText(this, error.getMessage(), Toast.LENGTH_SHORT).show();
    }
}
```

The example has been modified to display a `ListView`, which will be populated by the parsed items from the RSS feed. In the example, we add an `OnItemClickListener` to the list that will launch the news item's link in the browser.

Once the data is returned from the API in the response callback, Android's built-in SAX parser handles the job of traversing the XML string. `SAXParser.parse()` uses an instance of our `RSSHandler` to process the XML, which results in the handler's `feedItems` list being populated. The receiver then iterates through all the parsed items and adds them to an `ArrayAdapter` for display in the `ListView`.

XmlPullParser

The XmlPullParser provided by the framework is another efficient way of parsing incoming XML data. Like SAX, the parsing is stream-based so it does not require much memory to parse large document feeds as the entire XML data structure does not need to be loaded before parsing can begin. Let's see an example of using XmlPullParser to parse our RSS feed data. Unlike SAX, however, we must manually advance the parser through the data stream every step of the way, even over the tag elements we aren't interested in.

Listing 3-30 contains a factory class that iterates over the feed to construct model elements.

Listing 3-30. *Factory Class to Parse XML into Model Objects*

```
public class NewsItemFactory {

    /* Data Model Class */
    public static class NewsItem {
        public String title;
        public String link;
        public String description;

        @Override
        public String toString() {
            return title;
        }
    }

    /*
     * Parse the RSS feed out into a list of NewsItem elements
     */
    public static List<NewsItem> parseFeed(XmlPullParser parser)
            throws XmlPullParserException, IOException {
        List<NewsItem> items = new ArrayList<NewsItem>();

        while (parser.next() != XmlPullParser.END_TAG) {
            if (parser.getEventType() != XmlPullParser.START_TAG) {
                continue;
            }

            if (parser.getName().equals("rss") ||
                    parser.getName().equals("channel")) {
                //Skip these items, but allow to drill inside
            } else if (parser.getName().equals("item")) {
                NewsItem newsItem = readItem(parser);
                items.add(newsItem);
            } else {
                //Skip any other elements and their children
```

```
                skip(parser);
            }
        }

        //Return the parsed list
        return items;
    }

    /*
     * Parse each <item> element in the XML into a NewsItem
     */
    private static NewsItem readItem(XmlPullParser parser) throws
            XmlPullParserException, IOException {
        NewsItem newsItem = new NewsItem();

        //Must start with an <item> element to be valid
        parser.require(XmlPullParser.START_TAG, null, "item");
        while (parser.next() != XmlPullParser.END_TAG) {
            if (parser.getEventType() != XmlPullParser.START_TAG) {
                continue;
            }

            String name = parser.getName();
            if (name.equals("title")) {
                parser.require(XmlPullParser.START_TAG, null, "title");
                newsItem.title = readText(parser);
                parser.require(XmlPullParser.END_TAG, null, "title");
            } else if (name.equals("link")) {
                parser.require(XmlPullParser.START_TAG, null, "link");
                newsItem.link = readText(parser);
                parser.require(XmlPullParser.END_TAG, null, "link");
            } else if (name.equals("description")) {
                parser.require(XmlPullParser.START_TAG, null, "description");
                newsItem.description = readText(parser);
                parser.require(XmlPullParser.END_TAG, null, "description");
            } else {
                //Skip any other elements and their children
                skip(parser);
            }
        }

        return newsItem;
    }

    /*
     * Read the text content of the current element, which is the data
     * contained between the start and end tag
     */
    private static String readText(XmlPullParser parser) throws
            IOException, XmlPullParserException {
```

```
        String result = "";
        if (parser.next() == XmlPullParser.TEXT) {
            result = parser.getText();
            parser.nextTag();
        }
        return result;
    }

    /*
     * Helper method to skip over the current element and any children
     * it may have underneath it
     */
    private static void skip(XmlPullParser parser) throws
            XmlPullParserException, IOException {
        if (parser.getEventType() != XmlPullParser.START_TAG) {
            throw new IllegalStateException();
        }

        /*
         * For every new tag, increase the depth counter.  Decrease it for each
         * tag's end and return when we have reached an end tag that matches
         * the one we started with.
         */
        int depth = 1;
        while (depth != 0) {
            switch (parser.next()) {
            case XmlPullParser.END_TAG:
                depth--;
                break;
            case XmlPullParser.START_TAG:
                depth++;
                break;
            }
        }
    }
}
```

Pull parsing works by processing the data stream as a series of events. The application advances the parser to the next event by calling the `next()` method or one of the specialized variations. The following are the event types the parser will advance within:

- `START_DOCUMENT`: The parser will return this event when it is first initialized. It will only be in this state until the first call to `next()`, `nextToken()`, or `nextTag()`.

- START_TAG: The parser has just read a start tag element. The tag name can be retrieved with getName(), and any attributes that were present can be read with getAttributeValue() and associated methods.
- TEXT: Character data inside the tag element was read and can be obtained with getText().
- END_TAG: The parser has just read an end tag element. The tag name of the matching start tag can be retrieved with getName().
- END_DOCUMENT: The end of the data stream has been reached.

Because we must advance the parser ourselves, we have created a helper skip() method to assist in moving the parser past tags we aren't interested in. This method walks from the current position through all nested child elements until the matching end tag is reached, skipping over them. It does this through a depth counter that increments for each start tag and decrements for each end tag. When the depth counter reaches zero, we have reached the matching end tag for the initial position.

The parser in this example starts iterating through the tags in the stream looking for <item> tags that it can parse into a NewsItem when the parseFeed() method is called. Every element that is not one of these is skipped over with the exception of two: <rss> and <channel>. The reason is all the items are nested within these two tags, so while we aren't interested in them directly, we cannot hand them off to skip() or all our items will be skipped as well.

The task of parsing each <item> element is handled by readItem(), where a new NewsItem is constructed and filled in by the data found within. The method begins by calling require(), which is a security check to ensure the XML is formatted as we expect. The method will quietly return if the current parser event matches the namespace and tag name passed in, otherwise it will throw an exception. As we iterate through the child elements, we look specifically for the title, link, and description tags so we can read their values into the model data. After finding each tag, readText() advances the parser and pulls the enclosed character data out. Again, there are other elements inside of <item> that we aren't parsing, so we call skip() in the case of any tag we don't need.

You can see that XmlPullParser is extremely flexible because you control every step of the process, but this also requires more code to accomplish the same result. Listing 3-31 shows our feed display Activity reworked to use the new parser.

Listing 3-31. *Activity Displaying Parsed XML Feed*

```
public class PullFeedActivity extends Activity implements ResponseCallback {
    private static final String TAG = "FeedReader";
    private static final String FEED_URI =
            "http://news.google.com/?output=rss";

    private ListView mList;
    private ArrayAdapter<NewsItem> mAdapter;
    private ProgressDialog mProgress;

    @Override
    public void onCreate(Bundle savedInstanceState) {
        super.onCreate(savedInstanceState);

        mList = new ListView(this);
        mAdapter = new ArrayAdapter<NewsItem>(this,
                android.R.layout.simple_list_item_1,
                android.R.id.text1);
        mList.setAdapter(mAdapter);
        mList.setOnItemClickListener(new AdapterView.OnItemClickListener() {
            @Override
            public void onItemClick(AdapterView<?> parent, View v,
                    int position, long id) {
                NewsItem item = mAdapter.getItem(position);
                Intent intent = new Intent(Intent.ACTION_VIEW);
                intent.setData(Uri.parse(item.link));
                startActivity(intent);
            }
        });

        setContentView(mList);
    }

    @Override
    public void onResume() {
        super.onResume();
        //Retrieve the RSS feed
        try{
            HttpGet feedRequest = new HttpGet( new URI(FEED_URI) );
            RestTask task = new RestTask();
            task.setResponseCallback(this);
            task.execute(feedRequest);
            mProgress = ProgressDialog.show(this, "Searching",
                    "Waiting For Results...", true);
        } catch (Exception e) {
            Log.w(TAG, e);
        }
    }
```

```
    @Override
    public void onRequestSuccess(String response) {
        if (mProgress != null) {
            mProgress.dismiss();
            mProgress = null;
        }
        //Process the response data
        try {
            XmlPullParser parser = Xml.newPullParser();
            parser.setInput(new StringReader(response));
            //Jump to the first tag
            parser.nextTag();

            mAdapter.clear();
            for(NewsItem item : NewsItemFactory.parseFeed(parser)) {
                mAdapter.add(item);
            }
            mAdapter.notifyDataSetChanged();
        } catch (Exception e) {
            Log.w(TAG, e);
        }
    }

    @Override
    public void onRequestError(Exception error) {
        if (mProgress != null) {
            mProgress.dismiss();
            mProgress = null;
        }
        //Display the error
        mAdapter.clear();
        mAdapter.notifyDataSetChanged();
        Toast.makeText(this, error.getMessage(), Toast.LENGTH_SHORT).show();
    }
}
```

A fresh XmlPullParser can be instantiated using Xml.newPullParser(), and the input data source can be a Reader our InputStream instance with setInput(). In our case, the response data from the web service is already in a String, so we wrap that in a StringReader to have the parser consume. We can pass the parser to NewsItemFactory, which will then return a list of NewsItem elements that we can add to the ListAdapter and display just as we did before.

> **TIP:** You can also use `XmlPullParser` to parse local XML data you may want to bundle in your application. By placing your raw XML into resources (such as `res/xml/`) you can instantiate an `XmlResourceParser` preloaded with your local data with `Resources.getXml()`.

3–9. Receiving SMS

Problem

Your application must react to incoming SMS messages, commonly called text messages.

Solution

(API Level 1)

Register a `BroadcastReceiver` to listen for incoming messages, and process them in `onReceive()`. The operating system will fire a broadcast Intent with the `android.provider.Telephony.SMS_RECEIVED` action whenever there is an incoming SMS message. Your application can register a BroadcastReceiver to filter for this Intent and process the incoming data.

> **NOTE:** Receiving this broadcast does not prevent the rest of the system's applications from receiving it as well. The default messaging application will still receive and display any incoming SMS.

How It Works

In previous recipes, we defined `BroadcastReceivers` as private internal members to an Activity. In this case, it is probably best to define the receiver separately and register it in `AndroidManifest.xml` using the `<receiver>` tag. This will allow your receiver to process the incoming events even when your application is not active. Listings 3-31 and 3-32 show an example of a receiver that monitors all incoming SMS and raises a Toast when one arrives from the party of interest.

Listing 3-31. *Incoming SMS BroadcastReceiver*

```
public class SmsReceiver extends BroadcastReceiver {
    private static final String SHORTCODE = "55443";

    @Override
    public void onReceive(Context context, Intent intent) {
        Bundle bundle = intent.getExtras();

        Object[] messages = (Object[])bundle.get("pdus");
        SmsMessage[] sms = new SmsMessage[messages.length];
        //Create messages for each incoming PDU
        for(int n=0; n < messages.length; n++) {
            sms[n] = SmsMessage.createFromPdu((byte[]) messages[n]);
        }
        for(SmsMessage msg : sms) {
            //Verify if the message came from our known sender
            if(TextUtils.equals(msg.getOriginatingAddress(), SHORTCODE)) {
                Toast.makeText(context,
                        "Received message from the mothership: "
                        + msg.getMessageBody(),
                        Toast.LENGTH_SHORT).show();
            }
        }
    }
}
```

Listing 3-32. *Partial AndroidManifest.xml*

```
<?xml version="1.0" encoding="utf-8"?>
<manifest ...>
    <application ...>
      <receiver android:name=".SmsReceiver">
        <intent-filter>
          <action android:name="android.provider.Telephony.SMS_RECEIVED" />
        </intent-filter>
      </receiver>
    </application>
    <uses-permission android:name="android.permission.RECEIVE_SMS" />
</manifest>
```

> **IMPORTANT:** Receiving SMS messages requires that the `android.permission.RECEIVE_SMS` permission be declared in the manifest!

Incoming SMS messages are passed via the extras of the broadcast Intent as an Object array of byte arrays, each byte array representing an SMS packet data unit (PDU). `SmsMessage.createFromPdu()` is a convenience method allowing us to create SmsMessage objects from the raw PDU data. With the setup work complete, we can inspect each message to determine if there is something interesting to handle or process. In the example, we compare the originating address of each message against a known short code, and the user is notified when one arrives.

At the point in the example where the Toast is raised, you may wish to provide something more useful to the user. Perhaps the SMS message includes an offer code for your application, and you could launch the appropriate Activity to display this information to the user within the application.

3–10. Sending an SMS Message

Problem

Your application must issue outgoing SMS messages.

Solution

(API Level 4)

Use the SMSManager to send text and data SMS messages. SMSManager is a system service that handles sending SMS and providing feedback to the application about the status of the operation. SMSManager provides methods to send text messages using SmsManager.sendTextMessage() and SmsManager.sendMultipartTextMessage(), or data messages using SmsManager.sendDataMessage(). Each of these methods takes PendingIntent parameters to deliver status for the send operation and the message delivery back to a requested destination.

How It Works

Let's take a look at a simple example Activity that sends an SMS message and monitors its status (see Listing 3-33).

Listing 3-33. *Activity to Send SMS Messages*

```
public class SmsActivity extends Activity {
    private static final String SHORTCODE = "55443";
    private static final String ACTION_SENT = "com.examples.sms.SENT";
    private static final String ACTION_DELIVERED =
```

```
            "com.examples.sms.DELIVERED";

    @Override
    public void onCreate(Bundle savedInstanceState) {
        super.onCreate(savedInstanceState);

        Button sendButton = new Button(this);
        sendButton.setText("Hail the Mothership");
        sendButton.setOnClickListener(new View.OnClickListener() {
            @Override
            public void onClick(View v) {
                sendSMS("Beam us up!");
            }
        });

        setContentView(sendButton);
    }

    private void sendSMS(String message) {
        PendingIntent sIntent = PendingIntent.getBroadcast(this, 0,
            new Intent(ACTION_SENT), 0);
        PendingIntent dIntent = PendingIntent.getBroadcast(this, 0,
            new Intent(ACTION_DELIVERED), 0);
         //Monitor status of the operation
        registerReceiver(sent, new IntentFilter(ACTION_SENT));
        registerReceiver(delivered, new IntentFilter(ACTION_DELIVERED));
         //Send the message
        SmsManager manager = SmsManager.getDefault();
        manager.sendTextMessage(SHORTCODE, null, message, sIntent, dIntent);
    }

    private BroadcastReceiver sent = new BroadcastReceiver(){
        @Override
        public void onReceive(Context context, Intent intent) {
            switch (getResultCode()) {
            case Activity.RESULT_OK:
                //Handle sent success
                break;
            case SmsManager.RESULT_ERROR_GENERIC_FAILURE:
            case SmsManager.RESULT_ERROR_NO_SERVICE:
            case SmsManager.RESULT_ERROR_NULL_PDU:
            case SmsManager.RESULT_ERROR_RADIO_OFF:
                //Handle sent error
                break;
            }

            unregisterReceiver(this);
        }
    };
```

```
    private BroadcastReceiver delivered = new BroadcastReceiver(){
        @Override
        public void onReceive(Context context, Intent intent) {
            switch (getResultCode()) {
            case Activity.RESULT_OK:
                //Handle delivery success
                break;
            case Activity.RESULT_CANCELED:
                //Handle delivery failure
                break;
            }

            unregisterReceiver(this);
        }
    };
}
```

IMPORTANT: Sending SMS messages requires that the `android.permission.SEND_SMS` permission be declared in the manifest!

In the example, an SMS message is sent out via the `SMSManager` whenever the user taps the button. Because `SMSManager` is a system service, the static `SMSManager.getDefault()` method must be called to get a reference to it. `sendTextMessage()` takes the destination address (number), service center address, and message as parameters. The service center address should be null to allow `SMSManager` to use the system default.

Two `BroadcastReceivers` are registered to receive the callback Intents that will be sent: one for status of the send operation and the other for status of the delivery. The receivers are registered only while the operations are pending, and they unregister themselves as soon as the Intent is processed.

3–11. Communicating over Bluetooth

Problem

You want to leverage Bluetooth communication to transmit data between devices in your application.

Solution

(API Level 5)

Use the Bluetooth APIs introduced in API Level 5 to create a peer-to-peer connection. Bluetooth is a very popular wireless radio technology that is in almost all mobile devices today. Many users think of Bluetooth as a way for their mobile devices to connect with a wireless headset or integrate with a vehicle's stereo system. However, Bluetooth can also be a simple and effective way for developers to create peer-to-peer connections in their applications.

How It Works

> **IMPORTANT:** Bluetooth is not currently supported in the Android emulator. In order to execute the code in this example, it must be run on an Android device. Furthermore, to appropriately test the functionality, you need two devices running the application simultaneously.

Bluetooth Peer-To-Peer

Listings 3-34 through 3-36 illustrate an example that uses Bluetooth to find other users nearby and quickly exchange contact information (in this case, just an email address). Connections are made over Bluetooth by discovering available "services" and connecting to them by referencing their unique 128-bit UUID value. This means that the UUID of the service you want to use must either be discovered or known ahead of time.

In this example, the same application is running on both devices on each end of the connection, so we have the freedom to define the UUID in code as a constant because both devices will have a reference to it.

> **NOTE:** To ensure that the UUID you choose is unique, use one of the many free UUID generators available on the Web.

Listing 3-34. *AndroidManifest.xml*

```
<?xml version="1.0" encoding="utf-8"?>
<manifest xmlns:android="http://schemas.android.com/apk/res/android"
      android:versionCode="1"
```

```
    android:versionName="1.0" package="com.examples.bluetooth">
  <application android:icon="@drawable/icon"
      android:label="@string/app_name">
      <activity android:name=".ExchangeActivity"
                android:label="@string/app_name">
          <intent-filter>
              <action android:name="android.intent.action.MAIN" />
              <category android:name="android.intent.category.LAUNCHER" />
          </intent-filter>
      </activity>
  </application>
  <uses-sdk android:minSdkVersion="5" />

  <uses-permission android:name="android.permission.BLUETOOTH"/>
  <uses-permission android:name="android.permission.BLUETOOTH_ADMIN"/>
</manifest>
```

> **IMPORTANT:** Remember that `android.permission.BLUETOOTH` must be declared in the manifest to use these APIs. In addition, `android.permission.BLUETOOTH_ADMIN` must be declared to make changes to preferences like discoverability and to enable/disable the adapter.

Listing 3-35. *res/layout/main.xml*

```
<?xml version="1.0" encoding="utf-8"?>
<RelativeLayout xmlns:android="http://schemas.android.com/apk/res/android"
  android:layout_width="fill_parent"
  android:layout_height="fill_parent">
  <TextView
    android:id="@+id/label"
    android:layout_width="wrap_content"
    android:layout_height="wrap_content"
    android:textAppearance="?android:attr/textAppearanceLarge"
    android:text="Enter Your Email:"
  />
  <EditText
    android:id="@+id/emailField"
    android:layout_width="fill_parent"
    android:layout_height="wrap_content"
    android:layout_below="@id/label"
    android:singleLine="true"
    android:inputType="textEmailAddress"
  />
  <Button
    android:id="@+id/scanButton"
    android:layout_width="fill_parent"
    android:layout_height="wrap_content"
```

```
    android:layout_alignParentBottom="true"
    android:text="Connect and Share"
  />
  <Button
    android:id="@+id/listenButton"
    android:layout_width="fill_parent"
    android:layout_height="wrap_content"
    android:layout_above="@id/scanButton"
    android:text="Listen for Sharers"
  />
</RelativeLayout>
```

The user interface for this example consists of an EditText for the user to enter his or her email address, and two buttons to initiate communication. The button titled "Listen for Sharers" puts the device into Listen Mode. In this mode, the device will accept and communicate with any device that attempts to connect with it. The button titled "Connect and Share" puts the device into Search Mode. In this mode, the device searches for any device that is currently listening and makes a connection (see Listing 3-36).

Listing 3-36. *Bluetooth Exchange Activity*

```
public class ExchangeActivity extends Activity {

    // Unique UUID for this application (generated from the web)
    private static final UUID MY_UUID =
        UUID.fromString("321cb8fa-9066-4f58-935e-ef55d1ae06ec");
    //Friendly name to match while discovering
    private static final String SEARCH_NAME = "bluetooth.recipe";

    BluetoothAdapter mBtAdapter;
    BluetoothSocket mBtSocket;
    Button listenButton, scanButton;
    EditText emailField;

    @Override
    public void onCreate(Bundle savedInstanceState) {
        super.onCreate(savedInstanceState);
        requestWindowFeature(Window.FEATURE_INDETERMINATE_PROGRESS);
        setContentView(R.layout.main);

        //Check the system status
        mBtAdapter = BluetoothAdapter.getDefaultAdapter();
        if(mBtAdapter == null) {
            Toast.makeText(this, "Bluetooth is not supported.",
                Toast.LENGTH_SHORT).show();
            finish();
            return;
        }
```

```
        if (!mBtAdapter.isEnabled()) {
            Intent enableIntent =
                    new Intent(BluetoothAdapter.ACTION_REQUEST_ENABLE);
            startActivityForResult(enableIntent, REQUEST_ENABLE);
        }

        emailField = (EditText)findViewById(R.id.emailField);
        listenButton = (Button)findViewById(R.id.listenButton);
        listenButton.setOnClickListener(new View.OnClickListener() {
            @Override
            public void onClick(View v) {
                //Make sure the device is discoverable first
                if (mBtAdapter.getScanMode() !=
                        BluetoothAdapter.SCAN_MODE_CONNECTABLE_DISCOVERABLE) {
                    Intent discoverableIntent =
                            new Intent(
                                BluetoothAdapter.ACTION_REQUEST_DISCOVERABLE);
                    discoverableIntent.putExtra(BluetoothAdapter.
                            EXTRA_DISCOVERABLE_DURATION, 300);
                    startActivityForResult(discoverableIntent,
                            REQUEST_DISCOVERABLE);
                    return;
                }
                startListening();
            }
        });
        scanButton = (Button)findViewById(R.id.scanButton);
        scanButton.setOnClickListener(new View.OnClickListener() {
            @Override
            public void onClick(View v) {
                mBtAdapter.startDiscovery();
                setProgressBarIndeterminateVisibility(true);
            }
        });
    }

    @Override
    public void onResume() {
        super.onResume();
        //Register the activity for broadcast intents
        IntentFilter filter = new IntentFilter(BluetoothDevice.ACTION_FOUND);
        registerReceiver(mReceiver, filter);
        filter = new IntentFilter(BluetoothAdapter.ACTION_DISCOVERY_FINISHED);
        registerReceiver(mReceiver, filter);
    }

    @Override
    public void onPause() {
        super.onPause();
        unregisterReceiver(mReceiver);
```

```
    }

    @Override
    public void onDestroy() {
        super.onDestroy();
        try {
            if(mBtSocket != null) {
                mBtSocket.close();
            }
        } catch (IOException e) {
            e.printStackTrace();
        }
    }

    private static final int REQUEST_ENABLE = 1;
    private static final int REQUEST_DISCOVERABLE = 2;

    @Override
    protected void onActivityResult(int requestCode, int resultCode,
            Intent data) {
        switch(requestCode) {
        case REQUEST_ENABLE:
            if(resultCode != Activity.RESULT_OK) {
                Toast.makeText(this, "Bluetooth Not Enabled.",
                    Toast.LENGTH_SHORT).show();
                finish();
            }
            break;
        case REQUEST_DISCOVERABLE:
            if(resultCode == Activity.RESULT_CANCELED) {
                Toast.makeText(this, "Must be discoverable.",
                    Toast.LENGTH_SHORT).show();
            } else {
                startListening();
            }
            break;
        default:
            break;
        }
    }

    //Start a server socket and listen
    private void startListening() {
        AcceptTask task = new AcceptTask();
        task.execute(MY_UUID);
        setProgressBarIndeterminateVisibility(true);
    }

    //AsyncTask to accept incoming connections
    private class AcceptTask extends AsyncTask<UUID,Void,BluetoothSocket> {
```

```
        @Override
        protected BluetoothSocket doInBackground(UUID... params) {
            String name = mBtAdapter.getName();
            try {
                //While listening, set the discovery name to a specific value
                mBtAdapter.setName(SEARCH_NAME);
                BluetoothServerSocket socket =
                        mBtAdapter.listenUsingRfcommWithServiceRecord(
                            "BluetoothRecipe", params[0]);
                BluetoothSocket connected = socket.accept();
                //Reset the BT adapter name
                mBtAdapter.setName(name);
                return connected;
            } catch (IOException e) {
                e.printStackTrace();
                mBtAdapter.setName(name);
                return null;
            }
        }

        @Override
        protected void onPostExecute(BluetoothSocket socket) {
            if(socket == null) {
                return;
            }
            mBtSocket = socket;
            ConnectedTask task = new ConnectedTask();
            task.execute(mBtSocket);
        }

    }

    //AsyncTask to receive a single line of data and post
    private class ConnectedTask extends
            AsyncTask<BluetoothSocket,Void,String> {

        @Override
        protected String doInBackground(BluetoothSocket... params) {
            InputStream in = null;
            OutputStream out = null;
            try {
                //Send your data
                out = params[0].getOutputStream();
                out.write(emailField.getText().toString().getBytes());
                //Receive the other's data
                in = params[0].getInputStream();
                byte[] buffer = new byte[1024];
                in.read(buffer);
                //Create a clean string from results
```

```
                String result = new String(buffer);
                //Close the connection
                mBtSocket.close();
                return result.trim();
            } catch (Exception exc) {
                return null;
            }
        }

        @Override
        protected void onPostExecute(String result) {
            Toast.makeText(ExchangeActivity.this, result, Toast.LENGTH_SHORT)
                    .show();
            setProgressBarIndeterminateVisibility(false);
        }
    }

    // The BroadcastReceiver that listens for discovered devices
    private BroadcastReceiver mReceiver = new BroadcastReceiver() {
        @Override
        public void onReceive(Context context, Intent intent) {
            String action = intent.getAction();

            // When discovery finds a device
            if (BluetoothDevice.ACTION_FOUND.equals(action)) {
                // Get the BluetoothDevice object from the Intent
                BluetoothDevice device =
                    intent.getParcelableExtra(BluetoothDevice.EXTRA_DEVICE);
                if(TextUtils.equals(device.getName(), SEARCH_NAME)) {
                    //Matching device found, connect
                    mBtAdapter.cancelDiscovery();
                    try {
                        mBtSocket =
                           device.createRfcommSocketToServiceRecord(MY_UUID);
                        mBtSocket.connect();
                        ConnectedTask task = new ConnectedTask();
                        task.execute(mBtSocket);
                    } catch (IOException e) {
                        e.printStackTrace();
                    }
                }
            //When discovery is complete
            } else if (BluetoothAdapter.ACTION_DISCOVERY_FINISHED
                    .equals(action)) {
                setProgressBarIndeterminateVisibility(false);
            }

        }
    };
}
```

When the application first starts up, it runs some basic checks on the Bluetooth status of the device. If `BluetoothAdapter.getDefaultAdapter()` returns null, it is an indication that the device does not have Bluetooth support and the application will go no further. Even with Bluetooth on the device, it must be enabled for the application to use it. If Bluetooth is disabled, the preferred method for enabling the adapter is to send an Intent to the system with `BluetoothAdapter.ACTION_REQUEST_ENABLE` as the action. This notifies the user of the issue, and he or she can then enable Bluetooth. A `BluetoothAdapter` can be manually enabled with the `enable()` method, but we strongly discourage you from doing this unless you have requested the user's permission another way.

With Bluetooth validated, the application waits for user input. As mentioned previously, the example can be put into one of two modes on each device: Listen Mode or Search Mode. Let's look at the path each mode takes.

Listen Mode

Tapping the "Listen for Sharers" button starts the application listening for incoming connections. In order for a device to accept incoming connections from devices it may not know, it must be set as discoverable. The application verifies this by checking if the adapter's scan mode is equal to `SCAN_MODE_CONNECTABLE_DISCOVERABLE`. If the adapter does not meet this requirement, another Intent is sent to the system to notify the user that they should allow the device to be discoverable, similar to the method used to request Bluetooth be enabled. If the user accepts this request, the Activity will return a result equal to the length of time they allowed the device to be discoverable; if they cancel the request, the Activity will return `Activity.RESULT_CANCELED`. Our example monitors for a user canceling in `onActivityResult()`, and finishes under those conditions.

If the user allows discovery, or if the device was already discoverable, an `AcceptTask` is created and executed. This task creates a listener socket for the specified UUID of the service we defined, and it blocks the calling thread while waiting for an incoming connection request. Once a valid request is received, it is accepted and the application moves into Connected Mode.

During the period of time while the device is listening, its Bluetooth name is set to a known unique value (`SEARCH_NAME`) to speed up the discovery process (we'll see more about why in the "Search Mode" section). Once the connection is established, the default name given to the adapter is restored.

Search Mode

Tapping the "Connect and Share" button tells the application to begin searching for another device to connect with. It does this by starting a Bluetooth discovery process and handling the results in a BroadcastReceiver. When a discovery is started via `BluetoothAdapter.startDiscovery()`, Android will asynchronously call back with broadcasts under two conditions: when another device is found, and when the process is complete.

The private receiver `mReceiver` is registered at all times when the Activity is visible to the user, and it will receive a broadcast with each new discovered device. Recall from the discussion on Listen Mode that the device name of a listening device was set to a unique value. Upon each discovery made, the receiver checks that the device name matches our known value, and it attempts to connect when one is found. This is important to the speed of the discovery process because otherwise the only way to validate each device is to attempt a connection to the specific service UUID and see if the operation is successful. The Bluetooth connection process is heavyweight and slow and should only be done when necessary to keep things performing well.

This method of matching devices also relieves the user of the need to select manually which device they want to connect to. The application is smart enough to find another device that is running the same application and in a listening mode to complete the transfer. Removing the user also means that this value should be unique and obscure so as to avoid finding other devices that may accidentally have the same name.

With a matching device found, we cancel the discovery process (as it is also heavyweight and will slow down the connection) and then make a connection to the service's UUID. With a successful connection made, the application moves into Connected Mode.

Connected Mode

Once connected, the application on both devices will create a `ConnectedTask` to send and receive the user contact information. The connected `BluetoothSocket` has an `InputStream` and an `OutputStream` available to do data transfer. First, the current value of the email textfield is packaged up and written to the `OutputStream`. Then, the `InputStream` is read to receive the remote device's information. Finally, each device takes the raw data it received and packages this into a clean String to display for the user.

The `ConnectedTask.onPostExecute()` method is tasked with displaying the results of the exchange to the user; currently, this is done by raising a Toast with the received contents. After the transaction, the connection is closed and both devices are in the same mode and ready to execute another exchange.

For more information on this topic, take a look at the BluetoothChat sample application provided with the Android SDK. This application provides a great demonstration of making a long-lived connection for users to send chat messages between devices.

Bluetooth Beyond Android

As we mentioned in the beginning of this section, Bluetooth is found in many wireless devices besides mobile phones and tablets. RFCOMM interfaces also exist in devices like Bluetooth modems and serial adapters. The same APIs that were used to create the peer-to-peer connection between Android devices can also be used to connect to other embedded Bluetooth devices for the purposes of monitoring and control.

The key to establishing a connection with these embedded devices is obtaining the UUID of the RFCOMM services they support. As with the previous example, with the proper UUID we can create a BluetoothSocket and transmit data. However, since the UUID is not known as it was in the last example, we must have a way to discover and obtain it.

The capability to do this exists in the SDK, although prior to Android 4.0.3 (API Level 15) it was not part of the public SDK. There are two methods on `BluetoothDevice` that will provide this information; `fetchUuidsWithSdp()` and `getUuids()`. The latter simply returned the cached instances for the device that was found during discovery, while the former asynchronously connects to the device and does a fresh query. Because of this, when using `fetchUuidsWithSdp()`, you must register a `BroadcastReceiver` that will receive Intents set with the `BluetoothDevice.ACTION_UUID` action string to discover the UUID values.

Discover a UUID

A quick glance at the source code for BluetoothDevice (thanks to Android's open source roots) points out that these methods to return UUID information for a remote device have existed for awhile, and if necessary we can use reflection to call them in earlier Android versions now that they are part of the public API and won't change in the future. The simplest to use is the synchronous (blocking) method `getUuids()`, which returns an array of `ParcelUuid` objects referring to each service. Here is an example method for reading the UUIDs of service records from a remote device using reflection:

```
public ParcelUuid servicesFromDevice(BluetoothDevice device) {
    try {
        Class cl = Class.forName("android.bluetooth.BluetoothDevice");
        Class[] par = {};
        Method method = cl.getMethod("getUuids", par);
        Object[] args = {};
        ParcelUuid[] retval = (ParcelUuid[])method.invoke(device, args);
        return retval;
    } catch (Exception e) {
        e.printStackTrace();
        return null;
    }
}
```

You may also call `fetchUuidsWithSdp()`in the same fashion, but there were some variations in the Intent structure that was returned in early versions, so we would not recommend doing so for earlier Android versions.

3–12. Querying Network Reachability

Problem

Your application needs to be aware of changes in network connectivity.

Solution

(API Level 1)

Keep tabs on the device's connectivity with `ConnectivityManager`. One of the paramount issues to consider in mobile application design is that the network is not always available for use. As people move about, the speeds and capabilities of networks are subject to change. Because of this, an application that uses network resources should always be able to detect if those resources are reachable and then notify the user when they are not.

In addition to reachability, `ConnectivityManager` can provide the application with information about the connection type. This allows you to make decisions like whether to download a large file because the user is currently roaming and it may cost him or her a fortune.

How It Works

Listing 3-37 creates a wrapper method you can place in your code to check for network connectivity.

Listing 3-37. *ConnectivityManager Wrapper*

```
public boolean isNetworkReachable() {
    ConnectivityManager mManager =
            (ConnectivityManager)context.getSystemService(
                    Context.CONNECTIVITY_SERVICE);
    NetworkInfo current = mManager.getActiveNetworkInfo();
    if(current == null) {
        return false;
    }
    return (current.getState() == NetworkInfo.State.CONNECTED);
}
```

`ConnectivityManager` does pretty much all of the work in checking the network status, and this wrapper method is more to simplify having to check all possible network paths each time. Note that `ConnectivityManager.getActiveNetworkInfo()` will return null if there is no active data connection available, so we must check for that case first. If there is an active network, we can inspect its state, which will return one of the following:

- DISCONNECTED
- CONNECTING
- CONNECTED
- DISCONNECTING

When the state returns as CONNECTED, the network is considered stable and we can utilize it to access remote resources.

It is considered good practice to call a reachability check whenever a network request fails and to notify the user that his or her request failed due to a lack of connectivity. Listing 3-38 is an example of doing this when a network access fails.

Listing 3-38. *Notify User of Connectivity Failure*

```
try {
    //Attempt to access network resource
    //May throw HttpResponseException or some other IOException on failure
} catch (Exception e) {
    if( !isNetworkReachable() ) {
```

```
            AlertDialog.Builder builder = new AlertDialog.Builder(context);
            builder.setTitle("No Network Connection");
            builder.setMessage("The Network is unavailable."
                    + " Please try your request again later.");
            builder.setPositiveButton("OK",null);
            builder.create().show();
        }
    }
```

Determining Connection Type

In cases where it is also essential to know whether the user is connected to a network that charges for bandwidth, we can call `NetworkInfo.getType()` on the active network connection (see Listing 3-39).

Listing 3-39. *ConnectivityManager Bandwidth Checking*

```
public boolean isWifiReachable() {
    ConnectivityManager mManager =
            (ConnectivityManager)context.getSystemService(
                    Context.CONNECTIVITY_SERVICE);
    NetworkInfo current = mManager.getActiveNetworkInfo();
    if(current == null) {
        return false;
    }
    return (current.getType() == ConnectivityManager.TYPE_WIFI);
}
```

This modified version of the reachability check determines if the user is attached to a WiFi connection, typically indicating that he or she has a faster connection where bandwidth isn't tariffed.

3-13. Transferring Data with NFC

Problem

You have an application that must quickly transfer small data packets between two Android devices with minimal setup.

Solution

(API Level 16)

Make use of the NFC Beam APIs. NFC communication was originally added to the SDK in Android 2.3 and was expanded in 4.0 to include make short message transfer between devices painless through a process called Android Beam. In Android 4.1, even more was added to make the Beam APIs fully mature for transferring data between two devices.

One of the major additions in 4.1 was the ability to transfer large data over alternate connections. NFC is a great method of discovering devices and setting up an initial connection, but it is low bandwidth and inefficient for sending large data packets like full-color images. Previously, developers could use NFC to connect two devices but would need to manually negotiate a second connection over WiFi Direct or Bluetooth to actually transfer the file data. In Android 4.1, the framework now handles that entire process, and any application can share large files over any available connection with a single API call.

How It Works

Depending on the size of the content you wish to push, there are two mechanisms available to Beam data from one device to another.

Beaming with Foreground Push

If you want to send simple content between devices over NFC, you can use the foreground push mechanism to create an `NfcMessage` containing one or more `NfcRecord` instances. Listings 3-40 and 3-41 illustrate creating a simple `NfcMessage` to push to another device.

Listing 3-40. *AndroidManifest.xml*

```
<manifest xmlns:android="http://schemas.android.com/apk/res/android"
    package="com.examples.nfcbeam"
    android:versionCode="1"
    android:versionName="1.0" >

    <uses-sdk
        android:minSdkVersion="16"
        android:targetSdkVersion="16" />

    <uses-permission android:name="android.permission.NFC" />
```

```
    <application
        android:icon="@drawable/ic_launcher"
        android:label="NfcBeam">
        <activity
            android:name=".NfcActivity"
            android:label="NfcActivity"
            android:launchMode="singleTop">
            <intent-filter>
                <action android:name="android.intent.action.MAIN" />
                <category android:name="android.intent.category.LAUNCHER" />
            </intent-filter>
             <intent-filter>
                 <action android:name="android.nfc.action.NDEF_DISCOVERED" />
                 <category android:name="android.intent.category.DEFAULT" />
                 <data android:mimeType=
                         "application/com.example.androidrecipes.beamtext"/>
             </intent-filter>
        </activity>
    </application>
</manifest>
```

First notice that android.permission.NFC is required to work with the NFC service. Second, note the custom <intent-filter> placed on our Activity. This is how Android will know which application to launch in response to the content it receives.

Listing 3-41. *Activity Generating an NFC Foreground Push*

```
public class NfcActivity extends Activity implements
        CreateNdefMessageCallback, OnNdefPushCompleteCallback {
    private static final String TAG = "NfcBeam";
    private NfcAdapter mNfcAdapter;
    private TextView mDisplay;

    @Override
    public void onCreate(Bundle savedInstanceState) {
        super.onCreate(savedInstanceState);
        mDisplay = new TextView(this);
        setContentView(mDisplay);

        // Check for available NFC Adapter
        mNfcAdapter = NfcAdapter.getDefaultAdapter(this);
        if (mNfcAdapter == null) {
            mDisplay.setText("NFC is not available on this device.");
        } else {
            // Register callback to set NDEF message.  Setting this makes
            // NFC data push active while the Activity is in the foreground.
            mNfcAdapter.setNdefPushMessageCallback(this, this);
            // Register callback to listen for message-sent success
            mNfcAdapter.setOnNdefPushCompleteCallback(this, this);
```

```
        }
    }

    @Override
    public void onResume() {
        super.onResume();
        // Check to see if a Beam launched this Activity
        if (NfcAdapter.ACTION_NDEF_DISCOVERED
                .equals(getIntent().getAction())) {
            processIntent(getIntent());
        }
    }

    @Override
    public void onNewIntent(Intent intent) {
        // onResume gets called after this to handle the intent
        setIntent(intent);
    }

    void processIntent(Intent intent) {
        Parcelable[] rawMsgs =
                intent.getParcelableArrayExtra(NfcAdapter.EXTRA_NDEF_MESSAGES);
        // only one message sent during the beam
        NdefMessage msg = (NdefMessage) rawMsgs[0];
        // record 0 contains the MIME type
        mDisplay.setText(new String(msg.getRecords()[0].getPayload()));
    }

    @Override
    public NdefMessage createNdefMessage(NfcEvent event) {
        String text =
                String.format("Sending A Message From Android Recipes at %s",
                    DateFormat.getTimeFormat(this).format(new Date()));
        NdefMessage msg = new NdefMessage(NdefRecord.createMime(
                "application/com.example.androidrecipes.beamtext",
                text.getBytes()) );
        return msg;
    }

    @Override
    public void onNdefPushComplete(NfcEvent event) {
        //This callback happens on a binder thread, don't update
        // the UI directly from this method.
        Log.i(TAG, "Message Sent!");
    }
}
```

This example application encompasses both the sending and receiving of an NFC push, so the same application should be installed on both devices: the one that is sending and the one that is receiving the data. The Activity registers itself for foreground push using the setNdefPushMessageCallback() method on the NfcAdapter. This call does two things simultaneously. It tells the NFC service to call this Activity at the moment a transfer is initiated to receive the message it needs to send, and it also activates NFC push whenever this Activity is in the foreground. There is also an alternate version of this called setNdefPushMessage() that takes the message directly rather than implementing a callback.

The callback method constructs a single NdefMessage containing a single NDEF MIME record (created with the NdefRecord.createMime() method). MIME records are simple ways of passing application-specific data. The create method takes both a string for the MIME type and a byte array for the raw data. The information can be anything from a text string to a small image; your application is responsible for packing and unpacking it. Notice that the MIME type here matches the type defined in the manifest's <intent-filter>.

In order for the push to work, the sending device must have this Activity active in the foreground, and the receiving device must not be locked. When the user touches the two devices together, the sending screen will show Android's "Touch to beam" UI and a tap of the screen will send the message to the other device. As soon as the message is received, the application will launch on the receiving device, and the sending device's onNdefPushComplete() callback will be triggered.

On the receiving device, the Activity will be launched with the ACTION_NDEF_DISCOVERED Intent, so our example will inspect the Intent for the NdefMessage and unpack the payload, turning it back from bytes into a string. This method of using Intent matching to send NFC data is the most flexible, but sometimes you want your application to be explicitly called. This is where Android Application Records come in.

Android Application Records

Your application can provide an additional NdefRecord inside an NdefMessage that directs Android to call a specific package name on the receiving device. To include this in our previous example, we would simply modify the CreateNdefMessageCallback like so.

```
@Override
public NdefMessage createNdefMessage(NfcEvent event) {
    String text = String.format("Sending A Message From Android Recipes at %s",
            DateFormat.getTimeFormat(this).format(new Date()));
    NdefMessage msg = new NdefMessage(NdefRecord.createMime(
            "application/com.example.androidrecipes.beamtext", text.getBytes()),
             NdefRecord.createApplicationRecord("com.examples.nfcbeam") );
```

```
    return msg;
}
```

With the addition of NdefRecord.createApplicationRecord() this push message is now guaranteed to launch only our com.examples.nfcbeam package. The text information is still the first record in the message, so our unpacking of the received message remains unchanged.

Beaming Larger Content

We mentioned at the beginning of this recipe that sending large content blobs over NFC is not a great idea. However, Android Beam has the capability to handle that as well. Have a look at Listings 3-42 and 3-43 for examples of sending large image files over Beam.

Listing 3-42. *AndroidManifest.xml*

```
<manifest xmlns:android="http://schemas.android.com/apk/res/android"
    package="com.examples.nfcbeam"
    android:versionCode="1"
    android:versionName="1.0" >

    <uses-sdk
        android:minSdkVersion="16"
        android:targetSdkVersion="16" />

    <uses-permission android:name="android.permission.NFC" />
    <application
        android:icon="@drawable/ic_launcher"
        android:label="NfcBeam">
        <activity
            android:name=".BeamActivity"
            android:label="BeamActivity"
            android:launchMode="singleTop">
            <intent-filter>
                <action android:name="android.intent.action.MAIN" />
                <category android:name="android.intent.category.LAUNCHER" />
            </intent-filter>
            <intent-filter>
                <action android:name="android.intent.action.VIEW" />
                <data android:mimeType="image/*" />
            </intent-filter>
        </activity>
    </application>

</manifest>
```

Listing 3-43. *Activity to Beam an Image File*

```
public class BeamActivity extends Activity implements
        CreateBeamUrisCallback, OnNdefPushCompleteCallback {
    private static final String TAG = "NfcBeam";
    private static final int PICK_IMAGE = 100;

    private NfcAdapter mNfcAdapter;
    private Uri mSelectedImage;

    private TextView mUriName;
    private ImageView mPreviewImage;

    @Override
    protected void onCreate(Bundle savedInstanceState) {
        super.onCreate(savedInstanceState);
        setContentView(R.layout.main);

        mUriName = (TextView) findViewById(R.id.text_uri);
        mPreviewImage = (ImageView) findViewById(R.id.image_preview);

        // Check for available NFC Adapter
        mNfcAdapter = NfcAdapter.getDefaultAdapter(this);
        if (mNfcAdapter == null) {
            mUriName.setText("NFC is not available on this device.");
        } else {
            // Register callback to set NDEF message
            mNfcAdapter.setBeamPushUrisCallback(this, this);
            // Register callback to listen for message-sent success
            mNfcAdapter.setOnNdefPushCompleteCallback(this, this);
        }
    }

    @Override
    protected void onActivityResult(int requestCode, int resultCode,
            Intent data) {
        if (requestCode == PICK_IMAGE && resultCode == RESULT_OK
                && data != null) {
            mUriName.setText( data.getData().toString() );
            mSelectedImage = data.getData();
        }
    }

    @Override
    public void onResume() {
        super.onResume();
        // Check to see that the Activity started due to an Android Beam
        if (Intent.ACTION_VIEW.equals(getIntent().getAction())) {
            processIntent(getIntent());
        }
```

```
    }

    @Override
    public void onNewIntent(Intent intent) {
        // onResume gets called after this to handle the intent
        setIntent(intent);
    }

    void processIntent(Intent intent) {
        Uri data = intent.getData();
        if(data != null) {
            mPreviewImage.setImageURI(data);
        } else {
            mUriName.setText("Received Invalid Image Uri");
        }
    }

    public void onSelectClick(View v) {
        Intent intent = new Intent(Intent.ACTION_GET_CONTENT);
        intent.setType("image/*");
        startActivityForResult(intent, PICK_IMAGE);
    }

    @Override
    public Uri[] createBeamUris(NfcEvent event) {
        if (mSelectedImage == null) {
            return null;
        }
        return new Uri[] {mSelectedImage};
    }

    @Override
    public void onNdefPushComplete(NfcEvent event) {
        //This callback happens on a binder thread, don't update
        // the UI directly from this method.
        //This is a good time to tell your user they don't need to hold
        // their phones together anymore!
        Log.i(TAG, "Push Complete!");
    }
}
```

This example makes use of the `CreateBeamUrisCallback`, which allows an application to construct an array of `Uri` instances pointing to content you would like to transmit. Android will do the work of negotiating the initial connection over NFC but will then drop to a more suitable connection such as Bluetooth or WiFi Direct to finish the larger transfers.

In this case, the data on the receiving device is launched using the system's standard `Intent.ACTION_VIEW` action, so it actually is not necessary to load the application on both devices. However, our application does filter for `ACTION_VIEW` so the receiving device could use it to view the received image content if the user prefers.

Here, the user is asked to select an image from his or her device to Beam, and then the `Uri` of that content is displayed once selected. As soon as the user touches his or her device to another, the same "Touch to beam" UI (see Figure 3-4) displays and the transfer begins when the screen is tapped.

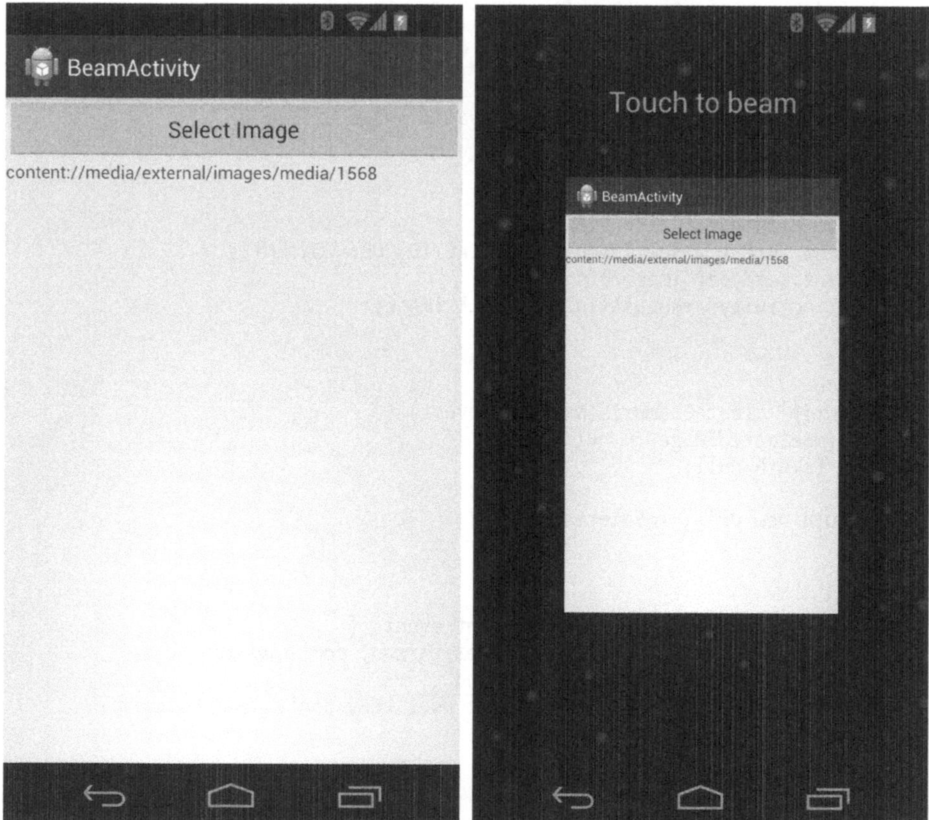

Figure 3-4. *Activity with Touch to Beam activated.*

Once the NFC portion of the transfer is complete, the `onNdefPushComplete()` method is called on the sending device. At this point, the transfer has moved to another connection, so the users don't need to hold their phones together anymore.

The receiving device will display a progress notification in the system's window shade while the file is transferring, and once complete the user can tap on the notification to view the content. If this application is chosen as the content viewer, the image will be shown in our application's `ImageView`. One possible disadvantage to registering your application with such a generic `Intent` is that every application on the device can then ask your application to view images, so choose your filters wisely!

3-14. Connecting over USB

Problem

Your application needs to communicate with a USB device for the purposes of control or transferring data.

Solution

(API Level 12)

Android has built-in support for devices that contain USB Host circuitry to allow them to enumerate and communicate with connected USB devices. `USBManager` is the system service that provides applications access to any external devices connected via USB, and we are going to see how you can use that service to establish a connection from your application.

USB Host circuitry is becoming more common on devices, but it is still rare. Initially, only tablet devices had this capability, but it is growing rapidly and may soon become a commonplace interface on commercial Android handsets as well. However, because of this you will certainly want to include the following element in your application manifest:

```
<uses-feature android:name="android.hardware.usb.host" />
```

This will limit your application to devices that actually have the available hardware to do the communications.

The APIs provided by Android are pretty much direct mirrors of the USB specification, without much in the way of higher-level abstraction. This means that if you would like to make use of them, you will need at least a basic knowledge of USB and how devices communicate.

USB Overview

Before looking at an example of how Android interacts with USB devices, let's take a moment to define some USB terms.

- Endpoint: The smallest building block of a USB device. These are what your application eventually connects to for the purpose of sending and receiving data. They can take the form of four main types:
  - Control: Used for configuration and status commands. Every device has at least one control endpoint, called "endpoint 0" that is not attached to any interface.
  - Interrupt: Used for small, high-priority control commands.
  - Bulk: Large data transfer. Commonly found in bidirectional pair (1 IN and 1 OUT).
  - Isochronous: Used for real-time data transfer such as audio. Not supported by the latest Android SDK as of this writing.
- Interface: A collection of endpoints to represent a "logical" device.
  - Physical USB devices can manifest themselves to the host as multiple logical devices, and they do this by exposing multiple interfaces.
- Configuration: Collection of one or more interfaces. The USB protocol enforces that only one configuration can be active at any one time on a device. In fact, most devices only have one configuration at all. Think of this as the device's operating mode.

How It Works

Listings 3-44 and 3-45 show examples that use `UsbManager` to inspect devices connected over USB and then uses control transfers to further query the configuration.

Listing 3-44. *res/layout/main.xml*

```
<LinearLayout xmlns:android="http://schemas.android.com/apk/res/android"
    android:layout_width="match_parent"
```

```
    android:layout_height="match_parent"
    android:orientation="vertical" >
    <Button
        android:id="@+id/button_connect"
        android:layout_width="match_parent"
        android:layout_height="wrap_content"
        android:text="Connect"
        android:onClick="onConnectClick" />
    <TextView
        android:id="@+id/text_status"
        android:layout_width="match_parent"
        android:layout_height="wrap_content" />
    <TextView
        android:id="@+id/text_data"
        android:layout_width="match_parent"
        android:layout_height="wrap_content" />

</LinearLayout>
```

Listing 3-45. *Activity on USB Host Querying Devices*

```
public class USBActivity extends Activity {
    private static final String TAG = "UsbHost";

    TextView mDeviceText, mDisplayText;
    Button mConnectButton;

    UsbManager mUsbManager;
    UsbDevice mDevice;
    PendingIntent mPermissionIntent;

    @Override
    public void onCreate(Bundle savedInstanceState) {
        super.onCreate(savedInstanceState);
        setContentView(R.layout.main);

        mDeviceText = (TextView) findViewById(R.id.text_status);
        mDisplayText = (TextView) findViewById(R.id.text_data);
        mConnectButton = (Button) findViewById(R.id.button_connect);

        mUsbManager = (UsbManager) getSystemService(Context.USB_SERVICE);
    }

    @Override
    protected void onResume() {
        super.onResume();
        mPermissionIntent =
            PendingIntent.getBroadcast(this, 0,
                new Intent(ACTION_USB_PERMISSION), 0);
        IntentFilter filter = new IntentFilter(ACTION_USB_PERMISSION);
```

```
        registerReceiver(mUsbReceiver, filter);

        //Check currently connected devices
        updateDeviceList();
    }

    @Override
    protected void onPause() {
        super.onPause();
        unregisterReceiver(mUsbReceiver);
    }

    public void onConnectClick(View v) {
        if (mDevice == null) {
            return;
        }
        mDisplayText.setText("---");

        //This will either prompt the user with a grant permission dialog,
        // or immediately fire the ACTION_USB_PERMISSION broadcast if the
        // user has already granted it to us.
        mUsbManager.requestPermission(mDevice, mPermissionIntent);
    }

    /*
     * Receiver to catch user permission responses, which are required in
     * order to actually interact with a connected device.
     */
    private static final String ACTION_USB_PERMISSION =
            "com.android.recipes.USB_PERMISSION";
    private final BroadcastReceiver mUsbReceiver = new BroadcastReceiver() {
        public void onReceive(Context context, Intent intent) {
            String action = intent.getAction();
            if (ACTION_USB_PERMISSION.equals(action)) {
                UsbDevice device = (UsbDevice) intent.getParcelableExtra(
                        UsbManager.EXTRA_DEVICE);

                if (intent.getBooleanExtra(UsbManager.EXTRA_PERMISSION_GRANTED,
                        false) && device != null) {
                        //Query the device's descriptor
                        getDeviceStatus(device);
                } else {
                    Log.d(TAG, "permission denied for device " + device);
                }
            }
        }
    };

    //Type: Indicates whether this is a read or write
    // Matches USB_ENDPOINT_DIR_MASK for either IN or OUT
```

```
private static final int REQUEST_TYPE = 0x80;
//Request: GET_CONFIGURATION_DESCRIPTOR = 0x06
private static final int REQUEST = 0x06;
//Value: Descriptor Type (High) and Index (Low)
// Configuration Descriptor = 0x2
// Index = 0x0 (First configuration)
private static final int REQ_VALUE = 0x200;
private static final int REQ_INDEX = 0x00;
private static final int LENGTH = 64;

/*
 * Initiate a control transfer to request the first configuration
 * descriptor of the device.
 */
private void getDeviceStatus(UsbDevice device) {
    UsbDeviceConnection connection = mUsbManager.openDevice(device);
    //Create a sufficiently large buffer for incoming data
    byte[] buffer = new byte[LENGTH];
    connection.controlTransfer(REQUEST_TYPE, REQUEST, REQ_VALUE, REQ_INDEX,
            buffer, LENGTH, 2000);
    //Parse received data into a description
    String description = parseConfigDescriptor(buffer);

    mDisplayText.setText(description);
    connection.close();
}

/*
 * Parse the USB configuration descriptor response per the
 * USB Specification.  Return a printable description of
 * the connected device.
 */
private static final int DESC_SIZE_CONFIG = 9;
private String parseConfigDescriptor(byte[] buffer) {
    StringBuilder sb = new StringBuilder();
    //Parse configuration descriptor header
    int totalLength = (buffer[3] &0xFF) << 8;
    totalLength += (buffer[2] & 0xFF);
    //Interface count
    int numInterfaces = (buffer[5] & 0xFF);
    //Configuration attributes
    int attributes = (buffer[7] & 0xFF);
    //Power is given in 2mA increments
    int maxPower = (buffer[8] & 0xFF) * 2;

    sb.append("Configuration Descriptor:\n");
    sb.append("Length: " + totalLength + " bytes\n");
    sb.append(numInterfaces + " Interfaces\n");
    sb.append(String.format("Attributes:%s%s%s\n",
            (attributes & 0x80) == 0x80 ? " BusPowered" : "",
```

```
            (attributes & 0x40) == 0x40 ? " SelfPowered" : "",
            (attributes & 0x20) == 0x20 ? " RemoteWakeup" : ""));
    sb.append("Max Power: " + maxPower + "mA\n");

    //The rest of the descriptor is interfaces and endpoints
    int index = DESC_SIZE_CONFIG;
    while (index < totalLength) {
        //Read length and type
        int len = (buffer[index] & 0xFF);
        int type = (buffer[index+1] & 0xFF);
        switch (type) {
        case 0x04: //Interface Descriptor
            int intfNumber = (buffer[index+2] & 0xFF);
            int numEndpoints = (buffer[index+4] & 0xFF);
            int intfClass = (buffer[index+5] & 0xFF);

            sb.append(String.format("- Interface %d, %s, %d Endpoints\n",
                    intfNumber, nameForClass(intfClass), numEndpoints));
            break;
        case 0x05: //Endpoint Descriptor
            int endpointAddr = ((buffer[index+2] & 0xFF));
            //Number is lower 4 bits
            int endpointNum = (endpointAddr & 0x0F);
            //Direction is high bit
            int direction = (endpointAddr & 0x80);

            int endpointAttrs = (buffer[index+3] & 0xFF);
            //Type is the lower two bits
            int endpointType = (endpointAttrs & 0x3);

            sb.append(String.format("-- Endpoint %d, %s %s\n",
                    endpointNum,
                    nameForEndpointType(endpointType),
                    nameForDirection(direction) ));
            break;
        }
        //Advance to next descriptor
        index += len;
    }

    return sb.toString();
}

private void updateDeviceList() {
    HashMap<String, UsbDevice> connectedDevices = mUsbManager
            .getDeviceList();
    if (connectedDevices.isEmpty()) {
        mDevice = null;
        mDeviceText.setText("No Devices Currently Connected");
        mConnectButton.setEnabled(false);
```

```
    } else {
        StringBuilder builder = new StringBuilder();
        for (UsbDevice device : connectedDevices.values()) {
            //Use the last device detected (if multiple) to open
            mDevice = device;
            builder.append(readDevice(device));
            builder.append("\n\n");
        }
        mDeviceText.setText(builder.toString());
        mConnectButton.setEnabled(true);
    }
}

/*
 * Enumerate the endpoints and interfaces on the connected device.
 * We do not need permission to do anything here, it is all "publicly
 * available" until we try to connect to an actual device.
 */
private String readDevice(UsbDevice device) {
    StringBuilder sb = new StringBuilder();
    sb.append("Device Name: " + device.getDeviceName() + "\n");
    sb.append(String.format(
            "Device Class: %s -> Subclass: 0x%02x -> Protocol: 0x%02x\n",
            nameForClass(device.getDeviceClass()),
            device.getDeviceSubclass(), device.getDeviceProtocol()));

    for (int i = 0; i < device.getInterfaceCount(); i++) {
        UsbInterface intf = device.getInterface(i);
        sb.append(String.format("+--Interface %d Class: %s -> "
                + "Subclass: 0x%02x -> Protocol: 0x%02x\n",
                        intf.getId(),
                        nameForClass(intf.getInterfaceClass()),
                        intf.getInterfaceSubclass(),
                        intf.getInterfaceProtocol()));

        for (int j = 0; j < intf.getEndpointCount(); j++) {
            UsbEndpoint endpoint = intf.getEndpoint(j);
            sb.append(String.format("  +---Endpoint %d: %s %s\n",
                    endpoint.getEndpointNumber(),
                    nameForEndpointType(endpoint.getType()),
                    nameForDirection(endpoint.getDirection())));
        }
    }

    return sb.toString();
}

/* Helper Methods to Provide Readable Names for USB Constants */

private String nameForClass(int classType) {
```

```
        switch (classType) {
        case UsbConstants.USB_CLASS_APP_SPEC:
            return String.format("Application Specific 0x%02x", classType);
        case UsbConstants.USB_CLASS_AUDIO:
            return "Audio";
        case UsbConstants.USB_CLASS_CDC_DATA:
            return "CDC Control";
        case UsbConstants.USB_CLASS_COMM:
            return "Communications";
        case UsbConstants.USB_CLASS_CONTENT_SEC:
            return "Content Security";
        case UsbConstants.USB_CLASS_CSCID:
            return "Content Smart Card";
        case UsbConstants.USB_CLASS_HID:
            return "Human Interface Device";
        case UsbConstants.USB_CLASS_HUB:
            return "Hub";
        case UsbConstants.USB_CLASS_MASS_STORAGE:
            return "Mass Storage";
        case UsbConstants.USB_CLASS_MISC:
            return "Wireless Miscellaneous";
        case UsbConstants.USB_CLASS_PER_INTERFACE:
            return "(Defined Per Interface)";
        case UsbConstants.USB_CLASS_PHYSICA:
            return "Physical";
        case UsbConstants.USB_CLASS_PRINTER:
            return "Printer";
        case UsbConstants.USB_CLASS_STILL_IMAGE:
            return "Still Image";
        case UsbConstants.USB_CLASS_VENDOR_SPEC:
            return String.format("Vendor Specific 0x%02x", classType);
        case UsbConstants.USB_CLASS_VIDEO:
            return "Video";
        case UsbConstants.USB_CLASS_WIRELESS_CONTROLLER:
            return "Wireless Controller";
        default:
            return String.format("0x%02x", classType);
        }
    }

    private String nameForEndpointType(int type) {
        switch (type) {
        case UsbConstants.USB_ENDPOINT_XFER_BULK:
            return "Bulk";
        case UsbConstants.USB_ENDPOINT_XFER_CONTROL:
            return "Control";
        case UsbConstants.USB_ENDPOINT_XFER_INT:
            return "Interrupt";
        case UsbConstants.USB_ENDPOINT_XFER_ISOC:
            return "Isochronous";
```

```
            default:
                return "Unknown Type";
            }
        }

        private String nameForDirection(int direction) {
            switch (direction) {
            case UsbConstants.USB_DIR_IN:
                return "IN";
            case UsbConstants.USB_DIR_OUT:
                return "OUT";
            default:
                return "Unknown Direction";
            }
        }
    }
```

When the Activity first comes into the foreground, it registers a BroadcastReceiver with a custom action (of which we'll discuss more shortly), and it queries the list of currently connected devices using UsbManager.getDeviceList(), which returns a HashMap of UsbDevice items that we can iterate over and interrogate. For each device connected, we query each interface and endpoint, building a description string to print to the user about what this device is. We then print all of that data to the user interface.

> **NOTE:** This application, as it stands, does not require any manifest permissions. We do not need to declare a permission simply to query information about devices connected to the host.

You can see that UsbManager provides APIs to inspect just about every piece of information you would need to discover if a connected device is the one you are interested in communicating with. All standard definitions for device classes, endpoint types, and transfer directions are also defined in UsbConstants, so you can match the types you want without defining all of this yourself.

So, what about that BroadcastReceiver we registered? The remainder of this example code takes action when the user presses the Connect button on the screen. At this point, we would like to actually talk to the connected device, which is an operation that does require user permission. Here, when the user clicks the button, we call UsbManager.requestPermission() to ask the user if we can connect. If permission has not yet been granted, the user will see a dialog asking him or her to grant permission to connect.

Upon saying yes, the PendingIntent passed along to the method will get fired. In our example, that Intent was a broadcast with a custom action string we defined, so this will trigger onReceive() in that BroadcastReceiver; any subsequent calls to requestPermission() will immediately trigger the receiver as well. Inside the receiver, we check to make sure that the result was a permission granted response, and we attempt to open a connection to the device with UsbManager.openDevice(), which returns a UsbDeviceConnection instance when successful.

With a valid connection made, we request some more detailed information about the device by requesting its configuration descriptor via a control transfer. Control transfers are requests always made on "endpoint 0" of the device. A configuration descriptor contains information about the configuration as well as each interface and endpoint, so its length is variable. We allocate a decent-sized buffer to ensure we capture everything.

Upon returning from controlTransfer(), the buffer is filled with the response data. Our application then processes the bytes, determining some more information about the device, like its maximum power draw and whether the device is configured to be powered from the USB post (bus-powered) or by an external source (self-powered). This example only parses out a fraction of the useful information that can be found inside these descriptors. Once again, all the parsed data is put into a string report and displayed to the user interface.

Much of the data read in the first section from the framework APIs and in the second section directly from the device is the same and should match up 1:1 between the two text reports displayed on the screen. One thing to note is that this application only works if the device is already connected when the application runs: it will not be notified if a connection happens while it is in the foreground. We will look at how to handle that scenario in the next section.

Getting Notified of Device Connections

In order for Android to notify your application when a particular device is connected, you need to register the device types you are interested in with an <intent-filter> in the manifest. Take a look at Listings 3-46 and 3-47 to see how this is done.

Listing 3-46. *Partial AndroidManifest.xml*

```
<activity
    android:name=".USBActivity"
    android:label="@string/title_activity_usb" >
    <intent-filter>
        <action android:name="android.intent.action.MAIN" />
        <category android:name="android.intent.category.LAUNCHER" />
    </intent-filter>
```

```
    <intent-filter>
        <action
            android:name="android.hardware.usb.action.USB_DEVICE_ATTACHED" />
    </intent-filter>

    <meta-data android:name="android.hardware.usb.action.USB_DEVICE_ATTACHED"
        android:resource="@xml/device_filter" />
</activity>
```

Listing 3-47. *res/xml/device_filter.xml*

```
<?xml version="1.0" encoding="utf-8"?>
<resources>
    <usb-device vendor-id="5432" product-id="9876" />
</resources>
```

The Activity you want to launch with a connection has a filter added to it with the USB_DEVICE_ATTACHED action string and with some XML metadata describing the devices you are interested in. There are several device attribute fields you can place into <usb-device> to filter which connection events notify your application.

- vendor-id
- product-id
- class
- subclass
- protocol

You can define as many of these as necessary to fit your application. For example, if you only want to communicate with one specific device, you might define both vendor-id and product-id as the example code did. If you are more interested in all devices of a given type (say, all mass storage devices) then you might only define the class attribute. It is even allowable to define *no* attributes, and have your application match on *any* device connected!

Summary

Connecting an Android application to the Web and web services is a great way to add user value in today's connected world. Android's framework for connecting to the Web and other remote hosts makes adding this functionality straightforward. We've explored how to bring the standards of the Web into your application, using HTML and JavaScript to interact with the user, but within a native context. You also saw how to use Android to download content from remote servers and consume it in your application. We also showed that a web server is not the only host worth connecting to, by using Bluetooth, NFC, and SMS to communicate directly from one device to another. In the next chapter, we will look at using the tools that Android provides to interact with a device's hardware resources.

Chapter 4

Interacting with Device Hardware and Media

Integrating application software with device hardware presents opportunities to create unique user experiences that only the mobile platform can provide. Capturing media using the microphone and camera allows applications to incorporate a personal touch through a photo or recorded greeting. Integration of sensor and location data can help you develop applications to answer relevant questions such as "Where am I?" and "What am I looking at?"

In this chapter, we are going to investigate how the location, media, and sensor APIs provided by Android can be used to add that unique value the mobile brings into your applications.

4-1. Integrating Device Location

Problem

You want to leverage the device's ability to report its current physical position in an application.

Solution

(API Level 1)

Utilize the background services provided by the Android `LocationManager`. One of the most powerful benefits that a mobile application can often provide to the user is the ability to add context by including information based on where they are currently located. Applications may ask the `LocationManager` to provide updates of a device's location either regularly or just when it is detected that the device has moved a significant distance.

When working with the Android location services, some care should be taken to respect both the device battery and the user's wishes. Obtaining a fine-grained location fix using a device's GPS is a power-intensive process, and this can quickly drain the battery in the user's device if left on continuously. For this reason, among others, Android allows the user to disable certain sources of location data, such as the device's GPS. These settings must be observed when your application decides how it will obtain location.

Each location source also comes with a trade-off degree of accuracy. The GPS will return a more exact location (within a few meters) but will take longer to fix and use more power, whereas the network location will usually be accurate to a few kilometers but is returned much faster and uses less power. Consider the requirements of the application when deciding which sources to access; if your application only wishes to display information about the local city, perhaps GPS fixes are not necessary.

> **IMPORTANT:** When using location services in an application, keep in mind that `android.permission.ACCESS_COARSE_LOCATION` or `android.permission.ACCESS_FINE_LOCATION` must be declared in the application manifest. If you declare `android.permission.ACCESS_FINE_LOCATION`, you do not need both because it includes coarse permissions as well.

How It Works

When creating a simple monitor for user location in an Activity or Service, there are a few actions that we need to consider:

1. Determine whether the source we want to use is enabled. If it's not, decide whether to ask the user to enable it or to try another source.
2. Register for updates using reasonable values for a minimum distance and update interval.
3. Unregister for updates when they are no longer needed to conserve device power.

In Listing 4-1, we register an Activity to listen for location updates while it is visible to the user and to display that location onscreen.

Listing 4-1. *Activity Monitoring Location Updates*

```
public class MyActivity extends Activity {

    LocationManager manager;
    Location currentLocation;

    TextView locationView;

    @Override
    public void onCreate(Bundle savedInstanceState) {
        super.onCreate(savedInstanceState);
        locationView = new TextView(this);
        setContentView(locationView);

        manager = (LocationManager)getSystemService(Context.LOCATION_SERVICE);
    }

    @Override
    public void onResume() {
        super.onResume();
        if(!manager.isProviderEnabled(LocationManager.GPS_PROVIDER)) {
            //Ask the user to enable GPS
            AlertDialog.Builder builder = new AlertDialog.Builder(this);
            builder.setTitle("Location Manager");
            builder.setMessage("We want to use your location, but GPS is disabled.\n"
                    +"Would you like to change these settings now?");
            builder.setPositiveButton("Yes",
                    new DialogInterface.OnClickListener() {
                @Override
                public void onClick(DialogInterface dialog, int which) {
                    //Launch settings, allowing user to make a change
                    Intent i =
                        new Intent(Settings.ACTION_LOCATION_SOURCE_SETTINGS);
                    startActivity(i);
                }
```

```
            });
            builder.setNegativeButton("No",
                    new DialogInterface.OnClickListener() {
                @Override
                public void onClick(DialogInterface dialog, int which) {
                    //No location service, no Activity
                    finish();
                }
            });
            builder.create().show();
        }

        //Get a cached location, if it exists
        currentLocation =
                manager.getLastKnownLocation(LocationManager.GPS_PROVIDER);
        updateDisplay();
        //Register for updates
        int minTime = 5000;
        float minDistance = 0;
        manager.requestLocationUpdates(LocationManager.GPS_PROVIDER,
                minTime, minDistance, listener);
    }

    @Override
    public void onPause() {
        super.onPause();
        manager.removeUpdates(listener);
    }

    //Update text view
    private void updateDisplay() {
        if(currentLocation == null) {
            locationView.setText("Determining Your Location...");
        } else {
            locationView.setText(String.format("Your Location:\n%.2f, %.2f",
                    currentLocation.getLatitude(),
                    currentLocation.getLongitude()));
        }
    }

    //Handle location callback events
    private LocationListener listener = new LocationListener() {

        @Override
        public void onLocationChanged(Location location) {
            currentLocation = location;
            updateDisplay();
        }
```

```
        @Override
        public void onProviderDisabled(String provider) { }

        @Override
        public void onProviderEnabled(String provider) { }

        @Override
        public void onStatusChanged(String provider, int status,
                Bundle extras) { }

    };
}
```

This example chooses to work strictly with the device's GPS to get location updates. Because it is a key element to the functionality of this Activity, the first major task undertaken after each resume is to check if the `LocationManager.GPS_PROVIDER` is still enabled. If, for any reason, the user has disabled this feature, we give them the opportunity to rectify this by asking if they would like to enable GPS. An application does not have the ability to do this for the user, so if they agree we launch an Activity using the Intent action `Settings.ACTION_LOCATION_SOURCE_SETTINGS`, which brings up the device settings so the user may enable GPS.

> **TIP:** If you are testing your application using the Android emulator, your application will not be able to receive real location data from any of the system providers. Using the DDMS tool in the SDK, you are able to inject location change events for the `GPS_PROVIDER` manually.

Once GPS is active and available, the Activity registers a `LocationListener` to be notified of location updates. The `LocationManager.requestLocationUpdates()` method takes two major parameters of interest in addition to the provider type and destination listener:

- `minTime`
  - The minimum time interval between updates, in milliseconds.
  - Setting this to nonzero allows the location provider to rest for approximately the specified period before updating again.
  - This is a parameter to conserve power, and it should not be set to a value any lower than the minimum acceptable update rate.

- `minDistance`
  - The distance the device must move before another update will be sent, in meters.
  - Setting this to nonzero will block updates until it is determined that the device has moved at least this much.

In the example, we request that updates be sent no more often than every five seconds, with no regard for whether the location has changed significantly or not. When these updates arrive, the `onLocationChanged()` method of the registered listener is called. Notice that a LocationListener will also be notified when the status of different providers changes, although we are not utilizing those callbacks here.

> **NOTE:** If you are receiving updates in a Service or other background operation, Google recommends that the minimum time interval should be no less than 60,000 (60 seconds).

The example keeps a running reference to the latest location it received. Initially, this value is set to the last known location that the provider has cached by calling `getLastKnownLocation()`, which may return null if the provider does not have a cached location value. With each incoming update, the location value is reset and the user interface display is updated to reflect the new change.

4-2. Mapping Locations

Problem

You would like to display one or more locations on a map for the user.

Solution

(API Level 1)

The simplest way to show the user a map is to create an Intent with the location data and pass it to the Android system to launch in a mapping application. We'll look more in depth at this method for doing a number of different tasks in a later chapter. In addition, maps can be embedded within your application by using the `MapView` and `MapActivity` provided by the Google Maps API SDK add-on.

The Maps API is an add-on module to the core SDK, although they are still bundled together. If you do not already have the Google APIs SDK, open the SDK manager and you will find a package for each API level listed under "Third-party Add-ons."

In order to use the Maps API in your application, an API key must first be obtained from Google. This key is built using the private key that your application is signed with. Without an API key, the mapping classes may be utilized, but no map tiles will be returned to the application.

> **NOTE:** For more information on the SDK, and to obtain an API key, visit http://code.google.com/android/add-ons/google-apis/mapkey.html.
> Notice also that Android uses the same signing key for all applications that run in debug mode (such as when they are run from the IDE), so one key can serve for all applications you develop while in the testing phase.

If you are running code in an emulator to test, that emulator must be built with an SDK target that includes the Google APIs for mapping to operate properly. If you create emulators from the command line, these targets are named "Google Inc.:Google APIs:X," where "X" is the API version indicator. If you create emulators from inside an IDE (such as Eclipse), the target has a similar naming convention of "Google APIs (Google Inc.) – X," where "X" is the API version indicator.

With the API key in hand and a suitable test platform in place, you are ready to begin.

How It Works

To display a map, simply create an instance of `MapView` inside a `MapActivity`. One of the required attributes that must be passed to the `MapView` in your XML layout is the API key that you obtained from Google. See Listing 4-2.

Listing 4-2. *Typical MapView in a Layout*

```
<com.google.android.maps.MapView
  android:layout_width="fill_parent"
  android:layout_height="fill_parent"
  android:enabled="true"
  android:clickable="true"
```

```
  android:apiKey="API_KEY_STRING_HERE"
/>
```

> **NOTE:** When adding `MapView` to an XML layout, the fully qualified package name must be included, because the class does not exist in `android.view` or `android.widget`.

Although `MapView` may be instantiated from code as well, the API key is still required as a constructor parameter:

```
MapView map = new MapView(this, "API_KEY_STRING_HERE");
```

In addition, the application manifest must declare its use of the Maps library, which dually acts as a Google Play filter to remove the application from devices that don't have this capability.

Now, let's look at an example that puts the last known user location on a map and displays it. See Listing 4-3.

Listing 4-3. *AndroidManifest.xml*

```
<?xml version="1.0" encoding="utf-8"?>
<manifest xmlns:android="http://schemas.android.com/apk/res/android"
    package="com.examples.mapper"
    android:versionCode="1"
    android:versionName="1.0">
    <uses-sdk android:minSdkVersion="3" />
    <uses-permission android:name="android.permission.ACCESS_FINE_LOCATION" />
    <uses-permission android:name="android.permission.INTERNET" />

    <application android:icon="@drawable/icon"
        android:label="@string/app_name">
        <activity android:name=".MyActivity"
            android:label="@string/app_name">
            <intent-filter>
                <action android:name="android.intent.action.MAIN" />
                <category android:name="android.intent.category.LAUNCHER" />
            </intent-filter>
        </activity>

        <uses-library android:name="com.google.android.maps"></uses-library>

    </application>
</manifest>
```

Notice the permissions declared for INTERNET and ACCESS_FINE_LOCATION. The latter is required only because this example is hooking back up to the

LocationManager to get the cached location value. The other key ingredient that must be present in the manifest is the <uses-library> tag, which references the Google Maps API. Android requires this item to properly link the external library into your application build, but it also serves another purpose. The library declaration is used by Google Play to filter out the application so it cannot be installed on devices that are not equipped with the proper mapping library. See Listing 4-4.

Listing 4-4. *res/layout/main.xml*

```
<?xml version="1.0" encoding="utf-8"?>
<LinearLayout xmlns:android="http://schemas.android.com/apk/res/android"
  android:orientation="vertical"
  android:layout_width="fill_parent"
  android:layout_height="fill_parent">
  <TextView
    android:layout_width="fill_parent"
    android:layout_height="wrap_content"
    android:gravity="center_horizontal"
    android:text="Map Of Your Location"
  />
  <com.google.android.maps.MapView
    android:id="@+id/map"
    android:layout_width="fill_parent"
    android:layout_height="fill_parent"
    android:enabled="true"
    android:clickable="true"
    android:apiKey="YOUR_API_KEY_HERE"
  />
</LinearLayout>
```

Note the location of the required API key that you must enter. Also, notice that the MapView does not have to be the only thing in the Activity layout, despite the fact that it must be inflated inside of a MapActivity. See Listing 4-5.

Listing 4-5. *MapActivity Displaying Cached Location*

```
public class MyActivity extends MapActivity {

    MapView map;
    MapController controller;

    @Override
    public void onCreate(Bundle savedInstanceState) {
        super.onCreate(savedInstanceState);
        setContentView(R.layout.main);

        map = (MapView)findViewById(R.id.map);
        controller = map.getController();
```

```
        LocationManager manager =
            (LocationManager)getSystemService(Context.LOCATION_SERVICE);
        Location location =
            manager.getLastKnownLocation(LocationManager.GPS_PROVIDER);
        int lat, lng;
        if(location != null) {
            //Convert to microdegrees
            lat = (int)(location.getLatitude() * 1000000);
            lng = (int)(location.getLongitude() * 1000000);
        } else {
            //Default to Google HQ
            lat = 37427222;
            lng = -122099167;
        }
        GeoPoint mapCenter = new GeoPoint(lat,lng);
        controller.setCenter(mapCenter);
        controller.setZoom(15);
    }

    //Required abstract method, return false
    @Override
    protected boolean isRouteDisplayed() {
        return false;
    }
}
```

This Activity takes the latest user location and centers the map on that point. All control of the map is done through a `MapController` instance, which we obtain by calling `MapView.getController()`; the controller can be used to pan, zoom, and otherwise adjust the map onscreen. In this example, we use the controller's `setCenter()` and `setZoom()` methods to adjust the map display.

`MapController.setCenter()` takes a `GeoPoint` as its parameter, which is slightly different than the `Location` we receive from the Android services. The primary difference is that `GeoPoint` expresses latitude and longitude in terms of microdegrees (or degrees * 1E6) instead of a decimal value representing whole degrees. Therefore, we must convert the `Location` values before applying them to the map.

`MapController.setZoom()` allows the map to be programmatically zoomed to a specified level, between 1 and 21. By default, the map will zoom to level 1, which the SDK documentation defines as being a global view, with each increasing level magnifying the map by two. See Figure 4-1.

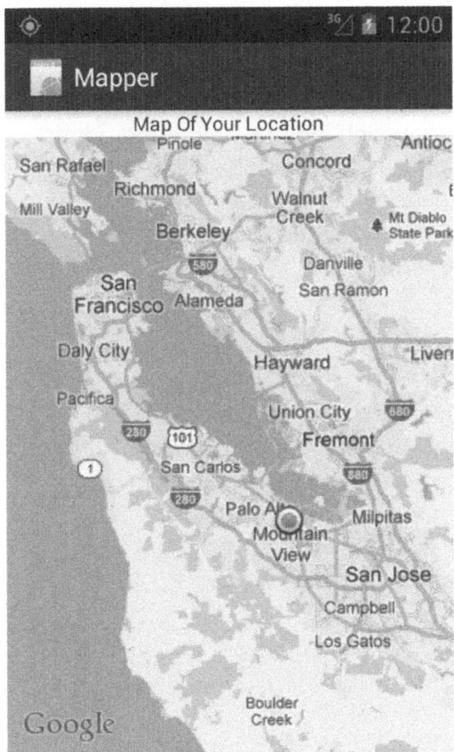

Figure 4-1. *Map of user location*

The first thing you will probably notice is that the map doesn't display any indicator on the location point (such as a pin). In Recipe 4-3 we will create these annotations and then describe how to customize them.

4-3. Annotating Maps

Problem

In addition to displaying a map centered on a specific location, your application needs to put an annotation down to mark the location more visibly.

Solution

(API Level 1)

Create a custom ItemizedOverlay for the map, which includes all of the points to mark. ItemizedOverlay is an abstract base class that handles all the drawing of the individual items on a MapView. The items themselves are instances of OverlayItem, which is a model class that defines the name, subtitle, and Drawable marker to describe the point on the map.

How It Works

Let's create an implementation of ItemizedOverlay that will take an array of GeoPoints and draw them on the map using the same Drawable marker for each. See Listing 4-6.

Listing 4-6. *Basic ItemizedOverlay Implementation*

```
public class LocationOverlay extends ItemizedOverlay<OverlayItem> {
    private List<GeoPoint> mItems;

    public LocationOverlay(Drawable marker) {
        super( boundCenterBottom(marker) );
    }

    public void setItems(ArrayList<GeoPoint> items) {
        mItems = items;
        populate();
    }

    @Override
    protected OverlayItem createItem(int i) {
        return new OverlayItem(mItems.get(i), null, null);
    }

    @Override
    public int size() {
        return mItems.size();
    }

    @Override
    protected boolean onTap(int i) {
        //Handle a tap event here
        return true;
    }
}
```

In this implementation, the constructor takes a Drawable to represent the marker placed on the map at each location. Drawables that are used in overlays must have proper bounds applied to them, and boundCenterBottom() is a convenience method that handles this for us. Specifically, it applies bounds, such that the point on the Drawable that touches the map location will be in the center of the bottom row of pixels.

ItemizedOverlay has two abstract methods that must be overridden: createItem(), which must return an object of the declared type, and size(), which returns the number of items managed. This example takes a list of GeoPoints and wraps them all into OverlayItems. The populate() method should be called on the overlay as soon as all the data is present and ready for display, which in this case is at the end of setItems().

Let's apply this overlay to a map to draw three custom locations around Google HQ, using the default app icon as the marker. See Listing 4-7.

Listing 4-7. *Activity Using Custom Map Overlay*

```
public class MyActivity extends MapActivity {

    MapView map;
    MapController controller;

    @Override
    public void onCreate(Bundle savedInstanceState) {
        super.onCreate(savedInstanceState);
        setContentView(R.layout.main);

        map = (MapView)findViewById(R.id.map);
        controller = map.getController();

        ArrayList<GeoPoint> locations = new ArrayList<GeoPoint>();
        //Google HQ @ 37.427,-122.099
        locations.add(new GeoPoint(37427222,-122099167));
        //Subtract 0.01 degrees
        locations.add(new GeoPoint(37426222,-122089167));
        //Add 0.01 degrees
        locations.add(new GeoPoint(37428222,-122109167));

        LocationOverlay myOverlay =
            new LocationOverlay(getResources().getDrawable(R.drawable.icon));
        myOverlay.setItems(locations);
        map.getOverlays().add(myOverlay);
        controller.setCenter(locations.get(0));
        controller.setZoom(15);

    }
```

```
    //Required abstract method, return false
    @Override
    protected boolean isRouteDisplayed() {
        return false;
    }

}
```

When run, this Activity produces the display shown in Figure 4-2.

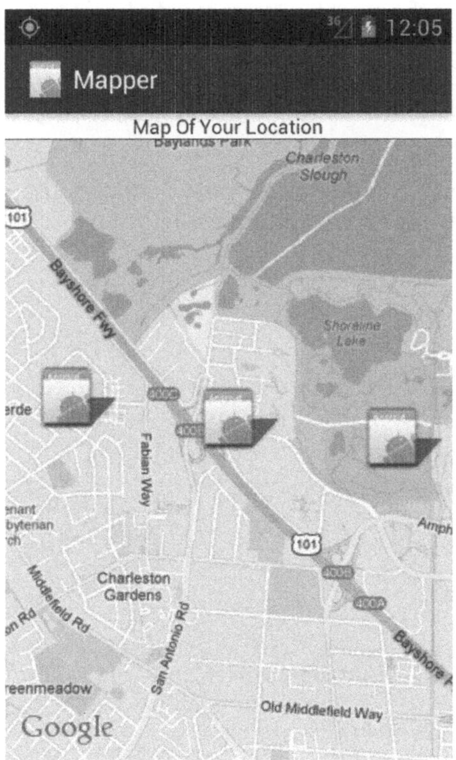

Figure 4-2. *Map with ItemizedOverlay*

Notice how the drawing of the drop shadow on the marker was handled for us by `MapView` and the `ItemizedOverlay`.

But what if we want to customize each item so it displays a different marker image? How would we do that? By explicitly setting the item's marker, a custom `Drawable` can be returned for each item. In this case, the `Drawable` provided to the `ItemizedOverlay` constructor is just a default value to be used if no custom override exists. Consider the modification to the implementation that is shown in Listing 4-8.

Listing 4-8. *ItemizedOverlay with Custom Markers*

```
public class LocationOverlay extends ItemizedOverlay<OverlayItem> {
    private List<GeoPoint> mItems;
    private List<Drawable> mMarkers;

    public LocationOverlay(Drawable marker) {
        super( boundCenterBottom(marker) );
    }

    public void setItems(ArrayList<GeoPoint> items,
            ArrayList<Drawable> drawables) {
        mItems = items;
        mMarkers = drawables;
        populate();
    }

    @Override
    protected OverlayItem createItem(int i) {
        OverlayItem item = new OverlayItem(mItems.get(i), null, null);
        item.setMarker( boundCenterBottom(mMarkers.get(i)) );
        return item;
    }

    @Override
    public int size() {
        return mItems.size();
    }

    @Override
    protected boolean onTap(int i) {
        //Handle a tap event here
        return true;
    }
}
```

With this modification, the OverlayItems created now receive a custom marker image in the form of a bounded `Drawable` matching the item's index in a list of images. If the `Drawable` that you set has states, the pressed and focused states will display when the item is selected or touched. Our example, when modified to use the new implementation, looks like Listing 4-9.

Listing 4-9. *Example Activity Providing Custom Markers*

```
public class MyActivity extends MapActivity {

    MapView map;
    MapController controller;
```

```
    @Override
    public void onCreate(Bundle savedInstanceState) {
        super.onCreate(savedInstanceState);
        setContentView(R.layout.main);

        map = (MapView)findViewById(R.id.map);
        controller = map.getController();

        ArrayList<GeoPoint> locations = new ArrayList<GeoPoint>();
        ArrayList<Drawable> images = new ArrayList<Drawable>();

        //Google HQ 37.427,-122.099
        locations.add(new GeoPoint(37427222,-122099167));
        images.add(getResources().getDrawable(R.drawable.logo));
        //Subtract 0.01 degrees
        locations.add(new GeoPoint(37426222,-122089167));
        images.add(getResources().getDrawable(R.drawable.icon));
        //Add 0.01 degrees
        locations.add(new GeoPoint(37428222,-122109167));
        images.add(getResources().getDrawable(R.drawable.icon));

        LocationOverlay myOverlay =
            new LocationOverlay(getResources().getDrawable(R.drawable.icon));
        myOverlay.setItems(locations, images);
        map.getOverlays().add(myOverlay);
        controller.setCenter(locations.get(0));
        controller.setZoom(15);

    }

    //Required abstract method, return false
    @Override
    protected boolean isRouteDisplayed() {
        return false;
    }
}
```

Now our example provides a discrete image for each item it wants to display on the map. Specifically, we have decided to represent the actual Google HQ location by a version of the Google logo, while keeping the other two points with the same marker. See Figure 4-3.

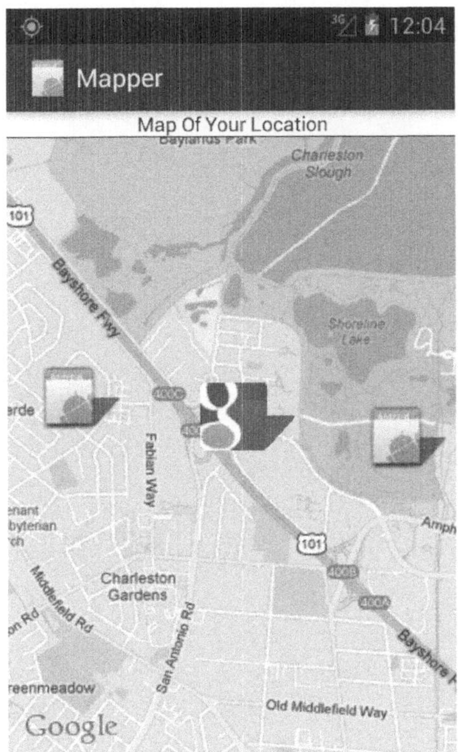

Figure 4-3. *Map overlay with custom markers*

Make Them Interactive

Perhaps you noticed the `onTap()` method that was defined in the LocationOverlay, but never mentioned. Another nice feature of the `ItemizedOverlay` base implementation is that it handles hit testing and has a convenience method when a specific item is tapped, referencing that item's index. From this method, you can raise a toast, show a dialog, start a new Activity, or perform any other action that fits the context of the user tapping on the annotation for more information.

What About Me?

The Maps API for Android also includes a special overlay to draw the user location, the `MyLocationOverlay`. This overlay is very straightforward to use, but it should only be enabled while the Activity it is present on is visible. Otherwise, unnecessary resource usage will cause poor performance and decreased battery life. See Listing 4-10.

Listing 4-10. *Adding a MyLocationOverlay*

```
public class MyActivity extends MapActivity {

    MapView map;
    MyLocationOverlay myOverlay;

    @Override
    public void onCreate(Bundle savedInstanceState) {
        super.onCreate(savedInstanceState);
        setContentView(R.layout.main);

        map = (MapView)findViewById(R.id.map);
        myOverlay = new MyLocationOverlay(this, map);
        map.getOverlays().add(myOverlay);
    }

    @Override
    public void onResume() {
        super.onResume();
        myOverlay.enableMyLocation();
    }

    @Override
    public void onPause() {
        super.onResume();
        myOverlay.disableMyLocation();
    }

    //Required abstract method, return false
    @Override
    protected boolean isRouteDisplayed() {
        return false;
    }
}
```

This will display a standard dot or arrow marker (depending on whether the compass is in use) on the user's latest location, and it will track as the user moves as long as the overlay is enabled.

The key to using the `MyLocationOverlay` is to disable its features when they are not in use (when the Activity is not visible) and to reenable them when they are needed. Just as with using the `LocationManager`, this ensures these services are not draining unnecessary power.

4-4. Capturing Images and Video

Problem

Your application needs to make use of the device's camera in order to capture media, whether it be still images or short video clips.

Solution

(API Level 3)

Send an Intent to Android to transfer control to the Camera application and to return the image the user captured. Android does contain APIs for directly accessing the camera hardware, previewing, and taking snapshots or videos. However, if your only goal is to simply get the media content using the camera with an interface the user is familiar with, there is no better solution than a handoff.

How It Works

Let's take a look at how to use the Camera application to take both still images and video clips.

Image Capture

Let's take a look at an example Activity that will activate the Camera application when the "Take a Picture" button is pressed; you will receive the result of this operation as a Bitmap. See Listings 4-11 and 4-12.

Listing 4-11. *res/layout/main.xml*

```
<?xml version="1.0" encoding="utf-8"?>
<LinearLayout xmlns:android="http://schemas.android.com/apk/res/android"
  android:orientation="vertical"
  android:layout_width="fill_parent"
  android:layout_height="fill_parent">
  <Button
    android:id="@+id/capture"
    android:layout_width="fill_parent"
    android:layout_height="wrap_content"
    android:text="Take a Picture"
  />
```

```
    <ImageView
      android:id="@+id/image"
      android:layout_width="fill_parent"
      android:layout_height="fill_parent"
      android:scaleType="centerInside"
    />
</LinearLayout>
```

Listing 4-12. *Activity to Capture an Image*

```
public class MyActivity extends Activity {

    private static final int REQUEST_IMAGE = 100;

    Button captureButton;
    ImageView imageView;

    @Override
    public void onCreate(Bundle savedInstanceState) {
        super.onCreate(savedInstanceState);
        setContentView(R.layout.main);

        captureButton = (Button)findViewById(R.id.capture);
        captureButton.setOnClickListener(listener);

        imageView = (ImageView)findViewById(R.id.image);
    }

    @Override
    protected void onActivityResult(int requestCode, int resultCode,
            Intent data) {
        if(requestCode == REQUEST_IMAGE && resultCode == Activity.RESULT_OK) {
            //Process and display the image
            Bitmap userImage = (Bitmap)data.getExtras().get("data");
            imageView.setImageBitmap(userImage);
        }
    }

    private View.OnClickListener listener = new View.OnClickListener() {
        @Override
        public void onClick(View v) {
            Intent intent = new Intent(MediaStore.ACTION_IMAGE_CAPTURE);
            startActivityForResult(intent, REQUEST_IMAGE);
        }
    };
}
```

This method captures the image and returns a scaled-down `Bitmap` as an extra in the "data" field. If you need to capture an image and need the full-sized image to be saved somewhere, insert a `Uri` for the image destination into the

MediaStore.EXTRA_OUTPUT field of the Intent before starting the capture. See Listing 4-13.

Listing 4-13. *Full-Size Image Capture to File*

```
public class MyActivity extends Activity {

    private static final int REQUEST_IMAGE = 100;

    Button captureButton;
    ImageView imageView;
    File destination;

    @Override
    public void onCreate(Bundle savedInstanceState) {
        super.onCreate(savedInstanceState);
        setContentView(R.layout.main);

        captureButton = (Button)findViewById(R.id.capture);
        captureButton.setOnClickListener(listener);

        imageView = (ImageView)findViewById(R.id.image);

        destination =
            new File(Environment.getExternalStorageDirectory(),"image.jpg");
    }

    @Override
    protected void onActivityResult(int requestCode, int resultCode,
            Intent data) {
        if(requestCode == REQUEST_IMAGE && resultCode == Activity.RESULT_OK) {
            try {
                FileInputStream in = new FileInputStream(destination);
                BitmapFactory.Options options = new BitmapFactory.Options();
                options.inSampleSize = 10; //Downsample by 10x

                Bitmap userImage =
                        BitmapFactory.decodeStream(in, null, options);
                imageView.setImageBitmap(userImage);
            } catch (Exception e) {
                e.printStackTrace();
            }
        }
    }
```

```
    private View.OnClickListener listener = new View.OnClickListener() {
        @Override
        public void onClick(View v) {
            Intent intent = new Intent(MediaStore.ACTION_IMAGE_CAPTURE);
            //Add extra to save full-image somewhere
            intent.putExtra(MediaStore.EXTRA_OUTPUT,
                    Uri.fromFile(destination));
            startActivityForResult(intent, REQUEST_IMAGE);
        }
    };
}
```

This method will instruct the Camera application to store the image elsewhere (in this case, on the device's SD card as "image.jpg") and the result will not be scaled down. When going to retrieve the image after the operation returns, we now go directly to the file location where we told the camera to store the image.

Using `BitmapFactory.Options`, however, we do still scale the image down prior to displaying to the screen to avoid from loading the full-size `Bitmap` into memory at once. Also note that this example chose a file location that was on the device's external storage, which requires the `android.permission.WRITE_EXTERNAL_STORAGE` permission to be declared in API Levels 4 and above. If your final solution writes the file elsewhere, this may not be necessary.

Video Capture

Capturing video clips using this method is just as straightforward, although the results produced are slightly different. There is no case under which the actual video-clip data is returned directly in the Intent extras, and it is always saved to a destination file location. The following two parameters may be passed along as extras:

1. `MediaStore.EXTRA_VIDEO_QUALITY`
    a. Integer value to describe the quality level used to capture the video.
    b. Allowed values are 0 for low quality and 1 for high quality.
2. `MediaStore.EXTRA_OUTPUT`
    c. Uri destination of where to save the video content.
    d. If this is not present, the video will be saved in a standard location for the device.

When the video recording is complete, the actual location where the data was saved is returned as a `Uri` in the data field of the result Intent. Let's take a look at a similar example that allows the user to record and save their videos and then display the saved location back to the screen. See Listings 4-14 and 4-15.

Listing 4-14. *res/layout/main.xml*

```
<?xml version="1.0" encoding="utf-8"?>
<LinearLayout xmlns:android="http://schemas.android.com/apk/res/android"
    android:orientation="vertical"
    android:layout_width="fill_parent"
    android:layout_height="fill_parent">
    <Button
        android:id="@+id/capture"
        android:layout_width="fill_parent"
        android:layout_height="wrap_content"
        android:text="Take a Video"
    />
    <TextView
        android:id="@+id/file"
        android:layout_width="fill_parent"
        android:layout_height="fill_parent"
    />
</LinearLayout>
```

Listing 4-15. *Activity to Capture a Video Clip*

```
public class MyActivity extends Activity {

    private static final int REQUEST_VIDEO = 100;

    Button captureButton;
    TextView text;
    File destination;

    @Override
    public void onCreate(Bundle savedInstanceState) {
        super.onCreate(savedInstanceState);
        setContentView(R.layout.main);

        captureButton = (Button)findViewById(R.id.capture);
        captureButton.setOnClickListener(listener);

        text = (TextView)findViewById(R.id.file);

        destination =
                new File(Environment.getExternalStorageDirectory(),"myVideo");
    }
```

```
    @Override
    protected void onActivityResult(int requestCode, int resultCode,
            Intent data) {
        if(requestCode == REQUEST_VIDEO && resultCode == Activity.RESULT_OK) {
            String location = data.getData().toString();
            text.setText(location);
        }
    }

    private View.OnClickListener listener = new View.OnClickListener() {
        @Override
        public void onClick(View v) {
            Intent intent = new Intent(MediaStore.ACTION_VIDEO_CAPTURE);
            //Add (optional) extra to save video to our file
            intent.putExtra(MediaStore.EXTRA_OUTPUT,
                    Uri.fromFile(destination));
            //Optional extra to set video quality
            intent.putExtra(MediaStore.EXTRA_VIDEO_QUALITY, 0);
            startActivityForResult(intent, REQUEST_VIDEO);
        }
    };
}
```

This example, like the previous example saving an image, puts the recorded video on the device's SD card (which requires the `android.permission.WRITE_EXTERNAL_STORAGE` permission for API Levels 4+). To initiate the process, we send an Intent with the `MediaStore.ACTION_VIDEO_CAPTURE` action string to the system. Android will launch the default Camera application to handle recording the video and return with an OK result when recording is complete. We retrieve the location where the data was stored as a Uri by calling `Intent.getData()` in the `onActivityResult()` callback method, and then display that location to the user.

This example requests explicitly that the video be shot using the low-quality setting, but this parameter is optional. If `MediaStore.EXTRA_VIDEO_QUALITY` is not present in the request Intent, the device will usually choose to shoot using high quality.

In cases where `MediaStore.EXTRA_OUTPUT` is provided, the `Uri` returned should match the location you requested, unless an error occurs that keeps the application from writing to that location. If this parameter is not provided, the returned value will be a `content:// Uri` to retrieve the media from the system's MediaStore Content Provider.

Later on, in Recipe 4-8, we will look at practical ways to play this media back in your application.

4-5. Making a Custom Camera Overlay

Problem

Many applications need more direct access to the camera, either for the purposes of overlaying a custom user interface (UI) for controls or displaying metadata about what is visible through information based on location and direction sensors (augmented reality).

Solution

(API Level 5)

Attach directly to the camera hardware in a custom Activity. Android provides APIs to directly access the device's camera for the purposes of obtaining the preview feed and taking photos. We can access these when the needs of the application grow beyond simply snapping and returning a photo for display.

> **NOTE:** Because we are taking a more direct approach to the camera here, the `android.permission.CAMERA` permission must be declared in the manifest.

How It Works

We start by creating a `SurfaceView`, a dedicated view for live drawing where we will attach the camera's preview stream. This provides us with a live preview inside a view that we can lay out any way we choose inside an Activity. From there, it's simply a matter of adding other views and controls that suit the context of the application. Let's take a look at the code (see Listings 4-16 and 4-17).

> **NOTE:** The `Camera` class used here is `android.hardware.Camera`, not to be confused with `android.graphics.Camera`. Ensure that you have imported the correct reference within your application.

Listing 4-16. *res/layout/main.xml*

```
<?xml version="1.0" encoding="utf-8"?>
<RelativeLayout xmlns:android="http://schemas.android.com/apk/res/android"
    android:layout_width="fill_parent"
    android:layout_height="fill_parent">
    <SurfaceView
        android:id="@+id/preview"
        android:layout_width="fill_parent"
        android:layout_height="fill_parent"
    />
</RelativeLayout>
```

Listing 4-17. *Activity Displaying Live Camera Preview*

```
import android.hardware.Camera;

public class PreviewActivity extends Activity implements SurfaceHolder.Callback {

    Camera mCamera;
    SurfaceView mPreview;

    @Override
    public void onCreate(Bundle savedInstanceState) {
        super.onCreate(savedInstanceState);
        setContentView(R.layout.main);

        mPreview = (SurfaceView)findViewById(R.id.preview);
        mPreview.getHolder().addCallback(this);
        mPreview.getHolder().setType(SurfaceHolder.SURFACE_TYPE_PUSH_BUFFERS);

        mCamera = Camera.open();
    }

    @Override
    public void onPause() {
        super.onPause();
        mCamera.stopPreview();
    }

    @Override
    public void onDestroy() {
        super.onDestroy();
        mCamera.release();
    }
```

```
    //Surface Callback Methods
    @Override
    public void surfaceChanged(SurfaceHolder holder, int format,
            int width, int height) {
        Camera.Parameters params = mCamera.getParameters();
        //Get the device's supported sizes and pick the first (largest)
        List<Camera.Size> sizes = params.getSupportedPreviewSizes();
        Camera.Size selected = sizes.get(0);
        params.setPreviewSize(selected.width,selected.height);
        mCamera.setParameters(params);

        mCamera.startPreview();
    }

    @Override
    public void surfaceCreated(SurfaceHolder holder) {
        try {
            mCamera.setPreviewDisplay(mPreview.getHolder());
        } catch (Exception e) {
            e.printStackTrace();
        }
    }

    @Override
    public void surfaceDestroyed(SurfaceHolder holder) { }
}
```

NOTE: If you are testing on an emulator, there may not be a camera to preview. Newer versions of the SDK have started to make use of cameras built into some host machines, but this is not universal. Where a camera is unavailable, the emulator displays a fake preview that looks slightly different depending on the version you are running. To verify that this code is working properly, open the Camera application on your specific emulator and take note of what the preview looks like. The same display should appear in this sample. It is always best to test code that integrates with device hardware on an actual device.

In the example, we create a `SurfaceView` that fills the window and tells it that our Activity is to be notified of all the `SurfaceHolder` callbacks. The camera cannot begin displaying preview information on the surface until it is fully initialized, so we wait until `surfaceCreated()` gets called to attach the `SurfaceHolder` of our view to the `Camera` instance. Similarly, we wait to size the preview and start drawing until the surface has been given its size, which occurs when `surfaceChanged()` is called.

The camera hardware resources are opened and claimed for this application by calling `Camera.open()`. There is an alternate version of this method introduced in Android 2.3 (API Level 9) that takes an integer parameter (valid values being from 0 to `getNumberOfCameras()-1`) to determine which camera you would like to access for devices that have more than one. On these devices, the version that takes no parameters will always default to the rear-facing camera.

> **IMPORTANT:** Some newer devices like Google's Nexus 7 tablet do not have a rear-facing camera, and so the old implementation of `Camera.open()` will return null. If you have a Camera application that supports older versions of Android, you will want to branch your code and use the newer API where available to get whatever camera the device has to offer.

Calling `Parameters.getSupportedPreviewSizes()` returns a list of all the sizes the device will accept, and they are typically ordered largest to smallest. In the example, we pick the first (and, thus, largest) preview resolution and use it to set the size.

> **NOTE:** In versions earlier than 2.0 (API Level 5), it was acceptable to directly pass the height and width parameters from this method as to `Parameters.setPreviewSize()`; but in 2.0, and later, the camera will only set its preview to one of the supported resolutions of the device. Attempts otherwise will result in an Exception.

`Camera.startPreview()` begins the live drawing of camera data on the surface. Notice that the preview always displays in a landscape orientation. Prior to Android 2.2 (API Level 8), there was no official way to adjust the rotation of the preview display. For that reason, it is recommended that an Activity using the camera preview have its orientation fixed with `android:screenOrientation="landscape"` in the manifest to match if you must support devices running older versions.

The Camera service can only be accessed by one application at a time. For this reason, it is important that you call `Camera.release()` as soon as the camera is no longer needed. In the example, we no longer need the camera when the Activity is finished, so this call takes place in `onDestroy()`.

Changing Capture Orientation

(API Level 8)

Starting with Android 2.2, the ability to rotate the actual camera preview was added. Applications can now call `Camera.setDisplayOrientation()` to rotate the incoming data to match the orientation of their Activity. Valid values are degrees of 0, 90, 180, and 270; 0 will map to the default landscape orientation. This method affects primarily how the preview data is drawn on the surface before the capture.

To rotate the output data from the camera, use the method `setRotation()` on `Camera.Parameters`. This method's implementation depends on the device; it will either rotate the actual image output, update the EXIF data with a rotation parameter, or both.

Photo Overlay

We can now add on to the previous example any controls or views that are appropriate to display on top of the camera preview. Let's modify the preview to include a Cancel button and a Snap Photo button. See Listings 4-18 and 4-19.

Listing 4-18. *res/layout/main.xml*

```
<?xml version="1.0" encoding="utf-8"?>
<RelativeLayout xmlns:android="http://schemas.android.com/apk/res/android"
    android:layout_width="fill_parent"
    android:layout_height="fill_parent">
    <SurfaceView
        android:id="@+id/preview"
        android:layout_width="fill_parent"
        android:layout_height="fill_parent"
    />
    <RelativeLayout
        android:layout_width="fill_parent"
        android:layout_height="100dip"
        android:layout_alignParentBottom="true"
        android:gravity="center_vertical"
        android:background="#A000">
        <Button
            android:layout_width="100dip"
            android:layout_height="wrap_content"
            android:text="Cancel"
            android:onClick="onCancelClick"
        />
        <Button
            android:layout_width="100dip"
```

```
            android:layout_height="wrap_content"
            android:layout_alignParentRight="true"
            android:text="Snap Photo"
            android:onClick="onSnapClick"
        />
    </RelativeLayout>
</RelativeLayout>
```

Listing 4-19. *Activity with Photo Controls Added*

```
public class PreviewActivity extends Activity implements
      SurfaceHolder.Callback, Camera.ShutterCallback, Camera.PictureCallback {

    Camera mCamera;
    SurfaceView mPreview;

    @Override
    public void onCreate(Bundle savedInstanceState) {
        super.onCreate(savedInstanceState);
        setContentView(R.layout.main);

        mPreview = (SurfaceView)findViewById(R.id.preview);
        mPreview.getHolder().addCallback(this);
        mPreview.getHolder().setType(SurfaceHolder.SURFACE_TYPE_PUSH_BUFFERS);

        mCamera = Camera.open();
    }

    @Override
    public void onPause() {
        super.onPause();
        mCamera.stopPreview();
    }

    @Override
    public void onDestroy() {
        super.onDestroy();
        mCamera.release();
        Log.d("CAMERA","Destroy");
    }

    public void onCancelClick(View v) {
        finish();
    }

    public void onSnapClick(View v) {
        //Snap a photo
        mCamera.takePicture(this, null, null, this);
    }
```

```
//Camera Callback Methods
@Override
public void onShutter() {
    Toast.makeText(this, "Click!", Toast.LENGTH_SHORT).show();
}

@Override
public void onPictureTaken(byte[] data, Camera camera) {

    //Store the picture off somewhere
    //Here, we chose to save to internal storage
    try {
        FileOutputStream out =
                openFileOutput("picture.jpg", Activity.MODE_PRIVATE);
        out.write(data);
        out.flush();
        out.close();
    } catch (FileNotFoundException e) {
        e.printStackTrace();
    } catch (IOException e) {
        e.printStackTrace();
    }

    //Must restart preview
    camera.startPreview();
}

//Surface Callback Methods
@Override
public void surfaceChanged(SurfaceHolder holder, int format,
        int width, int height) {
    Camera.Parameters params = mCamera.getParameters();
    List<Camera.Size> sizes = params.getSupportedPreviewSizes();
    Camera.Size selected = sizes.get(0);
    params.setPreviewSize(selected.width,selected.height);
    mCamera.setParameters(params);

    mCamera.setDisplayOrientation(90);
    mCamera.startPreview();
}

@Override
public void surfaceCreated(SurfaceHolder holder) {
    try {
        mCamera.setPreviewDisplay(mPreview.getHolder());
    } catch (Exception e) {
        e.printStackTrace();
    }
}
```

```
    @Override
    public void surfaceDestroyed(SurfaceHolder holder) { }
}
```

Here we have added a simple, partially transparent overlay to include a pair of controls for camera operation. The action taken by Cancel is nothing to speak of; we simply finish the Activity. However, Snap Photo introduces more of the Camera API in manually taking and returning a photo to the application. A user action will initiate the `Camera.takePicture()` method, which takes a series of callback pointers.

Notice that the Activity in this example implements two more interfaces: `Camera.ShutterCallback` and `Camera.PictureCallback`. The former is called as near as possible to the moment when the image is captured (when the "shutter" closes), while the latter can be called at multiple instances when different forms of the image are available.

The parameters of `takePicture()` are a single `ShutterCallback` and up to three `PictureCallback` instances. The `PictureCallbacks` will be called at the following times (in the order they appear as parameters):

1. After the image is captured with RAW image data
    a. This may return null on devices with limited memory.
2. After the image is processed with scaled image data (known as the POSTVIEW image)
    b. This may return null on devices with limited memory.
3. After the image is compressed with JPEG image data

This example only cares to be notified when the JPEG is ready. Consequently, that is also the last callback made and the point in time when the preview must be started back up again. If `startPreview()` is not called again after a picture is taken, then preview on the surface will remain frozen at the captured image.

> **TIP:** If you would like to guarantee that your application is downloaded only on devices that have the appropriate hardware, you can use the market filter for the camera in your manifest with the following line: `<uses-feature android:name="android.hardware.camera" />`

4-6. Recording Audio

Problem

You have an application that needs to use the device microphone to record audio input.

Solution

(API Level 1)

Use the MediaRecorder to capture the audio and store it out to a file.

How It Works

MediaRecorder is quite simple to use. All you need to provide is some basic information about the file format to use for encoding and where to store the data. Listings 4-20 and 4-21 provide examples of how to record an audio file to the device's SD card, monitoring user actions for when to start and stop.

> **IMPORTANT:** In order to use MediaRecorder to record audio input, you must also declare the android.permission.RECORD_AUDIO permission in the application manifest.

Listing 4-20. *res/layout/main.xml*

```
<?xml version="1.0" encoding="utf-8"?>
<LinearLayout xmlns:android="http://schemas.android.com/apk/res/android"
    android:orientation="vertical"
    android:layout_width="fill_parent"
    android:layout_height="fill_parent">
    <Button
        android:id="@+id/startButton"
        android:layout_width="fill_parent"
        android:layout_height="wrap_content"
        android:text="Start Recording"
    />
    <Button
        android:id="@+id/stopButton"
        android:layout_width="fill_parent"
        android:layout_height="wrap_content"
```

```
        android:text="Stop Recording"
        android:enabled="false"
    />
</LinearLayout>
```

Listing 4-21. *Activity for Recording Audio*

```
public class RecordActivity extends Activity {

    private MediaRecorder recorder;
    private Button start, stop;
    File path;

    @Override
    public void onCreate(Bundle savedInstanceState) {
        super.onCreate(savedInstanceState);
        setContentView(R.layout.main);

        start = (Button)findViewById(R.id.startButton);
        start.setOnClickListener(startListener);
        stop = (Button)findViewById(R.id.stopButton);
        stop.setOnClickListener(stopListener);

        recorder = new MediaRecorder();
        path = new File(Environment.getExternalStorageDirectory(),
                "myRecording.3gp");

        resetRecorder();
    }

    @Override
    public void onDestroy() {
        super.onDestroy();
        recorder.release();
    }

    private void resetRecorder() {
        recorder.setAudioSource(MediaRecorder.AudioSource.MIC);
        recorder.setOutputFormat(MediaRecorder.OutputFormat.THREE_GPP);
        recorder.setAudioEncoder(MediaRecorder.AudioEncoder.DEFAULT);
        recorder.setOutputFile(path.getAbsolutePath());
        try {
            recorder.prepare();
        } catch (Exception e) {
            e.printStackTrace();
        }
    }
```

```
    private View.OnClickListener startListener = new View.OnClickListener() {
        @Override
        public void onClick(View v) {
            try {
                recorder.start();

                start.setEnabled(false);
                stop.setEnabled(true);
            } catch (Exception e) {
                e.printStackTrace();
            }
        }
    };

    private View.OnClickListener stopListener = new View.OnClickListener() {
        @Override
        public void onClick(View v) {
            recorder.stop();
            resetRecorder();

            start.setEnabled(true);
            stop.setEnabled(false);
        }
    };
}
```

The UI for this example is very basic. There are two buttons, and their uses alternate based on the recording state. When the user presses Start, we enable the Stop button and begin recording. When the user presses Stop, we re-enable the Start button and reset the recorder to run again.

MediaRecorder setup is just as straightforward. We create a file on the SD card entitled "myRecording.3gp" and pass the path in `setOutputFile()`. The remaining setup methods tell the recorder to use the device microphone as input (AudioSource.MIC), and it will create a 3GP file format for the output using the default encoder.

For now, you could play this audio file using any of the device's file browser or media player applications. Later on, in Recipe 4-8, we will point out how to play audio back through the application as well.

4-7. Custom Video Capture

Problems

Your application requires video capture, but you need more control over the video recording process than Recipe 4-4 provides.

Solution

(API Level 8)

Use MediaRecorder and Camera directly in concert with each other to create your own video-capture Activity. This is slightly more complex than working with MediaRecorder in an audio-only context as we did with the previous recipe. We want the user to be able to see the camera preview even during the times that we aren't recording video, and to do this we must manage the access to the camera between the two objects.

How It Works

Listings 4-22 through 4-24 illustrate an example of recording video to the device's external storage.

Listing 4-22. *Partial AndroidManifest.xml*

```
<uses-permission android:name="android.permission.RECORD_AUDIO" />
<uses-permission android:name="android.permission.CAMERA" />
<uses-permission android:name="android.permission.WRITE_EXTERNAL_STORAGE" />

...

<activity
    android:name=".VideoCaptureActivity"
    android:screenOrientation="portrait" >
    <intent-filter>
        <action android:name="android.intent.action.MAIN" />
        <category android:name="android.intent.category.LAUNCHER" />
    </intent-filter>
</activity>
```

The key element to point out in the manifest is that we have set our Activity orientation to be fixed in portrait. There is also a small host of permissions required to access the camera and to make a recording that includes the audio track.

Listing 4-23. *res/layout/main.xml*

```
<RelativeLayout xmlns:android="http://schemas.android.com/apk/res/android"
    android:layout_width="match_parent"
    android:layout_height="match_parent" >

    <Button
        android:id="@+id/button_record"
        android:layout_width="match_parent"
        android:layout_height="wrap_content"
        android:layout_alignParentBottom="true"
        android:onClick="onRecordClick" />

    <SurfaceView
        android:id="@+id/surface_video"
        android:layout_width="match_parent"
        android:layout_height="match_parent"
        android:layout_above="@id/button_record" />
</RelativeLayout>
```

Listing 4-24. *Activity Capturing Video*

```
public class VideoCaptureActivity extends Activity implements SurfaceHolder.Callback {

    private Camera mCamera;
    private MediaRecorder mRecorder;

    private SurfaceView mPreview;
    private Button mRecordButton;

    private boolean mRecording = false;

    @Override
    public void onCreate(Bundle savedInstanceState) {
        super.onCreate(savedInstanceState);
        setContentView(R.layout.main);

        mRecordButton = (Button) findViewById(R.id.button_record);
        mRecordButton.setText("Start Recording");

        mPreview = (SurfaceView) findViewById(R.id.surface_video);
        mPreview.getHolder().addCallback(this);
        mPreview.getHolder().setType(SurfaceHolder.SURFACE_TYPE_PUSH_BUFFERS);

        mCamera = Camera.open();
        //Rotate the preview display to match portrait
        mCamera.setDisplayOrientation(90);
```

```
        mRecorder = new MediaRecorder();
    }

    @Override
    protected void onDestroy() {
        mCamera.release();
        mCamera = null;
        super.onDestroy();
    }

    public void onRecordClick(View v) {
        updateRecordingState();
    }

    /*
     * Initialize the camera and recorder.
     * The order of these methods is important because MediaRecorder is a
     * strict state machine that moves through states as each method is called.
     */
    private void initializeRecorder() throws IllegalStateException,
            IOException {
        //Unlock the camera to let MediaRecorder use it
        mCamera.unlock();
        mRecorder.setCamera(mCamera);
        //Update the source settings
        mRecorder.setAudioSource(MediaRecorder.AudioSource.CAMCORDER);
        mRecorder.setVideoSource(MediaRecorder.VideoSource.CAMERA);
        //Update the output settings
        File recordOutput = new File(Environment.getExternalStorageDirectory(),
                "recorded_video.mp4");
        if (recordOutput.exists()) {
            recordOutput.delete();
        }
        CamcorderProfile cpHigh =
                CamcorderProfile.get(CamcorderProfile.QUALITY_HIGH);
        mRecorder.setProfile(cpHigh);
        mRecorder.setOutputFile(recordOutput.getAbsolutePath());
        //Attach the surface to the recorder to allow preview while recording
        mRecorder.setPreviewDisplay(mPreview.getHolder().getSurface());

        //Optionally, set limit values on recording
        mRecorder.setMaxDuration(50000); // 50 seconds
        mRecorder.setMaxFileSize(5000000); // Approximately 5 megabytes

        mRecorder.prepare();
    }

    private void updateRecordingState() {
        if (mRecording) {
            mRecording = false;
```

```
            //Reset the recorder state for the next recording
            mRecorder.stop();
            mRecorder.reset();
            //Take the camera back to let preview continue
            mCamera.lock();
            mRecordButton.setText("Start Recording");
        } else {
            try {
                //Reset the recorder for the next session
                initializeRecorder();
                //Start recording
                mRecording = true;
                mRecorder.start();
                mRecordButton.setText("Stop Recording");
            } catch (Exception e) {
                //Error occurred initializing recorder
                e.printStackTrace();
            }
        }
    }

    @Override
    public void surfaceCreated(SurfaceHolder holder) {
        //When we get a surface, immediately start camera preview
        try {
            mCamera.setPreviewDisplay(holder);
            mCamera.startPreview();
        } catch (IOException e) {
            e.printStackTrace();
        }
    }

    @Override
    public void surfaceChanged(SurfaceHolder holder, int format, int width,
            int height) { }

    @Override
    public void surfaceDestroyed(SurfaceHolder holder) { }
}
```

When this Activity is first created, it obtains an instance of the device's camera and sets its display orientation to match the portrait orientation we defined in the manifest. This call will only affect how the preview content is displayed, not the recorded output; we will talk more about this later in the section. When the Activity becomes visible, we will receive the `surfaceCreated()` callback, at which point the `Camera` begins sending preview data.

When the user decides to press the button and start recording, the `Camera` is unlocked and handed over to `MediaRecorder` for use. The recorder is then set up with the proper sources and formats that it should use to capture video, including both a time and file-size limit to keep users from overloading their storage.

> **NOTE:** It is possible to record video with `MediaRecorder` without having to manage the `Camera` directly, but you will be unable to modify the display orientation and the application will display only preview frames while recording is taking place.

Once recording is finished, the file is automatically saved to external storage and we reset the recorder instance to be ready if the user wants to record again. We also regain control of the `Camera` so that preview frames will continue to draw.

Output Format Orientation

(API Level 9)

In our example we used `Camera.setDisplayOrientation()` to match the preview display orientation to our portrait Activity. However, in some cases if you play this video back on your computer the playback will still be in landscape. To fix this problem, we can use the `setOrientationHint()` method on `MediaRecorder`. This method takes a value in degrees that would match up with our display orientation and applies that value to the metadata of the video container file (i.e., the 3GP or MP4 file) to notify other video player applications that the video should be oriented a certain way.

This may not be necessary because some video players determine orientation based on which dimension of the video size is smaller. It is for this reason, and to keep compatibility with API Level 8, that we have not added it to the example here.

4-8. Adding Speech Recognition

Problem

Your application needs speech-recognition technology in order to interpret voice input.

Solution

(API Level 3)

Use the classes of the android.speech package to leverage the built-in speech-recognition technology of every Android device. Every Android device that is equipped with voice search (available since Android 1.5) provides applications with the ability to use the built-in SpeechRecognizer to process voice input.

To activate this process, the application needs only to send a RecognizerIntent to the system, where the recognition service will handle recording the voice input and processing it; then it returns to you a list of strings indicating what the recognizer thought it heard.

How It Works

Let's examine this technology in action. See Listing 4-25.

Listing 4-25. *Activity Launching and Processing Speech Recognition*

```
public class RecognizeActivity extends Activity {

    private static final int REQUEST_RECOGNIZE = 100;

    TextView tv;

    @Override
    public void onCreate(Bundle savedInstanceState) {
        super.onCreate(savedInstanceState);
        tv = new TextView(this);
        setContentView(tv);

        Intent intent = new Intent(RecognizerIntent.ACTION_RECOGNIZE_SPEECH);
        intent.putExtra(RecognizerIntent.EXTRA_LANGUAGE_MODEL,
                RecognizerIntent.LANGUAGE_MODEL_FREE_FORM);
        intent.putExtra(RecognizerIntent.EXTRA_PROMPT, "Tell Me Your Name");
        try {
            startActivityForResult(intent, REQUEST_RECOGNIZE);
        } catch (ActivityNotFoundException e) {
            //If no recognizer exists, download one from Google Play
            AlertDialog.Builder builder = new AlertDialog.Builder(this);
            builder.setTitle("Not Available");
            builder.setMessage("There is no recognition application installed."
                +" Would you like to download one?");
            builder.setPositiveButton("Yes",
                    new DialogInterface.OnClickListener() {
                @Override
```

```
                public void onClick(DialogInterface dialog, int which) {
                    //Download, for example, Google Voice Search
                    Intent marketIntent = new Intent(Intent.ACTION_VIEW);
                    marketIntent.setData(
                        Uri.parse(
                            "market://details?id=com.google.android.voicesearch"
                        ) );
                }
            });
            builder.setNegativeButton("No", null);
            builder.create().show();
        }
    }

    @Override
    protected void onActivityResult(int requestCode, int resultCode,
            Intent data) {
        if(requestCode == REQUEST_RECOGNIZE &&
                resultCode == Activity.RESULT_OK) {
            ArrayList<String> matches =
                data.getStringArrayListExtra(RecognizerIntent.EXTRA_RESULTS);
            StringBuilder sb = new StringBuilder();
            for(String piece : matches) {
                sb.append(piece);
                sb.append('\n');
            }
            tv.setText(sb.toString());
        } else {
            Toast.makeText(this, "Operation Canceled",
                    Toast.LENGTH_SHORT).show();
        }
    }
}
```

NOTE: If you are testing your application in the emulator, beware that neither Google Play nor any voice recognizers will likely be installed. It is best to test the operation of this example on a device.

This example automatically starts the speech-recognition Activity upon launch of the application and asks the user "Tell Me Your Name". Upon receiving speech from the user and processing the result, the Activity returns with a list of possible items the user could have said. This list is in order of probability, and so in many cases it would be prudent to simply call `matches.get(0)` as the best possible choice and move on. However, this Activity takes all the returned values and displays them on the screen for entertainment purposes.

When starting up the `SpeechRecognizer`, there are a number of extras that can be passed in the Intent to customize the behavior. This example uses the two that are most common:

- EXTRA_LANGUAGE_MODEL
  - A value to help fine-tune the results from the speech processor.
  - Typical speech-to-text queries should use the LANGUAGE_MODEL_FREE_FORM option.
  - If shorter request-type queries are being made, LANGUAGE_MODEL_WEB_SEARCH may produce better results.
- EXTRA_PROMPT
  - This string value displays as the prompt for user speech.

In addition to these, a handful of other parameters may be useful to pass along:

- EXTRA_MAX_RESULTS
  - This integer sets the maximum number of returned results.
- EXTRA_LANGUAGE
  - This requests that results be returned in a language other than the current system default.
  - The string value is a valid IETF tag, such as “en-US” or “es”.

4-9. Playing Back Audio/Video

Problem

An application needs to play audio or video content, either local or remote, on the device.

Solution

(API Level 1)

Use the MediaPlayer to play local or streamed media. Whether the content is audio or video, local or remote, MediaPlayer will connect, prepare, and play the associated media efficiently. In this recipe, we will also explore using MediaController and VideoView as simple ways to include interaction and video play in an Activity layout.

How It Works

> **NOTE:** Before expecting a specific media clip or stream to play, please read the "Android Supported Media Formats" section of the developer documentation to verify support.

Audio Playback

Let's look at a simple example of just using MediaPlayer to play a sound. See Listing 4-26.

Listing 4-26. *Activity Playing Local Sound*

```
public class PlayActivity extends Activity implements MediaPlayer.OnCompletionListener {

    Button mPlay;
    MediaPlayer mPlayer;

    @Override
    public void onCreate(Bundle savedInstanceState) {
        super.onCreate(savedInstanceState);

        mPlay = new Button(this);
        mPlay.setText("Play Sound");
        mPlay.setOnClickListener(playListener);

        setContentView(mPlay);
    }
```

```
    @Override
    public void onDestroy() {
        super.onDestroy();
        if(mPlayer != null) {
            mPlayer.release();
        }
    }

    private View.OnClickListener playListener = new View.OnClickListener() {

        @Override
        public void onClick(View v) {
            if(mPlayer == null) {
                try {
                    mPlayer = MediaPlayer.create(PlayActivity.this,
                            R.raw.sound);
                    mPlayer.start();
                } catch (Exception e) {
                    e.printStackTrace();
                }
            } else {
                mPlayer.stop();
                mPlayer.release();
                mPlayer = null;
            }
        }
    };

    //OnCompletionListener Methods
    @Override
    public void onCompletion(MediaPlayer mp) {
        mPlayer.release();
        mPlayer = null;
    }

}
```

This example uses a button to start and stop playback of a local sound file that is stored in the res/raw directory of a project. `MediaPlayer.create()` is a convenience method with several forms, intended to construct and prepare a player object in one step. The form used in this example takes a reference to a local resource ID, but `create()` can also be used to access and play a remote resource using MediaPlayer.create(Context context, Uri uri);.

Once created, the example starts playing the sound immediately. While the sound is playing, the user may press the button again to stop play. The Activity also implements the `MediaPlayer.OnCompletionListener` interface, so it receives a callback when the playing operation completes normally.

In either case, once play is stopped, the MediaPlayer instance is released. This method allows the resources to be retained only as long as they are in use, and the sound may be played multiple times. To be sure resources are not unnecessarily retained, the player is also released when the Activity is destroyed if it still exists.

If your application needs to play many different sounds, you may consider calling `reset()` instead of `release()` when playback is over. Remember, though, to still call `release()` when the player is no longer needed (or the Activity goes away).

Audio Player

Beyond just simple playback, what if the application needs to create an interactive experience for the user to be able to play, pause, and seek through the media? There are methods available on MediaPlayer to implement all these functions with custom UI elements, but Android also provides the MediaController view so you don't have to. See Listings 4-27 and 4-28.

Listing 4-27. *res/layout/main.xml*

```
<?xml version="1.0" encoding="utf-8"?>
<LinearLayout xmlns:android="http://schemas.android.com/apk/res/android"
    android:id="@+id/root"
    android:orientation="vertical"
    android:layout_width="fill_parent"
    android:layout_height="fill_parent">
    <TextView
        android:layout_width="wrap_content"
        android:layout_height="wrap_content"
        android:layout_gravity="center_horizontal"
        android:text="Now Playing..."
    />
    <ImageView
        android:id="@+id/coverImage"
        android:layout_width="fill_parent"
        android:layout_height="fill_parent"
        android:scaleType="centerInside"
    />
</LinearLayout>
```

Listing 4-28. *Activity Playing Audio with a MediaController*

```
public class PlayerActivity extends Activity implements
        MediaController.MediaPlayerControl,
        MediaPlayer.OnBufferingUpdateListener {
```

```
MediaController mController;
MediaPlayer mPlayer;
ImageView coverImage;

int bufferPercent = 0;

@Override
public void onCreate(Bundle savedInstanceState) {
    super.onCreate(savedInstanceState);
    setContentView(R.layout.main);

    coverImage = (ImageView)findViewById(R.id.coverImage);

    mController = new MediaController(this);
    mController.setAnchorView(findViewById(R.id.root));
}

@Override
public void onResume() {
    super.onResume();
    mPlayer = new MediaPlayer();
    //Set the audio data source
    try {
        mPlayer.setDataSource(this, Uri.parse("URI_TO_REMOTE_AUDIO"));
        mPlayer.prepare();
    } catch (Exception e) {
        e.printStackTrace();
    }
    //Set an image for the album cover
    coverImage.setImageResource(R.drawable.icon);

    mController.setMediaPlayer(this);
    mController.setEnabled(true);
}

@Override
public void onPause() {
    super.onPause();
    mPlayer.release();
    mPlayer = null;
}

@Override
public boolean onTouchEvent(MotionEvent event) {
    mController.show();
    return super.onTouchEvent(event);
}
```

```
    //MediaPlayerControl Methods
    @Override
    public int getBufferPercentage() {
        return bufferPercent;
    }

    @Override
    public int getCurrentPosition() {
        return mPlayer.getCurrentPosition();
    }

    @Override
    public int getDuration() {
        return mPlayer.getDuration();
    }

    @Override
    public boolean isPlaying() {
        return mPlayer.isPlaying();
    }

    @Override
    public void pause() {
        mPlayer.pause();
    }

    @Override
    public void seekTo(int pos) {
        mPlayer.seekTo(pos);
    }

    @Override
    public void start() {
        mPlayer.start();
    }

    //BufferUpdateListener Methods
    @Override
    public void onBufferingUpdate(MediaPlayer mp, int percent) {
        bufferPercent = percent;
    }

    //Android 2.0+ Target Callbacks
    public boolean canPause() {
        return true;
    }

    public boolean canSeekBackward() {
        return true;
    }
```

```
    public boolean canSeekForward() {
        return true;
    }
}
```

This example creates a simple audio player that displays an image for the artist or cover art associated with the audio being played (we just set it to the application icon here). The example still uses a MediaPlayer instance, but this time we are not creating it using the `create()` convenience method. Instead we use `setDataSource()` after the instance is created to set the content. When attaching the content in this manner, the player is not automatically prepared so we must also call `prepare()` to ready the player for use.

At this point, the audio is ready to start. We would like the `MediaController` to handle all playback controls, but `MediaController` can only attach to objects that implement the `MediaController.MediaPlayerControl` interface. Strangely, `MediaPlayer` alone does not implement this interface so we appoint the Activity to do that job instead. Six of the seven methods included in the interface are actually implemented by `MediaPlayer`, so we just call down to those directly.

> **LATE ADDITIONS:** If your application is targeting API Level 5 or later, there are three additional methods to implement in the `MediaController.MediaPlayerControl` interface:
>
> `canPause()`
>
> `canSeekBackward()`
>
> `canSeekForward()`
>
> These methods simply tell the system whether we want to allow these operations to occur inside of this control, so our example returns `true` for all three. These methods are not required if you target a lower API level (which is why we didn't provide `@Override` annotations above them), but you may implement them for best results when running on later versions.

The final method required to use `MediaController` is `getBufferPercentage()`. To obtain this data, the Activity is also tasked with implementing `MediaPlayer.OnBufferingUpdateListener`, which updates the buffer percentage as it changes.

MediaController has one trick to its implementation. It is designed as a widget that floats above an active view in its own Window and it is only visible for a few seconds at a time. As a result, we do not instantiate the widget in the XML layout of the content view, but rather in code. The link is made between the MediaController and the content view by calling `setAnchorView()`, which also determines where the controller will show up onscreen. In this example, we anchor it to the root layout object, so it will display at the bottom of the screen when visible. If the `MediaController` is anchored to a child view in the hierarchy, it will display next to that child instead.

Also, due to the controller's separate window, `MediaController.show()` must not be called from within `onCreate()`, and doing so will cause a fatal exception. `MediaController` is designed to be hidden by default and activated by the user. In this example, we override the `onTouchEvent()` method of the Activity to show the controller whenever the user taps the screen. Unless `show()` is called with a parameter of 0, it will fade out after the amount of time noted by the parameter. Calling `show()` without any parameter tells it to fade out after the default timeout, which is around three seconds. See Figure 4-4.

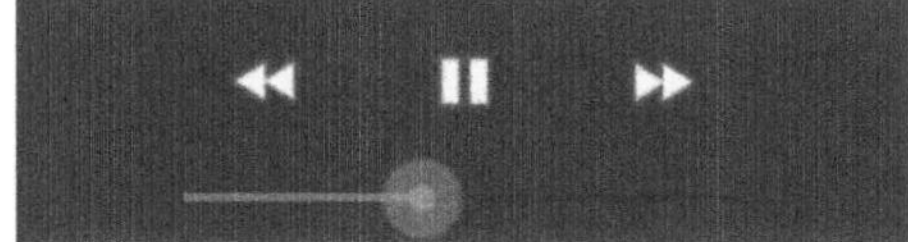

Figure 4-4. *Activity Using MediaController*

Now all features of the audio playback are handled by the standard controller widget. The version of setDataSource() used in this example takes a Uri, making it suitable for loading audio from a ContentProvider or a remote location. Keep in mind that all of this works just as well with local audio files and resources using the alternate forms of setDataSource().

Video Player

When playing video, typically a full set of playback controls is required to play, pause, and seek through the content. In addition, MediaPlayer must have a reference to a SurfaceHolder onto which it can draw the frames of the video. As we mentioned in the previous example, Android provides APIs to do all of this and create a custom video-playing experience. However, in many cases the most efficient path forward is to let the classes provided with the SDK, namely MediaController and VideoView, do all the heavy lifting.

Let's take a look at an example of creating a video player in an Activity. See Listing 4-29.

Listing 4-29. *Activity to Play Video Content*

```
public class VideoActivity extends Activity {

    VideoView videoView;
    MediaController controller;

    @Override
    public void onCreate(Bundle savedInstanceState) {
        super.onCreate(savedInstanceState);
        videoView = new VideoView(this);

        videoView.setVideoURI( Uri.parse("URI_TO_REMOTE_VIDEO") );
        controller = new MediaController(this);
        videoView.setMediaController(controller);
        videoView.start();

        setContentView(videoView);
    }

    @Override
    public void onDestroy() {
        super.onDestroy();
        videoView.stopPlayback();
    }
}
```

This example passes the URI of a remote video location to VideoView and tells it to handle the rest. VideoView can be embedded in larger XML layout hierarchies as well, although often it is the only thing and is displayed as full-screen, so setting it in code as the only view in the layout tree is not uncommon.

With `VideoView`, interaction with `MediaController` is much simpler. `VideoView` implements the `MediaController.MediaPlayerControl` interface, so no additional glue logic is required to make the controls functional. `VideoView` also internally handles the anchoring of the controller to itself, so it displays onscreen in the proper location.

Handling Redirects

We have one final note about using the MediaPlayer classes to handle remote content. Many media content servers on the Web today do not publicly expose a direct URL to the video container. Either for the purposes of tracking or security, public media URLs can often redirect one or more times before ending up at the true media content. MediaPlayer does not handle this redirect process, and it will return an error when presented with a redirected URL.

If you are unable to directly retrieve locations of the content you want to display in an application, that application must trace the redirect path before handing the URL to MediaPlayer. Listing 4-30 is an example of a simple AsyncTask tracer that will do the job.

Listing 4-30. *RedirectTracerTask*

```
public class RedirectTracerTask extends AsyncTask<Uri, Void, Uri> {

    private VideoView mVideo;
    private Uri initialUri;

    public RedirectTracerTask(VideoView video) {
        super();
        mVideo = video;
    }

    @Override
    protected Uri doInBackground(Uri... params) {
        initialUri = params[0];
        String redirected = null;
        try {
          URL url = new URL(initialUri.toString());
          HttpURLConnection connection =
                  (HttpURLConnection)url.openConnection();
          //Once connected, see where you ended up
```

```
            redirected = connection.getHeaderField("Location");

            return Uri.parse(redirected);
        } catch (Exception e) {
            e.printStackTrace();
            return null;
        }
    }

    @Override
    protected void onPostExecute(Uri result) {
        if(result != null) {
            mVideo.setVideoURI(result);
        } else {
            mVideo.setVideoURI(initialUri);
        }
    }

}
```

This helper class tracks down the final location by retrieving it out of the HTTP headers. If there were no redirects in the supplied Uri, the background operation will end up returning null, in which case the original Uri is passed to the VideoView. With this helper class, you can now pass the locations to the view as follows:

```
VideoView videoView = new VideoView(this);
RedirectTracerTask task = new RedirectTracerTask(videoView);
Uri location = Uri.parse("URI_TO_REMOTE_VIDEO");

task.execute(location);
```

4-10. Playing Sound Effects

Problem

Your application requires a handful of short sound effects that need to be played in response to user interaction with very low latency.

Solution

(API Level 1)

Use SoundPool to buffer load your sound files into memory and play them back quickly in response to the user's actions. The Android framework provides

SoundPool as a way to decode small sound files and hold them in memory for rapid and repeated playback. It also has some added features where the volume and playback speed of each sound can be controlled at runtime. The sounds themselves can be housed in assets, resources, or just in the device's filesystem.

How It Works

Let's take a look at how to use SoundPool to load up some sounds and attach them to Button clicks. See Listings 4-31 and 4-32.

Listing 4-31. *res/layout/main.xml*

```
<?xml version="1.0" encoding="utf-8"?>
<LinearLayout xmlns:android="http://schemas.android.com/apk/res/android"
    android:layout_width="fill_parent"
    android:layout_height="fill_parent"
    android:orientation="vertical" >
    <Button
        android:id="@+id/button_beep1"
        android:layout_width="fill_parent"
        android:layout_height="wrap_content"
        android:text="Play Beep 1" />
    <Button
        android:id="@+id/button_beep2"
        android:layout_width="fill_parent"
        android:layout_height="wrap_content"
        android:text="Play Beep 2" />
        <Button
        android:id="@+id/button_beep3"
        android:layout_width="fill_parent"
        android:layout_height="wrap_content"
        android:text="Play Beep 3" />
</LinearLayout>
```

Listing 4-32. *Activity with SoundPool*

```
public class SoundPoolActivity extends Activity implements
        View.OnClickListener {

    private AudioManager mAudioManager;
    private SoundPool mSoundPool;
    private SparseIntArray mSoundMap;

    @Override
    protected void onCreate(Bundle savedInstanceState) {
        super.onCreate(savedInstanceState);
        setContentView(R.layout.main);
```

```
        //Get the AudioManager system service
        mAudioManager = (AudioManager) getSystemService(AUDIO_SERVICE);
        //Set up pool to only play one sound at a time over the
        // standard speaker output.
        mSoundPool = new SoundPool(1, AudioManager.STREAM_MUSIC, 0);

        findViewById(R.id.button_beep1).setOnClickListener(this);
        findViewById(R.id.button_beep2).setOnClickListener(this);
        findViewById(R.id.button_beep3).setOnClickListener(this);

        //Load each sound and save their streamId into a map
        mSoundMap = new SparseIntArray();
        AssetManager manager = getAssets();
        try {
            int streamId;
            streamId = mSoundPool.load(manager.openFd("Beep1.ogg"), 1);
            mSoundMap.put(R.id.button_beep1, streamId);

            streamId = mSoundPool.load(manager.openFd("Beep2.ogg"), 1);
            mSoundMap.put(R.id.button_beep2, streamId);

            streamId = mSoundPool.load(manager.openFd("Beep3.ogg"), 1);
            mSoundMap.put(R.id.button_beep3, streamId);
        } catch (IOException e) {
            Toast.makeText(this, "Error Loading Sound Effects",
                    Toast.LENGTH_SHORT).show();
        }
    }

    @Override
    public void onDestroy() {
        super.onDestroy();
        mSoundPool.release();
        mSoundPool = null;
    }

    @Override
    public void onClick(View v) {
        //Retrieve the appropriate sound ID
        int streamId = mSoundMap.get(v.getId());
        if (streamId > 0) {
            float streamVolumeCurrent =
                  mAudioManager.getStreamVolume(AudioManager.STREAM_MUSIC);
            float streamVolumeMax =
                  mAudioManager.getStreamMaxVolume(AudioManager.STREAM_MUSIC);
            float volume = streamVolumeCurrent / streamVolumeMax;
```

```
            //Play the sound at the specified volume, with no loop
            // and at the standard playback rate
            mSoundPool.play(streamId, volume, volume, 1, 0, 1.0f);
        }
    }
}
```

This example is fairly straightforward. The Activity initially loads three sound files from the application's assets directory into the SoundPool. This step decodes them into raw PCM audio and buffers them in memory. Each time a sound is loaded into the pool with load(), a stream identifier is returned that will be used to play the sound later. We attach each sound to play with a particular button by storing them together as a key/value pair inside of a SparseIntArray.

> **NOTE:** SparseIntArray (and its sibling SparseBooleanArray) is a key/value store similar to a Map. However, it is significantly more efficient at storing primitive data like integers because it avoids unnecessary object creation caused by auto-boxing. Whenever possible, these classes should be chosen over Map for best performance.

When the user presses one of the buttons, the stream identifier to play and call SoundPool again to play the audio is retrieved. Because the maxStreams property of the SoundPool constructor was set to 1, if the user taps multiple buttons in quick succession, new sounds will cause older ones to stop. If this value is increased, multiple sounds can be played together.

The parameters of the play() method allow the sound to be configured with each access. Features such as looping the sound or playing it back slower or faster than the original source can be controlled from here.

- Looping supports any finite number of loops, or the value can be set to -1 to loop infinitely.
- Rate control supports any value between 0.5 and 2.0 (half-speed to double-speed).

If you want to use SoundPool to dynamically change which sounds are loaded into memory at a given time, without recreating the pool, you can use the unload() method to remove items from the pool in order to load() more in. When you are completely done with a SoundPool, call release() to relinquish its native resources.

4-11. Creating a Tilt Monitor

Problem

Your application requires feedback from the device's accelerometer that goes beyond just understanding whether the device is oriented in portrait or landscape.

Solution

(API Level 3)

Use `SensorManager` to receive constant feedback from the accelerometer sensor. `SensorManager` provides a generic abstracted interface for working with sensor hardware on Android devices. The accelerometer is just one of many sensors that an application can register to receive regular updates from.

How It Works

> **IMPORTANT:** Device sensors such as the accelerometer do not exist in the emulator. If you cannot test `SensorManager` code on an Android device, you will need to use a tool such as Sensor Simulator to inject sensor events into the system. Sensor Simulator requires modifying this example to use a different `SensorManager` interface for testing; see "Useful Tools to Know: Sensor Simulator" at the end of this chapter for more information.

This example Activity registers with `SensorManager` for accelerometer updates and displays the data onscreen. The raw X/Y/Z data is displayed in a `TextView` at the bottom of the screen, but in addition the device's "tilt" is visualized through a simple graph of four views in a `TableLayout`. See Listings 4-33 and 4-34.

> **NOTE:** It is also recommended that you add `android:screenOrientation="portrait"` or

android:screenOrientation="landscape" to the application's manifest to keep the Activity from trying to rotate as you move and tilt the device.

Listing 4-33. *res/layout/main.xml*

```
<?xml version="1.0" encoding="utf-8"?>
<RelativeLayout xmlns:android="http://schemas.android.com/apk/res/android"
    android:layout_width="fill_parent"
    android:layout_height="fill_parent">
    <TableLayout
        android:layout_width="fill_parent"
        android:layout_height="fill_parent"
        android:stretchColumns="0,1,2">
        <TableRow
            android:layout_weight="1">
            <View
                android:id="@+id/top"
                android:layout_column="1"
            />
        </TableRow>
        <TableRow
            android:layout_weight="1">
            <View
                android:id="@+id/left"
                android:layout_column="0"
            />
            <View
                android:id="@+id/right"
                android:layout_column="2"
            />
        </TableRow>
        <TableRow
            android:layout_weight="1">
            <View
                android:id="@+id/bottom"
                android:layout_column="1"
            />
        </TableRow>
    </TableLayout>
    <TextView
        android:id="@+id/values"
        android:layout_width="fill_parent"
        android:layout_height="wrap_content"
        android:layout_alignParentBottom="true"
    />
</RelativeLayout>
```

Listing 4-34. *Tilt Monitoring Activity*

```
public class TiltActivity extends Activity implements SensorEventListener {

    private SensorManager mSensorManager;
    private Sensor mAccelerometer;
    private TextView valueView;
    private View mTop, mBottom, mLeft, mRight;

    public void onCreate(Bundle savedInstanceState) {
        super.onCreate(savedInstanceState);
        setContentView(R.layout.main);

        mSensorManager = (SensorManager)getSystemService(SENSOR_SERVICE);
        mAccelerometer =
                mSensorManager.getDefaultSensor(Sensor.TYPE_ACCELEROMETER);

        valueView = (TextView)findViewById(R.id.values);
        mTop = findViewById(R.id.top);
        mBottom = findViewById(R.id.bottom);
        mLeft = findViewById(R.id.left);
        mRight = findViewById(R.id.right);
    }

    protected void onResume() {
        super.onResume();
        mSensorManager.registerListener(this, mAccelerometer,
            SensorManager.SENSOR_DELAY_UI);
    }

    protected void onPause() {
        super.onPause();
        mSensorManager.unregisterListener(this);
    }

    public void onAccuracyChanged(Sensor sensor, int accuracy) { }

    public void onSensorChanged(SensorEvent event) {
        float[] values = event.values;
        float x = values[0] / 10;
        float y = values[1] / 10;
        int scaleFactor;

        if(x > 0) {
            scaleFactor = (int)Math.min(x * 255, 255);
            mRight.setBackgroundColor(Color.TRANSPARENT);
            mLeft.setBackgroundColor(Color.argb(scaleFactor, 255, 0, 0));
        } else {
            scaleFactor = (int)Math.min(Math.abs(x) * 255, 255);
            mRight.setBackgroundColor(Color.argb(scaleFactor, 255, 0, 0));
```

```
            mLeft.setBackgroundColor(Color.TRANSPARENT);
        }

        if(y > 0) {
            scaleFactor = (int)Math.min(y * 255, 255);
            mTop.setBackgroundColor(Color.TRANSPARENT);
            mBottom.setBackgroundColor(Color.argb(scaleFactor, 255, 0, 0));
        } else {
            scaleFactor = (int)Math.min(Math.abs(y) * 255, 255);
            mTop.setBackgroundColor(Color.argb(scaleFactor, 255, 0, 0));
            mBottom.setBackgroundColor(Color.TRANSPARENT);
        }
        //Display the raw values
        valueView.setText(String.format("X: %1$1.2f, Y: %2$1.2f, Z: %3$1.2f",
                values[0], values[1], values[2]));
    }
}
```

The orientation of the three axes on the device accelerometer is as follows, from the perspective of looking at the device screen, upright in portrait:

- X: Horizontal axis with positive pointing to the right
- Y: Vertical axis with positive pointing up
- Z: Perpendicular axis with positive pointing back at you

When the Activity is visible to the user (between onResume() and onPause()), it registers with SensorManager to receive updates about the accelerometer. When registering, the last parameter to registerListener() defines the update rate. The chosen value, SENSOR_DELAY_UI, is the fastest recommended rate to receive updates and still directly modify the UI with each update.

With each new sensor value, the onSensorChanged() method of our registered listener is called with a SensorEvent value; this event contains the X/Y/Z acceleration values.

> **QUICK SCIENCE NOTE:** An accelerometer measures the acceleration due to forces applied. When a device is at rest, the only force operating on it is the force of gravity (~9.8 m/s^2). The output value on each axis is the product of this force (pointing down to the ground) and each orientation vector. When the two are parallel, the value will be at its maximum (~9.8–10). When the two are perpendicular, the value will be at its minimum (~0.0). Therefore, a device lying flat on a table will read ~0.0 for both X and Y, and ~9.8 for Z.

The example application displays the raw acceleration values for each axis in the TextView at the bottom of the screen. In addition, there is a grid of four `Views` arranged in a top/bottom/left/right pattern, and we proportionally adjust the background color of this grid based on the orientation. When the device is perfectly flat, both X and Y should be close to zero and the entire screen will be black. As the device tilts, the squares on the low side of the tilt will start to glow red until they are completely red once the device orientation reaches upright in either position.

> **TIP:** Try modifying this example with some of the other rate values, like `SENSOR_DELAY_NORMAL`. Notice how the change affects the update rate in the example.

In addition, you can shake the device and see alternating grid boxes highlight as the device accelerates in each direction.

4-12. Monitoring Compass Orientation

Problem

Your application wants to know which major direction the user is facing by monitoring the device's compass sensor.

Solution

(API Level 3)

`SensorManager` comes to the rescue once again. Android doesn't provide a "compass" sensor exactly; instead it includes the necessary methods to infer where the device is pointing based on other sensor data. In this case, the device's magnetic field sensor will be used with the accelerometer to ascertain in which direction the user is facing.

We can then ask SensorManager for the user's orientation with respect to the Earth using `getOrientation()`.

How It Works

> **IMPORTANT:** Device sensors such as the accelerometer do not exist in the emulator. If you cannot test SensorManager code on an Android device, you will need to use a tool such as Sensor Simulator to inject sensor events into the system. Sensor Simulator requires modifying this example to use a different SensorManager interface for testing; see "Useful Tools to Know: Sensor Simulator" at the end of this chapter for more information.

As with the previous accelerometer example, we use SensorManager to register for updates on all sensors of interest (in this case, there are two) and to then process the results in onSensorChanged(). This example calculates and displays the user orientation from the device camera's point of view, as it would be required for an application such as augmented reality. See Listings 4-35 and 4-36.

Listing 4-35. *res/layout/main.xml*

```
<?xml version="1.0" encoding="utf-8"?>
<RelativeLayout xmlns:android="http://schemas.android.com/apk/res/android"
    android:layout_width="fill_parent"
    android:layout_height="fill_parent">
    <TextView
        android:id="@+id/direction"
        android:layout_width="wrap_content"
        android:layout_height="wrap_content"
        android:layout_centerInParent="true"
        android:textSize="64dip"
        android:textStyle="bold"
    />
    <TextView
        android:id="@+id/values"
        android:layout_width="wrap_content"
        android:layout_height="wrap_content"
        android:layout_alignParentBottom="true"
    />
</RelativeLayout>
```

Listing 4-36. *Activity Monitoring User Orientation*

```
public class CompassActivity extends Activity implements SensorEventListener {

    private SensorManager mSensorManager;
    private Sensor mAccelerometer, mField;
```

```
private TextView valueView, directionView;

private float[] mGravity;
private float[] mMagnetic;

public void onCreate(Bundle savedInstanceState) {
    super.onCreate(savedInstanceState);
    setContentView(R.layout.main);

    mSensorManager = (SensorManager)getSystemService(SENSOR_SERVICE);
    mAccelerometer =
            mSensorManager.getDefaultSensor(Sensor.TYPE_ACCELEROMETER);
    mField = mSensorManager.getDefaultSensor(Sensor.TYPE_MAGNETIC_FIELD);

    valueView = (TextView)findViewById(R.id.values);
    directionView = (TextView)findViewById(R.id.direction);
}

protected void onResume() {
    super.onResume();
    mSensorManager.registerListener(this, mAccelerometer,
            SensorManager.SENSOR_DELAY_UI);
    mSensorManager.registerListener(this, mField,
            SensorManager.SENSOR_DELAY_UI);
}

protected void onPause() {
    super.onPause();
    mSensorManager.unregisterListener(this);
}

private void updateDirection() {
    float[] temp = new float[9];
    float[] R = new float[9];
    //Load rotation matrix into R
    SensorManager.getRotationMatrix(temp, null, mGravity, mMagnetic);
    //Map to camera's point of view
    SensorManager.remapCoordinateSystem(temp, SensorManager.AXIS_X,
        SensorManager.AXIS_Z, R);
    //Return the orientation values
    float[] values = new float[3];
    SensorManager.getOrientation(R, values);
    //Convert to degrees
    for (int i=0; i < values.length; i++) {
        Double degrees = (values[i] * 180) / Math.PI;
        values[i] = degrees.floatValue();
    }
    //Display the compass direction
    directionView.setText( getDirectionFromDegrees(values[0]) );
    //Display the raw values
```

```
        valueView.setText(
                String.format("Azimuth: %1$1.2f, Pitch: %2$1.2f, Roll: %3$1.2f",
                values[0], values[1], values[2]));
    }

    private String getDirectionFromDegrees(float degrees) {
        if(degrees >= -22.5 && degrees < 22.5) { return "N"; }
        if(degrees >= 22.5 && degrees < 67.5) { return "NE"; }
        if(degrees >= 67.5 && degrees < 112.5) { return "E"; }
        if(degrees >= 112.5 && degrees < 157.5) { return "SE"; }
        if(degrees >= 157.5 || degrees < -157.5) { return "S"; }
        if(degrees >= -157.5 && degrees < -112.5) { return "SW"; }
        if(degrees >= -112.5 && degrees < -67.5) { return "W"; }
        if(degrees >= -67.5 && degrees < -22.5) { return "NW"; }

        return null;
    }

    public void onAccuracyChanged(Sensor sensor, int accuracy) { }
    public void onSensorChanged(SensorEvent event) {
        switch(event.sensor.getType()) {
        case Sensor.TYPE_ACCELEROMETER:
            mGravity = event.values.clone();
            break;
        case Sensor.TYPE_MAGNETIC_FIELD:
            mMagnetic = event.values.clone();
            break;
        default:
            return;
        }

        if(mGravity != null && mMagnetic != null) {
            updateDirection();
        }
    }
}
```

This example Activity displays the three raw values returned by the sensor calculation at the bottom of the screen in real time. In addition, the compass direction associated with where the user is currently facing is converted and displayed center-stage. As updates are received from the sensors, local copies of the latest values from each are maintained. As soon as we have received at least one reading from both sensors of interest, we allow the UI to begin updating.

`updateDirection()` is where all the heavy lifting takes place. `SensorManager.getOrientation()` provides the output information we require to display direction. The method returns no data, and instead an empty float array is passed in for the method to fill in three angle values, and they represent (in order):

- Azimuth
  - Angle of rotation about an axis pointing directly into the Earth.
  - This is the value of interest to the example.
- Pitch
  - Angle of rotation about an axis pointing west.
- Roll
  - Angle of rotation about an axis pointing at magnetic north.

One of the parameters passed to `getOrientation()` is a float array representing a rotation matrix. The rotation matrix is a representation of how the current coordinate system of the devices is oriented, so the method may provide appropriate rotation angles based on its reference coordinates. The rotation matrix for the device orientation is obtained by using `getRotationMatrix()`, which takes the latest values from the accelerometer and magnetic field sensor as input. Like `getOrientation()`, it also returns void; an empty float array of length 9 or 16 (to represent a 3x3 or 4x4 matrix) must be passed in as the first parameter for the method to fill in.

Finally, we want the output of the orientation calculation to be specific to the camera's point of view. To further transform the obtained rotation, we use the `remapCoordinateSystem()` method. This method takes four parameters (in order):

1. Input array representing the matrix to transform
2. How to transform the device's x axis with respect to world coordinates
3. How to transform the device's y axis with respect to world coordinates
4. Empty array to fill in the result

In our example, we want to leave the x axis untouched, so we map X to X. However, we would like to align the device's y axis (vertical axis) to the world's z axis (the one pointing into the Earth). This orients the rotation matrix we receive to match up with the device being held vertically upright as if the user is using the camera and looking at the preview on the screen.

With the angular data calculated, we do some data conversion and display the result on the screen. The unit output of `getOrientation()` is radians, so we first have to convert each result to degrees before displaying it. In addition, we need to convert the azimuth value to a compass direction; `getDirectionFromDegrees()` is a helper method to return the proper direction based on the range the current reading falls within. Going in a full clockwise circle, the azimuth will read from 0 to 180 degrees from north to south. Continuing around the circle, the azimuth will read -180 to 0 degrees rotating from south to north.

4-13. Retrieving Metadata from Media Content

Problem

Your application needs to gather thumbnail screenshots or other metadata from media content on the device.

Solution

(API Level 10)

Use `MediaMetadataRetriever` to read media files and return useful information. This class can read and track information like album and artist data or data about the content itself, such as the size of a video. In addition, you can use it to grab a screenshot of any frame within a video file, either at a specific time or just any frame that Android considers representative.

MediaMetadataRetriever is a great option for applications that work with lots of media content from the device and that need to display extra data about the media to enrich the user interface.

How It Works

Listings 4-37 and 4-38 show how to access this extra metadata on the device.

Listing 4-37. *res/layout/main.xml*

```
<RelativeLayout xmlns:android="http://schemas.android.com/apk/res/android"
    android:layout_width="match_parent"
    android:layout_height="match_parent" >
```

```
    <Button
        android:id="@+id/button_select"
        android:layout_width="match_parent"
        android:layout_height="wrap_content"
        android:text="Pick Video"
        android:onClick="onSelectClick" />
    <TextView
        android:id="@+id/text_metadata"
        android:layout_width="wrap_content"
        android:layout_height="wrap_content"
        android:layout_below="@id/button_select"
        android:layout_margin="15dp" />
    <ImageView
        android:id="@+id/image_frame"
        android:layout_width="wrap_content"
        android:layout_height="wrap_content"
        android:layout_alignParentBottom="true"
        android:layout_centerHorizontal="true"
        android:layout_margin="10dp" />
</RelativeLayout>
```

Listing 4-28. *Activity with MediaMetadataRetriever*

```
public class MetadataActivity extends Activity {
    private static final int PICK_VIDEO = 100;

    private ImageView mFrameView;
    private TextView mMetadataView;

    @Override
    public void onCreate(Bundle savedInstanceState) {
        super.onCreate(savedInstanceState);
        setContentView(R.layout.main);

        mFrameView = (ImageView) findViewById(R.id.image_frame);
        mMetadataView = (TextView) findViewById(R.id.text_metadata);
    }

    @Override
    protected void onActivityResult(int requestCode, int resultCode,
            Intent data) {
        if (requestCode == PICK_VIDEO && resultCode == RESULT_OK
                && data != null) {
            Uri video = data.getData();
            MetadataTask task = new MetadataTask(this, mFrameView,
                    mMetadataView);
            task.execute(video);
        }
    }
```

```
public void onSelectClick(View v) {
    Intent intent = new Intent(Intent.ACTION_GET_CONTENT);
    intent.setType("video/*");
    startActivityForResult(intent, PICK_VIDEO);
}

public static class MetadataTask extends AsyncTask<Uri, Void, Bundle> {
    private Context mContext;
    private ImageView mFrame;
    private TextView mMetadata;
    private ProgressDialog mProgress;

    public MetadataTask(Context context, ImageView frame,
            TextView metadata) {
        mContext = context;
        mFrame = frame;
        mMetadata = metadata;
    }

    @Override
    protected void onPreExecute() {
        mProgress = ProgressDialog.show(mContext, "",
                "Analyzing Video File...", true);
    }

    @Override
    protected Bundle doInBackground(Uri... params) {
        Uri video = params[0];
        MediaMetadataRetriever retriever = new MediaMetadataRetriever();
        retriever.setDataSource(mContext, video);

        Bitmap frame = retriever.getFrameAtTime();

        String date = retriever.extractMetadata(
                MediaMetadataRetriever.METADATA_KEY_DATE);
        String duration = retriever.extractMetadata(
                MediaMetadataRetriever.METADATA_KEY_DURATION);
        String width = retriever.extractMetadata(
                MediaMetadataRetriever.METADATA_KEY_VIDEO_WIDTH);
        String height = retriever.extractMetadata(
                MediaMetadataRetriever.METADATA_KEY_VIDEO_HEIGHT);

        Bundle result = new Bundle();
        result.putParcelable("frame", frame);
        result.putString("date", date);
        result.putString("duration", duration);
        result.putString("width", width);
        result.putString("height", height);
```

```
            return result;
        }

        @Override
        protected void onPostExecute(Bundle result) {
            if (mProgress != null) {
                mProgress.dismiss();
                mProgress = null;
            }

            Bitmap frame = result.getParcelable("frame");
            mFrame.setImageBitmap(frame);
            String metadata = String.format(
                    "Video Date: %s\nVideo Duration: %s\nVideo Size: %s x %s",
                    result.getString("date"),
                    result.getString("duration"),
                    result.getString("width"),
                    result.getString("height") );
            mMetadata.setText(metadata);
        }
    }

}
```

In this example, the user can select a video file from the device to process. Upon receipt of a valid video `Uri`, the Activity starts an `AsyncTask` to parse some metadata out of the video. The reason we create an `AsyncTask` for this purpose is because the process can take a few seconds or more to complete, and we don't want to block the UI thread while this is going on.

The background task creates a new MediaMetadataRetriever and sets the selected video as its data source. We then call the method `getFrameAtTime()` to return a `Bitmap` image of a frame in the video. This method is useful for creating thumbnails for a video in your UI. The version we call takes no parameters, and the frame it returns is semirandom. If you are more interested in a specific frame, there is an alternate version of the method that takes the presentation time (in microseconds) of the video where you would like a frame. In this case, it will return a key frame in the video that is closest to the requested time.

In addition to the frame image, we also gather some basic information about the video, including when it was created, how long it is, and how big it is. All the resulting data is packaged into a `bundle` and passed back from the background thread. The `onPostExecute()` method of the task is called on the main thread, so we use it to update the UI with the data we retrieved.

Useful Tools to Know: Sensor Simulator

Google's Android emulator doesn't directly support sensors because most computers don't have compasses, accelerometers, or even light sensors that the emulator can leverage. Instead the SDK tools allow developers to tether an Android device to a machine and run a special application called SdkController while forwarding data into the emulator over ADB. The interesting paradox this creates is that if a developer is using the emulator for testing, he likely won't have a device to tether for sensor input (unless he is using the emulator to test a newer version of Android than the device will support).

> **NOTE:** For more information about SdkController and device tethering for sensor or multitouch support, visit http://tools.android.com/tips/hardware-emulation.

Although this limitation can be problematic for apps that need to interact with sensors, and where the pure emulator is the only viable testing option, it can be overcome by working with Sensor Simulator.

Sensor Simulator (`http://code.google.com/p/openintents/wiki/SensorSimulator`) is an open source tool that lets you simulate sensor data and make this data available to your apps for testing purposes. It currently supports accelerometer, compass/magnetic field, orientation, temperature, light, proximity, pressure, gravity, linear acceleration, rotation vector, and gyroscope sensors. These sensors can be configured.

Obtaining Sensor Simulator

Sensor Simulator is distributed in a single ZIP archive. Point your browser to `http://code.google.com/p/openintents/downloads/list?q=sensorsimulator` and click the `sensorsimulator-2.0-rc1.zip` link followed by the `sensorsimulator-2.0-rc1.zip` link on the subsequent page (or scan the barcode) to download this 692 KB file.

After unzipping the archive, you'll discover a `sensorsimulator-2.0-rc1` home directory with the following subdirectories:

- bin: Contains the executables SensorRecordFromDevice-2.0-rc1.apk (an app for recording sensor data from a real Android device), sensorsimulator-2.0-rc1.jar (a Java-based desktop application for choosing and configuring sensors to simulate, and for sending test data to the emulator), and SensorSimulatorSettings-2.0-rc1.apk (an app for communicating with the desktop application and for launching a test) along with their readme files
- lib: Contains the library sensorsimulator-lib-2.0-rc1.jar
- release: Contains the build script to assemble the release distribution file (such as sensorsimulator-2.0-rc1.zip)
- samples: Contains examples for how to include the Sensor Simulator in your Android apps
- SensorRecordFromDevice: Contains an Eclipse project for building SensorRecordFromDevice-2.0-rc1.apk
- SensorSimulator: Contains an Eclipse project for building sensorsimulator-2.0-rc1.jar
- SensorSimulatorSettings: Contains an Eclipse project for building SensorSimulatorSettings-2.0-rc1.apk

Launching Sensor Simulator Settings and Sensor Simulator

Now that you've downloaded and unarchived the Sensor Simulator distribution, you'll want to launch this software. Complete the following steps to accomplish this task:

1. Start the Android emulator if not already running; for example, execute `emulator -avd AVD1` at the command line. This example assumes that you've previously created AVD1 in Chapter 1.

2. Install SensorSimulatorSettings-2.0-rc1.apk on the emulator; for example, execute `adb install SensorSimulatorSettings-2.0-rc1.apk`. This example assumes that the adb tool is accessible via your PATH environment variable and that the bin directory is current. It outputs a success message when the APK is successfully installed on the emulator. (You might also want to install SensorRecordFromDevice-2.0-rc1.apk, but doing so is not necessary.)
3. Click the app launcher screen's Sensor Simulator icon to start the app.
4. Start the bin directory's Sensor Simulator desktop application, which is located in sensorsimulator-2.0-rc1.jar. For example, under Windows, double-click this filename.

Figure 4-5 reveals the emulator's app launcher screen with the Sensor Simulator icon highlighted.

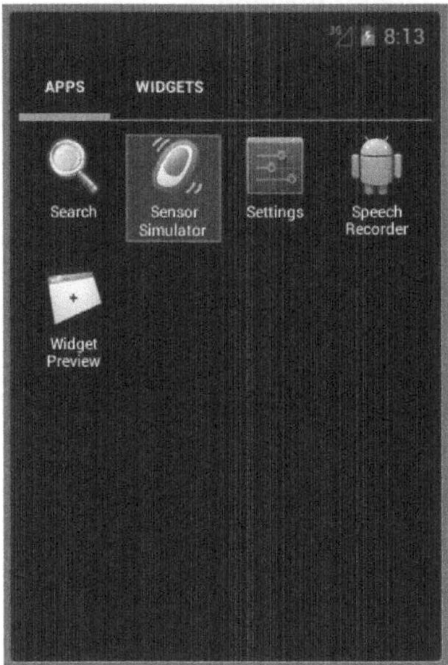

Figure 4-5. *The Sensor Simulator icon is highlighted on the app launcher screen.*

Click the icon. Figure 4-6 reveals the Sensor Simulator Settings activity divided into two screens: Settings and Testing.

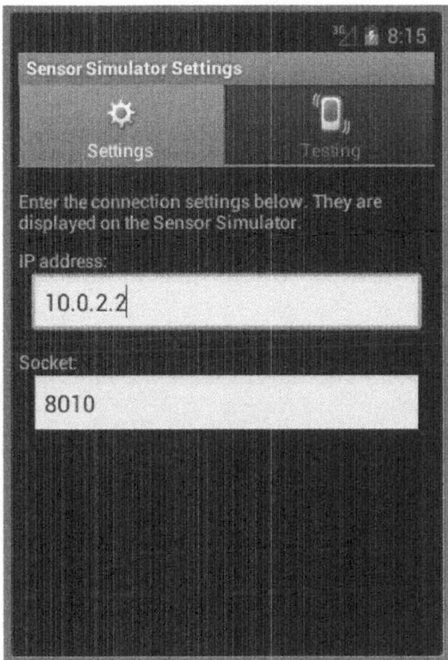

Figure 4-6. *The IP address defaults to 10.0.2.2 and the socket port number defaults to 8010.*

The Settings screen lets you enter connection information for communicating with the Sensor Simulator application. Figure 4-7 reveals this application's UI.

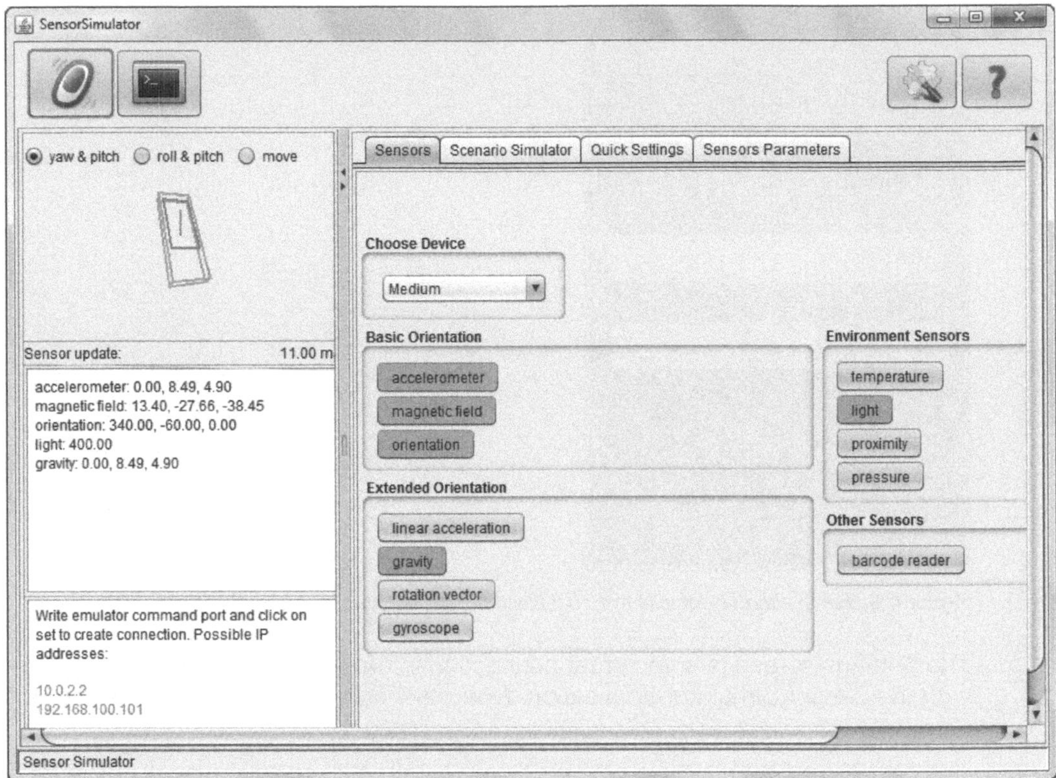

Figure 4-7. *Use the Sensor Simulator application's UI to configure sensors and send sensor data to the emulator.*

Sensor Simulator presents a button menu near the top where the buttons, from left to right, let you switch between Sensor Simulator, Telnet, and Settings screens. You can also launch your browser to display help information:

- The Sensor Simulator screen presents the device representation, enabled sensors, and a list of IP addresses for communicating with the emulator. It also presents Sensors, Scenario Simulator, Quick Settings, and Sensors Parameters tabs:
  - Sensors let you choose which sensors to enable. You can select desired sensors individually or choose a group of sensors in the context of a device.

- Scenario Simulator lets you record a simulation scenario from a real device or create and edit a simulation, and you can play back a recorded simulation on the device or emulator. (You will need to install the `SensorRecordFromDevice-2.0-rc1.apk` app.)
- Quick Settings lets you choose an orientation for the device along with temperature, light, and pressure settings.
- Sensors Parameters lets you further parameterize orientation, temperature, light, and pressure; you can also parameterize the barcode reader.

- The Telnet screen lets you control the emulator GPS position and the battery level.
- The Settings screen lets you provide additional configuration, such as the duration between internal sensor updates.
- The Help button points your browser to the web page at `http://openintents.org/en/node/885`.

The Testing screen lets you connect to the Sensor Simulator application and obtain sensor data. Figure 4-8 reveals this screen.

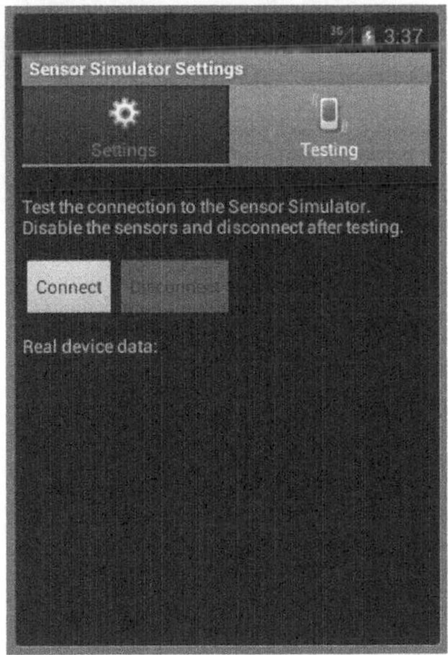

Figure 4-8. *Click Connect to connect to the Sensor Simulator application and start receiving test data.*

According to this screen, you must click the Connect button to establish a connection with Sensor Simulator, which must be running at this point. (You can later click Disconnect to break the connection.)

After clicking Connect, the Testing screen reveals sensors and their values. This information is updated by interacting with the Sensor Simulator application. Figure 4-9 shows this interaction.

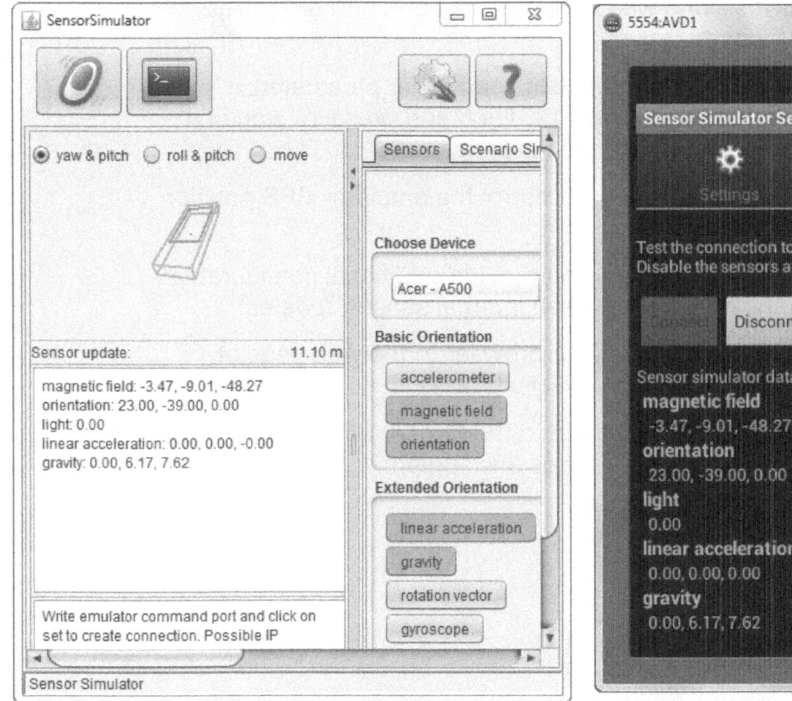

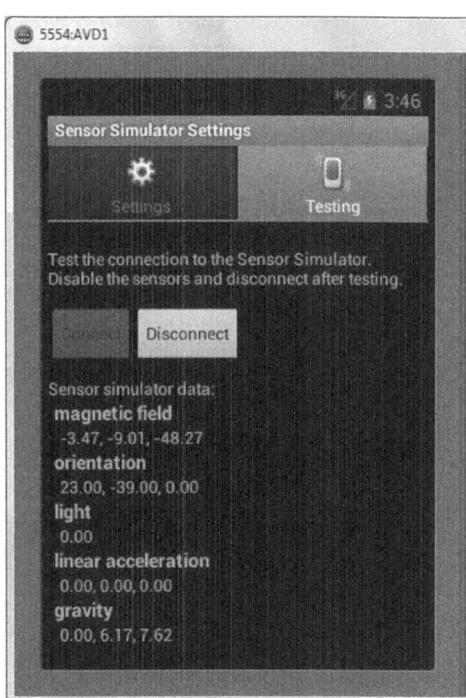

Figure 4-9. *The Sensor Simulator application is sending sensor data to the Sensor Simulator Settings app.*

Accessing Sensor Simulator from Your Apps

Although Sensor Simulator Settings helps you learn how to use Sensor Simulator to send test data to an app, it's no substitute for your own apps. At some point, you'll want to incorporate code into your activities that accesses this tool. Google provides the following guidelines for modifying your app to access Sensor Simulator:

1. Add the lib directory's JAR file (sensorsimulator-lib-2.0-rc1.jar, for example) to your project.
2. Import the following Sensor Simulator types from this library into your source code:

```
import org.openintents.sensorsimulator.hardware.Sensor;
import org.openintents.sensorsimulator.hardware.SensorEvent;
import org.openintents.sensorsimulator.hardware.SensorEventListener;
import org.openintents.sensorsimulator.hardware.SensorManagerSimulator;
```

3. Replace your activity's onCreate() method's existing SensorManager.getSystemService() method calls with equivalent SensorManagerSimulator.getSystemService() method calls. For example, you might replace mSensorManager = (SensorManager) getSystemService(SENSOR_SERVICE); with mSensorManager = SensorManagerSimulator.getSystemService(this, SENSOR_SERVICE);.
4. Connect to the Sensor Simulator desktop application by using the settings that have been set previously with SensorSimulatorSettings: mSensorManager.connectSimulator();, for example.
5. All other code remains untouched. However, remember to register the sensors in onResume() and unregister them in onStop():

```
@Override
protected void onResume()
{
   super.onResume();
   mSensorManager.registerListener(this,
                    mSensorManager.getDefaultSensor(Sensor.TYPE_ACCELEROMETER),
                    SensorManager.SENSOR_DELAY_FASTEST);
   mSensorManager.registerListener(this,
                    mSensorManager.getDefaultSensor(Sensor.TYPE_MAGNETIC_FIELD),
                    SensorManager.SENSOR_DELAY_FASTEST);
   mSensorManager.registerListener(this,
                    SensorManager.getDefaultSensor(Sensor.TYPE_ORIENTATION),
                    SensorManager.SENSOR_DELAY_FASTEST);
   mSensorManager.registerListener(this,
                    mSensorManager.getDefaultSensor(Sensor.TYPE_TEMPERATURE),
                    SensorManager.SENSOR_DELAY_FASTEST);
```

```
}
@Override
protected void onStop()
{
   mSensorManager.unregisterListener(this);
   super.onStop();
}
```

6. Finally, you must implement the `SensorEventListener` interface:

```
class MySensorActivity extends Activity implements SensorEventListener
{
   @Override
   public void onAccuracyChanged(Sensor sensor, int accuracy)
   {
   }
   @Override
   public void onSensorChanged(SensorEvent event)
   {
      int sensor = event.type;
      float[] values = event.values;
      // do something with the sensor data
   }
}
```

> **NOTE:** `SensorManagerSimulator` is derived from the Android `SensorManager` class and implements exactly the same methods as `SensorManager`. For the callback, the new `SensorEventListener` interface has been implemented to resemble the standard Android `SensorEventListener` interface.
>
> Whenever you are not connected to the Sensor Simulator desktop application, you'll get real device sensor data: the `org.openintents.hardware.SensorManagerSimulator` class transparently calls the `SensorManager` instance that's returned by the system service to make this happen.

Summary

This collection of recipes exposed how to use Android to use maps, user location, and device sensor data to integrate information about the user's surroundings into your applications. We also discussed how to utilize the device's camera and microphone, allowing users to capture, and sometimes interpret, what's around them. Finally, using the media APIs, you learned how to take media content, either captured locally by the user or downloaded remotely from the Web, and play it back from within your applications. In the next chapter, we will discuss how to use Android's many persistence techniques to store nonvolatile data on the device.

Chapter 5

Persisting Data

Even in the midst of grand architectures designed to shift as much user data into the cloud as possible, the transient nature of mobile applications will always require that at least some user data be persisted locally on the device. This data may range from cached responses from a web service guaranteeing offline access to preferences that the user has set for specific application behaviors. Android provides a series of helpful frameworks to take the pain out of using files and databases to persist information.

5–1. Making a Preference Screen

Problem

You need to create a simple way to store, change, and display user preferences and settings within your application.

Solution

(API Level 1)

Use the `PreferenceActivity` and an XML `Preference` hierarchy to provide the user interface, key/value combinations, and persistence all at once. Using this method will create a user interface that is consistent with the Settings application on Android devices, and it will keep users' experiences consistent with what they expect.

Within the XML, an entire set of one or more screens can be defined with the associated settings displayed and grouped into categories using the PreferenceScreen, PreferenceCategory, and associated Preference elements. The Activity can then load this hierarchy for the user using very little code.

How It Works

Listings 5-1 and 5-2 show the basic settings for an Android application. The XML defines two screens with a variety of all the common preference types that this framework supports. Notice that one screen is nested inside of the other; the internal screen will be displayed when the user clicks on its associated list item from the root screen.

Listing 5-1. *res/xml/settings.xml*

```
<?xml version="1.0" encoding="utf-8"?>
<PreferenceScreen xmlns:android="http://schemas.android.com/apk/res/android">
  <EditTextPreference
    android:key="namePref"
    android:title="Name"
    android:summary="Tell Us Your Name"
    android:defaultValue="Apress"
  />
  <CheckBoxPreference
      android:key="morePref"
      android:title="Enable More Settings"
      android:defaultValue="false"
  />
  <PreferenceScreen
    android:key="moreScreen"
    android:title="More Settings"
    android:dependency="morePref">
    <ListPreference
      android:key="colorPref"
      android:title="Favorite Color"
      android:summary="Choose your favorite color"
      android:entries="@array/color_names"
      android:entryValues="@array/color_values"
      android:defaultValue="GRN"
    />
    <PreferenceCategory
      android:title="Location Settings">
      <CheckBoxPreference
        android:key="gpsPref"
        android:title="Use GPS Location"
        android:summary="Use GPS to Find You"
        android:defaultValue="true"
```

```
        />
        <CheckBoxPreference
          android:key="networkPref"
          android:title="Use Network Location"
          android:summary="Use Network to Find You"
          android:defaultValue="true"
        />
      </PreferenceCategory>
    </PreferenceScreen>
</PreferenceScreen>
```

Listing 5-2. *res/values/arrays.xml*

```
<?xml version="1.0" encoding="utf-8"?>
<resources>
    <string-array name="color_names">
      <item>Black</item>
      <item>Red</item>
      <item>Green</item>
    </string-array>
    <string-array name="color_values">
      <item>BLK</item>
      <item>RED</item>
      <item>GRN</item>
    </string-array>
</resources>
```

Notice first the convention used to create the XML file. Although this resource could be inflated from any directory (such as res/layout), the convention is to put them into a generic directory for the project titled simply "xml."

Also, notice that we provide an `android:key` attribute for each `Preference` object instead of `android:id`. When each stored value is referenced elsewhere in the application through a `SharedPreferences` object, it will be accessed using the key. In addition, `PreferenceActivity` includes the `findPreference()` method for obtaining a reference to an inflated `Preference` in Java code, which is more efficient than using `findViewById()`; `findPreference()` also takes the key as a parameter.

When inflated, the root PreferenceScreen presents a list with the following three options (in order):

1. An item titled "Name"
    - This is an instance of `EditTextPreference`, which stores a string value.
    - Tapping this item will present a text box so that the user can type a new preference value.

2. An item titled "Enable More Settings" with a check box beside it
   - This is an instance of CheckBoxPreference, which stores a boolean value.
   - Tapping this item will toggle the checked status of the check box.
3. An item titled "More Settings"
   - Tapping this item will load another PreferenceScreen with more items.

When the user taps the "More Settings" item, a second screen is displayed with three more items: a `ListPreference` item and two more `CheckBoxPreferences` grouped together by a `PreferenceCategory`. `PreferenceCategory` is simply a way to create section breaks and headers in the list for grouping actual preference items.

The `ListPreference` is the final preference type used in the example. This item requires two array parameters (although they can both be set to the same array) that represent a set of choices the user may pick from. The `android:entries` array is the list of human-readable items to display, while the `android:entryValues` array represents the actual value to be stored.

All the preference items may optionally have a default value set for them as well. This value is not automatically loaded, however. It will load the first time this XML file is inflated when the `PreferenceActivity` is displayed OR when a call to `PreferenceManager.setDefaultValues()` is made.

Now let's take a look at how a `PreferenceActivity` would load and manage this. See Listing 5-3.

Listing 5-3. *PreferenceActivity in Action*

```
public class SettingsActivity extends PreferenceActivity {

    @Override
    public void onCreate(Bundle savedInstanceState) {
        super.onCreate(savedInstanceState);
        //Load preference data from XML
        addPreferencesFromResource(R.xml.settings);
    }
}
```

All that is required to display the preferences to the user and allow him or her to make changes is a call to `addPreferencesFromResource()`. There is no need to call `setContentView()` with `PreferenceActivity`, as `addPreferencesFromResource()` inflates the XML and displays it as well. However a custom layout may be provided as long as it contains a `ListView` with the `android:id="@android:id/list"` attribute set, which is where `PreferenceActivity` will load the preference items.

Preference items can also be placed in the list for the sole purpose of controlling access. In the example, we put the "Enable More Settings" item in the list just to allow the user to enable or disable access to the second `PreferenceScreen`. In order to accomplish this, our nested `PreferenceScreen` includes the `android:dependency` attribute, which links its enabled state to the state of another preference. Whenever the referenced preference is either not set or false, this preference will be disabled.

When this Activity loads, you see something like Figure 5-1.

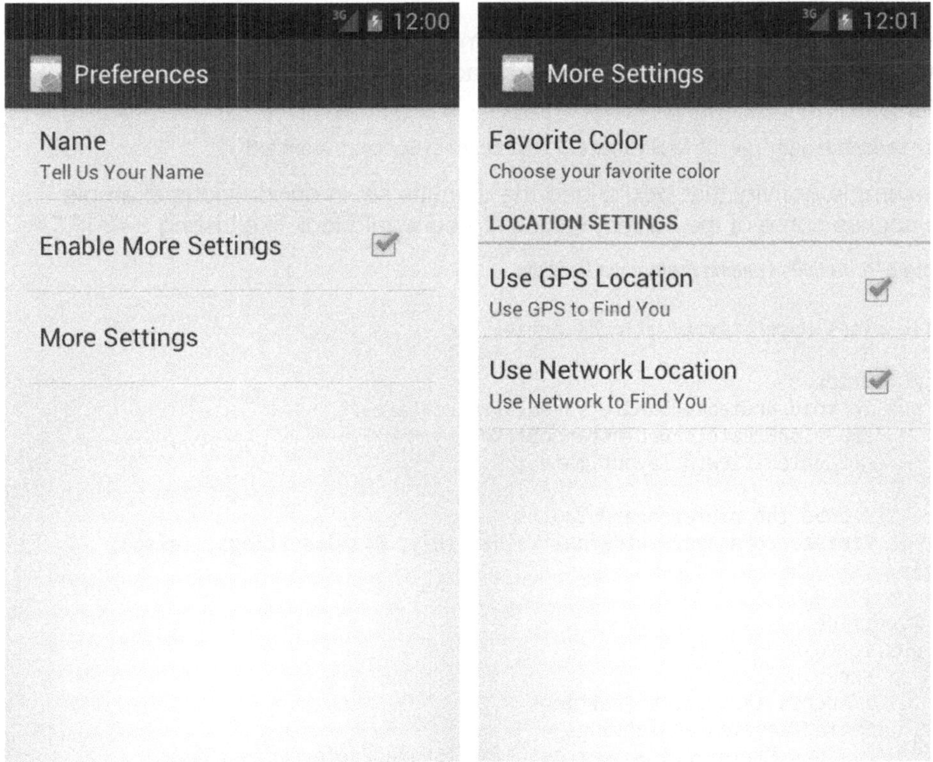

Figure 5-1. *PreferenceScreen in action.*

The root `PreferenceScreen` (left) displays first. If the user taps on "More Settings," the secondary screen (right) displays.

Loading Defaults and Accessing Preferences

Typically, a `PreferenceActivity` such as this one is not the root of an application. Often, if default values are set they may need to be accessed by the rest of the application before the user ever visits Settings (the first case under which the defaults will load). Therefore, it can be helpful to put a call to the following method elsewhere in your application to ensure that the defaults are loaded prior to being used.

```
PreferenceManager.setDefaultValues(Context context, int resId, boolean readAgain);
```

This method may be called multiple times, and the defaults will not get loaded over again. It may be placed in the main Activity so it is called on first launch, or perhaps it could be in a common place where the application can call it before any access to shared preferences.

Preferences that are stored by using this mechanism are put into the default shared preferences object, which can be accessed with any `Context` pointer using

```
PreferenceManager.getDefaultSharedPreferences(Context context);
```

An example Activity that would load the defaults set in our previous example and access some of the current values stored would look like Listing 5-4.

Listing 5-4. ***Activity Loading Preference Defaults***

```
public class HomeActivity extends Activity {

    @Override
    public void onCreate(Bundle savedInstanceState) {
        super.onCreate(savedInstanceState);
        setContentView(R.layout.main);

        //Load the preference defaults
        PreferenceManager.setDefaultValues(this, R.xml.settings, false);
    }

    @Override
    public void onResume() {
        super.onResume();
        //Access the current settings
        SharedPreferences settings =
                PreferenceManager.getDefaultSharedPreferences(this);

        String name = settings.getString("namePref", "");
        boolean isMoreEnabled = settings.getBoolean("morePref", false);
    }
}
```

Calling setDefaultValues() will create a value in the preference store for any item in the XML file that includes an android:defaultValue attribute. This will make them accessible to the application, even if the user has not yet visited the settings screen.

These values can then be accessed using a set of typed accessor functions on the SharedPreferences object. Each of these accessor methods requires both the name of the preference key and a default value to be returned if a value for the preference key does not yet exist.

PreferenceFragment

(API Level 11)

Starting with Android 3.0, a new method of creating preference screens was introduced in the form of PreferenceFragment. This class is not in the support library, so it can only be used as a replacement for PreferenceActivity if your application targets a minimum of API Level 11. Listings 5-5 and 5-6 modify the previous example to use PreferenceFragment instead.

Listing 5-5. *Activity Containing Fragments*

```
public class MainActivity extends Activity {

    @Override
    protected void onCreate(Bundle savedInstanceState) {
        super.onCreate(savedInstanceState);

        FragmentTransaction ft = getFragmentManager().beginTransaction();
        ft.add(android.R.id.content, new PreferenceFragment());
        ft.commit();
    }
}
```

Listing 5-6. *New PreferenceFragment*

```
public class SettingsFragment extends PreferenceFragment {

    @Override
    public void onCreate(Bundle savedInstanceState) {
        super.onCreate(savedInstanceState);
        //Load preference data from XML
        addPreferencesFromResource(R.xml.settings);
    }
}
```

Now the preferences themselves are housed inside of a `PreferenceFragment`, which manages them in the same way as before. The other required change is that a `Fragment` cannot live on its own; it must be contained inside an `Activity` so we have created a new root `Activity` where the `Fragment` is attached.

5-2. Persisting Simple Data

Problem

Your application needs a simple, low-overhead method of storing basic data, such as numbers and strings, in persistent storage.

Solution

(API Level 1)

Using `SharedPreferences` objects, applications can quickly create one or more persistent stores where data can be saved and retrieved at a later time. Underneath the hood, these objects are actually stored as XML files in the application's user data area. However, unlike directly reading and writing data from files, `SharedPreferences` provide an efficient framework for persisting basic data types.

Creating multiple SharedPreferences as opposed to dumping all your data in the default object can be a good habit to get into, especially if the data you are storing will have a shelf life. Keeping in mind that all preferences stored using the XML and `PreferenceActivity` framework are also stored in the default location, what if you wanted to store a group of items related to, say, a logged-in user? When that user logs out, you will need to remove all the persisted data that goes along with that. If you store all that data in default preferences, you will most likely need to remove each item individually. However, if you create a preference object just for those settings, logging out can be as simple as calling `SharedPreferences.Editor.clear()`.

How It Works

Let's look at a practical example of using `SharedPreferences` to persist simple data. Listings 5-7 and 5-8 create a data entry form for the user to send a simple message to a remote server. To aid the user, we will remember all the data he or she enters for each field until a successful request is made. This will allow the user to leave the screen (or be interrupted by a text message or phone call) without having to enter all the information again.

Listing 5-7. *res/layout/form.xml*

```
<?xml version="1.0" encoding="utf-8"?>
<LinearLayout xmlns:android="http://schemas.android.com/apk/res/android"
  android:orientation="vertical"
  android:layout_width="fill_parent"
  android:layout_height="fill_parent">
  <TextView
    android:layout_width="fill_parent"
    android:layout_height="wrap_content"
    android:text="Email:"
    android:padding="5dip"
  />
  <EditText
    android:id="@+id/email"
    android:layout_width="fill_parent"
    android:layout_height="wrap_content"
    android:singleLine="true"
  />
  <CheckBox
    android:id="@+id/age"
    android:layout_width="fill_parent"
    android:layout_height="wrap_content"
    android:text="Are You Over 18?"
  />
  <TextView
    android:layout_width="fill_parent"
    android:layout_height="wrap_content"
    android:text="Message:"
    android:padding="5dip"
  />
  <EditText
    android:id="@+id/message"
    android:layout_width="fill_parent"
    android:layout_height="wrap_content"
    android:minLines="3"
    android:maxLines="3"
  />
  <Button
    android:id="@+id/submit"
    android:layout_width="fill_parent"
    android:layout_height="wrap_content"
    android:text="Submit"
  />
</LinearLayout>
```

Listing 5-8. *Entry Form with Persistence*

```
public class FormActivity extends Activity implements View.OnClickListener {

    EditText email, message;
    CheckBox age;
    Button submit;

    SharedPreferences formStore;

    boolean submitSuccess = false;

    @Override
    public void onCreate(Bundle savedInstanceState) {
        super.onCreate(savedInstanceState);
        setContentView(R.layout.form);

        email = (EditText)findViewById(R.id.email);
        message = (EditText)findViewById(R.id.message);
        age = (CheckBox)findViewById(R.id.age);

        submit = (Button)findViewById(R.id.submit);
        submit.setOnClickListener(this);

        //Retrieve or create the preferences object
        formStore = getPreferences(Activity.MODE_PRIVATE);
    }

    @Override
    public void onResume() {
        super.onResume();
        //Restore the form data
        email.setText(formStore.getString("email", ""));
        message.setText(formStore.getString("message", ""));
        age.setChecked(formStore.getBoolean("age", false));
    }

    @Override
    public void onPause() {
        super.onPause();
        if(submitSuccess) {
            //Editor calls can be chained together
            formStore.edit().clear().commit();
        } else {
            //Store the form data
            SharedPreferences.Editor editor = formStore.edit();
            editor.putString("email", email.getText().toString());
            editor.putString("message", message.getText().toString());
            editor.putBoolean("age", age.isChecked());
            editor.commit();
```

```
        }
    }

    @Override
    public void onClick(View v) {

        //DO SOME WORK SUBMITTING A MESSAGE

        //Mark the operation successful
        submitSuccess = true;
        //Close
        finish();
    }
}
```

We start with a typical user form containing two simple EditText entry fields and a check box. When the Activity is created, we gather a SharedPreferences object using Activity.getPreferences(), and this is where all the persisted data will be stored. If at any time the Activity is paused for a reason other than a successful submission (controlled by the boolean member), the current state of the form will be quickly loaded into the preferences and persisted.

> **NOTE:** When saving data into SharedPreferences using an Editor, always remember to call commit() or apply() after the changes are made. Otherwise, your changes will not be saved.

Conversely, whenever the Activity becomes visible, onResume() loads the user interface with the latest information stored in the preferences object. If no preferences exist, either because they were cleared or never created (first launch), then the form is set to blank.

When a user presses Submit and the fake form submits successfully, the subsequent call to onPause() will clear any stored form data in preferences. Because all these operations were done on a private preferences object, clearing the data does not affect any user settings that may have been stored using other means.

> **NOTE:** Methods called from an Editor always return the same Editor object, allowing them to be chained together in places where doing so makes your code more readable.

Creating Common SharedPreferences

The previous example illustrated how to use a single SharedPreferences object within the context of a single Activity with an object obtained from Activity.getPreferences(). Truth be told, this method is really just a convenience wrapper for Context.getSharedPreferences(), in which it passes the Activity name as the preference store name. If the data you are storing are best shared between two or more Activity instances, it might make sense to call getSharedPreferences() instead and pass a more common name so it can be accessed easily from different places in code. See Listing 5-9.

Listing 5-9. *Two Activities Using the Same Preferences*

```
public class ActivityOne extends Activity {
    public static final String PREF_NAME = "myPreferences";
    private SharedPreferences mPreferences;

    @Override
    public void onCreate(Bundle savedInstanceState) {
        super.onCreate(savedInstanceState);
        mPreferences = getSharedPreferences(PREF_NAME, Activity.MODE_PRIVATE);
    }
}

public class ActivityTwo extends Activity {

    private SharedPreferences mPreferences;

    @Override
    public void onCreate(Bundle savedInstanceState) {
        super.onCreate(savedInstanceState);
        mPreferences = getSharedPreferences(ActivityOne.PREF_NAME,
            Activity.MODE_PRIVATE);
    }

}
```

In this example, both Activity classes retrieve the SharedPreferences object using the same name (defined as a constant string): thus they will be accessing the same set of preference data. Furthermore, both references are even pointing at the same *instance* of preferences, as the framework creates a singleton object for each set of SharedPreferences (a set being defined by its name). This means that changes made on one side will immediately be reflected on the other.

A Note About Mode

`Context.getSharedPreferences()` also takes a mode parameter. Passing 0 or `MODE_PRIVATE` provides the default behavior of allowing only the application that created the preferences (or another application with the same user ID) to gain read/write access. This method supports two more mode parameters: `MODE_WORLD_READABLE` and `MODE_WORLD_WRITEABLE`. These modes allow other applications to gain access to these preferences by setting the user permissions on the file it creates appropriately. However, the external application still requires a valid Context pointing back to the package where the preference file was created.

For example, let's say you created `SharedPreferences with world-readable permission` in an application with the package `com.examples.myfirstapplication`. In order to access those preferences from a second application, the second application would obtain them using the following code:

```
Context otherContext = createPackageContext("com.examples.myfirstapplication", 0);
SharedPreferences externalPreferences = otherContext.getSharedPreferences(PREF_NAME, 0);
```

> **CAUTION:** If you choose to use the mode parameter to allow external access, be sure that you are consistent in the mode you provide everywhere `getSharedPreferences()` is called. This mode is only used the first time the preference file gets created, so calling up `SharedPreferences` with different mode parameters at different times will only lead to confusion on your part.

5–3. Reading and Writing Files

Problem

Your application needs to read data in from an external file or write more complex data out for persistence.

Solution

(API Level 1)

Sometimes, there is no substitute for working with a filesystem. Working with files allows your application to read and write data that does not lend itself well to other persistence options like key/value preferences and databases. Android also provides a number of cache locations for files you can use to place data that you need to persist on a temporary basis.

Android supports all the standard Java File I/O APIs for create, read, update, and delete (CRUD) operations, along with some additional helpers to make accessing those files in specific locations a little more convenient. There are three main locations in which an application can work with files:

- Internal storage
  - Protected directory space to read and write file data.
- External storage
  - Externally mountable space to read and write file data.
  - Requires the `WRITE_EXTERNAL_STORAGE` permission in API Level 4+.
  - Often, this is a physical SD card in the device.
- Assets
  - Protected read-only space inside the APK bundle.
  - Good for local resources that can't/shouldn't be compiled.

While the underlying mechanism to work with file data remains the same, we will look at the details that make working with each destination slightly different.

How It Works

As we stated earlier, the traditional Java `FileInputStream` and `FileOutputStream` classes constitute the primary method of accessing file data. In fact, you can create a `File` instance at any time with an absolute path location and use one of these streams to read and write data. However, with root paths varying on different devices and certain directories being protected from your application, we recommend some slightly more efficient ways to work with files.

Internal Storage

In order to create or modify a file's location on internal storage, utilize the Context.openFileInput() and Context.openFileOutput() methods. These methods require only the name of the file as a parameter, instead of the entire path, and will reference the file in relation to the application's protected directory space, regardless of the exact path on the specific device. See Listing 5-10.

Listing 5-10. *CRUD a File on Internal Storage*

```
public class InternalActivity extends Activity {

    private static final String FILENAME = "data.txt";

    @Override
    public void onCreate(Bundle savedInstanceState) {
        super.onCreate(savedInstanceState);
        TextView tv = new TextView(this);
        setContentView(tv);

        //Create a new file and write some data
        try {
            FileOutputStream mOutput = openFileOutput(FILENAME, Activity.MODE_PRIVATE);
            String data = "THIS DATA WRITTEN TO A FILE";
            mOutput.write(data.getBytes());
            mOutput.close();
        } catch (FileNotFoundException e) {
            e.printStackTrace();
        } catch (IOException e) {
            e.printStackTrace();
        }

        //Read the created file and display to the screen
        try {
            FileInputStream mInput = openFileInput(FILENAME);
            byte[] data = new byte[128];
            mInput.read(data);
            mInput.close();

            String display = new String(data);
            tv.setText(display.trim());
        } catch (FileNotFoundException e) {
            e.printStackTrace();
        } catch (IOException e) {
            e.printStackTrace();
        }
```

```
        //Delete the created file
        deleteFile(FILENAME);
    }
}
```

This example uses Context.openFileOutput() to write some simple string data out to a file. When using this method, the file will be created if it does not already exist. It takes two parameters: a file name and an operating mode. In this case, we use the default operation by defining the mode as MODE_PRIVATE. This mode will overwrite the file with each new write operation; use MODE_APPEND if you prefer that each write append to the end of the existing file.

After the write is complete, the example uses Context.openFileInput(), which only requires the file name again as a parameter to open an InputStream and read the file data. The data will be read into a byte array and displayed to the user interface through a TextView. Upon completing the operation, Context.deleteFile() is used to remove the file from storage.

> **NOTE:** Data is written to the file streams as bytes, so higher-level data (even strings) must be converted into and out of this format.

This example leaves no traces of the file behind, but we encourage you to try the same example without running deleteFile() at the end in order to keep the file in storage. Using the SDK's DDMS tool with an emulator or unlocked device, you may view the filesystem and can find the file this application creates in its respective application data folder.

Because these methods are a part of Context, and not bound to an Activity, this type of file access can occur anywhere in an application that you require, such as a BroadcastReceiver or even a custom class. Many system constructs either are a subclass of Context or will pass a reference to one in their callbacks. This allows the same open/close/delete operations to take place anywhere.

External Storage

The key differentiator between internal and external storage lies in the fact that external storage is mountable. This means that the user can connect his or her device to a computer and have the option of mounting that external storage as a removable disk on the PC. Often, the storage itself is physically removable (such as an SD card), but this is not a requirement of the platform.

> **IMPORTANT:** Writing to the external storage of the device will require that you add a declaration for `android.permission.WRITE_EXTERNAL_STORAGE` to the application manifest.

During periods where the device's external storage is either mounted externally or physically removed, it is not accessible to an application. Because of this, it is always prudent to check whether or not external storage is ready by checking `Environment.getExternalStorageState()`.

Let's modify the file example to do the same operation with the device's external storage. See Listing 5-11.

Listing 5-11. *CRUD a File on External Storage*

```
public class ExternalActivity extends Activity {

    private static final String FILENAME = "data.txt";

    @Override
    public void onCreate(Bundle savedInstanceState) {
        super.onCreate(savedInstanceState);
        TextView tv = new TextView(this);
        setContentView(tv);

        //Create the file reference
        File dataFile = new File(Environment.getExternalStorageDirectory(), FILENAME);

        //Check if external storage is usable
        if(!Environment.getExternalStorageState().equals(Environment.MEDIA_MOUNTED)) {
            Toast.makeText(this, "Cannot use storage.", Toast.LENGTH_SHORT).show();
            finish();
            return;
        }

        //Create a new file and write some data
        try {
            FileOutputStream mOutput = new FileOutputStream(dataFile, false);
            String data = "THIS DATA WRITTEN TO A FILE";
            mOutput.write(data.getBytes());
            mOutput.close();
        } catch (FileNotFoundException e) {
            e.printStackTrace();
        } catch (IOException e) {
            e.printStackTrace();
        }
```

```
        //Read the created file and display to the screen
        try {
            FileInputStream mInput = new FileInputStream(dataFile);
            byte[] data = new byte[128];
            mInput.read(data);
            mInput.close();

            String display = new String(data);
            tv.setText(display.trim());
        } catch (FileNotFoundException e) {
            e.printStackTrace();
        } catch (IOException e) {
            e.printStackTrace();
        }

        //Delete the created file
        dataFile.delete();
    }
}
```

With external storage, we utilize a little more of the traditional Java File I/O. The key to working with external storage is calling `Environment.getExternalStorageDirectory()` to retrieve the root path to the device's external storage location.

Before any operations can take place, the status of the device's external storage is first checked with `Environment.getExternalStorageState()`. If the value returned is anything other than `Environment.MEDIA_MOUNTED`, we do not proceed because the storage cannot be written to, so the Activity is closed. Otherwise, a new file can be created and the operations may commence.

The input and output streams must now use default Java constructors, as opposed to the `Context` convenience methods. The default behavior of the output stream will be to overwrite the current file or to create it if it does not exist. If your application must append to the end of the existing file with each write, change the boolean parameter in the `FileOutputStream` constructor to true.

Often, it makes sense to create a special directory on external storage for your application's files. We can accomplish this simply by using more of Java's File API. See Listing 5-12.

Listing 5-12. *CRUD a File Inside New Directory*

```
public class ExternalActivity extends Activity {

    private static final String FILENAME = "data.txt";
    private static final String DNAME = "myfiles";
```

```
    @Override
    public void onCreate(Bundle savedInstanceState) {
        super.onCreate(savedInstanceState);
        TextView tv = new TextView(this);
        setContentView(tv);

        //Create a new directory on external storage
        File rootPath = new File(Environment.getExternalStorageDirectory(), DNAME);
        if(!rootPath.exists()) {
            rootPath.mkdirs();
        }
        //Create the file reference
        File dataFile = new File(rootPath, FILENAME);

        //Create a new file and write some data
        try {
            FileOutputStream mOutput = new FileOutputStream(dataFile, false);
            String data = "THIS DATA WRITTEN TO A FILE";
            mOutput.write(data.getBytes());
            mOutput.close();
        } catch (FileNotFoundException e) {
            e.printStackTrace();
        } catch (IOException e) {
            e.printStackTrace();
        }

        //Read the created file and display to the screen
        try {
            FileInputStream mInput = new FileInputStream(dataFile);
            byte[] data = new byte[128];
            mInput.read(data);
            mInput.close();

            String display = new String(data);
            tv.setText(display.trim());
        } catch (FileNotFoundException e) {
            e.printStackTrace();
        } catch (IOException e) {
            e.printStackTrace();
        }

        //Delete the created file
        dataFile.delete();
    }
}
```

In this example we created a new directory path within the external storage directory and used that new location as the root location for the data file. Once the file reference is created using the new directory location, the remainder of the example is the same.

External System Directories

(API Level 8)

There are additional methods in `Environment` and `Context` that provide standard locations on external storage where specific files can be written. Some of these locations have additional properties as well.

- `Environment.getExternalStoragePublicDirectory(String type)`
  - Returns a common directory where all applications store media files. The contents of these directories are visible to users and other applications. In particular, the media placed here will likely be scanned and inserted into the device's `MediaStore` for applications like the Gallery.
  - Valid type values include `DIRECTORY_PICTURES`, `DIRECTORY_MUSIC`, `DIRECTORY_MOVIES`, and `DIRECTORY_RINGTONES`.
- `Context.getExternalFilesDir(String type)`
  - Returns a directory on external storage for media files that are specific to the application. Media placed here will not be considered public, however, and won't show up in `MediaStore`.
  - This is still external storage, however, so it is still possible for users and other applications to see and edit the files directly: there is no security enforced.
  - Files placed here will be removed when the application is uninstalled, so it can be a good location in which to place large content files the application needs that one may not want on internal storage.
  - Valid type values include `DIRECTORY_PICTURES`, `DIRECTORY_MUSIC`, `DIRECTORY_MOVIES`, and `DIRECTORY_RINGTONES`.

- `Context`.getExternalCacheDir()
  - Returns a directory on internal storage for app-specific temporary files. The contents of this directory are visible to users and other applications.
  - Files placed here will be removed when the application is uninstalled, so it can be a good location in which to place large content files the application needs that one may not want on internal storage.

5–4. Using Files as Resources

Problem

Your application must utilize resource files that are in a format Android cannot compile into a resource ID.

Solution

(API Level 1)

Use the Assets directory to house files your application needs to read from, such as local HTML, Comma Separated Values (CSV), or proprietary data. The Assets directory is a protected resource location for files in an Android application. The files placed in this directory will be bundled with the final APK but will not be processed or compiled. Like all other application resources, the files in Assets are read-only.

How It Works

There are a few specific instances that we've seen already in this book where Assets can be used to load content directly into widgets, like `WebView` and `MediaPlayer`. However, in most cases, Assets is best accessed through a traditional `InputStream`. Listings 5-13 and 5-14 provide an example in which a private CSV file is read from Assets and displayed onscreen.

Listing 5-13. *assets/data.csv*

```
John,38,Red
Sally,42,Blue
Rudy,31,Yellow
```

Listing 5-14. *Reading from an Asset File*

```
public class AssetActivity extends Activity {

    @Override
    public void onCreate(Bundle savedInstanceState) {
        super.onCreate(savedInstanceState);
        TextView tv = new TextView(this);
        setContentView(tv);

        try {
            //Access application assets
            AssetManager manager = getAssets();
            //Open our data file
            InputStream mInput = manager.open("data.csv");
            //Read data in
            byte[] data = new byte[128];
            mInput.read(data);
            mInput.close();

            //Parse the CSV data and display
            String raw = new String(data);
            ArrayList<Person> cooked = parse(raw.trim());
            StringBuilder builder = new StringBuilder();
            for(Person piece : cooked) {
              builder.append(String.format("%s is %s years old, and likes the color %s",
                        piece.name, piece.age, piece.color));
              builder.append('\n');
            }
            tv.setText(builder.toString());

        } catch (FileNotFoundException e) {
            e.printStackTrace();
        } catch (IOException e) {
            e.printStackTrace();
        }

    }

    /* Simple CSV Parser */
    private static final int COL_NAME = 0;
    private static final int COL_AGE = 1;
    private static final int COL_COLOR = 2;

    private ArrayList<Person> parse(String raw) {
        ArrayList<Person> results = new ArrayList<Person>();
        Person current = null;

        StringTokenizer st = new StringTokenizer(raw,",\n");
        int state = COL_NAME;
```

```
        while(st.hasMoreTokens()) {
            switch(state) {
            case COL_NAME:
                current = new Person();
                current.name = st.nextToken();
                state = COL_AGE;
                break;
            case COL_AGE:
                current.age = st.nextToken();
                state = COL_COLOR;
                break;
            case COL_COLOR:
                current.color = st.nextToken();
                results.add(current);
                state = COL_NAME;
                break;
            }
        }

        return results;
    }

    private class Person {
        public String name;
        public String age;
        public String color;

        public Person() { }
    }
}
```

The key to accessing files in Assets lies in using `AssetManager`, which will allow the application to open any resource currently residing in the Assets directory. Passing the name of the file we are interested in to `AssetManager.open()` returns an InputStream for us to read the file data. Once the stream is read into memory, the example passes the raw data off to a parsing routine and displays the results to the user interface.

Parsing the CSV

This example also illustrates a simple method of taking data from a CSV file and parsing it into a model object (called `Person` in this case). The method used here takes the entire file and reads it into a byte array for processing as a single string. This method is not the most memory efficient when the amount of data to be read is quite large, but for small files like this one it works just fine.

The raw string is passed into a StringTokenizer instance, along with the required characters to use as breakpoints for the tokens: comma and new line. At this point, each individual chunk of the file can be processed in order. Using a basic state machine approach, the data from each line is inserted into new `Person` instances and loaded into the resulting list.

5–5. Managing a Database

Problem

Your application needs to persist data that can later be queried or modified as subsets or individual records.

Solution

(API Level 1)

Create an `SQLiteDatabase` with the assistance of an `SQLiteOpenHelper` to manage your data store. SQLite is a fast and lightweight database technology that utilizes SQL syntax to build queries and manage data. Support for SQLite is baked in to the Android SDK, making it very easy to set up and use in your applications.

How It Works

Customizing `SQLiteOpenHelper` allows you to manage the creation and modification of the database schema itself. It is also an excellent place to insert any initial or default values you may want into the database while it is created. Listing 5-15 is an example of how to customize the helper in order to create a database with a single table that stores basic information about people.

Listing 5-15. *Custom SQLiteOpenHelper*

```
public class MyDbHelper extends SQLiteOpenHelper {

    private static final String DB_NAME = "mydb";
    private static final int DB_VERSION = 1;

    public static final String TABLE_NAME = "people";
    public static final String COL_NAME = "pName";
    public static final String COL_DATE = "pDate";
```

```
    private static final String STRING_CREATE =
        "CREATE TABLE "+TABLE_NAME+" (_id INTEGER PRIMARY KEY AUTOINCREMENT, "
        +COL_NAME+" TEXT, "+COL_DATE+" DATE);";

    public MyDbHelper(Context context) {
        super(context, DB_NAME, null, DB_VERSION);
    }

    @Override
    public void onCreate(SQLiteDatabase db) {
        //Create the database table
        db.execSQL(STRING_CREATE);

        //You may also load initial values into the database here
        ContentValues cv = new ContentValues(2);
        cv.put(COL_NAME, "John Doe");
        //Create a formatter for SQL date format
        SimpleDateFormat dateFormat = new SimpleDateFormat("yyyy-MM-dd HH:mm:ss");
        cv.put(COL_DATE, dateFormat.format(new Date())); //Insert 'now' as the date
        db.insert(TABLE_NAME, null, cv);
    }

    @Override
    public void onUpgrade(SQLiteDatabase db, int oldVersion, int newVersion) {
        //For now, clear the database and re-create
        db.execSQL("DROP TABLE IF EXISTS "+TABLE_NAME);
        onCreate(db);
    }
}
```

They key pieces of information you will need for your database are a name and version number. Creating and upgrading an SQLiteDatabase does require some light knowledge of SQL, so we recommend glancing at an SQL reference briefly if you are unfamiliar with some of the syntax. The helper will call onCreate() any time this particular database is accessed, using either SQLiteOpenHelper.getReadableDatabase() or SQLiteOpenHelper.getWritableDatabase(), if it does not already exist.

The example abstracts the table and column names as constants for external use (a good practice to get into). Here is the actual SQL create string that is used in onCreate() to make our table:

```
CREATE TABLE people (_id INTEGER PRIMARY KEY AUTOINCREMENT, pName TEXT, pAge INTEGER,
pDate DATE);
```

When using SQLite in Android, there is a small amount of formatting that the database must have in order for it to work properly with the framework. Most of it is created for you, but one piece that the tables you create must have is a column for _id. The remainder of this string creates two more columns for each record in the table:

- A textfield for the person's name
- A date field for the date this record was entered

Data is inserted into the database by using ContentValues objects. The example illustrates how to use ContentValues to insert some default data into the database when it is created. SQLiteDatabase.insert() takes a table name, null column hack, and ContentValues representing the record to insert as parameters.

The null column hack is not used here but serves a purpose that may be vital to your application. SQL cannot insert an entirely empty value into the database, and attempting to do so will cause an error. If there is a chance that your implementation may pass an empty ContentValues to insert(), the null column hack is used to instead insert a record where the value of the referenced column is NULL.

A Note About Upgrading

SQLiteOpenHelper also does a great job of assisting you with migrating your database schema in future versions of the application. Whenever the database is accessed, but the version on disk does not match the current version (meaning the version passed in the constructor), onUpgrade() will be called.

In our example, we took the lazy way out and simply dropped the existing database and recreated it. In practice, this may not be a suitable method if the database contains user-entered data; a user probably won't be too happy to see it disappear. So let's digress for a moment and look at an example of onUpgrade() that may be more useful. Take, for example, the following three databases used throughout the lifetime of an application:

- Version 1: First release of the application
- Version 2: Application upgrade to include phone number field
- Version 3: Application upgrade to include date entry inserted

We can leverage onUpgrade() to alter the existing database instead of erasing all the current information in place. See Listing 5-16.

Listing 5-16. *Sample of onUpgrade()*

```
@Override
public void onUpgrade(SQLiteDatabase db, int oldVersion, int newVersion) {
    //Upgrade from v1. Adding phone number
    if(oldVersion <= 1) {
        db.execSQL("ALTER TABLE "+TABLE_NAME+" ADD COLUMN phone_number INTEGER;");
    }
    //Upgrade from v2. Add entry date
    if(oldVersion <= 2) {
        db.execSQL("ALTER TABLE "+TABLE_NAME+" ADD COLUMN entry_date DATE;");
    }
}
```

In this example, if the user's existing database version is 1, both statements will be called to add columns to the database. If a user already has version 2, just the latter statement is called to add the entry date column. In both cases, any existing data in the application database is preserved.

Using the Database

Looking back to our original sample, let's take a look at how an Activity would utilize the database we've created. See Listings 5-17 and 5-18.

Listing 5-17. *res/layout/main.xml*

```
<?xml version="1.0" encoding="utf-8"?>
<LinearLayout xmlns:android="http://schemas.android.com/apk/res/android"
  android:orientation="vertical"
  android:layout_width="fill_parent"
  android:layout_height="fill_parent">
  <EditText
    android:id="@+id/name"
    android:layout_width="fill_parent"
    android:layout_height="wrap_content"
  />
  <Button
    android:id="@+id/add"
    android:layout_width="fill_parent"
    android:layout_height="wrap_content"
    android:text="Add New Person"
  />
  <ListView
    android:id="@+id/list"
    android:layout_width="fill_parent"
    android:layout_height="fill_parent"
  />
</LinearLayout>
```

Listing 5-18. *Activity to View and Manage Database*

```
public class DbActivity extends Activity implements View.OnClickListener,
        AdapterView.OnItemClickListener {

    EditText mText;
    Button mAdd;
    ListView mList;

    MyDbHelper mHelper;
    SQLiteDatabase mDb;
    Cursor mCursor;
    SimpleCursorAdapter mAdapter;

    @Override
    public void onCreate(Bundle savedInstanceState) {
        super.onCreate(savedInstanceState);
        setContentView(R.layout.main);

        mText = (EditText)findViewById(R.id.name);
        mAdd = (Button)findViewById(R.id.add);
        mAdd.setOnClickListener(this);
        mList = (ListView)findViewById(R.id.list);
        mList.setOnItemClickListener(this);

        mHelper = new MyDbHelper(this);
    }

    @Override
    public void onResume() {
        super.onResume();
        //Open connections to the database
        mDb = mHelper.getWritableDatabase();
        String[] columns = new String[] {"_id", MyDbHelper.COL_NAME,
MyDbHelper.COL_DATE};
        mCursor = mDb.query(MyDbHelper.TABLE_NAME, columns, null, null, null, null,
                null);
        //Refresh the list
        String[] headers = new String[] {MyDbHelper.COL_NAME, MyDbHelper.COL_DATE};
        mAdapter = new SimpleCursorAdapter(this, android.R.layout.two_line_list_item,
                mCursor, headers, new int[]{android.R.id.text1, android.R.id.text2});
        mList.setAdapter(mAdapter);
    }

    @Override
    public void onPause() {
        super.onPause();
        //Close all connections
        mDb.close();
        mCursor.close();
```

```
    }

    @Override
    public void onClick(View v) {
        //Add a new value to the database
        ContentValues cv = new ContentValues(2);
        cv.put(MyDbHelper.COL_NAME, mText.getText().toString());
        //Create a formatter for SQL date format
        SimpleDateFormat dateFormat = new SimpleDateFormat("yyyy-MM-dd HH:mm:ss");
        //Insert 'now' as the date
        cv.put(MyDbHelper.COL_DATE, dateFormat.format(new Date()));
        mDb.insert(MyDbHelper.TABLE_NAME, null, cv);
        //Refresh the list
        mCursor.requery();
        mAdapter.notifyDataSetChanged();
        //Clear the edit field
        mText.setText(null);
    }

    @Override
    public void onItemClick(AdapterView<?> parent, View v, int position, long id) {
        //Delete the item from the database
        mCursor.moveToPosition(position);
         //Get the id value of this row
        String rowId = mCursor.getString(0); //Column 0 of the cursor is the id
        mDb.delete(MyDbHelper.TABLE_NAME, "_id = ?", new String[]{rowId});
        //Refresh the list
        mCursor.requery();
        mAdapter.notifyDataSetChanged();
    }
}
```

In this example, we utilize our custom SQLiteOpenHelper to give us access to a database instance, and it displays each record in that database as a list to the user interface. Information from the database is returned in the form of a Cursor, an interface designed to read, write, and traverse the results of a query.

When the Activity becomes visible, a database query is made to return all records in the “people” table. An array of column names must be passed to the query to tell the database which values to return. The remaining parameters of query() are designed to narrow the selection data set, and we will investigate this further in the next recipe. It is important to close all database and cursor connections when they are no longer needed. In the example, we do this in onPause(), when the Activity is no longer in the foreground.

SimpleCursorAdapter is used to map the data from the database to the standard Android two-line list item view. The string and int array parameters constitute the mapping; the data from each item in the string array will be inserted into the view with the corresponding id value in the int array. The list of column names passed here is slightly different than the array passed to the query. This is because we will need to know the record id for other operations, but it is not necessary in mapping the data to the user interface.

The user may enter a name in the textfield and then press the "Add New Person" button to create new ContentValues and insert it into the database. At that point, in order for the UI to display the change, we call `Cursor.requery()` and `ListAdapter.notifyDataSetChanged()`.

Conversely, tapping on an item in the list will remove that specified item from the database. In order to accomplish this, we must construct a simple SQL statement telling the database to remove only records where the _id value matches this selection. At that point, the cursor and list adapter are refreshed again.

The _id value of the selection is obtained by moving the cursor to the selected position and calling `getString(0)` to get the value of column index zero. This request returns the _id because the first parameter (index 0) passed in the columns list to the query was "_id." The delete statement is comprised of two parameters: the statement string and the arguments. An argument from the passed array will be inserted in the statement for each question mark that appears in the string.

5–6. Querying a Database

Problem

Your application uses an SQLiteDatabase, and you need to return specific subsets of the data contained therein.

Solution

(API Level 1)

Using fully structured SQL queries, it is very simple to create filters for specific data and return those subsets from the database. There are several overloaded forms of `SQLiteDatabase.query()` to gather information from the database. We'll examine the most verbose of them here.

```
public Cursor query(String table, String[] columns, String selection, String[]
selectionArgs, String groupBy, String having, String orderBy, String limit)
```

The first two parameters simply define the table in which to query data, as well as the columns for each record that we would like to have access to. The remaining parameters define how we will narrow the scope of the results.

- selection
  - SQL WHERE clause for the given query.
- selectionArgs
  - If question marks are in the selection, these items fill in those fields.
- groupBy
  - SQL GROUP BY clause for the given query.
- having
  - SQL ORDER BY clause for the given query.
- orderBy
  - SQL ORDER BY clause for the given query.
- limit
  - Maximum number of results returned from the query.

As you can see, all of these parameters are designed to provide the full power of SQL to the database queries.

How It Works

Let's look at some example queries that can be constructed to accomplish some common practical queries.

- Return all rows where the value matches a given parameter.

```
String[] COLUMNS = new String[] {COL_NAME, COL_DATE};
String selection = COL_NAME+" = ?";
String[] args = new String[] {"NAME_TO_MATCH"};
Cursor result = db.query(TABLE_NAME, COLUMNS, selection, args, null, null, null, null);
```

This query is fairly straightforward. The selection statement just tells the database to match any data in the name column with the argument supplied (which is inserted in place of "?" in the selection string).

- Return the last 10 rows inserted into the database.

```
String orderBy = "_id DESC";
String limit = "10";
Cursor result = db.query(TABLE_NAME, COLUMNS, null, null, null, null, orderBy, limit);
```

This query has no special selection criteria but instead tells the database to order the results by the auto-incrementing _id value, with the newest (highest _id) records first. The limit clause sets the maximum number of returned results to 10.

- Return rows where a date field is within a specified range (within the year 2000, in this example).

```
String[] COLUMNS = new String[] {COL_NAME, COL_DATE};
String selection = "datetime("+COL_DATE+") > datetime(?)"+
        " AND datetime("+COL_DATE+") < datetime(?)";
String[] args = new String[] {"2000-1-1 00:00:00","2000-12-31 23:59:59"};
Cursor result = db.query(TABLE_NAME, COLUMNS, selection, args, null, null, null, null);
```

SQLite does not reserve a specific data type for dates, although they allow DATE as a declaration type when creating a table. However, the standard SQL date and time functions can be used to create representations of the data as TEXT, INTEGER, or REAL. Here, we compare the return values of `datetime()` for both the value in the database and a formatted string for the start and end dates of the range.

- Return rows where an integer field is within a specified range (between 7 and 10 in the example).

```
String[] COLUMNS = new String[] {COL_NAME, COL_AGE};
String selection = COL_AGE+" > ? AND "+COL_AGE+" < ?";
String[] args = new String[] {"7","10"};
Cursor result = db.query(TABLE_NAME, COLUMNS, selection, args, null, null, null, null);
```

This is similar to the previous example but is much less verbose. Here, we simply have to create the selection statement to return values greater than the low limit, but less than the high limit. Both limits are provided as arguments to be inserted so they can be dynamically set in the application.

5–7. Backing Up Data

Problem

Your application persists data on the device, and you need to provide users with a way to back up and restore this data in cases where they change devices or are forced to reinstall the application.

Solution

(API Level 1)

Use the device's external storage as a safe location to copy databases and other files. External storage is often physically removable, allowing the user to place it in another device and do a restore. Even in cases where this is not possible, external storage can always be mounted when the user connects his or her device to a computer, allowing data transfer to take place.

How It Works

Listing 5-19 shows an implementation of AsyncTask that copies a database file back and forth between the device's external storage and its location in the application's data directory. It also defines an interface for an Activity to implement to get notified when the operation is complete. File operations like copy can take some time to complete, so you can implement this by using an AsyncTask so it can happen in the background and not block the main thread.

Listing 5-19. *AsyncTask for Backup and Restore*

```
public class BackupTask extends AsyncTask<String,Void,Integer> {

    public interface CompletionListener {
        void onBackupComplete();
        void onRestoreComplete();
        void onError(int errorCode);
    }

    public static final int BACKUP_SUCCESS = 1;
    public static final int RESTORE_SUCCESS = 2;
    public static final int BACKUP_ERROR = 3;
    public static final int RESTORE_NOFILEERROR = 4;

    public static final String COMMAND_BACKUP = "backupDatabase";
    public static final String COMMAND_RESTORE = "restoreDatabase";

    private Context mContext;
    private CompletionListener listener;

    public BackupTask(Context context) {
        super();
        mContext = context;
    }

    public void setCompletionListener(CompletionListener aListener) {
        listener = aListener;
```

```
    }

    @Override
    protected Integer doInBackground(String... params) {

        //Get a reference to the database
        File dbFile = mContext.getDatabasePath("mydb");
        //Get a reference to the directory location for the backup
        File exportDir =
                new File(Environment.getExternalStorageDirectory(), "myAppBackups");
        if (!exportDir.exists()) {
            exportDir.mkdirs();
        }
        File backup = new File(exportDir, dbFile.getName());

        //Check the required operation
        String command = params[0];
        if(command.equals(COMMAND_BACKUP)) {
            //Attempt file copy
            try {
                backup.createNewFile();
                fileCopy(dbFile, backup);

                return BACKUP_SUCCESS;
            } catch (IOException e) {
                return BACKUP_ERROR;
            }
        } else if(command.equals(COMMAND_RESTORE)) {
            //Attempt file copy
            try {
                if(!backup.exists()) {
                    return RESTORE_NOFILEERROR;
                }
                dbFile.createNewFile();
                fileCopy(backup, dbFile);
                return RESTORE_SUCCESS;
            } catch (IOException e) {
                return BACKUP_ERROR;
            }
        } else {
            return BACKUP_ERROR;
        }
    }

    @Override
    protected void onPostExecute(Integer result) {

        switch(result) {
        case BACKUP_SUCCESS:
            if(listener != null) {
```

```
                listener.onBackupComplete();
            }
            break;
        case RESTORE_SUCCESS:
            if(listener != null) {
                listener.onRestoreComplete();
            }
            break;
        case RESTORE_NOFILEERROR:
            if(listener != null) {
                listener.onError(RESTORE_NOFILEERROR);
            }
            break;
        default:
            if(listener != null) {
                listener.onError(BACKUP_ERROR);
            }
        }
    }

    private void fileCopy(File source, File dest) throws IOException {
        FileChannel inChannel = new FileInputStream(source).getChannel();
        FileChannel outChannel = new FileOutputStream(dest).getChannel();
        try {
            inChannel.transferTo(0, inChannel.size(), outChannel);
        } finally {
            if (inChannel != null)
                inChannel.close();
            if (outChannel != null)
                outChannel.close();
        }
    }
}
```

As you can see, BackupTask operates by copying the current version of a named database to a specific directory in external storage when `COMMAND_BACKUP` is passed to `execute()`, and it copies the file back when `COMMAND_RESTORE` is passed.

Once executed, the task uses `Context.getDatabasePath()` to retrieve a reference to the database file we need to back up. This line could easily be replaced with a call to `Context.getFilesDir()`, accessing a file on the system's internal storage to back up instead. A reference to a backup directory we've created on external storage is also obtained.

The files are copied using traditional Java File I/O, and if all is successful the registered listener is notified. During the process, any exceptions thrown are caught and an error is returned to the listener instead. Now let's take a look at an Activity that utilizes this task to back up a database: see Listing 5-20.

Listing 5-20. *Activity Using BackupTask*

```
public class BackupActivity extends Activity implements
BackupTask.CompletionListener {

    @Override
    public void onCreate(Bundle savedInstanceState) {
        super.onCreate(savedInstanceState);
        setContentView(R.layout.main);
        //Dummy example database
        SQLiteDatabase db = openOrCreateDatabase("mydb", Activity.MODE_PRIVATE, null);
        db.close();
    }

    @Override
    public void onResume() {
        super.onResume();
        if( Environment.getExternalStorageState().equals(Environment.MEDIA_MOUNTED) ) {
            BackupTask task = new BackupTask(this);
            task.setCompletionListener(this);
            task.execute(BackupTask.COMMAND_RESTORE);
        }
    }

    @Override
    public void onPause() {
        super.onPause();
        if( Environment.getExternalStorageState().equals(Environment.MEDIA_MOUNTED) ) {
            BackupTask task = new BackupTask(this);
            task.execute(BackupTask.COMMAND_BACKUP);
        }
    }

    @Override
    public void onBackupComplete() {
        Toast.makeText(this, "Backup Successful", Toast.LENGTH_SHORT).show();
    }

    @Override
    public void onError(int errorCode) {
        if(errorCode == BackupTask.RESTORE_NOFILEERROR) {
            Toast.makeText(this, "No Backup Found to Restore",
                Toast.LENGTH_SHORT).show();
        } else {
            Toast.makeText(this, "Error During Operation: "+errorCode,
                Toast.LENGTH_SHORT).show();
        }
    }
```

```
    @Override
    public void onRestoreComplete() {
        Toast.makeText(this, "Restore Successful", Toast.LENGTH_SHORT).show();
    }
}
```

The Activity implements the CompletionListener defined by BackupTask, so it may be notified when operations are finished or an error occurs. For the purposes of the example, a dummy database is created in the application's database directory. We call openOrCreateDatabase() only to allow a file to be created, so the connection is immediately closed afterward. Under normal circumstances, this database would already exist and these lines would not be necessary.

The example does a restore operation each time the Activity is resumed, registering itself with the task so it can be notified and raise a toast to the user of the status result. Notice that the task of checking whether external storage is usable falls to the Activity as well, and no tasks are executed if external storage is not accessible. When the Activity is paused a backup operation is executed, this time without registering for callbacks. This is because the Activity is no longer interesting to the user, so we won't need to raise a toast to point out the operation results.

Extra Credit

This background task could be extended to save the data to a cloud-based service for maximum safety and data portability. There are many options available to accomplish this, including Google's own set of web APIs, and we recommend you give this a try.

Android, as of API Level 8, also includes an API for backing up data to a cloud-based service. This API may suit your purposes; however, we will not discuss it here. The Android framework cannot guarantee that this service will be available on all Android devices, and there is no API as of this writing to determine whether the device the user has will support the Android backup, so it is not recommended for critical data.

5–8. Sharing Your Database

Problem

Your application would like to provide the database content it maintains to other applications on the device.

Solution

(API Level 4)

Create a ContentProvider to act as an external interface for your application's data. ContentProvider exposes an arbitrary set of data to external requests through a database-like interface of query(), insert(), update(), and delete(), though the implementer is free to design how the interface maps to the actual data model. Creating a ContentProvider to expose the data from an SQLiteDatabase is straightforward and simple. With some minor exceptions, the developer needs only to pass calls from the provider down to the database.

Arguments about which data set to operate on are typically encoded in the Uri passed to the ContentProvider. For example, sending a query Uri such as

```
content://com.examples.myprovider/friends
```

would tell the provider to return information from the "friends" table within its data set, while

```
content://com.examples.myprovider/friends/15
```

would instruct just the record id 15 to return from the query. It should be noted that these are only the conventions used by the rest of the system, and that you are responsible for making the ContentProvider you create behave in this manner. There is nothing inherent about ContentProvider that provides this functionality for you.

How It Works

First of all, to create a ContentProvider that interacts with a database, we must have a database in place to interact with. Listing 5-21 is a sample SQLiteOpenHelper implementation that we will use to create and access the database itself.

Listing 5-21. *Sample SQLiteOpenHelper*

```
public class ShareDbHelper extends SQLiteOpenHelper {

    private static final String DB_NAME = "frienddb";
    private static final int DB_VERSION = 1;

    public static final String TABLE_NAME = "friends";
    public static final String COL_FIRST = "firstName";
    public static final String COL_LAST = "lastName";
    public static final String COL_PHONE = "phoneNumber";

    private static final String STRING_CREATE =
        "CREATE TABLE "+TABLE_NAME+" (_id INTEGER PRIMARY KEY AUTOINCREMENT, "
        +COL_FIRST+" TEXT, "+COL_LAST+" TEXT, "+COL_PHONE+" TEXT);";

    public ShareDbHelper(Context context) {
        super(context, DB_NAME, null, DB_VERSION);
    }

    @Override
    public void onCreate(SQLiteDatabase db) {
        //Create the database table
        db.execSQL(STRING_CREATE);

        //Inserting example values into database
        ContentValues cv = new ContentValues(3);
        cv.put(COL_FIRST, "John");
        cv.put(COL_LAST, "Doe");
        cv.put(COL_PHONE, "8885551234");
        db.insert(TABLE_NAME, null, cv);
        cv = new ContentValues(3);
        cv.put(COL_FIRST, "Jane");
        cv.put(COL_LAST, "Doe");
        cv.put(COL_PHONE, "8885552345");
        db.insert(TABLE_NAME, null, cv);
        cv = new ContentValues(3);
        cv.put(COL_FIRST, "Jill");
        cv.put(COL_LAST, "Doe");
        cv.put(COL_PHONE, "8885553456");
        db.insert(TABLE_NAME, null, cv);
    }

    @Override
    public void onUpgrade(SQLiteDatabase db, int oldVersion, int newVersion) {
        //For now, clear the database and re-create
        db.execSQL("DROP TABLE IF EXISTS "+TABLE_NAME);
        onCreate(db);
    }
}
```

Overall this helper is fairly simple, creating a single table to keep a list of our friends with just three columns for housing text data. For the purposes of this example, three row values are inserted. Now let's take a look at a ContentProvider that will expose this database to other applications: see Listings 5-22 and 5-23.

Listing 5-22. *Manifest Declaration for ContentProvider*

```
<manifest xmlns:android="http://schemas.android.com/apk/res/android" …>
    <application …>
      <provider android:name=".FriendProvider"
          android:authorities="com.examples.sharedb.friendprovider">
      </provider>
    </application>
</manifest>
```

Listing 5-23. *ContentProvider for a Database*

```
public class FriendProvider extends ContentProvider {

    public static final Uri CONTENT_URI =
            Uri.parse("content://com.examples.sharedb.friendprovider/friends");

    public static final class Columns {
        public static final String _ID = "_id";
        public static final String FIRST = "firstName";
        public static final String LAST = "lastName";
        public static final String PHONE = "phoneNumber";
    }

    /* Uri Matching */
    private static final int FRIEND = 1;
    private static final int FRIEND_ID = 2;

    private static final UriMatcher matcher = new UriMatcher(UriMatcher.NO_MATCH);
    static {
        matcher.addURI(CONTENT_URI.getAuthority(), "friends", FRIEND);
        matcher.addURI(CONTENT_URI.getAuthority(), "friends/#", FRIEND_ID);
    }

    SQLiteDatabase db;

    @Override
    public int delete(Uri uri, String selection, String[] selectionArgs) {
        int result = matcher.match(uri);
        switch(result) {
        case FRIEND:
            return db.delete(ShareDbHelper.TABLE_NAME, selection, selectionArgs);
        case FRIEND_ID:
```

```
            return db.delete(ShareDbHelper.TABLE_NAME, "_ID = ?",
                    new String[]{uri.getLastPathSegment()});
        default:
            return 0;
        }
    }

    @Override
    public String getType(Uri uri) {
        return null;
    }

    @Override
    public Uri insert(Uri uri, ContentValues values) {
        long id = db.insert(ShareDbHelper.TABLE_NAME, null, values);
        if(id >= 0) {
            return Uri.withAppendedPath(uri, String.valueOf(id));
        } else {
            return null;
        }
    }

    @Override
    public boolean onCreate() {
        ShareDbHelper helper = new ShareDbHelper(getContext());
        db = helper.getWritableDatabase();
        return true;
    }

    @Override
    public Cursor query(Uri uri, String[] projection, String selection,
        String[] selectionArgs, String sortOrder) {
        int result = matcher.match(uri);
        switch(result) {
        case FRIEND:
            return db.query(ShareDbHelper.TABLE_NAME, projection, selection,
                selectionArgs, null, null, sortOrder);
        case FRIEND_ID:
            return db.query(ShareDbHelper.TABLE_NAME, projection, "_ID = ?",
                    new String[]{uri.getLastPathSegment()}, null, null, sortOrder);
        default:
            return null;
        }
    }

    @Override
    public int update(Uri uri, ContentValues values, String selection,
        String[] selectionArgs) {
        int result = matcher.match(uri);
        switch(result) {
```

```
            case FRIEND:
                return db.update(ShareDbHelper.TABLE_NAME, values, selection,
                    selectionArgs);
            case FRIEND_ID:
                return db.update(ShareDbHelper.TABLE_NAME, values, "_ID = ?",
                        new String[]{uri.getLastPathSegment()});
            default:
                return 0;
            }
        }
}
```

A ContentProvider must be declared in the application's manifest with the authority string that it represents. This allows the provider to be accessed from external applications, but the declaration is still required even if you only use the provider internally within your application. The authority is what Android uses to match Uri requests to the provider, so it should match the authority portion of the public CONTENT_URI.

The six required methods to override when extending ContentProvider are query(), insert(), update(), delete(), getType(), and onCreate(). The first four of these methods have direct counterparts in SQLiteDatabase, so the database method is simply called with the appropriate parameters. The primary difference between the two is that the ContentProvider method passes in a Uri, which the provider should inspect to determine which portion of the database to operate on.

These four primary CRUD methods are called on the provider when an Activity or other system component calls the corresponding method on its internal ContentResolver (you see this in action in Listing 5-23).

To adhere to the Uri convention mentioned in the first part of this recipe, insert() returns a Uri object created by appending the newly created record id onto the end of the path. This Uri should be considered by its requester to be a direct reference back to the record that was just created.

The remaining methods (query(), update(), and delete()) adhere to the convention by inspecting the incoming Uri to see if it refers to a specific record or to the whole table. This task is accomplished with the help of the UriMatcher convenience class. The UriMatcher.match() method compares a Uri to a set of supplied patterns and returns the matching pattern as an int, or UriMatcher.NO_MATCH if one is not found. If a Uri is supplied with a record id appended, the call to the database is modified to affect only that specific row.

A UriMatcher should be initialized by supplying a set of patterns with UriMatcher.addURI(); Google recommends that this all be done in a static context within the ContentProvider, so it will be initialized the first time the class is loaded into memory. Each pattern added is also given a constant identifier that will be the return value when matches are made. There are two wildcard characters that may be placed in the supplied patterns: the pound (#) character will match any number, and the asterisk (*) will match any text.

Our example has created two patterns to match. The initial pattern matches the supplied CONTENT_URI directly, and it is taken to reference the entire database table. The second pattern looks for an appended number to the path, which will be taken to reference just the record at that id.

Access to the database is obtained through a reference given by the ShareDbHelper in onCreate(). The size of the database that is used should be considered when deciding if this method will be appropriate for your application. Our database is quite small when it is created, but larger databases may take a long time to create, in which case the main thread should not be tied up while this operation is taking place; getWritableDatabase() may need to be wrapped in an AsyncTask and done in the background in these cases. Now let's take a look at a sample Activity accessing the data: see Listings 5-24 and 5-25.

Listing 5-24. *AndroidManifest.xml*

```
<?xml version="1.0" encoding="utf-8"?>
<manifest xmlns:android="http://schemas.android.com/apk/res/android"
    package="com.examples.sharedb" android:versionCode="1" android:versionName="1.0">
    <uses-sdk android:minSdkVersion="4" />
    <application android:icon="@drawable/icon" android:label="@string/app_name">
      <activity android:name=".ShareActivity" android:label="@string/app_name">
        <intent-filter>
          <action android:name="android.intent.action.MAIN" />
          <category android:name="android.intent.category.LAUNCHER" />
        </intent-filter>
      </activity>
      <provider android:name=".FriendProvider"
          android:authorities="com.examples.sharedb.friendprovider">
      </provider>
    </application>
</manifest>
```

Listing 5-25. *Activity Accessing the ContentProvider*

```
public class ShareActivity extends FragmentActivity implements
    LoaderManager.LoaderCallbacks<Cursor>, AdapterView.OnItemClickListener {
    private static final int LOADER_LIST = 100;
    SimpleCursorAdapter mAdapter;

    @Override
    public void onCreate(Bundle savedInstanceState) {
```

```
        super.onCreate(savedInstanceState);
        getSupportLoaderManager().initLoader(LOADER_LIST, null, this);

        mAdapter = new SimpleCursorAdapter(this,
                android.R.layout.simple_list_item_1, null,
                new String[]{FriendProvider.Columns.FIRST},
                new int[]{android.R.id.text1}, 0);

        ListView list = new ListView(this);
        list.setOnItemClickListener(this);
        list.setAdapter(mAdapter);

        setContentView(list);
    }

    @Override
    public void onItemClick(AdapterView<?> parent, View v, int position, long id) {
        Cursor c = mAdapter.getCursor();
        c.moveToPosition(position);

        Uri uri = Uri.withAppendedPath(FriendProvider.CONTENT_URI, c.getString(0));
        String[] projection = new String[]{FriendProvider.Columns.FIRST,
                FriendProvider.Columns.LAST,
                FriendProvider.Columns.PHONE};
        //Get the full record
        Cursor cursor = getContentResolver().query(uri, projection, null, null, null);
        cursor.moveToFirst();

        String message = String.format("%s %s, %s", cursor.getString(0),
                cursor.getString(1), cursor.getString(2));
        Toast.makeText(this, message, Toast.LENGTH_SHORT).show();
        cursor.close();
    }

    @Override
    public Loader<Cursor> onCreateLoader(int id, Bundle args) {
        String[] projection = new String[]{FriendProvider.Columns._ID,
                FriendProvider.Columns.FIRST};
        return new CursorLoader(this, FriendProvider.CONTENT_URI,
                projection, null, null, null);
    }

    @Override
    public void onLoadFinished(Loader<Cursor> loader, Cursor data) {
        mAdapter.swapCursor(data);
    }

    @Override
    public void onLoaderReset(Loader<Cursor> loader) {
        mAdapter.swapCursor(null);
```

```
    }
}
```

> **IMPORTANT:** This example requires the support library to provide access to the `Loader` pattern in Android 1.6 and above. If you are targeting Android 3.0+ in your application, you may replace `FragmentActivity` with `Activity` and `getSupportLoaderManager()` with `getLoaderManager()`.

This example queries the `FriendsProvider` for all its records and places them into a list, displaying only the first name column. In order for the `Cursor` to adapt properly into a list, our projection must include the ID column, even though it is not displayed.

If the user taps any of the items in the list, another query is made of the provider using a Uri constructed with the record ID appended to the end, forcing the provider to return only that one record. In addition, an expanded projection is provided to get all the column data about this friend.

The returned data is placed into a `Toast` and raised for the user to see. Individual fields from the cursor are accessed by their *column index*, corresponding to the index in the projection passed to the query. The `Cursor.getColumnIndex()` method may also be used to query the cursor for the index associated with a given column name.

A `Cursor` should always be closed when it is no longer needed, as we do with the `Cursor` created after a user click. The only exceptions to this are `Cursor` instances created and managed by the Loader.

Figure 5–2 shows the result of running this sample to display the provider content.

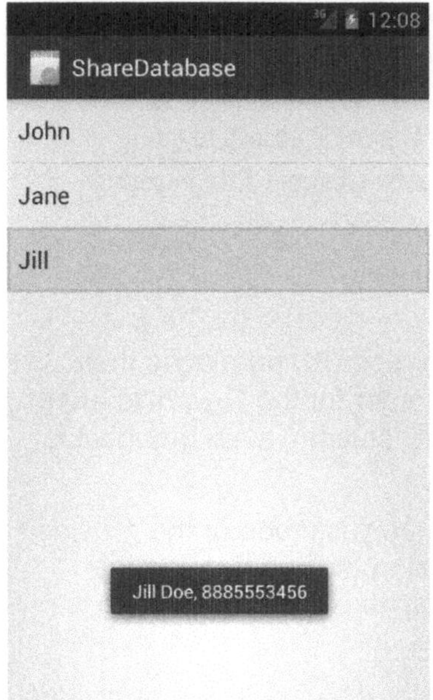

Figure 5–2. *Information from a ContentProvider.*

5–9. Sharing Your SharedPreferences

Problem

You would like your application to provide the settings values it has stored in SharedPreferences to other applications of the system and even to allow those applications to modify those settings if they have permission to do so.

Solution

(API Level 1)

Create a `ContentProvider` to interface your application's `SharedPreferences` to the rest of the system. The settings data will be delivered using a `MatrixCursor`, which is an implementation that can be used for data that does not reside in a database. The `ContentProvider` will be protected by separate permissions to read/write the data within so that only permitted applications will have access.

How It Works

To properly demonstrate the permissions aspect of this recipe, we need to create two separate applications: one that actually contains our preference data and one that wants to read and modify it through the ContentProvider interface. This is because Android does not enforce permissions on anything operating within the same application. Let's start with the provider, shown in Listing 5-26.

Listing 5-26. *ContentProvider for Application Settings*

```
public class SettingsProvider extends ContentProvider {

    public static final Uri CONTENT_URI =
        Uri.parse("content://com.examples.sharepreferences.settingsprovider/settings");

    public static class Columns {
        public static final String _ID = Settings.NameValueTable._ID;
        public static final String NAME = Settings.NameValueTable.NAME;
        public static final String VALUE = Settings.NameValueTable.VALUE;
    }

    private static final String NAME_SELECTION = Columns.NAME + " = ?";

    private SharedPreferences mPreferences;

    @Override
    public int delete(Uri uri, String selection, String[] selectionArgs) {
        throw new UnsupportedOperationException(
                "This ContentProvider is does not support removing Preferences");
    }

    @Override
    public String getType(Uri uri) {
        return null;
    }

    @Override
    public Uri insert(Uri uri, ContentValues values) {
        throw new UnsupportedOperationException(
                "This ContentProvider is does not support adding new Preferences");
    }

    @Override
    public boolean onCreate() {
        mPreferences = PreferenceManager.getDefaultSharedPreferences(getContext());
        return true;
    }
```

```
@Override
public Cursor query(Uri uri, String[] projection, String selection,
        String[] selectionArgs, String sortOrder) {
    MatrixCursor cursor = new MatrixCursor(projection);
    Map<String, ?> preferences = mPreferences.getAll();
    Set<String> preferenceKeys = preferences.keySet();

    if(TextUtils.isEmpty(selection)) {
        //Get all items
        for(String key : preferenceKeys) {
            //Insert only the columns they requested
            MatrixCursor.RowBuilder builder = cursor.newRow();
            for(String column : projection) {
                if(column.equals(Columns._ID)) {
                    //Generate a unique id
                    builder.add(key.hashCode());
                }
                if(column.equals(Columns.NAME)) {
                    builder.add(key);
                }
                if(column.equals(Columns.VALUE)) {
                    builder.add(preferences.get(key));
                }
            }
        }
    } else if (selection.equals(NAME_SELECTION)) {
        //Parse the key value and check if it exists
        String key = selectionArgs == null ? "" : selectionArgs[0];
        if(preferences.containsKey(key)) {
            //Get the requested item
            MatrixCursor.RowBuilder builder = cursor.newRow();
            for(String column : projection) {
                if(column.equals(Columns._ID)) {
                    //Generate a unique id
                    builder.add(key.hashCode());
                }
                if(column.equals(Columns.NAME)) {
                    builder.add(key);
                }
                if(column.equals(Columns.VALUE)) {
                    builder.add(preferences.get(key));
                }
            }
        }
    }

    return cursor;
}
```

```
    @Override
    public int update(Uri uri, ContentValues values, String selection,
            String[] selectionArgs) {
        //Check if the key exists, and update its value
        String key = values.getAsString(Columns.NAME);
        if (mPreferences.contains(key)) {
            Object value = values.get(Columns.VALUE);
            SharedPreferences.Editor editor = mPreferences.edit();
            if (value instanceof Boolean) {
                editor.putBoolean(key, (Boolean)value);
            } else if (value instanceof Number) {
                editor.putFloat(key, ((Number)value).floatValue());
            } else if (value instanceof String) {
                editor.putString(key, (String)value);
            } else {
                //Invalid value, do not update
              return 0;
            }
            editor.commit();
            //Notify any observers
            getContext().getContentResolver().notifyChange(CONTENT_URI, null);
            return 1;
        }
        //Key not in preferences
        return 0;
    }
}
```

Upon creation of this ContentProvider we obtain a reference to the application's default SharedPreferences rather than opening up a database connection as in the previous example. We only support two methods in this provider—query() and update()—and throw exceptions for the rest. This allows read/write access to the preference values without allowing any ability to add or remove new preference types.

Inside the query() method we check the selection string to determine if we should return all preference values or just the requested value. There are three fields defined for each preference: _id, name, and value. The value of _id may not be related to the preference itself, but if the client of this provider wants to display the results in a list using CursorAdapter, this field will need to exist and have a unique value for each record, so we generate one. Notice that we obtain the preference value as an Object to insert in the cursor; we want to minimize the amount of knowledge the provider should have about the types of data it contains.

The cursor implementation used in this provider is a MatrixCursor, which is a cursor designed to be built around data not held inside a database. The example iterates through the list of columns requested (the projection) and builds each row according to these columns it contains. Each row is created by calling `MatrixCursor.newRow()`, which also returns a `Builder` instance that will be used to add the column data. Care should always be taken to match the order of the column data that is added to the order of the requested projection. They should always match.

The implementation of `update()` inspects only the incoming `ContentValues` for the preference it needs to update. Because this is enough to describe the exact item we need, we don't implement any further logic using the selection arguments. If the name value of the preference already exists, the value for it is updated and saved. Unfortunately, there is no method to simply insert an `Object` back into `SharedPreferences`, so you must inspect it based on the valid types that `ContentValues` can return and call the appropriate setter method to match. Finally we call `notifyObservers()` so any registered `ContentObserver` objects will be notified of the data change.

You may have noticed that there is no code in the `ContentProvider` to manage the read/write permissions we promised to implement! This is actually handled by Android for us: we just need to update the manifest appropriately. Have a look at Listing 5-27.

Listing 5-27. *AndroidManifest.xml*

```
<manifest xmlns:android="http://schemas.android.com/apk/res/android"
    package="com.examples.sharepreferences"
    android:versionCode="1"
    android:versionName="1.0" >

    <uses-sdk ... />

    <permission
        android:name="com.examples.sharepreferences.permission.READ_PREFERENCES"
        android:label="Read Application Settings"
        android:protectionLevel="normal" />
    <permission
        android:name="com.examples.sharepreferences.permission.WRITE_PREFERENCES"
        android:label="Write Application Settings"
        android:protectionLevel="dangerous" />

    <uses-permission
        android:name="com.examples.sharepreferences.permission.READ_PREFERENCES" />
    <uses-permission
        android:name="com.examples.sharepreferences.permission.WRITE_PREFERENCES" />

    <application ... >
        <activity android:name=".SettingsActivity" >
```

```
            <intent-filter>
                <action android:name="android.intent.action.MAIN" />
                <category android:name="android.intent.category.LAUNCHER" />
            </intent-filter>
            <intent-filter>
                <action android:name="com.examples.sharepreferences.ACTION_SETTINGS" />
                <category android:name="android.intent.category.DEFAULT" />
            </intent-filter>
        </activity>

        <provider
            android:name=".SettingsProvider"
            android:authorities="com.examples.sharepreferences.settingsprovider"
            android:readPermission=
                    "com.examples.sharepreferences.permission.READ_PREFERENCES"
            android:writePermission=
                    "com.examples.sharepreferences.permission.WRITE_PREFERENCES" >
        </provider>
    </application>

</manifest>
```

Here you can see two custom `<permission>` elements declared and attached to our `<provider>` declaration. This is the only code we need to add, and Android knows to enforce the read permissions for operations like `query()`, and the write permission for `insert()`, `update()`, and `delete()`. We have also declared a custom `<intent-filter>` on the `Activity` in this application, which will come in handy for any external applications that may want to launch the settings UI directly. Listings 5-28 through 5-30 define the rest of this example.

Listing 5-28. *res/xml/preferences.xml*

```
<?xml version="1.0" encoding="utf-8"?>
<PreferenceScreen xmlns:android="http://schemas.android.com/apk/res/android" >
    <CheckBoxPreference
        android:key="preferenceEnabled"
        android:title="Set Enabled"
        android:defaultValue="true"/>
    <EditTextPreference
        android:key="preferenceName"
        android:title="User Name"
        android:defaultValue="John Doe"/>
    <ListPreference
        android:key="preferenceSelection"
        android:title="Selection"
        android:entries="@array/selection_items"
        android:entryValues="@array/selection_items"
        android:defaultValue="Four"/>
</PreferenceScreen>
```

Listing 5-29. *res/values/arrays.xml*

```
<?xml version="1.0" encoding="utf-8"?>
<resources>
    <string-array name="selection_items">
        <item>One</item>
        <item>Two</item>
        <item>Three</item>
        <item>Four</item>
    </string-array>
</resources>
```

Listing 5-30. *Preferences Activity*

```
//Note the package for this application
package com.examples.sharepreferences;

public class SettingsActivity extends PreferenceActivity {

    @Override
    protected void onCreate(Bundle savedInstanceState) {
        super.onCreate(savedInstanceState);
        //Load the preferences defaults on first run
        PreferenceManager.setDefaultValues(this, R.xml.preferences, false);

        addPreferencesFromResource(R.xml.preferences);
    }
}
```

The settings values for this example application are manageable directly via a simple `PreferenceActivity`, whose data are defined in the `preferences.xml` file.

> **NOTE:** `PreferenceActivity` was deprecated in Android 3.0 in favor of `PreferenceFragment`, but at the time of this book's publication `PreferenceFragment` has not yet been added to the support library. Therefore, we use it here to allow support for earlier versions of Android.

Usage Example

Next let's take a look at Listings 5-31 through 5-33, which define a second application that will attempt to access our preferences data by using this `ContentProvider` interface.

Listing 5-31. *AndroidManifest.xml*

```
<manifest xmlns:android="http://schemas.android.com/apk/res/android"
    package="com.examples.accesspreferences"
    android:versionCode="1"
    android:versionName="1.0">

    <uses-sdk ... />

    <uses-permission
        android:name="com.examples.sharepreferences.permission.READ_PREFERENCES" />
    <uses-permission
        android:name="com.examples.sharepreferences.permission.WRITE_PREFERENCES" />

    <application ... >
        <activity android:name=".MainActivity" >
            <intent-filter>
                <action android:name="android.intent.action.MAIN" />
                <category android:name="android.intent.category.LAUNCHER" />
            </intent-filter>
        </activity>
    </application>

</manifest>
```

The key point here is that this application declares the use of both our custom permissions as `<uses-permission>` elements. This is what allows it to have access to the external provider. Without these, a request through `ContentResolver` would result in a `SecurityException`.

Listing 5-32. *res/layout/main.xml*

```
<RelativeLayout xmlns:android="http://schemas.android.com/apk/res/android"
    android:layout_width="match_parent"
    android:layout_height="match_parent" >
    <Button
        android:id="@+id/button_settings"
        android:layout_width="match_parent"
        android:layout_height="wrap_content"
        android:text="Show Settings"
        android:onClick="onSettingsClick" />
    <CheckBox
        android:id="@+id/checkbox_enable"
        android:layout_width="wrap_content"
        android:layout_height="wrap_content"
        android:layout_below="@id/button_settings"
        android:text="Set Enable Setting"/>
    <LinearLayout
        android:layout_width="wrap_content"
```

```
        android:layout_height="wrap_content"
        android:layout_centerInParent="true"
        android:orientation="vertical">
        <TextView
            android:id="@+id/value_enabled"
            android:layout_width="wrap_content"
            android:layout_height="wrap_content" />
        <TextView
            android:id="@+id/value_name"
            android:layout_width="wrap_content"
            android:layout_height="wrap_content" />
        <TextView
            android:id="@+id/value_selection"
            android:layout_width="wrap_content"
            android:layout_height="wrap_content" />
    </LinearLayout>
</RelativeLayout>
```

Listing 5-33. *Activity Interacting with the Provider*

```
//Note the package as this is a different application
package com.examples.accesspreferences;

public class MainActivity extends Activity implements OnCheckedChangeListener {

    public static final String SETTINGS_ACTION =
        "com.examples.sharepreferences.ACTION_SETTINGS";
    public static final Uri SETTINGS_CONTENT_URI =
        Uri.parse("content://com.examples.sharepreferences.settingsprovider/settings");
    public static class SettingsColumns {
        public static final String _ID = Settings.NameValueTable._ID;
        public static final String NAME = Settings.NameValueTable.NAME;
        public static final String VALUE = Settings.NameValueTable.VALUE;
    }

    TextView mEnabled, mName, mSelection;
    CheckBox mToggle;

    private ContentObserver mObserver = new ContentObserver(new Handler()) {
        public void onChange(boolean selfChange) {
            updatePreferences();
        }
    };

    @Override
    public void onCreate(Bundle savedInstanceState) {
        super.onCreate(savedInstanceState);
        setContentView(R.layout.main);

        mEnabled = (TextView) findViewById(R.id.value_enabled);
```

```
        mName = (TextView) findViewById(R.id.value_name);
        mSelection = (TextView) findViewById(R.id.value_selection);
        mToggle = (CheckBox) findViewById(R.id.checkbox_enable);
        mToggle.setOnCheckedChangeListener(this);
    }

    @Override
    protected void onResume() {
        super.onResume();
        //Get the latest provider data
        updatePreferences();
        //Register an observer for changes that will
        // happen while we are active
        getContentResolver().registerContentObserver(SETTINGS_CONTENT_URI,
                false, mObserver);
    }

    @Override
    public void onCheckedChanged(CompoundButton buttonView, boolean isChecked) {
        ContentValues cv = new ContentValues(2);
        cv.put(SettingsColumns.NAME, "preferenceEnabled");
        cv.put(SettingsColumns.VALUE, isChecked);

        //Update the provider, which will trigger our observer
        getContentResolver().update(SETTINGS_CONTENT_URI, cv, null, null);
    }

    public void onSettingsClick(View v) {
        try {
            Intent intent = new Intent(SETTINGS_ACTION);
            startActivity(intent);
        } catch (ActivityNotFoundException e) {
            Toast.makeText(this,
                    "You do not have the Android Recipes Settings App installed.",
                    Toast.LENGTH_SHORT).show();
        }
    }

    private void updatePreferences() {
        Cursor c = getContentResolver().query(SETTINGS_CONTENT_URI,
                new String[] {SettingsColumns.NAME, SettingsColumns.VALUE},
                null, null, null);
        if (c == null) {
            return;
        }

        while (c.moveToNext()) {
            String key = c.getString(0);
```

```
                if ("preferenceEnabled".equals(key)) {
                    mEnabled.setText( String.format("Enabled Setting = %s",
                        c.getString(1)) );
                    mToggle.setChecked( Boolean.parseBoolean(c.getString(1)) );
                } else if ("preferenceName".equals(key)) {
                    mName.setText( String.format("User Name Setting = %s",
                        c.getString(1)) );
                } else if ("preferenceSelection".equals(key)) {
                    mSelection.setText( String.format("Selection Setting = %s",
                        c.getString(1)) );
                }
            }

            c.close();
        }
    }
```

Because this is a separate application, it may not have access to the constants defined in the first (unless you control both applications and use a library project or some other method), so we have redefined them here for this example. If you were producing an application with an external provider you would like other developers to use, it would be prudent to also provide a JAR library that contains the constants necessary to access the Uri and column data in the provider; similar to the API provided by `ContactsContract` and `CalendarContract`.

In this example the `Activity` queries the provider for the current values of the settings each time it returns to the foreground and displays them in a `TextView`. The results are returned in a `Cursor` with two values in each row: the preference name and its value. The `Activity` also registers a `ContentObserver` so that if the values change while this `Activity` is active, the displayed values can be updated as well. When the user changes the value of the `CheckBox` onscreen, this calls the provider's update() method, which will trigger this observer to update the display.

Finally, if the user would like to, he or she may launch the `SettingsActivity` from the external application directly by clicking the "Show Settings" button. This calls `startActivity()` with an `Intent` containing the custom action string for which `SettingsActivity` is set to filter.

5–10. Sharing Your Other Data

Problem

You would like your application to provide the files or other data it maintains to other applications on the device.

Solution

(API Level 3)

Create a ContentProvider to act as an external interface for your application's data. ContentProvider exposes an arbitrary set of data to external requests through a database-like interface of query(), insert(), update(), and delete(), though the implementation is free to design how the data passes to the actual model from these methods.

ContentProvider can be used to expose any type of application data, including the application's resources and assets, to external requests.

How It Works

Let's take a look at a ContentProvider implementation that exposes two data sources: an array of strings located in memory, and a series of image files stored in the application's Assets directory. As before, we must declare our provider to the Android system using a <provider> tag in the manifest. See Listings 5-34 and 5-35.

Listing 5-34. *Manifest Declaration for ContentProvider*

```
<?xml version="1.0" encoding="utf-8"?>
<manifest xmlns:android="http://schemas.android.com/apk/res/android" …>
    <application …>
      <provider android:name=".ImageProvider"
          android:authorities="com.examples.share.imageprovider">
      </provider>
    </application>
</manifest>
```

Listing 5-35. *Custom ContentProvider Exposing Assets*

```
public class ImageProvider extends ContentProvider {

    public static final Uri CONTENT_URI =
        Uri.parse("content://com.examples.share.imageprovider");

    public static final String COLUMN_NAME = "nameString";
    public static final String COLUMN_IMAGE = "imageUri";

    private String[] mNames;

    @Override
    public int delete(Uri uri, String selection, String[] selectionArgs) {
        throw new UnsupportedOperationException("This ContentProvider is read-only");
    }

    @Override
    public String getType(Uri uri) {
        return null;
    }

    @Override
    public Uri insert(Uri uri, ContentValues values) {
        throw new UnsupportedOperationException("This ContentProvider is read-only");
    }

    @Override
    public boolean onCreate() {
        mNames = new String[] {"John Doe", "Jane Doe", "Jill Doe"};
        return true;
    }

    @Override
    public Cursor query(Uri uri, String[] projection, String selection,
        String[] selectionArgs, String sortOrder) {
        MatrixCursor cursor = new MatrixCursor(projection);
        for(int i = 0; i < mNames.length; i++) {
            //Insert only the columns they requested
            MatrixCursor.RowBuilder builder = cursor.newRow();
            for(String column : projection) {
                if(column.equals("_id")) {
                    //Use the array index as a unique id
                    builder.add(i);
                }
                if(column.equals(COLUMN_NAME)) {
                    builder.add(mNames[i]);
                }
                if(column.equals(COLUMN_IMAGE)) {
                    builder.add(Uri.withAppendedPath(CONTENT_URI, String.valueOf(i)));
```

```
                }
            }
        }
        return cursor;
    }

    @Override
    public int update(Uri uri, ContentValues values, String selection,
        String[] selectionArgs) {
        throw new UnsupportedOperationException("This ContentProvider is read-only");
    }

    @Override
    public AssetFileDescriptor openAssetFile(Uri uri, String mode) throws
        FileNotFoundException {
        int requested = Integer.parseInt(uri.getLastPathSegment());
        AssetFileDescriptor afd;
        AssetManager manager = getContext().getAssets();
        //Return the appropriate asset for the requested item
        try {
            switch(requested) {
            case 0:
                afd = manager.openFd("logo1.png");
                break;
            case 1:
                afd = manager.openFd("logo2.png");
                break;
            case 2:
                afd = manager.openFd("logo3.png");
                break;
            default:
                afd = manager.openFd("logo1.png");
            }
            return afd;
        } catch (IOException e) {
            e.printStackTrace();
            return null;
        }
    }
}
```

As you may have guessed, the example exposes three logo image assets. The images we have chosen for this example are shown in Figure 5-3.

Figure 5–3. *Examples of logo1.png (left), logo2.png (center), and logo3.png (right) stored in Assets.*

Because we are exposing read-only content in the Assets directory, there is no need to support the inherited methods insert(), update(), or delete(), so we have these methods simply throw an UnsupportedOperationException.

When the provider is created, the string array that holds people's names is created and onCreate() returns true; this signals to the system that the provider was created successfully. The provider exposes constants for its Uri and all readable column names. These values will be used by external applications to make requests for data.

This provider only supports a query for all the data within it. To support conditional queries for specific records or a subset of all the content, an application can process the values passed in to query() for selection and selectionArgs. In this example, any call to query() will build a cursor with all three elements contained within.

The cursor implementation used in this provider is a MatrixCursor, which is a cursor designed to be built around data that is not held inside a database. The example iterates through the list of columns requested (the projection) and builds each row according to these columns it contains. Each row is created by calling MatrixCursor.newRow(), which also returns a Builder instance that will be used to add the column data. Care should always be taken to match the order that the column data is added to the order of the requested projection. They should always match.

The value in the name column is the respective string in the local array, and the _id value, which Android requires to utilize the returned cursor with most ListAdapters, is simply returned as the array index. The information presented in the image column for each row is actually a content Uri representing the image file for each row, created with the provider's content Uri as the base, with the array index appended to it.

When an external application actually goes to retrieve this content, through ContentResolver.openInputStream(), a call will be made to openAssetFile(), which has been overridden to return an AssetFileDescriptor pointing to one of the image files in the Assets directory. This implementation determines which image file to return by deconstructing the content Uri once again and retrieving the appended index value from the end.

Usage Example

Let's take a look at how this provider should be implemented and accessed in the context of the Android application. See Listing 5-36.

Listing 5-36. *AndroidManifest.xml*

```
<?xml version="1.0" encoding="utf-8"?>
<manifest xmlns:android="http://schemas.android.com/apk/res/android"
    package="com.examples.share"
    android:versionCode="1"
    android:versionName="1.0">
    <uses-sdk android:minSdkVersion="3" />

    <application android:icon="@drawable/icon" android:label="@string/app_name">
        <activity android:name=".ShareActivity"
                  android:label="@string/app_name">
            <intent-filter>
                <action android:name="android.intent.action.MAIN" />
                <category android:name="android.intent.category.LAUNCHER" />
            </intent-filter>
        </activity>
        <provider android:name=".ImageProvider"
          android:authorities="com.examples.share.imageprovider">
        </provider>
    </application>
</manifest>
```

To implement this provider, the manifest of the application that owns the content must declare a `<provider>` tag pointing out the `ContentProvider` name and the authority to match when requests are made. The authority value should match the base portion of the exposed content `Uri`. The provider must be declared in the manifest so the system can instantiate and run it, even when the owning application is not running. See Listings 5-37 and 5-38.

Listing 5-37. *res/layout/main.xml*

```
<?xml version="1.0" encoding="utf-8"?>
<LinearLayout xmlns:android="http://schemas.android.com/apk/res/android"
  android:orientation="vertical"
  android:layout_width="fill_parent"
  android:layout_height="fill_parent">
  <TextView
    android:id="@+id/name"
    android:layout_width="wrap_content"
    android:layout_height="20dip"
    android:layout_gravity="center_horizontal"
  />
  <ImageView
    android:id="@+id/image"
    android:layout_width="wrap_content"
    android:layout_height="50dip"
    android:layout_gravity="center_horizontal"
  />
```

```
  <ListView
    android:id="@+id/list"
    android:layout_width="fill_parent"
    android:layout_height="fill_parent"
  />
</LinearLayout>
```

Listing 5-38. *Activity Reading from ImageProvider*

```
public class ShareActivity extends FragmentActivity implements
        LoaderManager.LoaderCallbacks<Cursor>, AdapterView.OnItemClickListener {
    private static final int LOADER_LIST = 100;
    SimpleCursorAdapter mAdapter;

    @Override
    public void onCreate(Bundle savedInstanceState) {
        super.onCreate(savedInstanceState);
        getSupportLoaderManager().initLoader(LOADER_LIST, null, this);
        setContentView(R.layout.main);

        mAdapter = new SimpleCursorAdapter(this, android.R.layout.simple_list_item_1,
                null, new String[]{ImageProvider.COLUMN_NAME},
                new int[]{android.R.id.text1}, 0);

        ListView list = (ListView)findViewById(R.id.list);
        list.setOnItemClickListener(this);
        list.setAdapter(mAdapter);
    }

    @Override
    public void onItemClick(AdapterView<?> parent, View v, int position, long id) {
        //Seek the cursor to the selection
        Cursor c = mAdapter.getCursor();
        c.moveToPosition(position);

        //Load the name column into the TextView
        TextView tv = (TextView)findViewById(R.id.name);
        tv.setText(c.getString(1));

        ImageView iv = (ImageView)findViewById(R.id.image);
        try {
            //Load the content from the image column into the ImageView
            InputStream in =
                    getContentResolver().openInputStream(Uri.parse(c.getString(2)));
            Bitmap image = BitmapFactory.decodeStream(in);
            iv.setImageBitmap(image);
        } catch (FileNotFoundException e) {
            e.printStackTrace();
        }
    }
```

```
    @Override
    public Loader<Cursor> onCreateLoader(int id, Bundle args) {
        String[] projection = new String[]{"_id",
                ImageProvider.COLUMN_NAME,
                ImageProvider.COLUMN_IMAGE};
        return new CursorLoader(this, ImageProvider.CONTENT_URI,
                projection, null, null, null);
    }

    @Override
    public void onLoadFinished(Loader<Cursor> loader, Cursor data) {
        mAdapter.swapCursor(data);
    }

    @Override
    public void onLoaderReset(Loader<Cursor> loader) {
        mAdapter.swapCursor(null);
    }
}
```

IMPORTANT: This example requires the support library to provide access to the `Loader` pattern in Android 1.6 and above. If you are targeting Android 3.0+ in your application, you may replace `FragmentActivity` with `Activity` and `getSupportLoaderManager()` with `getLoaderManager()`.

In this example a managed cursor is obtained from the custom `ContentProvider`, referencing the exposed Uri and column names for the data. The data is then connected to a `ListView` through a `SimpleCursorAdapter` to display only the name value.

When the user taps any of the items in the list, the cursor is moved to that position and the respective name and image are displayed above. This is where the Activity calls `ContentResolver.openInputStream()` to access the asset images through the Uri that was stored in the column field.

Figure 5-4 displays the result of running this application and selecting the last item in the list (Jill Doe).

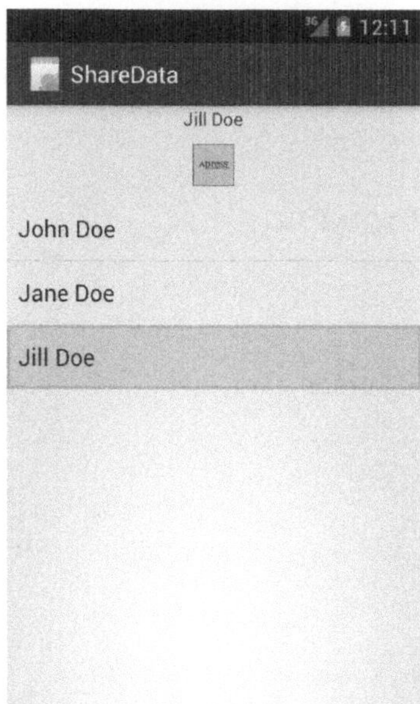

Figure 5–4. *Activity drawing resources from ContentProvider.*

Note that the connection to the `Cursor` is not closed explicitly because it was created by the `Loader`, which means it is also the job of the `Loader` to manage it.

Useful Tools to Know: SQLite3

Android provides the `sqlite3` tool (in the `tools` subdirectory of the Android SDK's home directory) for creating new databases and managing existing databases on your hosting platform or (when used with `adb`, the Android Debug Bridge tool) on an Android device. If you're not familiar with `sqlite3`, point your browser to `http://sqlite.org/sqlite.html` and read the short tutorial on this command-line tool.

You can specify `sqlite3` with a database file name argument (`sqlite3 employees`, for example) to create the database file when it doesn't exist (you must create a table at least) or open the existing file, and enter this tool's shell from where you can execute `sqlite3`-specific dot-prefixed commands and SQL statements. As Figure 5-5 shows, you can also specify `sqlite3` without an argument and enter the shell.

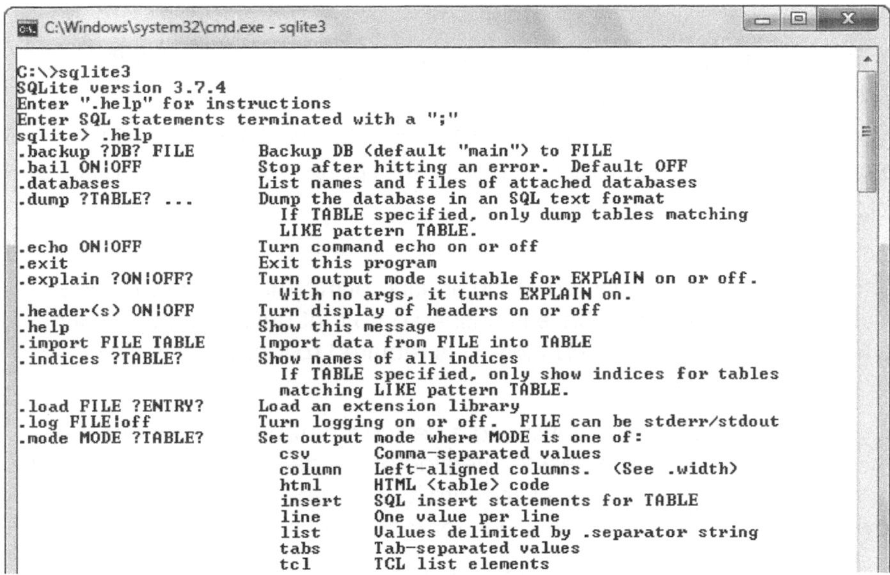

Figure 5-5. *Invoking `sqlite3` without a database file name argument.*

Figure 5-5 reveals the prologue that greets you after entering the `sqlite3` shell, which is indicated by the `sqlite>` prompt from where you enter commands. It also reveals part of the help text that's presented when you type the `sqlite3`-specific "`.help`" command.

> **TIP:** You can create a database after specifying `sqlite3` without an argument by entering the appropriate SQL statements to create and populate desired tables (and possibly create indexes), and then invoking `.backup` *file name* (where *file name* identifies the file that stores the database) before exiting `sqlite3`.

After you've created the database on your hosting platform, you can upload it to your Android device. Accomplish this task by invoking the `adb` tool with its `push` command according to the following command-line syntax (split across two lines for readability):

```
adb [-s <serialNumber>] push local.db
    /data/data/<application package>/databases/remote.db
```

This command pushes the locally hosted database identified as *local*.db to a file named *remote*.db that's located in the /data/data/<*application package*>/databases directory on the connected Android device.

> **NOTE:** *local* and *remote* are placeholders for the actual database file names. By convention, the file name is associated with a .db file extension (although an extension isn't mandatory). Also, /data/data/<*application package*> refers to the application's own private storage area, and *application package* refers to an application's unique package name.

When only one device is connected to the hosting platform, -s <*serialNumber*> isn't required and the local database is pushed onto that device. When multiple devices are connected, -s <*serialNumber*> is required to identify a device (-s emulator-5556, for example).

Alternatively, you might want to download a device's database to your hosting platform, perhaps to use with a desktop version of the device's application. You can accomplish this task by invoking adb with its pull command according to the following syntax (split across two lines for readability):

```
adb [-s <serialNumber>] pull /data/data/<application
package>/databases/remote.db
    local.db
```

If you want to use sqlite3 to manage SQLite databases that are stored on a device, you'll need to invoke this tool from within an adb remote shell for that device. You can accomplish this task by invoking adb and sqlite3 according to the following syntax:

```
adb [-s <serialNumber>] shell
# sqlite3 /data/data/<application package>/databases/remote.db
```

The adb shell is indicated by the # prompt. Enter sqlite3 followed by either the path and name of the existing device-hosted database file to manipulate the database or the path of the new database to create. Alternatively, you can enter sqlite3 without an argument.

The sqlite3 command presents the same prologue that you saw in Figure 5-5. Enter sqlite3 commands and issue SQL statements to manage *remote*.db (or create a new database), and then exit sqlite3 (.exit or .quit) followed by the adb shell (exit).

> **NOTE:** When running sqlite3 after running adb shell, you will probably observe a version number that differs from the number that is presented when you run the sqlite3 tool.

Univerter and SQLite3

Chapter 1 introduced you to `Univerter`. This units-conversion app lets you perform conversions between various units (degrees Fahrenheit to degrees Celsius, for example).

> **NOTE:** Appendix D presents a thorough discussion of `Univerter`'s architecture, in terms of source code, resources, and the manifest. Read this appendix now if you have not done so.

Although useful, `Univerter` is flawed because its conversions are hard-coded. This app must be rebuilt each time a new conversion is added to its conversions list. We can eliminate this flaw by storing additional conversions in a database and then adding these conversions to the hard-coded list at runtime.

This section improves `Univerter` by augmenting this app's conversions with additional conversions that are stored in a database. At startup, if the database exists, its conversions are added to those already built into `Univerter`. If the database does not exist, `Univerter` proceeds with its 200 hard-coded conversions without alerting the user.

Before making this enhancement, several questions need to be answered:

- How extensively will existing source code need to be changed, and do any resources need to be modified?
- Although simple conversions, where an input value is multiplied by a multiplier, can be stored easily in a database (by storing the multiplier), how are more complex conversions (such as converting from Celsius to Fahrenheit), which require several calculations, stored?
- `Univerter` is fairly responsive with its hard-coded list of conversions. However, this responsiveness is bound to decrease (and frustrate the user, especially as the number of conversions increases) if `Univerter` has to access the database and create its conversions list each time its activity is created. How can responsiveness be improved?

- A conversion includes a string resource ID (identifying the conversion name), which makes it possible to localize the app to support multiple languages (a feature that may be utilized in the future). Because string resources and their IDs cannot be created dynamically at runtime, how will new conversion and category name strings be handled?

These questions are answered as follows:

- Only two changes need to be made to `Univerter`, and these changes are not significant. Also, a few constructors and methods and a private field need to be added to `Category` and `Conversion`; also, a small amount of existing code in these classes needs to be enhanced. Finally, a new `SQLiteOpenHelper` class is needed.
- The second question has not been addressed in the enhancement. However, it could be addressed by creating a simple expression language, and storing strings representing calculations and exception-throwing logic in the database. When the database is accessed, these strings could be parsed into dynamically created `Converter` objects.
- Performance can be improved by not extracting conversions from the database each time the `onCreate(Bundle)` method is called (when an activity is created). Instead, a `static boolean` field would be interrogated to determine whether or not the database has been accessed before; execution would proceed based on its value.
- No additional string resource IDs can be created at runtime. However, localized text can be stored in the database (perhaps in different tables or in different table columns), and the correct text can be extracted by interrogating the current device locale and using this value to access the proper table/column.

Perhaps a better way to attack the performance issue is to present the default list of 200 conversions and, on a background thread at startup, build a parallel list with all possible conversions. The next time the user clicks the CAT or CON button (after the parallel list has been built), the default list is replaced with the parallel list by changing a reference.

> **TIP:** You will find the `android.os.AsyncTask` class to be handy for creating a parallel list in the background (via a worker thread), and assigning its reference to a `Category[]` variable in the foreground (via the activity thread). This variable's reference would be assigned to `categories` in response to a CAT or CON button click.

There is one more question to answer: How is a database with additional conversions distributed to the user?

The app should not access a server and download the database each time it starts running; doing so is often unnecessary (how frequently will the database be updated?) and will only waste battery power. Perhaps a better choice is to introduce an "Upgrade" button to the user interface so that the user can decide when to upgrade the database.

Creating the Database

The first step in enhancing `Univerter` is to design the database. What will be the database name and structure (in terms of tables and table structures)?

Conversions will be stored in a database called `conversions.db`. This file will be stored in the `/data/data/ca.tutortutor.univerter/databases/` directory.

The following tables will be created:

- *`categories`*: This table will contain an `id` column (of type `text`) that stores the nonlocalized identifiers of category tables. This table will also contain a `name_en` column (of type `text`) that stores English text for category names. Later, more columns (such as `name_en_GB` and `name_fr`) could be added as necessary.
- *`category name`*: This table is named after one of the entries in the `id` column of the `categories` table. It will contain a `name_en` column (of type `text`), which stores English conversion names, and a `multiplier` column (of type `real`), which stores multipliers. Later, a column for storing custom converter strings could be added. (The converter string column could be accessed when the `multiplier` contains a 0 entry.)

The sqlite3 tool lets us create this database with sample entries, which is facilitated when the SQL commands are stored in a separate file (see Listing 5-39).

Listing 5-39. *A Batch of Commands for Populating* conversions.db

```
create table categories(id text, name_en text);
insert into categories(id, name_en) values('density', 'DENSITY');
insert into categories(id, name_en) values('energy', 'ENERGY AND WORK');

create table density(name_en text, multiplier real);
insert into density(name_en, multiplier)
   values("EARTH'S DENSITY (MEAN) > PSI/1000 FEET", 2392.204767079);
insert into density(name_en, multiplier)
   values("PSI/1000 FEET > EARTH'S DENSITY (MEAN)", 0.000418024);

create table energy(name_en text, multiplier real);
insert into energy(name_en, multiplier)
   values('WATT-HOURS > TONS (EXPLOSIVE)', 0.00000086);
insert into energy(name_en, multiplier)
   values('TONS (EXPLOSIVE) > WATT-HOURS', 1162222.2222222);
```

Listing 5-39 presents the contents of an init.sql file (the extension is optional), which consists of create table and insert commands (each insert command is split across two lines for readability). The following Windows command uses sqlite3 with this file to create and populate conversions.db:

```
type init.sql | sqlite3 conversions.db
```

This command first executes type init.sql to output the contents of init.sql to standard output. The pipe symbol (|) pipes this output to the standard input of the sqlite3 command, which executes each SQL statement in its standard input to populate conversions.db, which is also created.

> **TIP:** Before rebuilding conversions.db, execute erase conversions.db. Otherwise, you will encounter errors about tables already existing.

Extending the Category and Conversion Classes

The second step in enhancing Univerter is to refactor the Conversion and Category classes so that they can be used by the aforementioned DBHelper class.

Listing 5-40 presents the refactored Conversion class. Changes between this class and the Conversion class shown in Appendix D are bolded.

Listing 5-40. *The Refactored* `Conversion` *Class*

```
package ca.tutortutor.univerter;

import android.content.Context;

class Conversion {
   private int nameID;
   private String name;
   private Converter converter;
   private boolean canBeNegative;

   Conversion(int nameID, final double multiplier) {
      this(nameID,
           new Converter() {
              @Override
              public double convert(Context ctx, double value) {
                 return value*multiplier;
              }
           },
           false);
   }

   Conversion(int nameID, Converter converter, boolean canBeNegative) {
      this.nameID = nameID;
      this.converter = converter;
      this.canBeNegative = canBeNegative;
   }

   Conversion(String name, final double multiplier) {
      this(name, new Converter() {
              @Override
              public double convert(Context ctx, double value) {
                 return value*multiplier;
              }
           },
           false);
   }

   Conversion(String name, Converter converter, boolean canBeNegative) {
      this.name = name;
      this.converter = converter;
      this.canBeNegative = canBeNegative;
   }

   boolean canBeNegative() {
      return canBeNegative;
   }
```

```
   Converter getConverter() {
      return converter;
   }

   String getName(Context ctx) {
      return (name == null) ? ctx.getString(nameID) : name;
   }
}
```

The name field, the new constructors, and the enhanced getName(Context) method that returns this field when it does not contain the null reference are present to address conversions that do not have string resource IDs. (Conversions stored in the database do not have string resource IDs.)

Listing 5-41 presents the refactored Category class. Changes between this class and the Category class shown in Appendix D are bolded.

Listing 5-41. *The Refactored Category Class*

```
package ca.tutortutor.univerter;

import android.content.Context;

class Category {
   private int nameID;
   private String name;
   private Conversion[] conversions;
   private String[] conversionNames;

   Category(int nameID, Conversion[] conversions) {
      this.nameID = nameID;
      this.conversions = conversions;
   }

   Category(String name, Conversion[] conversions) {
      this.name = name;
      this.conversions = conversions;
   }

   Conversion getConversion(int index) {
      return conversions[index];
   }

   String[] getConversionNames(Context ctx) {
      if (conversionNames == null) {
         conversionNames = new String[conversions.length];
         for (int i = 0; i < conversionNames.length; i++) {
            conversionNames[i] = conversions[i].getName(ctx);
         }
      }
```

```
      return conversionNames;
   }

   String getName(Context ctx) {
      return (name == null) ? ctx.getString(nameID) : name;
   }

   int getNumConversions() {
      return conversions.length;
   }

   void setConversions(Conversion[] conversions) {
      this.conversions = conversions;
   }
}
```

As well as addressing the case where new category names stored in the database do not have string resource IDs, Listing 5-41 introduces the following methods:

- `int getNumConversions()`: This method returns the number of `Conversion` instances stored in the `Category` instance. `DBHelper` calls this method when merging additional `Conversion` instances (based on new conversions in the same category) obtained from the database with existing `Conversion` instances.
- `void setConversions(Conversion[] conversions)`: This method replaces, in the `Category` instance, the previous `Conversion` instance's array with `conversions`. `DBHelper` calls this method after merging the existing and additional `Conversion` instances into a temporary array of `Conversion` instances.

Introducing the DBHelper Class

The third step in enhancing `Univerter` is to introduce a `DBHelper` class that encapsulates database access, to minimally impact `Univerter.java`. See Listing 5-42.

Listing 5-42. *The `DBHelper` Class*

```
package ca.tutortutor.univerter;

import android.content.Context;
```

```
import android.database.Cursor;
import android.database.SQLException;

import android.database.sqlite.SQLiteDatabase;
import android.database.sqlite.SQLiteOpenHelper;

import java.util.ArrayList;
import java.util.Comparator;
import java.util.List;
import java.util.Set;
import java.util.TreeSet;

public class DBHelper extends SQLiteOpenHelper {
   private final static String DB_PATH =
      "data/data/ca.tutortutor.univerter/databases/";
   private final static String DB_NAME = "conversions.db";

   private final static int CATEGORIES_ID_COLUMN_ID = 0;
   private final static int CATEGORIES_NAME_EN_COLUMN_ID = 1;

   private final static int CATTABLE_NAME_EN_COLUMN_ID = 0;
   private final static int CATTABLE_MULTIPLIER_COLUMN_ID = 1;

   private Context ctx;
   private SQLiteDatabase db;

   public DBHelper(Context ctx) {
      super(ctx, DB_NAME, null, 1);
      this.ctx = ctx;
   }

   @Override
   public void onCreate(SQLiteDatabase db) {
      // Do nothing ... we don't create a new database.
   }

   @Override
   public void onUpgrade(SQLiteDatabase db, int oldver, int newver) {
      // Do nothing ... we don't upgrade a database.
   }

   public Category[] updateCategories(Category[] categories) {
      try {
         String path = DB_PATH+DB_NAME;
         db = SQLiteDatabase.openDatabase(path, null,
                                          SQLiteDatabase.OPEN_READONLY|
                                          SQLiteDatabase.NO_LOCALIZED_COLLATORS);
         Cursor cur = db.query("categories", null, null, null, null, null, null);
         if (cur.getCount() == 0) {
            return categories;
```

```
      }
      Comparator<Category> cmpCat;
      cmpCat = new Comparator<Category>() {
                @Override
                public int compare(Category c1, Category c2) {
                   return c1.getName(ctx).compareTo(c2.getName(ctx));
                }
             };
      Set<Category> catSet = new TreeSet<Category>(cmpCat);
      Comparator<Conversion> cmpCon;
      cmpCon = new Comparator<Conversion>() {
                @Override
                public int compare(Conversion c1, Conversion c2) {
                   return c1.getName(ctx).compareTo(c2.getName(ctx));
                }
             };
      Set<Conversion> conSet = new TreeSet<Conversion>(cmpCon);
      while (cur.moveToNext()) {
         String catID = cur.getString(CATEGORIES_ID_COLUMN_ID);
         String catEn = cur.getString(CATEGORIES_NAME_EN_COLUMN_ID);
         Conversion[] conversions = getConversions(catID);
         for (int i = 0; i < categories.length; i++) {
            Category cat = categories[i];
            catSet.add(cat);
            if (catEn.equals(cat.getName(ctx))) {
               int numCon = cat.getNumConversions();
               for (int j = 0; j < numCon; j++) {
                  conSet.add(cat.getConversion(j));
               }
               for (int j = 0; j < conversions.length; j++) {
                  conSet.add(conversions[j]);
               }
               cat.setConversions(conSet.toArray(new Conversion[0]));
               conSet.clear();
            }
            if (i == categories.length-1) {
               catSet.add(new Category(catEn, conversions));
            }
         }
      }
      return catSet.toArray(new Category[0]);
   } catch (SQLException sqle) {
      //Do nothing
   } finally {
      if (db != null)
         db.close();
   }
   return categories;
}
```

```
    private Conversion[] getConversions(String catID) {
        try {
            Cursor cur = db.query(catID, null, null, null, null, null, null);
            if (cur.getCount() == 0) {
                return new Conversion[0];
            }
            List<Conversion> conList = new ArrayList<Conversion>();
            while (cur.moveToNext()) {
                String name_en = cur.getString(CATTABLE_NAME_EN_COLUMN_ID);
                double multiplier = cur.getDouble(CATTABLE_MULTIPLIER_COLUMN_ID);
                Conversion con = new Conversion(name_en, multiplier);
                conList.add(con);
            }
            return conList.toArray(new Conversion[0]);
        } catch (SQLException sqle) {
            //Do nothing
        }
        return null;
    }
}
```

DBHelper extends android.database.sqlite.SQLiteOpenHelper and overrides its abstract onCreate() and onUpgrade() methods. The overriding methods do nothing; all that's important is whether or not the database can be opened.

The database is opened in Category[] updateCategories(Category[] categories), which merges additional Category and/or Conversion instances into its categories array argument. This array is subsequently returned.

After the database is successfully opened, db.query("categories", null, null, null, null, null, null) is invoked to return an android.database.Cursor object for iterating over all rows in the categories table. This object represents a *cursor* (table row pointer).

Iteration consists of successive calls to Cursor's boolean moveToNext() method, which positions the cursor to the start of the next row (the cursor is initially positioned before the first row). Each iteration first retrieves the row's id and name_en column values.

> **NOTE:** Although expedient for this short exercise, accessing the name_en column directly is not a smart solution in the long term where multiple locales will most likely be used. A better solution would involve accessing the default locale (by calling the java.util.Locale class's Locale getDefault() class method), and identifying the appropriate column based on this value. Perhaps name_en could be used to supply a default value when a suitable locale-specific column is not found.

After obtaining these values, the private Conversion[] getConversions(String catID) method is called with the id value (in catID) to load the contents of all conversion rows from the category-specific table and return them as a Conversion array.

It is now a simple matter of iterating over all current categories to determine whether the conversions belong to an existing category (and must be appended to the category's conversions) or whether a new category must be created that stores these conversions.

A pair of java.util.TreeSet instances is created to store Category and Conversion instances. TreeSet is used because it prevents duplicate objects from being stored and also because it allows its contained objects to be sorted.

Two java.util.Comparator objects are created for comparing Category objects or Conversion objects based on their names. These comparators are passed to TreeSet's constructor to ensure that objects are sorted in ascending order based on their names.

It is possible that an android.database.SQLException instance might be thrown. Should this happen, no message is printed out to avoid alarming the user. The database is closed regardless of a thrown exception.

> **CAUTION:** DBHelper offers a quick, but far from optimal, solution for updating the array of categories. Furthermore, it is problematic. For instance, this code can fail when you change the database organization. Also, the array of categories and their conversions may be left in an inconsistent state should an android.database.SQLException instance be thrown.

Extending the Univerter Class

The final step in reimplementing Univerter is to refactor the Univerter class to work with DBHelper. First, a categoriesUpdated class field is introduced, as shown below:

```
public class Univerter extends Activity {
   private static boolean categoriesUpdated;
   private static Category[] categories;
   static {
      categories = new Category[]
```

Continuing, onCreate(Bundle) is modified to instantiate DBHelper and invoke its updateCategories(Category[]) method, as follows:

```
public void onCreate(Bundle savedInstanceState) {
   super.onCreate(savedInstanceState);

   if (!categoriesUpdated) {
      DBHelper dbh = new DBHelper(this);
      categories = dbh.updateCategories(categories);
      categoriesUpdated = true;
   }

   catNames = new String[categories.length];
   for (int i = 0; i < catNames.length; i++) {
      catNames[i] = categories[i].getName(Univerter.this);
   }
```

And that is it. You now have an implementation of `Univerter` that can accommodate additional conversions.

> **TIP:** If you store many conversions in the database, it is possible that you could end up with the dreaded *Application Not Responding* dialog box. If this happens, consider creating a parallel `Category[]` array on a background thread, and you can assign this array to `categories` on the activity thread in response to a CAT or CON button click.

Running the Enhanced Univerter App

You can run `Univerter` with or without `conversions.db` being present on the device. When this file is absent, `Univerter` behaves as normal with 200 conversions. However, when this file is present, `Univerter` expands into a more useful app.

The following command (split across two lines for readability) stores `conversions.db` on the device and in the proper location:

```
adb push conversions.db
 /data/data/ca.tutortutor.univerter/databases/conversions.db
```

> **NOTE:** If you make changes to `conversion.db`, you must uninstall `Univerter` and then reinstall it before pushing the updated database onto the device.

Launch `Univerter` and click the CAT button. You should observe the new DENSITY category shown in Figure 5-6.

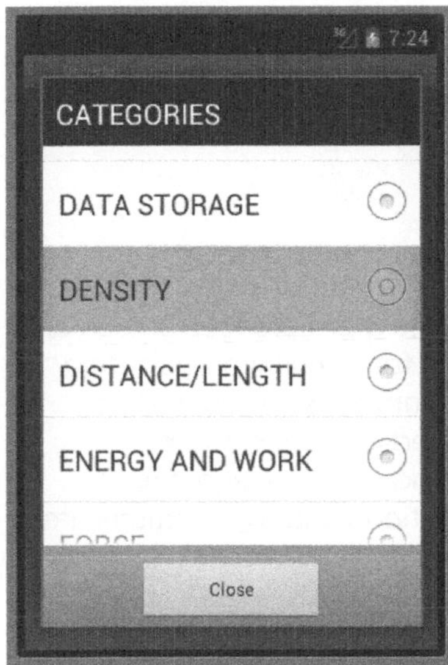

Figure 5-6. *A new DENSITY category is added to the CATEGORIES list.*

Close this dialog box and click the CON button. You should see the same list of density-specific conversions that is shown in Figure 5-7.

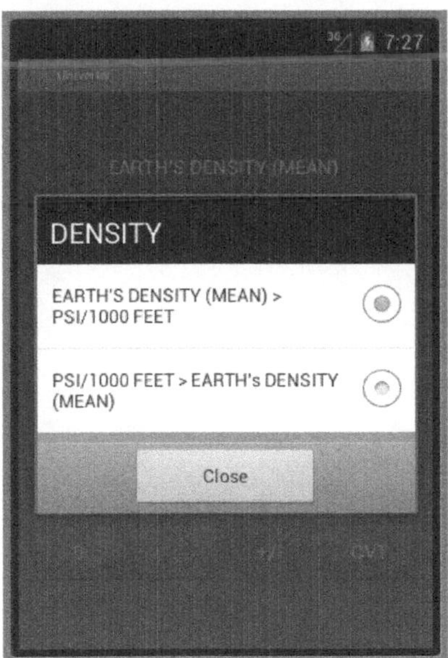

Figure 5-7. *Conversions appear in sorted order.*

While you are at it, you might want to change the category to “ENERGY AND WORK”. You should observe new “TONS (EXPLOSIVE) > WATT-HOURS” and “WATT-HOURS > TONS (EXPLOSIVE)” conversions (and in alphabetic order).

Summary

In this chapter, you investigated a number of practical methods to persist data on Android devices. You learned how to quickly create a preferences screen as well as how to use preferences and a simple method for persisting basic data types. You saw how and where files can be placed, for reference as well as storage. You even learned how to share your persisted data with other applications. In the next chapter, we will investigate how to leverage the operating system’s services to do background operations and to communicate between applications.

Chapter 6

Interacting with the System

The Android operating system provides a number of useful services that applications can leverage. Many of these services are designed to allow your application to function within the mobile system in ways beyond just interacting briefly with a user. Applications can schedule themselves for alarms, run background services, and send messages to each other; all of which allows an Android application to integrate to the fullest extent with the mobile device. In addition, Android provides a set of standard interfaces that are designed to expose all the data collected by its core applications to your software. Through these interfaces, any application may integrate with, add to, and improve upon the core functionality of the platform, thereby enhancing the experience for the user.

6–1. Notifying from the Background

Problem

Your application is running in the background, with no currently visible interface to the user, but must notify the user of an important event that has occurred.

Solution

(API Level 4)

Use NotificationManager to post a status bar notification. Notifications are an unobtrusive way of telling the user that you want his or her attention. Perhaps new messages have arrived, an update is available, or a long-running job is complete; notifications are perfect for accomplishing these tasks.

How It Works

A Notification can be posted to the NotificationManager from just about any system component, such as a Service, BroadcastReceiver, or Activity. In Listing 6-1, we will look at an Activity that uses a delay to simulate a long-running operation, resulting in a Notification when it is complete.

Listing 6-1. *Activity Firing a Notification*

```
public class NotificationActivity extends Activity implements
View.OnClickListener {

    private static final int NOTE_ID = 100;

    @Override
    public void onCreate(Bundle savedInstanceState) {
        super.onCreate(savedInstanceState);
        Button button = new Button(this);
        button.setText("Post New Notification");
        button.setOnClickListener(this);
        setContentView(button);
    }

    @Override
    public void onClick(View v) {
        //Run 10 seconds after click
        handler.postDelayed(task, 10000);
        Toast.makeText(this, "Notification will post in 10 seconds",
            Toast.LENGTH_SHORT).show();
    }

    private Handler handler = new Handler();
    private Runnable task = new Runnable() {
        @Override
        public void run() {
            NotificationManager manager =
                (NotificationManager)getSystemService(Context.NOTIFICATION_SERVICE);
```

```
            Intent launchIntent =
                new Intent(getApplicationContext(), NotificationActivity.class);
            PendingIntent contentIntent =
                PendingIntent.getActivity(getApplicationContext(), 0, launchIntent, 0);

            //Create notification with the time it was fired
            NotificationCompat.Builder builder =
                    new NotificationCompat.Builder(NotificationActivity.this);

            builder.setSmallIcon(R.drawable.icon)
                .setTicker("Something Happened")
                .setWhen(System.currentTimeMillis())
                .setAutoCancel(true)
                .setDefaults(Notification.DEFAULT_SOUND)
                .setContentTitle("We're Finished!")
                .setContentText("Click Here!")
                .setContentIntent(contentIntent);
            Notification note = builder.build();

            //Post the notification
            manager.notify(NOTE_ID, note);
        }
    };
}
```

This example makes use of a `Handler` to schedule a task to post the `Notification` 10 seconds after the button is clicked by calling `Handler.postDelayed()` in the button listener. This task will execute regardless of whether the Activity is in the foreground, so if the user gets bored and leaves the application, he or she will still get notified.

When the scheduled task executes, a new `Notification` is created using `Notification.Builder`. An icon resource and title string may be provided, and these items will display in the status bar at the time the notification occurs. In addition, we pass a time value (in milliseconds) to display in the notification list as the event time. Here, we are setting that value to the time the notification fired, but it may take on a different meaning in your application.

> **IMPORTANT:** We are using `NotificationCompat.Builder` in this example, which is part of the support library and allows us to use the new API, which was introduced in Android 3.0 (API Level 11), going back to Android 1.6. If you are targeting Android 3.0+ only, you can replace `NotificationCompat.Builder` with `Notification.Builder` within the code.

Prior to creating the `Notification`, we can fill it out with some other useful parameters, such as more detailed text to be displayed in the Notifications list when the user pulls down the status bar.

One of the parameters passed to the builder is a `PendingIntent` that points back to our Activity. This Intent makes the `Notification` interactive, allowing the user to tap it in the list and launch the Activity.

> **NOTE:** This Intent will launch a new Activity with each event. If you would rather an existing instance of the Activity respond to the launch, if one exists in the stack, be sure to include Intent flags and manifest parameters appropriately to accomplish this, such as `Intent.FLAG_ACTIVITY_CLEAR_TOP` and `android:launchMode="singleTop."`

To enhance the `Notification` beyond the visual animation in the status bar, the `Notification` defaults are modified to include that the system's default notification sound be played when the `Notification` fires. Values such as `Notification.DEFAULT_VIBRATION` and `Notification.DEFAULT_LIGHTS` may also be added.

> **TIP:** If you would like to customize the sound played with a `Notification`, set the `Notification.sound` parameter to a `Uri` that references a file or `ContentProvider` to read from.

We finally add a series of flags to the `Notification` for further customization. This example enables `Notification.FLAG_AUTO_CANCEL` to signify that the notification should be canceled, or removed from the list, as soon as the user selects it. Without this flag, the notification remains in the list until it is manually canceled by calling `NotificationManager.cancel()` or `NotificationManager.cancelAll()`.

The following are some other useful flags to apply:

- `FLAG_INSISTENT`
  - Repeats the `Notification` sounds until the user responds.

- FLAG_NO_CLEAR
  - Does not allow the Notification to be cleared with the user's "Clear Notifications" button, only through a call to cancel().

Once the Notification is prepared, it is posted to the user with NotificationManager.notify(), which takes an ID parameter as well. Each Notification type in your application should have a unique ID. The manager will only allow one Notification with the same ID in the list at a time, and new instances with the same ID will take the place of those existing. In addition, the ID is required to cancel a specific Notification manually.

When we run this example, an Activity like Figure 6-1 displays a button to the user. Upon pressing the button, you can see the Notification post sometime later, even if the Activity is no longer visible (see Figure 6-2).

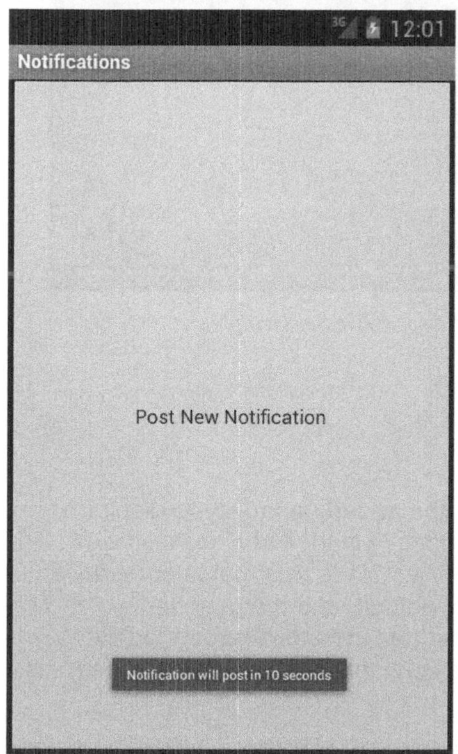

Figure 6-1. *Notification posted from button press.*

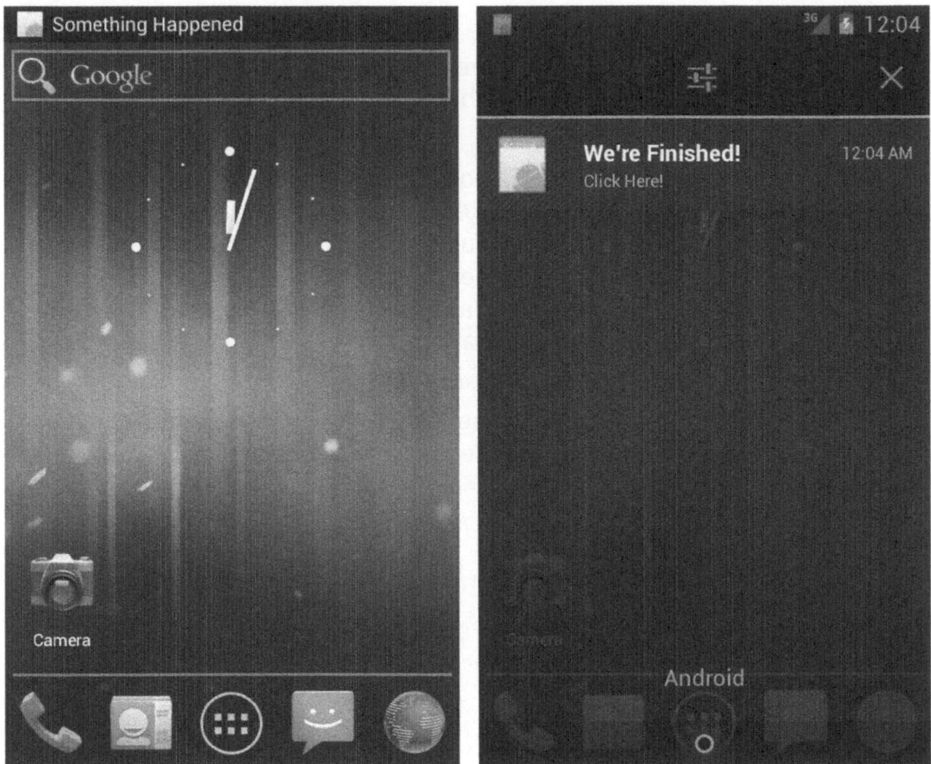

Figure 6-2. *Notification that is occurring (left) and being displayed in the list (right).*

Expanded Notification Styles

(API Level 16)

Starting with Android 4.1, a notification has the added capability to display additional rich information with interactivity directly in the `Notification` view. These are known as `Notification` styles. Any `Notification` that is currently at the top of the window shade is expanded by default, and the user can expand any other `Notification` with a two-finger gesture. Therefore, expanded views don't replace the traditional view; rather, they enhance the experience at certain times.

There are three default styles (implementations of `Notification.Style`) provided by the platform:

- `BigTextStyle`: Displays an extended amount of text, such as the full contents of a message or post.

- BigPictureStyle: Displays a large, full-color image.
- InboxStyle: Provides a list of items, similar to the inbox view from an application like Gmail.

You are not limited to using these, however. Notification.Style is an interface that your application can implement to display any custom expanded layout that may best fit your needs.

In addition to styles, Android 4.1 added inline actions for an expanded Notification. This means that you can add multiple action items for the user to take directly from the window shade view rather than just the single callback Intent when the user clicks the whole Notification item. These items will show up on top of the expanded view, lined up at the bottom. Listing 6-2 illustrates how to modify the previous example to add a BigTextStyle expanded notification, and Figure 6-3 shows the result.

Listing 6-2. *BigTextStyle Notification*

```
//Create notification with the time it was fired
NotificationCompat.Builder builder =
        new NotificationCompat.Builder(NotificationActivity.this);

builder.setSmallIcon(R.drawable.icon)
       .setTicker("Something Happened")
       .setWhen(System.currentTimeMillis())
       .setAutoCancel(true)
       .setDefaults(Notification.DEFAULT_SOUND)
       .setContentTitle("We're Finished!")
       .setContentText("Click Here!")
       .setContentIntent(contentIntent);

//Add some custom actions
builder.addAction(android.R.id.drawable.ic_menu_call, "Call Back", contentIntent);
builder.addAction(android.R.id.drawable.ic_menu_recent_history,
        "Call History", contentIntent);

//Apply an expanded style
NotificationCompat.BigTextStyle expandedStyle =
        new NotificationCompat.BigTextStyle(builder);
expandedStyle.bigText("Here is some additional text to be displayed when"
    + " the notification is in expanded mode.  "
    + " I can fit so much more content into this giant view!");

Notification note = expandedStyle.build();

//Post the notification
manager.notify(NOTE_ID, note);
```

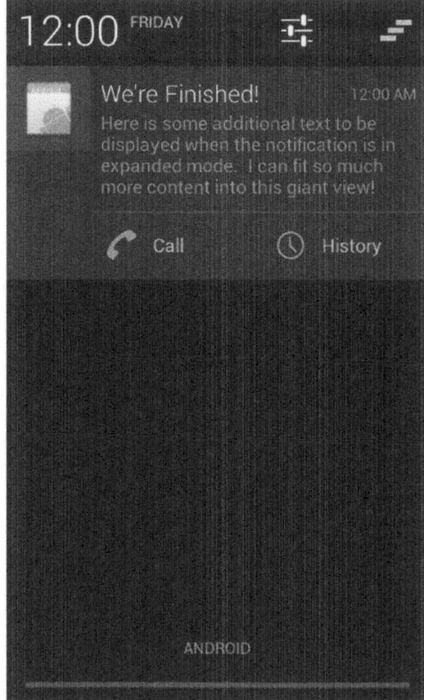

Figure 6-3. *BigTextStyle in the window shade.*

You can attach custom actions by using the addAction() method on the builder. You can see here how the actions that are added lay out with respect to the overall view. In this example each action goes to the same place, but you can attach any PendingIntent to each action to make them travel to different places in your application.

The only necessary modification to the previous example is that we wrap our existing Builder object in the BigTextStyle and apply any specific customizations there. In this case, the only additional piece of information is setting bigText() with the text to display in expanded mode. Then the notification is created from the build() method on the style, rather than the builder.

Let's take a look at BigPictureStyle in Listing 6-3 and Figure 6-4.

Listing 6-3. *BigPictureStyle Notification*

```
//Create notification with the time it was fired
NotificationCompat.Builder builder =
        new NotificationCompat.Builder(NotificationActivity.this);
```

```
builder.setSmallIcon(R.drawable.icon)
        .setTicker("Something Happened")
        .setWhen(System.currentTimeMillis())
        .setAutoCancel(true)
        .setDefaults(Notification.DEFAULT_SOUND)
        .setContentTitle("We're Finished!")
        .setContentText("Click Here!")
        .setContentIntent(contentIntent);

//Add some custom actions
builder.addAction(android.R.id.drawable.ic_menu_compass,
        "View Location", contentIntent);

//Apply an expanded style
NotificationCompat.BigPictureStyle expandedStyle =
        new NotificationCompat.BigPictureStyle(builder);
expandedStyle.bigPicture(
        BitmapFactory.decodeResource(getResources(), R.drawable.icon) );

Notification note = expandedStyle.build();

//Post the notification
manager.notify(NOTE_ID, note);
```

Figure 6-4. *BigPictureStyle in the window shade.*

This code is almost identical to BigTextStyle, except that here we use the `bigPicture()` method to pass in the `Bitmap` that will be used as the full-color image. Finally, take a look at InboxStyle in Listing 6-4 and Figure 6-5.

Listing 6-4. *InboxStyle Notification*

```
//Create notification with the time it was fired
NotificationCompat.Builder builder =
        new NotificationCompat.Builder(NotificationActivity.this);

builder.setSmallIcon(R.drawable.icon)
       .setTicker("Something Happened")
       .setWhen(System.currentTimeMillis())
       .setAutoCancel(true)
       .setDefaults(Notification.DEFAULT_SOUND)
       .setContentTitle("We're Finished!")
       .setContentText("Click Here!")
       .setContentIntent(contentIntent);

//Apply an expanded style
NotificationCompat.InboxStyle expandedStyle =
        new NotificationCompat.InboxStyle(builder);
expandedStyle.setSummaryText("4 New Tasks");
expandedStyle.addLine("Make Dinner");
expandedStyle.addLine("Call Mom");
expandedStyle.addLine("Call Wife First");
expandedStyle.addLine("Pick up Kids");

Notification note = expandedStyle.build();

//Post the notification
manager.notify(NOTE_ID, note);
```

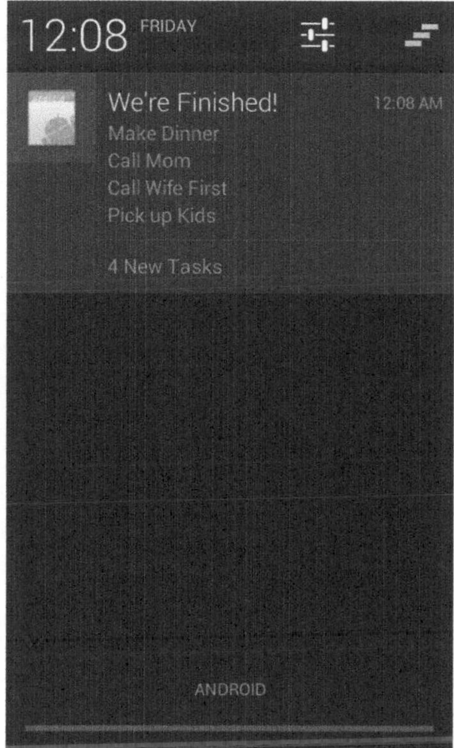

Figure 6-5. *InboxStyle in the window shade.*

With `Notification.InboxStyle`, multiple items are added to the list by using the `addLine()` method. We also topped off the example with a summary line noting how many items there were with `setSummaryText()`, a method that is actually available for use with all the previous styles as well.

As before, we've made use of the support library's `NotificationCompat` class, which allows us to call all these methods in an application running back to API Level 4. If your application is targeting Android 4.1 as the minimum platform, you can replace this with the native `Notification.Builder`.

One of the real powers of the support library is shown in this particular case. We are calling methods that are not available until API Level 16, but the support library takes care of version checking for us under the hood and simply ignores methods that a certain platform doesn't support; we don't have to branch our code to use new APIs.

As a result, when this same code is used on a device running Android 4.0 or earlier the traditional notification will simply appear as if we hadn't taken advantage of the new features.

> **NOTE:** One of the great powers of the support library is that you can use new APIs in applications running on older Android devices, and you don't have to branch your own code to do so.

6–2. Creating Timed and Periodic Tasks

Problem

Your application needs to run an operation on a timer, such as updating the UI on a scheduled basis.

Solution

(API Level 1)

Use the timed operations provided by a `Handler`. With `Handler`, operations can efficiently be scheduled to occur at a specific time or after a specified delay.

How It Works

Let's look at an example Activity that displays the current time in a `TextView`. See Listing 6-5.

Listing 6-5. *Activity Updated with a Handler*

```
public class TimingActivity extends Activity {

    TextView mClock;

    @Override
    public void onCreate(Bundle savedInstanceState) {
        super.onCreate(savedInstanceState);
        mClock = new TextView(this);
        setContentView(mClock);
    }
```

```
    private Handler mHandler = new Handler();
    private Runnable timerTask = new Runnable() {
        @Override
        public void run() {
            Calendar now = Calendar.getInstance();
            mClock.setText(String.format("%02d:%02d:%02d",
                    now.get(Calendar.HOUR),
                    now.get(Calendar.MINUTE),
                    now.get(Calendar.SECOND)) );
            //Schedule the next update in one second
            mHandler.postDelayed(timerTask,1000);
        }
    };

    @Override
    public void onResume() {
        super.onResume();
        mHandler.post(timerTask);
    }

    @Override
    public void onPause() {
        super.onPause();
        mHandler.removeCallbacks(timerTask);
    }
}
```

Here we've wrapped up the operation of reading the current time and updating the UI into a Runnable named timerTask, which will be triggered by the Handler that has also been created. When the Activity becomes visible, the task is executed as soon as possible with a call to Handler.post(). After the TextView has been updated, the final operation of timerTask is to invoke the Handler to schedule another execution one second (1,000 milliseconds) from now by using Handler.postDelayed().

As long as the Activity remains uninterrupted, this cycle will continue, with the UI being updated every second. As soon as the Activity is paused (the user leaves or something else grabs his or her attention), Handler.removeCallbacks() removes all pending operations and ensures the task will not be called further until the Activity becomes visible once more.

> **TIP:** In this example, we are safe to update the UI because the Handler was created on the main thread. Operations will always execute on the same thread as the Handler that posted them is attached to.

6–3. Scheduling a Periodic Task

Problem

Your application needs to register to run a task periodically, such as checking a server for updates or reminding the user to do something.

Solution

(API Level 1)

Utilize the AlarmManager to manage and execute your task. AlarmManager is useful for scheduling future single or repeated operations that need to occur even if your application is not running. AlarmManager is handed a PendingIntent to fire whenever an alarm is scheduled. This Intent can point to any system component, such as an Activity, BroadcastReceiver, or Service, that can be executed when the alarm triggers.

It should be noted that this method is best suited to operations that need to occur even when the application code may not be running. The AlarmManager requires too much overhead to be useful for simple timing operations that may be needed while an application is in use. These are better handled using the postAtTime() and postDelayed() methods of a Handler.

How It Works

Let's take a look at how AlarmManager can be used to trigger a BroadcastReceiver on a regular basis. See Listings 6-6 through 6-8.

Listing 6-6. *BroadcastReceiver to Be Triggered*

```
public class AlarmReceiver extends BroadcastReceiver {
    @Override
    public void onReceive(Context context, Intent intent) {
        //Perform an interesting operation, we'll just display the current time
        Calendar now = Calendar.getInstance();
        DateFormat formatter = SimpleDateFormat.getTimeInstance();
        Toast.makeText(context, formatter.format(now.getTime()),
            Toast.LENGTH_SHORT).show();
    }
}
```

> **REMINDER:** BroadcastReceiver (`AlarmReceiver`, in this case) must be declared in the manifest with a `<receiver>` tag in order for `AlarmManager` to be able to trigger it. Be sure to include one within your `<application>` tag like so:
>
> ```
> <application>
>   ...
>   <receiver android:name=".AlarmReceiver"></receiver>
> </application>
> ```

Listing 6-7. *res/layout/main.xml*

```
<?xml version="1.0" encoding="utf-8"?>
<LinearLayout xmlns:android="http://schemas.android.com/apk/res/android"
  android:orientation="vertical"
  android:layout_width="fill_parent"
  android:layout_height="fill_parent">
  <Button
    android:id="@+id/start"
    android:layout_width="fill_parent"
    android:layout_height="wrap_content"
    android:text="Start Alarm"
  />
  <Button
    android:id="@+id/stop"
    android:layout_width="fill_parent"
    android:layout_height="wrap_content"
    android:text="Cancel Alarm"
  />
</LinearLayout>
```

Listing 6-8. *Activity to Register/Unregister Alarms*

```
public class AlarmActivity extends Activity implements View.OnClickListener {

    private PendingIntent mAlarmIntent;

    @Override
    public void onCreate(Bundle savedInstanceState) {
        super.onCreate(savedInstanceState);
        setContentView(R.layout.main);
        //Attach the listener to both buttons
        findViewById(R.id.start).setOnClickListener(this);
        findViewById(R.id.stop).setOnClickListener(this);
        //Create the launch sender
        Intent launchIntent = new Intent(this, AlarmReceiver.class);
        mAlarmIntent = PendingIntent.getBroadcast(this, 0, launchIntent, 0);
```

```
    }

    @Override
    public void onClick(View v) {
        AlarmManager manager = (AlarmManager)getSystemService(Context.ALARM_SERVICE);
        long interval = 5*1000; //5 seconds

        switch(v.getId()) {
        case R.id.start:
            Toast.makeText(this, "Scheduled", Toast.LENGTH_SHORT).show();
            manager.setRepeating(AlarmManager.ELAPSED_REALTIME,
                    SystemClock.elapsedRealtime()+interval,
                    interval,
                    mAlarmIntent);
            break;
        case R.id.stop:
            Toast.makeText(this, "Canceled", Toast.LENGTH_SHORT).show();
            manager.cancel(mAlarmIntent);
            break;
        default:
            break;
        }
    }
}
```

In this example, we have provided a very basic BroadcastReceiver that, when triggered, will simply display the current time as a Toast. That receiver must be registered in the application's manifest with a <receiver> tag. Otherwise, AlarmManager—which is external to your application—will not be aware of how to trigger it. The sample Activity presents two buttons: one to begin firing regular alarms, and the other to cancel them.

The operation to trigger is referenced by a PendingIntent, which will be used to both set and cancel the alarms. We create an Intent referencing the application's BroadcastReceiver directly, and then we use a PendingIntent from that using getBroadcast() (because we are creating a reference to a BroadcastReceiver).

> **REMINDER:** PendingIntent has the creator methods getActivity() and getService() as well. Be sure to reference the correct application component you are triggering when creating this piece.

When the start button is pressed, the Activity registers a repeating alarm using AlarmManager.setRepeating(). In addition to PendingIntent, this method takes some parameters to determine when to trigger the alarms. The first parameter defines the alarm type, in terms of the units of time to use and whether or not the alarm should occur when the device is in sleep mode. In the example, we chose ELAPSED_REALTIME, which indicates a value (in milliseconds) since the last device boot. In addition, there are three other modes that may be used:

- ELAPSED_REALTIME_WAKEUP
  - The alarm times are referenced to time elapsed and will wake the device to trigger if it is asleep.
- RTC
  - The alarm times are referenced to UTC time.
- RTC_WAKEUP
  - The alarm times are referenced to UTC time and will wake the device to trigger if it is asleep.

The following parameters (respectively) refer to the first time the alarm will trigger and the interval on which it should repeat. Because the chosen alarm type is ELAPSED_REALTIME, the start time must also be relative to elapsed time; SystemClock.elapsedRealtime() provides the current time in this format.

The alarm in the example is registered to trigger five seconds after the button is pressed, and then every five seconds after that. Every five seconds, a Toast will come onscreen with the current time value, even if the application is no longer running or in front of the user. When the user displays the Activity and presses the stop button, any pending alarms matching our PendingIntent are immediately canceled and will stop the flow of Toasts.

A More Precise Example

What if we wanted to schedule an alarm to occur at a specific time? Perhaps once per day at 9:00 AM? Setting AlarmManager with some slightly different parameters could accomplish this. See Listing 6-9.

Listing 6-9. *Precision Alarm*

```
long oneDay = 24*3600*1000; //24 hours
long firstTime;

//Get a Calendar (defaults to today)
//Set the time to 09:00:00
Calendar startTime = Calendar.getInstance();
startTime.set(Calendar.HOUR_OF_DAY, 9);
startTime.set(Calendar.MINUTE, 0);
startTime.set(Calendar.SECOND, 0);
```

```
//Get a Calendar at the current time
Calendar now = Calendar.getInstance();

if(now.before(startTime)) {
    //It's not 9AM yet, start today
    firstTime = startTime.getTimeInMillis();
} else {
    //Start 9AM tomorrow
    startTime.add(Calendar.DATE, 1);
    firstTime = startTime.getTimeInMillis();
}

//Set the alarm
 manager.setRepeating(AlarmManager.RTC_WAKEUP,
                firstTime,
                oneDay,
                mAlarmIntent);
```

This example uses an alarm that is referenced to real time. A determination is made whether the next occurrence of 9:00 AM will be today or tomorrow, and that value is returned as the initial trigger time for the alarm. The calculated value of 24 hours in terms of milliseconds is then passed as the interval so that the alarm triggers once per day from that point forward.

IMPORTANT: Alarms do not persist through a device reboot. If a device is powered off and then back on, any previously registered alarms must be rescheduled.

6–4. Creating Sticky Operations

Problem

Your application needs to execute one or more background operations that will run to completion even if the user suspends the application.

Solution

(API Level 3)

Create an IntentService to handle the work. IntentService is a wrapper around Android's base Service implementation, the key component to doing work in the background without interaction from the user. IntentService queues incoming work (expressed using Intents), processing each request in turn, and then stops itself when the queue is empty.

IntentService also handles creation of the worker thread needed to do the work in the background, so it is not necessary to use AsyncTask or Java Threads to ensure that the operation is properly in the background.

This recipe provides an example of using IntentService to create a central manager of background operations. In the example, the manager will be invoked externally with calls to Context.startService(). The manager will queue up all requests received, and process them individually with a call to onHandleIntent().

How It Works

Let's take a look at how to construct a simple IntentService implementation to handle a series of background operations. See Listing 6-10.

Listing 6-10. *IntentService Handling Operations*

```
public class OperationsManager extends IntentService {

    public static final String ACTION_EVENT = "ACTION_EVENT";
    public static final String ACTION_WARNING = "ACTION_WARNING";
    public static final String ACTION_ERROR = "ACTION_ERROR";
    public static final String EXTRA_NAME = "eventName";

    private static final String LOGTAG = "EventLogger";

    private IntentFilter matcher;

    public OperationsManager() {
        super("OperationsManager");
        //Create the filter for matching incoming requests
        matcher = new IntentFilter();
        matcher.addAction(ACTION_EVENT);
        matcher.addAction(ACTION_WARNING);
        matcher.addAction(ACTION_ERROR);
    }

    @Override
    protected void onHandleIntent(Intent intent) {
        //Check for a valid request
        if(!matcher.matchAction(intent.getAction())) {
            Toast.makeText(this, "OperationsManager: Invalid Request",
                    Toast.LENGTH_SHORT).show();
            return;
        }
```

```
        //Handle each request directly in this method. Don't create more threads.
        if(TextUtils.equals(intent.getAction(), ACTION_EVENT)) {
            logEvent(intent.getStringExtra(EXTRA_NAME));
        }
        if(TextUtils.equals(intent.getAction(), ACTION_WARNING)) {
            logWarning(intent.getStringExtra(EXTRA_NAME));
        }
        if(TextUtils.equals(intent.getAction(), ACTION_ERROR)) {
            logError(intent.getStringExtra(EXTRA_NAME));
        }
    }

    private void logEvent(String name) {
        try {
            //Simulate a long network operation by sleeping
            Thread.sleep(5000);
            Log.i(LOGTAG, name);
        } catch (InterruptedException e) {
            e.printStackTrace();
        }
    }

    private void logWarning(String name) {
        try {
            //Simulate a long network operation by sleeping
            Thread.sleep(5000);
            Log.w(LOGTAG, name);
        } catch (InterruptedException e) {
            e.printStackTrace();
        }
    }

    private void logError(String name) {
        try {
            //Simulate a long network operation by sleeping
            Thread.sleep(5000);
            Log.e(LOGTAG, name);
        } catch (InterruptedException e) {
            e.printStackTrace();
        }
    }
}
```

IntentService does not have a default constructor (one that takes no parameters), so a custom implementation must implement a constructor that calls through to super with a service name. This name is of little technical importance, as it is only useful for debugging; Android uses the name provided to name the worker thread that it creates.

All requests are processed by the service through the onHandleIntent() method. This method is called on the provided worker thread, so all work should be done directly here; no new threads or operations should be created. When onHandleIntent() returns, this is the signal to the IntentService to begin processing the next request in the queue.

This example provides three logging operations that can be requested using different action strings on the request Intents. For demonstration purposes, each operation writes the provided message out to the device log by using a specific logging level (INFO, WARNING, or ERROR). Note that the message itself is passed as an extra of the request Intent. Use the data and extra fields of each Intent to hold any parameters for the operation, leaving the action field to define the operation type.

The service in the example maintains an IntentFilter, which is used for convenience to determine whether a valid request has been made. All of the valid actions are added to the filter when the service is created, allowing us to call IntentFilter.matchAction() on any incoming request to determine if it includes an action we can process here.

Listings 6-11 and 6-12 reveal an example including an Activity calling in to this service to perform work.

Listing 6-11. *AndroidManifest.xml*

```
<?xml version="1.0" encoding="utf-8"?>
<manifest xmlns:android="http://schemas.android.com/apk/res/android"
    package="com.examples.sticky"
    android:versionCode="1"
    android:versionName="1.0">
    <uses-sdk android:minSdkVersion="3" />

    <application android:icon="@drawable/icon" android:label="@string/app_name">
        <activity android:name=".ReportActivity"
                  android:label="@string/app_name">
            <intent-filter>
                <action android:name="android.intent.action.MAIN" />
                <category android:name="android.intent.category.LAUNCHER" />
            </intent-filter>
        </activity>
        <service android:name=".OperationsManager"></service>
    </application>
</manifest>
```

REMINDER: The package attribute in AndroidManifest.xml must match the package you have chosen for your application; "`com.examples.sticky`" is simply the chosen package for our example here.

NOTE: Because `IntentService` is invoked as a `Service`, it must be declared in the application manifest with a `<service>` tag.

Listing 6-12. *Activity Calling IntentService*

```
public class ReportActivity extends Activity {

    @Override
    public void onCreate(Bundle savedInstanceState) {
        super.onCreate(savedInstanceState);
        logEvent("CREATE");
    }

    @Override
    public void onStart() {
        super.onStart();
        logEvent("START");
    }

    @Override
    public void onResume() {
        super.onResume();
        logEvent("RESUME");
    }

    @Override
    public void onPause() {
        super.onPause();
        logWarning("PAUSE");
    }

    @Override
    public void onStop() {
        super.onStop();
        logWarning("STOP");
    }
```

```
    @Override
    public void onDestroy() {
        super.onDestroy();
        logWarning("DESTROY");
    }

    private void logEvent(String event) {
        Intent intent = new Intent(this, OperationsManager.class);
        intent.setAction(OperationsManager.ACTION_EVENT);
        intent.putExtra(OperationsManager.EXTRA_NAME, event);

        startService(intent);
    }

    private void logWarning(String event) {
        Intent intent = new Intent(this, OperationsManager.class);
        intent.setAction(OperationsManager.ACTION_WARNING);
        intent.putExtra(OperationsManager.EXTRA_NAME, event);

        startService(intent);
    }
}
```

This Activity isn't much to look at, as all the interesting events are sent out through the device log instead of to the user interface. Nevertheless, it helps illustrate the queue-processing behavior of the service we created in the previous example. As the Activity becomes visible, it will call through all of its normal life-cycle methods, resulting in three requests made of the logging service. As each request is processed, a line will output to the log and the service will move on.

> **TIP:** These log statements are visible through the `logcat` tool provided with the SDK. The `logcat` output from a device or emulator is visible from within most development environments (including Eclipse) or from the command line by typing `adb logcat`.

Notice also that when the service is finished with all three requests, a notification is logged out that the service has been stopped. `IntentServices` are only around in memory for as long as is required to complete the job; this is a very useful feature for your services to have, making them good citizens of the system.

Pressing either the HOME or BACK buttons will cause more of the life-cycle methods to generate requests of the service, and the Pause/Stop/Destroy portion calls a separate operation in the service, causing their messages to be logged as warnings; simply setting the action string of the request intent to a different value controls this.

Notice that messages continue to be output to the log, even after the application is no longer visible (or even if another application is opened instead). This is the power of the Android Service component at work. These operations are protected from the system until they are complete, regardless of user behavior.

A Possible Drawback

In each of the operation methods, a five-second delay has been placed to simulate the time required for an actual request to be made of a remote API or some similar operation. When running this example, it also helps to illustrate that `IntentService` handles all requests sent to it in a serial fashion with a single worker thread. The example queues multiple requests in succession from each life-cycle method; however, the result will still be a log message every five seconds, because `IntentService` does not start a new request until the current one is complete (essentially, when `onHandleIntent()` returns).

If your application requires concurrency from sticky background tasks, you may need to create a more customized `Service` implementation that uses a pool of threads to execute work. The beauty of Android being an open source project is that you can go directly to the source code for `IntentService` and use it as a starting point for such an implementation if it is required, minimizing the amount of time and custom code required.

6–5. Running Persistent Background Operations

Problem

Your application has a component that must be running in the background indefinitely, performing some operation or monitoring certain events to occur.

Solution

(API Level 1)

Build the component into a `Service`. Services are designed as background components that an application may start and leave running for an indefinite amount of time. Services are also given elevated status above other background processes in terms of protection from being killed in low-memory conditions.

Services may be started and stopped explicitly for operations that do not require a direct connection to another component (like an Activity). However, if the application must interact directly with the Service, a binding interface is provided to pass data. In these instances, the service may be started and stopped implicitly by the system as is required to fulfill its requested bindings.

The key thing to remember with Service implementations is to always be user-friendly. An indefinite operation most likely should not be started unless the user explicitly requests it. The overall application should probably contain an interface or setting that allows the user to control enabling or disabling such a Service.

How It Works

Listing 6-13 is an example of a persisted service that is used to track and log the user's location over a certain period.

Listing 6-13. *Persistent Tracking Service*

```
public class TrackerService extends Service implements LocationListener {

    private static final String LOGTAG = "TrackerService";

    private LocationManager manager;
    private ArrayList<Location> storedLocations;

    private boolean isTracking = false;

    /* Service Setup Methods */
    @Override
    public void onCreate() {
        manager = (LocationManager)getSystemService(LOCATION_SERVICE);
        storedLocations = new ArrayList<Location>();
        Log.i(LOGTAG, "Tracking Service Running...");
    }

    @Override
    public void onDestroy() {
        manager.removeUpdates(this);
        Log.i(LOGTAG, "Tracking Service Stopped...");
    }
```

```
public void startTracking() {
    if(!manager.isProviderEnabled(LocationManager.GPS_PROVIDER)) {
        return;
    }
    Toast.makeText(this, "Starting Tracker", Toast.LENGTH_SHORT).show();
    manager.requestLocationUpdates(LocationManager.GPS_PROVIDER, 30000, 0, this);

    isTracking = true;
}

public void stopTracking() {
    Toast.makeText(this, "Stopping Tracker", Toast.LENGTH_SHORT).show();
    manager.removeUpdates(this);
    isTracking = false;
}

public boolean isTracking() {
    return isTracking;
}

/* Service Access Methods */
public class TrackerBinder extends Binder {
    TrackerService getService() {
        return TrackerService.this;
    }
}

private final IBinder binder = new TrackerBinder();

@Override
public IBinder onBind(Intent intent) {
    return binder;
}

public int getLocationsCount() {
    return storedLocations.size();
}

public ArrayList<Location> getLocations() {
    return storedLocations;
}

/* LocationListener Methods */
@Override
public void onLocationChanged(Location location) {
    Log.i("TrackerService", "Adding new location");
    storedLocations.add(location);
}
```

```
    @Override
    public void onProviderDisabled(String provider) { }

    @Override
    public void onProviderEnabled(String provider) { }

    @Override
    public void onStatusChanged(String provider, int status, Bundle extras) { }
}
```

This Service monitors and tracks the updates it receives from the LocationManager. When the Service is created, it prepares a blank list of Location items and waits to begin tracking. An external component, such as an Activity, can call startTracking() and stopTracking() to enable and disable the flow of location updates to the Service. In addition, methods are exposed to access the list of locations that the Service has logged.

Because this Service requires direct interaction from an Activity or other component, a Binder interface is required. The Binder concept can get complex when a Service has to communicate across process boundaries, but for instances like this, where everything is local to the same process, a very simple Binder is created with one method, getService(), to return the Service instance itself to the caller. We'll look at this in more detail from the Activity's perspective in a moment.

When tracking is enabled on the service, it registers for updates with LocationManager, and it stores every update received in its locations list. Notice that requestLocationUpdates() was called with a minimum time of 30 seconds. Because this Service is expected to be running for a long time, it is prudent to space out the updates to give the GPS (and consequently the battery) a little rest.

Now let's take a look at a simple Activity that allows the user access into this Serviceservice. See Listings 6-14 through 6-16.

Listing 6-14. *AndroidManifest.xml*

```
<?xml version="1.0" encoding="utf-8"?>
<manifest xmlns:android="http://schemas.android.com/apk/res/android"
    package="com.examples.service"
    android:versionCode="1"
    android:versionName="1.0">
    <uses-sdk android:minSdkVersion="1" />
    <application android:icon="@drawable/icon" android:label="@string/app_name">
        <activity android:name=".ServiceActivity"
                  android:label="@string/app_name">
            <intent-filter>
                <action android:name="android.intent.action.MAIN" />
```

```
                <category android:name="android.intent.category.LAUNCHER" />
            </intent-filter>
        </activity>
        <service android:name=".TrackerService"></service>
    </application>
    <uses-permission android:name="android.permission.ACCESS_FINE_LOCATION"/>
</manifest>
```

REMINDER: The `Service` must be declared in the application manifest using a `<service>` tag so Android knows how and where to call on it. Also, for this example the permission `android.permission.ACCESS_FINE_LOCATION` is required because we are working with the GPS.

Listing 6-15. *res/layout/main.xml*

```
<?xml version="1.0" encoding="utf-8"?>
<LinearLayout xmlns:android="http://schemas.android.com/apk/res/android"
  android:orientation="vertical"
  android:layout_width="fill_parent"
  android:layout_height="fill_parent">
  <Button
    android:id="@+id/enable"
    android:layout_width="fill_parent"
    android:layout_height="wrap_content"
    android:text="Start Tracking"
  />
  <Button
    android:id="@+id/disable"
    android:layout_width="fill_parent"
    android:layout_height="wrap_content"
    android:text="Stop Tracking"
  />
  <TextView
    android:id="@+id/status"
    android:layout_width="fill_parent"
    android:layout_height="wrap_content"
  />
</LinearLayout>
```

Listing 6-16. *Activity Interacting with Service*

```
public class ServiceActivity extends Activity implements View.OnClickListener {

    Button enableButton, disableButton;
    TextView statusView;
```

```
TrackerService trackerService;
Intent serviceIntent;

@Override
public void onCreate(Bundle savedInstanceState) {
    super.onCreate(savedInstanceState);
    setContentView(R.layout.main);
    enableButton = (Button)findViewById(R.id.enable);
    enableButton.setOnClickListener(this);
    disableButton = (Button)findViewById(R.id.disable);
    disableButton.setOnClickListener(this);
    statusView = (TextView)findViewById(R.id.status);

    serviceIntent = new Intent(this, TrackerService.class);
}

@Override
public void onResume() {
    super.onResume();
    //Starting the service makes it stick, regardless of bindings
    startService(serviceIntent);
    //Bind to the service
    bindService(serviceIntent, serviceConnection, Context.BIND_AUTO_CREATE);
}

@Override
public void onPause() {
    super.onPause();
    if(!trackerService.isTracking()) {
        //Stopping the service lets it die once unbound
        stopService(serviceIntent);
    }
    //Unbind from the service
    unbindService(serviceConnection);
}

@Override
public void onClick(View v) {
    switch(v.getId()) {
    case R.id.enable:
        trackerService.startTracking();
        break;
    case R.id.disable:
        trackerService.stopTracking();
        break;
    default:
        break;
    }
    updateStatus();
}
```

```
    private void updateStatus() {
        if(trackerService.isTracking()) {
            statusView.setText(
                String.format("Tracking enabled. %d locations
                    logged.",trackerService.getLocationsCount()));
        } else {
            statusView.setText("Tracking not currently enabled.");
        }
    }

    private ServiceConnection serviceConnection = new ServiceConnection() {
        public void onServiceConnected(ComponentName className, IBinder service) {
            trackerService = ((TrackerService.TrackerBinder)service).getService();
            updateStatus();
        }

        public void onServiceDisconnected(ComponentName className) {
            trackerService = null;
        }
    };
}
```

Figure 6-6 displays the basic Activity with two buttons for the user to enable and disable location tracking behavior, and a text display for the current service status.

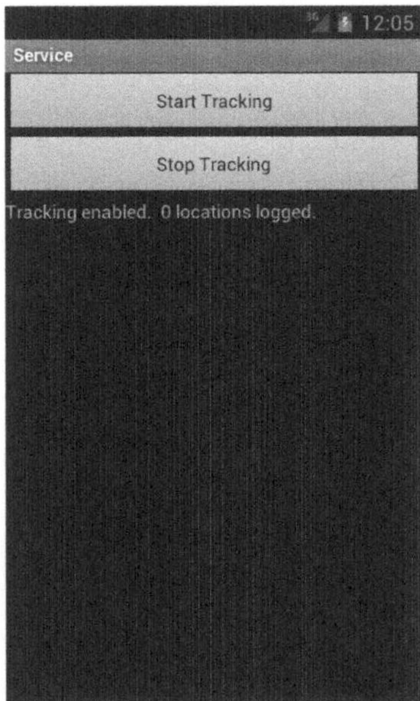

Figure 6-6. *ServiceActivity layout.*

While the Activity is visible, it is bound to the TrackerService. This is done with the help of the ServiceConnection interface, which provides callback methods when the binding and unbinding operations are complete. With the Service bound to the Activity, you can now make direct calls on all the public methods exposed by the Service.

However, bindings alone will not allow the Service to run for the long term; accessing the Service solely through its Binder interface causes it to be created and destroyed automatically along with the life cycle of this Activity. In this case, we want the Service to persist beyond when this Activity is in memory. In order to accomplish this, the Service is explicitly started via startService() before it is bound. There is no harm in sending start commands to a service that is already running, so we can safely do this in onResume() as well.

The Service will now continue running in memory, even after the Activity unbinds itself. In onPause() the example always checks whether the user has activated tracking, and if not it stops the service first. This allows the Service to die if it is not required for tracking, which keeps the Service from perpetually hanging out in memory if it has no real work to do.

Running this example and pressing the Start Tracking button will spin up the persisted service and the LocationManager. The user may leave the application at this point and the service will remain running, all the while logging all incoming location updates from the GPS. When the user returns to this application, he or she can see that the Service is still running and the current number of stored location points is displayed. Pressing Stop Tracking will end the process and allow the Service to die as soon as the user leaves the Activity once more.

6–6. Launching Other Applications

Problem

Your application requires a specific function that another application on the device is already programmed to do. Instead of overlapping functionality, you would like to launch the other application for the job instead.

Solution

(API Level 1)

Use an implicit Intent to tell the system what you are looking to do, and determine if any applications exist to meet the need. Most often, developers use Intents in an explicit fashion to start another Activity or Service, like so:

```
Intent intent = new Intent(this, NewActivity.class);
startActivity(intent);
```

By declaring the specific component we want to launch, the Intent is very explicit in its delivery. We also have the power to define an Intent in terms of its action, category, data, and type to define a more implicit requirement of what task we want to accomplish.

External applications are always launched within the same Android task as your application when fired in this fashion, so once the operation is complete (or if the user backs out) the user is returned to your application. This keeps the experience seamless, allowing multiple applications to act as one from the user's perspective.

How It Works

When defining Intents in this fashion, it can be unclear what information you must include, because there is no published standard and it is possible for two applications offering the same service (reading a PDF file, for example) to define slightly different filters to listen for incoming Intents. You want to make sure to provide enough information for the system (or the user) to pick the best application to handle the required task.

The core piece of information to define on almost any implicit Intent is the action: a string value that is passed either in the constructor or via `Intent.setAction()`. This value tells Android what you want to do, whether it is to view a piece of content, send a message, select a choice, and so on. From there, the fields provided are scenario specific, and often multiple combinations can arrive at the same result. Let's take a look at some useful examples.

Read a PDF File

Components to display PDF documents are not included in the core SDK, although almost every consumer Android device on the market today ships with a PDF reader application, and many more are available through Google Play.

Because of this, it may not make sense to go through the trouble of embedding PDF display capabilities in your application.

Instead, Listing 6-17 illustrates how to find and launch another app to view the PDF.

Listing 6-17. *Method to View PDF*

```
private void viewPdf(Uri file) {
        Intent intent;
        intent = new Intent(Intent.ACTION_VIEW);
        intent.setDataAndType(file, "application/pdf");
        try {
            startActivity(intent);
        } catch (ActivityNotFoundException e) {
            //No application to view, ask to download one
            AlertDialog.Builder builder = new AlertDialog.Builder(this);
            builder.setTitle("No Application Found");
            builder.setMessage("We could not find an application to view PDFs."
                    +"  Would you like to download one from Android Market?");
            builder.setPositiveButton("Yes, Please",
                new DialogInterface.OnClickListener() {
                @Override
                public void onClick(DialogInterface dialog, int which) {
                    Intent marketIntent = new Intent(Intent.ACTION_VIEW);
                    marketIntent.setData(
                            Uri.parse("market://details?id=com.adobe.reader"));
                    startActivity(marketIntent);
                }
            });
            builder.setNegativeButton("No, Thanks", null);
            builder.create().show();
        }
    }
```

This example will open any local PDF file on the device (internal or external storage) by using the best application found. If no application is found on the device to view PDFs, a message will encourage the user to go to Google Play and download one.

The Intent we create for this is constructed with the generic `Intent.ACTION_VIEW` action string, telling the system we want to view the data provided in the Intent. The data file itself and its MIME type are also set to tell the system what kind of data we want to view.

> **TIP:** `Intent.setData()` and `Intent.setType()` clear each other's previous values when used. If you need to set both simultaneously, use `Intent.setDataAndType()`, as in the example.

If `startActivity()` fails with an `ActivityNotFoundException`, it means the user does not have an application installed on his or her device that can view PDFs. We want users to have the full experience, so if this happens, a dialog box will tell them of the problem and ask if he or she would like to go to Market and get a reader. If the user presses Yes, another implicit Intent will request that Google Play be opened directly to the application page for Adobe Reader, a free application the user may download to view PDF files. We'll discuss the `Uri` scheme used for this Intent in the next recipe.

Notice that the example method takes a `Uri` parameter to the local file. Here is an example of how to retrieve a `Uri` for files located on internal storage:

```
String filename = NAME_OF_YOUR_FILE;
File internalFile = getFileStreamPath(filename);
Uri internal = Uri.fromFile(internalFile);
```

The method `getFileStreamPath()` is called from a `Context`, so if this code is not in an Activity you must have reference to a `Context` object to call on. Here's how to create a `Uri` for files located on external storage:

```
String filename = NAME_OF_YOUR_FILE;
File externalFile = new File(Environment.getExternalStorageDirectory(),
filename);
Uri external = Uri.fromFile(externalFile);
```

This same example will work for any other document type as well by simply changing the MIME type attached to the Intent.

Share with Friends

Another popular feature for developers to include in their applications is a method of sharing the application content with others, either through e-mail, text messaging, or prominent social networks. All Android devices include applications for e-mail and text messaging, and most users who wish to share via a social network (like Facebook or Twitter) also have those mobile applications on their devices.

As it turns out, this task can also be accomplished using an implicit Intent because most of these applications respond to the `Intent.ACTION_SEND` action string in some way. Listing 6-18 is an example of allowing a user to post to any medium with a single Intent request.

Listing 6-18. *Sharing Intent*

```
private void shareContent(String update) {
    Intent intent = new Intent(Intent.ACTION_SEND);
    intent.setType("text/plain");
    intent.putExtra(Intent.EXTRA_TEXT, update);
    startActivity(Intent.createChooser(intent, "Share..."));
}
```

Here, we tell the system that we have a piece of text that we would like to send, passed in as an extra. This is a very generic request, and we expect more than one application to be able to handle it. By default, Android will present the user with a list of applications to select which he or she would like to open. In addition, some devices provide the user with a check box to set a selection as a default so the list is never shown again.

We would prefer to have a little more control over this process because we also expect multiple results every time. Therefore, instead of passing the Intent directly to `startActivity()`, we first pass it through `Intent.createChooser()`, which allows us to customize the title and guarantee the selection list will always be displayed.

When the user selects a choice, that specific application will launch with the `EXTRA_TEXT` prepopulated into the message entry box, ready for sharing!

ShareActionProvider

(API Level 14)

Starting with Android 4.0, a new widget was introduced to assist applications in sharing content by using a common mechanism called `ShareActionProvider`. It is designed to be added to an item in the options menu to show up either on the `ActionBar` or in the overflow. It also has an added feature for the users in that, by default, it ranks the share options it provides by usage. This means that options users click on most frequently will always be at the top of the list.

Implementing `ShareActionProvider` in a menu is quite simple, and it requires only a few more lines of code than creating the share `Intent` itself. Listing 6-19 shows how to attach the provider to a menu item.

Listing 6-19. *res/menu/options.xml*

```
<menu xmlns:android="http://schemas.android.com/apk/res/android">
    <item android:id="@+id/menu_share"
        android:showAsAction="ifRoom"
        android:title="Share"
        android:actionProviderClass="android.widget.ShareActionProvider"/>
</menu>
```

> **NOTE:** If you do not define your Menu in XML, you can still attach the ShareActionProvider by calling setActionProvider() inside your Java code.

Listing 6-20 shows how to attach the share Intent to the provider widget inside of an Activity.

Listing 6-20. *Providing the Share Intent*

```
@Override
public boolean onCreateOptionsMenu(Menu menu) {
    //Inflate the menu
    getMenuInflater().inflate(R.menu.options, menu);

    //Find the item and set the share Intent
    MenuItem item = menu.findItem(R.id.menu_share);
    ShareActionProvider provider = (ShareActionProvider) item.getActionProvider();

    Intent intent = new Intent(Intent.ACTION_SEND);
    intent.setType("text/plain");
    intent.putExtra(Intent.EXTRA_TEXT, update);
    provider.setShareIntent(intent);

    return true;
}
```

And that's it! The provider handles all the user interaction so your application doesn't even need to handle the user selection events for that MenuItem.

6–7. Launching System Applications

Problem

Your application requires a specific function that one of the system applications on the device is already programmed to do. Instead of overlapping functionality, you would like to launch the system application for the job instead.

Solution

(API Level 1)

Use an implicit Intent to tell the system which application you are interested in. Each system application subscribes to a custom `Uri` scheme that can be inserted as data into an implicit Intent to signify the specific application you need to launch.

External applications are always launched in the same task as your application when fired in this fashion, so once the task is complete (or if the user backs out) the user is returned to your application. This keeps the experience seamless, allowing multiple applications to act as one from the user's perspective.

How It Works

All of the following examples will construct Intents that can be used to launch system applications in various states. Once constructed, you should launch these applications by passing the Intent to `startActivity()`.

Browser

The browser application may be launched to display a web page or run a web search.

To display a web page, construct and launch the following Intent:

```
Intent pageIntent = new Intent();
pageIntent.setAction(Intent.ACTION_VIEW);
pageIntent.setData(Uri.parse("http://WEB_ADDRESS_TO_VIEW"));

startActivity(pageIntent);
```

This replaces the Uri in the data field with the page you would like to view. To launch a web search inside the browser, construct and launch the following Intent:

```
Intent searchIntent = new Intent();
searchIntent.setAction(Intent.ACTION_WEB_SEARCH);
searchIntent.putExtra(SearchManager.QUERY, STRING_TO_SEARCH);

startActivity(searchIntent);
```

This places the search query you want to execute as an extra in the Intent.

Phone Dialer

The dialer application may be launched to place a call to a specific number by using the following Intent:

```
Intent dialIntent = new Intent();
dialIntent.setAction(Intent.ACTION_DIAL);
dialIntent.setData(Uri.Parse("tel:8885551234");

startActivity(dialIntent);
```

This replaces the phone number in the data Uri with the number to call.

> **NOTE:** This action just brings up the dialer; it does not actually place the call. `Intent.ACTION_CALL` can be used to actually place the call directly, although Google discourages using this in most cases. Using `ACTION_CALL` will also require that the `android.permission.CALL_PHONE` permission be declared in the manifest.

Maps

The Maps application on the device can be launched to display a location or to provide directions between two points. If you know the latitude and longitude of the location you want to map, then create the following Intent:

```
Intent mapIntent = new Intent();
mapIntent.setAction(Intent.ACTION_VIEW);
mapIntent.setData(Uri.parse("geo:latitude,longitude"));

startActivity(mapIntent);
```

This replaces the coordinates for latitude and longitude of your location. For example, the Uri

```
"geo:37.422,122.084"
```

would map the location of Google's headquarters. If you know the address of the location to display, then create the following Intent:

```
Intent mapIntent = new Intent();
mapIntent.setAction(Intent.ACTION_VIEW);
mapIntent.setData(Uri.parse("geo:0,0?q=ADDRESS"));

startActivity(mapIntent);
```

This inserts the address you would like to map. For example, the Uri

```
"geo:0,0?q=1600 Amphitheatre Parkway, Mountain View, CA 94043"
```

would map the address of Google's headquarters.

> **TIP:** The Maps application will also accept a Uri where spaces in the Address query are replaced with the "+" character. If you are having trouble encoding a string with spaces in it, try replacing them with "+" instead.

If you would like to display directions between two locations, create the following Intent:

```
Intent mapIntent = new Intent();
mapIntent.setAction(Intent.ACTION_VIEW);
mapIntent.setData(Uri.parse("http://maps.google.com/maps?saddr=lat,lng&daddr=lat,lng"));

startActivity(mapIntent);
```

This inserts the locations for the start and end addresses.

It is also allowed for only one of the parameters to be included if you would like to open the Maps application with one address being open-ended. For example, the Uri

```
"http://maps.google.com/maps?&daddr=37.422,122.084"
```

would display the Maps application with the destination location prepopulated, but it would allow the user to enter his or her own start address.

E-mail

Any e-mail application on the device can be launched into compose mode by using the following Intent:

```
Intent mailIntent = new Intent();
mailIntent.setAction(Intent.ACTION_SEND);
mailIntent.setType("message/rfc822");
mailIntent.putExtra(Intent.EXTRA_EMAIL, new String[] {"recipient@gmail.com"});
mailIntent.putExtra(Intent.EXTRA_CC, new String[] {"carbon@gmail.com"});
mailIntent.putExtra(Intent.EXTRA_BCC, new String[] {"blind@gmail.com"});
mailIntent.putExtra(Intent.EXTRA_SUBJECT, "Email Subject");
mailIntent.putExtra(Intent.EXTRA_TEXT, "Body Text");
mailIntent.putExtra(Intent.EXTRA_STREAM, URI_TO_FILE);

startActivity(mailIntent);
```

In this scenario, the action and type fields are the only required pieces to bring up a blank e-mail message. All the remaining extras prepopulate specific fields of the e-mail message. Notice that `EXTRA_EMAIL` (which fills the To: field), `EXTRA_CC`, and `EXTRA_BCC` are passed string arrays, even if there is only one recipient to be placed there. File attachments may also be specified in the Intent using `EXTRA_STREAM`. The value passed here should be a `Uri` pointing to the local file to be attached.

If you need to attach more than one file to an e-mail, the requirements change slightly to the following:

```
Intent mailIntent = new Intent();
mailIntent.setAction(Intent.ACTION_SEND_MULTIPLE);
mailIntent.setType("message/rfc822");
mailIntent.putExtra(Intent.EXTRA_EMAIL, new String[] {"recipient@gmail.com"});
mailIntent.putExtra(Intent.EXTRA_CC, new String[] {"carbon@gmail.com"});
mailIntent.putExtra(Intent.EXTRA_BCC, new String[] {"blind@gmail.com"});
mailIntent.putExtra(Intent.EXTRA_SUBJECT, "Email Subject");
mailIntent.putExtra(Intent.EXTRA_TEXT, "Body Text");

ArrayList<Uri> files = new ArrayList<Uri>();
files.add(URI_TO_FIRST_FILE);
files.add(URI_TO_SECOND_FILE);
//...Repeat add() as often as necessary to add all the files you need
mailIntent.putParcelableArrayListExtra(Intent.EXTRA_STREAM, files);

startActivity(mailIntent);
```

Notice that the Intent's action string is now `ACTION_SEND_MULTIPLE`. All the primary fields remain the same as before, except for the data that gets added as the `EXTRA_STREAM`. This example creates a list of Uris pointing to the files you want to attach and adds them using `putParcelableArrayListExtra()`.

It is not uncommon for users to have multiple applications on their devices that can handle this content, so it is usually prudent to wrap either of these constructed Intents with `Intent.createChooser()` before passing it on to `startActivity()`.

SMS (Messages)

The messages application can be launched into compose mode for a new SMS message by using the following Intent:

```
Intent smsIntent = new Intent();
smsIntent.setAction(Intent.ACTION_VIEW);
smsIntent.setType("vnd.android-dir/mms-sms");
smsIntent.putExtra("address", "8885551234");
smsIntent.putExtra("sms_body", "Body Text");

startActivity(smsIntent);
```

As with composing e-mail, you must set the action and type at a minimum to launch the application with a blank message. Including the address and `sms_body extras` allows the application to prepopulate the recipient (address) and `body text (sms_body)` of the message.

Neither of these keys has a constant defined in the Android framework, which means that they are subject to change in the future. However, as of this writing, the keys behave as expected on all versions of Android.

Contact Picker

An application may launch the default contact picker for the user in order to make a selection from his or her contacts database using the following Intent:

```
static final int REQUEST_PICK = 100;

Intent pickIntent = new Intent();
pickIntent.setAction(Intent.ACTION_PICK);
pickIntent.setData(URI_TO_CONTACT_TABLE);

startActivityForResult(pickIntent, REQUEST_PICK);
```

This Intent requires the `CONTENT_URI` of the Contacts table you are interested in to be passed in the data field. Because of the major changes to the Contacts API in API Level 5 (Android 2.0) and later, this may not be the same `Uri` if you are supporting versions across that boundary.

For example, to pick a person from the contacts list on a device previous to 2.0, we would pass

```
android.provider.Contacts.People.CONTENT_URI
```

However, in 2.0 and later, similar data would be gathered by passing

```
android.provider.ContactsContract.Contacts.CONTENT_URI
```

Be sure to consult the API documentation with regards to the contact data you need to access. This Activity is also designed to return back a `Uri` representing the selection the user made, so you will want to launch this using `startActivityForResult()`.

Google Play

Google Play can be launched from within an application to display a specific application's details page or to run a search for specific keywords. To launch a specific applications market page, use the following Intent:

```
Intent marketIntent = new Intent();
marketIntent.setAction(Intent.ACTION_VIEW);
marketIntent.setData(Uri.parse("market://details?id=PACKAGE_NAME_HERE"));

startActivity(marketIntent);
```

This inserts the unique package name (such as "com.adobe.reader") of the application you want to display. If you would like to open the market with a search query, use this Intent:

```
Intent marketIntent = new Intent();
marketIntent.setAction(Intent.ACTION_VIEW);
marketIntent.setData(Uri.parse("market://search?q=SEARCH_QUERY"));

startActivity(marketIntent);
```

This will insert the query string you would like to search on. The search query itself can take one of three main forms:

- `q=<simple text string here>`
  - In this case, the search will be a keyword-style search of the market.
- `q=pname:<package name here>`
  - In this case, the package names will be searched, and only exact matches will be returned.
- `q=pub:<developer name here>`
  - In this case, the developer name field will be searched, and only exact matches will be returned.

6–8. Letting Other Applications Launch Your Application

Problem

You've created an application that is absolutely the best at doing a specific task, and you would like to expose an interface for other applications on the device to be able to run your application.

Solution

(API Level 1)

Create an `IntentFilter` on the Activity or Service you would like to expose, then publicly document the actions, data types, and extras that are required to access it properly. Recall that the action, category, and data/type of an Intent can all be used as criteria to match requests to your application. Any additional required or optional parameters should be passed in as extras.

How It Works

Let's say that you have created an application that includes an Activity to play a video and will marquee the video's title at the top of the screen during playback. You want to allow other applications to play video using your application, so we need to define a useful Intent structure for applications to pass in the required data and then create an `IntentFilter` on the Activity in the applications manifest to match.

This hypothetical Activity requires two pieces of data to do its job:

1. The Uri of a video, either local or remote
2. A string representing the video's title

If the application specializes in a certain type of video, we could define that a generic action (such as ACTION_VIEW) be used and filter more specifically on the data type of the video content we want to handle. Listing 6-21 is an example of how the Activity would be defined in the manifest to filter Intents in this manner.

Listing 6-21. *AndroidManifest.xml <activity> Element with Data Type Filter*

```
<activity android:name=".PlayerActivity">
    <intent-filter>
    <action android:name="android.intent.action.VIEW" />
    <category android:name="android.intent.category.DEFAULT" />
    <data android:mimeType="video/h264" />
    </intent-filter>
</activity>
```

This filter will match any Intent with Uri data that is either explicitly declared as an H.264 video clip or is determined to be H.264 upon inspecting the Uri file. An external application would then be able to call on this Activity to play a video using the following lines of code:

```
Uri videoFile = A_URI_OF_VIDEO_CONTENT;
Intent playIntent = new Intent(Intent.ACTION_VIEW);
playIntent.setDataAndType(videoFile, "video/h264");
playIntent.putExtra(Intent.EXTRA_TITLE, "My Video");
startActivity(playIntent);
```

In some cases, it may be more useful for an external application to directly reference this player as the target, regardless of the type of video they want to pass in. In this case, we would create a unique custom action string for Intents to implement. The filter attached to the Activity in the manifest would then only need to match the custom action string. See Listing 6-22.

Listing 6-22. *AndroidManifest.xml <activity> Element with Custom Action Filter*

```
<activity android:name=".PlayerActivity">
    <intent-filter>
    <action android:name="com.examples.myplayer.PLAY" />
    <category android:name="android.intent.category.DEFAULT" />
    </intent-filter>
</activity>
```

An external application could call on this Activity to play a video by using the following code:

```
Uri videoFile = A_URI_OF_VIDEO_CONTENT;
Intent playIntent = new Intent("com.examples.myplayer.PLAY");
playIntent.setData(videoFile);
playIntent.putExtra(Intent.EXTRA_TITLE, "My Video");
startActivity(playIntent);
```

Processing a Successful Launch

Regardless of how the Intent is matched to the Activity, once it is launched, we want to inspect the incoming Intent for the two pieces of data the Activity needs to complete its intended purpose. See Listing 6-23.

Listing 6-23. *Activity Inspecting Intent*

```
public class PlayerActivity extends Activity {

    public static final String ACTION_PLAY = "com.examples.myplayer.PLAY";

    @Override
    public void onCreate(Bundle savedInstanceState) {
        super.onCreate(savedInstanceState);
        setContentView(R.layout.main);

        //Inspect the Intent that launched us
        Intent incoming = getIntent();
        //Get the video URI from the data field
        Uri videoUri = incoming.getData();
        //Get the optional title extra, if it exists
        String title;
        if(incoming.hasExtra(Intent.EXTRA_TITLE)) {
            title = incoming.getStringExtra(Intent.EXTRA_TITLE);
        } else {
            title = "";
        }

        /* Begin playing the video and displaying the title */
    }

    /* Remainder of the Activity Code */

}
```

When the Activity is launched, the calling Intent can be retrieved with `Activity.getIntent()`. Because the `Uri` for the video content is passed in the data field of the Intent, it is unpacked by calling `Intent.getData()`. The video's title is an optional value for calling Intents, so we check the extras bundle to first see if the caller decided to pass it in; if it exists, that value is unpacked from the Intent as well.

Notice that the `PlayerActivity` in this example did define the custom action string as a constant, but it was not referenced in the sample Intent we constructed above to launch the Activity. Since this call is coming from an external application, it does not have access to the shared public constants defined in this application.

For this reason, it is also a good idea to reuse the Intent extra keys already in the SDK whenever possible, as opposed to defining new constants. In this example, we chose the standard Intent.EXTRA_TITLE to define the optional extra to be passed instead of creating a custom key for this value.

6–9. Interacting with Contacts

Problem

Your application needs to interact directly with the `ContentProvider` exposed by Android to the user's contacts to add, view, change, or remove information from the database.

Solution

(API Level 5)

Use the interface exposed by `ContactsContract` to access the data. `ContactsContract` is a vast `ContentProvider` API that attempts to aggregate the contact information stored in the system from multiple user accounts into a single data store. The result is a maze of `Uris`, tables, and columns, from which data may be accessed and modified.

The Contact structure is a hierarchy with three tiers: Contacts, RawContacts, and Data.

- A Contact conceptually represents a person, and it is an aggregation of all `RawContacts` believed by Android to represent that same person.
- `RawContacts` represents a collection of data stored in the device from a specific device account, such as the user's e-mail address book, Facebook account, or otherwise.
- Data elements are the specific pieces of information attached to `RawContacts`, such as an e-mail address, phone number, or postal address.

The complete API has too many combinations and options for us to cover them all here, so consult the SDK documentation for all possibilities. We will investigate how to construct the basic building blocks for performing queries and making changes to the contacts data set.

How It Works

The Android Contacts API boils down to a complex database with multiple tables and joins. Therefore, the methods for accessing the data are no different than those used to access any other SQLite database from an application.

Listing/Viewing Contacts

Let's look at an example Activity that lists all contact entries in the database, and it displays more detail when an item is selected. See Listing 6-24.

> **IMPORTANT:** In order to display information from the Contacts API in your application, you will need to declare `android.permission.READ_CONTACTS` in the application manifest.

Listing 6-24. *Activity Displaying Contacts*

```
public class ContactsActivity extends ListActivity implements
        AdapterView.OnItemClickListener {

    Cursor mContacts;

    @Override
    public void onCreate(Bundle savedInstanceState) {
        super.onCreate(savedInstanceState);
        // Return all contacts, ordered by name
        String[] projection = new String[] { ContactsContract.Contacts._ID,
                ContactsContract.Contacts.DISPLAY_NAME };
        mContacts = managedQuery(ContactsContract.Contacts.CONTENT_URI,
                projection, null, null, ContactsContract.Contacts.DISPLAY_NAME);

        // Display all contacts in a ListView
        SimpleCursorAdapter mAdapter = new SimpleCursorAdapter(this,
                android.R.layout.simple_list_item_1, mContacts,
                new String[] { ContactsContract.Contacts.DISPLAY_NAME },
                new int[] { android.R.id.text1 });
        setListAdapter(mAdapter);
        // Listen for item selections
        getListView().setOnItemClickListener(this);
    }

    @Override
    public void onItemClick(AdapterView<?> parent, View v, int position, long id) {
        if (mContacts.moveToPosition(position)) {
            int selectedId = mContacts.getInt(0); // _ID column
```

```
// Gather email data from email table
Cursor email = getContentResolver().query(
        CommonDataKinds.Email.CONTENT_URI,
        new String[] { CommonDataKinds.Email.DATA },
        ContactsContract.Data.CONTACT_ID + " = " + selectedId, null, null);
// Gather phone data from phone table
Cursor phone = getContentResolver().query(
        CommonDataKinds.Phone.CONTENT_URI,
        new String[] { CommonDataKinds.Phone.NUMBER },
        ContactsContract.Data.CONTACT_ID + " = " + selectedId, null, null);
// Gather addresses from address table
Cursor address = getContentResolver().query(
        CommonDataKinds.StructuredPostal.CONTENT_URI,
        new String[] { CommonDataKinds.StructuredPostal.FORMATTED_ADDRESS },
        ContactsContract.Data.CONTACT_ID + " = " + selectedId, null, null);

//Build the dialog message
StringBuilder sb = new StringBuilder();
sb.append(email.getCount() + " Emails\n");
if (email.moveToFirst()) {
    do {
        sb.append("Email: " + email.getString(0));
        sb.append('\n');
    } while (email.moveToNext());
    sb.append('\n');
}
sb.append(phone.getCount() + " Phone Numbers\n");
if (phone.moveToFirst()) {
    do {
        sb.append("Phone: " + phone.getString(0));
        sb.append('\n');
    } while (phone.moveToNext());
    sb.append('\n');
}
sb.append(address.getCount() + " Addresses\n");
if (address.moveToFirst()) {
    do {
        sb.append("Address:\n" + address.getString(0));
    } while (address.moveToNext());
    sb.append('\n');
}

AlertDialog.Builder builder = new AlertDialog.Builder(this);
builder.setTitle(mContacts.getString(1)); // Display name
builder.setMessage(sb.toString());
builder.setPositiveButton("OK", null);
builder.create().show();

// Finish temporary cursors
email.close();
```

```
                phone.close();
                address.close();
            }
        }
}
```

As you can see, referencing all the tables and columns in this API can result in very verbose code. All of the references to Uris, tables, and columns in this example are inner classes stemming off of ContactsContract. It is important to verify when interacting with the Contacts API that you are referencing the proper classes, as any Contacts classes not stemming from ContactsContract are deprecated and incompatible.

When the Activity is created, we make a simple query on the core Contacts table by calling Activity.managedQuery() with Contacts.CONTENT_URI, requesting only the columns we need to wrap the cursor in a ListAdapter. The resulting cursor is displayed in a list on the user interface. The example leverages the convenience behavior of ListActivity to provide a ListView as the content view so that we do not have to manage these components.

At this point, the user may scroll through all the contact entries on the device, and he or she can tap on one to get more information. When a list item is selected, the _ID value of that particular contact is recorded and the application goes out to the other ContactsContract.Data tables to gather more detailed information. Notice that the information for this single contact is spread across multiple tables (e-mails in an e-mail table, phone numbers in a phone table, and so on), requiring multiple queries to obtain.

Each CommonDataKinds table has a unique CONTENT_URI for the query to reference, as well as a unique set of column aliases for requesting the data. All of the rows in these data tables are linked to the specific contact through the Data.CONTACT_ID, so each cursor asks to return only rows where the values match.

With all the data collected for the selected contact, we iterate through the results to display in a dialog to the user. Because the data in these tables are an aggregation of multiple sources, it is not uncommon for all of these queries to return multiple results. With each cursor, we display the number of results, and then append each value included. When all the data is composed, the dialog is created and shown to the user.

As a final step, all temporary and unmanaged cursors are closed as soon as they are no longer required.

Running the Application

The first thing that you may notice when running this application on a device that has any number of accounts set up is that the list seems insurmountably long, certainly much longer than what shows up when running the Contacts application bundled with the device. The Contacts API allows for the storage of grouped entries that may be hidden from the user and are used for internal purposes. Gmail often uses this to store incoming e-mail addresses for quick access, even if an address is not associated with a true contact.

In the next example, we will show how to filter this list, but for now marvel at the amount of data truly stored in the Contacts table.

Changing/Adding Contacts

Now let's look at an example Activity that manipulates the data for a specific contact. See Listing 6-25.

> **IMPORTANT:** In order to interact with the Contacts API in your application, you must declare `android.permission.READ_CONTACTS` and `android.permission.WRITE_CONTACTS` in the application manifest.

Listing 6-25. *Activity Writing to Contacts API*

```
public class ContactsEditActivity extends ListActivity implements
            AdapterView.OnItemClickListener, DialogInterface.OnClickListener {

    private static final String TEST_EMAIL = "test@email.com";

    private Cursor mContacts, mEmail;
    private int selectedContactId;

    @Override
    public void onCreate(Bundle savedInstanceState) {
        super.onCreate(savedInstanceState);
        // Return all contacts, ordered by name
        String[] projection = new String[] { ContactsContract.Contacts._ID,
                ContactsContract.Contacts.DISPLAY_NAME };
        //List only contacts visible to the user
        mContacts = managedQuery(ContactsContract.Contacts.CONTENT_URI,
                projection,
                ContactsContract.Contacts.IN_VISIBLE_GROUP+" = 1",
                null, ContactsContract.Contacts.DISPLAY_NAME);
```

```
    // Display all contacts in a ListView
    SimpleCursorAdapter mAdapter = new SimpleCursorAdapter(this,
            android.R.layout.simple_list_item_1, mContacts,
            new String[] { ContactsContract.Contacts.DISPLAY_NAME },
            new int[] { android.R.id.text1 });

    setListAdapter(mAdapter);
    // Listen for item selections
    getListView().setOnItemClickListener(this);
}

@Override
public void onItemClick(AdapterView<?> parent, View v, int position, long id) {
    if (mContacts.moveToPosition(position)) {
        selectedContactId = mContacts.getInt(0); // _ID column
        // Gather email data from email table
        String[] projection = new String[] { ContactsContract.Data._ID,
                ContactsContract.CommonDataKinds.Email.DATA };
        mEmail = getContentResolver().query(
                ContactsContract.CommonDataKinds.Email.CONTENT_URI,
                projection,
                ContactsContract.Data.CONTACT_ID+" = "+selectedContactId,
                null, null);
        AlertDialog.Builder builder = new AlertDialog.Builder(this);
        builder.setTitle("Email Addresses");
        builder.setCursor(mEmail, this,
                ContactsContract.CommonDataKinds.Email.DATA);
        builder.setPositiveButton("Add", this);
        builder.setNegativeButton("Cancel", null);
        builder.create().show();
    }
}

@Override
public void onClick(DialogInterface dialog, int which) {
    //Data must be associated with a RAW contact, retrieve the first raw ID
    Cursor raw = getContentResolver().query(
            ContactsContract.RawContacts.CONTENT_URI,
            new String[] { ContactsContract.Contacts._ID },
            ContactsContract.Data.CONTACT_ID+" = "+selectedContactId, null, null);
    if(!raw.moveToFirst()) {
        return;
    }

    int rawContactId = raw.getInt(0);
    ContentValues values = new ContentValues();
    switch(which) {
    case DialogInterface.BUTTON_POSITIVE:
        //User wants to add a new email
        values.put(ContactsContract.CommonDataKinds.Email.RAW_CONTACT_ID,
```

```
                    rawContactId);
            values.put(ContactsContract.Data.MIMETYPE,
                    ContactsContract.CommonDataKinds.Email.CONTENT_ITEM_TYPE);
            values.put(ContactsContract.CommonDataKinds.Email.DATA, TEST_EMAIL);
            values.put(ContactsContract.CommonDataKinds.Email.TYPE,
                    ContactsContract.CommonDataKinds.Email.TYPE_OTHER);
            getContentResolver().insert(ContactsContract.Data.CONTENT_URI, values);
            break;
        default:
            //User wants to edit selection
            values.put(ContactsContract.CommonDataKinds.Email.DATA, TEST_EMAIL);
            values.put(ContactsContract.CommonDataKinds.Email.TYPE,
                    ContactsContract.CommonDataKinds.Email.TYPE_OTHER);
            getContentResolver().update(ContactsContract.Data.CONTENT_URI, values,
                    ContactsContract.Data._ID+" = "+mEmail.getInt(0), null);
            break;
        }

        //Don't need the email cursor anymore
        mEmail.close();
    }
}
```

In this example, we start out as before, performing a query for all entries in the Contacts database. This time, we provide a single selection criterion:

```
ContactsContract.Contacts.IN_VISIBLE_GROUP+" = 1"
```

The effect of this line is to limit the returned entries to only those that include entries that are visible to the user through the Contacts user interface. This will (drastically, in some cases) reduce the size of the list displayed in the Activity and will make it more closely match the list displayed in the Contacts application.

When the user selects a contact from this list, a dialog is displayed with a list of all the e-mail entries attached to that contact. If a specific address is selected from the list, that entry is edited; if the add button is pressed a new e-mail address entry is added. For the purposes of simplifying the example, we do not provide an interface to enter a new e-mail address. Instead, a constant value is inserted, either as a new record or as an update to the selected one.

Data elements, such as e-mail addresses, can only be associated with a `RawContact`. Therefore, when we want to add a new e-mail address, we must obtain the ID of one of the RawContacts represented by the higher-level contact that the user selected. For the purposes of the example we aren't terribly interested in which one, so we retrieve the ID of the first RawContact that matches. This value is only required for doing an insert, because the update references the distinct row ID of the e-mail record already present in the table.

The Uri provided in CommonDataKinds that was used as an alias to read this data cannot be used to make updates and changes. Inserts and updates must be called directly on the ContactsContract.Data Uri. What this means (besides referencing a different Uri in the operation method) is that an extra piece of metadata, the MIMETYPE, must also be specified. Without setting the MIMETYPE field for inserted data, subsequent queries made may not recognize it as a contact's e-mail address.

Aggregating at Work

Because this example updates records by adding or editing e-mail addresses with the same value, it offers a unique opportunity to see Android's aggregation operations in real time. As you run this example application, you may take notice of the fact that adding or editing contacts to give them the same e-mail address often triggers Android to start thinking that previously separate contacts are now the same people. Even in this sample application, as the managed query attached to the core Contacts table updates, notice that certain contacts will disappear as they become aggregated together.

> **NOTE:** Contact aggregation behavior is not implemented fully on the Android emulator. To see this effect in full you will need to run the code on a real device.

Maintaining a Reference

The Android Contacts API introduces one more concept that can be important depending on the scope of the application. Because of this aggregation process that occurs, the distinct row ID that refers to a contact becomes quite volatile; a certain contact may receive a new _ID when it is aggregated together with another one.

If your application requires a long-standing reference to a specific contact, it is recommended that your application persist the ContactsContract.Contacts.LOOKUP_KEY instead of the row ID. When querying for a Contact using this key, a special Uri is also provided as the ContactsContract.Contacts.CONTENT_LOOKUP_URI. Using these values to query records over the long term will protect your application from getting confused by the automatic aggregation process.

6–10. Picking Device Media

Problem

Your application needs to import a user-selected media item (audio, video, or image) for display or playback.

Solution

(API Level 1)

Use an implicit Intent targeted with `Intent.ACTION_GET_CONTENT` to bring up a system media picker interface. Firing this Intent with a matching content type for the media of interest (audio, video, or image) will present the user with a picker interface to select an item, and the Intent result will include a Uri pointing to the selection he or she made.

How It Works

Let's take a look at this technique used in the context of an example Activity. See Listings 6-26 and 6-27.

Listing 6-26. *res/layout/main.xml*

```
<?xml version="1.0" encoding="utf-8"?>
<LinearLayout xmlns:android="http://schemas.android.com/apk/res/android"
    android:orientation="vertical"
    android:layout_width="fill_parent"
    android:layout_height="fill_parent">
    <Button
        android:id="@+id/imageButton"
        android:layout_width="fill_parent"
        android:layout_height="wrap_content"
        android:text="Images"
    />
    <Button
         android:id="@+id/videoButton"
         android:layout_width="fill_parent"
         android:layout_height="wrap_content"
         android:text="Video"
    />
    <Button
        android:id="@+id/audioButton"
        android:layout_width="fill_parent"
```

```
        android:layout_height="wrap_content"
        android:text="Audio"
    />
</LinearLayout>
```

Listing 6-27. *Activity to Pick Media*

```
public class MediaActivity extends Activity implements View.OnClickListener {

    private static final int REQUEST_AUDIO = 1;
    private static final int REQUEST_VIDEO = 2;
    private static final int REQUEST_IMAGE = 3;

    @Override
    public void onCreate(Bundle savedInstanceState) {
        super.onCreate(savedInstanceState);
        setContentView(R.layout.main);

        Button images = (Button)findViewById(R.id.imageButton);
        images.setOnClickListener(this);
        Button videos = (Button)findViewById(R.id.videoButton);
        videos.setOnClickListener(this);
        Button audio = (Button)findViewById(R.id.audioButton);
        audio.setOnClickListener(this);

    }

    @Override
    protected void onActivityResult(int requestCode, int resultCode, Intent data) {

        if(resultCode == Activity.RESULT_OK) {
            //Uri to user selection returned in the Intent
            Uri selectedContent = data.getData();

            if(requestCode == REQUEST_IMAGE) {
                //Display the image
            }
            if(requestCode == REQUEST_VIDEO) {
                //Play the video clip
            }
            if(requestCode == REQUEST_AUDIO) {
                //Play the audio clip
            }
        }
    }

    @Override
    public void onClick(View v) {
        Intent intent = new Intent();
        intent.setAction(Intent.ACTION_GET_CONTENT);
```

```
        switch(v.getId()) {
        case R.id.imageButton:
            intent.setType("image/*");
            startActivityForResult(intent, REQUEST_IMAGE);
            return;
        case R.id.videoButton:
            intent.setType("video/*");
            startActivityForResult(intent, REQUEST_VIDEO);
            return;
        case R.id.audioButton:
            intent.setType("audio/*");
            startActivityForResult(intent, REQUEST_AUDIO);
            return;
        default:
            return;
        }
    }
}
```

This example has three buttons for the user to press, each targeting a specific type of media. When the user presses any one of these buttons, an Intent with the `Intent.ACTION_GET_CONTENT` action string is fired to the system, launching the proper picker Activity. If the user selects a valid item, a content `Uri` pointing to that item is returned in the result Intent with a status of `RESULT_OK`. If the user cancels or otherwise backs out of the picker, the status will be `RESULT_CANCELED` and the Intent's data field will be null.

With the `Uri` of the media received, the application is now free to play or display the content as is deemed appropriate. Classes like `MediaPlayer` and `VideoView` will take a Uri directly to play media content, and the `Uri.getPath()` method will return a file path for images that can be passed to `BitmapFactory.decodeFile()`.

6–11. Saving to the MediaStore

Problem

Your application would like to store media and insert it into the device's global MediaStore so that it is visible to all applications.

Solution

(API Level 1)

Utilize the ContentProvider interface exposed by MediaStore to perform inserts. In addition to the media content itself, this interface allows you to insert metadata to tag each item, such as a title, description, or time created. The result of the ContentProvider insert operation is a Uri that the application may use as a destination for the new media.

How It Works

Let's take a look at an example of inserting an image or video clip into MediaStore. See Listings 6-28 and 6-29.

Listing 6-28. *res/layout/main.xml*

```
<?xml version="1.0" encoding="utf-8"?>
<LinearLayout xmlns:android="http://schemas.android.com/apk/res/android"
    android:orientation="vertical"
    android:layout_width="fill_parent"
    android:layout_height="fill_parent">
    <Button
        android:id="@+id/imageButton"
        android:layout_width="fill_parent"
        android:layout_height="wrap_content"
        android:text="Images"
    />
    <Button
        android:id="@+id/videoButton"
        android:layout_width="fill_parent"
        android:layout_height="wrap_content"
        android:text="Video"
    />
</LinearLayout>
```

Listing 6-29. *Activity Saving Data in the MediaStore*

```
public class StoreActivity extends Activity implements View.OnClickListener {

    private static final int REQUEST_CAPTURE = 100;

    @Override
    public void onCreate(Bundle savedInstanceState) {
        super.onCreate(savedInstanceState);
        setContentView(R.layout.main);
```

```
        Button images = (Button)findViewById(R.id.imageButton);
        images.setOnClickListener(this);
        Button videos = (Button)findViewById(R.id.videoButton);
        videos.setOnClickListener(this);
    }

    @Override
    protected void onActivityResult(int requestCode, int resultCode, Intent data) {
        if(requestCode == REQUEST_CAPTURE && resultCode == Activity.RESULT_OK) {
            Toast.makeText(this, "All Done!", Toast.LENGTH_SHORT).show();
        }
    }

    @Override
    public void onClick(View v) {
        ContentValues values;
        Intent intent;
        Uri storeLocation;

        switch(v.getId()) {
        case R.id.imageButton:
            //Create any metadata for image
            values = new ContentValues(2);
            values.put(MediaStore.Images.ImageColumns.DATE_TAKEN,
System.currentTimeMillis());
            values.put(MediaStore.Images.ImageColumns.DESCRIPTION, "Sample Image");
            //Insert metadata and retrieve Uri location for file
            storeLocation = getContentResolver().insert(
                    MediaStore.Images.Media.EXTERNAL_CONTENT_URI, values);
            //Start capture with new location as destination
            intent = new Intent(MediaStore.ACTION_IMAGE_CAPTURE);
            intent.putExtra(MediaStore.EXTRA_OUTPUT, storeLocation);
            startActivityForResult(intent, REQUEST_CAPTURE);
            return;
        case R.id.videoButton:
            //Create any metadata for video
            values = new ContentValues(2);
            values.put(MediaStore.Video.VideoColumns.ARTIST, "Yours Truly");
            values.put(MediaStore.Video.VideoColumns.DESCRIPTION, "Sample Video Clip");
            //Insert metadata and retrieve Uri location for file
            storeLocation = getContentResolver().insert(
                    MediaStore.Video.Media.EXTERNAL_CONTENT_URI, values);
            //Start capture with new location as destination
            intent = new Intent(MediaStore.ACTION_VIDEO_CAPTURE);
            intent.putExtra(MediaStore.EXTRA_OUTPUT, storeLocation);
            startActivityForResult(intent, REQUEST_CAPTURE);
            return;
        default:
            return;
```

```
        }
    }
}
```

> **NOTE:** Because this example interacts with the Camera hardware, you should run it on a real device to get the full effect. In fact, there is a known bug in emulators running Android 2.2 or later that will cause this example to crash if the camera is accessed. Earlier emulators will execute the code appropriately, but without real hardware the example is less interesting.

In this example, when the user clicks on either button, metadata that are associated with the media itself are inserted into a ContentValues instance. Some of the more common metadata columns that are common to both image and video are the following:

- TITLE: String value for the content title
- DESCRIPTION: String value for the content description
- DATE_TAKEN: Integer value describing the date the media item was captured. Fill this field with System.currentTimeMillis() to indicate a time of "now"

The ContentValues are then inserted into the MediaStore using the appropriate CONTENT_URI reference. Notice that the metadata are inserted before the media item itself is actually captured. The return value from a successful insert is a fully qualified Uri that the application may use as the destination for the media content.

In the previous example, we are using the simplified methods from Chapter 4 of capturing audio and video by requesting that the system applications handle this process. Recall from Chapter 4 that both the audio and video capture Intent can be passed with an extra, declaring the destination for the result. This is where we pass the Uri that was returned from the insert.

Upon a successful return from the capture Activity, there is nothing more for the application to do. The external application has saved the captured image or video into the location referenced by our MediaStore insert. This data is now visible to all applications, including the system's Gallery application.

6-12. Interacting with the Calendar

Problem

Your application needs to interact directly with the ContentProvider exposed by the Android framework to add, view, change, or remove calendar events on the device.

Solution

(API Level 14)

Use the CalendarContract interface to read/write data to the system's ContentProvider for event data. CalendarContract exposes the API that is necessary to gain access to the device's calendars, events, attendees, and reminders. Much like ContactsContract, this interface defines mostly the data that is necessary to perform queries. The methods used will be the same as when working with any other system ContentProvider.

How It Works

Working with CalendarContract is very similar to working with ContactsContract; they both provide identifiers for the Uri and column values you will need to construct queries through the ContentResolver. Listing 6-30 illustrates an Activity that obtains and displays a list of the calendars present on the device.

Listing 6-30. *Activity Listing Calendars on the Device*

```
public class CalendarListActivity extends ListActivity implements
        LoaderManager.LoaderCallbacks<Cursor>, AdapterView.OnItemClickListener {
    private static final int LOADER_LIST = 100;

    SimpleCursorAdapter mAdapter;

    @Override
    public void onCreate(Bundle savedInstanceState) {
        super.onCreate(savedInstanceState);
        getLoaderManager().initLoader(LOADER_LIST, null, this);

        // Display all calendars in a ListView
        mAdapter = new SimpleCursorAdapter(this,
```

```
                android.R.layout.simple_list_item_2, null,
                new String[] {
                        CalendarContract.Calendars.CALENDAR_DISPLAY_NAME,
                        CalendarContract.Calendars.ACCOUNT_NAME },
                new int[] {
                        android.R.id.text1, android.R.id.text2 }, 0);
        setListAdapter(mAdapter);
        // Listen for item selections
        getListView().setOnItemClickListener(this);
    }

    @Override
    public void onItemClick(AdapterView<?> parent, View view, int position,
            long id) {
        Cursor c = mAdapter.getCursor();
        if (c != null && c.moveToPosition(position)) {
            Intent intent = new Intent(this, CalendarDetailActivity.class);
            // Pass the _ID and TITLE of the selected calendar to the next
            // Activity
            intent.putExtra(Intent.EXTRA_UID, c.getInt(0));
            intent.putExtra(Intent.EXTRA_TITLE, c.getString(1));
            startActivity(intent);
        }
    }

    @Override
    public Loader<Cursor> onCreateLoader(int id, Bundle args) {
        // Return all calendars, ordered by name
        String[] projection = new String[] { CalendarContract.Calendars._ID,
                CalendarContract.Calendars.CALENDAR_DISPLAY_NAME,
                CalendarContract.Calendars.ACCOUNT_NAME };

        return new CursorLoader(this, CalendarContract.Calendars.CONTENT_URI,
                projection, null, null,
                CalendarContract.Calendars.CALENDAR_DISPLAY_NAME);
    }

    @Override
    public void onLoadFinished(Loader<Cursor> loader, Cursor data) {
        mAdapter.swapCursor(data);
    }

    @Override
    public void onLoaderReset(Loader<Cursor> loader) {
        mAdapter.swapCursor(null);
    }
}
```

In contrast to our contacts example, here we use Android's `Loader` pattern to query the data and load the resulting `Cursor` into the list. This pattern provides a lot of benefit over managedCursor(), primarily in that all queries are automatically made on background threads to keep the UI responsive. The Loader pattern also has built-in reuse, so multiple clients wanting the same data can actually gain access to the same Loader through the LoaderManager.

With Loaders, our Activity receives a series of callback methods when new data is available. Under the hood, CursorLoader also registers as a ContentObserver, so we will get a callback with a new Cursor when the underlying data set changes without even having to request a reload. But back to the Calendar...

To obtain a list of the device calendars, we construct a query to the Calendars.CONTENT_URI with the column names we are interested in (here, the record ID, calendar name, and owning account name). When the query is complete, onLoadFinished() is called with a new Cursor pointing to the result data, which we then pass to our list adapter. When the user taps on a particular calendar item, a new Activity is initialized to look at the specific events it contains. We will see this in more detail in the next section.

Viewing/Modifying Calender Events

Listing 6-31 shows the contents of the second Activity in this example that displays a list of all the events for the selected calendar.

Listing 6-31. *Activity Listing and Modifying Calendar Events*

```
public class CalendarDetailActivity extends ListActivity implements
        LoaderManager.LoaderCallbacks<Cursor>, AdapterView.OnItemClickListener,
        AdapterView.OnItemLongClickListener {
    private static final int LOADER_DETAIL = 101;

    SimpleCursorAdapter mAdapter;

    int mCalendarId;

    @Override
    protected void onCreate(Bundle savedInstanceState) {
        super.onCreate(savedInstanceState);

        mCalendarId = getIntent().getIntExtra(Intent.EXTRA_UID, -1);

        String title = getIntent().getStringExtra(Intent.EXTRA_TITLE);
        setTitle(title);

        getLoaderManager().initLoader(LOADER_DETAIL, null, this);
```

```
    // Display all events in a ListView
    mAdapter = new SimpleCursorAdapter(this,
            android.R.layout.simple_list_item_2, null,
            new String[] {
                    CalendarContract.Events.TITLE,
                    CalendarContract.Events.EVENT_LOCATION },
            new int[] {
                    android.R.id.text1, android.R.id.text2 }, 0);
    setListAdapter(mAdapter);
    // Listen for item selections
    getListView().setOnItemClickListener(this);
    getListView().setOnItemLongClickListener(this);
}

@Override
public boolean onCreateOptionsMenu(Menu menu) {
    menu.add("Add Event")
        .setIcon(android.R.drawable.ic_menu_add)
        .setShowAsAction(MenuItem.SHOW_AS_ACTION_ALWAYS);

    return true;
}

@Override
public boolean onOptionsItemSelected(MenuItem item) {
    showAddEventDialog();
    return true;
}

// Display a dialog to add a new event
private void showAddEventDialog() {
    final EditText nameText = new EditText(this);
    AlertDialog.Builder builder = new AlertDialog.Builder(this);
    builder.setTitle("New Event");
    builder.setView(nameText);
    builder.setNegativeButton("Cancel", null);
    builder.setPositiveButton("Add Event",
            new DialogInterface.OnClickListener() {
                @Override
                public void onClick(DialogInterface dialog, int which) {
                    addEvent(nameText.getText().toString());
                }
            });
    builder.show();
}

// Add an event to the calendar with the specified name
// and the current time as the start date
private void addEvent(String eventName) {
    long start = System.currentTimeMillis();
```

```
        // End 1 hour from now
        long end = start + (3600 * 1000);

        ContentValues cv = new ContentValues(5);
        cv.put(CalendarContract.Events.CALENDAR_ID, mCalendarId);
        cv.put(CalendarContract.Events.TITLE, eventName);
        cv.put(CalendarContract.Events.DESCRIPTION,
                "Event created by Android Recipes");
        cv.put(CalendarContract.Events.EVENT_TIMEZONE,
                Time.getCurrentTimezone());
        cv.put(CalendarContract.Events.DTSTART, start);
        cv.put(CalendarContract.Events.DTEND, end);

        getContentResolver().insert(CalendarContract.Events.CONTENT_URI, cv);
    }

    // Remove the selected event from the calendar
    private void deleteEvent(int eventId) {
        String selection = CalendarContract.Events._ID + " = ?";
        String[] selectionArgs = { String.valueOf(eventId) };
        getContentResolver().delete(CalendarContract.Events.CONTENT_URI,
                selection, selectionArgs);
    }

    @Override
    public void onItemClick(AdapterView<?> parent, View view, int position,
            long id) {
        Cursor c = mAdapter.getCursor();
        if (c != null && c.moveToPosition(position)) {
            // Show a dialog with more detailed data about the event when
            // clicked
            SimpleDateFormat sdf = new SimpleDateFormat("yyyy-MM-dd HH:mm:ss");
            StringBuilder sb = new StringBuilder();

            sb.append("Location: "
                    + c.getString(
                            c.getColumnIndex(CalendarContract.Events.EVENT_LOCATION))
                    + "\n\n");
            int startDateIndex = c.getColumnIndex(CalendarContract.Events.DTSTART);
            Date startDate = c.isNull(startDateIndex) ? null
                    : new Date( Long.parseLong(c.getString(startDateIndex)) );
            if (startDate != null) {
                sb.append("Starts At: " + sdf.format(startDate) + "\n\n");
            }
            int endDateIndex = c.getColumnIndex(CalendarContract.Events.DTEND);
            Date endDate = c.isNull(endDateIndex) ? null
                    : new Date( Long.parseLong(c.getString(endDateIndex)) );
            if (endDate != null) {
                sb.append("Ends At: " + sdf.format(endDate) + "\n\n");
            }
```

```
            AlertDialog.Builder builder = new AlertDialog.Builder(this);
            builder.setTitle(
                    c.getString(c.getColumnIndex(CalendarContract.Events.TITLE)) );
            builder.setMessage(sb.toString());
            builder.setPositiveButton("OK", null);
            builder.show();
        }
    }

    @Override
    public boolean onItemLongClick(AdapterView<?> parent, View view,
            int position, long id) {
        Cursor c = mAdapter.getCursor();
        if (c != null && c.moveToPosition(position)) {
            // Allow the user to delete the event on a long-press
            final int eventId = c.getInt(
                    c.getColumnIndex(CalendarContract.Events._ID));
            String eventName = c.getString(
                    c.getColumnIndex(CalendarContract.Events.TITLE));
            AlertDialog.Builder builder = new AlertDialog.Builder(this);
            builder.setTitle("Delete Event");
            builder.setMessage(String.format(
                    "Are you sure want to delete %s?",
                    TextUtils.isEmpty(eventName) ? "this event" : eventName));
            builder.setNegativeButton("Cancel", null);
            builder.setPositiveButton("Delete Event",
                    new DialogInterface.OnClickListener() {
                        @Override
                        public void onClick(DialogInterface dialog, int which) {
                            deleteEvent(eventId);
                        }
                    });
            builder.show();
        }

        return true;
    }

    @Override
    public Loader<Cursor> onCreateLoader(int id, Bundle args) {
        // Return all calendars, ordered by name
        String[] projection = new String[] { CalendarContract.Events._ID,
                CalendarContract.Events.TITLE, CalendarContract.Events.DTSTART,
                CalendarContract.Events.DTEND,
                CalendarContract.Events.EVENT_LOCATION };
        String selection = CalendarContract.Events.CALENDAR_ID + " = ?";
        String[] selectionArgs = { String.valueOf(mCalendarId) };
```

```
        return new CursorLoader(this, CalendarContract.Events.CONTENT_URI,
                projection, selection, selectionArgs,
                CalendarContract.Events.DTSTART + " DESC");
    }

    @Override
    public void onLoadFinished(Loader<Cursor> loader, Cursor data) {
        mAdapter.swapCursor(data);
    }

    @Override
    public void onLoaderReset(Loader<Cursor> loader) {
        mAdapter.swapCursor(null);
    }
}
```

You can see that the code to query the list of events and display them is very similar; in this case you query the `Events.CONTENT_URI` with the ID of the selected calendar as a selection parameter. Here when the user taps on an event, he or she is presented with a simple dialog with more details about the event itself. In addition, though, this Activity includes a few more methods to create and delete events on this calendar.

To add a new event, an item is added to the options menu, which will show up in the overhead `ActionBar` if the device has one visible. When pressed, a dialog appears, allowing the user to enter a name for this event. If he or she elects to continue, a `ContentValues` object is created with the bare necessities required to create a new event. Because this event is nonrecurring, it must have both start and end times, as well as a valid time zone. We must also supply the ID of the calendar we are looking at so the event is properly attached. From there the data is handed back to `ContentResolver` to be inserted into the Events table.

To delete an event, the user may long-press on a particular item in the list and then confirm the deletion through a dialog. In this case, all we need is the unique record ID of the selected event to pass in a selection string to `ContentResolver`.

Did you notice in both of these cases that we didn't write any code after the insert/delete to refresh the `Cursor` or the `CursorAdapter`? That's the power of the `Loader` pattern! Because the `CursorLoader` is observing the data set, when a change occurred it automatically refreshed itself and handed a new `Cursor` to the adapter, which refreshes the display.

> **NOTE:** Loaders may have been introduced in Android 3.0 (API Level 11), but they are also part of the support library. You can use them in your applications supporting all the way back to Android 1.6.

6-13. Logging Code Execution

Problem

You need to place log statements into your code for debugging or testing purposes, and they should be removed before shipping the code to production.

Solution

(API Level 1)

Leverage the `BuildConfig.DEBUG` flag to protect statements in the `Log` class so they print only on debug builds of the application. It can be extremely convenient to keep logging statements in your code for future testing and development, even after the application has shipped to your users. But if those statements are unchecked, you might risk printing private information to the console on a user's device. By creating a simple wrapper class around `Log` that monitors `BuildConfig.DEBUG`, you can leave log statements in place without fear of what they will show in the field.

How It Works

Listing 6-32 illustrates a simple wrapper class around the default Android `Log` functionality.

Listing 6-32. *Logger Wrapper*

```
public class Logger {
    private static final String LOGTAG = "AndroidRecipes";

    private static String getLogString(String format, Object... args) {
        //Minor optimization, only call String.format if necessary
        if(args.length == 0) {
            return format;
        }

        return String.format(format, args);
    }

    /* The INFO, WARNING, ERROR log levels print always */

    public static void e(String format, Object... args) {
        Log.e(LOGTAG, getLogString(format, args));
```

```
    }

    public static void w(String format, Object... args) {
        Log.w(LOGTAG, getLogString(format, args));
    }

    public static void w(Throwable throwable) {
        Log.w(LOGTAG, throwable);
    }

    public static void i(String format, Object... args) {
        Log.i(LOGTAG, getLogString(format, args));
    }

    /* The DEBUG and VERBOSE log levels are protected by DEBUG flag */

    public static void d(String format, Object... args) {
        if(!BuildConfig.DEBUG) return;

        Log.d(LOGTAG, getLogString(format, args));
    }

    public static void v(String format, Object... args) {
        if(!BuildConfig.DEBUG) return;

        Log.v(LOGTAG, getLogString(format, args));
    }
}
```

This class provides a few simple optimizations around the framework's version to make logging a bit more civilized. First, it consolidates the log tag so your entire application prints under one consistent tag heading in logcat. Second, it takes input in the form of a format string so variables can be logged out cleanly without needing to break up the log string. The one additional optimization to this is that `String.format()` can be slow, so we only want to call it when there are actually parameters to format. Otherwise we can just pass the raw string along directly.

Finally, it protects two of the five main log levels with the `BuildConfig.DEBUG` flag, so that log statements set to these levels print only in debug versions of the application. There are many cases where we want log statements to be output in the production application as well (such as error conditions), so it is prudent not to hide all the log levels behind the debug flag. Listing 6-33 quickly shows how this wrapper can take the place of traditional logging.

Listing 6-33. *Activity Using Logger*

```
public class LoggerActivity extends Activity {

    @Override
    public void onCreate(Bundle savedInstanceState) {
        super.onCreate(savedInstanceState);
        setContentView(R.layout.main);

        //This statement only printed in debug
        Logger.d("Activity Created");
    }

    @Override
    protected void onResume() {
        super.onResume();

        //This statement only printed in debug
        Logger.d("Activity Resume at %d", System.currentTimeMillis());
        //This statement always printed
        Logger.i("It is now %d", System.currentTimeMillis());
    }

    @Override
    protected void onPause() {
        super.onPause();

        //This statement only printed in debug
        Logger.d("Activity Pause at %d", System.currentTimeMillis());
        //This always printed
        Logger.w("No, don't leave!");
    }
}
```

6-14. Creating a Background Worker

Problem

You need to create a long-running background thread that sits waiting for work to execute and that can be terminated easily when it is no longer needed.

Solution

(API Level 1)

Let HandlerThread assist you in creating a background thread with a working Looper that can be attached to a Handler for processing work inside of its MessageQueue. One of the most popular backgrounding methods in Android is AsyncTask, which is a fabulous class and should be used in your applications. However, it has some drawbacks that may make other implementations more efficient in certain cases. One of those drawbacks is that AsyncTask execution is one-shot and finite. If you want to do the same task repeatedly or indefinitely for the life cycle of a component like an Activity or Service, AsyncTask can be a bit heavyweight. Often, you will need to create multiple instances to accomplish that goal.

The advantage of HandlerThread in cases like this is we can create one worker object to accept multiple tasks to handle in the background and it will process them serially through the built-in queue that Looper maintains.

How It Works

Listing 6-34 contains an extension of HandlerThread used to do some simple manipulation of image data. Because modifying images can take some time, we want to task this to a background operation to keep the application UI responsive.

Listing 6-34. *Background Worker Thread*

```
public class ImageProcessor extends HandlerThread implements Handler.Callback {
    public static final int MSG_SCALE = 100;
    public static final int MSG_CROP = 101;

    private Context mContext;
    private Handler mReceiver, mCallback;

    public ImageProcessor(Context context) {
        this(context, null);
    }

    public ImageProcessor(Context context, Handler callback) {
        super("AndroidRecipesWorker");
        mCallback = callback;
        mContext = context;
    }
```

```
@Override
protected void onLooperPrepared() {
    mReceiver = new Handler(getLooper(), this);
}

@Override
public boolean handleMessage(Message msg) {
    Bitmap source, result;
    //Retrieve arguments from the incoming message
    int scale = msg.arg1;
    switch (msg.what) {
    case MSG_SCALE:
        source = BitmapFactory.decodeResource(mContext.getResources(),
                R.drawable.ic_launcher);
        //Create a new, scaled up image
        result = Bitmap.createScaledBitmap(source,
                source.getWidth() * scale, source.getHeight() * scale, true);
        break;
    case MSG_CROP:
        source = BitmapFactory.decodeResource(mContext.getResources(),
                R.drawable.ic_launcher);
        int newWidth = source.getWidth() / scale;
        //Create a new, horizontally cropped image
        result = Bitmap.createBitmap(source,
                (source.getWidth() - newWidth) / 2, 0,
                newWidth, source.getHeight());
        break;
    default:
        throw new IllegalArgumentException("Unknown Worker Request");
    }

    // Return the image to the main thread
    if (mCallback != null) {
        mCallback.sendMessage(Message.obtain(null, 0, result));
    }
    return true;
}

//Add/Remove a callback handler
public void setCallback(Handler callback) {
    mCallback = callback;
}

/* Methods to Queue Work */

// Scale the icon to the specified value
public void scaleIcon(int scale) {
    Message msg = Message.obtain(null, MSG_SCALE, scale, 0, null);
    mReceiver.sendMessage(msg);
```

```
    }

    //Crop the icon in the center and scale the result to the specified value
    public void cropIcon(int scale) {
        Message msg = Message.obtain(null, MSG_CROP, scale, 0, null);
        mReceiver.sendMessage(msg);
    }
}
```

The name HandlerThread may be a bit of a misnomer, as it does not actually contain a Handler that you can use to process input. Instead it is a thread designed to work externally with a Handler to create a background process. Because of that we have to still provide a customized implementation of Handler to actually execute the work we want done. In this example, our custom processor implements the Handler.Callback interface, which we pass into a new Handler owned by the thread. We do this simply to avoid the need to subclass Handler, which would have worked just as well. The receiver Handler is not created until the onLooperPrepared() callback because we need to have the Looper object that HandlerThread creates to send work to the background thread.

The external API we create to allow other objects to queue work all create a Message and send it to the receiver Handler to be processed in handleMessage(), which inspects the Message contents and creates the appropriate modified image. Any code that goes through handleMessage() is running on our background thread.

Once the work is complete, we need to have a second Handler attached to the main thread so we can send our results and modify the UI.

> **REMINDER:** Any code that touches UI elements *must* be called from the main thread *only*. This cannot be overstated.

This callback Handler receives a second Message containing the Bitmap result from the image code. This is one of the great features about using the Message interface to pass data between threads; each instance can take with it two integer arguments as well as any arbitrary Object so no additional code is necessary to pass in parameters or access your results. In our case, one integer is passed in as a parameter for the scale value of the transformation, and the Object field is used to return the image as a Bitmap. To see how this is used in practice, take a look at the sample application in Listings 6-35 and 6-36.

Listing 6-35. *res/layout/main.xml*

```
<LinearLayout xmlns:android="http://schemas.android.com/apk/res/android"
    android:layout_width="match_parent"
    android:layout_height="match_parent"
    android:orientation="vertical" >

    <Button
        android:layout_width="match_parent"
        android:layout_height="wrap_content"
        android:text="Scale Icon"
        android:onClick="onScaleClick" />
    <Button
        android:layout_width="match_parent"
        android:layout_height="wrap_content"
        android:text="Crop Icon"
        android:onClick="onCropClick" />

    <ImageView
        android:id="@+id/image_result"
        android:layout_width="match_parent"
        android:layout_height="match_parent"
        android:scaleType="center" />
</LinearLayout>
```

Listing 6-36. *Activity Interacting with Worker*

```
public class WorkerActivity extends Activity implements Handler.Callback {

    private ImageProcessor mWorker;
    private Handler mResponseHandler;

    private ImageView mResultView;

    @Override
    public void onCreate(Bundle savedInstanceState) {
        super.onCreate(savedInstanceState);
        setContentView(R.layout.main);

        mResultView = (ImageView) findViewById(R.id.image_result);
        //Handler to map background callbacks to this Activity
        mResponseHandler = new Handler(this);
    }

    @Override
    protected void onResume() {
        super.onResume();
        //Start a new worker
        mWorker = new ImageProcessor(this, mResponseHandler);
        mWorker.start();
```

```
    }

    @Override
    protected void onPause() {
        super.onPause();
        //Terminate the worker
        mWorker.setCallback(null);
        mWorker.quit();
        mWorker = null;
    }

    /*
     * Callback method for background results.
     * This is called on the UI thread.
     */
    @Override
    public boolean handleMessage(Message msg) {
        Bitmap result = (Bitmap) msg.obj;
        mResultView.setImageBitmap(result);
        return true;
    }

    /* Action Methods to Post Background Work */

    public void onScaleClick(View v) {
        for(int i=1; i < 10; i++) {
            mWorker.scaleIcon(i);
        }
    }

    public void onCropClick(View v) {
        for(int i=1; i < 10; i++) {
            mWorker.cropIcon(i);
        }
    }
}
```

This sample makes use of our worker by creating a single running instance while the `Activity` is in the foreground and passing image requests to it when the user clicks the buttons. To further illustrate the scale of this pattern, we queue up several requests with each button click. The `Activity` also implements `Handler.Callback` and owns a simple `Handler` (which is running on the main thread) to receive result messages from the worker.

To start the processor, we just have to call start() on the `HandlerThread`, which sets up the `Looper` and `Handler`, and it begins waiting for input. Terminating it is just as simple; calling `quit()` stops the `Looper` and immediately drops any unprocessed messages. We also set the callback to null just so that any work that may be in process currently doesn't try to call the `Activity` after this point.

Run this application and you can see how the background work doesn't slow the UI no matter how fast or how often the buttons are pressed. Each request just gets added to the queue and processed if possible before the user leaves the `Activity`. The visible result is that each created image will be displayed below the buttons as that request finishes.

6-15. Customizing the Task Stack

Problem

Your application allows external applications to launch certain Activities directly, and you need to implement the proper BACK versus UP navigation patterns.

Solution

(API Level 4)

The `NavUtils` and `TaskStackBuilder` classes in the support library allow you to easily construct and launch the appropriate navigation stacks from within your application. The functionality of both these classes is actually native to the SDK in Android 4.1 and later, but for applications that need to target earlier platform versions as well, the support library implementation provides a compatible API that will still call the native methods whenever they are present.

BACK Versus UP

Android screen navigation provides for two specific user actions. The first is the action taken when the user presses the BACK button. The second is the action taken when the user presses the Home icon in the `ActionBar`, which is known as the UP action. For developers who are new to the platforms, the distinction can often be confusing, especially since in many cases both actions always perform the same function.

Conceptually, BACK should always take the user to the content screen he or she had been viewing prior to the current screen. The UP action, on the other hand, should navigate to the hierarchical parent screen of the current screen. For most applications where the user drills down from the home screen to subsequent screens with more specific content, BACK and UP will go to the same place, and so their usefulness may be called into question.

Consider, though, an application where one or more Activity elements can be launched directly by an external application. Say, for example, an Activity is designed to view an image file. Or perhaps the application posts Notification messages that allow the user to go directly to a lower-level Activity when an event occurs. In these cases, the BACK action should take the user back to the application task he or she was using before jumping into your application. But the UP action provides the user with a way to move back up your application's stack if he or she decides to continue using this application rather than going back to the original task. In this instance, the entire stack of Activity elements that your application normally has constructed to get to this point may not exist, and that is where TaskStackBuilder and some key attributes in your application's manifest can help.

How It Works

Let's define two applications to illustrate how this recipe works. First, look at Listing 6-37, which shows the <application> element of the manifest.

Listing 6-37. *AndroidManifest.xml Application Tag*

```
<application
    android:icon="@drawable/ic_launcher"
    android:label="TaskStack"
    android:theme="@style/AppTheme" >
    <activity
        android:name=".RootActivity"
        android:label="@string/title_activity_root" >
        <intent-filter>
            <action android:name="android.intent.action.MAIN" />
            <category android:name="android.intent.category.LAUNCHER" />
        </intent-filter>
    </activity>
    <activity android:name=".ItemsListActivity"
        android:parentActivityName=".RootActivity">
        <!-- Parent definition for the support library -->
        <meta-data android:name="android.support.PARENT_ACTIVITY"
            android:value=".RootActivity" />
    </activity>
    <activity android:name=".DetailsActivity"
        android:parentActivityName=".ItemsListActivity">
        <!-- Parent definition for the support library -->
        <meta-data android:name="android.support.PARENT_ACTIVITY"
            android:value=".ItemsListActivity" />
        <!-- Supply a filter to allow external launches -->
        <intent-filter>
            <action android:name="com.examples.taskstack.ACTION_NEW_ARRIVAL" />
            <category android:name="android.intent.category.DEFAULT" />
```

```
        </intent-filter>
    </activity>
</application>
```

The first step in defining ancestral navigation is to define the parent-child relationship hierarchy between each Activity. In Android 4.1, the android:parentActivityName attribute was introduced to create this link. To support the same functionality in older platforms, the support library defines a <meta-data> value that can be attached to each Activity to define the parent. Our example defines both attributes for each lower-level Activity to work with both the native API and the support library.

We have also defined a custom <intent-filter> on the DetailsActivity, which will allow an external application to launch this Activity directly.

> **NOTE:** If you are only supporting Android 4.1 and later with your application, you can actually stop here. All the remaining functionality to build the stack and navigate are built into Activity in these versions and the default behavior happens without any extra code. In this case, you would only need to implement TaskStackBuilder if you want to somehow customize the task stack in certain situations.

With our hierarchy defined, we can create the code for each Activity. See Listings 6-38 through 6-40.

Listing 6-38. *Root Activity*

```
public class RootActivity extends Activity implements View.OnClickListener {

    @Override
    public void onCreate(Bundle savedInstanceState) {
        super.onCreate(savedInstanceState);
        Button listButton = new Button(this);
        listButton.setText("Show Family Members");
        listButton.setOnClickListener(this);

        setContentView(listButton,
                new ViewGroup.LayoutParams(LayoutParams.MATCH_PARENT,
                        LayoutParams.WRAP_CONTENT));
    }

    public void onClick(View v) {
        //Launch the next Activity
        Intent intent = new Intent(this, ItemsListActivity.class);
        startActivity(intent);
    }
}
```

Listing 6-39. *Second-Level Activity*

```
public class ItemsListActivity extends Activity implements OnItemClickListener {

    private static final String[] ITEMS = {"Mom", "Dad", "Sister", "Brother", "Cousin"};

    @Override
    protected void onCreate(Bundle savedInstanceState) {
        super.onCreate(savedInstanceState);
        //Enable ActionBar home button with up arrow
        getActionBar().setDisplayHomeAsUpEnabled(true);
        //Create and display a list of family members
        ListView list = new ListView(this);
        ArrayAdapter<String> adapter = new ArrayAdapter<String>(this,
                android.R.layout.simple_list_item_1, ITEMS);
        list.setAdapter(adapter);
        list.setOnItemClickListener(this);

        setContentView(list);
    }

    @Override
    public boolean onOptionsItemSelected(MenuItem item) {
        switch (item.getItemId()) {
        case android.R.id.home:
            //Create an intent for the parent Activity
            Intent upIntent = NavUtils.getParentActivityIntent(this);
            //Check if we need to create the entire stack
            if (NavUtils.shouldUpRecreateTask(this, upIntent)) {
                //This stack doesn't exist yet, so it must be synthesized
                TaskStackBuilder.create(this)
                        .addParentStack(this)
                        .startActivities();
            } else {
                //Stack exists, so just navigate up
                NavUtils.navigateUpFromSameTask(this);
            }
            return true;
        default:
            return super.onOptionsItemSelected(item);
        }
    }

    @Override
    public void onItemClick(AdapterView<?> parent, View v, int position, long id) {
        //Launch the final Activity, passing in the selected item name
        Intent intent = new Intent(this, DetailsActivity.class);
        intent.putExtra(Intent.EXTRA_TEXT, ITEMS[position]);
        startActivity(intent);
    }
```

```
}
```

Listing 6-40. *Third-Level Activity*

```
public class DetailsActivity extends Activity {
    //Custom Action String for external Activity launches
    public static final String ACTION_NEW_ARRIVAL =
            "com.examples.taskstack.ACTION_NEW_ARRIVAL";

    @Override
    protected void onCreate(Bundle savedInstanceState) {
        super.onCreate(savedInstanceState);
        //Enable ActionBar home button with up arrow
        getActionBar().setDisplayHomeAsUpEnabled(true);

        TextView text = new TextView(this);
        text.setGravity(Gravity.CENTER);
        String item = getIntent().getStringExtra(Intent.EXTRA_TEXT);
        text.setText(item);

        setContentView(text);
    }

    @Override
    public boolean onOptionsItemSelected(MenuItem item) {
        switch (item.getItemId()) {
        case android.R.id.home:
            //Create an intent for the parent Activity
            Intent upIntent = NavUtils.getParentActivityIntent(this);
            //Check if we need to create the entire stack
            if (NavUtils.shouldUpRecreateTask(this, upIntent)) {
                //This stack doesn't exist yet, so it must be synthesized
                TaskStackBuilder.create(this)
                    .addParentStack(this)
                    .startActivities();
            } else {
                //Stack exists, so just navigate up
                NavUtils.navigateUpFromSameTask(this);
            }
            return true;
        default:
            return super.onOptionsItemSelected(item);
        }
    }
}
```

This example application consists of three screens. The root screen just has a button to launch the next `Activity`. The second `Activity` contains a `ListView` with several options to select from. When any item in the list is selected, the third `Activity` is launched, which displays the selection made in the center of the view. As you might expect, the user can use the BACK button to navigate back through this stack of screens. However, in this case we have also enabled the UP action to provide the same navigation.

There is some common code in the two lower-level Activities that enables the UP navigation. The first is a call to `setDisplayHomeAsUpEnabled()` on `ActionBar`. This enables the home icon in the bar to be clickable and also to display with the default back arrow that indicates an UP action is possible. Whenever this item is clicked by the user, `onOptionsItemSelected()` will trigger and the item's ID will be `android.R.id.home`, so we use this information to filter out when the user taps requests to navigate UP.

When navigating UP, we have to make the determination about whether the Activity stack we need already exists, or we need to create it; the `shouldUpRecreateTask()` method does this for us. On platform versions prior to Android 4.1, it does this by checking if the target `Intent` has a valid action string that isn't `Intent.ACTION_MAIN`. On Android 4.1 and later, it decides this by checking the `taskAffinity` of the target `Intent` against the rest of the application.

If the task stack does not exist, primarily because this Activity was launched directly rather than being navigated to from within its own application, we must create it. `TaskStackBuilder` contains a host of methods to allow the stack to be created in any way that fits your application's needs. We are using the convenience method `addParentStack()`, which traverses all of the `parentActivityName` attributes (or `PARENT_ACTIVITY` on support platforms) and every Intent necessary to recreate the path from this `Activity` to the root. With the stack built, we just need to call `startActivities()` to have it build the stack and navigate to the next level up.

If the stack already exists, we can call on `NavUtils` to take us up one level with `navigateUpFromSameTask()`. This is really just a convenience method for `navigateUpTo()` that constructs the target `Intent` by calling `getParentActivityIntent()` for us.

Now we have an application that is properly compliant with the BACK/UP navigation pattern, but how do we test it? Running this application as is will produce the same results for each BACK and UP action. Let's construct a simple second application to launch our `DetailsActivity` to better illustrate the navigation pattern. See Listings 6-41 and 6-42.

Listing 6-41. *res/layout/main.xml*

```
<?xml version="1.0" encoding="utf-8"?>
<LinearLayout xmlns:android="http://schemas.android.com/apk/res/android"
    android:layout_width="match_parent"
```

```
    android:layout_height="match_parent"
    android:orientation="vertical" >
    <Button
        android:id="@+id/button_nephew"
        android:layout_width="match_parent"
        android:layout_height="wrap_content"
        android:text="Add a New Nephew" />
    <Button
        android:id="@+id/button_niece"
        android:layout_width="match_parent"
        android:layout_height="wrap_content"
        android:text="Add a New Niece" />
    <Button
        android:id="@+id/button_twins"
        android:layout_width="match_parent"
        android:layout_height="wrap_content"
        android:text="Add Twin Nieces!" />
</LinearLayout>
```

Listing 6-42. *Activity Launching into the Task Stack*

```
public class MainActivity extends Activity implements View.OnClickListener {
    //Custom Action String for external Activity launches
    public static final String ACTION_NEW_ARRIVAL =
            "com.examples.taskstack.ACTION_NEW_ARRIVAL";

    @Override
    protected void onCreate(Bundle savedInstanceState) {
        super.onCreate(savedInstanceState);
        setContentView(R.layout.main);
        //Attach the button listeners
        findViewById(R.id.button_nephew).setOnClickListener(this);
        findViewById(R.id.button_niece).setOnClickListener(this);
        findViewById(R.id.button_twins).setOnClickListener(this);
    }

    @Override
    public void onClick(View v) {
        String newArrival;
        switch(v.getId()) {
        case R.id.button_nephew:
            newArrival = "Baby Nephew";
            break;
        case R.id.button_niece:
            newArrival = "Baby Niece";
            break;
        case R.id.button_twins:
            newArrival = "Twin Nieces!";
            break;
        default:
            return;
```

```
        }

        Intent intent = new Intent(ACTION_NEW_ARRIVAL);
        intent.putExtra(Intent.EXTRA_TEXT, newArrival);
        startActivity(intent);
    }
}
```

This application provides a few options for name values to pass in, and it then launches our previous application's `DetailActivity` directly. In this case, we see different behavior exhibited between BACK and UP. Pressing the BACK button will take the user back to the options selection screen, because that is the `Activity` that launched it. But pressing the UP action button will launch the user into the original application's task stack, so it will go to the screen with the `ListView` of items instead. From this point forward, the user's task has changed, so BACK button actions will now also traverse the original stack, thus matching subsequent UP actions. Figure 6-7 illustrates this use case.

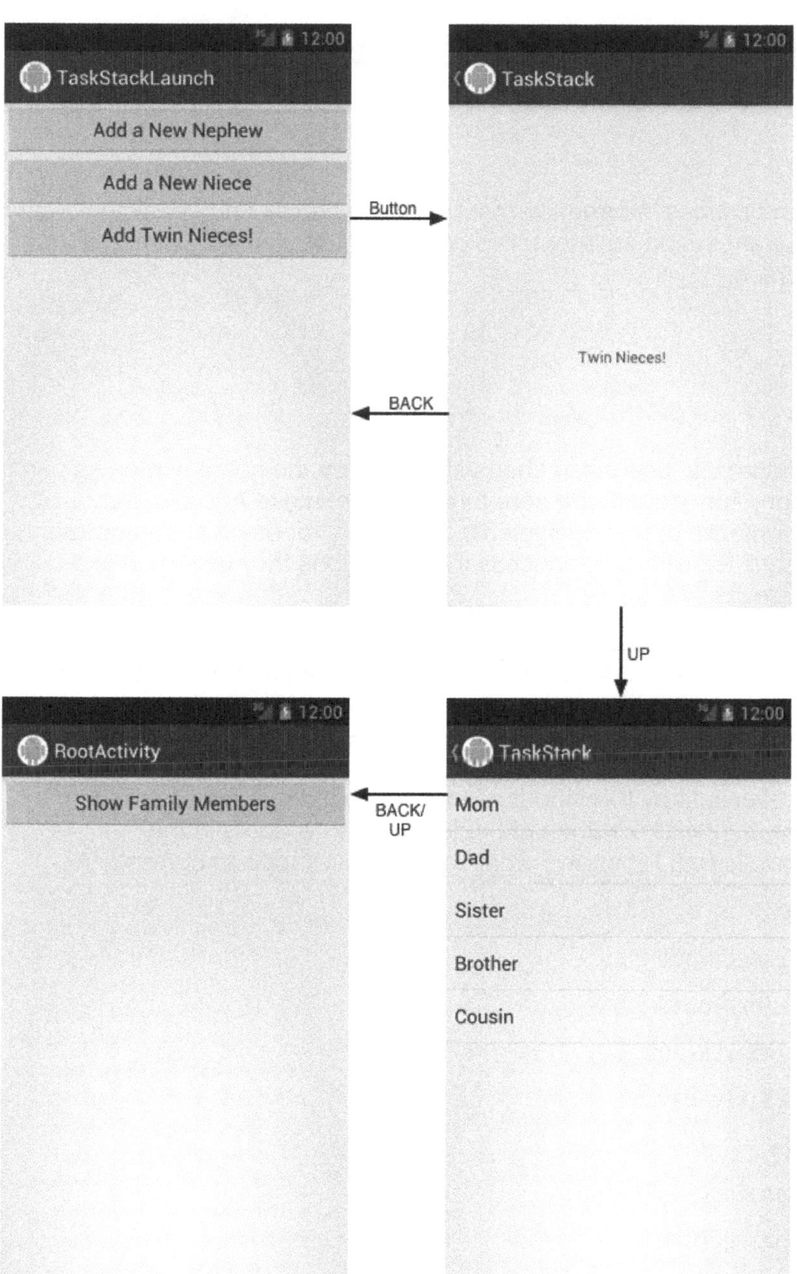

Figure 6-7. *BACK versus UP navigation.*

6-16. Implementing AppWidgets

Problem

Your application provides information that users need quick and consistent access to. You want to add an interactive component of your application to the user's home screen.

Solution

(API Level 3)

Build an AppWidget that users can choose to install on the home screen as part of the application. AppWidgets are core functions that make Android stand apart from other mobile operating systems. The ability for users to customize their Home experience with quick access to applications they use most is a strong draw for many.

An AppWidget is a view element that is designed to run in the Launcher application's process but is controlled from your application's process. Because of this, special pieces of the framework that are designed to support remote process connections must be used. In particular, the view hierarchy of the widget must be provided wrapped in a `RemoteViews` object, which has methods to update view elements by ID without needing to gain direct access to them. `RemoteViews` only supports a subset of the layouts and widgets in the framework. The following list shows what `RemoteViews` supports currently:

- Layouts
  - `FrameLayout`
  - `GridLayout`
  - `LinearLayout`
  - `RelativeLayout`
- Widgets
  - `AdapterViewFlipper`
  - `AnalogClock`
  - `Button`
  - `Chronometer`

- `GridView`
- `ImageButton`
- `ImageView`
- `ListView`
- `ProgressBar`
- `StackView`
- `TextView`
- `ViewFlipper`

The view for your AppWidget must be composed of these objects only, or the view will not properly display.

Working in a remote process also means that most user interaction must be handled through `PendingIntent` instances, rather than traditional listener interfaces. The `PendingIntent` allows your application to freeze `Intent` action along with the `Context` that has permission to execute it so the action can be freely handed off to another process and be run at the specified time as if it had come directly from the originating application `Context`.

Sizing

Android Launcher screens on handsets are typically made from a 4x4 grid of spaces in which you can fit your AppWidget. While tablets will have considerably greater space, this should be the design metric to keep in mind when determining the minimum height or width of your widget. Android 3.1 introduced the ability for a user to also resize an AppWidget after it had been placed, but prior to that a widget's size was fixed to these values. Taken from the Android documentation, Table 6-1 defines a good rule of thumb to use in determining how many cells a given minimum size will occupy:

Table 6-1. *Home Screen Grid Cell Sizes.*

Number of Cells	Available Space
1	40dp
2	110dp
3	180dp

Number of Cells	Available Space
4	250dp
n	70 * *n* - 30

So, as an example, if your widget needed to be at least 200dp x 48dp in size, it would require three columns and one row in order to display on the Launcher.

How It Works

Let's first take a look at constructing a simple AppWidget that can be updated from either the widget itself or the associated Activity. This example constructs a random number generator (something I'm sure we all wish could be on our Launcher screen) that can be placed as an AppWidget. Let's start with the application's manifest in Listing 6-43.

Listing 6-43. *AndroidManifest.xml*

```
<application android:label="@string/app_name"
        android:icon="@drawable/ic_launcher">
        <!-- Simple AppWidget Components -->
        <activity android:name=".MainActivity">
            <intent-filter>
                <action android:name="android.intent.action.MAIN" />
                <category android:name="android.intent.category.LAUNCHER" />
            </intent-filter>
        </activity>

        <receiver android:name=".SimpleAppWidget">
            <intent-filter>
                <action android:name="android.appwidget.action.APPWIDGET_UPDATE" />
            </intent-filter>
            <!-- This data required to configure the AppWidget -->
            <meta-data android:name="android.appwidget.provider"
                android:resource="@xml/simple_appwidget" />
        </receiver>

        <service android:name=".RandomService" />
</application>
```

The only required component here to produce the AppWidget is the `<receiver>` marked `SimpleAppWidget`. This element must point to a subclass of `AppWidgetProvider`, which, as you might expect, is a customized `BroadcastReceiver`. It must register in the manifest for the `APPWIDGET_UPDATE` broadcast action. There are several other broadcasts that it processes, but this is the only one that must be declared in the manifest. You must also attach a `<meta-data>` element that points to an `<appwidget-provider>`, which will eventually be inflated into `AppWidgetProviderInfo`. Let's have a look at that element now in Listing 6-44.

Listing 6-44. *res/xml/simple_appwidget.xml*

```
<?xml version="1.0" encoding="utf-8"?>
<appwidget-provider xmlns:android="http://schemas.android.com/apk/res/android"
    android:minWidth="180dp"
    android:minHeight="40dp"
    android:updatePeriodMillis="86400000"
    android:initialLayout="@layout/simple_widget_layout"/>
```

These attributes define the configuration for the AppWidget. Besides the size metrics, `updatePeriodMillis` defines the period on which Android should automatically call an update on this widget to refresh it. Be judicious with this value, and do not set it higher than you need to. In many cases, it is more efficient to have other Services or observers notifying you of changes that require an AppWidget update. In fact, Android will not deliver updates to an AppWidget more frequently than 30 seconds. We have set our AppWidget to only update once per day. This example also defines an `initialLayout` attribute, which points to the layout that should be used for the AppWidget.

There are a number of other useful attributes you can apply here as well:

- `android:configure` provides an `Activity` that should be launched to configure the AppWidget before it is added to the Launcher.
- `android:icon` references a resource to be displayed at the widget icon on the system's selection UI.
- `android:previewImage` references a resource to display a full-size preview of the AppWidget in the system's selection UI (API Level 11).
- `android:resizeMode` defines how the widget should be resizable on platforms that support it: horizontally, vertically, or both (API Level 12).

Listings 6-45 and 6-46 reveal what the AppWidget layout looks like.

Listing 6-45. *res/layout/simple_widget_layout.xml*

```
<?xml version="1.0" encoding="utf-8"?>
<LinearLayout xmlns:android="http://schemas.android.com/apk/res/android"
    android:layout_width="match_parent"
    android:layout_height="match_parent"
    android:background="@drawable/widget_background"
```

```
    android:orientation="horizontal"
    android:padding="10dp" >
    <LinearLayout
        android:id="@+id/container"
        android:layout_width="0dp"
        android:layout_height="wrap_content"
        android:layout_weight="1"
        android:layout_gravity="center_vertical"
        android:orientation="vertical">
        <TextView
            android:id="@+id/text_title"
            android:layout_width="wrap_content"
            android:layout_height="wrap_content"
            android:layout_gravity="center_horizontal"
            android:textAppearance="?android:attr/textAppearanceMedium"
            android:text="Random Number" />
        <TextView
            android:id="@+id/text_number"
            android:layout_width="wrap_content"
            android:layout_height="wrap_content"
            android:layout_gravity="center_horizontal"
            android:textStyle="bold"
            android:textAppearance="?android:attr/textAppearanceLarge"/>
    </LinearLayout>

    <ImageButton
        android:id="@+id/button_refresh"
        android:layout_width="55dp"
        android:layout_height="55dp"
        android:layout_gravity="center_vertical"
        android:background="@null"
        android:src="@android:drawable/ic_menu_rotate" />

</LinearLayout>
```

Listing 6-46. *res/drawable/widget_background.xml*

```
<?xml version="1.0" encoding="utf-8"?>
<shape xmlns:android="http://schemas.android.com/apk/res/android"
    android:shape="rectangle">
    <corners
        android:radius="10dp" />
    <solid
        android:color="#A333" />
    <stroke
        android:width="2dp"
        android:color="#333" />
</shape>
```

It is always good practice with an AppWidget, especially in later platform versions where they can be resized, to define layouts that easily stretch and adapt to a changing container size. In this case, we have defined the background for the widget as a semitransparent rounded rectangle in XML, which could fill any size necessary. The children of the layout are also defined by using weight, so they will fill excess space. This layout is made of two `TextView` elements and an `ImageButton`. We have applied `android:id` attributes to all of these views because there will be no other way to access them once wrapped in a `RemoteViews` instance later. Listing 6-47 reveals our `AppWidgetProvider` mentioned earlier.

Listing 6-47. *AppWidgetProvider Instance*

```
public class SimpleAppWidget extends AppWidgetProvider {

    /*
     * This method is called to update the widgets created by this provider.
     * Normally, this will get called:
     * 1. Initially when the widget is created
     * 2. When the updatePeriodMillis defined in the AppWidgetProviderInfo expires
     * 3. Manually when updateAppWidget() is called on AppWidgetManager
     */
    @Override
    public void onUpdate(Context context, AppWidgetManager appWidgetManager,
            int[] appWidgetIds) {
        //Start the background service to update the widget
        context.startService(new Intent(context, RandomService.class));
    }
}
```

The only required method to implement here is `onUpdate()`, which will get called initially when the user selects the widget to be added and subsequently when either the framework or your application requests another update. In many cases, you can create the views and update your AppWidget directly inside this method. Because `AppWidgetProvider` is a `BroadcastReceiver`, it is not considered good practice to do long operations inside of it. If you must do intensive work to set up your AppWidget, you should start a `Service` instead and perhaps a background thread as well to do the work, which is what we have done here.

For convenience, this method is passed an `AppWidgetManager` instance, which is necessary for updating the AppWidget if you do so from this method. It is also possible to have multiple AppWidgets loaded on a single Launcher screen. The array of IDs references each individual AppWidget so you can update them all at once. Let's have a look at that `Service` in Listing 6-48.

Listing 6-48. *AppWidget Service*

```
public class RandomService extends Service {
    /* Broadcast Action When Updates Complete */
    public static final String ACTION_RANDOM_NUMBER =
            "com.examples.appwidget.ACTION_RANDOM_NUMBER";

    /* Current Data Saved as a static value */
    private static int sRandomNumber;
    public static int getRandomNumber() {
        return sRandomNumber;
    }

    @Override
    public int onStartCommand(Intent intent, int flags, int startId) {
        //Update the random number data
        sRandomNumber = (int)(Math.random() * 100);

        //Create the AppWidget view
        RemoteViews views = new RemoteViews(getPackageName(),
                R.layout.simple_widget_layout);
        views.setTextViewText(R.id.text_number, String.valueOf(sRandomNumber));

        //Set an Intent for the refresh button to start this service again
        PendingIntent refreshIntent = PendingIntent.getService(this, 0,
                new Intent(this, RandomService.class), 0);
        views.setOnClickPendingIntent(R.id.button_refresh, refreshIntent);

        //Set an Intent so tapping the widget text will open the Activity
        PendingIntent appIntent = PendingIntent.getActivity(this, 0,
                new Intent(this, MainActivity.class), 0);
        views.setOnClickPendingIntent(R.id.container, appIntent);

        //Update the widget
        AppWidgetManager manager = AppWidgetManager.getInstance(this);
        ComponentName widget = new ComponentName(this, SimpleAppWidget.class);
        manager.updateAppWidget(widget, views);

        //Fire a broadcast to notify listeners
        Intent broadcast = new Intent(ACTION_RANDOM_NUMBER);
        sendBroadcast(broadcast);

        //This service should not continue to run
        stopSelf();
        return START_NOT_STICKY;
    }

    /*
     * We are not binding to this Service, so this method should
     * just return null.
```

```
     */
    @Override
    public IBinder onBind(Intent intent) {
        return null;
    }
}
```

This RandomService does two operations when started. First, it regenerates and saves the random number data into a static field. Second, it constructs a new view for our AppWidget. In this way, we can use this Service to refresh our AppWidget on demand. We must first create a RemoteViews instance, passing in our widget layout. We use setTextViewText() to update a TextView in the layout with the new number, and setOnClickPendingIntent() attaches click listeners. The first PendingIntent is attached to the refresh button on the AppWidget, and the Intent that it is set to fire will restart this same Service. The second PendingIntent is attached to the main layout of the widget, allowing the user to click anywhere inside it, and it fires an Intent to launch the application's main Activity.

The final step with our RemoteViews initialized is to update the AppWidget. We do this by obtaining the AppWidgetManager instance and calling updateAppWidget(). We do not have the ID values for each AppWidget attached to the provider here, which is one method of updating them. Instead, we can pass a ComponentName that references our AppWidgetProvider and this update will apply to all AppWidgets attached to that provider.

To finish up, we send a broadcast to any listeners that a new random number has been generated and we stop the service. At this point we have all the code in place for our AppWidget to be live and working on a device. But let's add one more component and include an Activity that interacts with the same data. See Listings 6-49 and 6-50.

Listing 6-49. *res/layout/main.xml*

```
<?xml version="1.0" encoding="utf-8"?>
<LinearLayout xmlns:android="http://schemas.android.com/apk/res/android"
    android:layout_width="match_parent"
    android:layout_height="match_parent"
    android:orientation="vertical" >
    <Button
        android:layout_width="match_parent"
        android:layout_height="wrap_content"
        android:text="Generate New Number"
        android:onClick="onRandomClick" />
    <TextView
        android:layout_width="wrap_content"
        android:layout_height="wrap_content"
        android:layout_gravity="center_horizontal"
```

```
        android:textAppearance="?android:attr/textAppearanceLarge"
        android:text="Current Random Number" />
    <TextView
        android:id="@+id/text_number"
        android:layout_width="wrap_content"
        android:layout_height="wrap_content"
        android:layout_gravity="center_horizontal"
        android:textSize="55dp"
        android:textStyle="bold" />

</LinearLayout>
```

Listing 6-50. *Main Application Activity*

```
public class MainActivity extends Activity {

    private TextView mCurrentNumber;

    @Override
    protected void onCreate(Bundle savedInstanceState) {
        super.onCreate(savedInstanceState);
        setContentView(R.layout.main);

        mCurrentNumber = (TextView) findViewById(R.id.text_number);
    }

    @Override
    protected void onResume() {
        super.onResume();
        updateNumberView();
        //Register a receiver to receive updates when the service finishes
        IntentFilter filter = new IntentFilter(RandomService.ACTION_RANDOM_NUMBER);
        registerReceiver(mReceiver, filter);
    }

    @Override
    protected void onPause() {
        super.onPause();
        //Unregister our receiver
        unregisterReceiver(mReceiver);
    }

    public void onRandomClick(View v) {
        //Call the service to update the number data
        startService(new Intent(this, RandomService.class));
    }

    private void updateNumberView() {
        //Update the view with the latest number
        mCurrentNumber.setText(String.valueOf(RandomService.getRandomNumber()));
    }
```

```
    private BroadcastReceiver mReceiver = new BroadcastReceiver() {
        @Override
        public void onReceive(Context context, Intent intent) {
            //Update the view with the new number
            updateNumberView();
        }
    };
}
```

This `Activity` displays the current value of the random number provided by our `RandomService`. It also responds to button clicks by starting the service to generate a new number. The nice side effect is that this will also update our AppWidget so the two will stay in sync. We also register a `BroadcastReceiver` to listen for the event when the `Service` has finished generating new data so that we can update the user interface here as well. Figure 6-8 shows the application Activity, and the corresponding AppWidget added to the home screen.

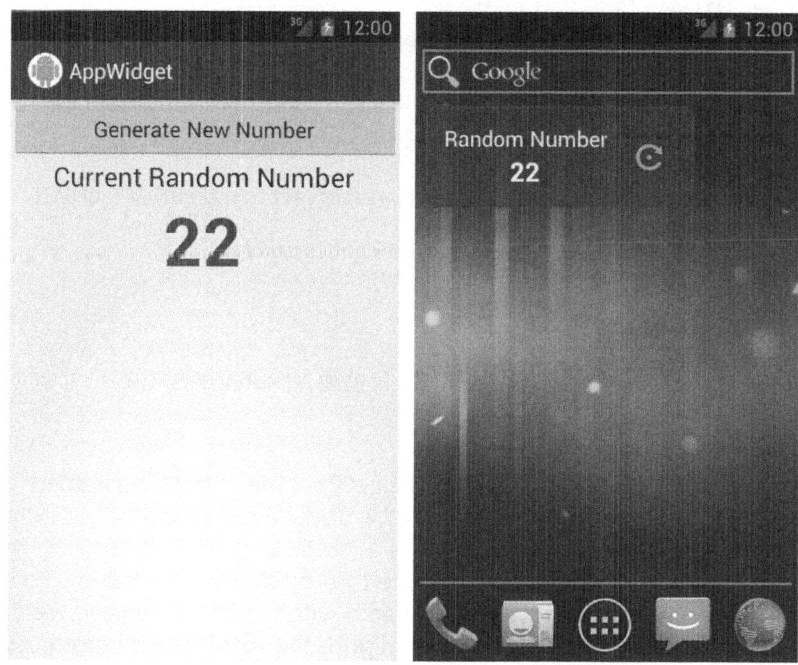

Figure 6-8. *The Random Number Activity app (left) and AppWidget (right).*

Collection-Based AppWidgets

(API Level 12)

Starting in Android 3.0, the things an AppWidget can display got a boost when collection views were added to the AppWidget framework. This allows applications to display information in a list, grid, or stack. In Android 3.1, AppWidgets also received the ability to be resized after being placed. Let's take a look at an example of an AppWidget that allows the user to see his or her media collection. Again, we'll start with the manifest in Listing 6-51.

Listing 6-51. *AndroidManifest.xml*

```
<application android:label="@string/app_name"
        android:icon="@drawable/ic_launcher">
        <!-- Collection AppWidget Components -->
        <activity android:name=".ListWidgetConfigureActivity">
            <intent-filter>
                <action android:name="android.appwidget.action.APPWIDGET_CONFIGURE"/>
            </intent-filter>
        </activity>

        <receiver android:name=".ListAppWidget">
            <intent-filter>
                <action android:name="android.appwidget.action.APPWIDGET_UPDATE" />
            </intent-filter>
            <meta-data android:name="android.appwidget.provider"
                android:resource="@xml/list_appwidget" />
        </receiver>

        <service android:name=".ListWidgetService"
            android:permission="android.permission.BIND_REMOTEVIEWS" />
        <service android:name=".MediaService" />
</application>
```

This example has a similar definition to the `AppWidgetProvider`, this time named `ListAppWidget`. We have defined a `Service` with the special permission `BIND_REMOTEVIEWS`. You will see shortly that this is actually a `RemoteViewsService`, which the framework will use to provide data for the AppWidget's list, similar to how a `ListAdapter` works with `ListView`. Finally, we have defined an `Activity` that will be used to configure the AppWidget before the user adds it. For this to take place, the `Activity` must include an `<intent-filter>` for the `APPWIDGET_CONFIGURE` action. The `AppWidgetProviderInfo` attached to our AppWidget is defined in Listing 6-52.

Listing 6-52. *res/xml/list_appwidget.xml*

```
<?xml version="1.0" encoding="utf-8"?>
<appwidget-provider xmlns:android="http://schemas.android.com/apk/res/android"
    android:minWidth="110dp"
    android:minHeight="110dp"
    android:updatePeriodMillis="86400000"
    android:initialLayout="@layout/list_widget_layout"
    android:configure="com.examples.appwidget.ListWidgetConfigureActivity"
    android:resizeMode="horizontal|vertical"/>
```

In addition to the standard attributes we discussed in the previous example, we have added android:configure to point to our configuration Activity, and android:resizeMode will enable this AppWidget to be resized in both directions. Listings 6-53 through 6-55 show the layouts we will use for both the AppWidget itself and for each row of the ListView.

Listing 6-53. *res/layout/list_widget_layout.xml*

```
<?xml version="1.0" encoding="utf-8"?>
<LinearLayout xmlns:android="http://schemas.android.com/apk/res/android"
    android:layout_width="match_parent"
    android:layout_height="match_parent"
    android:orientation="vertical"
    android:background="@drawable/list_widget_background">
    <TextView
        android:id="@+id/text_title"
        android:layout_width="match_parent"
        android:layout_height="45dp"
        android:gravity="center"
        android:textAppearance="?android:attr/textAppearanceMedium" />
    <FrameLayout
        android:layout_width="match_parent"
        android:layout_height="match_parent" >
        <ListView
            android:id="@+id/list"
            android:layout_width="match_parent"
            android:layout_height="match_parent" />
        <TextView
            android:id="@+id/list_empty"
            android:layout_width="wrap_content"
            android:layout_height="wrap_content"
            android:layout_gravity="center"
            android:text="No Items Available" />
    </FrameLayout>
</LinearLayout>
```

Listing 6-54. *res/drawable/list_widget_background.xml*

```
<?xml version="1.0" encoding="utf-8"?>
<shape xmlns:android="http://schemas.android.com/apk/res/android"
    android:shape="rectangle">
    <solid
        android:color="#A333" />
</shape>
```

Listing 6-55. *res/layout/list_widget_item.xml*

```
<?xml version="1.0" encoding="utf-8"?>
<LinearLayout xmlns:android="http://schemas.android.com/apk/res/android"
    android:id="@+id/list_widget_item"
    android:layout_width="match_parent"
    android:layout_height="?android:attr/listPreferredItemHeight"
    android:paddingLeft="10dp"
    android:gravity="center_vertical"
    android:orientation="vertical" >

    <TextView
        android:id="@+id/line1"
        android:layout_width="wrap_content"
        android:layout_height="wrap_content" />

    <TextView
        android:id="@+id/line2"
        android:layout_width="wrap_content"
        android:layout_height="wrap_content" />

</LinearLayout>
```

The layout of the AppWidget is a simple `ListView` with a `TextView` above it for a title. We have encapsulated the list into a `FrameLayout` so that we can also supply a sibling empty view as well.

> **TIP:** Try as you might, you will be unsuccessful using most of the Android standard row layouts for `ListView` in an AppWidget, such as `android.R.id.simple_list_item_1`. This is because these elements typically contain views like `CheckedTextView` that are not supported by `RemoteViews`. You will have to create your own layout for each row.

Before we look at the `AppWidgetProvider` for this example, let's first look at the configuration `Activity`. This is the first thing the user will see after dropping the AppWidget onto the home screen, but before it is installed. The result from this

Activity will actually govern if the AppWidgetProvider gets called at all! See Listings 6-56 and 6-57.

Listing 6-56. *res/layout/configure.xml*

```
<?xml version="1.0" encoding="utf-8"?>
<RelativeLayout xmlns:android="http://schemas.android.com/apk/res/android"
    android:layout_width="match_parent"
    android:layout_height="match_parent">
    <TextView
        android:id="@+id/text_title"
        android:layout_width="wrap_content"
        android:layout_height="wrap_content"
        android:textAppearance="?android:attr/textAppearanceLarge"
        android:text="Select Media Type:" />
    <RadioGroup
        android:id="@+id/group_mode"
        android:layout_width="wrap_content"
        android:layout_height="wrap_content"
        android:layout_below="@id/text_title"
        android:orientation="vertical">
        <RadioButton
            android:id="@+id/mode_image"
            android:layout_width="wrap_content"
            android:layout_height="wrap_content"
            android:text="Images"/>
        <RadioButton
            android:id="@+id/mode_video"
            android:layout_width="wrap_content"
            android:layout_height="wrap_content"
            android:text="Videos"/>
    </RadioGroup>

    <Button
        android:layout_width="match_parent"
        android:layout_height="wrap_content"
        android:layout_alignParentBottom="true"
        android:text="Add Widget"
        android:onClick="onAddClick" />

</RelativeLayout>
```

Listing 6-57. *Configuration Activity*

```
public class ListWidgetConfigureActivity extends Activity {

    private int mAppWidgetId;
    private RadioGroup mModeGroup;
```

```
@Override
protected void onCreate(Bundle savedInstanceState) {
    super.onCreate(savedInstanceState);
    setContentView(R.layout.configure);

    mModeGroup = (RadioGroup) findViewById(R.id.group_mode);

    mAppWidgetId = getIntent()
            .getIntExtra(AppWidgetManager.EXTRA_APPWIDGET_ID,
                    AppWidgetManager.INVALID_APPWIDGET_ID);

    setResult(RESULT_CANCELED);
}

public void onAddClick(View v) {
    SharedPreferences.Editor prefs =
            getSharedPreferences(String.valueOf(mAppWidgetId), MODE_PRIVATE)
                    .edit();
    RemoteViews views = new RemoteViews(getPackageName(),
            R.layout.list_widget_layout);
    switch (mModeGroup.getCheckedRadioButtonId()) {
    case R.id.mode_image:
        prefs.putString(ListWidgetService.KEY_MODE,
                ListWidgetService.MODE_IMAGE).commit();
        views.setTextViewText(R.id.text_title, "Image Collection");
        break;
    case R.id.mode_video:
        prefs.putString(ListWidgetService.KEY_MODE,
                ListWidgetService.MODE_VIDEO).commit();
        views.setTextViewText(R.id.text_title, "Video Collection");
        break;
    default:
        Toast.makeText(this, "Please Select a Media Type.",
                Toast.LENGTH_SHORT).show();
        return;
    }

    Intent intent = new Intent(this, ListWidgetService.class);
    intent.putExtra(AppWidgetManager.EXTRA_APPWIDGET_ID, mAppWidgetId);
    intent.setData(Uri.parse(intent.toUri(Intent.URI_INTENT_SCHEME)));

    //Attach the adapter to populate the data for the list in
    //the form of an Intent that points to our RemoveViewsService
    views.setRemoteAdapter(mAppWidgetId, R.id.list, intent);
    //Set the empty view for the list
    views.setEmptyView(R.id.list, R.id.list_empty);

    Intent viewIntent = new Intent(Intent.ACTION_VIEW);
    PendingIntent pendingIntent = PendingIntent.getActivity(this, 0, viewIntent, 0);
    views.setPendingIntentTemplate(R.id.list, pendingIntent);
```

```
        AppWidgetManager manager = AppWidgetManager.getInstance(this);
        manager.updateAppWidget(mAppWidgetId, views);

        Intent data = new Intent();
        data.putExtra(AppWidgetManager.EXTRA_APPWIDGET_ID, mAppWidgetId);
        setResult(RESULT_OK, data);
        finish();
    }
}
```

The layout for this Activity provides a single RadioGroup to choose between images and videos, which will be the selected media type that the AppWidget displays in its list and on an add button. By convention, when we enter the Activity we immediately set the result to RESULT_CANCELED. This is because if the user ever leaves this Activity without going through the process of hitting Add, we don't want the AppWidget to show up on the screen. The framework checks the result of this Activity to decide whether or not to add the AppWidget. We are also passed the ID of this AppWidget by the framework, which we save for later.

Once the user had made a selection and clicks Add, his or her selection is saved in a specific SharedPreferences instance named by the AppWidget's ID. We want to be able to allow the application to handle multiple widgets, and we want their configuration values to be separate, so we avoid using the default SharedPreferences to persist this data.

> **NOTE:** In Android 4.1 the ability to pass configuration data to the AppWidget as a Bundle of "options" was introduced. However, to keep compatibility with previous versions, we can use the SharedPreferences approach instead.

We also can begin to construct the RemoteViews for this AppWidget, setting the title based on the user's type selection. For a collection-based AppWidget, we must construct an Intent that will launch an instance of RemoteViewsService to act as the adapter for the collection data, similar to a ListAdapter. This is attached to the RemoteViews with setRemoteAdapter(), which also takes the ID of the ListView we want the adapter to connect with. We also use setEmptyView() to attach the ID of our sibling TextView to display when the list is empty.

Each list item must have a PendingIntent attached to fire when the user clicks on it. The framework is aware that you may need to supply specific information for every item, so it uses the pattern of a PendingIntent template that gets filled in by each item. Here we are creating the base Intent for each item to fill in as a simple ACTION_VIEW, and attaching it via setPendingIntentTemplate(); the data and extras fields will be filled in later.

With all this in place, we call updateAppWidget() on the AppWidgetManager. In this case, we called a version of this method that takes a single ID rather than a ComponentName because we only want to call update for this specific AppWidget. We then set the result to RESULT_OK and finish, allowing the framework to add the AppWidget to the screen. Let's look briefly now at the AppWidgetProvider, which is shown in Listing 6-58.

Listing 6-58. *List AppWidgetProvider*

```
public class ListAppWidget extends AppWidgetProvider {

    /*
     * This method is called to update the widgets created by this provider.
     * Because we supplied a configuration Activity, this method will not get called
     * for the initial adding of the widget, but will still be called:
     * 1. When the updatePeriodMillis defined in the AppWidgetProviderInfo expires
     */
    @Override
    public void onUpdate(Context context, AppWidgetManager appWidgetManager,
            int[] appWidgetIds) {
        //Update each widget created by this provider
        for (int i=0; i < appWidgetIds.length; i++) {
            Intent intent = new Intent(context, ListWidgetService.class);
            intent.putExtra(AppWidgetManager.EXTRA_APPWIDGET_ID, appWidgetIds[i]);
            intent.setData(Uri.parse(intent.toUri(Intent.URI_INTENT_SCHEME)));

            RemoteViews views = new RemoteViews(context.getPackageName(),
                    R.layout.list_widget_layout);
            //Set the title view based on the widget configuration
            SharedPreferences prefs =
                    context.getSharedPreferences(String.valueOf(appWidgetIds[i]),
                            Context.MODE_PRIVATE);
            String mode = prefs.getString(ListWidgetService.KEY_MODE,
                    ListWidgetService.MODE_IMAGE);
            if (ListWidgetService.MODE_VIDEO.equals(mode)) {
                views.setTextViewText(R.id.text_title, "Video Collection");
            } else {
                views.setTextViewText(R.id.text_title, "Image Collection");
            }

            //Attach the adapter to populate the data for the list in
            //the form of an Intent that points to our RemoveViewsService
            views.setRemoteAdapter(appWidgetIds[i], R.id.list, intent);

            //Set the empty view for the list
            views.setEmptyView(R.id.list, R.id.list_empty);
```

```
            //Set the template Intent for item clicks that each item will fill-in
            Intent viewIntent = new Intent(Intent.ACTION_VIEW);
            PendingIntent pendingIntent = PendingIntent.getActivity(context, 0,
                    viewIntent, 0);
            views.setPendingIntentTemplate(R.id.list, pendingIntent);

            appWidgetManager.updateAppWidget(appWidgetIds[i], views);
        }
    }

    /*
     * Called when the first widget is added to the provider
     */
    @Override
    public void onEnabled(Context context) {
        //Start the service to monitor the MediaStore
        context.startService(new Intent(context, MediaService.class));
    }

    /*
     * Called when all widgets have been removed from this provider
     */
    @Override
    public void onDisabled(Context context) {
        //Stop the service that is monitoring the MediaStore
        context.stopService(new Intent(context, MediaService.class));
    }

    /*
     * Called when one or more widgets attached to this provider are removed
     */
    @Override
    public void onDeleted(Context context, int[] appWidgetIds) {
        //Remove the SharedPreferences we created for each widget removed
        for (int i=0; i < appWidgetIds.length; i++) {
            context.getSharedPreferences(String.valueOf(appWidgetIds[i]),
                    Context.MODE_PRIVATE)
                .edit()
                .clear()
                .commit();
        }

    }
}
```

The onUpdate() method of this provider is identical to the code found in the configuration Activity, except that the provider is reading the current values of the user configuration settings rather than updating them. The code must be the same because we want to have the same AppWidget result from a subsequent update.

This provider also overrides onEnabled() and onDisabled(). These methods are called when the very first widget is added to the provider and after the very last widget is removed. The provider is using them to start and stop a long-running Service that we will look at in more detail shortly, but its purpose is to monitor the MediaStore for changes so we can update our AppWidget. Finally, the onDeleted() callback is called for each AppWidget that gets removed. In our example, we make use of this to clear out the SharedPreferences we had created when the AppWidget was added.

Now look at Listing 6-59, which defines our RemoteViewsService for serving data to the AppWidget list.

Listing 6-59. *RemoteViews Adapter*

```
public class ListWidgetService extends RemoteViewsService {

    public static final String KEY_MODE = "mode";
    public static final String MODE_IMAGE = "image";
    public static final String MODE_VIDEO = "video";

    @Override
    public RemoteViewsFactory onGetViewFactory(Intent intent) {
        return new ListRemoteViewsFactory(this, intent);
    }

    private class ListRemoteViewsFactory implements
            RemoteViewsService.RemoteViewsFactory {
        private Context mContext;
        private int mAppWidgetId;

        private Cursor mDataCursor;

        public ListRemoteViewsFactory(Context context, Intent intent) {
            mContext = context.getApplicationContext();
            mAppWidgetId = intent.getIntExtra(AppWidgetManager.EXTRA_APPWIDGET_ID,
                    AppWidgetManager.INVALID_APPWIDGET_ID);
        }

        @Override
        public void onCreate() {
            //Load preferences to get settings user set while adding the widget
            SharedPreferences prefs =
                    mContext.getSharedPreferences(String.valueOf(mAppWidgetId),
                            MODE_PRIVATE);
            //Get the user's config setting, defaulting to image mode
            String mode = prefs.getString(KEY_MODE, MODE_IMAGE);
```

```
        //Set the media type to query based on the user configuration setting
        if (MODE_VIDEO.equals(mode)) {
            //Query for video items in the MediaStore
            String[] projection = {MediaStore.Video.Media.TITLE,
                    MediaStore.Video.Media.DATE_TAKEN,
                    MediaStore.Video.Media.DATA};
            mDataCursor = MediaStore.Images.Media.query(getContentResolver(),
                    MediaStore.Video.Media.EXTERNAL_CONTENT_URI, projection);
        } else {
            //Query for image items in the MediaStore
            String[] projection = {MediaStore.Images.Media.TITLE,
                    MediaStore.Images.Media.DATE_TAKEN,
                    MediaStore.Images.Media.DATA};
            mDataCursor = MediaStore.Images.Media.query(getContentResolver(),
                    MediaStore.Images.Media.EXTERNAL_CONTENT_URI, projection);
        }
    }

    /*
     * This method gets called after onCreate(), but also if an external call
     * to AppWidgetManager.notifyAppWidgetViewDataChanged() indicates that the
     * data for a widget should be refreshed.
     */
    @Override
    public void onDataSetChanged() {
        //Refresh the Cursor data
        mDataCursor.requery();
    }

    @Override
    public void onDestroy() {
        //Close the cursor when we no longer need it.
        mDataCursor.close();
        mDataCursor = null;
    }

    @Override
    public int getCount() {
        return mDataCursor.getCount();
    }

    /*
     * If your data comes from the network or otherwise may take a while to load,
     * you can return a loading view here.  This view will be shown while
     * getViewAt() is blocked until it returns
     */
    @Override
    public RemoteViews getLoadingView() {
        return null;
    }
```

```
        /*
         * Return a view for each item in the collection.  You can safely perform long
         * operations in this method.  The loading view will be displayed until this
         * method returns.
         */
        @Override
        public RemoteViews getViewAt(int position) {
            mDataCursor.moveToPosition(position);

            RemoteViews views = new RemoteViews(getPackageName(),
                    R.layout.list_widget_item);
            views.setTextViewText(R.id.line1, mDataCursor.getString(0));
            views.setTextViewText(R.id.line2, DateFormat.format("MM/dd/yyyy",
                    mDataCursor.getLong(1)));

            SharedPreferences prefs = mContext
                .getSharedPreferences(String.valueOf(mAppWidgetId), MODE_PRIVATE);
            String mode = prefs.getString(KEY_MODE, MODE_IMAGE);
            String type;
            if (MODE_VIDEO.equals(mode)) {
                type = "video/*";
            } else {
                type = "image/*";
            }

            Uri data = Uri.fromFile(new File(mDataCursor.getString(2)));

            Intent intent = new Intent();
            intent.setDataAndType(data, type);
            views.setOnClickFillInIntent(R.id.list_widget_item, intent);

            return views;
        }

        @Override
        public int getViewTypeCount() {
            return 1;
        }

        @Override
        public boolean hasStableIds() {
            return false;
        }

        @Override
        public long getItemId(int position) {
            return position;
        }
    }
}
```

The RemoteViewsFactory implementation that RemoteViewsService must return looks very much like a ListAdapter. Many of the methods like getCount() and getViewTypeCount() perform the same functions as they do for local lists. When the RemoteViewsFactory is first created, we check the setting value the user had selected during configuration, and we then retrieve the appropriate Cursor from the system's MediaStore Content Provider to display either images or videos. When the factory is destroyed because it's no longer needed, that is our opportunity to close the Cursor. When an external stimulus tells AppWidgetManager that the data need to be refreshed, onDataSetChanged() will be called. To refresh our data, all we need to do is requery() the Cursor.

The getViewAt() method is where we obtain a view for each row in the list. This method is safe to call long-running operations in (such as network I/O); the framework will display whatever is returned from getLoadingView() instead until getViewAt() returns. In the example, we update the RemoteViews version of our row layout with the title and a text representation of the date for the given item. We must then fill in the PendingIntent template that was set in our original update. We set the file path of the image or video and the appropriate MIME type as the data field. Combined with ACTION_VIEW, this will open the file in the device's Gallery app (or any other application capable of handling the media) when the item is clicked.

You may notice in this example we didn't use explicit column names when retrieving the Cursor data. This is primarily because the projections between the two types have different names, so it is more efficient to access them by index. Finally, look at Listing 6-60, which reveals the background service that was started and stopped by the AppWidgetProvider.

Listing 6-60. *Update Monitoring Service*

```
public class MediaService extends Service {

    private ContentObserver mMediaStoreObserver;

    @Override
    public void onCreate() {
        super.onCreate();
        //Create a register a new observer on the MediaStore when this Service begins
        mMediaStoreObserver = new ContentObserver(new Handler()) {
            @Override
            public void onChange(boolean selfChange) {
                //Update all the widgets currently attached to our AppWidgetProvider
                AppWidgetManager manager =
                        AppWidgetManager.getInstance(MediaService.this);
                ComponentName provider = new ComponentName(MediaService.this,
                        ListAppWidget.class);
                int[] appWidgetIds = manager.getAppWidgetIds(provider);
```

```
                //This method triggers onDataSetChanged() in the RemoteViewsService
                manager.notifyAppWidgetViewDataChanged(appWidgetIds, R.id.list);
            }
        };
        //Register for Images and Video
        getContentResolver().registerContentObserver(
            MediaStore.Images.Media.EXTERNAL_CONTENT_URI, true, mMediaStoreObserver);
        getContentResolver().registerContentObserver(
            MediaStore.Video.Media.EXTERNAL_CONTENT_URI, true, mMediaStoreObserver);
    }

    @Override
    public void onDestroy() {
        super.onDestroy();
        //Unregister the observer when the Service stops
        getContentResolver().unregisterContentObserver(mMediaStoreObserver);
    }


    /*
     * We are not binding to this Service, so this method should
     * just return null.
     */
    @Override
    public IBinder onBind(Intent intent) {
        return null;
    }

}
```

The purpose of this Service is to register a ContentObserver with the MediaStore while any AppWidgets are active. This way, when a photo or video is added or removed, we can update the list of our widget to reflect that. Whenever the ContentObserver triggers, we will call notifyAppWidgetViewDataChanged() on AppWidgetManager for every widget currently attached. This will trigger the onDataSetChanged() callback in the RemoveViewsService to refresh the lists. You can see the result of all this working together in Figures 6-9 and 6-10.

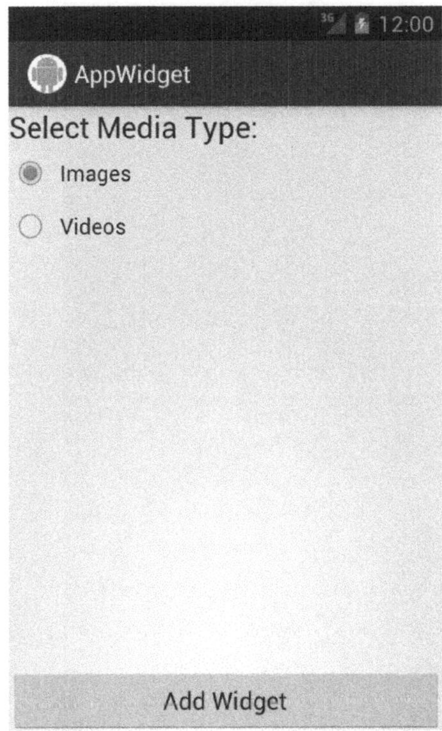

Figure 6-9. *Configuration Activity prior to AppWidget being added.*

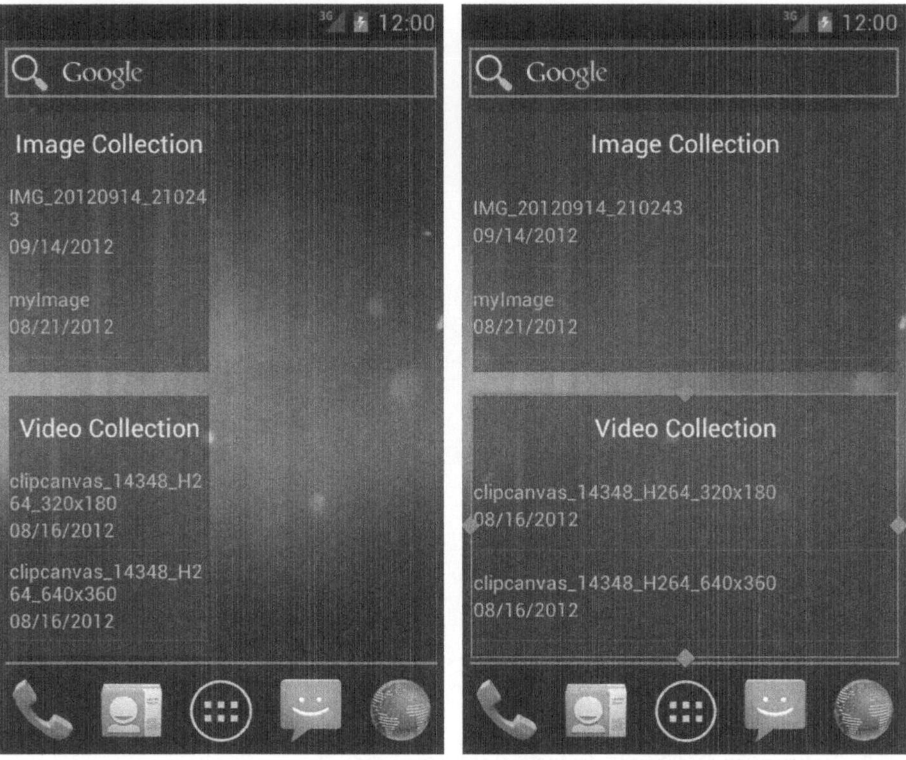

Figure 6-10. *AppWidget added for both types (left) and after being resized (right).*

You can see that by simply adding the resize attributes to the `AppWidgetProviderInfo`, the size of the AppWidget can be modified by the user. Each list can be scrolled, and a tap on any item will bring up the default viewing application to view the image or play the video.

Summary

In this chapter, you learned how your application can interact directly with the Android operating system. We discussed several methods of placing operations into the background for various lengths of time. You learned how applications can share responsibility, launching each other to best accomplish the task at hand. Finally, we presented how the system exposes the content gathered by its core application suite for your application's use. In the next chapter, we will look at how you can use the wide array of publicly available Java libraries to further enhance your application.

Chapter 7

Working with Libraries

Smart Android developers deliver their apps to market faster by taking advantage of libraries, which reduce development time by providing previously created and tested code. Developers may create and use their own libraries, use libraries created by others, or do both.

This chapter's initial recipes show you how to create and use your own libraries. Subsequent recipes introduce you to Kidroid's kiChart charting library for presenting bar, line, and pie charts; to IBM's Message Queue Telemetry Transport (MQTT) library for implementing lightweight push messaging in your apps; and to Google's Support Package, which offers various libraries that apps can use to access various new Android features on older Android platforms where these features are not supported.

> **TIP:** OpenIntents.org publishes a list of libraries from various vendors that you might find helpful in your app development (`http://openintents.org/en/libraries`). Examples include AdWhirl for serving ads in your app from any number of ad networks as well as providing your own ads, and the previously mentioned kiChart.

7-1. Creating Java Library JARs

Problem

You want to create a library that stores Android-agnostic code and that can be used in your Android and non-Android projects.

Solution

Create a JAR-based library that accesses only Java 5 (and earlier) APIs via JDK command-line tools or Eclipse.

How It Works

Suppose you plan to create a simple library of math-oriented utilities. This library will consist of a single `MathUtils` class with various `static` methods. Listing 7-1 presents an early version of this class.

Listing 7-1. *`MathUtils` Implementing Math-Oriented Utilities via `static` Methods*

```
package ca.tutortutor.mathutils;

public class MathUtils
{
   public static long factorial(long n)
   {
      if (n <= 0)
         return 1;
      else
         return n*factorial(n-1);
   }
}
```

`MathUtils` currently consists of a single `long factorial(long n)` class method for computing and returning factorials (perhaps for use in calculating permutations and combinations). You might eventually expand this class to support fast Fourier transforms and other math operations not supported by the `java.lang.Math` class.

> **CAUTION:** When creating a library that stores Android-agnostic code, make sure to access only standard Java APIs (such as the collections framework) that are supported by Android. Don't access unsupported Java APIs (such as Swing) or Android-specific APIs (such as Android widgets).

Creating MathUtils with the JDK

Developing a JAR-based library with the JDK is easy. Complete the following steps to create a `mathutils.jar` file that contains the `MathUtils` class:

1. Within the current directory, create a package directory structure consisting of a ca subdirectory that contains a tutortutor subdirectory that contains a mathutils subdirectory.

2. Copy Listing 7-1's MathUtils.java source code to a MathUtils.java file stored in mathutils.

3. Assuming that the current directory contains the ca subdirectory, execute javac ca/tutortutor/mathutils/MathUtils.java to compile MathUtils.java. A MathUtils.class file is stored in ca/tutortutor/mathutils.

4. Create mathutils.jar by executing the jar cfv mathutils.jar ca/tutortutor/mathutils/*.class. The resulting mathutils.jar file contains a ca/tutortutor/mathutils/MathUtils.class entry.

NOTE: If you're using JDK 7, execute one of the following command lines to compile MathUtils.java:

```
javac -source 1.5 -target 1.5
ca/tutortutor/mathutils/MathUtils.java
```

```
javac -source 1.6 -target 1.6
ca/tutortutor/mathutils/MathUtils.java
```

Each command line results in a harmless "bootclasspath" warning message that is explained at https://blogs.oracle.com/darcy/entry/bootclasspath_older_source

Fail to do this and you will see the following warning messages when executing ant debug to build an APK that references this library:

```
[dx] trouble processing:

[dx] bad class file magic (cafebabe) or version (0033.0000)

[dx] ...while parsing ca/tutortutor/mathutils/MathUtils.class

[dx] ...while processing
ca/tutortutor/mathutils/MathUtils.class

[dx] 1 warning
```

> Furthermore, after installing the APK, an attempt to run `UseMathUtils` will result in a dialog box stating "Unfortunately, UseMathUtils has stopped." Although JDK 7 is a somewhat problematic environment for developing Android apps (as first pointed out in Chapter 1) and libraries, it is not impossible to create them, as you have seen in Chapter 1 and above.

Creating MathUtils with Eclipse

Developing a JAR-based library with Eclipse is a bit more involved. Complete the following steps to create a `mathutils.jar` file that contains the `MathUtils` class:

1. Assuming that you've installed the Eclipse version discussed in Chapter 1, start this IDE if it is not already running.
2. Select New from the File menu and Java Project from the resulting pop-up menu.
3. On the resulting *New Java Project* dialog box, enter **`mathutils`** into the Project name textfield. If the execution environment JRE setting (in the JRE section) is set to JavaSE-1.7, change this setting to JavaSE-1.6. Click the Finish button.
4. Expand Package Explorer's mathutils node. Then right-click the src node (underneath mathutils) and select New, followed by Package from the resulting pop-up menus.
5. On the resulting *New Java Package* dialog box, enter **`ca.tutortutor.mathutils`** into the Name textfield and click Finish.
6. Right-click the resulting ca.tutortutor.mathutils node and select New, followed by Class on the resulting pop-up menus.
7. On the resulting *New Java Class* dialog box, enter **`MathUtils`** into the Name field and click Finish.
8. Replace the skeletal contents in the resulting MathUtils.java editor window with Listing 7-1.

9. Right-click the mathutils project node and select Build Project from the resulting pop-up menu. (You might have to deselect Build Automatically from the project menu first.) Ignore any "Build path specifies execution environment JavaSE-1.6. There are no JREs installed in the workspace that are strictly compatible with this environment" warning message.
10. Right-click the mathutils project node and select Export from the resulting pop-up menu.
11. On the resulting *Export* dialog box, select JAR file under the Java node (if not selected), and click the Next button.
12. On the resulting *JAR Export* dialog box, keep the defaults but enter `mathutils.jar` into the JAR file textfield. Click Finish. (At this point, you will see a *Save Modified Resources* dialog box if you have not saved the source code entered in Step 8. Click OK to dismiss this dialog box.) The resulting `mathutils.jar` file is created in your Eclipse workspace's root directory.

7-2. Using Java Library JARs

Problem

You've successfully built `mathutils.jar` and want to learn how to integrate this JAR file into your command-line-based or Eclipse-based Android projects.

Solution

You'll create a command-line-based or Eclipse-based Android project with a `libs` directory and copy `mathutils.jar` into this directory.

> **NOTE:** It's common practice to store libraries (`.jar` files and Linux shared object libraries, `.so` files) in a `libs` subdirectory of the Android project directory. The Android build system automatically takes files found in `libs` and integrates them into APKs. When the library is a shared object library, it is stored in the `.apk` file with an entry starting with `lib` (not `libs`).

How It Works

Now that you've created `mathutils.jar`, you'll need an Android app to try out this library. Listing 7-2 presents the source code to a `UseMathUtils` single-activity-based app that computes 5-factorial, which the activity subsequently outputs.

Listing 7-2. *`UseMathUtils` Invoking `MathUtil`'s `factorial()` Method to Compute 5-factorial*

```
package ca.tutortutor.usemathutils;

import android.app.Activity;

import android.os.Bundle;

import android.widget.TextView;

import ca.tutortutor.mathutils.MathUtils;

public class UseMathUtils extends Activity
{
   @Override
   public void onCreate(Bundle savedInstanceState)
   {
      super.onCreate(savedInstanceState);
      TextView tv = new TextView(this);
      tv.setText("5! = "+MathUtils.factorial(5));
      setContentView(tv);
   }
}
```

Creating and Running UseMathUtils with the Android SDK

Execute the following command (spread across two lines for readability) to create a `UseMathUtils` project:

```
android create project -t 1 -p C:\prj\dev\UseMathUtils -a UseMathUtils
                       -k ca.tutortutor.usemathutils
```

This command assumes an Android 4.1 target, a Windows platform, and a `C:\prj\dev` hierarchy in which projects are stored.

Now, replace the skeletal `src/ca/tutortutor/usemathutils/UseMathUtils.java` source file with the contents of Listing 7-2.

Continue by copying `mathutils.jar` into the project's `libs` subdirectory.

At this point, execute the following command to build this project in debug mode:

```
ant debug
```

Assuming success, execute the following command from the project's `bin` subdirectory to install the `UseMathUtils-debug.apk` file onto AVD1, which should be running:

```
adb install UseMathUtils-debug.apk
```

Finally, launch the app. You should see the output shown in Figure 7-1.

Figure 7-1. *`UseMathUtils`'s simple user interface could be expanded to let the user enter an arbitrary number.*

Creating and Running UseMathUtils with Eclipse

Complete the following steps to create the `UseMathUtils` project in Eclipse:

1. Assuming that you've installed the Eclipse version discussed in Chapter 1, start this IDE if it is not already running.
2. Select New from the File menu, and select Project from the resulting pop-up menu.
3. On the resulting *New Project* dialog box, expand the Android node in the wizard tree (if not expanded), select the Android Application Project branch below this node (if not selected), and click the Next button.
4. On the resulting *New Android App* dialog box, enter **`UseMathUtils`** into the Application Name textfield. This entered name also appears in the Project Name textfield, and it identifies the folder/directory in which the `UseMathUtils` project is stored.
5. Enter **`ca.tutortutor.usemathutils`** into the Package Name textfield.

6. Via Build SDK, select the appropriate Android SDK to target. This selection identifies the Android platform you'd like your app to be built against. Assuming that you've installed only the Android 4.1 platform, only this choice should appear and be selected.
7. Via Minimum SDK, select the minimum Android SDK on which your app runs, or keep the default setting.
8. Leave the "Create custom launcher icon" check box checked if you want a custom launcher icon to be created. Otherwise, uncheck this check box when you supply your own launcher icon.
9. Leave the "Mark this project as a library" check box unchecked because you are not creating a library.
10. Leave the "Create Project in Workspace" check box checked, and click Next.
11. On the resulting Configure Launcher Icon pane, make suitable adjustments to the custom launcher icon; click Next.
12. On the resulting Create Activity pane, leave the Create Activity check box checked, make sure that BlankActivity is selected, and click Next.
13. On the resulting New Blank Activity pane, enter **`UseMathUtils`** into the Activity Name textfield. Keep all other settings and click Next (if enabled). Otherwise, click Finish.
14. If Next is enabled, click this button. You will observe an Install Dependencies pane telling you to install Google's support library (discussed in this chapter's final recipe). Click the Install/Upgrade button to install this library, and then follow the instructions on the resulting dialog boxes. Click Finish to complete the project.

Eclipse creates a UseMathUtils node in the Package Explorer window. Complete the following steps to set up all files:

1. Expand the UseMathUtils node (if not expanded), followed by the src node, followed by the ca.tutortutor.usemathutils node.

2. Double-click the UseMathUtils.java node (underneath ca.tutortutor.usemathutils) and replace the skeletal contents in the resulting window with Listing 7-2. Ignore any error messages; they will disappear shortly.
3. Use your platform's file manager program to select and drag the previously created `mathutils.jar` file to the libs node. If a *File Operation* dialog box appears, keep the Copy files radio button selected and click the OK button.
4. Expand the libs node, right-click mathutils.jar, and select Build Path followed by Configure Build Path on the resulting pop-up menus.
5. On the resulting *Properties for UseMathUtils* dialog box, select the Libraries tab and click the Add Jars button.
6. On the resulting *JAR Selection* dialog box, expand the UseMathUtils node followed by the libs node. Select mathutils.jar and click OK to close *JAR Selection*. Click OK a second time to close *Properties for UseMathUtils*.

Build this project by right-clicking the UseMathUtils node and selecting Build Project from the pop-up menu. Then, with the UseMathUtils node selected, select Run from the menubar followed by Run from the drop-down menu. (Click Yes on the resulting *Save Resource* dialog box if you are prompted to save changes to `UseMathUtils.java`.) If a *Run As* dialog box appears, select Android Application and click OK. Eclipse starts the emulator, installs the project's APK, and runs the app. Figure 7-2 shows its output.

Figure 7-2. *`UseMathUtils`'s user interface looks different because of an Eclipse-generated custom theme..*

> **NOTE:** Examine this app's `UseMathUtils.apk` file (`jar tvf UseMathUtils.apk`) and you won't find a `mathutils.jar` entry. Instead, you'll find `classes.dex`, which contains the app's Dalvik-executable bytecode.

> `classes.dex` also contains the Dalvik equivalent of the `MathUtils` classfile, because the Android build system unpacks JAR files, processes their contents with the `dx` tool to convert their Java bytecodes to Dalvik bytecodes, and merges the equivalent Dalvik code into `classes.dex`. (The same is true of `UseMathUtils-debug.apk`.)

7-3. Creating Android Library Projects

Problem

You want to create a library that stores Android-specific code, such as custom widgets or activities with or without resources.

Solution

You can create *Android library projects*, which are projects containing shareable Android source code and resources and which you can reference in other Android projects. This is useful when you want to reuse common code. Library projects cannot be installed onto a device. They are pulled into the `.apk` file at build time.

> **NOTE:** The Android 4.0 SDK (r14) features changes to Android library projects. Previously, library projects were handled as extra resource and source code folders for use when compiling the resources and the app's source, respectively. Because developers wanted to distribute a library as one JAR file of compiled code and resources, and because library project implementations were extremely fragile in Eclipse, r14 based Android library projects on a compiled-code library mechanism. Check out the "Changes to Library Projects in Android SDK Tools, r14" blog post (`http://android-developers.blogspot.ca/2011/10/changes-to-library-projects-in-android.html`) for more information.

How It Works

Suppose you want to create a library that contains a single reusable custom view describing a game board (for playing chess, checkers, or even tic-tac-toe). Listing 7-3 reveals this view's GameBoard class.

Listing 7-3. *GameBoard Describing a Reusable Custom View for Drawing Different Game Boards*

```
package ca.tutortutor.gameboard;

import android.content.Context;

import android.graphics.Canvas;
import android.graphics.Paint;

import android.view.View;

public class GameBoard extends View
{
   private int nSquares, colorA, colorB;

   private Paint paint;
   private int squareDim;

   public GameBoard(Context context, int nSquares, int colorA, int colorB)
   {
      super(context);
      this.nSquares = nSquares;
      this.colorA = colorA;
      this.colorB = colorB;
      paint = new Paint();
   }

   @Override
   protected void onDraw(Canvas canvas)
   {
      for (int row = 0; row < nSquares; row++)
      {
         paint.setColor(((row & 1) == 0) ? colorA : colorB);
         for (int col = 0; col < nSquares; col++)
         {
            int a = col*squareDim;
            int b = row*squareDim;
            canvas.drawRect(a, b, a+squareDim, b+squareDim, paint);
            paint.setColor((paint.getColor() == colorA) ? colorB : colorA);
         }
      }
   }
```

```
    @Override
    protected void onMeasure(int widthMeasuredSpec, int heightMeasuredSpec)
    {
       // keep the view squared
       int width = MeasureSpec.getSize(widthMeasuredSpec);
       int height = MeasureSpec.getSize(heightMeasuredSpec);
       int d = (width == 0) ? height : (height == 0) ? width :
               (width < height) ? width : height;
       setMeasuredDimension(d, d);
       squareDim = width/nSquares;
    }
}
```

Android custom views subclass android.view.View or one of its subclasses (such as android.widget.TextView). GameBoard subclasses View directly because it doesn't need any subclass functionality.

GameBoard declares the following fields:

- nSquares stores the number of squares on each side of the game board. Typical values include 3 (for a 3-by-3 board) and 8 (for an 8-by-8 board).
- colorA stores the color of even-numbered squares on even-numbered rows, and the color of odd-numbered squares on odd-numbered rows—row and column numbering starts at 0.
- colorB stores the color of odd-numbered squares on even-numbered rows, and the color of even-numbered squares on odd-numbered rows.
- paint stores a reference to an android.graphics.Paint object that is used to specify the square color (colorA or colorB) when the game board is drawn.
- squareDim stores the dimension of a square—the number of pixels on each side.

GameBoard's constructor initializes this widget by storing its nSquares, colorA, and colorB arguments in same-named fields, and it also instantiates the Paint class. Before doing so, however, it passes its context argument to its View superclass.

NOTE: View subclasses are required to pass an android.content.Context instance to their View superclass. Doing so identifies the context (an activity, for example) in which the custom view is running. Custom view subclasses can

> subsequently call View's Context getContext() method to return this Context object, so that they can call Context methods to access the current theme, resources, and so on.

Android tells a custom view to draw itself by calling the view's overriding protected void onDraw(Canvas canvas) method. GameBoard's onDraw(Canvas) method responds by invoking android.graphics.Canvas's void drawRect(float left, float top, float right, float bottom, Paint paint) method to paint each square for each row/column intersection. The final paint argument determines the color of that square.

Before Android invokes onDraw(Canvas), it must measure the view. It accomplishes this task by invoking the view's overriding protected void onMeasure(int widthMeasureSpec, int heightMeasureSpec) method, where the passed arguments specify the horizontal and vertical space requirements that are imposed by the parent view. The custom view typically passes these arguments to the View.MeasureSpec nested class's static int getSize(int measureSpec) method to return the exact width or height of the view based on the passed measureSpec argument. The returned values or a modified version of these values must then be passed to View's void setMeasuredDimension(int measuredWidth, int measuredHeight) method to store the measured width and height. Failure to call this method results in a thrown exception at runtime. Because game boards should be square, GameBoard's onMeasure(int, int) method passes the minimum of the width and height to setMeasuredDimension(int, int) to ensure a square game board.

Creating GameBoard with the Android SDK

You create an Android library project in much the same way as you create a standard app project. However, instead of specifying a command line beginning with "android create project" (see Chapter 1), you specify a command line starting with "android create lib-project", according to the following syntax:

```
android create lib-project --target target_ID
                          --name your_project_name
                          --path /path/to/your/project/project_name
                          --package your_library_package_namespace
```

This command creates a standard project structure, adding the following line to the project's project.properties file indicating that the project is a library:

```
android.library=true
```

Once the command completes, the library project is created and you can begin moving source code and resources into it.

> **TIP:** To convert an existing app project to a library project for other apps to use, add the `android.library=true` property to the app's `project.properties` file.

Execute the following command (spread across two lines for readability) to create a `GameBoard` library project:

```
android create lib-project -t 1 -p C:\prj\dev\GameBoard
                           -k ca.tutortutor.gameboard
```

Continue by creating a `ca/tutortutor/gameboard` hierarchy under the `src` directory, and store a `GameBoard.java` source file containing Listing 7-3's code in this directory.

Although you can build the library by executing `ant debug` or `ant release` (it doesn't matter which command you use, because the same `classes.jar` file is created in the `bin` directory), there is no need to do so because this library will be built automatically when referenced from another project (as demonstrated in the next recipe).

Creating GameBoard with Eclipse

Complete the following steps to create the `GameBoard` project in Eclipse:

1. Assuming that you've installed the Eclipse version discussed in Chapter 1, start this IDE if it is not already running.
2. Select New from the File menu, and select Project from the resulting pop-up menu.
3. On the resulting *New Project* dialog box, expand the Android node in the wizard tree (if not expanded), select the Android Application Project branch below this node (if not selected), and click the Next button.
4. On the resulting *New Android App* dialog box, enter **`GameBoard`** into the Application Name textfield. This entered name also appears in the Project Name textfield, and it identifies the folder/directory in which the `GameBoard` project is stored.
5. Enter **`ca.tutortutor.gameboard`** into the Package Name textfield.

6. Via Build SDK, select the appropriate Android SDK to target. This selection identifies the Android platform you'd like your library to be built against. Assuming that you've installed only the Android 4.1 platform, only this choice should appear and be selected.
7. Via Minimum SDK, select the minimum Android SDK on which your library runs, or keep the default setting.
8. Uncheck the "Create custom launcher icon" check box because a custom launcher icon is not used with a library.
9. Check the "Mark this project as a library" check box.
10. Leave the "Create Project in Workspace" check box checked, and click Next.
11. On the resulting Create Activity pane, uncheck the Create Activity check box and click Finish.

The `GameBoard` project is marked as an Android library project. However, it doesn't yet contain a `GameBoard.java` source file containing Listing 7-3's contents.

Introduce a ca.tutortutor.gameboard node under Package Explorer's GameBoard/src node (right-click src, select New followed by Package on the resulting pop-up menus, enter **`ca.tutortutor.gameboard`** into the Name textfield on the resulting *New Java Package* dialog box, and click the Finish button), introduce a GameBoard.java node under ca.tutortutor.gameboard (right-click ca.tutortutor.gameboard, select New followed by Class from the resulting pop-up menus, enter **`GameBoard`** into the Name textfield on the resulting *New Java Class* dialog box, and click the Finish button), double-click the GameBoard.java node, and replace its skeletal contents with Listing 7-3.

Although you can build the library by right-clicking the GameBoard node and selecting Build Project from the pop-up menu (a `gameboard.jar` file is created in the `bin` directory), there is no need to do so because this library will be built automatically when referenced from another project (as demonstrated in the next recipe).

7-4. Using Android Library Projects

Problem

You've successfully built the GameBoard library and want to learn how to integrate this library into your command-line-based or Eclipse-based Android projects.

Solution

Identify the GameBoard library in the properties of the app project being built and build the app.

How It Works

Now that you've created GameBoard, you'll need an Android app to try out this library. Listing 7-4 presents the source code to a UseGameBoard single-activity-based app that instantiates this library's GameBoard class and places it in the activity's view hierarchy.

Listing 7-4. *UseGameBoard Placing the GameBoard View into the Activity's View Hierarchy*

```
package ca.tutortutor.usegameboard;

import android.app.Activity;

import android.graphics.Color;

import android.os.Bundle;

import ca.tutortutor.gameboard.GameBoard;

public class UseGameBoard extends Activity
{
   @Override
   public void onCreate(Bundle savedInstanceState)
   {
      super.onCreate(savedInstanceState);
      GameBoard gb = new GameBoard(this, 8, Color.BLUE, Color.WHITE);
      setContentView(gb);
   }
}
```

Creating and Running UseGameBoard with the Android SDK

Execute the following command (spread across two lines for readability) to create a UseGameBoard project:

```
android create project -t 1 -p C:\prj\dev\UseGameBoard -a UseGameBoard
                       -k ca.tutortutor.usegameboard
```

Now replace the skeletal src/ca/tutortutor/usegameboard/UseGameBoard.java source file with the contents of Listing 7-4.

Continue by executing the following command (spread across two lines for readability) to reference the GameBoard library project:

```
android update project -t 1 -p C:\prj\dev\UseGameBoard
                       -l ..\GameBoard
```

The "android update project" command updates the UseGameBoard app project to reference the GameBoard library project via the -l (--library) option. (You must specify a relative reference to the library project; otherwise, you will probably observe a failed build along with a message that starts with "Failed to resolve library path".) The following reference to the GameBoard library project is stored in the project.properties file:

```
android.library.reference.1=..\\GameBoard
```

> **NOTE:** References to library projects have the form android.library.reference.*n*, where *n* is an integer starting at 1.
>
> Multiple library references can be specified via repeated applications of the "android update project" command, where each command references a different library. Each successor reference appearing in project.properties is given an incrementally higher integer (2, 3, and so on).
>
> Holes between numbers (such as android.library.reference.1=... and android.library.reference.3=... without an android.library.reference.2=...) are not allowed. References that appear in the index after a hole are ignored. (android.library.reference.3=... would be ignored.)
>
> At build time, the libraries are merged with the app one at a time, starting from the lowest-priority library reference (the smallest integer) to the highest-priority library reference (the highest integer). Note that a library cannot reference another library

> and that, at build time, libraries are not merged with each other before being merged with the app.

At this point, execute the following command to build this project in debug mode:

```
ant debug
```

Assuming success, execute the following command from the project's `bin` subdirectory to install the `UseGameboard-debug.apk` file onto AVD1, which should be running:

```
adb install UseGameBoard-debug.apk
```

Finally, launch the app. You should see the output shown in Figure 7-3.

Figure 7-3. *`UseGameBoard` reveals a blue-and-white checkered game board that could be used as the background for a game such as checkers or chess.*

Creating and Running UseGameBoard with Eclipse.

Complete the following steps to create the `UseGameBoard` project in Eclipse:

1. Assuming that you've installed the Eclipse version discussed in Chapter 1, start this IDE if it is not already running.
2. Select New from the File menu, and select Project from the resulting pop-up menu.

3. On the resulting *New Android App* dialog box, enter **`UseGameBoard`** into the Application Name textfield. This entered name also appears in the Project Name textfield, and it identifies the folder/directory in which the `UseGameBoard` project is stored.
4. Enter **`ca.tutortutor.usegameboard`** into the Package Name textfield.
5. Via Build SDK, select the appropriate Android SDK to target. This selection identifies the Android platform you'd like your app to be built against. Assuming that you've installed only the Android 4.1 platform, only this choice should appear and be selected.
6. Via Minimum SDK, select the minimum Android SDK on which your app runs, or keep the default setting.
7. Leave the "Create custom launcher icon" check box checked if you want a custom launcher icon to be created. Otherwise, uncheck this check box when you supply your own launcher icon.
8. Leave the "Mark this project as a library" check box unchecked because you are not creating a library.
9. Leave the "Create Project in Workspace" check box checked, and click Next.
10. On the resulting Configure Launcher Icon pane, make suitable adjustments to the custom launcher icon; click Next.
11. On the resulting Create Activity pane, leave the Create Activity check box checked, make sure that BlankActivity is selected, and click Next.
12. On the resulting New Blank Activity pane, enter **`UseGameBoard`** into the Activity Name textfield. Keep all other settings and click Finish.

Eclipse creates a UseGameBoard node in the Package Explorer window. Complete the following steps to set up all files:

1. Expand the UseGameBoard node (if necessary), followed by the src node, followed by the ca.tutortutor.usegameboard node.

2. Double-click the UseGameBoard.java node (underneath ca.tutortutor.usegameboard) and replace the skeletal contents in the resulting window with Listing 7-4.
3. Right-click the UseGameBoard node and select Properties from the resulting pop-up menu.
4. On the resulting *Properties for UseGameBoard* dialog box, select the Android category and click the Add button.
5. On the resulting *Project Selection* dialog box, select GameBoard and click OK.
6. Click Apply, and then click OK to close *Properties for UseGameBoard*.

To build and run this project, select Run from the menubar, followed by Run from the drop-down menu. (Click OK if the *Save Resources* dialog box appears.) If a *Run As* dialog box appears, select Android Application and click OK. Eclipse starts the emulator, installs this project's APK, and runs the app, whose output appears in Figure 7-4.

Figure 7-4. *`UseGameBoard`'s user interface looks different because of an Eclipse-generated custom theme.*

> **NOTE:** If you're interested in creating and using an Android library project-based library that incorporates an activity, check out Google's "Setting Up a Library Project" (`http://developer.android.com/tools/projects/projects-eclipse.html#SettingUpLibraryProject`) and "Referencing a Library Project" (`http://developer.android.com/tools/projects/projects-eclipse.html#ReferencingLibraryProject`) documentation.

7-5. Charting

Problem

You're looking for a simple library that lets your app generate bar, line, or pie charts.

Solution

Although several Android libraries exist for generating charts, you might prefer the simplicity of Kidroid.com's kiChart product (`www.kidroid.com/kichart/`). Version 0.3 supports bar, line, and pie charts; Kidroid promises to add new chart types in subsequent releases.

The above link to kiChart's home page presents links for downloading `kiChart-0.3.jar` (the library) and `kiChart-manual-0.3.pdf` (documentation describing the library).

How It Works

kiChart's documentation states that its charts support multiple series of data. Furthermore, it states that charts can be exported to image files and that you can define chart parameters (such as font color, font size, margin, and so on).

The documentation then presents a trio of screenshots to the sample line, bar, and pie charts rendered by a demo app. These screenshots are followed by a code exert from this demo—specifically, the `LineChart` chart activity class.

`LineChart`'s source code reveals the basics of establishing a chart, explained here:

1. Create an activity that extends the `com.kidroid.kichart.ChartActivity` class. This activity renders either a bar, line, or pie chart.
2. Within the activity's `onCreate(Bundle)` method, create a `String` array of horizontal axis labels, and create a floating-point array of data for each set of bars or lines (or a single floating-point item for each pie wedge).
3. Create an array of `com.kidroid.kichart.model.Aitem` (axis item) instances and populate this array with `Aitem` objects that store the data arrays. Each `Aitem` constructor call requires you to pass an `android.graphics.Color` value to identify the color associated with the data array (whose displayed values and bars or lines are displayed in that color), a `String` value that associates a label with the color and data array, and the data array itself. (For a pie chart, you would use the `com.kidroid.kichart.model.Bitem` class instead.)
4. Instantiate the `com.kidroid.kichart.view.BarView` class if you want to display a bar chart, the `com.kidroid.kichart.view.LineView` class if you want to display a line chart, or the `com.kidroid.kichart.view.PieView` class if you want to display a pie chart.
5. Call the class's `public void setTitle(String title)` method to specify a title for the chart.
6. Call the `BarView` or `LineView` class's `public void setAxisValueX(String[] labels)` method to specify the bar or line chart's horizontal labels.
7. Call the `BarView` or `LineView` class's `public void setItems(Aitem[] items)` method to specify the chart's arrays of data items, or call the `PieView` class's `public void setItems(Bitem[] items)` method to specify the chart's data items.
8. Call `setContentView()` with the chart instance as its argument to display the chart.

9. You don't have to worry about selecting a range of values for the vertical axis because kiChart takes care of this task on your behalf.

A class diagram that presents kiChart's classes and shows their relationships follows the source code. This diagram shows that com.kidroid.kichart.view.ChartView is the superclass of com.kidroid.kichart.view.AxisView, which superclasses BarView and LineView. Although not shown, ChartView is also the superclass of PieView.

Each class's properties and ChartView's public boolean exportImage(String filename) method are then documented. This method lets you output a chart to a PNG file, returning "true" if successful and "false" if unsuccessful.

> **TIP:** To influence the range of values displayed on the vertical axis, you will need to work with AxisView's intervalCount, intervalValue, and valueGenerate properties.

In practice, you'll find kiChart easy to use. For example, consider a ChartDemo app whose main activity (also named ChartDemo) presents a user interface that lets the user enter quarterly sales figures for each of the years 2010 and 2011 via its eight textfields. The main activity also presents a pair of buttons that let the user view this data in the context of a bar, line, or pie chart via separate BarChart, LineChart, and PieChart activities.

Listing 7-5 presents ChartDemo's source code.

Listing 7-5. *ChartDemo Describing an Activity for Entering Chart Data Values and Launching the BarChart, LineChart, or PieChart Activity*

```
package ca.tutortutor.chartdemo;

import android.app.Activity;

import android.content.Intent;

import android.os.Bundle;

import android.view.View;

import android.widget.AdapterView;
import android.widget.Button;
import android.widget.EditText;
```

```
public class ChartDemo extends Activity
{
   @Override
   public void onCreate(Bundle savedInstanceState)
   {
      super.onCreate(savedInstanceState);
      setContentView(R.layout.main);

      Button btnViewBC = (Button) findViewById(R.id.viewbc);
      AdapterView.OnClickListener ocl;
      ocl = new AdapterView.OnClickListener()
      {
         @Override
         public void onClick(View v)
         {
            final float[] data2010 = new float[4];
            int[] ids = { R.id.data2010_1, R.id.data2010_2, R.id.data2010_3,
                          R.id.data2010_4 };
            for (int i = 0; i < ids.length; i++)
            {
               EditText et = (EditText) findViewById(ids[i]);
               String s = et.getText().toString();
               try
               {
                  float input = Float.parseFloat(s);
                  data2010[i] = input;
               }
               catch (NumberFormatException nfe)
               {
                  data2010[i] = 0;
               }
            }
            final float[] data2011 = new float[4];
            ids = new int[] { R.id.data2011_1, R.id.data2011_2,
                              R.id.data2011_3, R.id.data2011_4 };
            for (int i = 0; i < ids.length; i++)
            {
               EditText et = (EditText) findViewById(ids[i]);
               String s = et.getText().toString();
               try
               {
                  float input = Float.parseFloat(s);
                  data2011[i] = input;
               }
               catch (NumberFormatException nfe)
               {
                  data2011[i] = 0;
               }
            }
```

```
            Intent intent = new Intent(ChartDemo.this, BarChart.class);
            intent.putExtra("2010", data2010);
            intent.putExtra("2011", data2011);
            startActivity(intent);
         }
      };
      btnViewBC.setOnClickListener(ocl);

      Button btnViewLC = (Button) findViewById(R.id.viewlc);
      ocl = new AdapterView.OnClickListener()
      {
         @Override
         public void onClick(View v)
         {
            final float[] data2010 = new float[4];
            int[] ids = { R.id.data2010_1, R.id.data2010_2, R.id.data2010_3,
                          R.id.data2010_4 };
            for (int i = 0; i < ids.length; i++)
            {
               EditText et = (EditText) findViewById(ids[i]);
               String s = et.getText().toString();
               try
               {
                  float input = Float.parseFloat(s);
                  data2010[i] = input;
               }
               catch (NumberFormatException nfe)
               {
                  data2010[i] = 0;
               }
            }
            final float[] data2011 = new float[4];
            ids = new int[] { R.id.data2011_1, R.id.data2011_2,
                              R.id.data2011_3, R.id.data2011_4 };
            for (int i = 0; i < ids.length; i++)
            {
               EditText et = (EditText) findViewById(ids[i]);
               String s = et.getText().toString();
               try
               {
                  float input = Float.parseFloat(s);
                  data2011[i] = input;
               }
               catch (NumberFormatException nfe)
               {
                  data2011[i] = 0;
               }
            }
            Intent intent = new Intent(ChartDemo.this, LineChart.class);
            intent.putExtra("2010", data2010);
```

```
            intent.putExtra("2011", data2011);
            startActivity(intent);
         }
      };
      btnViewLC.setOnClickListener(ocl);

      Button btnViewPC = (Button) findViewById(R.id.viewpc);
      ocl = new AdapterView.OnClickListener()
      {
         @Override
         public void onClick(View v)
         {
            final float[] data2010 = new float[4];
            int[] ids = { R.id.data2010_1, R.id.data2010_2, R.id.data2010_3,
                          R.id.data2010_4 };
            for (int i = 0; i < ids.length; i++)
            {
               EditText et = (EditText) findViewById(ids[i]);
               String s = et.getText().toString();
               try
               {
                  float input = Float.parseFloat(s);
                  data2010[i] = input;
               }
               catch (NumberFormatException nfe)
               {
                  data2010[i] = 0;
               }
            }
            final float[] data2011 = new float[4];
            ids = new int[] { R.id.data2011_1, R.id.data2011_2,
                              R.id.data2011_3, R.id.data2011_4 };
            for (int i = 0; i < ids.length; i++)
            {
               EditText et = (EditText) findViewById(ids[i]);
               String s = et.getText().toString();
               try
               {
                  float input = Float.parseFloat(s);
                  data2011[i] = input;
               }
               catch (NumberFormatException nfe)
               {
                  data2011[i] = 0;
               }
            }
            Intent intent = new Intent(ChartDemo.this, PieChart.class);
            intent.putExtra("2010", data2010);
            intent.putExtra("2011", data2011);
            startActivity(intent);
```

```
            }
        };
        btnViewPC.setOnClickListener(ocl);
    }
}
```

ChartDemo implements all of its logic in its onCreate(Bundle) method. This method largely concerns itself with setting its content view and attaching a click listener to each of the view's three buttons.

Because the bar and line chart listeners are nearly identical, we'll consider only the code for the listener attached to the viewbc (view bar chart) button. (The code for the pie chart listener, which differs more significantly, will be presented later.) In response to this button being clicked, the listener's onClick(View) method is called to perform the following tasks:

1. Populate a data2010 floating-point array with the values from the four textfields corresponding to 2010 data.
2. Populate a data2011 floating-point array with the values from the four textfields corresponding to 2011 data.
3. Create an Intent object that specifies BarChart.class as the classfile of the activity to launch.
4. Store the data2010 and data2011 arrays in this object so that they can be accessed from the BarChart activity.
5. Launch the BarChart activity.

Listing 7-6 presents BarChart's source code.

Listing 7-6. *Describing the BarChart Activity*

```
package ca.tutortutor.chartdemo;

import com.kidroid.kichart.ChartActivity;

import com.kidroid.kichart.model.Aitem;

import com.kidroid.kichart.view.BarView;

import android.graphics.Color;

import android.os.Bundle;

public class BarChart extends ChartActivity
{
   @Override
```

```
    public void onCreate(Bundle savedInstanceState)
    {
       super.onCreate(savedInstanceState);
       Bundle bundle = getIntent().getExtras();
       float[] data2010 = bundle.getFloatArray("2010");
       float[] data2011 = bundle.getFloatArray("2011");
       String[] arrX = new String[4];
       arrX[0] = "2010.1";
       arrX[1] = "2010.2";
       arrX[2] = "2010.3";
       arrX[3] = "2010.4";
       Aitem[] items = new Aitem[2];
       items[0] = new Aitem(Color.RED, "2010", data2010);
       items[1] = new Aitem(Color.GREEN, "2011", data2011);
       BarView bv = new BarView(this);
       bv.setTitle("Quarterly Sales (Billions)");
       bv.setAxisValueX(arrX);
       bv.setItems(items);
       setContentView(bv);
    }
}
```

BarChart first obtains a reference to the Intent object passed to it by calling its inherited Intent getIntent() method. It then uses this method to retrieve a reference to the Intent object's Bundle object, which stores the floating-point arrays of data items. Each array is retrieved by invoking Bundle's float[] getFloatArray(String key) method.

BarChart next builds a String array of labels for the chart's X-axis and creates an Aitem array populated with two Aitem objects. The first object stores the 2010 data values and associates these values with the color red and 2010 as the legend value; the second object stores 2011 data values with the color green and the legend value 2011.

After instantiating BarView, BarChart calls this object's setTitle(String) method to establish the chart's title, setAxisValueX(String[]) method to pass the array of X-axis labels to the object, and setItems(Aitem[]) method to pass the Aitem array to the object. The BarView object is then passed to setContentView() to display the bar chart.

> **NOTE:** Because LineChart is nearly identical to BarChart, its source code is not presented in this chapter. You can easily create LineChart by changing the line that reads BarView bv = new BarView(this); to LineView bv = new LineView(this);. Also, you should probably rename the variable bv to lv (as

> appropriate) for best practices. And don't forget to change `import com.kidroid.kichart.view.BarView;` to `import com.kidroid.kichart.view.LineView;`.

Listing 7-7 presents `PieChart`'s source code.

Listing 7-7. *Describing the `PieChart` Activity*

```
package ca.tutortutor.chartdemo;

import com.kidroid.kichart.ChartActivity;

import com.kidroid.kichart.model.Bitem;

import com.kidroid.kichart.view.PieView;

import android.graphics.Color;

import android.os.Bundle;

public class PieChart extends ChartActivity
{
   @Override
   public void onCreate(Bundle savedInstanceState)
   {
      super.onCreate(savedInstanceState);
      Bundle bundle = getIntent().getExtras();
      float[] data2010 = bundle.getFloatArray("2010");
      float[] data2011 = bundle.getFloatArray("2011");
      Bitem[] items = new Bitem[data2010.length];
      items[0] = new Bitem(Color.RED, "2010.1", data2010[0]);
      items[1] = new Bitem(Color.GREEN, "2010.2", data2010[1]);
      items[2] = new Bitem(Color.BLUE, "2010.3", data2010[2]);
      items[3] = new Bitem(Color.MAGENTA, "2010.4", data2010[3]);
      PieView pv = new PieView(this);
      pv.setTitle("Quarterly Sales (Billions)");
      pv.setItems(items);
      setContentView(pv);
   }
}
```

`PieChart` is similar to `BarChart` in how it obtains information from its intent object. Although it doesn't use the `data2011` array, this array is available for use should `PieChart` be upgraded.

Unlike `BarChart`, which relies on the `Aitem` class to store axis information, `PieChart` relies on a `Bitem` class for its pie wedge information. The chief difference between these classes is that the final argument passed to `Aitem`'s constructor is a `float[]` array, whereas the final argument passed to `Bitem`'s constructor is a single `float` value.

Listing 7-8 presents `main.xml`, which describes the layout and widgets that comprise `ChartDemo`'s user interface.

Listing 7-8. *`main.xml` Describing the `ChartDemo` Activity's Layout*

```
<?xml version="1.0" encoding="utf-8"?>
<TableLayout xmlns:android="http://schemas.android.com/apk/res/android"
             android:layout_width = "match_parent"
             android:layout_height="match_parent"
             android:stretchColumns="*">
  <TableRow>
    <TextView android:text=""/>
    <TextView android:text="2010"
              android:layout_gravity="center"/>
    <TextView android:text="2011"
              android:layout_gravity="center"/>
  </TableRow>

  <TableRow>
    <TextView android:text="1st Quarter"/>
    <EditText android:id="@+id/data2010_1"
              android:inputType="numberDecimal"
              android:maxLines="1"/>
    <EditText android:id="@+id/data2011_1"
              android:inputType="numberDecimal"
              android:maxLines="1"/>
  </TableRow>

  <TableRow>
    <TextView android:text="2nd Quarter"/>
    <EditText android:id="@+id/data2010_2"
              android:inputType="numberDecimal"
              android:maxLines="1"/>
    <EditText android:id="@+id/data2011_2"
              android:inputType="numberDecimal"
              android:maxLines="1"/>
  </TableRow>

  <TableRow>
    <TextView android:text="3rd Quarter"/>
    <EditText android:id="@+id/data2010_3"
              android:inputType="numberDecimal"
              android:maxLines="1"/>
    <EditText android:id="@+id/data2011_3"
              android:inputType="numberDecimal"
```

```
               android:maxLines="1"/>
  </TableRow>

  <TableRow>
    <TextView android:text="4th Quarter"/>
    <EditText android:id="@+id/data2010_4"
              android:inputType="numberDecimal"
              android:maxLines="1"/>
    <EditText android:id="@+id/data2011_4"
              android:inputType="numberDecimal"
              android:maxLines="1"/>
  </TableRow>

  <TableRow>
    <Button android:id="@+id/viewbc"
            android:text="View Barchart"
            android:layout_weight="1"/>
    <Button android:id="@+id/viewlc"
            android:text="View Linechart"
            android:layout_weight="1"/>
    <Button android:id="@+id/viewpc"
            android:text="View Piechart"
            android:layout_weight="1"/>
  </TableRow>
</TableLayout>
```

main.xml describes a tabular layout via the <TableLayout> element, where the user interface is laid out in six rows and three columns. The "match_parent" assignment to each of <TableLayout>'s layout_width and layout_height attributes tells this layout to occupy the activity's entire screen. The "*" assignment to <TableLayout>'s stretchColumns attribute tells this layout to give each column an identical width.

> **NOTE:** A *stretchable column* is a column that can expand in width to fit any available space. To specify which columns are stretchable, assign a comma-delimited list of 0-based integers to stretchColumns. For example, "0, 1" specifies that column 0 (the leftmost column) and column 1 are stretchable. The "*" assignment indicates that all columns are equally stretchable, which gives them identical widths.

Nested inside <TableLayout> and its </TableLayout> partner are a series of <TableRow> elements. Each <TableRow> element describes the contents of a single row in the tabular layout, and these contents are a variety of zero or more view elements (such as <TextView> and <EditText>), where each view constitutes one column.

> **NOTE:** For brevity, string values are stored directly in `main.xml` instead of being stored in a separate `strings.xml` file. Consider it an exercise to introduce `strings.xml` and replace these literal strings with references to strings stored in `strings.xml`.

Listing 7-9 presents this app's `AndroidManifest.xml` file, which describes the app and its activities.

Listing 7-9. *`AndroidManifest.xml` Pulling Everything Together for the `ChartDemo` App*

```
<?xml version="1.0" encoding="utf-8"?>
<manifest xmlns:android="http://schemas.android.com/apk/res/android"
          package="ca.tutortutor.chartdemo"
          android:versionCode="1"
          android:versionName="1.0">
  <uses-sdk android:minSdkVersion="10"/>
  <application android:label="@string/app_name"
               android:icon="@drawable/ic_launcher">
    <activity android:name="ChartDemo"
              android:label="@string/app_name">
      <intent-filter>
        <action android:name="android.intent.action.MAIN"/>
        <category android:name="android.intent.category.LAUNCHER"/>
      </intent-filter>
    </activity>
    <activity android:name="BarChart"/>
    <activity android:name="LineChart"/>
    <activity android:name="PieChart"/>
  </application>
</manifest>
```

It's important to include `<activity>` tags for each of the `BarChart`, `LineChart`, and `PieChart` activities in the manifest. Failure to do so results in a runtime dialog box that displays a message about the app no longer working.

Create a `ChartDemo` project (`android create project -t 1 -p C:\prj\dev\ChartDemo -a ChartDemo -k ca.tutortutor.chartdemo`); copy the previously presented source files (including the `LineChart.java` equivalent of `BarChart.java`), `main.xml` resource file, and `AndroidManifest.xml` manifest file to the `src/ca/tutortutor/chartdemo` directory; copy `kiChart-03.jar` to the `libs` directory; build the project (`ant debug`); install it onto AVD1 (`adb install ChartDemo-debug.apk`); and launch this app.

Figure 7-5 reveals `ChartDemo`'s main activity with sample values entered for each quarter.

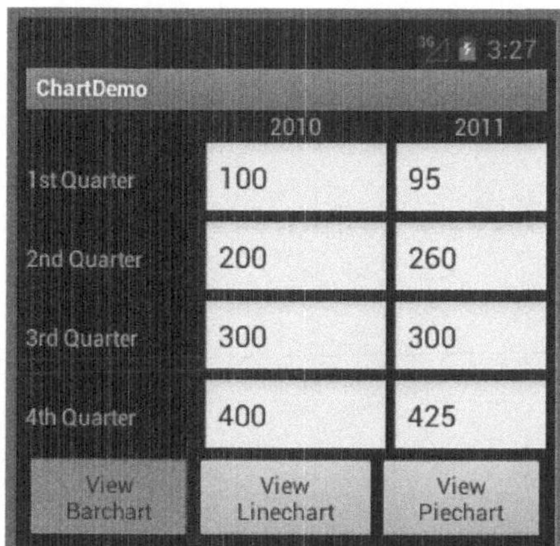

Figure 7-5. *`ChartDemo` lets you enter eight data values, and you can choose either to display these values via a bar chart or a line chart or to display only the 2010 column's values via a pie chart.*

Clicking the View Barchart button after entering the aforementioned data values launches the `BarChart` activity, which displays the bar chart shown in Figure 7-6.

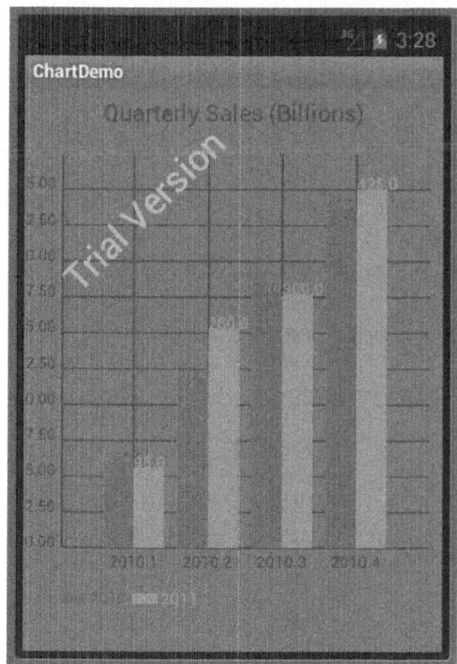

Figure 7-6. *`BarChart` displays each array's data values via a series of colored bars.*

In addition to presenting a barchart, Figure 7-6 reveals that a trial version of kiChart is being used. You'll need to contact Kidroid.com and find out about licensing and how to obtain a version of kiChart that doesn't display this message.

Click the View Linechart button to launch the `LineChart` activity, which displays the line chart shown in Figure 7-7.

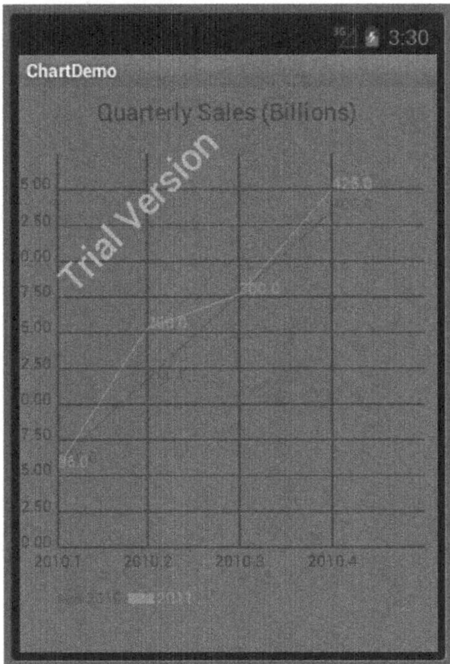

Figure 7-7. ***`LineChart` displays each array's data values via a series of colored lines.***

Finally, click the View Piechart button to launch the `PieChart` activity, which displays the pie chart shown in Figure 7-8.

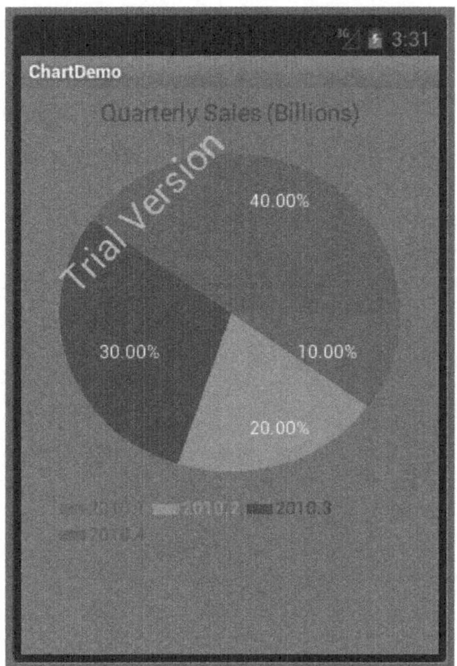

Figure 7-8. *`PieChart` displays only the 2010 array's data values via a series of colored wedges.*

7-6. Practical Push Messaging

Problem

Google's Cloud Messaging for Android (GCM) framework (`http://developer.android.com/guide/google/gcm/index.html`), which is designed to implement push messaging to the device, has several drawbacks that can impact it as a practical solution for push messaging. Your app needs a more universal push solution.

THE LIMITATIONS OF GOOGLE'S GCM

GCM is a technology fostered by Google to run on Android devices over the Extensible Messaging and Presence Protocol (XMPP), a common implementation for chat clients. Upon further inspection, there are a number of required attributes for GCM that often diminish its usefulness in apps:

- *Requires a minimum of API Level 8*: While this restriction will not remain a significant limitation forever, apps looking to support push messaging now on Android devices running versions earlier than Android 2.2 will not be able to use GCM.
- *Requires a Google account and Google APIs on the device*: GCM runs over the XMPP channel created by the GTalk chat service. If the user is running on an Android device that does not include the Google APIs (and, thus, the GTalk application), or if a user had not entered a valid Google account into the device, your app will be unable to register for GCM messaging on that device.
- *Utilizes HTTP POST for transactions between host app and GCM servers*: From the server side of the app, messages that are to be sent down to devices are handed over to the GCM servers by using individual HTTP POST requests for each message. As the required number of messages to be sent increases, this mechanism becomes increasingly slow, to the point where GCM may not be a viable option in certain time-critical apps.

Solution

Utilize IBM's MQTT library to implement lightweight push messaging in your apps. The MQTT client library is offered from IBM in a pure Java implementation, meaning it can be utilized on any Android device, without limitation on specific API levels.

An MQTT system consists of three main components:

- *Client app:* Runs on the device and registers with the message broker for a given set of "topics" on which to receive messages.
- *Message broker:* Handles registration of clients and distributes incoming messages from the server app to each client based on its "topic."
- *Server application*: Publishes messages to the broker.

Messages are filtered by topic. Topics are defined in a tree format, represented by a path string. Clients may subscribe to specific topics or to subtopic groups by providing the appropriate path. For example, suppose we define two topics for our app like so:

```
examples/one
examples/two
```

A client may subscribe to either topic by subscribing to the exact full path string. However, if the client prefers to subscribe to both topics (and any others that may be created later in this group), it may conveniently do so by subscribing as follows:

```
examples/#
```

The '#' wildcard character indicates that all topics in the examples group are of interest to this client.

In this recipe we'll focus on implementing the client app using the MQTT library on the Android device. IBM provides excellent tools for development and testing of the other components, which we'll expose here as well.

How It Works

The MQTT Java library may be freely downloaded from IBM at the following location: `www-01.ibm.com/support/docview.wss?uid=swg24006006`. The download archive contains sample code, API Javadoc, and usage documentation, in addition to the library JAR.

Locate the `wmqtt.jar` file from within the download archive. This is the library that must be included into the Android project. By convention, this means a `/libs` directory should be created in your project directory, and this JAR should be inserted there.

For testing your client implementation, IBM provides the Really Small Message Broker (RSMB). RSMB may be downloaded at the following location: `www.alphaworks.ibm.com/tech/rsmb`.

RSMB is a multiplatform download that includes command-line tools for both the message broker and an application to publish messages. The license provided by IBM for this tool forbids it from being used in a production environment; at that point you will need to roll your own or use one of the many open source implementations available. However, for development of the mobile client, RSMB couldn't be more perfect.

Client Sample

Because monitoring for incoming push messages is an indefinite, long-standing operation, let's take a look at an example that puts the basic functionality into a service.

> **NOTE:** As a reminder, you should have `libs/wmqtt.jar` in your project directory and referenced in your project build path.

Listing 7-10 presents the source code to an example MQTT service.

Listing 7-10. *MQTT Example Service*

```
import com.ibm.mqtt.IMqttClient;
import com.ibm.mqtt.MqttClient;
import com.ibm.mqtt.MqttException;
import com.ibm.mqtt.MqttPersistenceException;
import com.ibm.mqtt.MqttSimpleCallback;

public class ClientService extends Service implements MqttSimpleCallback {

    //Location where broker is running
    private static final String HOST = HOSTNAME_STRING_HERE;
    private static final String PORT = "1883";
    //30 minute keep-alive ping
    private static final short KEEP_ALIVE = 60 * 30;
    //Unique identifier of this device
    private static final String CLIENT_ID =
"apress/"+System.currentTimeMillis();
    //Topic we want to watch for
    private static final String TOPIC = "apress/examples";

    private static final String ACTION_KEEPALIVE =
"com.examples.pushclient.ACTION_KEEPALIVE";

    private IMqttClient mClient;
    private AlarmManager mManager;
    private PendingIntent alarmIntent;

    @Override
    public void onCreate() {
        super.onCreate();
        mManager = (AlarmManager)getSystemService(Context.ALARM_SERVICE);

        Intent intent = new Intent(ACTION_KEEPALIVE);
        alarmIntent = PendingIntent.getBroadcast(this, 0, intent, 0);

        registerReceiver(mReceiver, new IntentFilter(ACTION_KEEPALIVE));

        try {
            //Format: tcp://hostname@port
            String connectionString = String.format("%s%s@%s",
MqttClient.TCP_ID, HOST, PORT);
```

```
            mClient = MqttClient.createMqttClient(connectionString, null);
        } catch (MqttException e) {
            e.printStackTrace();
            //Can't continue without a client
            stopSelf();
        }
    }

    @Override
    public void onStart(Intent intent, int startId) {
        //Callback on Android devices prior to 2.0
        handleCommand(intent);
    }

    @Override
    public int onStartCommand(Intent intent, int flags, int startId) {
        //Callback on Android devices 2.0 and later
        handleCommand(intent);
        //If Android kills this service, we want it back when possible
        return START_STICKY;
    }

    private void handleCommand(Intent intent) {
        try {
            //Make a connection
            mClient.connect(CLIENT_ID, true, KEEP_ALIVE);
            //Target MQTT callbacks here
            mClient.registerSimpleHandler(this);
            //Subscribe to a topic
            String[] topics = new String[] { TOPIC };
            //QoS of 0 indicates fire once and forget
            int[] qos = new int[] { 0 };
            mClient.subscribe(topics, qos);

            //Schedule a ping
            scheduleKeepAlive();
        } catch (MqttException e) {
            e.printStackTrace();
        }
    }

    @Override
    public void onDestroy() {
        super.onDestroy();
        unregisterReceiver(mReceiver);
        unscheduleKeepAlive();

        if(mClient != null) {
            try {
                mClient.disconnect();
```

```
                mClient.terminate();
            } catch (MqttPersistenceException e) {
                e.printStackTrace();
            }
            mClient = null;
        }
    }

    //Handle incoming message from remote
    private Handler mHandler = new Handler() {
        @Override
        public void handleMessage(Message msg) {
            String incoming = (String)msg.obj;
            Toast.makeText(ClientService.this, incoming,
Toast.LENGTH_SHORT).show();
        }
    };

    //Handle ping alarms to keep the connection alive
    private BroadcastReceiver mReceiver = new BroadcastReceiver() {
        @Override
        public void onReceive(Context context, Intent intent) {
            if(mClient == null) {
                return;
            }
            //Ping the MQTT service
            try {
                mClient.ping();
            } catch (MqttException e) {
                e.printStackTrace();
            }
            //Schedule the next alarm
            scheduleKeepAlive();
        }
    };

    private void scheduleKeepAlive() {
        long nextWakeup = System.currentTimeMillis() + (KEEP_ALIVE * 1000);
        mManager.set(AlarmManager.RTC_WAKEUP, nextWakeup, alarmIntent);
    }

    private void unscheduleKeepAlive() {
        mManager.cancel(alarmIntent);
    }

    /* MqttSimpleCallback Methods */

    @Override
    public void connectionLost() throws Exception {
        mClient.terminate();
```

```
        mClient = null;
        stopSelf();
    }

    @Override
    public void publishArrived(String topicName, byte[] payload, int qos,
boolean retained) throws Exception {
        //Be wary of UI related code here!
        //Best to use a Handler for UI or Context operations

        StringBuilder builder = new StringBuilder();
        builder.append(topicName);
        builder.append('\n');
        builder.append(new String(payload));
        //Pass the message up to our handler
        Message receipt = Message.obtain(mHandler, 0, builder.toString());
        receipt.sendToTarget();
    }

    /*Unused method*/
    //We are not using this service as bound
    //It is explicitly started and stopped with no direct connection
    @Override
    public IBinder onBind(Intent intent) { return null; }
}
```

> **CAUTION:** This service will most likely be communicating with a remote server, so you must declare android.permission.INTERNET in the application manifest, as well as the service itself with a <service> tag.

In order to subclass Service, an implementation of onBind() must be provided. In this case, our example does not need to provide a Binder interface because activities will never need to hook directly into call methods. Therefore, this required method simply returns null. This Service is designed to receive explicit instructions to start and stop, running for an indeterminate amount of time in between.

When the Service is created, an MqttClient object is also instantiated using createMqttClient(); this client takes the location of the message broker host as a string. The connection string is in the format of tcp://hostname@port. In the example, the chosen port number is 1883, which is the default port number for MQTT communication. If you choose a different port number, you should verify that your server implementation is running on a matching port.

From this point forward, the Service remains idle until a start command is issued. Upon receipt of a start command (issued externally by a call to

`Context.startService()`), either `onStart()` or `onStartCommand()` will be called (depending on the version of Android running on the device). In the latter case, the service returns `START_STICKY`, a constant telling the system that it should leave this service running, and restart it if it's prematurely killed for memory reasons.

Once started, the service will register with the MQTT message broker, passing a unique client ID and a keep-alive time. For simplicity, this example defines the client ID in terms of the current time when the service was created. In production, a more unique identifier such as the WiFi MAC Address or `TelephonyManager.getDeviceId()` might be more appropriate, keeping in mind that neither of those choices is guaranteed to appear on all devices.

The keep-alive parameter is the time (in seconds) that the broker should use to time out the connection to this client. In order to avoid this time-out, clients should post a message or regularly ping the broker. We will shortly discuss this task more fully.

During startup, the client is also subscribed to a single topic. Notice that the `subscribe()` method takes arrays as parameters; a client may subscribe to multiple topics within a single method call. Each topic is also subscribed with a requested quality of service (QoS) value. The most tactful value to request for mobile devices is zero, telling the broker to send a message only once without requiring confirmation. Doing so reduces the amount of handshaking required between the broker and the device.

With the connection live and registered, any incoming messages from the remote broker will result in a call to `publishArrived()`, with the data about the message passed in. This method may be called on any of the background threads that `MqttClient` creates and maintains, so it's important to not do anything related to the main thread directly here. In the example's case, all incoming messages are passed to a local `Handler`, to guarantee that the resulting `Toast` is posted on the main thread for display.

There's one upkeep task required when implementing an MQTT client, and that is pinging the broker to keep the connection alive. To accomplish this task, the `Service` registers with the `AlarmManager` to trigger a broadcast on a schedule matching the keep-alive parameter. This task must be done even if the device is currently asleep, so the alarm is set each time with `AlarmManager.RTC_WAKEUP`. When each alarm triggers, the `Service` simply calls `MqttClient.ping()` and schedules the next keep-alive update.

Due to the persistent nature of this requirement, it is prudent to select a low-frequency interval for the keep-alive timer; we chose 30 minutes in this example. This timer value represents a balance between reducing the frequency of required updates on the device (to save power and bandwidth), and the latency before the remote broker becomes aware that a remote device is no longer there and times it out.

When the push service is no longer required, an external call to `Context.stopService()` will result in a call to `onDestroy()`. Here, the `Service` tears down the MQTT connection, removes any pending alarms, and releases all resources. The second callback implemented as part of the `MqttSimpleCallback` interface is `onConnectionLost()`, indicating an unexpected disconnect. In these cases, the `Service` stops itself much in the same way as a manual stop request.

Testing the Client

In order to test messaging with the device, you will need to start up an instance of RSMB on your machine. From the command line, navigate into the location where you unarchived the download, and then find the directory that matches your computer's platform (Windows, Linux, Mac OS X). From here, simply execute the `broker` command and the broker service will begin running on your machine, located at `localhost:1883`:

```
CWNAN9999I Really Small Message Broker
CWNAN9997I Licensed Materials - Property of IBM
CWNAN9996I Copyright IBM Corp. 2007, 2010 All Rights Reserved
…
CWNAN0014I MQTT protocol starting, listening on port 1883
```

At this point, you may connect to the service and publish messages or register to receive messages. To put this `Service` to the test, let's create a simple `Activity` that may be used to start and stop the service.

Listing 7-11. *res/menu/home.xml*

```
<?xml version="1.0" encoding="utf-8"?>
<menu xmlns:android="http://schemas.android.com/apk/res/android">
  <item
    android:id="@+id/menu_start"
    android:title="Start Service" />
  <item
    android:id="@+id/menu_stop"
    android:title="Stop Service" />
</menu>
```

Listing 7-12. *Activity Controlling MQTT Service*

```
//ClientActivity.java
package com.apress.pushclient;
```

```
import android.app.Activity;
import android.content.Intent;
import android.os.Bundle;
import android.view.Menu;
import android.view.MenuItem;

public class ClientActivity extends Activity {
    private Intent serviceIntent;

    @Override
    public void onCreate(Bundle savedInstanceState) {
        super.onCreate(savedInstanceState);
        serviceIntent = new Intent(this, ClientService.class);
    }

    @Override
    public boolean onCreateOptionsMenu(Menu menu) {
        getMenuInflater().inflate(R.menu.home, menu);
        return true;
    }

    @Override
    public boolean onOptionsItemSelected(MenuItem item) {
        switch(item.getItemId()) {
        case R.id.menu_start:
            startService(serviceIntent);
            return true;
        case R.id.menu_stop:
            stopService(serviceIntent);
            return true;
        }

        return super.onOptionsItemSelected(item);
    }
}
```

Listing 7-12 creates an Intent that will be used by two menu options to start and stop the service at will (see Figure 7-9). By pressing the MENU button and selecting "Start Service", the MQTT connection will start up and register the device for messages with the topic "apress/examples".

Figure 7-9. *This activity controls the service*

> **NOTE:** The HOST value in the example service needs to point to the machine where your RSMB instance is running. Even if you are testing in the emulator on the same machine, this value is **NOT** `localhost`! At the very least, you must point the emulator or device to the IP address of the machine where your broker is running.

With the Android device successfully registered for push messages from the broker, open up another command-line window and navigate to the same directory from where `broker` was executed. Another command, `stdinpub`, can be used to connect to the broker instance and publish messages down to the device. From the command line, type the following command:

```
stdinpub apress/examples
```

This command will register a client to publish messages with a topic matching our example. You will see the following as a result:

```
Using topic apress/examples
Connecting
```

Now you may type any message you like and then press Enter. Upon pressing Enter, the message will be sent to the broker and pushed out to the registered device. Do this as many times as you like, and then use Ctrl-C to break out of the program. Ctrl-C will also work to terminate the broker service.

> **TIP:** RSMB also includes a third command, `stdoutsub`, to subscribe to a set of topics with your local broker service. This command lets you completely close the loop, and you can test whether problems are occurring in the test suite or in your Android app.

7-7. Using Google's Support Package

Problem

Google keeps improving Android by offering new features (such as fragments) in SDK upgrades. Furthermore, Google lets you use some of these features on older Android platforms where they are not supported. You want to use Google's solution to retrofit your apps to support fragments and/or other previously unsupported features.

Solution

Google has anticipated the need for apps to access newer Android features on older versions of Android by introducing the Support Package. This collection of static support libraries can be added to an app to use APIs that are not available on older Android platforms or to use utility APIs that are not part of the framework APIs.

The Support Package introduces various new capabilities, including the following:

- Fragments (introduced in Chapter 1).
- Recommended Android user interface navigation patterns.
- Support classes that ease the implementation of Android Dreams in a backward-compatible fashion. First introduced in Android 4.0 (Ice Cream Sandwich), *Android Dreams* (also known as Rocket Launcher) is a new screen-saver feature.

Google discusses the Support Package on its "Support Library" page at `http://developer.android.com/tools/extras/support-library.html`. This page points out that each of the static support libraries has a specific minimum API level. (An app using a specific library will not work on Android platforms with a lower API level.)

Three libraries are currently targeted:

- *Level 4*: This level corresponds to Android 1.6 (Donut). An app including this library has access to all capabilities except for those belonging to Level 7 and Level 13.
- *Level 7*: This level corresponds to Android 2.1 (Éclair). An app including this library has access to an equivalent `android.widget.GridLayout` class, which was introduced in Level 14.
- *Level 13*: This level corresponds to Android 3.2 (Honeycomb). An app including this library has access to fragment features introduced after Level 13 and Android Dreams.

You need to run the `SDK Manager` tool to download and install the Support Package. Run this tool from the command line (as shown in Chapter 1) or from within Eclipse (by selecting Android SDK Manager from the Window menu). Figure 7-10 shows the Android Support Library entry checked in the Extras section.

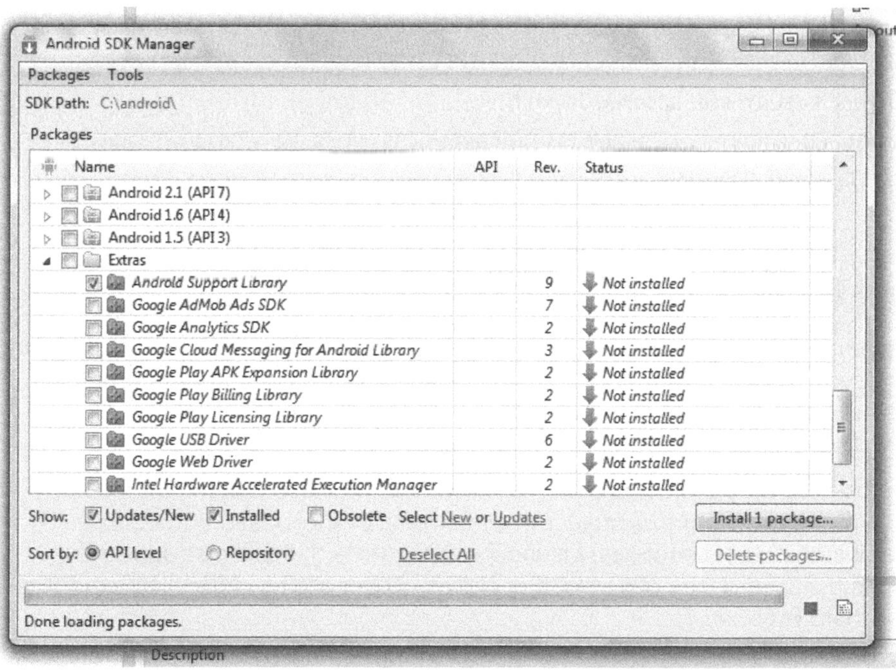

Figure 7-10. *Android Support Library corresponds to the Support Package.*

Click the "Install 1 package" button, followed by the Install button on the subsequent *Choose Packages to Install* dialog box. The Support Package Revision 9 (current at the time of this writing) is installed to the *<Android_home_directory>*/extras/android/support directory, which includes text files along with samples, v4, v7, and v13 directories.

The v4 directory contains an android-support-v4.jar file. Similarly, the v13 directory contains an android-support-v13.jar file. In contrast, the v7 directory contains a library project whose libs subdirectory contains an android-support-v7-gridlayout.jar file and whose res subdirectory contains accompanying resource files.

> **NOTE:** The android-support-v7-gridlayout.jar library file contains an android.support.v7.widget.GridLayout class and its related Space and ViewGroup classes. GridLayout is a viewgroup that organizes its child views in a rectangular grid.
>
> The v7 support library introduces GridLayout as a compatible alternative to the android.widget.GridLayout class that was introduced in API Level 14 (Android 4.0). Instead of specifying import android.widget.GridLayout;, a pre-Level 14 app's source code specifies import android.support.v7.widget.GridLayout; to access the v7 support library's GridLayout equivalent.

How It Works

To use the v4 or v13 library, copy the JAR file to your project's libs directory. In Eclipse, you must also add the JAR file to the project build path. Accomplish this task by right-clicking the JAR file's node, and then select Build Path followed by Add to Build Path from the resulting pop-up menus.

Using the v7 library project is a bit more involved. For this reason, this recipe focuses on referencing this project from command-line-based and Eclipse-based UseGridLayout projects. Listing 7-13 presents the source code to this project's UseGridLayout.java file. (For brevity, there are no other files except for AndroidManifest.xml.)

Listing 7-13. *UseGridLayout Presenting a Grid of Buttons*

```
package ca.tutortutor.usegridlayout;

import android.app.Activity;

import android.os.Bundle;

import android.support.v7.widget.GridLayout;

import android.widget.Button;

public class UseGridLayout extends Activity
{
    @Override
    public void onCreate(Bundle savedInstanceState)
    {
        super.onCreate(savedInstanceState);
        GridLayout gl = new GridLayout(this);
        gl.setRowCount(2);
        gl.setColumnCount(2);
        Button btn = new Button(this);
        btn.setText("1");
        gl.addView(btn);
        btn = new Button(this);
        btn.setText("2");
        gl.addView(btn);
        btn = new Button(this);
        btn.setText("3");
        gl.addView(btn);
        btn = new Button(this);
        btn.setText("4");
        gl.addView(btn);
        setContentView(gl);
    }
}
```

Also for brevity, Listing 7-13 hard-codes the layout and includes literal text. After instantiating `GridLayout`, it invokes this class's `void setRowCount(int rowCount)` and `void setColumnCount(int columnCount)` methods to establish the grid dimensions. Lastly, it sets the activity's view hierarchy to the grid layout and its child view.

Creating and Running UseGridLayout with the Android SDK

Execute the following command (spread across two lines for readability) to create a `UseGridLayout` project:

```
android create project -t 2 -p C:\prj\dev\UseGridLayout -a UseGridLayout
                       -k ca.tutortutor.usegridlayout
```

This command assumes an Android 2.3.3 target identified as ID 2. It is also assumed that you have created an AVD2 device with Android 2.3.3 as the target platform.

Now replace the skeletal `src/ca/tutortutor/usegridlayout/UseGridLayout.java` source file with the contents of Listing 7-13.

Continue by executing the following command (spread across two lines for readability) to reference the `GridLayout` library project:

```
android update project -t 2 -p C:\prj\dev\UseGridLayout -l
                       ..\..\..\android\extras\android\support\v7\gridlayout
```

This command assumes that `C:\prj\dev` is the current directory where this command is executed. It also assumes that `C:\android\extras\android\support\v7\gridlayout` is the location of the library project.

At this point, execute the following command to build this project in debug mode:

```
ant debug
```

The output should reveal the following error message:

```
Invalid file: C:\android\extras\android\support\v7\gridlayout\build.xml
```

The error message results from the absence of a `build.xml` file in the `C:\android\extras\android\support\v7\gridlayout` directory.

To create this file, switch to this directory and execute the following command:

```
android update lib-project -t 2 -p .
```

You could replace `lib-project` with `project` for this example. Assuming that `build.xml` is created, re-execute `ant debug`.

Assuming success, execute the following command from the project's `bin` subdirectory to install the `UseGridLayout-debug.apk` file onto AVD2, which should be running:

```
adb install UseGridLayout-debug.apk
```

Finally, launch the app. You should see the output shown in Figure 7-11.

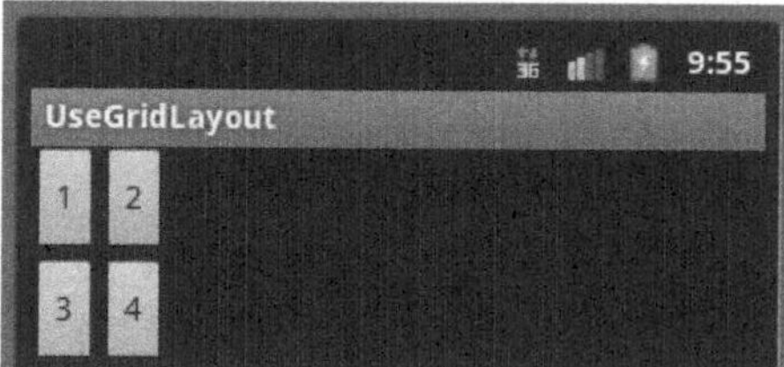

Figure 7-11. *The buttons appear small because the default values of gridlayout's width and height properties are each set to* `WRAP_CONTENT`.

Creating and Running UseGridLayout with Eclipse

Complete the following steps to create the `UseGridLayout` project that references the `GridLayout` library project in Eclipse:

1. Assuming that you've installed the Eclipse version discussed in Chapter 1, start this IDE if it is not already running.
2. Select Import from the File menu, followed by "Existing Android Code Into Workspace" on the resulting *Import* dialog box. Click Next.
3. On the resulting dialog box, click the Browse button and locate `C:\android\extras\android\support\v7\gridlayout` (or the equivalent directory). Exit these dialog boxes by clicking OK, followed by Finish.
4. Select New from the File menu, and select Project from the resulting pop-up menu.
5. On the resulting *New Project* dialog box, expand the Android node in the wizard tree (if not expanded), select the Android Application Project branch below this node (if not selected), and click the Next button.
6. On the resulting *New Android App* dialog box, enter **`UseGridLayout`** into the Application Name textfield. This entered name also appears in the Project Name textfield, and it identifies the folder/directory in which the `UseGridLayout` project is stored.
7. Enter **`ca.tutortutor.usegridlayout`** into the Package Name textfield.

8. Via Build SDK, select the appropriate Android SDK to target. This selection identifies the Android platform you'd like your app to be built against. Assuming that you've installed Android 2.3.3, select this platform.
9. Via Minimum SDK, select the minimum Android SDK on which your app runs, or keep the default setting. (Do not select an SDK whose API level is less than Level 10.)
10. Leave the "Create custom launcher icon" check box checked if you want a custom launcher icon to be created. Otherwise, uncheck this check box when you supply your own launcher icon.
11. Leave the "Mark this project as a library" check box unchecked because you are not creating a library.
12. Leave the "Create Project in Workspace" check box checked, and click Next.
13. On the resulting Configure Launcher Icon pane, make suitable adjustments to the custom launcher icon; click Next.
14. On the resulting Create Activity pane, leave the Create Activity check box checked, make sure that BlankActivity is selected, and click Next.
15. On the resulting New Blank Activity pane, enter **`UseGridLayout`** into the Activity Name textfield. Keep all other settings and click Finish.

Eclipse creates a UseGridLayout node in the Package Explorer window. Complete the following steps to set up all files:

1. Expand the UseGridLayout node (if not expanded), followed by the src node, followed by the ca.tutortutor.usegridlayout node.
2. Double-click the UseGridLayout.java node (underneath ca.tutortutor.usegridlayout) and replace the skeletal contents in the resulting window with Listing 7-13. Ignore any error messages; they will disappear shortly.
3. Right-click the UseGridLayout node and select Properties from the resulting pop-up menu.

4. On the resulting *Properties for UseGridLayout* dialog box, select the Android category and click the Add button.
5. On the resulting *Project Selection* dialog box, select gridlayout and click OK.
6. Click Apply, and then OK to close *Properties for UseGridLayout*.

To build and run this project, select Run from the menubar, followed by Run from the drop-down menu. (Click OK if the *Save Resources* dialog box appears.) If a *Run As* dialog box appears, select Android Application and click OK. Eclipse starts the emulator, installs this project's APK, and runs the app, whose output appears in Figure 7-12.

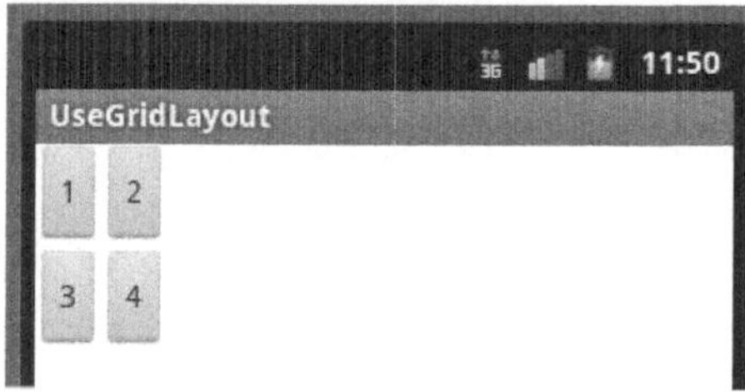

Figure 7-12. *`UseGridLayout`'s user interface looks different because of an Eclipse-generated custom theme.*

Summary

Smart Android developers deliver their apps to market faster by taking advantage of libraries, which reduce development time by providing previously created and tested code.

This chapter's initial recipes introduced you to the topics of creating and using your own libraries. Specifically, you learned how to create and use Java library JARs, whose code was restricted to Java 5 (or earlier version) APIs, and Android library projects.

Although you'll probably create your own libraries to save yourself from reinventing the wheel, you might also need to use someone else's library. For example, if you need a simple charting library, you might want to look at kiChart, which facilitates the creation and display of bar, line, and pie charts.

If you're working with the cloud, you might decide to use Google's GCM framework. However, because this framework has a number of drawbacks (such as requiring a minimum of API level 8), you might consider utilizing IBM's MQTT library to implement lightweight push messaging in your apps.

You can use Google's support library (also known as the Support Package) to introduce the equivalents of newer Android APIs (such as the `android.widget.GridLayout` equivalent) to older Android platforms that don't support them.

Apart from the appendixes, Chapter 8 completes this book by introducing you to the Android Native Development Kit and Renderscript.

Chapter 8

Working with Android NDK and Renderscript

Developers typically write Android apps entirely in Java. However, situations arise where it's desirable (or even necessary) to express at least part of the code in another language (notably C or C++). Google addresses these situations by providing the Android Native Development Kit (NDK) and Renderscript.

Android NDK

The Android NDK complements the Android SDK by providing a toolset that lets you implement parts of your app using native code languages such as C and C++. The NDK provides headers and libraries for building native activities, handling user input, using hardware sensors, and more.

Many developers believe that the NDK exists to boost app performance. Although performance can improve, it can also worsen because transitions from the Dalvik virtual machine (VM) equivalent of compiled Java code to native code via the Java Native Interface (JNI) will add overhead, which impacts performance.

> **NOTE:** Code running inside of Dalvik already experiences a performance boost thanks to the Just-In-Time compiler that was integrated with Dalvik in Android 2.2.

The NDK is used in the following scenarios:

- Your app contains CPU-intensive code that doesn't allocate much memory. Code examples include physics simulation, signal processing, huge factorial calculations, and testing huge integers for primeness. Renderscript (discussed later in this chapter) is probably more appropriate for addressing at least some of these examples.
- You want to ease the porting of existing C/C++-based source code to your app. Using the NDK can help to speed up app development by letting you keep most or all of your app's code in C/C++. Furthermore, working with the NDK can help you keep code changes synchronized between Android and non-Android projects.

> **CAUTION:** Think carefully about integrating native code into your app. Basing even part of an app on native code increases its complexity and makes it harder to debug.

Installing the NDK

If you believe that your app can benefit from being at least partly expressed in native code, you'll need to install the NDK. Before doing so, you need to be aware of the following software and system requirements:

- A complete Android SDK installation (including all dependencies) is required. Version 1.5 or later of the SDK is supported.
- The following operating systems are supported: Windows XP (32-bit), Windows Vista (32- or 64-bit), Windows 7 (32- or 64-bit), Mac OS X 10.4.8 or later (x86 only), and Linux (32- or 64-bit; Ubuntu 8.04, or other Linux distributions using glibc 2.7 or later).
- For all platforms, GNU Make 3.81 or later is required. Earlier versions of GNU Make might work but have not been tested. Also, GNU Awk or Nawk is required.
- For Windows platforms, Cygwin (1.7 or higher) is required to support debugging. Before Revision 7 of the NDK, Cygwin was also required to build projects by supplying `make` and `awk` tools.

- The native libraries created by the Android NDK can be used only on devices running specific minimum Android platform versions. The minimum required platform version depends on the CPU architecture of the devices you are targeting. Table 8-1 details which Android platform versions are compatible with native code developed for specific CPU architectures.

Table 8-1. *Mappings Between Native Code CPU Architectures and Compatible Android Platforms*

Native Code CPU Architecture Used	Compatible Android Platforms
ARM, ARM-NEON	Android 1.5 (API Level 3) and higher
x86	Android 2.3 (API Level 9) and higher
MIPS	Android 2.3 (API Level 9) and higher

These requirements mean that you can use native libraries created via the NDK in apps that are deployable to ARM-based devices running Android 1.5 or later. If you are deploying native libraries to x86- and MIPS-based devices, your app must target Android 2.3 or later.

- To ensure compatibility, an app using a native library created via the NDK must declare a `<uses-sdk>` element in its manifest file, with an `android:minSdkVersion` attribute value of `"3"` or higher. Example:

```
<manifest>
  <uses-sdk android:minSdkVersion="3" />
  ...
</manifest>
```

- If you use the NDK to create a native library that uses the OpenGL ES APIs, the app containing the library can be deployed only to devices running the minimum platform versions described in Table 8-2. To ensure compatibility, make sure that your app declares the proper `android:minSdkVersion` attribute value.

Table 8-2. *Mappings Between OpenGL ES Versions, Compatible Android Platforms, and Uses-SDK*

OpenGL ES Version Used	Compatible Android Platforms	Required `uses-sdk` Attribute
OpenGL ES 1.1	Android 1.6 (API Level 4) and higher	`android:minSdkVersion ="4"`
OpenGL ES 2.0	Android 2.0 (API Level 5) and higher	`android:minSdkVersion ="5"`

- Additionally, an app using the OpenGL ES APIs should declare a `<uses-feature>` element in its manifest, with an `android:glEsVersion` attribute that specifies the minimum OpenGL ES version required by the app. This ensures that Google Play will show your app only to users whose devices can support your app. Example:

```
<manifest>
  <uses-feature android:glEsVersion="0x00020000" />
  ...
</manifest>
```

- If you use the NDK to create a native library that uses the Android API to access `android.graphics.Bitmap` pixel buffers, or utilizes native activities, the app containing the library can be deployed only to devices running Android 2.2 (API level 8) or higher. To ensure compatibility, make sure that your app declares a `<uses-sdk android:minSdkVersion="8" />` element in its manifest.

Point your browser to `http://developer.android.com/tools/sdk/ndk/index.html` and download one of the following NDK packages for your platform—Revision 8b is the latest version at the time of writing:

- `android-ndk-r8b-windows.zip` (Windows)
- `android-ndk-r8b-darwin-x86.tar.bz2` (Mac OS X: Intel)
- `android-ndk-r8b-linux-x86.tar.bz2` (Linux 32-/64-bit: x86)

After downloading your chosen package, unarchive it and move its `android-ndk-r8b` home directory to a more suitable location, perhaps to the same directory that contains the Android SDK's home directory.

INSTALLING CYGWIN

Cygwin is a collection of tools that provides a Linux look-and-feel environment for Windows. Complete the following steps to install Cygwin 1.7 or higher when Windows is your platform:

1. Point your browser to http://cygwin.com/.
2. Click the setup.exe link and save this file to your hard drive.
3. Run this program on your Windows platform to begin installing Cygwin version 1.7.16-1 (the latest version at the time of writing). If you choose a different install location (C:\cygwin is the default), make sure that the directory path contains no spaces.
4. When you reach the Select Packages screen, select the Devel category and look for an entry in this category whose Package column presents make: The GNU version of the "make" utility. In the entry's New column, click the word Skip; this word should change to 3.82.90-1. Also, the Bin? column's check box should be checked—see Figure 8-1.

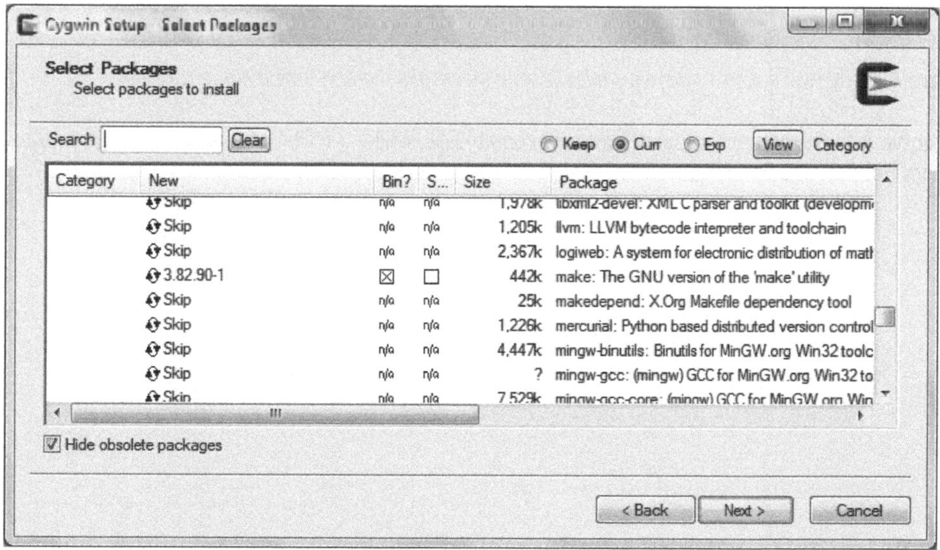

Figure 8-1. *Make sure that 3.82.90-1 appears in the New column and that the check box in the Bin? column is checked before clicking Next.*

5. Click the Next button and continue the installation.

When installation finishes, Cygwin gives you the opportunity to override its defaults of creating an icon on the desktop and of adding an icon to the Start Menu. After choosing to override these or not, click Finish.

Assuming that you've kept the defaults, click the desktop icon. You should see the Cygwin console (which is based on the Bash shell) shown in Figure 8-2.

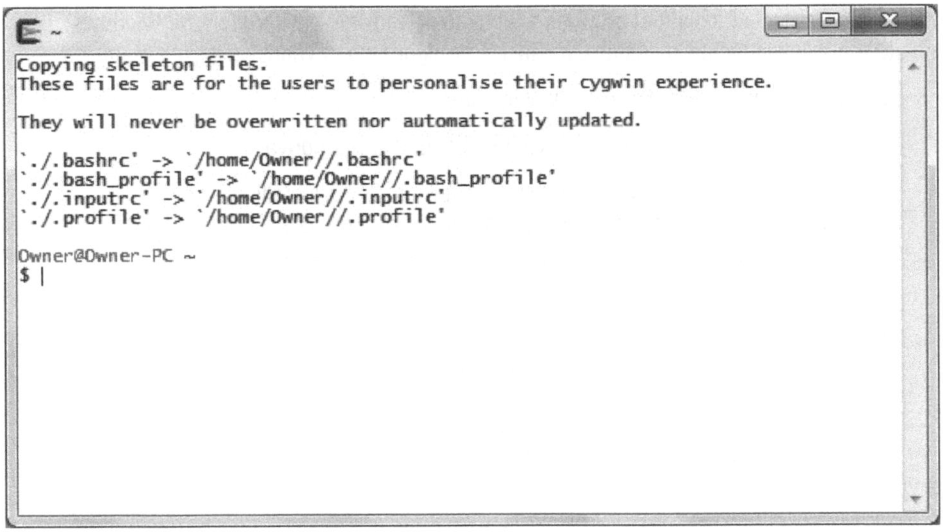

```
Copying skeleton files.
These files are for the users to personalise their cygwin experience.

They will never be overwritten nor automatically updated.

`./.bashrc' -> `/home/Owner//.bashrc'
`./.bash_profile' -> `/home/Owner//.bash_profile'
`./.inputrc' -> `/home/Owner//.inputrc'
`./.profile' -> `/home/Owner//.profile'

Owner@Owner-PC ~
$ |
```

Figure 8-2. *Cygwin's console displays initialization messages the first time it starts running.*

If you want to verify that Cygwin provides access to GNU Make 3.81 or later and GNU Awk, enter the commands shown in Figure 8-3.

```
Owner@Owner-PC ~
$ make -v
GNU Make 3.82.90
Built for i686-pc-cygwin
Copyright (C) 2010  Free Software Foundation, Inc.
License GPLv3+: GNU GPL version 3 or later <http://gnu.org/licenses/gpl.html>
This is free software: you are free to change and redistribute it.
There is NO WARRANTY, to the extent permitted by law.

Owner@Owner-PC ~
$ awk
Usage: awk [POSIX or GNU style options] -f progfile [--] file ...
Usage: awk [POSIX or GNU style options] [--] 'program' file ...
POSIX options:          GNU long options: (standard)
        -f progfile             --file=progfile
        -F fs                   --field-separator=fs
        -v var=val              --assign=var=val
Short options:          GNU long options: (extensions)
        -b                      --characters-as-bytes
        -c                      --traditional
        -C                      --copyright
        -d[file]                --dump-variables[=file]
        -e 'program-text'       --source='program-text'
        -E file                 --exec=file
```

Figure 8-3. *The Awk tool doesn't display a version number.*

You can learn more about Cygwin by checking out http://cygwin.com as well as Wikipedia's Cygwin entry (http://en.wikipedia.org/wiki/Cygwin).

Exploring the NDK

Now that you've installed the NDK on your platform, you might want to explore its home directory to discover what the NDK offers. The following list describes those directories and files that are located in the home directory for the Windows-based NDK:

- `build` contains the files that compose the NDK's build system.
- `docs` contains the NDK's HTML-based documentation files.
- `platforms` contains subdirectories that contain header files and shared libraries for each of the Android SDK's installed Android platforms.
- `prebuilt` contains binaries (notably `make.exe` and `awk.exe`) that let you build NDK source code without requiring Cygwin.
- `samples` contains various sample apps that demonstrate different aspects of the NDK.

- `sources` contains the source code and prebuilt binaries for various shared libraries, such as `cpufeatures` (detect the target device's CPU family and the optional features it supports) and `stlport` (multiplatform C++ standard library). Android NDK 1.5 required that developers organize their native code library projects under this directory. Starting with Android NDK 1.6, native code libraries are stored in `jni` subdirectories of their Android app project directories.
- `tests` contains scripts and sources to perform automated testing of the NDK. They are useful for testing a custom-built NDK.
- `toolchains` contains compilers, linkers, and other tools for generating native ARM (Advanced RISC Machine, the CPU used by Android—`http://en.wikipedia.org/wiki/ARM_architecture`) binaries on Linux, OS X, and Windows (with Cygwin) platforms.
- `documentation.html` is the entry point into the NDK's documentation.
- `GNUmakefile` is the default make file used by GNU Make.
- `ndk-build` is a shell script that simplifies building machine code.
- `ndk-build.cmd` is a Windows `cmd.exe` script that invokes the `prebuilt\windows\bin\make.exe` executable.
- `ndk-gdb` is a shell script that easily launches a native debugging session for your NDK-generated machine code. (Cygwin is required to run this script on Windows platforms.)
- `ndk-stack.exe` lets you filter stack traces as they appear in the output generated by `adb logcat` and replace any address inside a shared library with the corresponding values. In essence, it lets you observe more readable crash dump information.
- `README.TXT` welcomes you to the NDK, and it refers you to various documentation files that inform you about changes in the current release (and more).
- `RELEASE.TXT` contains the NDK's release number (`r8b`).

Each of the platforms directory's subdirectories contains header files that target stable native APIs. Google guarantees that all later platform releases will support the following APIs (see also http://developer.android.com/tools/sdk/ndk/overview.html#tools):

- Android logging (liblog)
- Android native app APIs
- C library (libc)
- C++ minimal support (stlport)
- JNI interface APIs
- Math library (libm)
- OpenGL ES 1.1 and OpenGL ES 2.0 (3D graphics libraries) APIs
- OpenSL ES native audio library APIs
- Pixel buffer access for Android 2.2 and above (libjnigraphics)
- Zlib compression (libz)

> **CAUTION:** Native system libraries that are not in this list are not stable and may change in future versions of the Android platform. Do not use them.

Greetings from the NDK

Perhaps the easiest way to become familiar with NDK programming is to create a small app that calls a native function that returns a Java String object. For example, Listing 8-1's NDKGreetings single-activity-based app calls a native getGreetingMessage() method to return a greeting message, which it displays via a dialog box.

Listing 8-1. *Receiving Greetings from the NDK*

```
package ca.tutortutor.ndkgreetings;

import android.app.Activity;
import android.app.AlertDialog;

import android.os.Bundle;
```

```
public class NDKGreetings extends Activity
{
   static
   {
      System.loadLibrary("NDKGreetings");
   }

   private native String getGreetingMessage();

   @Override
   public void onCreate(Bundle savedInstanceState)
   {
      super.onCreate(savedInstanceState);
      setContentView(R.layout.main);
      String greeting = getGreetingMessage();
      new AlertDialog.Builder(this).setMessage(greeting).show();
   }
}
```

Listing 8-1's `NDKGreetings` class reveals the following three important features of every app that incorporates native code:

- Native code is stored in an external library that must be loaded before its code can be invoked. Libraries are typically loaded at class-loading time via `System.loadLibrary()`. This method takes a single `String` argument that identifies the library without its `lib` prefix and `.so` suffix. In this example, the actual library file is named `libNDKGreetings.so`. (If the library cannot be located, an instance of the `java.lang.UnsatisfiedLinkError` class is thrown, which causes Android to terminate your app.)
- One or more native methods are declared that correspond to functions located within the library. A native method is identified to Java by prefixing its return type with the keyword `native`.
- A native method is invoked like any other Java method. Behind the scenes, Dalvik makes sure that the corresponding native function (expressed in C/C++) is invoked in the library.

Listing 8-2 presents the C source code to a native code library that implements `getGreetingMessage()` via the JNI.

Listing 8-2. *Implementing a Greetings Response to Dalvik*

```
#include <jni.h>

jstring
   Java_ca_tutortutor_ndkgreetings_NDKGreetings_getGreetingMessage(JNIEnv* env,
                                                                  jobject this)
{
   return (*env)->NewStringUTF(env, "Greetings from the NDK!");
}
```

Listing 8-2 first specifies an `#include` preprocessor directive that includes the contents of the `jni.h` header file when the source code is compiled. This file specifies various JNI constants, types, and function prototypes.

Listing 8-2 then declares the native function equivalent of Listing 8-1's `getGreetingMessage()` method. This native function's header reveals several important items:

- The native function's return type is specified as `jstring`. This type is defined in `jni.h` and represents Java's `java.lang.String` object type at the native code level.
- The function's name must begin with the Java package and class names that identify where the associated native method is declared.
- The type of the function's first parameter, `env`, is specified as a `JNIEnv` pointer. `JNIEnv`, which is defined in `jni.h`, is a C struct that identifies JNI functions that can be called to interact with Java.
- The type of the function's second parameter, `this`, is specified as `jobject`. This type, which is defined in `jni.h`, identifies an arbitrary Java object at the native code level. The argument passed to this parameter is the implicit `this` instance that the Java VM passes to any Java instance method.

The function de-references its `env` parameter in order to call the `NewStringUTF()` JNI function. `NewStringUTF()` converts its second argument, a C string, to its `jstring` equivalent (where the string is encoded via the Unicode UTF encoding standard), and it returns this equivalent Java string, which is then returned to Java.

> **NOTE:** When working with the JNI in the context of the C language, you must de-reference the JNIEnv parameter (*env, for example) in order to call a JNI function. Also, you must pass the JNIEnv parameter as the first argument to the JNI function. In contrast, C++ doesn't require this verbosity: you don't have to de-reference the JNIEnv parameter, and you don't have to pass this parameter as the first argument to the JNI function. For example, Listing 8-2's C-based (*env)->NewStringUTF(env, "Greetings from the NDK!") function call is expressed as env->NewStringUTF("Greetings from the NDK!") in C++.

Building and Running NDKGreetings with the Android SDK

To build NDKGreetings with the Android SDK, first use the SDK's android tool to create an NDKGreetings project. Assuming a Windows platform, a C:\prj\dev hierarchy in which the NDKGreetings project is to be stored (in C:\prj\dev\NDKGreetings), and an Android 4.1 platform target that corresponds to integer ID 1 (execute android list targets to obtain the correct ID), execute the following command (spread across two lines for readability) to create NDKGreetings:

```
android create project -t 1 -p C:\prj\dev\NDKGreetings -a NDKGreetings
                       -k ca.tutortutor.ndkgreetings
```

This command creates various directories and files within C:\prj\dev\NDKGreetings. For example, the src directory contains the ca\tutortutor\ndkgreetings directory structure, and the final ndkgreetings directory contains a skeletal NDKGreetings.java source file. Replace this skeletal file's contents with Listing 8-1.

Then create a jni directory within C:\prj\dev\NDKGreetings, and copy Listing 8-2 to C:\prj\dev\NDKGreetings\jni\NDKGreetings.c. Also, copy Listing 8-3 to C:\prj\dev\NDKGreetings\jni\Android.mk, which is a GNU Make file (explained in the NDK documentation) that's used to create the libNDKGreetings.so library.

Listing 8-3. *A Make File for NDKGreetings*

```
LOCAL_PATH := $(call my-dir)

include $(CLEAR_VARS)

LOCAL_MODULE    := NDKGreetings
LOCAL_SRC_FILES := NDKGreetings.c
```

```
include $(BUILD_SHARED_LIBRARY)
```

Execute the following command from within the C:\prj\dev\NDKGreetings directory:

```
\android-ndk-r8b\ndk-build
```

This command launches (on Windows) the ndk-build.cmd script to build the library. When the build is successful, the following messages are output:

```
Compile thumb  : NDKGreetings <= NDKGreetings.c
SharedLibrary  : libNDKGreetings.so
Install        : libNDKGreetings.so => libs/armeabi/libNDKGreetings.so
```

This output indicates that libNDKGreetings.so is located in the armeabi subdirectory of your NDKGreetings project directory's libs subdirectory.

> **NOTE:** If you observe a "No rule to make target" message instead of the output above, the cause is most likely extra spaces in Android.mk.

Alternatively, you can use Cygwin (assuming that it has been installed as previously discussed) to accomplish this task. Run Cygwin (if it is not running) and, from within the Cygwin command window, set the current directory to C:\prj\dev\NDKGreetings. See Figure 8-4.

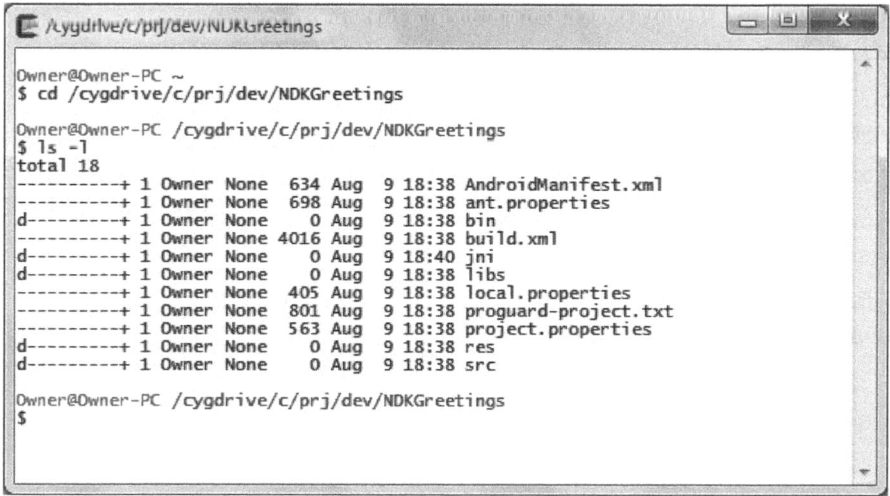

Figure 8-4. *The path to /prj/dev/NDKGreetings begins with a /cygdrive/c prefix.*

Assuming that the NDK home directory is `android-ndk-r8b` and that it's located in the root directory of the C drive, execute the following command (in Cygwin) to build the library:

```
../../../android-ndk-r8b/ndk-build
```

You should observe the same output messages as previously shown.

Assuming that `C:\prj\dev\NDKGreetings` is current, execute the following command (from Cygwin's shell or the normal Windows command window) to create `NDKGreetings-debug.apk`:

```
ant debug
```

This APK file is placed in the `NDKGreetings` project directory's `bin` subdirectory. To verify that `libNDKGreetings.so` is part of this APK, run the following command from `bin`:

```
jar tvf NDKGreetings-debug.apk
```

You should observe a line containing `lib/armeabi/libNDKGreetings.so` among the `jar` command's output.

To verify that the app works, start the emulator, which you can accomplish at the command line by executing the following command:

```
emulator -avd AVD1
```

This command assumes that you've created the AVD1 device configuration as specified in Chapter 1.

Install `NDKGreetings-debug.apk` on the emulated device via the following command:

```
adb install NDKGreetings-debug.apk
```

This command assumes that `adb` is located in your path. It also assumes that `bin` is the current directory.

When `adb` indicates that `NDKGreetings-debug.apk` has been installed, navigate to the app launcher screen and click the NDKGreetings icon. Figure 8-5 shows you the result.

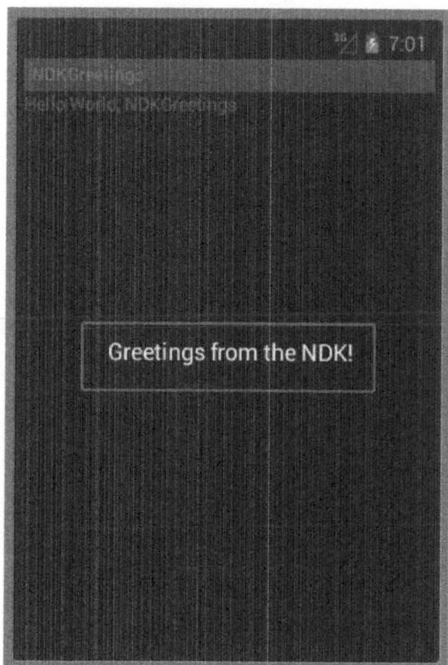

Figure 8-5. *Press the Esc key (in Windows) to make the dialog box go away.*

The dialog box displays the "Greetings from the NDK!" message that was obtained by calling the native function in the native code library. It also reveals a faint "Hello World, NDKGreetings" message near the top of the screen. This message originates in the project's default `main.xml` file that's created by the `android` tool.

Building and Running NDKGreetings with Eclipse

To build `NDKGreetings` with Eclipse, first create a new Android project as described in Chapter 1's Recipe 1-10. For your convenience, the steps that you need to follow to accomplish this task are provided here:

1. Start Eclipse if it is not running.
2. Select New from the File menu, and select Project from the resulting pop-up menu.
3. On the resulting *New Project* dialog box, expand the Android node in the wizard tree (if necessary), select the Android Application Project branch below this node (if necessary), and click the Next button.

4. On the resulting *New Android App* dialog box, enter **`NDKGreetings`** into the Application Name textfield. This entered name also appears in the Project Name textfield, and it identifies the folder/directory in which the `NDKGreetings` project is stored.
5. Enter **`ca.tutortutor.ndkgreetings`** into the Package Name textfield.
6. Via Build SDK, select the appropriate Android SDK to target. This selection identifies the Android platform you'd like your app to be built against. Assuming that you've installed only the Android 4.1 platform, only this choice should appear and be selected.
7. Via Minimum SDK, either select the minimum Android SDK on which your app runs or keep the default setting.
8. Leave the "Create custom launcher icon" check box checked if you want a custom launcher icon to be created. Otherwise, uncheck this check box when you supply your own launcher icon.
9. Leave the "Mark this project as a library" check box unchecked because you are not creating a library.
10. Leave the "Create Project in Workspace" check box checked, and click Next.
11. On the resulting Configure Launcher Icon pane, make suitable adjustments to the custom launcher icon and then click Next.
12. On the resulting Create Activity pane, leave the Create Activity check box checked, make sure that BlankActivity is selected, and click Next.
13. On the resulting New Blank Activity pane, enter **`NDKGreetings`** into the Activity Name textfield, and **`main`** into the Layout Name textfield. Keep all other settings and click Finish.

Then use Eclipse's Package Explorer to locate the `NDKGreetings.java` source file node. Double-click this node and replace the skeletal contents shown in the resulting edit window with Listing 8-1.

Using Package Explorer, create a jni folder node below the NDKGreetings project node, add an `NDKGreetings.c` file subnode of jni, replace this node's empty contents with Listing 8-2, add a new `Android.mk` file subnode of jni, and replace its empty contents with Listing 8-3.

At this point, you can use Cygwin to create the library file, or you can create a builder to do this for you. To use Cygwin, launch this tool if it is not running, and use the `cd` command to change to the project's folder (for example, `cd /cygdrive/c/users/owner/workspace/NDKGreetings`). Then execute `ndk-build` as demonstrated in the previous section (for example, `/cygdrive/c/android-ndk-r8b/ndk-build`). If all goes well, the `NDKGreetings` project directory's `libs` subdirectory should contain an `armeabi` subdirectory, which should contain a `libNDKGreetings.so` library file.

Complete the following steps to create a builder:

1. Right-click the NDKGreetings node, and select Properties from the resulting pop-up menu.
2. Select Builders on the resulting *Properties for NDKGreetings* dialog box.
3. On the resulting Builders pane, click the New button.
4. On the resulting *Choose configuration type* dialog box, select Program and click OK.
5. On the resulting *Edit Configuration* dialog box, choose whatever name you want for the builder (or keep the default), enter **`C:\android-ndk-r8b\ndk-build.cmd`** (or your equivalent) into the Location textfield, enter **`${workspace_loc:/NDKGreetings}`** into the Working Directory textfield, and click the OK button to close this dialog box.
6. Click the OK button to close the *Properties for NDKGreetings* dialog box.

To run `NDKGreetings` from Eclipse, select Run from the menubar, and then select Run from the drop-down menu. If a *Run As* dialog box appears, select Android Application and click OK. Eclipse launches `emulator` with the AVD1 device, installs `NDKGreetings.apk`, and runs this app, whose output appears in Figure 8-6.

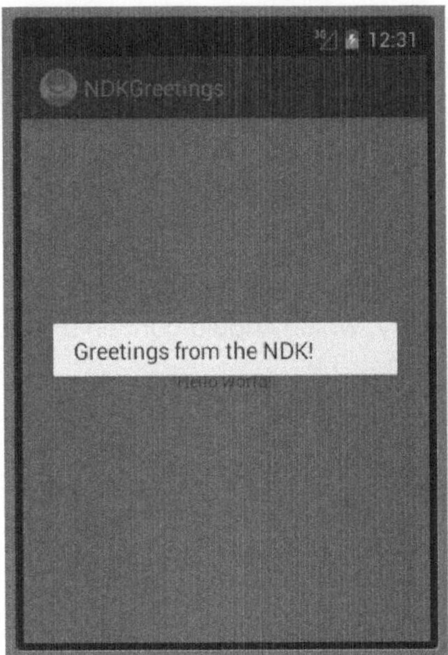

Figure 8-6. *NDKGreetings's user interface looks different because of an Eclipse-generated custom theme.*

Sampling the NDK

The `samples` subdirectory of the NDK installation's home directory contains several sample apps that demonstrate different aspects of the NDK:

- `bitmap-plasma`: An app that demonstrates how to access the pixel buffers of Android `android.graphics.Bitmap` objects from native code, and uses this capability to generate an old-school "plasma" effect.
- `hello-gl2`: An app that renders a triangle using OpenGL ES 2.0 vertex and fragment shaders. (If you run this app on the Android emulator, you will receive an error message stating that the app has stopped unexpectedly when the emulator doesn't support OpenGL ES 2.0 hardware emulation.)
- `hello-jni`: An app that loads a string from a native method implemented in a shared library and then displays it in the app's user interface. This app is similar to `NDKGreetings`.

- hello-neon: An app that shows how to use the cpufeatures library to check CPU capabilities at runtime, and then uses NEON (a marketing name of a SIMD instruction set for the ARM architecture) intrinsics if supported by the CPU. Specifically, the app implements two versions of a tiny benchmark for an FIR filter loop (http://en.wikipedia.org/wiki/Finite_impulse_response): a C version and a NEON-optimized version for devices that support it.
- native-activity: An app that demonstrates how to use the native-app-glue static library to create a *native activity* (an activity implemented entirely in native code).
- native-audio: An app that demonstrates how to use native methods to play sounds via OpenSL ES.
- native-plasma: A version of bitmap-plasma implemented with a native activity.
- san-angeles: An app that renders 3D graphics through the native OpenGL ES APIs, while managing the activity life cycle with an android.opengl.GLSurfaceView object.
- two-libs: An app that loads a shared library dynamically and calls a native method provided by the library. In this case, the method is implemented in a static library imported by the shared library.

You can use Eclipse to build these apps. For example, carry out the following steps to build san-angeles:

1. Start Eclipse if it is not running.
2. Select New from the File menu, and select Project from the resulting pop-up menu.
3. On the resulting *New Project* dialog box, expand the Android node in the wizard tree (if necessary), select the Android Project from Existing Code branch below this node, and click the Next button.
4. On the resulting Import Projects pane, click the Browse button.
5. On the resulting *Browse for Folder* dialog box, select the NDK's san-angeles directory, which is under the samples directory. Click OK to close this dialog box.

6. Back on the Import Projects pane, check the "Copy projects into workspace" check box and click the Finish button. A `com.example.SanAngeles.DemoActivity` node should appear in Package Explorer. Furthermore, a `com.example.SanAngeles.DemoActivity` project directory should appear in the workspace. This directory contains a separate copy of the NDK's `san-angeles` project.
7. Right-click the `com.example.SanAngeles.DemoActivity` node, and select Properties from the resulting pop-up menu.
8. On the resulting *Properties for com.example.SanAngeles.DemoActivity* dialog box, select Builders.
9. On the resulting Builders pane, click the New button.
10. On the resulting *Choose configuration type* dialog box, select Program and click OK.
11. On the resulting *Edit Configuration* dialog box, choose whatever name you want for the builder (or keep the default), enter **`C:\android-ndk-r8b\ndk-build.cmd`** (or your equivalent) into the Location textfield, enter **`${workspace_loc:/com.example.SanAngeles.DemoActivity}`** into the Working Directory textfield, and click the OK button to close this dialog box.
12. Close the Properties for com.example.SanAngeles.DemoActivity dialog box by clicking OK.

With `com.example.SanAngelese.DemoActivity` as the selected node in Package Explorer, select Run from the menubar and Run from the drop-down menu. If a *Run As* dialog box appears, select Android Application and click OK. If you encounter a dialog box claiming that your project has errors, close this dialog box and select Run again.

This time, Eclipse should launch `emulator` with the AVD1 device that you created in Chapter 1. It should install `DemoActivity.apk` on this device and run this app. After unlocking the home screen, you should see a continuously moving screen with content similar to that shown in Figure 8-7 (it may take a few moments to appear).

Figure 8-7. `DemoActivity` *takes you on a tour of a three-dimensional city.*

8-1. Discovering Native Activities

Problem

You know that Android supports native activities and you want to learn more about them.

Solution

A *native activity* is an activity that's implemented entirely in native code. First appearing in Android 2.3 (API Level 9) via the `android.app.NativeActivity` class, and in Revision 5 of the NDK, which provides support for developing them, native activities let you implement apps in C/C++ without writing any Java code.

> **NOTE:** A `NativeActivity` instance is equivalent to an `android.app.Activity` instance that performs JNI calls to native code.

How It Works

`NativeActivity` is a helper class that lets you write a completely native activity and, by extension, a completely native app. It handles communication between the Android framework and your native code. You don't have to subclass it or call its methods. Instead, create your native app and declare it to be native in `AndroidManifest.xml`.

Native activities don't change the fact that Android apps still run in their own VMs, where they are sandboxed from other apps. Because of this, you can still access Android framework APIs through the JNI. However, there are also native interfaces that you can use to access sensors, input events and assets, and so on.

> **NOTE:** To learn what APIs can be accessed by native activities, check out the list of stable native APIs that was presented earlier in this chapter.

The NDK offers two choices for developing a native activity:

- *Low-level*: The `native_activity.h` header file (located in `platforms/android-9/arch-arm/usr/include/android` and similar subdirectories of the NDK's home directory) defines the native version of the `NativeActivity` class. It contains the callback interface and data structures that you need to create your native activity. Because your app's main thread handles callbacks, your callback implementations must not be blocking. If they block, you might receive "Application Not Responding" errors because the main thread will be unresponsive until the callback returns. Check out the comments in `native_activity.h` for more information.

- *High-level*: The android_native_app_glue.h header file (located in the sources/android/native_app_glue subdirectory of the NDK's home directory) defines a static helper library built on top of native_activity.h. It spawns another thread to handle callbacks and input events. This spawned thread is used to prevent any callbacks from blocking the main thread, and it adds some flexibility in how you implement callbacks, so you might find this programming model a bit easier to implement. You can modify the android_native_app_glue.c source file (located in the same directory) when you need to change its functionality. Check out the comments in android_native_app_glue.h for more information.

You will learn more about native activities in the next two recipes, which show you how to develop similar native activities in low-level and high-level contexts. Furthermore, each recipe shows you how to develop its low-level or high-level native activity by using the Android SDK and Eclipse.

8-2. Developing Low-Level Native Activities

Problem

You want to learn how to develop low-level native activities, which are based on the native_activity.h header file.

Solution

Create a low-level native activity project as if it were a regular Android app project. Then modify its AndroidManifest.xml file appropriately, and introduce a jni subdirectory of the project directory that contains the native activity's C/C++ source code along with an Android.mk make file.

The modified AndroidManifest.xml file differs from the regular AndroidManifest.xml file in the following ways:

- A <uses-sdk android:minSdkVersion="9"/> element precedes the <application> element; native activities require at least API Level 9.
- An android:hasCode="false" attribute appears in the <application> tag because native activities don't contain source code.

- The <activity> element's `android:name` attribute contains the value `"android.app.NativeActivity"`. When Android discovers this value, it locates the appropriate entry point in the native activity's library.
- A <meta-data> element precedes the <intent-filter> element. <meta-data> specifies an `android:name="android.app.lib_name"` attribute and an `android:value` attribute whose value is the name of the native activity's library (without a `lib` prefix and a `.so` suffix).

Your native activity's C/C++ source file must define the following entry-point method:

```
void ANativeActivity_onCreate(ANativeActivity* activity, void* savedState,
                              size_t savedStateSize)
```

This method declares the following parameters:

- `activity`: This is the address of an `ANativeActivity` structure. `ANativeActivity` is defined in the NDK's `native_activity.h` header file, and it declares various members, including `callbacks` (an array of pointers to callback functions; you can set these pointers to your own callbacks), `internalDataPath` (the path to the app's internal data directory), `externalDataPath` (the path to the app's external [removable/mountable] data directory), `sdkVersion` (the platform's SDK version number), and `assetManager` (a pointer to an instance of the native equivalent of the app's `android.content.res.AssetManager` class for accessing binary assets bundled into the app's APK file).
- `savedState`: This is your activity's previously saved state. If the activity is being instantiated from a previously saved instance, `savedState` will be non-`NULL` and will point to the saved data. You must make a copy of this data when you need to access it later, because memory allocated to `savedState` will be released after you return from this function.
- `savedStateSize`: This is the size (in bytes) of the data pointed to by `savedState`.

> **NOTE:** When you launch an app that is based on a native activity, an instance of the `android.app.NativeActivity` class is created. Its `onCreate(Bundle)` method uses the JNI to call `void ANativeActivity_onCreate(ANativeActivity*, void*, size_t)`.

`void ANativeActivity_onCreate(ANativeActivity*, void*, size_t)` should override any needed callbacks. It must also create a thread that promptly responds to input events in order to prevent an "Application Not Responding" error from occurring.

> **NOTE:** `void ANativeActivity_onCreate(ANativeActivity*, void*, size_t)` and your callback methods must not delay their execution; otherwise, an "Application Not Responding" error will occur.

Finally, the `Android.mk` file is nearly identical to what you've already seen. However, this file will most likely include a `LOCAL_LDLIBS` entry that identifies any required libraries. (These libraries will undoubtedly include the standard `libandroid.so` library.)

How It Works

Consider an `LLNADemo` project that demonstrates low-level native activities. Listing 8-4 presents the contents of this project's solitary `llnademo.c` source file.

Listing 8-4. *Examining a Native Activity from a Low Perspective*

```
#include <android/log.h>
#include <android/native_activity.h>
#include <pthread.h>

#define LOGI(...) ((void)__android_log_print(ANDROID_LOG_INFO, \
                                             "llnademo", \
                                             __VA_ARGS__))

AInputQueue* _queue;
pthread_t thread;
pthread_cond_t cond;
pthread_mutex_t mutex;
```

```
static void onConfigurationChanged(ANativeActivity* activity)
{
   LOGI("ConfigurationChanged: %p\n", activity);
}

static void onDestroy(ANativeActivity* activity)
{
   LOGI("Destroy: %p\n", activity);
}

static void onInputQueueCreated(ANativeActivity* activity, AInputQueue* queue)
{
   LOGI("InputQueueCreated: %p -- %p\n", activity, queue);
   pthread_mutex_lock(&mutex);
   _queue = queue;
   pthread_cond_broadcast(&cond);
   pthread_mutex_unlock(&mutex);
}

static void onInputQueueDestroyed(ANativeActivity* activity, AInputQueue* queue)
{
   LOGI("InputQueueDestroyed: %p -- %p\n", activity, queue);
   pthread_mutex_lock(&mutex);
   _queue = NULL;
   pthread_mutex_unlock(&mutex);
}

static void onLowMemory(ANativeActivity* activity)
{
   LOGI("LowMemory: %p\n", activity);
}

static void onNativeWindowCreated(ANativeActivity* activity,
                                  ANativeWindow* window)
{
   LOGI("NativeWindowCreated: %p -- %p\n", activity, window);
}

static void onNativeWindowDestroyed(ANativeActivity* activity,
                                    ANativeWindow* window)
{
   LOGI("NativeWindowDestroyed: %p -- %p\n", activity, window);
}

static void onPause(ANativeActivity* activity)
{
   LOGI("Pause: %p\n", activity);
}
```

```
static void onResume(ANativeActivity* activity)
{
   LOGI("Resume: %p\n", activity);
}

static void* onSaveInstanceState(ANativeActivity* activity, size_t* outLen)
{
   LOGI("SaveInstanceState: %p\n", activity);
   return NULL;
}

static void onStart(ANativeActivity* activity)
{
   LOGI("Start: %p\n", activity);
}

static void onStop(ANativeActivity* activity)
{
   LOGI("Stop: %p\n", activity);
}

static void onWindowFocusChanged(ANativeActivity* activity, int focused)
{
   LOGI("WindowFocusChanged: %p -- %d\n", activity, focused);
}

static void* process_input(void* param)
{
   while (1)
   {
      pthread_mutex_lock(&mutex);
      if (_queue == NULL)
         pthread_cond_wait(&cond, &mutex);
      AInputEvent* event = NULL;
      while (AInputQueue_getEvent(_queue, &event) >= 0)
      {
         if (AInputQueue_preDispatchEvent(_queue, event))
            break;
         AInputQueue_finishEvent(_queue, event, 0);
      }
      pthread_mutex_unlock(&mutex);
   }
}

void ANativeActivity_onCreate(ANativeActivity* activity,
                              void* savedState,
                              size_t savedStateSize)
{
   LOGI("Creating: %p\n", activity);
   LOGI("Internal data path: %s\n", activity->internalDataPath);
```

```
    LOGI("External data path: %s\n", activity->externalDataPath);
    LOGI("SDK version code: %d\n", activity->sdkVersion);
    LOGI("Asset Manager: %p\n", activity->assetManager);

    activity->callbacks->onConfigurationChanged = onConfigurationChanged;
    activity->callbacks->onDestroy = onDestroy;
    activity->callbacks->onInputQueueCreated = onInputQueueCreated;
    activity->callbacks->onInputQueueDestroyed = onInputQueueDestroyed;
    activity->callbacks->onLowMemory = onLowMemory;
    activity->callbacks->onNativeWindowCreated = onNativeWindowCreated;
    activity->callbacks->onNativeWindowDestroyed = onNativeWindowDestroyed;
    activity->callbacks->onPause = onPause;
    activity->callbacks->onResume = onResume;
    activity->callbacks->onSaveInstanceState = onSaveInstanceState;
    activity->callbacks->onStart = onStart;
    activity->callbacks->onStop = onStop;
    activity->callbacks->onWindowFocusChanged = onWindowFocusChanged;

    pthread_mutex_init(&mutex, NULL);
    pthread_cond_init(&cond, NULL);
    pthread_create(&thread, NULL, process_input, NULL);
}
```

Listing 8-4 begins with three `#include` directives that (before compilation) include the contents of three NDK header files for logging, native activities, and Portable Operating System Interface (POSIX) threading.

> **NOTE:** If you are unfamiliar with POSIX, check out Wikipedia's "POSIX" entry (http://en.wikipedia.org/wiki/POSIX).

Listing 8-4 next declares a `LOGI` macro for logging information messages to the Android device's log (you can view this log by executing `adb logcat`). This macro refers to the `int __android_log_print(int prio, const char* tag, const char* fmt, ...)` function (prototyped in the `log.h` header file) that performs the actual writing. Each logged message must have a priority (such as `ANDROID_LOG_INFO`), a tag (such as `llnademo`), and a format string defining the message. Additional arguments are specified when the format string contains format specifiers (such as `%d`).

Listing 8-4 then declares a `_queue` variable of type `AInputQueue*`. (`AInputQueue` is defined in the `input.h` header file, which is included by the `native_activity.h` header file.) This variable is assigned a reference to the input queue when the queue is created, or it is assigned `NULL` when the queue is destroyed. The native activity must process all input events from this queue to avoid an "Application Not Responding" error.

Three POSIX thread global variables are now created: `thread`, `cond`, and `mutex`. The variable `thread` identifies the thread that is created later on in the listing, and the variables `cond` and `mutex` are used to avoid busy waiting and to ensure synchronized access to the shared `_queue` variable, respectively.

A series of "`on`"-prefixed callback functions follows. Each function is declared `static` to hide it from outside of its module. (The use of `static` isn't essential but is present for good form.)

Each "`on`"-prefixed callback function is called on the main thread and logs some information for viewing in the device log. However, the `void onInputQueueCreated(ANativeActivity* activity, AInputQueue* queue)` and `void onInputQueueDestroyed(ANativeActivity* activity, AInputQueue* queue)` functions have a little more work to accomplish:

- `onInputQueueCreated(ANativeActivity*, AInputQueue*)` must assign its queue argument address to the `_queue` variable. Because `_queue` is also accessed from a thread apart from the main thread, synchronization is required to ensure that there is no conflict between these threads. Synchronization is achieved by accessing `_queue` between `pthread_mutex_lock(&mutex)` and `pthread_mutex_unlock(&mutex)` calls. The former call locks a *mutex* (a program object used to prevent multiple threads from simultaneously accessing a shared variable); the latter call unlocks the mutex. Because the non-main thread waits until `_queue` contains a non-`NULL` value, a `pthread_cond_broadcast(&cond)` call is also present to wake up this waiting thread.
- `onInputQueueDestroyed(ANativeActivity*, AInputQueue*)` is simpler, assigning `NULL` to `_queue` (within a locked region) when the input queue is destroyed.

The non-main thread executes the `void* process_input(void* param)` function. This function repeatedly executes `int32_t AInputQueue_getEvent(AInputQueue* queue, AInputEvent** outEvent)` to return the next input event. The integer return value is negative when no events are available or when an error occurs. When an event is returned, it is referenced by `outEvent`.

Assuming that an event has been returned, `int32_t AInputQueue_preDispatchEvent(AInputQueue* queue, AInputEvent* event)` is called to send the event (if it is a keystroke-related event) to the current input method editor to be consumed before the app. This function returns 0 when the event was not predispatched, which means that you can process it right now.

When a nonzero value is returned, you must not process the current event so that the event can appear again in the event queue (assuming that it does not get consumed during predispatching).

At this point, you could do something with the event (when it is not predispatched). Regardless, you lastly call `void AInputQueue_finishEvent(AInputQueue* queue, AInputEvent* event, int handled)` to finish the dispatching of the given event. A `0` value is passed to `handled` to indicate that the event has not been handled in your code.

Finally, Listing 8-4 declares `void ANativeActivity_onCreate(ANativeActivity*, void*, size_t)`, which logs a message, overrides most of the default callbacks (you could also override the rest when desired), initializes the mutex and the condition variable, and finally creates and starts the thread that runs `void* process_input(void*)`.

Listing 8-5 presents this project's `Android.mk` file.

Listing 8-5. *A Make File for `LLNADemo`*

```
LOCAL_PATH := $(call my-dir)
include $(CLEAR_VARS)
LOCAL_MODULE    := llnademo
LOCAL_SRC_FILES := llnademo.c
LOCAL_LDLIBS := -llog -landroid
include $(BUILD_SHARED_LIBRARY)
```

This make file presents a `LOCAL_LDLIBS` entry, which identifies the `liblog.so` and `libandroid.so` standard libraries that are to be linked against.

Building and Running LLNADemo with the Android SDK

To build `LLNADemo` with the Android SDK, first use the SDK's `android` tool to create an `LLNADemo` project. Assuming a Windows platform, a `C:\prj\dev` hierarchy in which the `LLNADemo` project is to be stored (in `C:\prj\dev\LLNADemo`), and an Android 4.1 platform target corresponding to integer ID 1 (execute `android list targets` to obtain the correct ID), execute the following command (spread across two lines for readability) to create `LLNADemo`:

```
android create project -t 1 -p C:\prj\dev\LLNADemo -a LLNADemo
                       -k ca.tutortutor.llnademo
```

This command creates various directories and files within `C:\prj\dev\LLNADemo`. To reduce the size of the APK file, you can delete the `src` directory because this directory and its contents will not be needed. Also, you can delete all directories underneath res except for values, because they and their contents will not be needed.

Create a jni directory underneath LLNADemo, and copy Listings 8-4 and 8-5 to the llnademo.c and Android.mk files, respectively, which are stored in this directory. Then replace the contents of AndroidManifest.xml file with Listing 8-6.

Listing 8-6. *A Manifest File for* LLNADemo

```
<?xml version="1.0" encoding="utf-8"?>
<manifest xmlns:android="http://schemas.android.com/apk/res/android"
          package="ca.tutortutor.llnademo"
          android:versionCode="1"
          android:versionName="1.0">
  <uses-sdk android:minSdkVersion="9"/>
  <application android:label="@string/app_name" android:hasCode="false">
    <activity android:name="android.app.NativeActivity"
              android:label="@string/app_name"
              android:configChanges="orientation">
      <meta-data android:name="android.app.lib_name"
                 android:value="llnademo"/>
      <intent-filter>
        <action android:name="android.intent.action.MAIN" />
        <category android:name="android.intent.category.LAUNCHER"/>
      </intent-filter>
    </activity>
  </application>
</manifest>
```

An android:configChanges="orientation" attribute has been added to the <activity> tag so that void onConfigurationChanged(ANativeActivity* activity) is invoked when the device orientation changes (from portrait to landscape, for example). As an exercise, remove this attribute and observe how the log messages change.

With the C:\prj\dev\LLNADemo (or your equivalent) directory current, execute a command similar to that shown below to build the library:

```
\android-ndk-r8b\ndk-build
```

If all goes well, you should see the following messages:

```
Compile thumb : llnademo <= llnademo.c
SharedLibrary  : libllnademo.so
Install        : libllnademo.so => libs/armeabi/libllnademo.so
```

You should also observe an armeabi directory in libs, and a libllnademo.so file should be in armeabi.

Now execute the following command to build the project:

```
ant debug
```

Assuming success, execute the following command to install the `LLNADemo-debug.apk` file on the current device:

```
adb install bin\LLNADemo-debug.apk
```

Before launching this app, start AVD1 (created in Chapter 1). Then execute the following command in a separate window so that you can view the log output:

```
adb logcat
```

Launch `LLNADemo` and you should observe a black screen. Press the Esc key and you should revert to the app launcher. Figure 8-8 shows you a portion of the log related to these events.

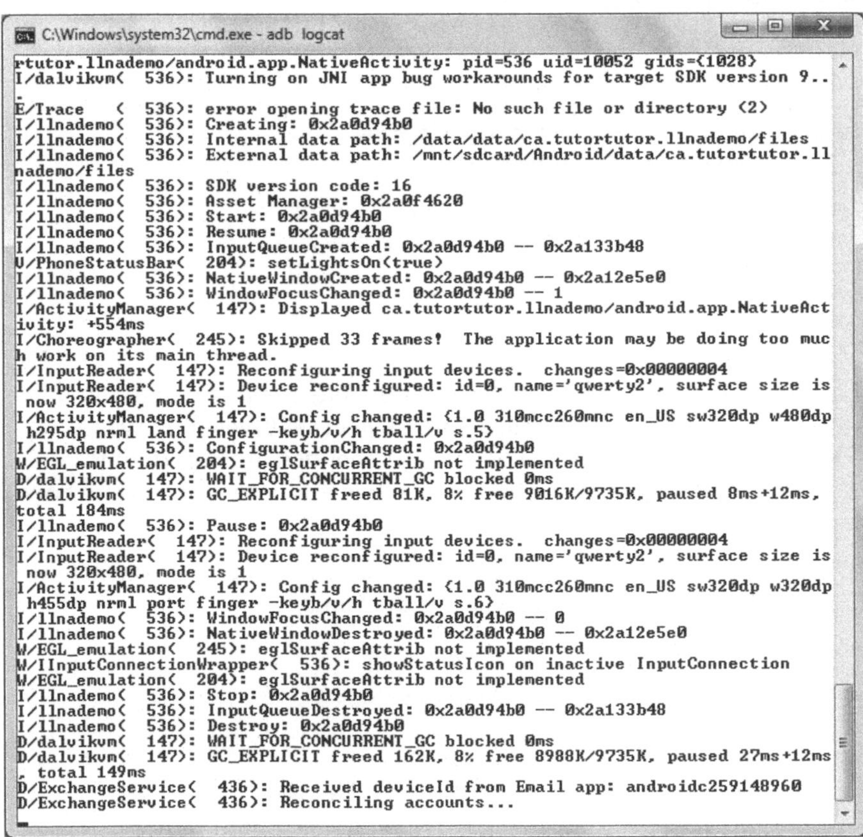

C:\Windows\system32\cmd.exe - adb logcat
rtutor.llnademo/android.app.NativeActivity: pid=536 uid=10052 gids={1028}
I/dalvikvm(536): Turning on JNI app bug workarounds for target SDK version 9..
.
E/Trace (536): error opening trace file: No such file or directory (2)
I/llnademo(536): Creating: 0x2a0d94b0
I/llnademo(536): Internal data path: /data/data/ca.tutortutor.llnademo/files
I/llnademo(536): External data path: /mnt/sdcard/Android/data/ca.tutortutor.ll
nademo/files
I/llnademo(536): SDK version code: 16
I/llnademo(536): Asset Manager: 0x2a0f4620
I/llnademo(536): Start: 0x2a0d94b0
I/llnademo(536): Resume: 0x2a0d94b0
I/llnademo(536): InputQueueCreated: 0x2a0d94b0 -- 0x2a133b48
V/PhoneStatusBar(204): setLightsOn(true)
I/llnademo(536): NativeWindowCreated: 0x2a0d94b0 -- 0x2a12e5e0
I/llnademo(536): WindowFocusChanged: 0x2a0d94b0 -- 1
I/ActivityManager(147): Displayed ca.tutortutor.llnademo/android.app.NativeAct
ivity: +554ms
I/Choreographer(245): Skipped 33 frames! The application may be doing too muc
h work on its main thread.
I/InputReader(147): Reconfiguring input devices. changes=0x00000004
I/InputReader(147): Device reconfigured: id=0, name='qwerty2', surface size is
now 320x480, mode is 1
I/ActivityManager(147): Config changed: {1.0 310mcc260mnc en_US sw320dp w480dp
h295dp nrml land finger -keyb/v/h tball/v s.5}
I/llnademo(536): ConfigurationChanged: 0x2a0d94b0
W/EGL_emulation(204): eglSurfaceAttrib not implemented
D/dalvikvm(147): WAIT_FOR_CONCURRENT_GC blocked 0ms
D/dalvikvm(147): GC_EXPLICIT freed 81K, 8% free 9016K/9735K, paused 8ms+12ms,
total 184ms
I/llnademo(536): Pause: 0x2a0d94b0
I/InputReader(147): Reconfiguring input devices. changes=0x00000004
I/InputReader(147): Device reconfigured: id=0, name='qwerty2', surface size is
now 320x480, mode is 1
I/ActivityManager(147): Config changed: {1.0 310mcc260mnc en_US sw320dp w320dp
h455dp nrml port finger -keyb/v/h tball/v s.6}
I/llnademo(536): WindowFocusChanged: 0x2a0d94b0 -- 0
I/llnademo(536): NativeWindowDestroyed: 0x2a0d94b0 -- 0x2a12e5e0
W/EGL_emulation(245): eglSurfaceAttrib not implemented
W/IInputConnectionWrapper(536): showStatusIcon on inactive InputConnection
W/EGL_emulation(204): eglSurfaceAttrib not implemented
I/llnademo(536): Stop: 0x2a0d94b0
I/llnademo(536): InputQueueDestroyed: 0x2a0d94b0 -- 0x2a133b48
I/llnademo(536): Destroy: 0x2a0d94b0
D/dalvikvm(147): WAIT_FOR_CONCURRENT_GC blocked 0ms
D/dalvikvm(147): GC_EXPLICIT freed 162K, 8% free 8988K/9735K, paused 27ms+12ms
, total 149ms
D/ExchangeService(436): Received deviceId from Email app: androidc259148960
D/ExchangeService(436): Reconciling accounts...

Figure 8-8. *`LLNADemo` logs various messages during its execution.*

Building and Running LLNADemo with Eclipse

To build LLNADemo with Eclipse, first create a new Android project as described in Chapter 1's Recipe 1-10. For your convenience, the steps that you need to follow to accomplish this task are provided here:

1. Start Eclipse if it is not running.
2. Select New from the File menu, and select Project from the resulting pop-up menu.
3. On the resulting *New Project* dialog box, expand the Android node in the wizard tree (if necessary), select the Android Application Project branch below this node (if necessary), and click the Next button.
4. On the resulting *New Android App* dialog box, enter **LLNADemo** into the Application Name textfield. This entered name also appears in the Project Name textfield, and it identifies the folder/directory in which the LLNADemo project is stored.
5. Enter **ca.tutortutor.llnademo** into the Package Name textfield.
6. Via Build SDK, select the appropriate Android SDK to target. This selection identifies the Android platform you'd like your app to be built against. Assuming that you've installed only the Android 4.1 platform, only this choice should appear and be selected.
7. Via Minimum SDK, either select the minimum Android SDK on which your app runs or keep the default setting. (Don't go lower than API Level 9.)
8. Leave the "Create custom launcher icon" check box checked if you want a custom launcher icon to be created. Otherwise, uncheck this check box when you supply your own launcher icon.
9. Leave the "Mark this project as a library" check box unchecked because you are not creating a library.
10. Leave the "Create Project in Workspace" check box checked, and click Next.

11. On the resulting Configure Launcher Icon pane, make suitable adjustments to the custom launcher icon; click Next.
12. On the resulting Create Activity pane, leave the Create Activity check box checked, make sure that BlankActivity is selected, and click Next.
13. On the resulting New Blank Activity pane, enter **`LLNADemo`** into the Activity Name textfield. Keep all other settings and click Finish.

Using Package Explorer, create a jni folder node below the LLNADemo project node, add an `LLNADemo.c` file subnode of jni, replace this node's empty contents with Listing 8-4, add a new `Android.mk` file subnode of jni, and replace its empty contents with Listing 8-5.

Let's create a builder to create the library file. Complete the following steps:

1. Right-click the LLNADemo node, and select Properties from the resulting pop-up menu.
2. Select Builders on the resulting *Properties for LLNADemo* dialog box.
3. On the resulting Builders pane, click the New button.
4. On the resulting *Choose configuration type* dialog box, select Program and click OK.
5. On the resulting *Edit Configuration* dialog box, choose whatever name you want for the builder (or keep the default), enter **`C:\android-ndk-r8b\ndk-build.cmd`** (or your equivalent) into the Location textfield, enter **`${workspace_loc:/LLNADemo}`** into the Working Directory textfield, and click the OK button to close this dialog box.
6. Click the OK button to close the *Properties for LLNADemo* dialog box.

Finally, using Eclipse's built-in manifest editor, make the necessary changes to `AndroidManifest.xml` that were presented earlier in this recipe.

To run `LLNADemo` from Eclipse, select Run from the menubar, and then select Run from the drop-down menu. If a *Run As* dialog box appears, select Android Application and click OK. Eclipse launches `emulator` with the AVD1 device, installs `LLNADemo.apk`, and runs this app, whose output appears in Figure 8-9.

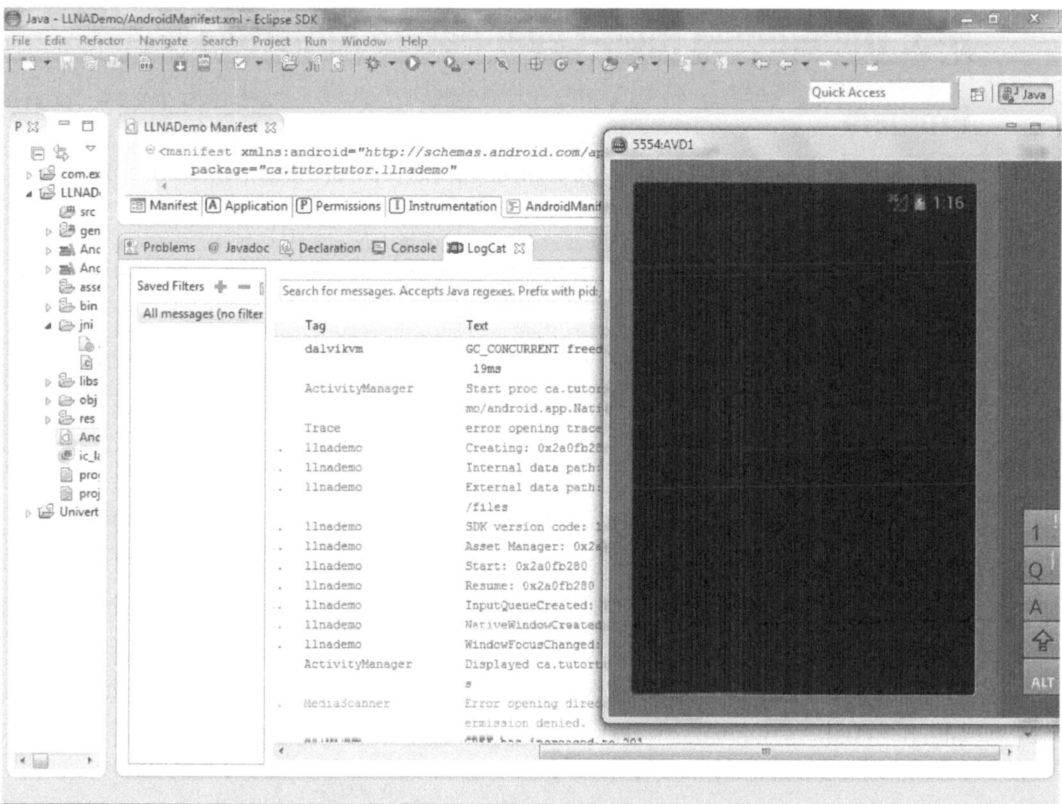

Figure 8-9. *LLNADemo logs various messages during its execution.*

> **NOTE:** When the target SDK is set to API Level 13 or higher (Eclipse defaults the target SDK to 15) and you haven't included `screenSize` with `orientation` in the value assigned to `<activity>`'s `configChanges` attribute (`"orientation|screenSize"`), you will not see "ConfigurationChanged" messages in the log when you change the device orientation.

8-3. Developing High-Level Native Activities

Problem

You want to learn how to develop high-level native activities, which are based on the android_native_app_glue.h header file.

Solution

The development of a high-level native activity is very similar to that of a low-level native activity. However, a new source file and a new Android.mk file are required.

How It Works

Consider an HLNADemo project that demonstrates high-level native activities. Listing 8-7 presents the contents of this project's solitary hlnademo.c source file.

Listing 8-7. *Examining a Native Activity from a High Perspective*

```
#include <android/log.h>
#include <android_native_app_glue.h>

#define LOGI(...) ((void)__android_log_print(ANDROID_LOG_INFO, \
                                             "hlnademo", \
                                             __VA_ARGS__))

static void handle_cmd(struct android_app* app, int32_t cmd)
{
   switch (cmd)
   {
      case APP_CMD_SAVE_STATE:
           LOGI("Save state");
           break;

      case APP_CMD_INIT_WINDOW:
           LOGI("Init window");
           break;

      case APP_CMD_TERM_WINDOW:
           LOGI("Terminate window");
           break;

      case APP_CMD_PAUSE:
           LOGI("Pausing");
           break;
```

```
        case APP_CMD_RESUME:
             LOGI("Resuming");
             break;

        case APP_CMD_STOP:
             LOGI("Stopping");
             break;

        case APP_CMD_DESTROY:
             LOGI("Destroying");
             break;

        case APP_CMD_LOST_FOCUS:
             LOGI("Lost focus");
             break;

        case APP_CMD_GAINED_FOCUS:
             LOGI("Gained focus");
   }
}

static int32_t handle_input(struct android_app* app, AInputEvent* event)
{
   if (AInputEvent_getType(event) == AINPUT_EVENT_TYPE_MOTION)
   {
      size_t pointerCount = AMotionEvent_getPointerCount(event);
      size_t i;
      for (i = 0; i < pointerCount; ++i)
      {
         LOGI("Received motion event from %zu: (%.2f, %.2f)", i,
              AMotionEvent_getX(event, i), AMotionEvent_getY(event, i));
      }
      return 1;
   }
   else if (AInputEvent_getType(event) == AINPUT_EVENT_TYPE_KEY)
   {
      LOGI("Received key event: %d", AKeyEvent_getKeyCode(event));
      if (AKeyEvent_getKeyCode(event) == AKEYCODE_BACK)
         ANativeActivity_finish(app->activity);
      return 1;
   }
   return 0;
}

void android_main(struct android_app* state)
{
   app_dummy(); // prevent glue from being stripped

   state->onAppCmd = &handle_cmd;
```

```
   state->onInputEvent = &handle_input;

   while(1)
   {
      int ident;
      int fdesc;
      int events;
      struct android_poll_source* source;

      while ((ident = ALooper_pollAll(0, &fdesc, &events, (void**)&source)) >=
0)
      {
         if (source)
            source->process(state, source);

         if (state->destroyRequested)
            return;
      }
   }
}
```

Listing 8-7 begins in a nearly identical fashion to Listing 8-4. However, the previous native_activity.h header file has been replaced by android_native_app_glue.h, which includes native_activity.h (along with pthread.h). A similar LOGI macro is also provided.

The void handle_cmd(struct android_app* app, int32_t cmd) function is called (on a thread other than the main thread) in response to an activity command. The app parameter references an android_app struct (defined in android_native_app_glue.h) that provides access to app-related data, and the cmd parameter identifies a command.

> **NOTE:** Commands are integer values that correspond to the low-level native activity functions that were presented earlier (void onDestroy(ANativeActivity* activity), for example). The android_native_app_glue.h header file defines integer constants for these commands (APP_CMD_DESTROY, for example).

The int32_t handle_input(struct android_app* app, AInputEvent* event) function is called (on a thread other than the main thread) in response to an input event. The event parameter references an AInputEvent struct (defined in input.h) that provides access to various kinds of event-related information.

The input.h header file declares several useful input functions, beginning with AInputEvent_getType(const AInputEvent* event), which returns the type of the event. The return value is one of AINPUT_EVENT_TYPE_KEY for a key event and AINPUT_EVENT_TYPE_MOTION for a motion event.

For a motion event, the size_t AMotionEvent_getPointerCount(const AInputEvent* motion_event) function is called to return the number of *pointers* (active touch points) of data contained in this event (this value is greater than or equal to 1). This count is repeated, with each touch point's coordinates being obtained and logged.

> **NOTE:** Active touch points and AMotionEvent_getPointerCount(const AInputEvent*) are related to *multitouch*. To learn more about this Android feature, check out "Making Sense of Multitouch" (http://android-developers.blogspot.ca/2010/06/making-sense-of-multitouch.html).

For a key event, the int32_t AKeyEvent_getKeyCode(const AInputEvent* key_event) function returns the code of the physical key that was pressed. Physical key codes are defined in the keycodes.h header file. For example, AKEYCODE_BACK corresponds to the back button on the device.

The key code is logged and is then compared with AKEYCODE_BACK to find out if the user wants to terminate the activity (and, by extension, the single-activity app). If so, the void ANativeActivity_finish(ANativeActivity* activity) function (defined in native_activity.h) is invoked with app->activity referencing the activity to be finished.

After processing a mouse or key event, handle_input(struct android_app*, AInputEvent*) returns 1 to indicate that it has handled the event. If the event was not handled (and should be handled by default processing in the background), this function returns 0.

> **NOTE:** You can comment out handle_input(struct android_app*, AInputEvent*)'s if (AKeyEvent_getKeyCode(event) == AKEYCODE_BACK), followed by ANativeActivity_finish(app->activity);, followed by return 1; statements, and let return 0; cause default processing to finish the activity when the back button is pressed.

The void android_main(struct android_app* state) function is the entry point. It first invokes a native glue function called app_dummy(), which doesn't do anything. However, app_dummy() must be present to ensure that the Android build system includes the android_native_app_glue.o module in the library.

> **NOTE:** See http://blog.beuc.net/posts/Make_sure_glue_isn__39__t_stripped to learn more about this oddity.

The android_app struct provides an onAppCmd field of type void (*onAppCmd)(struct android_app* app, int32_t cmd) and an onInputEvent field of type int32_t (*onInputEvent)(struct android_app* app, AInputEvent* event). The addresses of the aforementioned functions are assigned to these fields.

A pair of nested loops is now entered. The inner loop repeatedly invokes the int ALooper_pollAll(int timeoutMillis, int* outFd, int* outEvents, void** outData) function (defined in looper.h) to return the next event; this function returns a value greater than or equal to 0 when an event is ready for processing.

The event is recorded in an android_poll_source structure, whose address is stored in outData. Assuming that outData contains a non-NULL address, android_poll_source's void (*process)(struct android_app* app, struct android_poll_source* source) function is invoked to process the event. Behind the scenes, either handle_cmd(struct android_app*, int32_t) or handle_input(struct android_app*, AInputEvent*) is invoked; it depends on which function is appropriate for handling the event.

Finally, the destroyRequested member of the android_app structure is set to a nonzero value, as a result of a call to ANativeActivity_finish(ANativeActivity*) (or default processing in lieu of this function). This member is checked during each loop iteration to ensure that execution exits quickly from the nested loops and android_main(struct android_app*), because the app is ending. Failure to exit android_main(struct android_app*) in a timely fashion can result in an "Application Not Responding" error.

Listing 8-8 presents this project's Android.mk file.

Listing 8-8. *A Make File for HLNADemo*

```
LOCAL_PATH := $(call my-dir)
include $(CLEAR_VARS)
LOCAL_MODULE    := hlnademo
LOCAL_SRC_FILES := hlnademo.c
LOCAL_LDLIBS := -landroid
LOCAL_STATIC_LIBRARIES := android_native_app_glue
include $(BUILD_SHARED_LIBRARY)
$(call import-module,android/native_app_glue)
```

This make file is similar to the make file presented in Listing 8-5. However, there are some differences:

- The `LOCAL_LDLIBS` entry no longer contains `-llog` because the logging library is linked to the `android_native_app_glue` library when this library is built.
- A `LOCAL_STATIC_LIBRARIES` entry identifies `android_native_app_glue` as a library to be linked to the `hlnademo` module.
- A `$(call import-module,android/native_app_glue)` entry includes the `Android.mk` file associated with the `android_native_app_glue` module so that this library can be built.

Building and Running HLNADemo with the Android SDK

Build `HLNADemo` as if you were building `LLNADemo` (change each `llnademo` reference to `hlnademo` in the manifest and use the updated `Android.mk` file presented in Listing 8-8). Then launch `HLNADemo` and you should observe a black screen. Figure 8-10 shows you a portion of the log that reveals messages presented in Listing 8-7.

Figure 8-10. *HLNADemo logs various messages during its execution.*

Building and Running HLNADemo with Eclipse

Build `HLNADemo` as if you were building `LLNADemo` (change each `llnademo` reference to `hlnademo` in the manifest and use the updated `Android.mk` file presented in Listing 8-8). Then launch `HLNADemo` and you should observe a black screen. Figure 8-11 shows you a portion of the log that reveals messages presented in Listing 8-7.

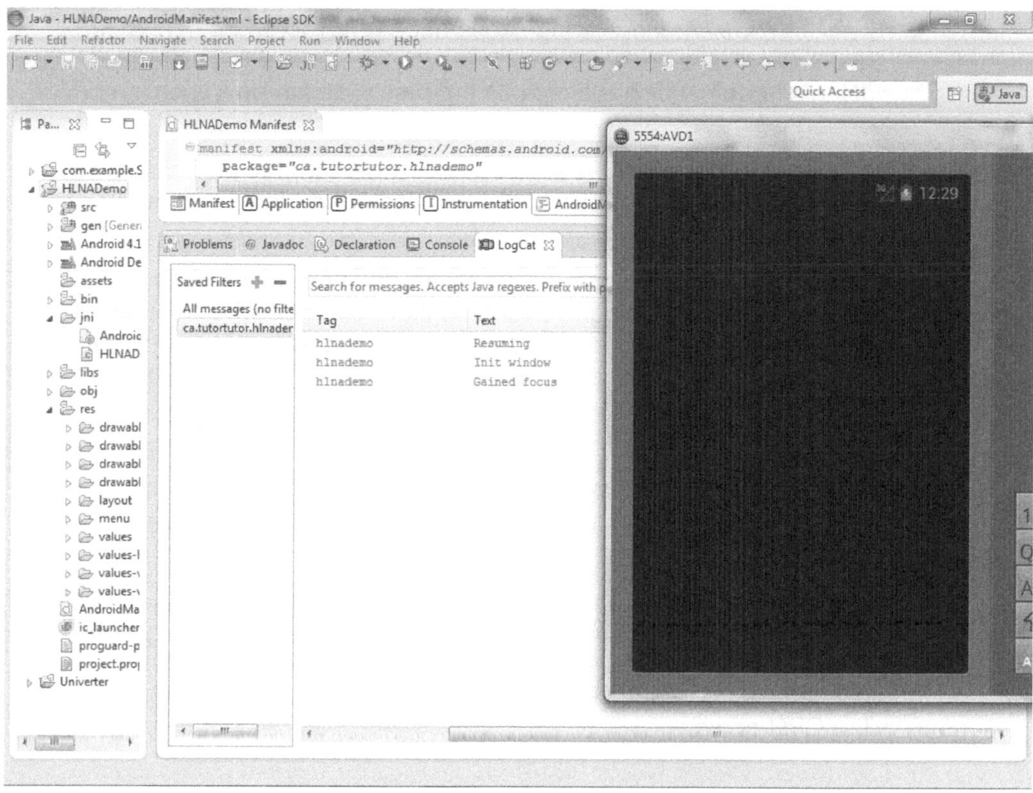

Figure 8-11. *HLNADemo logs various messages during its execution.*

Renderscript

You can use the Android NDK to perform rendering and data-processing operations quickly. However, there are three major problems with this approach:

- *Lack of portability*: Your apps are constrained to run on only those devices to which the native code targets. For example, a native library that runs on an ARM-based device won't run on an x86-based device.
- *Lack of performance*: Ideally, your code should run on multiple cores, be they CPU, GPU, or DSP cores. However, identifying cores, farming out work to them, and dealing with synchronization issues isn't easy.

- *Lack of usability*: Developing native code is harder than developing Java code. For example, you often need to create JNI glue code, which is a tedious process that can be a source of bugs.

Google's Android development team created Renderscript to address these problems, starting with lack of portability, then lack of performance, and finally lack of usability.

Renderscript consists of a language based on C99 (a modern dialect of the C language), a pair of compilers, and a runtime that collectively help you achieve high performance and visually compelling graphics via native code but in a portable manner. You get native app speed along with SDK app portability, and you don't have to use the JNI.

> **NOTE:** Although it has been present since Android 2.0, Renderscript was not made public until Android 3.0, where it is used to implement live wallpapers and more.

Renderscript combines a graphics engine with a compute engine. The graphics engine helps you achieve fast 2D/3D rendering, and the compute engine helps you achieve fast data processing. Performance is achieved by running threads on multiple CPU, GPU, and DSP cores. (The compute engine is currently confined to CPU cores.)

> **TIP:** The compute engine is not limited to processing graphics data. For example, it could be used to model weather data.

Exploring Renderscript Architecture

Renderscript adopts an architecture in which the low-level Renderscript runtime is controlled by the higher-level Android framework. Figure 8-12 presents this architecture.

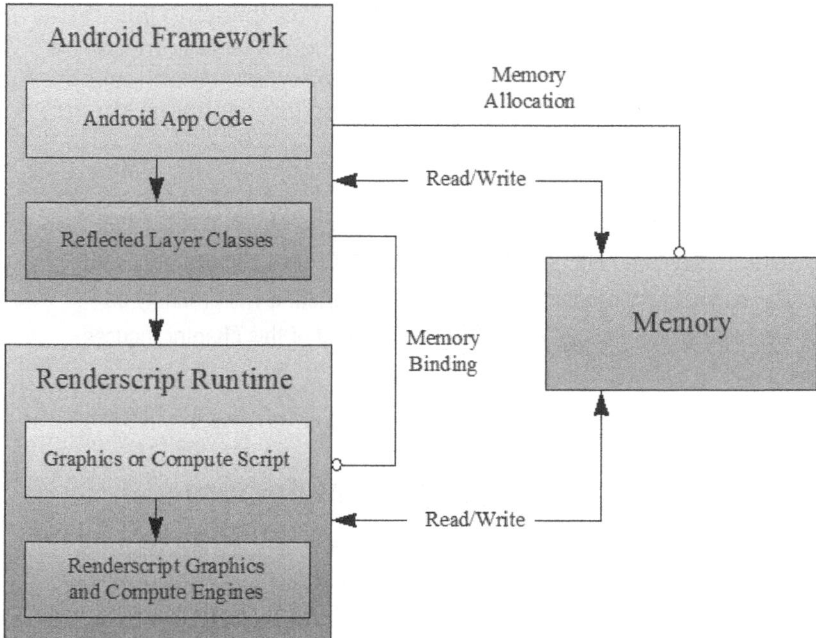

Figure 8-12. *Renderscript architecture is based on the Android framework and the Renderscript runtime.*

The Android framework consists of Android apps running in the Dalvik VM that communicate with graphics or compute scripts running in the Renderscript runtime via instances of reflected layer classes. These classes serve as wrappers around their scripts that make this communication possible. The Android build tools automatically generate the classes for this layer during the build process. These classes eliminate the need to write JNI glue code, which is commonly done when working with the NDK.

Memory management is controlled at the VM level. The app is responsible for allocating memory and binding this memory to the Renderscript runtime so that the memory can be accessed by the script. (The script can define simple [nonarray] fields for its own use, but that's about it.)

Apps make asynchronous calls to the Renderscript runtime (via the reflected layer classes) to make allocated memory available to and start executing their scripts. They can subsequently obtain results from these scripts without having to worry about whether or not the scripts are still running.

When you build an APK, the LLVM (Low-Level Virtual Machine) front-end compiler (see the `llvm-rs-cc` tool in Appendix B) compiles the script into a file of device-independent bitcode that is stored in the APK. (The reflected layer class is also created.) When the app launches, a small LLVM back-end compiler on the device compiles the bitcode into device-specific code, and it caches the code on the device so that it doesn't have to be recompiled each time you run the app. This is how portability is achieved.

> **NOTE:** As of Android 4.1, the graphics engine has been deprecated. App developers told the Android development team that they prefer to use OpenGL directly because of its familiarity. Although the graphics engine is still supported, it will probably be removed in a future Android release. For this reason, the rest of this chapter focuses only on the compute engine.

Exploring Compute Engine-Based App Architecture

A compute engine-based app consists of Java code and an `.rs` file that defines the compute script. The Java code interacts with this script by using APIs defined in the `android.renderscript` package. Key classes in this package are `RenderScript` and `Allocation`:

- `RenderScript` defines a context that is used in further interactions with Renderscript APIs (and also the compute script's reflected layer class). A `RenderScript` instance is returned by invoking this class's `static RenderScript create(Context ctx)` factory method.
- `Allocation` defines the means for moving data into and out of the compute script. Instances of this class are known as *allocations*, where an allocation combines an `android.renderscript.Type` instance with the memory needed to provide storage for user data and objects.

The Java code also interacts with the compute script by instantiating a reflected layer class. The name of the class begins with `ScriptC_` and continues with the name of the `.rs` file containing the compute script. For example, if you had a file named `gray.rs`, the name of this class would be `ScriptC_gray`.

The C99-based `.rs` file begins with two `#pragmas` that identify the Renderscript version number (currently 1) and the app's Java package name. Several additional items follow:

- `rs_allocation` directives that identify the input and output allocations created by the app and bound to the Renderscript code
- an `rs_script` directive that provides a link to the app's `ScriptC_`*`script`* instance so that compute results can be returned to this instance
- optional simple variable declarations whose values are supplied by the app
- a `root()` function that is called by each core to perform part of the overall computation
- a `noargument init` function with a `void` return type that's indirectly invoked from the Java code to execute `root()` on multiple CPU cores

At runtime, a Java-based activity creates a `Renderscript` context, creates input and output allocations, instantiates the `ScriptC_`-prefixed layer class, uses this object to bind the allocations and `ScriptC_` instance, and invokes the compute script, which results in the script's `init` function being invoked.

The `init` function performs additional initialization (as necessary) and executes the `rsForEach()` function with the `rs_script` value and the `rs_allocation` input/output allocations. `rsForEach()` causes the `root()` function to be executed on the device's available CPU cores. Results are then sent back to the app via the output allocation.

Figure 8-13 illustrates this scenario.

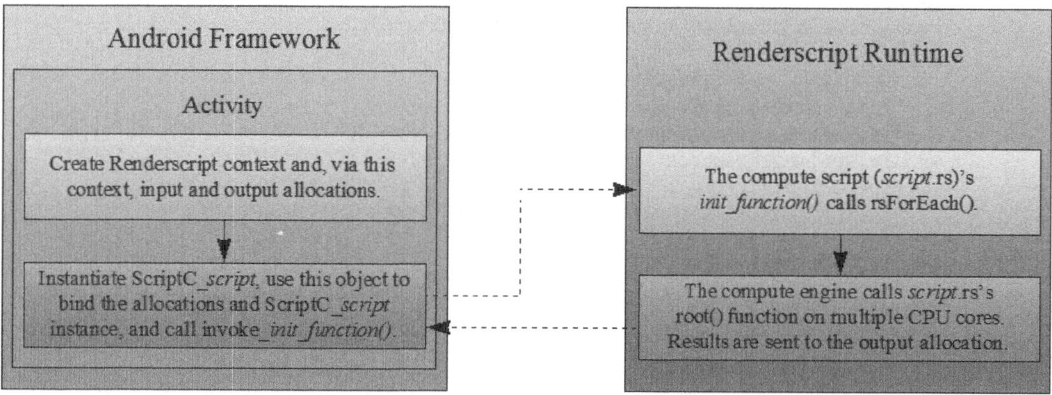

Figure 8-13. *Compute engine–based app architecture can be partitioned into four major tasks.*

Grayscaling Images with Renderscript

Perhaps the easiest way to become familiar with the compute side of Renderscript is to create a small app that performs a simple image-processing operation, such as grayscaling an image. Listing 8-9 presents the source code to a GrayScale app that lets you view an image of the Sun, grayscale the image, and view the result.

Listing 8-9. *Viewing Original and Grayscaled Images of the Sun*

```
package ca.tutortutor.grayscale;

import android.app.Activity;

import android.os.Bundle;

import android.graphics.Bitmap;
import android.graphics.BitmapFactory;

import android.renderscript.Allocation;
import android.renderscript.RenderScript;

import android.view.View;

import android.widget.ImageView;

public class GrayScale extends Activity
{
   boolean original = true;

   @Override
   public void onCreate(Bundle savedInstanceState)
   {
      super.onCreate(savedInstanceState);
      final ImageView iv = new ImageView(this);
      iv.setScaleType(ImageView.ScaleType.CENTER_CROP);
      iv.setImageResource(R.drawable.sol);
      setContentView(iv);
      iv.setOnClickListener(new View.OnClickListener()
                            {
                               @Override
                               public void onClick(View v)
                               {
                                  if (original)
                                     drawGS(iv, R.drawable.sol);
                                  else
                                     iv.setImageResource(R.drawable.sol);
                                  original = !original;
                               }
```

```
                    });
   }

   private void drawGS(ImageView iv, int imID)
   {
      Bitmap bmIn = BitmapFactory.decodeResource(getResources(), imID);
      Bitmap bmOut = Bitmap.createBitmap(bmIn.getWidth(), bmIn.getHeight(),
                                         bmIn.getConfig());
      RenderScript rs = RenderScript.create(this);
      Allocation allocIn;
      allocIn = Allocation.createFromBitmap(rs, bmIn,
                                            Allocation.MipmapControl.MIPMAP_NONE,
                                            Allocation.USAGE_SCRIPT);
      Allocation allocOut = Allocation.createTyped(rs, allocIn.getType());
      ScriptC_grayscale script = new ScriptC_grayscale(rs, getResources(),
                                                       R.raw.grayscale);
      script.set_in(allocIn);
      script.set_out(allocOut);
      script.set_script(script);
      script.invoke_filter();
      allocOut.copyTo(bmOut);
      iv.setImageBitmap(bmOut);
   }
}
```

Listing 8-9 declares an activity class named GrayScale. This class overrides the onCreate(Bundle) method, declares a void drawGS(ImageView iv, int imID) method that grayscales an image identified by resource ID imID, and then assigns the result to the android.widget.ImageView instance identified by iv.

onCreate(Bundle) creates the activity's user interface based on an ImageView instance whose contents are set to the drawable resource identified by R.drawable.sol. The image is scaled uniformly (maintaining the image's aspect ratio) so that each dimension is at least as large as the corresponding screen dimension (less any padding).

A click listener is registered with the imageview widget. An initial click on this widget causes the listener to invoke drawGS(ImageView, int)and to grayscale the image and update the widget with the grayscaled result. A second click causes the original image to be displayed. Subsequent clicks continue this alternating pattern of behavior.

drawGS(ImageView, int) first invokes the android.graphics.BitmapFactory class's static Bitmap decodeResource(Resources res, int id) method. When passed an android.content.res.Resources instance (obtained via android.content.Context's Resources getResources() method) and the resource ID of the desired drawable resource (R.drawable.sol), this method returns an `android.graphics.Bitmap` instance containing the contents of this resource.

`drawGS(ImageView, int)` next invokes `BitMap`'s `static Bitmap createBitmap(int width, int height, Bitmap.Config config)` method to create and return an empty bitmap with the same dimensions and configuration as the previous bitmap (which contains the contents of the Sun image).

A `RenderScript` context object is created. This object is then passed as the first argument to `Allocation`'s `static Allocation createFromBitmap(RenderScript rs, Bitmap b, Allocation.MipmapControl mips, int usage)` method, which creates an allocation that stores the drawable's bitmap. Three additional arguments are passed:

- `bmIn` identifies the bitmap source of the allocation.
- `Allocation.MipmapControl.MIPMAP_NONE` specifies that no *mipmaps* (precalculated, optimized collections of images that accompany a main texture, which are intended to increase rendering speed and reduce aliasing artifacts) will be generated, and the type generated from the incoming bitmap will not contain additional levels of detail.
- `Allocation.USAGE_SCRIPT` specifies that the allocation is to be bound to and accessed by the compute script.

The created `Allocation` object serves as the input allocation, from where the compute script obtains its input data for processing. A second `Allocation` object for storing computed output is now created, by invoking `Allocation`'s `static Allocation createTyped(RenderScript rs, Type type)` method with the following arguments:

- `rs` identifies the Renderscript context.
- `allocIn.getType()` returns the type of the input allocation. The type describes the layout of the input allocation's bitmap.

At this point, the reflected `ScriptC_grayscale` class, which provides communication between the app and the compute script, is instantiated with the following arguments:

- `rs` identifies the Renderscript context.
- `getResources()` returns a `Resources` instance for accessing resources.
- `R.raw.grayscale` identifies a `grayscale.bc` bitcode resource file that is stored in the APK's `res/raw` directory.

As you will soon discover, the compute script contains `in`, `out`, and `script` fields. These fields are accessible to the app (for initialization) via `ScriptC_grayscale`'s `set_in()`, `set_out()`, and `set_script()` methods. These methods are called to communicate the input/output allocations and the `ScriptC_grayscale` instance to the compute script.

Along with `set_in()`, `set_out()`, and `set_script()` methods, the LLVM front-end compiler creates an `invoke_filter()` method that is now called to execute the compute script. (The `filter` portion of this name matches the `noargument` `init` function in the compute script.)

One of the nice things about Renderscript is that the app can immediately request script output without having to wait for the script to finish. In this case, the app invokes `Allocation`'s `void copyTo(Bitmap b)` method to copy results from the output allocation to the `Bitmap` instance passed to this method, which happens to be the empty bitmap.

Finally, the formerly empty bitmap is assigned to the imageview widget via `ImageView`'s `void setImageBitmap(Bitmap bm)` method, and the grayscaled result is seen.

Now that you've explored the Java side of this app, Listing 8-10 introduces you to the C99 compute script side.

Listing 8-10. *Grayscaling an Image*

```
#pragma version(1)
#pragma rs java_package_name(ca.tutortutor.grayscale)

rs_allocation in;
rs_allocation out;
rs_script script;

const static float3 gsVector = {0.3f, 0.6f, 0.1f};

void root(const uchar4* v_in, uchar4* v_out)
{
   float4 f4 = rsUnpackColor8888(*v_in);
   *v_out = rsPackColorTo8888((float3) dot(f4.rgb, gsVector));
}

void filter()
{
   rsDebug("RS_VERSION = ", RS_VERSION);
#if !defined(RS_VERSION) || (RS_VERSION < 14)
   rsForEach(script, in, out, 0);
#else
   rsForEach(script, in, out);
```

```
#endif
}
```

Listing 8-10 first presents two #pragmas that respectively identify the Renderscript version number and ca.tutortutor.grayscale as the Java package with which this compute script associates.

A pair of rs_allocation directives and an rs_script directive follow. These directives introduce variables that will reference the input/output allocations and the ScriptC_grayscale instance.

Next, gsVector, a vector of three floating-point values (indicated by the float3 type), is defined. gsVector is initialized to 0.3f (red), 0.6f (green), and 0.1f (blue), which indicate the percentages of pixel color components that contribute to the overall gray value.

The subsequent void root(const uchar4* v_in, uchar4* v_out) function is invoked for each pixel and on each available CPU core. Each pixel is processed independently of other pixels.

The v_in parameter is a pointer to a uchar4 structure that holds the four eight-bit values (red, green, blue, and alpha color components) of the incoming pixel. The v_out parameter is a pointer to a similar structure for storing the pixel's resulting components.

root(const uchar4*, uchar4*) first unpacks *v_in to a float4 value (float4 identifies a vector of four floating-point values). This task is accomplished by invoking Renderscript's float4 rsUnpackColor8888(uchar4 color) function.

The RGB components of this vector are accessed by specifying f4.rgb and are then multiplied by gsVector's three components, by invoking Renderscript's float dot(float lhs, float rhs) (dot product) function.

> **NOTE:** dot() follows a pattern in which it accepts 1, 2, 3, or 4 components as arguments. This pattern lets you specify scalar values (such as float result = dot(1.0f, 2.0f);) or vectors with no more than four components (such as float3 result = dot(f4.rgb, gsVector);).

The final task is to pack dot()'s return value into a uchar4 value by invoking Renderscript's uchar4 rsPackColorTo8888(float3 color) function; then assign this value to *v_out. The (float3) cast is redundant but necessary.

Finally, the void filter() function is invoked as a result of the app executing script.invoke_filter();. (Note the pattern in which the name of this function is appended to invoke_.)

filter() first executes rsDebug("RS_VERSION = ", RS_VERSION); to output the value of the RS_VERSION constant to the log. You can invoke one of Renderscript's overloaded rsDebug() functions to output debugging information.

RS_VERSION is a special constant that is set to the SDK version number. filter() contains #if and #else directives that help the compiler choose a different version of rsForEach() to call based on this constant's existence and value.

Assuming that RS_VERSION exists and has a value less than 14, the simplest variant of rsForEach() that can be called is void rsForEach(rs_script script, rs_allocation input, rs_allocation output, const void* usrData).

> **NOTE:** usrData lets you pass a pointer to additional script-specific data to the root() function. You will see how to obtain this pointer in a root() context in Recipe 8-4.

If RS_VERSION contains a value that is 14 or higher, the simplest variant of the rsForEach() function that can be called is void rsForEach(rs_script script, rs_allocation input, rs_allocation output).

> **NOTE:** You will encounter rsForEach() call examples on the Internet that do not consult RS_VERSION. However, not testing this constant via #if and #else means that you can run into a situation where the script compiles okay under the Android SDK or Eclipse but then fails to compile on the other development platform, with output messages similar to the following:
>
> ```
> note: candidate function not viable: requires 4 arguments, but
> 3 were provided
>
> note: candidate function not viable: requires 5 arguments, but
> 3 were provided
> ```

Regardless of the rsForEach() function that is called, its first argument is a reference to the script object on the Java side; its second argument, in, corresponds to v_in; and its third argument, out, corresponds to v_out.

Building and Running GrayScale with the Android SDK

To build GrayScale with the Android SDK, first use the SDK's android tool to create a GrayScale project. Assuming a Windows platform, a C:\prj\dev hierarchy in which the GrayScale project is to be stored (in C:\prj\dev\GrayScale), and an Android 4.1 platform target that corresponds to integer ID 1 (execute android list targets to obtain the correct ID), execute the following command (spread across two lines for readability) to create GrayScale:

```
android create project -t 1 -p C:\prj\dev\GrayScale -a GrayScale
                       -k ca.tutortutor.grayscale
```

Replace the contents of the src\ca\tutortutor\grayscale\GrayScale.java file with Listing 8-9. Also, create a grayscale.rs file with Listing 8-10's contents, and store this file in the src directory. (Renderscript source files are given the .rs extension and are stored in a project's src directory.) Finally, create a drawable-nodpi directory and copy a file named sol.jpg (presumably containing an image of the Sun) to this directory. (Android does not scale images stored in drawable-nodpi; the app takes care of the scaling.)

Execute the following command to build the project:

```
ant debug
```

You will probably discover the following warning message (spread across multiple lines for readability) and a failed build:

```
WARNING: RenderScript include directory
         'C:\prj\dev\GrayScale\${android.renderscript.include.path}'
         does not exist!
[llvm-rs-cc.exe] <built-in>:2:10: fatal: 'rs_core.rsh' file not found
```

Issue 34569 in Google's Android issues database (http://code.google.com/p/android/issues/detail?id=34569) offers a workaround: Add the following property (spread across multiple lines for readability) to the build.xml file that's located in the tools\ant subdirectory of your Android SDK home directory:

```
<property name="android.renderscript.include.path"
          location="${android.platform.tools.dir}/renderscript/include:
                    ${android.platform.tools.dir}/renderscript/clang-include"/>
```

Place this <property> element after the following <path> element:

```
<!-- Renderscript include Path -->
<path id="android.renderscript.include.path">
  <pathelement location="${android.platform.tools.dir}/renderscript/include" />
  <pathelement location="${android.platform.tools.dir}/renderscript/clang-
```

```
include" />
</path>
```

Reexecute `ant debug` and the build should succeed. Finally, install the `grayscale-debug.apk` file on AVD1 (see Chapter 1) and run the app. Figure 8-14 shows the result.

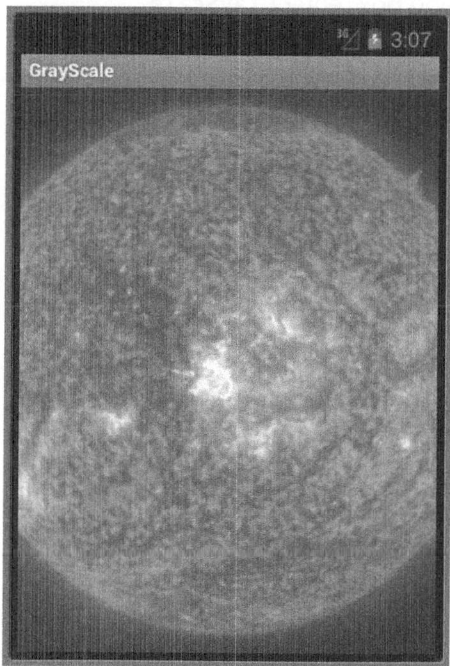

Figure 8-14. *Click this orange-colored Sun image to see the Sun in grayscale.*

Building and Running GrayScale with Eclipse

To build `GrayScale` with Eclipse, first create a new Android project as described in Chapter 1's Recipe 1-10. For your convenience, the steps that you need to follow to accomplish this task are provided here:

1. Start Eclipse if it is not running.
2. Select New from the File menu, and select Project from the resulting pop-up menu.

3. On the resulting *New Project* dialog box, expand the Android node in the wizard tree (if necessary), select the Android Application Project branch below this node (if necessary), and click the Next button.
4. On the resulting *New Android App* dialog box, enter **`GrayScale`** into the Application Name textfield. This entered name also appears in the Project Name textfield, and it identifies the folder/directory in which the `GrayScale` project is stored.
5. Enter **`ca.tutortutor.grayscale`** into the Package Name textfield.
6. Via Build SDK, select the appropriate Android SDK to target. This selection identifies the Android platform you'd like your app to be built against. Assuming that you've installed only the Android 4.1 platform, only this choice should appear and be selected.
7. Via Minimum SDK, either select the minimum Android SDK on which your app runs or keep the default setting.
8. Leave the "Create custom launcher icon" check box checked if you want a custom launcher icon to be created. Otherwise, uncheck this check box when you supply your own launcher icon.
9. Leave the "Mark this project as a library" check box unchecked because you are not creating a library.
10. Leave the "Create Project in Workspace" check box checked, and click Next.
11. On the resulting Configure Launcher Icon pane, make suitable adjustments to the custom launcher icon, and click Next.
12. On the resulting Create Activity pane, leave the Create Activity check box checked, make sure that BlankActivity is selected, and click Next.
13. On the resulting New Blank Activity pane, enter **`GrayScale`** into the Activity Name textfield. Keep all other settings and click Finish.

Use Eclipse's Package Explorer to locate the `GrayScale.java` source file node. Double-click this node and replace the skeletal contents shown in the resulting edit window with Listing 8-9.

Next, create a `grayscale.rs` file node with Listing 8-10's contents under the `src` node, and introduce a `drawable-nodpi` directory node under the `res` directory node into which you must introduce a `sol.jpg` file.

To run `GrayScale` from Eclipse, select Run from the menubar, and then select Run from the drop-down menu. If a *Run As* dialog box appears, select Android Application and click OK. Eclipse launches `emulator` with the AVD1 device, installs `GrayScale.apk`, and runs this app, whose output appears in Figure 8-15.

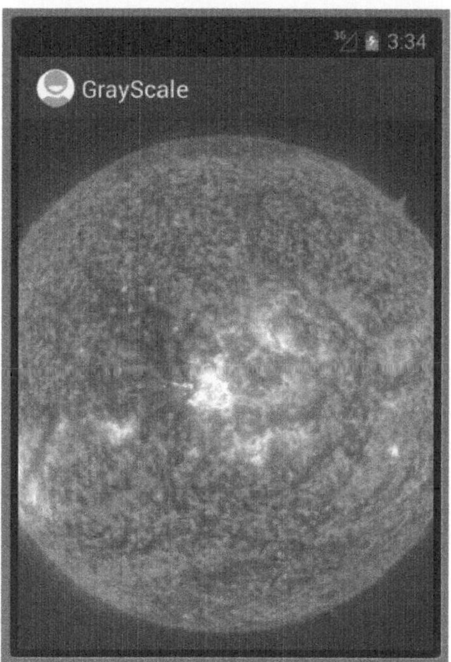

Figure 8-15. *The Sun in grayscale emerges after you click its orange-colored counterpart image.*

8-4. Learning More About Renderscript

Problem

You're intrigued by Renderscript and want to learn more about it. For example, you want to learn how to receive `rsForEach()`'s `usrData` value in the `root()` function.

Solution

The following resources will help you learn more about Renderscript:

- Romain Guy's and Chet Haase's "Learn about Renderscript" video (`http://youtube.com/watch?v=5jz0kSuR2j4`). This one-and-one-half-hour video covers the graphics and compute sides of Renderscript, and it is well worth your time.
- The Android documentation's Renderscript page (`http://developer.android.com/guide/topics/renderscript/index.html`) provides access to important compute information. It also provides access to Renderscript-oriented blog posts.
- The `android.renderscript` package documentation (`http://developer.android.com/reference/android/renderscript/package-summary.html`) can help you to explore the various types, with emphasis on the `RenderScript` and `Allocation` classes.
- The Renderscript reference page (`http://developer.android.com/reference/renderscript/index.html`) provides documentation on all of the functions that Renderscript makes available to your compute script.

Regarding `root()`, this function is minimally declared with two parameters that identify the input/output allocations, as in `void root(const uchar4* v_in, uchar4* v_out)`. However, you can specify three more parameters to obtain a `usrData` value and the x/y coordinates of the value passed to `v_in` in the input allocation, as follows:

```
void root(const uchar4* v_in, uchar4* v_out, const void* usrData, uint32_t x,
        uint32_t y)
```

How It Works

Although the void root(const uchar4*, uchar4*, const void*, uint32_t, uint32_t) function may look a little intimidating, it's not hard to use. For example, Listing 8-11 presents source code to a compute script that uses this expanded function to give an image a wavy appearance as if being seen in water.

Listing 8-11. *Waving an Image*

```
#pragma version(1)
#pragma rs java_package_name(ca.tutortutor.wavyimage)

rs_allocation in;
rs_allocation out;
rs_script script;

int height;

void root(const uchar4* v_in, uchar4* v_out, const void* usrData, uint32_t x,
          uint32_t y)
{
   float scaledy = y/(float) height;
   *v_out = *(uchar4*) rsGetElementAt(in, x, (uint32_t) ((scaledy+
                                      sin(scaledy*100)*0.03)*height));
}

void filter()
{
   rsDebug("RS_VERSION = ", RS_VERSION);
#if !defined(RS_VERSION) || (RS_VERSION < 14)
   rsForEach(script, in, out, 0);
#else
   rsForEach(script, in, out);
#endif
}
```

Listing 8-11's root() function ignores usrData (which isn't required), but it uses the values passed to x and y. It also uses the value passed to height, which represents the height of the image.

The function first uses height to scale the value passed to y to a floating-point value between 0 and 1. It then invokes Renderscript's const void* rsGetElementAt(rs_allocation, uint32_t x, uint32_t y) function to return the input allocation element that's located at position x and y, which is then assigned to *v_out.

The value passed to x, which happens to be the value in `root()`'s x parameter, is self-evident. However, the value passed to y may be a little harder to grasp. The idea is to vary the argument in a sinusoidal pattern so that returned pixels from the original image are chosen to yield a wavy appearance.

Listing 8-12 presents the source code to a `WavyImage` app that communicates with the compute script stored in `wavy.rs`.

Listing 8-12. *Viewing Original and Watery Images of the Sun*

```
package ca.tutortutor.wavyimage;

import android.app.Activity;

import android.os.Bundle;

import android.graphics.Bitmap;
import android.graphics.BitmapFactory;

import android.renderscript.Allocation;
import android.renderscript.RenderScript;

import android.view.View;

import android.widget.ImageView;

public class WavyImage extends Activity
{
   boolean original = true;

   @Override
   public void onCreate(Bundle savedInstanceState)
   {
      super.onCreate(savedInstanceState);
      final ImageView iv = new ImageView(this);
      iv.setScaleType(ImageView.ScaleType.CENTER_CROP);
      iv.setImageResource(R.drawable.sol);
      setContentView(iv);
      iv.setOnClickListener(new View.OnClickListener()
                            {
                               @Override
                               public void onClick(View v)
                               {
                                  if (original)
                                     drawWavy(iv, R.drawable.sol);
                                  else
                                     iv.setImageResource(R.drawable.sol);
                                  original = !original;
```

```
                        }
                    });
    }

    private void drawWavy(ImageView iv, int imID)
    {
        Bitmap bmIn = BitmapFactory.decodeResource(getResources(), imID);
        Bitmap bmOut = Bitmap.createBitmap(bmIn.getWidth(), bmIn.getHeight(),
                                          bmIn.getConfig());
        RenderScript rs = RenderScript.create(this);
        Allocation allocIn;
        allocIn = Allocation.createFromBitmap(rs, bmIn,

Allocation.MipmapControl.MIPMAP_NONE,
                                             Allocation.USAGE_SCRIPT);
        Allocation allocOut = Allocation.createTyped(rs, allocIn.getType());
        ScriptC_wavy script = new ScriptC_wavy(rs, getResources(), R.raw.wavy);
        script.set_in(allocIn);
        script.set_out(allocOut);
        script.set_script(script);
        script.set_height(bmIn.getHeight());
        script.invoke_filter();
        allocOut.copyTo(bmOut);
        iv.setImageBitmap(bmOut);
    }
}
```

Listing 8-12 differs from Listing 8-9 mainly via `script.set_height(bmIn.getHeight());`, which passes the bitmap's height to the script's height field so that the script can scale the y value.

If you were to build and run this app (in the same manner as with `GrayScale`), and if you were to click the image of the Sun, you would see the result that's shown in Figure 8-16.

Figure 8-16. *The Sun has a wavy (or possibly watery) appearance.*

Summary

The Android NDK complements the Android SDK by providing a toolset that lets you implement parts of your app by using native code languages such as C and C++. The NDK provides headers and libraries for building native activities, handling user input, using hardware sensors, and more.

Renderscript consists of a language based on C99 (a modern dialect of the C language), a pair of compilers, and a runtime that collectively help you achieve high performance and visually compelling graphics via native code but in a portable manner. You get native app speed along with SDK app portability, and you don't have to use the JNI.

Appendix

Scripting Layer for Android

Scripting Layer for Android (SL4A), which was previously known as Android Scripting Environment, is a platform for installing scripting language interpreters on Android devices and running scripts via these interpreters. Scripts can access many of the APIs that are available to Android apps, but with a greatly simplified interface that makes it easier to get things done.

> **NOTE:** SL4A currently supports Python, Perl, JRuby, Lua, BeanShell, Rhino JavaScript, Tcl, and shell.
>
> You can run scripts interactively in a *terminal window* (command window), in the background, or via Locale (`http://www.twofortyfouram.com/`). *Locale* is an Android app that lets you run scripts at predetermined times or when other criteria are met (running a script to change your phone's ringer mode to vibrate when you enter a theater or a courtroom, for example).

Installing SL4A

Before you can use SL4A, you must install it. You can download the latest release's APK file (`sl4a_r6.apk` at time of writing) from its Google-hosted project website (`http://code.google.com/p/android-scripting`) to your device. Do so by using your barcode reader app to scan the website's displayed barcode image.

If you're using the Android emulator, click the barcode image to download `sl4a_r6.apk`. Then execute `adb install sl4a_r6.apk` to install this app on the currently running emulated device. (You might have to make several attempts should you receive a device offline message.) Figure A-1 reveals SL4A's icon on the app launcher screen.

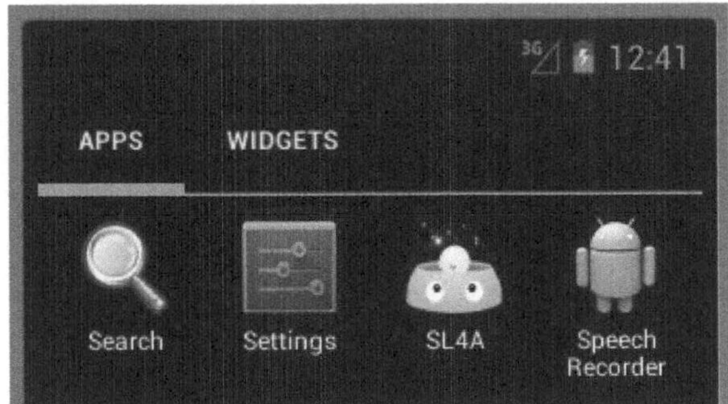

Figure A-1. *Click the SL4A icon to start exploring the Scripting Layer for Android app.*

Exploring SL4A

Now that you've installed SL4A, you'll want to learn how to use this app. Click the SL4A icon, and you'll be taken to the Scripts screen shown in Figure A-2.

Figure A-2. *Accept or refuse usage tracking.*

A Usage Tracking dialog box appears the first time you run SL4A. You can either accept or refuse to have your usage information collected anonymously.

The Scripts screen presents an initially empty list of installed scripts. Click the MENU button and SL4A reveals the options menu for this screen. See Figure A-3.

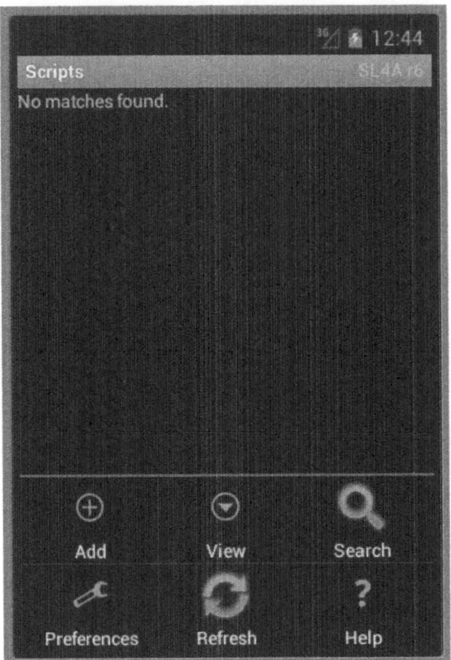

Figure A-3. *The options menu lets you add scripts and other items to the Scripts screen and perform other tasks.*

The options menu is organized into six categories:

- **Add**: Add folders (for organizing scripts), HTML pages with embedded JavaScript code, shell scripts, and scripts obtained by scanning barcode images to the Scripts screen. Folders and other items are stored in the device's `/sdcard/sl4a/scripts` directory.
- **View**: View installed interpreters (such as Python), *triggers* (a kind of intent for running scripts repeatedly whether or not the device is sleeping, or for running scripts conditionally based on ringer mode changes), and *logcat* (a tool for viewing system debug output). SL4A comes with a Bash-like shell and "HTML and JavaScript".
- **Search**: Create and display a list of only those scripts and other items that match entered search text. The search logic outputs "No matches found" when there are no matches.

- **Preferences**: Configure general, script manager, script editor, terminal, and trigger behavior options.
- **Refresh**: Redisplay the Scripts screen to reveal any changes; perhaps a script running in the background has updated this list.
- **Help**: Obtain help on using SL4A from SL4A's wiki documentation (`http://code.google.com/p/android-scripting/wiki/TableOfContents?tm=6`), YouTube screencasts, terminal help documentation, and API reference.

Adding a Shell Script

Let's add a simple shell script to the Scripts screen. Accomplish this task by completing the following steps:

1. Click the MENU button in the phone controls.
2. Click the Add menu item in the options menu that appears at the bottom of the screen.
3. Click Shell from the pop-up Add context menu.
4. Enter `hw.sh` into the single-line textfield at the top of the resulting script editor screen; this is the shell script's filename.
5. Enter `#! /system/bin/sh` followed by `echo "hello, world"` and `sleep 3` into the multiline textfield on separate lines. The first line tells Android where to find `sh` (the shell program), but isn't essential with SL4A (it has been included for good form); the second line tells Android to output some text to the standard output device; and the third line causes the script thread to sleep for three seconds to ensure that the text will be visible. (According to information at `http://bit.ly/MRFrlU`, two threads are used to display the terminal window and run the script. The thread that runs the script finishes before the thread that displays the terminal window; no output is seen unless the `sleep` command is used.)
6. Click the MENU button in the phone controls.
7. Click the Save & Exit or Save & Run menu item from the resulting menu.

Figure A-4 shows you what the edit screen looks like before clicking Save & Exit.

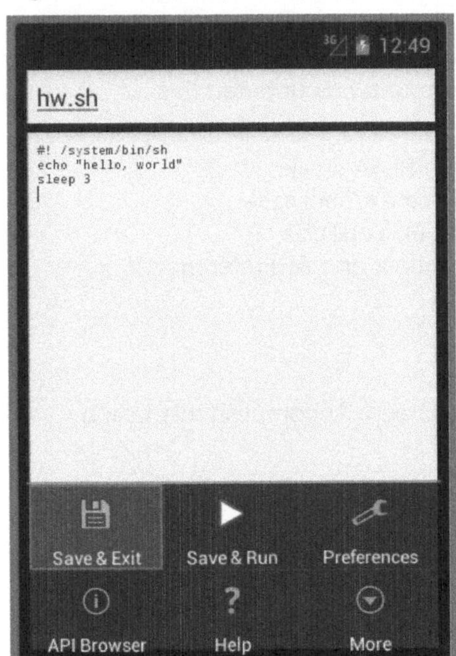

Figure A-4. ***SL4A's script editor screen prompts for a filename and a script.***

The Scripts screen should now present a single hw.sh item. Click this item and you'll see the icon menu that appears in Figure A-5.

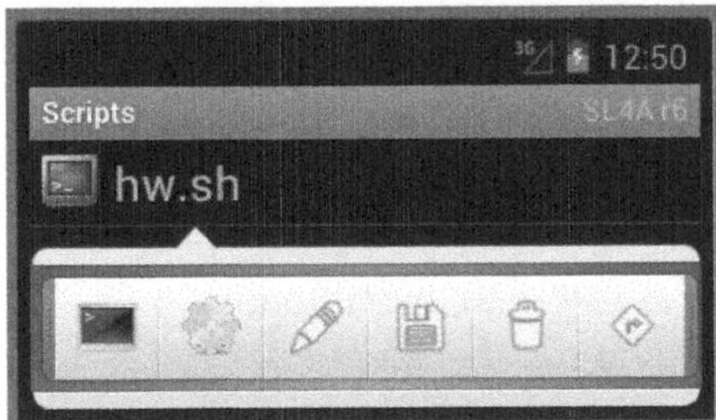

Figure A-5. ***The icon menu lets you run a script in a terminal window, run a script in the background, edit the script, rename the script, or delete the script.***

You have the option of running the script in a terminal window (the leftmost icon) or in the background (the next-to-leftmost "gear" icon). Click either icon to run this shell script. Although you won't see output when the script runs in the background, you should see the output that's shown in Figure A-6 when it runs in the terminal window.

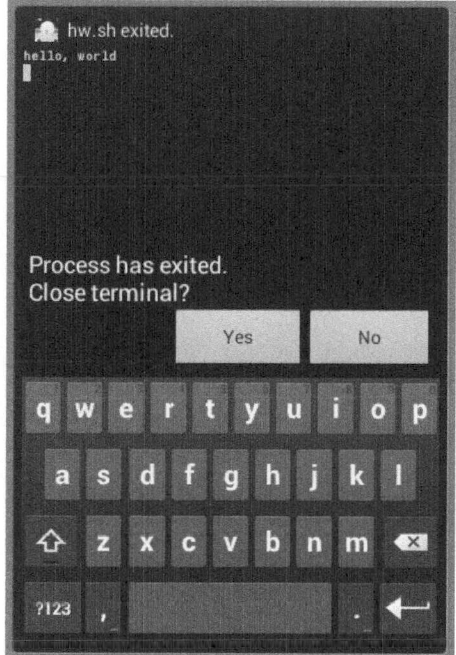

Figure A-6. *Click Yes to close the terminal window.*

The `sleep` command results in the "Process has exited. Close terminal?" message along with the Yes and No buttons. Click the Yes button to close the terminal window.

Accessing the Linux Shell

Another way to observe `hw.sh`'s output is to run this script via the Linux bash-like shell. Follow the steps below to accomplish this task:

1. Select View from the Scripts screen's options menu.
2. Select Interpreters from the View context menu.
3. Select Shell from the Interpreters screen to present a terminal window.

4. Execute `cd /sdcard/sl4a/scripts` at the terminal window's $ prompt to switch to the directory containing `hw.sh`.
5. Execute `sh hw.sh` at the $ prompt to run `hw.sh`.

Figure A-7 shows you how to run `hw.sh` from the shell. It also reveals what happens when you execute the `exit` command (or click the BACK button in the phone controls).

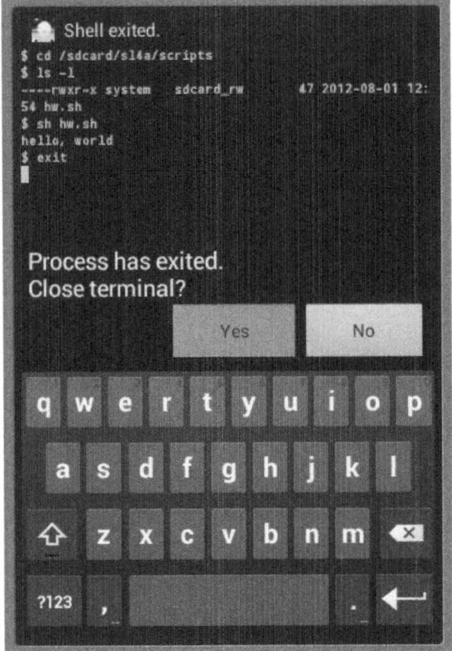

Figure A-7. *Execute the* `exit` *command or click the BACK button to obtain a "Process has exited. Close terminal?" message, and click the Yes button to exit the shell.*

> **NOTE:** Most shell commands (such as `cpio` and `fdisk`) are off limits without rooting the emulator. For information on how to accomplish this task, check out "Learn to root Android using emulator" at `http://allencch.wordpress.com/2012/02/29/learn-to-root-android-using-emulator/`.

Installing the Python Interpreter

Although you can't do much with SL4A, you can use this special app to install Python or another scripting language. Complete the following steps to install Python:

1. Select View from the Scripts screen options menu.
2. Select Interpreters from the View context menu.
3. Press the MENU phone control button.
4. Select Add from the Interpreters screen options menu. Figure A-8 reveals part of Add's interpreters list.

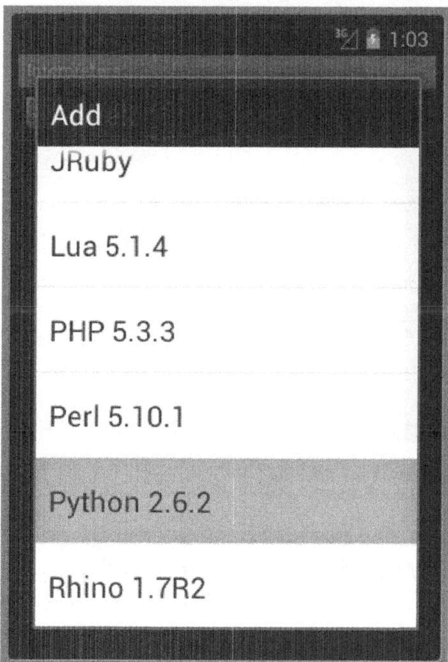

Figure A-8. *The Add context menu lets you choose the scripting language interpreter that you want to install.*

5. Click Python 2.6.2. SL4A displays a white screen with a thin lightblue horizontal line along the top that serves as a progress bar. After the download finishes, this screen disappears and you are taken back to the Interpreters screen. Also, you observe the notification icon in the upperleft corner of the screen. Drag this icon downward and you should observe Figure A-9's notification.

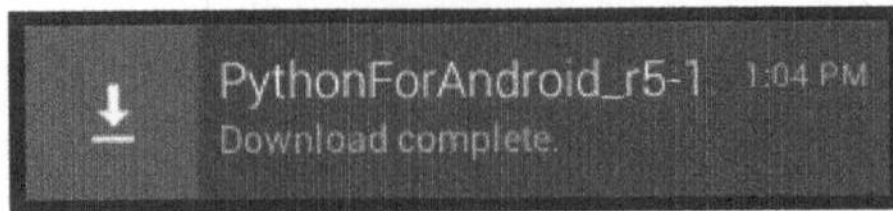

Figure A-9. *A notification tells you that Python's APK file has downloaded.*

6. Launch the shell interpreter and execute the commands shown in Figure A-10.

```
$ cd ../Download
$ ls -l
----rwxr-x system   sdcard_rw   127271 2012-08-01 13:
04 PythonForAndroid_r5-1.apk
$ adb install PythonForAndroid_r5-1.apk
* daemon not running. starting it now on port 5038 *
* daemon started successfully *
1029 KB/s (127271 bytes in 0.120s)
        pkg: /data/local/tmp/PythonForAndroid_r5-1.ap
k
Success
$
```

Figure A-10. *Python's APK file is stored in the* `/SDCard/Download` *directory.*

Python's APK file is stored in the `/SDCard/Download` directory. After changing to this directory, execute `adb install PythonForAndroid_r5-1.apk` to install this APK.

7. Exit the shell and SL4A. You should now observe a Python for Android icon on the app launcher screen (see Figure A-11).

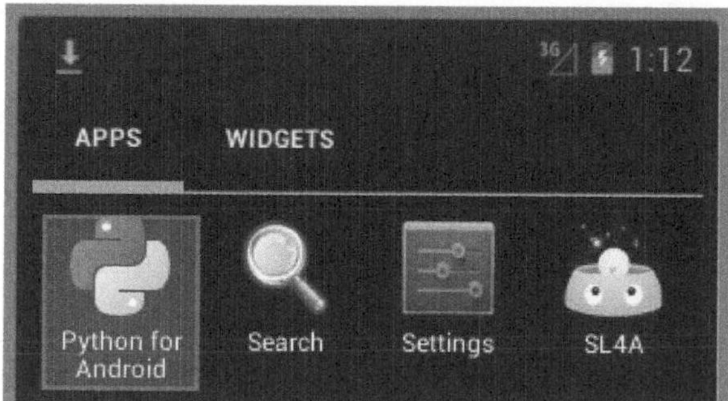

Figure A-11. *SL4A presents a Python for Android icon on the app launcher screen.*

8. Click Python for Android. Figure A-12 shows the resulting screen.

Figure A-12. *Click the Install button to download and install the latest release of Python.*

9. Click the Install button. SL4A presents Figure A-13's downloading screen.

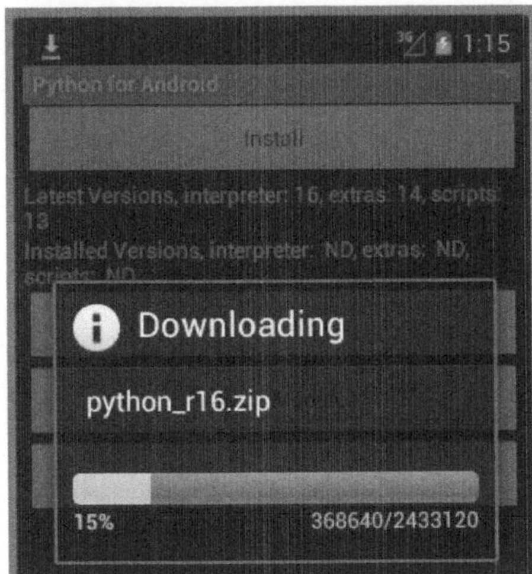

Figure A-13. *It takes a couple of minutes to download and extract contents from all Python-related archives on the Android emulator.*

10. Several archives are downloaded and their contents extracted. When finished, the Install button changes to Uninstall. Close Python for Android and return to the app launcher.

Scripting with Python

Now that you've installed Python 2.6.2, you'll want to try out this interpreter. Click the SL4A icon and you'll notice several script filenames with `.py` extensions populating the Scripts screen -- see Figure A-14.

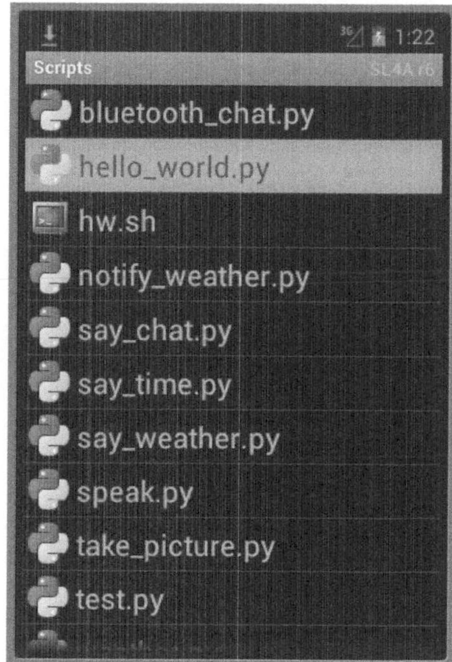

Figure A-14. *Select an appropriate script to run.*

Select one of these filenames (such as `hello_world.py`) and run it. You will see the same list of options that were previously presented in Figure A-5. Click the leftmost (terminal window) icon and you should see the content in Figure A-15.

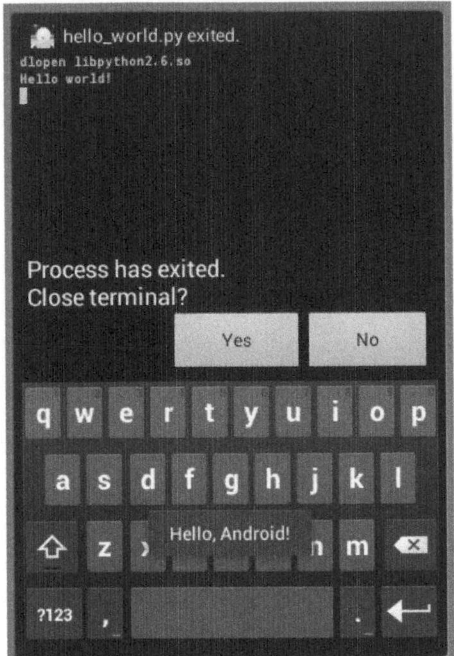

Figure A-15. *The script output includes a toast message over the keyboard.*

The script displays a toast message along with additional output. Once again, highlight the script's filename, but select the pencil icon to edit the script. Figure A-16 reveals the script's contents.

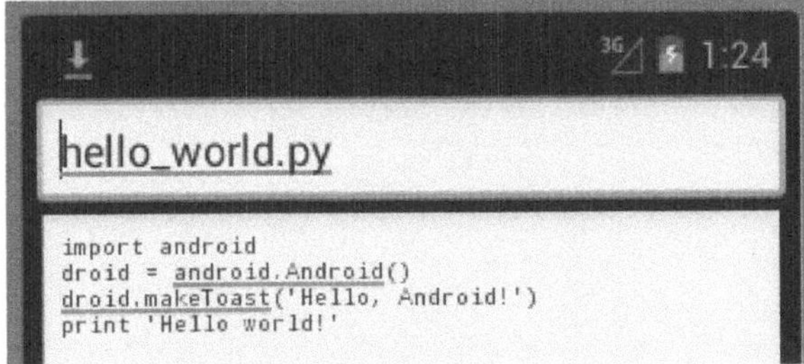

Figure A-16. *Python is based on modules that need to be imported.*

Python is based on modules that need to be imported. The `import` statement imports the `android` module, which provides an `Android` class that must be instantiated before you can call `makeToast()` and other methods.

> **NOTE:** The `Android` class's methods return `Result` objects. Each object provides `id`, `result`, and `error` fields: `id` uniquely identifies the object, `result` contains the method's return value (or None when the method doesn't return a value), and `error` identifies any error that may have occurred (or None when no error occurred).

You can also access the Python interpreter in much the same way as when accessing the Linux shell:

1. Select View from the Scripts screen's options menu.
2. Select Interpreters from the View context menu.
3. Select Python 2.6.2 from the Interpreters screen.

Figure A-17 reveals a sample session with Python, which consists of printing the version number (obtained from the `sys` module's `version` member), printing the `math` module's `pi` constant, and executing the `exit()` function to terminate the Python interpreter.

```
dlopen libpython2.6.so
Python 2.6.2 (r262:71600, Mar 20 2011, 16:54:21)
[GCC 4.4.3] on linux-armv7l
Type "help", "copyright", "credits" or "license" for
more information.
>>> import sys
>>> print(sys.version)
2.6.2 (r262:71600, Mar 20 2011, 16:54:21)
[GCC 4.4.3]
>>> import math
>>> print(math.pi)
3.14159265359
>>> exit()
```

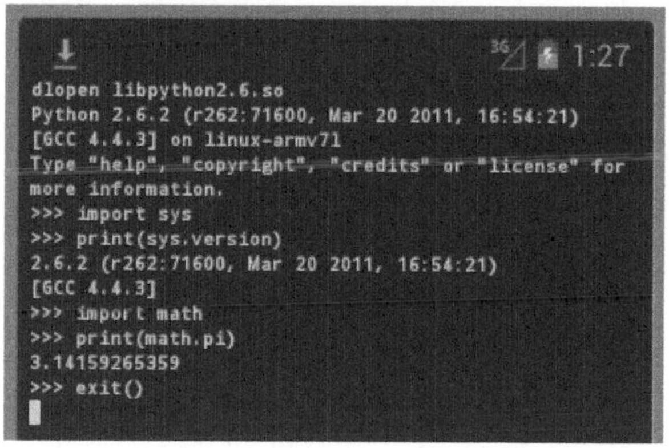

Figure A-17. *One way to terminate the Python interpreter is to execute Python's* `exit()` *function.*

> **NOTE:** As well as trying out other sample scripts, you should check out Google's "android-scripting Tutorials" page at `http://code.google.com/p/android-scripting/wiki/Tutorials`, to learn more about working with the Python interpreter in particular and SL4A in general.

Appendix B

Android Tools Overview

Apache Ant, the Eclipse IDE with Google's Android Development Tools (ADT) Plugin, Google's SDK Manager and AVD Manager, and its SDK tools and platform tools form the foundation of the Android app development ecosystem. Each of the SDK tools and platform tools is described in this appendix.

> **NOTE:** This appendix refers to booting in several places. To learn how an Android system boots up (and specifically how this happens for the Android Developer Phone 1), check out "Android Booting" (http://elinux.org/Android_Booting).

SDK Tools

SDK tools are the basic tools that are included in the SDK distribution file, and which are stored in the tools directory. This section introduces you to all basic tools as of Android SDK Revision 20.

android

android (one of several command-line tools) lets you create, delete, and view Android Virtual Devices (AVDs); create and update Android projects; and update your Android SDK with new platforms, add-ons, and documentation.

> **NOTE:** android's features are integrated into the Android Development Tools (ADT) Plugin.

android has the following usage syntax:

```
android [global options] action [action options]
```

You may specify various global options that apply to the command as a whole. These options include the following:

- -h or --help: Obtain help on a command. Examples: android -h create, android --help create avd, android -h create identity
- -s or --silent: Run in silent mode (only show errors).
- -v or --verbose: Output errors, warnings, and informational messages.

Following the global options is an action that tells android to perform some task. Most actions have options that further qualify the action. Table B-1 presents all actions.

Table B-1. *Supported Actions*

Action	Description	Options
avd	Launch AVD Manager.	none
create avd	Create new AVD.	-a --snapshot Place snapshots file in the AVD, to enable persistence. -b --abi ABI to use for the AVD. The default is to auto-select the ABI when the platform has only one ABI for its system images. -f --force Force creation, overwriting an existing AVD. -n --name Name of the new AVD. Required. -p --path Directory where new AVD will be created. -s --skin Skin for the new AVD.

		`-t --target` Target ID of the new AVD. Required.

`create identity`	Create identity file.	`-a --account`
		Publisher account. Required.
		`-k --alias`
		Key alias. Required.
		`-p --storepass`
		Keystore password. Default is to prompt.
		`-s --keystore`
		Keystore path. Required.
		`-w --keypass`
		Alias password. Default is to prompt.

`create lib-project`	Create library project.	`-k --package`
		Android package name for the library. Required.
		`-n --name`
		Project name.
		`-p --path`
		New project directory. Required.
		`-t --target`
		Target ID of the new project. Required.

`create project`	Create app project.	`-a --activity`
		Name of the default activity that is created. Required.
		`-k --package`
		Android package name for the app. Required.
		`-n --name`
		Project name.
		`-p --path`
		New project directory. Required.

		-t --target Target ID of the new project. Required.
create test-project	Create project for a test package.	-m --main Path of directory to the app under test, relative to the test project directory. Required. -n --name Project name. -p --path New project directory. Required.
delete avd	Delete existing AVD.	-n --name Name of AVD to delete. Required.
list	List existing targets and AVDs.	none
list avd	List existing AVDs.	-0 --null Terminate lines with \0 instead of \n. Only used by --compact. -c --compact Compact output (suitable for scripts).
list sdk	List remote SDK repository.	-a --all List all available packages (including those that are obsolete and installed). -e --extended Display extended details on each package. -o --obsolete Deprecated. Use --all instead. -s --no-https Use HTTP instead of HTTPS (the default) for downloads. -u --no-ui Display list result on console (no GUI). The default is true.

`list target`	List existing targets.	`-0 --null`
		Terminate lines with \0 instead of \n. Only used by `--compact`.
		`-c --compact`
		Compact output (suitable for scripts).

`move avd`	Move or rename an AVD.	`-n --name`
		Name of the AVD to move or rename. Required.
		`-p --path`
		Path to the AVD's new directory.
		`-r --rename`
		New name of the AVD.

`sdk`	Launch SDK Manager.	none
update adb	Update Android Debug Bridge tool (`adb`) to support the USB devices declared in the SDK add-ons.	none
update avd	Update an AVD to match a new SDK's directories.	`-n --name` Name of the AVD to update. Required.

update lib-project	Update an Android library project. Must have an `AndroidManifest.xml` file.	`-p --path`
		Project directory. Required.
		`-t --target`
		Target ID to set for the project.

update project	Update an Android project. Must have an `AndroidManifest.xml` file.	`-l --library`
		Directory of an Android library to add, relative to this project's directory.
		`-n --name`
		Project name.
		`-p --path`
		Project directory. Required.

		`-s --subprojects`
		Also updates any projects in subdirectories, such as test projects.
		`-t --target`
		Target ID to set for the project.

update sdk	Update the SDK by suggesting new platforms to install when available.	`--proxy-host`
		HTTP/HTTPS proxy host (overrides any defined setting)
		`--proxy-port`
		HTTP/HTTPS proxy port (overrides any defined setting)
		`-a --all`
		Include all packages, including those that are obsolete and non-dependent.
		`-f --force`
		Force replacement of a package or its parts, even when something has been modified.
		`-n --dry-mode`
		Simulate the update but do not download or install anything.
		`-p --obsolete`
		Deprecated. Use `--all` instead.
		`-s --no-https`
		Use HTTP instead of HTTPS (the default) for downloads.
		`-t --filter`
		A filter that limits the update to the specified types of packages in the form of a comma-separated list of [platform, system-image, tool, platform-tool, doc, sample, source]. This option also accepts the identifiers returned by `list sdk --extended`.

update test-project	Update Android project for a test package. Must have an `AndroidManifest.xml` file.	`-m --main`
		Path of directory to the app under test, relative to the test project directory. Required.
		`-p --path`
		Project directory. Required.

apkbuilder

`apkbuilder` is a deprecated tool that was formerly used to build APK files. For more information on this tool and its Java package replacement, run `apkbuilder` by itself at the command line.

> **NOTE:** Check out "How to build Android application package (.apk) from the command line using the SDK tools + continuously integrated using CruiseControl" at `http://asantoso.wordpress.com/2009/09/15/how-to-build-android-application-package-apk-from-the-command-line-using-the-sdk-tools-continuously-integrated-using-cruisecontrol/`, to learn how `apkbuilder` is used to build APKs.

ddms

`ddms` (Dalvik Debug Monitor Server) provides port-forwarding services, screen capture on the device, thread and heap information on the device, logcat, process, and radio state information, incoming call and SMS spoofing, location data spoofing, and more.

`ddms` has the following usage syntax:

```
ddms
```

> **NOTE:** Check out Google's "Using DDMS" page (`http://developer.android.com/tools/debugging/ddms.html`) for a thorough discussion on how to use this tool.

dmtracedump

dmtracedump provides an alternate way of generating graphical call-stack diagrams from trace log files (instead of using traceview).

dmtracedump has the following usage syntax (spread across two lines for readability):

```
dmtracedump [-ho] [-s sortable] [-d trace-file-name] [-g outfile]
            trace-file-name
```

This tool loads trace log data from *trace-file-name*.data and *trace-file-name*.key. Table B-2 describes the various options.

Table B-2. *Supported Options*

Option	Description
-d *trace-file-name*	Perform a diff with this trace.
-g *outfile*	Write a graph to *outfile*.
-h	Enable HTML output.
-k	Keep the intermediate DOT file when writing a graph.
-o	Dump the dmtrace file instead of profiling.
-s *sortable*	Provide the URL base to where the sortable javascript file is located.
-t *threshold*	Provide the threshold percentage for including nodes in the graph.

draw9patch

draw9patch is a GUI-based tool that lets you easily create *nine-patches* (resizable graphics). Google's "Nine-patch" documentation (http://developer.android.com/guide/topics/graphics/2d-graphics.html#nine-patch) provides an introduction to nine-patches.

draw9patch has the following usage syntax:

```
draw9patch
```

> **NOTE:** Check out Google's "Draw 9-patch" page (`http://developer.android.com/tools/help/draw9patch.html`) for a thorough discussion on how to use this tool.

emulator

`emulator` starts up an emulated device described by an AVD. You can install and run apps on this device.

`emulator` has the following usage syntax:

```
emulator -avd avd_name [-option [value]] ... [-qemu args]
```

Table B-3 describes the various options.

Table B-3. *Supported Options*

Option	Description
`-audio` *backend*	Use the specific audio *backend*.
`-avd` *name*	Use the specific AVD. This required option specifies the AVD to load for this emulator instance.
`-bootchart` *timeout*	Enable bootcharting. For more information, see `http://elinux.org/Using_Bootchart_on_Android`.
`-cache` *filepath*	Use *filepath* as the working cache partition image. The value passed as *filepath* is an absolute or relative path to the current working directory. If no cache file is specified, the emulator's default behavior is to use a temporary file instead.
`-cache-size` *size*	Specify the cache partition size (in megabytes).
`-camera-back` *mode*	Set emulation mode for a camera facing back.
`-camera-front` *mode*	Set emulation mode for a camera facing front.
`-charmap` *file*	Select the key character map stored in *file*.
`-cpu-delay` *cpudelay*	Slow down emulated CPU speed by *delay*. Supported values for *delay* are integers between 0 and 1000. The

	delay value does not correlate to clock speed or other absolute metrics — it simply represents an abstract, relative delay factor applied nondeterministically in the emulator. Effective performance does not always scale in direct relationship with *delay* values.
`-data` *filepath*	Use *filepath* as the working user-data disk image. Optionally, you can specify a path relative to the current working directory. If `-data` is not used, the emulator looks for a file named `userdata-qemu.img` in the storage area of the AVD being used (see `-avd`).
`-datadir` *dir*	Identify the location of the current user-data disk image.
`-debug` *tags*	Enable/disable debug messages for the specified debug *tags*, which is a space/comma/column-separated list of debug component names. Use `-help-debug-tags` to print a list of debug component names that you can use. Example: `-debug init`
`-debug-no-`*tag*	Disable debug messages for *tag*.
`-debug-`*tag*	Enable debug messages for *tag*. Use `-help-debug-tags` to print a list of debug component names that you can use in *tag*.
`-dns-server` *servers*	Use the specified DNS server(s) in the emulated system. The value of *servers* must be a comma-separated list of up to four DNS server names or IP addresses.
`-dpi-device` *dpi*	Scale the resolution of the emulator to match the screen size of a physical device. The default value is 165. See also `-scale`.
`-force-32bit`	Always use the 32-bit emulator.
`-gps` *device*	Redirect NMEA GPS to character device. Use this command to emulate an NMEA-compatible GPS unit connected to an external character device or socket. The format of *device* must agree with the Quick Emulator (QEMU)-specific serial device specification.
`-gpu on`	Turn on graphics acceleration for the emulator. This option is only available for emulators using a system image with API Level 15, revision 3 and higher.

`-help`	Print a list of all emulator options.
`-help-`*`option`*	Print help for a specific startup *`option`*.
`-help-all`	Print help for all startup options.
`-help-build-images`	Print help about disk images when building Android.
`-help-char-devices`	Print help about character devices that hook into an emulated device or communication channel. Examples include `stdio` and `pipe:`*`filename`*.
`-help-debug-tags`	Print help about debug tags for the `-debug` *`tags`* option.
`-help-disk-images`	Print help for using emulator disk images.
`-help-environment`	Print help on emulator environment variables.
`-help-keys`	Print the current mapping of keys.
`-help-keyset-file`	Print help for defining a custom key mappings file.
`-help-sdk-images`	Print help about disk images when using the SDK.
`-help-virtual-device`	Print help about virtual device management.
`-http-proxy` *`proxy`*	Make all TCP connections through a specified HTTP/HTTPS *`proxy`*. The value of *`proxy`* can be one of `http://`*`server`*`:`*`port`* or `http://`*`username`*`:`*`password`*`@`*`server`*`:`*`port`*. The `http://` prefix can be omitted. If the `-http-proxy` *`proxy`* option is not supplied, the emulator looks up the HTTP_PROXY environment variable and automatically uses any value matching the *`proxy`* format described above.
`-image` *`file`*	Obsolete. Use `-system` *`file`* option instead.
`-initdata` *`filepath`*	Identify a file whose contents are copied to the new user-data disk image when the `-wipe-data` option is specified. By default, the emulator copies from *`system`*`/userdata.img`. Optionally, you can specify a path relative to the current working directory. See also `-wipe-data`. Note that `-initdata` is equivalent to `-init-data`.

`-kernel` *`filepath`*	Use the kernel located at *`filepath`*.
`-keyset` *`file`*	Use the specified keyset *`file`* instead of the default. The keyset file defines the list of key bindings between the emulator and the host keyboard.
`-logcat` *`logtags`*	Enable logcat output with given *`logtags`*. If the environment variable ANDROID_LOG_TAGS is defined and not empty, its value will be used to enable `logcat` output by default.
`-memcheck` *`flags`*	Enable memory access checking.
`-memory` *`size`*	Specify physical RAM size (in megabytes).
`-netdelay` *`delay`*	Set network latency emulation to *`delay`*. Default value is `none`. See `http://developer.android.com/tools/devices/emulator.html#netspeed` for additional values.
`-netfast`	A shortcut for `-netspeed full -netdelay none`.
`-netspeed` *`speed`*	Set network speed emulation to *`speed`*. Default value is `full`. See `http://developer.android.com/tools/devices/emulator.html#netspeed` for additional values.
`-no-audio`	Disable audio support in the current emulator instance.
`-no-boot-anim`	Disable the boot animation during emulator startup. Disabling the boot animation can speed the startup time for the emulator.
`-no-cache`	Start the emulator without a cache partition.
`-no-jni`	Disable JNI checks in the Dalvik runtime.
`-no-skin`	Prevent any emulator skin from being used.
`-no-window`	Disable the emulator's graphical window display.
`-noaudio`	Same as `-no-audio`.
`-nocache`	Same as `-no-cache`.
`-nojni`	Same as `-no-jni`.

-noskin	Same as -no-skin.
-no-snapshot	Perform a full boot without auto-saving. However, QEMU vmload and vmsave instructions operate on snapstorage.
-no-snapshot-load	Does not auto-start from snapshot: performs a full boot.
-no-snapshot-save	Does not auto-save to snapshot on exit: abandons changed state.
-no-snapshot-update-time	Does not try to correct snapshot time on restore.
-no-snapstorage	Does not mount a snapshot storage file (all snapshot functionality is disabled).
-onion *image*	Use overlay PNG image over screen.
-onion-alpha *percent*	Specify onion skin translucency value (as percent). Default value is 50.
-onion-rotation *position*	Specify onion-skin rotation. The value passed to *position* must be 0, 1, 2, or 3.
-partition-size *size*	Specify system/data partition size (in megabytes).
-port *port*	Set the console port number for this emulator instance to *port*. The console port number must be an even integer between 5554 and 5584, inclusive. *port*+1 must also be free and will be reserved for adb.
-ports *consoleport*, *adbport*	Specify the TCP ports that will be used for the console and adb.
-prop *name=value*	Set the specified system property on boot.
-qemu *arguments...*	Pass *arguments* to the QEMU software. **IMPORTANT:** When using this option, make sure it is the *last option* specified, because all subsequent options are interpretted as QEMU-specific options.
-qemu -h	Display QEMU help.
-radio *device*	Redirect radio mode to the specified character device. The format of *device* must be QEMU-specific serial device

	specification.
`-ramdisk` *`filepath`*	Use *`filepath`* as the ramdisk image. Default value is *`system/`*`ramdisk.img`. Optionally, you can specify a path relative to the current working directory. For more information on disk images, use `-help-disk-images`.
`-raw-keys`	Disable Unicode keyboard reverse-mapping.
`-report-console` *`socket`*	Report the assigned console port for this emulator instance to a remote third party before starting the emulation. The *`socket`* format must be one of `tcp:`*`port`* `[,` *`server`*`] [, max=`*`seconds`*`]` or `unix:`*`port`* `[,` *`server`*`] [, max=`*`seconds`*`]`. Use `-help-report-console` to view more information about this topic.
`-scale` *`scale`*	Scale the emulator window. *`scale`* is a number between 0.1 and 3 that represents the desired scaling factor. You can also specify *`scale`* as a DPI value by adding the suffix `dpi` to the *`scale`* value. A value of `auto` tells the emulator to select the best window size.
`-screen` *`mode`*	Set emulated screen mode.
`-sdcard` *`filepath`*	Use *`filepath`* as the SD card image. Default value is *`system/`*`sdcard.img`. Optionally, you can specify a path relative to the current working directory. For more information on disk images, use `-help-disk-images`.
`-shared-net-id` *`number`*	Join the shared network, using IP address 10.1.2.*number*.
`-shell`	Create a root shell console on the current terminal. You can use this command even when the ADB daemon in the emulated system is broken. Pressing Ctrl-c from the shell stops the emulator instead of the shell.
`-shell-serial` *`device`*	Enable the root shell (as in `-shell`) and specify the QEMU character device to use for communication with the shell. *`device`* must be a QEMU device type. Examples include `-shell-serial stdio`, which is identical to `-shell`, and `-shell-serial tcp::4444,server,nowait`, which lets you communicate with the shell over TCP port 4444.
`-show-kernel` *`name`*	Display kernel messages.

`-skin` *skinID*	Deprecated. Set skin options using AVDs rather than via this emulator option. Using this option may yield unexpected and in some cases misleading results, since the density with which to render the skin may not be defined. AVDs let you associate each skin with a default density and override the default as needed.
`-skindir` *dir*	Deprecated. See `-skin` description for the reason.
`-snapshot` *name*	Provide the name of a snapshot within the storage file for auto-start and auto-save (default name is `default-boot`).
`-snapshot-list`	Show a list of available snapshots.
`-snapstorage` *file*	Specify the file that contains all state snapshots (default is *datadir*`/snapshots.img`).
`-sysdir` *dir*	Search for system disk images in *dir*.
`-system` *filepath*	Read the initial system image from *filepath*.
`-tcpdump` *filepath*	Capture network packets to *filepath*.
`-trace` *name*	Enable code profiling (press F9 to start), written to a specified file.
`-timezone` *timezone*	Set the timezone for the emulated device to *timezone*, instead of the host's timezone. *timezone* must be specified in zoneinfo format. Examples: `America/Los_Angeles` and `Europe/Paris`.
`-verbose`	Enable verbose output. Equivalent to `-debug-init`. You can define the default verbose output options used by emulator instances in the Android environment variable ANDROID_VERBOSE. Define the options you want to use in a comma-delimited list, specifying only the stem of each option (see `-debug-`*tags*). For example, set `ANDROID_VERBOSE=init,modem` defines ANDROID_VERBOSE with the `-debug-init` and `-debug-modem` options. For more information about debug tags, use `-help-debug-tags`.
`-version`	Display the emulator's version number.
`-webcam-list`	List all web cameras available for emulation.

-wipe-data	Reset the current user-data disk image (that is, the file specified by -datadir and -data, or the default file). The emulator deletes all data from the user data image file, then copies the contents of the file specified by -initdata to the image file before starting. See also -initdata. For more information on disk images, use -help-disk-images.

etc1tool

etc1tool lets you encode PNG images to the Ericsson Texture Compression (ETC1) compression standard and decode ETC1-compressed images back to PNG.

etc1tool has the following usage syntax (spread across two lines for readability):

```
etc1tool infile [--help | --encode | --encodeNoHeader | --decode]
                [--showDifference diff-file] [-o outfile]
```

This syntax presents the following items:

- *infile* identifies the input file to compress or containing compressed data.
- --help prints usage information.
- --encode creates an ETC1 file from a PNG file. This is the default mode for the tool when nothing is specified.
- --encodeNoHeader creates a raw ETC1 data file (without a header) from a PNG file.
- --decode creates a PNG file from an ETC1 file.
- --showDifference *diff-file* writes the difference between the original and encoded image to *diff-file* (only valid when encoding).
- -o *outfile* specifies the name of the output file. When *outfile* is not specified, the output file is constructed from the input filename with the appropriate suffix (.pkm or .png).

hierarchyviewer

`hierarchyviewer` is a GUI-based tool that lets you to debug and optimize your user interface. It provides a visual representation of the layout's View hierarchy (the Layout View) and a magnified inspector of the display (the Pixel Perfect View).

`hierarchyviewer` has the following usage syntax:

```
hierarchyviewer
```

> **NOTE:** Check out Google's "Optimizing Your UI" page (`http://developer.android.com/tools/debugging/debugging-ui.html`) and elsewhere in this book for a thorough discussion on how to use this tool.

hprof-conv

`hprof-conv` converts the HPROF file that's generated by SDK tools to a standard format so you can view the file in a profiling tool of your choice

`hprof-conv` has the following usage syntax:

```
hprof-conv infile outfile
```

You can use "`-`" for *`infile`* or *`outfile`* to specify stdin or stdout.

lint

`lint` is a static checker that analyzes Android projects for issues around correctness, security, performance, usability and accessibility, checking XML resources, bitmaps, ProGuard configuration files, source files and even compiled bytecode.

`lint` has the following usage syntax:

```
lint [flags] project directories
```

Table B-4 describes the various options.

Table B-4. *Supported Options*

Option	Description
`--check` *`list`*	Only check the specific *`list`* of issues. This will disable everything and re-enable the given *`list`* of issues. The *`list`* should be a comma-separated list of issue IDs or categories.
`--config` *`filename`*	Use the given configuration file to determine whether issues are enabled or disabled. If a project contains a `lint.xml` file, then this config file will be used as a fallback.
`--disable` *`list`*	Disable the *`list`* of categories or specific issue IDs. The *`list`* should be a comma-separated list of issue IDs or categories.
`--enable` *`list`*	Enable the specific *`list`* of issues. This checks all of the default issues plus the specifically enabled issues. The *`list`* should be a comma-separated list of issue IDs or categories.
`--exitcode`	Set the exit code to 1 when errors are found.
`--fullpath`	Use full paths in the error output.
`--help`	Print a detailed help message.
`--help` *`topic`*	Print help on the specified *`topic`*.
`--html` *`filename`*	Create an HTML report instead. If the *`filename`* is a directory (or a new filename without an extension), `lint` will create a separate report for each scanned project.
`--list`	List available issue IDs and exit.
`--nolines`	Do not include the source file lines with errors in the output. By default, the error output includes snippets of source code on the line containing the error, but this flag turns it off.
`--quiet`	Do not show progress.
`--show`	List available issues along with full explanations.
`--show` *`ids`*	Show full explanations for the given list of issue IDs.

`--showall`	Do not truncate long messages, lists of alternate locations, and so on.
`--simplehtml` *filename*	Create a simple HTML report.
`--url` *filepath=url*	Add links to HTML report, replacing local path prefixes with *url* prefix. The mapping can be a comma-separated list of path prefixes to corresponding URL prefixes, such as `C:\temp\Proj1=http://buildserver/sources/temp/Proj1`. To turn off linking to files, use `--url none`.
`--version`	Print version information and exit.
`-w --nowarn`	Only check for errors (ignore warnings).
`-Wall`	Check all warnings, including those that are off by default.
`-Werror`	Treat all warnings as errors.
`--xml` *filename*	Create an XML report instead.

`lint` also returns one of the following exit status codes:

- 0: Success.
- 1: Lint errors detected.
- 2: Lint usage.
- 3: Cannot clobber existing file.
- 4: Lint help.
- 5: Invalid command-line argument.

mksdcard

`mksdcard` lets you quickly create a FAT32 disk image that you can load into the emulator, to simulate the presence of an SD card in the device. Because you can specify an SD card while creating an AVD with `AVD Manager`, you usually use that feature to create an SD card. This tool creates an SD card that is not bundled with an AVD, so it is useful for situations where you need to share a virtual SD card between multiple emulators.

`mksdcard` has the following usage syntax:

```
mksdcard -l label size file
```

This syntax presents the following items:

- `-l` *`label`* specifies a volume label for the disk image to create.
- *`size`* specifies an integer identifying the size (in bytes) of the disk image to create. You can also specify *`size`* in kilobytes, megabytes, or gigabytes by appending a `K`, `M`, or `G` to the *`size`* value. Examples: `1048576K`, `1024M`, `1000G`.
- *`file`* specifies the path/filename of the disk image to create.

After you have created the disk image file, you can load it into the emulator at startup by using `emulator`'s `-sdcard` option. The usage for the `-sdcard` option is as follows:

```
emulator -sdcard file
```

monitor

`monitor` (Android Debug Monitor) provides a GUI for several Android app debugging and analysis tools. `monitor` does not require installation of a integrated development environment, such as Eclipse, and encapsulates the following tools (described elsewhere in this appendix):

- `ddms`
- `hierarchyviewer`
- `traceview`
- Tracer for OpenGL ES

`monitor` has the following usage syntax:

```
monitor
```

Start an Android emulator or connect an Android device via a USB cable, and connect `monitor` to the device by selecting it in the Devices window.

monkeyrunner

`monkeyrunner` (a tool that is good for functional testing) provides an API for writing programs that control an Android device or emulator from outside of Android code.

> **NOTE:** `monkeyrunner` is used for functional testing. To functionally test a single activity, you can also use the `android.test.ActivityInstrumentationTestCase2` class.

With `monkeyrunner`, you can write a Python program that installs an Android app or test package, runs it, sends keystrokes to it, takes screenshots of its user interface, and stores screenshots on the workstation.

> **NOTE:** Check out Google's "monkeyrunner" page (`http://developer.android.com/tools/help/monkeyrunner_concepts.html`) for a thorough discussion on how to use this tool.

sqlite3

`sqlite3` lets you manage SQLite databases created by Android apps, and lets you do so from a remote shell to your device or from your host machine. It includes many useful commands, such as `.dump` to print out the contents of a table and `.schema` to print the SQL CREATE statement for an existing table. `sqlite3` also gives you the ability to execute SQLite commands on the fly.

`sqlite3` has the following usage syntax:

```
sqlite3 [OPTIONS] [DATABASENAME]
```

`sqlite3` can be run by itself or it can be run with options and/or the name of a database file. A new database is created when the file does not exist.

Table B-5 describes the various options.

Table B-5. *Supported Options*

Option	Description
`-bail`	Stop after hitting an error.
`-batch`	Force batch I/O.
`-column`	Set output mode to column.
`-csv`	Set output mode to csv.

`-echo`	Print commands before execution.
`-help`	Print help.
`-html`	Set output mode to HTML.
`-init` *`filename`*	Read and process named file.
`-interactive`	Force interactive I/O.
`-line`	Set output mode to line.
`-list`	Set output mode to list.
`-[no]header`	Turn headers on or off.
`-nullvalue '`*`text`*`'`	Set *text* string for NULL values.
`-separator '`*`x`*`'`	Set output file separator to *x*.
`-stats`	Print memory stats before each finalize.
`-version`	Show SQLite version number.

> **NOTE:** Check out Google's "sqlite3" page (`http://developer.android.com/tools/help/sqlite3.html`) and elsewhere in this book for a thorough discussion on how to use this tool.

systrace

`systrace` is a Python script that invokes a Linux program called `atrace` (located on an Android device/emulator) to collect trace data about system and user behavior from the Linux kernel. `systrace` then generates an HTML file that presents this data (via the Google Chrome browser) as a group of vertically stacked time-series graphs.

The `systrace` subdirectory of the SDK's `tools` directory contains `systrace.py` along with a few other files that are used in generating an HTML page containing the graphs. You will need to install a Python interpreter to run `systrace.py` unless you already have one installed.

Before running this script, you will also need to enable various trace settings on the device. Accomplish this task as follows:

1. Click the MENU button on the home screen.
2. Select System settings from the pop-up menu.
3. Select Developer options from the SYSTEM section of the resulting Settings screen.
4. Select Enable traces from the MONITORING section of the resulting Developer options screen.
5. Select the traces that you want to enable from the resulting Select enabled traces pop-up menu. For example, you might select Graphics and View.
6. Click OK to enable these traces.

Figure B-1 shows the screen where you enable traces.

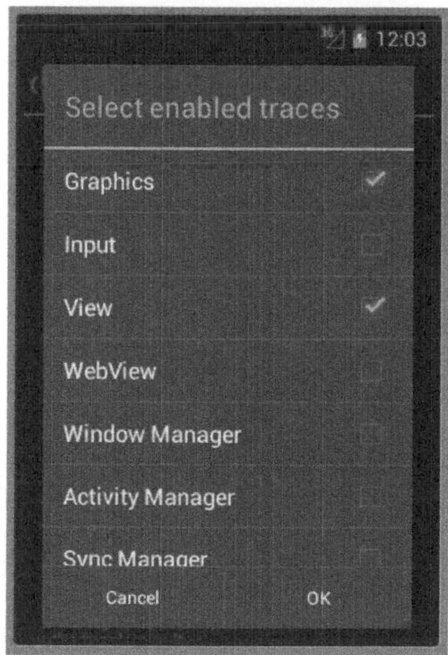

Figure B-1. *The Graphics and View traces are enabled.*

Switch to the `systrace` directory and execute a command such as the command shown below:

```
python systrace.py
```

The tool runs for about 5 seconds (the default setting, but you can change this by passing the `-t` or `--time` option to `systrace.py`). During this interval, you would launch an app to trace and interact with that app.

`systrace` generates the following messages:

```
capturing trace... done
downloading trace... done
```

It also generates a message about writing a `trace.html` file to the `systrace` directory. (You can change the name of this file by passing the `-o` option to `systrace.py`.)

Now that you have the `trace.html` file, you can view the results. Figure B-2 shows you what the resulting graph might look like.

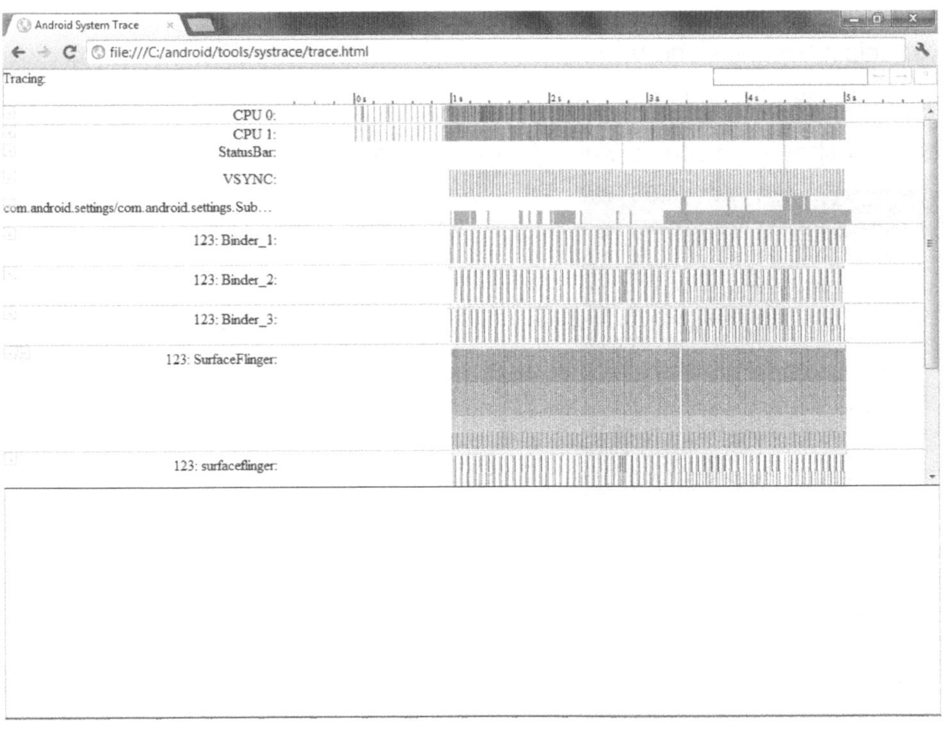

Figure B-2. *Trace results are shown in Google Chrome. Double-click a colored area to zoom into the results.*

Although you can run systrace on an actual device, you cannot run it on the Android emulator. When you try to do so, systrace generates the following output (the last line has been reformatted for readability):

```
Traceback (most recent call last):
  File "systrace.py", line 212, in <module>
    main()
  File "systrace.py", line 124, in main
    ready = select.select([adb.stdout, adb.stderr], [], [adb.stdout,
adb.stderr])
select.error: (10093, 'Either the application has not called WSAStartup, or
                      WSAStartup failed')
```

This error message results from atrace, which generates error messages when attempting to create/open files in subdirectories of the /sys/kernel/debug directory. It turns out that there is no debug subdirectory on the Android emulator.

You cannot simply execute a mkdir /sys/kernel/debug command to create this directory. Instead, you must enable kernel extensions for debugging, and you can only do so when rebuilding the kernel. (Execute emulator -help-build-images to obtain more information on this task.)

traceview

traceview is a GUI-based tool for viewing execution logs that your app creates by using the android.os.Debug class to log tracing information in its code. traceview can help you debug your app and profile its performance.

traceview has the following usage syntax:

```
traceview
```

> **NOTE:** Check out Google's "Profiling with Traceview and dmtracedump" page (http://developer.android.com/tools/debugging/debugging-tracing.html) for a thorough discussion on how to use this tool.

Tracer for OpenGL ES

Tracer is a tool for analyzing OpenGL for Embedded Systems (ES) code in your Android app. The tool allows you to capture OpenGL ES commands and frame by frame images to help you understand how your graphics commands are being executed.

Tracer is not a standalone tool, but is part of the ADT Plugin, and is also part of Android Device Monitor (`monitor`).

> **NOTE:** Check out Google's "Tracer for OpenGL ES" page (`http://developer.android.com/tools/help/gltracer.html`) for a thorough discussion on how to use this tool.

zipalign

`zipalign` is an archive alignment tool that provides important optimization to Android APKs. The purpose is to ensure that all uncompressed data starts with a particular alignment relative to the start of the file.

`zipalign` causes all uncompressed data within the APK (such as images or raw files) to be aligned on 4-byte boundaries. Doing so allows all portions to be accessed directly with the `mmap()` function, which maps files or devices into memory, even when they contain binary data with alignment restrictions. The benefit is a reduction in the amount of RAM consumed when running the app.

> **CAUTION:** Use `zipalign` only after the APK has been signed with your private key. If you run `zipalign` before signing, the signing procedure will undo the alignment. Also, do not make alterations to the aligned package. Alterations to the archive, such as renaming or deleting entries, will potentially disrupt the alignment of the modified entry and all later entries. Furthermore, any files added to an "aligned" archive will not be aligned.

`zipalign` has the following usage syntax:

```
zipalign [-f] [-v] alignment infile.apk outfile.apk
```

This syntax aligns *`infile`*`.apk` and saves it as *`outfile`*`.apk`.

`zipalign` also has the following usage syntax:

```
zipalign -c -v alignment existing.apk
```

This syntax confirms the alignment of *`existing`*`.apk`.

The *`alignment`* is an integer that defines the byte-alignment boundaries. This must always be 4 (which provides 32-bit alignment) or else it effectively does nothing.

Table B-6 describes the various options.

Table B-6. *Supported Options*

Option	Description
`-c`	Confirm the alignment of the given file.
`-f`	Overwrite existing *`outfile.apk`*.
`-v`	Print verbose output.

Platform Tools

SDK Platform-tools are platform-dependent tools for developing apps. These tools support the latest features of the Android platform and are typically updated only when a new platform becomes available. They are always backward compatible with older platforms, but you must make sure that you have the latest version of these tools when you install a new platform.

aapt

`aapt` (Android Asset Packaging Tool) lets you view, create, and update Zip-compatible archives (ZIP, JAR, APK). It can also compile resources into binary assets. When compiling resources, an `R.java` file is also created so that you can reference your resources from your Java code.

Although you probably won't often use `aapt` directly, build scripts and IDE plugins can use this tool to package the APK file that constitutes an Android app.

`aapt` has multiple usage syntaxes, with the following being the simplest:

```
aapt l[ist] [-v] [-a] file.{zip,jar,apk}
```

This syntax is used to list the contents of a Zip-compatible archive. Option `-v` produces verbose output and option `-a` prints Android-specific data (resources, manifest) when listing archive contents.

adb

`adb` lets you communicate with an emulator instance or a connected Android-powered device. It is a client-server program that includes three components:

- A client, which runs on your development machine. You can invoke a client from a shell by issuing an `adb` command. Other Android tools such as the ADT plugin and `ddms` also create `adb` clients.
- A server, which runs as a background process on your development machine. The server manages communication between the client and the ADB daemon running on an emulator or a device.
- A daemon, which runs as a background process on each emulator or device instance.

`adb` has the following usage syntax:

```
adb [-d|-e|-s serialNumber|-p product_name_or_path] command
```

This syntax shows that `adb` is used to submit *command*s. Table B-7 describes the various options that can preceed a *command*.

Table B-7. *Supported Options*

Option	Description
`-d`	Direct a command to the only attached USB device. Return an error when more than one USB device is attached.
`-e`	Direct a command to the only running emulator instance. Return an error when more than one emulator instance is running.
`-p`	Specify a simple product name (such as `sooner`) or a relative/absolute path to a product out directory (such as `out/target/product/sooner`). When `-p` is not specified, the ANDROID_PRODUCT_OUT environment variable is used, and it must specify an absolute path.
`-s`	Direct a command to a specific emulator/device instance, referred to by its `adb`-assigned serial number (such as "emulator-5556").

The following list identifies a few of the many commands that are available:

- `adb devices` prints a list of all attached emulator/device instances.

- `adb help` prints a list of supported commands.
- `adb install` *path-to-APK* pushes an Android app (specified as a full path to an APK file) to the data file of an emulator/device.
- `adb logcat` lets you view the device log.
- `adb pull` *remote local* copies a specified file from an emulator/device instance to your development computer.
- `adb push` *local remote* copies a specified file from your development computer to an emulator/device instance.
- `adb shell` starts a remote shell in the target emulator/device instance.
- `adb shell` *shellcommand* issues a *shellcommand* in the target emulator/device instance and then exits the remote shell.
- `adb uninstall` *package* removes an APK from a device. *package* is the fully-qualified Java package name of the app.
- `adb version` prints the `adb` version number.

> **NOTE:** Check out Google's "Android Debug Bridge" page (`http://developer.android.com/tools/help/adb.html`) for a thorough discussion on how to use this tool.

aidl

`aidl` (Android Interface Definition Language) is similar to other IDLs you might have worked with. It allows you to define the programming interface that both the client and service agree upon in order to communicate with each other using interprocess communication (IPC). On Android, one process cannot normally access the memory of another process. So to talk, they need to decompose their objects into primitives that the operating system can understand, and marshall the objects across that boundary for you. The code to do that marshalling is tedious to write, so Android handles it for you with `aidl`.

`aidl` has one of the following usage syntaxes:

```
aidl OPTIONS INPUT [OUTPUT]
aidl --preprocess OUTPUT INPUT...
```

OPTIONS is a combination of the following:

- -a: Generate a dependency file next to the output file with the name based on the input file.
- -b: Fail when trying to compile a parcelable.
- -d *FILE*: Generate dependency file.
- -I *DIR*: Search path for import statements.
- -o *DIRECTORY*: Specify base output directory for generated files.
- -p *FILE*: Specify file created by --preprocess to import.

INPUT is an aidl interface file. *OUTPUT* refers to the generated interface files. If omitted and if the -o option is not used, the input filename is used, with the .aidl extension changed to a .java extension. If the -o option is used, the generated files will be placed in the base output directory, under their package directory.

> **NOTE:** Check out Google's "Android Interface Definition Language (AIDL)" page (http://developer.android.com/guide/components/aidl.html) for a thorough discussion on how to use this tool.

dexdump

dexdump is used to output the contents of a Dalvik Executable (typically the classes.dex file stored in an APK file).

dexdump has the following usage syntax:

dexdump [-c] [-d] [-f] [-h] [-i] [-l *layout*] [-m] [-t *tempfile*] *dexfile...*

Table B-8 describes the various options.

Table B-8. *Supported Options*

Option	Description
-c	Verify checksum and exit.
-d	Disassemble code sections.

`-f`	Display summary information from file header.
`-h`	Display file header details.
`-i`	Ignore checksum failures.
`-l` *layout*	Specify output *layout*, either `plain` or `xml`.
`-m`	Dump register maps (and nothing else).
`-t`	Specify temp file name (defaults to `/sdcard/dex-temp-*`).

NOTE: Check out "Disassembling DEX files" at `http://mylifewithandroid.blogspot.ca/2009/01/disassembling-dex-files.html`, to learn how to use dexdump to dump the context of `classes.dex`.

dx

`dx` converts compiled `.class` files to executable `.dex` files. It has several usage syntaxes with the simplest being the following:

```
dx --help
```

Obtain a detailed help message on how to use `dx`.

fastboot

`fastboot` is used to update the flash filesystem in Android devices from a host over USB.

`fastboot` has the following usage syntax:

```
fastboot [option] command
```

This usage syntax suggests that you can specify various options before executing a command. Table B-9 describes the various options.

Table B-9. *Supported Options*

Option	Description
`-b` *baseAddr*	Specify a custom kernel *baseAddr*ESS.
`-c` *commandline*	Override the kernel *commandline*.
`-i` *vendorID*	Specify a custom USB *vendorID*.
`-n` *pageSize*	Specify the nand *pageSize*. Default is 2048 bytes.
`-p` *product*	Specify *product* name.
`-s` *serialNumber*	Specify device *serialNumber*.
`-l` *layout*	Specify output layout, either `plain` or `xml`.
`-w`	Wipe (erase) userdata and cache.

Table B-10 describes the various commands.

Table B-10. *Supported Commands*

Command	Description
`boot` *kernel* [*ramdisk*]	Download and boot kernel.
`continue`	Continue with autoboot.
`devices`	List all connected devices.
`erase` *partition*	Erase a flash *partition*.
`flash` *partition* [*filename*]	Write a file to a flash partition.
`flash:raw boot` *kernel* [*ramdisk*]	Create bootimage and flash it.
`flashall`	Flash boot plus recovery plus system.
`format` *partition*	Format a flash *partition*.
`getvar` *variable*	Display a bootloader *variable*.

help	Show this help message.
reboot	Reboot device normally.
reboot-bootloader	Reboot device into bootloader.
update *filename*	Reflash device from update.zip.

llvm-rs-cc

llvm-rs-cc is a RenderScript (see Chapter 8) source code compiler.

llvm-rs-cc has the following usage syntax:

```
llvm-rs-cc [options] inputs
```

This usage syntax suggests that you can specify various *options* before specifying *inputs*. Table B-11 describes the various *options*.

Table B-11. *Supported Options*

Option	Description
-additional-dep-target *value*	Additional targets to show up in dependencies output.
-allow-rs-prefix	Allow user-defined function prefixed with rs.
-bitcode-storage *value*	*value* should be ar or jc.
-emit-asm	Emit target assembly files.
-emit-bc	Build Abstract Syntax Trees (ASTs), then convert to LLVM, and finally emit .bc file.
-emit-llvm	Build ASTs, then convert to LLVM, and finally emit .ll file.
-emit-nothing	Build ASTs, then convert to LLVM, but emit nothing.
-g	Emit LLVM Debug Metadata.
-help	Print this help text.
-I *directory*	Add *directory* to include search path.

`-java-reflection-package-name` *value*	Specify the package name to which reflected Java files belong.
`-java-reflection-path-base` *directory*	Specify base *directory* in which to output reflected Java files.
`-O` *optimization-level*	*optimization-level* can be one of `0` or `3` (the default).
`-o` *directory*	Specify output *directory*.
`-output-dep-dir` *directory*	Specify output *directory* for dependencies output.
`-reflect-c++`	Reflect C++ classes.
`-target-api` *value*	Specify target API level (such as 14).
`-version`	Print the assembler version.
`-w`	Suppress all warnings.

Appendix C

App Design Guidelines

This book focuses on the mechanics of developing apps using various Android technologies. However, knowing how to create an app is not enough when you want to succeed as an Android developer. You must also know how to design apps that are only available to users with compatible devices, that perform well, that are responsive to their users, that interact properly with other apps, and that are secure. This appendix's recipes give you the necessary design knowledge so your apps shine.

Designing Filtered Apps

Problem

When you publish your app to Google Play, you don't want the app to be installable on incompatible devices. You want Google Play to filter your app so that users of these incompatible devices cannot download and install the app.

Solution

Android runs on many devices, which gives developers a huge potential market. However, not all devices contain the same features (for example, some devices have cameras, whereas other devices don't), so certain apps might not run properly on some devices.

Recognizing this problem, Google provides filters that are triggered whenever a user visits Google Play via an Android device. If an app doesn't satisfy a filter, the app cannot be downloaded to and subsequently installed on a device. Table

C-1 identifies three filters that are triggered when specific elements are present in an app's manifest file.

Table C-1. *Filters Based on Manifest Elements*

Filter Name	Manifest Element	How the Filter Works
Minimum Framework Version (minSdkVersion)	<uses-sdk>	An app requires a minimum API level. Devices that don't support that level won't be able to run the app. API levels are expressed as integers. For example, integer 9 corresponds to Android 2.3 (API Level 9). (For a complete list of API levels and associated platform version numbers, check out http://developer.android.com/guide/topics/manifest/uses-sdk-element.html#ApiLevels.) Example: <uses-sdk android:minSdkVersion="9"/> tells Google Play that the app only supports Android 2.3 and higher. If you don't declare this attribute, Google Play assumes a default value of "1", which indicates that the app is compatible with all versions of Android.
Device Features (name)	<uses-feature>	An app can require certain device features to be present on the device. This functionality was introduced in Android 2.0 (API Level 5). Example: <uses-feature android:name="android.hardware.sensor.compass"/> tells Google Play that the device must have a compass. The abstract android.content.pm.PackageManager class defines Java constants for "android.hardware.sensor.compass" and other feature IDs.
Screen Size	<supports-screens>	An app indicates the screen sizes that it supports by setting attributes of the <supports-screens> element (undefined under API Level 3 and lower). When the app is published, Google Play uses those attributes to determine whether to make the app available to users, based on the screen sizes of their devices. Example: <supports-screens android:smallScreens="false"/> tells Google Play that the app won't run on devices with QVGA (240-

by-320-pixel) screens.

Google Play generally assumes that the platform on the device can adapt smaller layouts to larger screens, but cannot adapt larger layouts to smaller screens. As a result, if an app declares support for "normal" screen size only, Google Play makes the app available to normal- and large-screen devices, but filters the app so that it's not available to small-screen devices.

Google Play also filters apps based on advanced manifest elements. For example, when `<supports-gl-texture>` is present, Google Play prevents an app from being downloaded to a device unless one or more of the GL texture compression formats supported by the app are also supported by the device.

Finally, Google Play uses other app characteristics (such as the country in which the user with the device is currently located) to determine whether to show or hide an app. Table C-2 identifies three filters that are triggered when some of these additional characteristics are present.

Table C-2. *Filters Based on Additional Characteristics*

Filter Name	How the Filter Works
Publishing Status	Only published apps will appear in searches and browsing from within Google Play. Even if an app is unpublished, it can be installed when users can see it in their Downloads area among their purchased, installed, or recently uninstalled apps. When an app has been suspended, users won't be able to reinstall or update it, even when it appears in their Downloads.
Priced Status	Not all users can see paid apps. To show paid apps, a device must have a SIM card and be running Android 1.1 or later, and it must be in a country (as determined by the SIM carrier) in which paid apps are available.
Country / Carrier Targeting	When you upload your app to Google Play, you can select specific countries to target. The app will be visible only to the countries (carriers) that you select, as follows: ▪ A device's carrier (when available) determines its country. When no carrier can be determined, Google Play tries to determine the country based on IP. ▪ The carrier is determined based on the device's SIM (for GSM devices), not the current roaming carrier.

> **NOTE:** For more information on filters, check out Google's "Filters on Google Play" (`http://developer.android.com/guide/google/play/filters.html`) document.

Designing High-Performance Apps

Problem

Apps should perform well, especially on devices with limited amounts of memory. Furthermore, better-performing apps provide less drain on battery power. You want to know how to design your app to have good performance.

Solution

Android devices differ in significant ways. Some devices may have a faster processor than others, some devices may have more memory than others, and some devices may include a Just-In-Time (JIT) compiler, whereas other devices don't have this technology for speeding up executable code by converting sequences of bytecode instructions to equivalent native code sequences on the fly. The following list identifies some things to consider when writing code so that your apps will perform well on any device:

- **Optimize your code carefully**: Strive to write apps with a solid architecture that doesn't impede performance before thinking about optimizing the code. Once the app is running correctly, profile its code (via a tool such as `traceview`, see Appendix B) on various devices and look for bottlenecks that slow the app down. Keep in mind that the emulator will give you a false impression of your app's performance. For example, its network connection is based on your development platform's network connection, which is much faster than what you'll probably encounter on many Android devices.

- **Minimize object creation**: Object creation impacts performance, especially where garbage collection is concerned. You should try to reuse existing objects as much as possible to minimize garbage collection cycles that can temporarily slow down an app. For example, use a `java.lang.StringBuilder` object (or a `java.lang.StringBuffer` object when multiple threads might access this object) to build strings instead of using the string concatentation operator in a loop, which results in unnecessary intermediate `String` objects being created.
- **Minimize floating-point operations**: Floating-point operations are about twice as slow as integer operations on Android devices; for example, the floating-point-unit-less and JIT-less G1 device. Also, keep in mind that some devices lack a hardware-based integer division instruction, which means that integer division is performed in software. The resulting slowness is especially bothersome where hashtables (that rely on the remainder operator) are concerned.
- **Use `System.arraycopy()` wherever you need to perform a copy**: The `java.lang.System` class's `static void arraycopy(Object src, int srcPos, Object dest, int destPos, int length)` method is around nine times faster than a hand-coded loop on a Nexus One with the JIT.
- **Use the enhanced for loop syntax**: In general, the enhanced for loop (such as `for (String s: strings) {}`) is faster than the regular for loop (such as `for (int i = 0; i < strings.length; i++)`) on a device without a JIT and no slower then a regular for loop when a JIT is involved. Because the enhanced for loop tends to be slower when iterating over a `java.util.ArrayList` instance, however, a regular for loop should be used instead for arraylist traversal.

NOTE: The previous version of this book recommended that you avoid using enums, which was based on advice in Google's performance documentation. The rationale for this advice was that enums add to the size of a `.dex` file and can impact performance. For example, `public enum Directions { UP, DOWN, LEFT, RIGHT }` can add several hundred bytes to a `.dex` file, compared to the equivalent class with four `public static final ints`. Google removed its "avoid enum"

> advice because enums are no longer problematic. To learn why, check out `http://stackoverflow.com/questions/5143256/why-was-avoid-enums-where-you-only-need-ints-removed-from-androids-performanc`.

You'll also want to choose algorithms and data structures carefully. For example, the linear search algorithm (which searches a sequence of items from start to finish, comparing each item to a search value) examines half of the items on average, whereas the binary search algorithm uses a recursive division technique to locate the search value with few comparisons. For example, where a linear search of 4 billion items averages 2 billion comparisons, binary search performs 32 comparisons at most.

Designing Responsive Apps

Problem

Apps that are slow to respond to users, or that appear to hang or freeze, risk triggering the *Application Not Responding* dialog box (see Figure C-1), which gives the user the opportunity to kill the app (and probably uninstall it) or keep waiting in the hope that the app will eventually respond.

Figure C-1. *The dreaded Application Not Responding dialog box may result in users uninstalling the app.*

You want to know how to design responsive apps so that you can avoid this dialog box (and quite likely a bad reputation from unimpressed users).

Solution

Android displays the *Application Not Responding* dialog box when an app cannot respond to user input. For example, an app blocking on an I/O operation (often a network access) prevents the main app thread from processing incoming user input events. After an Android-determined length of time, Android concludes that the app is frozen, and displays this dialog box to give the user the option to kill the app.

NOTE: The activity manager and window manager (see Chapter 1, Figure 1-1) monitor app responsiveness. When they detect no response to an input event (a key press or a screen touch, for example) within 5 seconds, or that a broadcast receiver has not finished executing within 10 seconds, they conclude that the app has frozen and display the *Application Not Responding* dialog box.

Similarly, when an app spends too much time building an elaborate in-memory data structure, or perhaps the app is performing an intensive computation (such as calculating the next move in chess or some other game), Android concludes that the app has hung. Therefore, it's always important to make sure these computations are efficient by using techniques such as those described in Recipe C-2.

In these situations, the app should create another thread and perform most of its work on that thread. This is especially true for activities, which should do as little work as possible in key lifecycle callback methods, such as `onCreate(Bundle)` and `onResume()`. As a result, the main thread (which drives the user interface event loop) keeps running and Android doesn't conclude that the app has frozen.

TIP: Use a progress bar to keep the user informed about the progress of a lengthy operation.

Designing Seamless Apps

Problem

You want to know how to design your apps to interact properly with other apps. Specifically, you want to know what things your app should avoid doing so that it doesn't cause problems for the user (and face the possibility of being uninstalled).

Solution

Your apps must play fair with other apps so that they don't disrupt the user by doing something such as popping up a dialog box when the user is interacting with some activity. Also, you don't want one of your app's activities to lose state when it's paused, leaving the user confused as to why previously entered data is missing when the user returns to the activity. In other words, you want your app to work well with other apps so that it doesn't disrupt the user's experience.

An app that achieves a seamless experience must take the following rules into account:

- **Don't drop data**: Because Android is a mobile platform, another activity can pop up over your app's activity (perhaps an incoming phone call has triggered the Phone app). When this happens, your activity's `void onSaveInstanceState(Bundle outState)` and `onPause()` callback methods are called, and your app will probably be killed. If the user was editing data at the time, the data will be lost unless saved via `onSaveInstanceState(Bundle)`. The data is later restored in the `onCreate(Bundle)` or `void onRestoreInstanceState(Bundle savedInstanceState)` method.
- **Don't expose raw data**: It's not a good idea to expose raw data because other apps must understand your data format. If you change the format, these other apps will break unless updated to take the format changes into account. Instead, you should create a `ContentProvider` instance that exposes the data via a carefully designed API.
- **Don't interrupt the user**: When the user is interacting with an activity, the user won't be happy when interrupted by a pop-up dialog box (perhaps activated via a background service as a result of a `startActivity(Intent)` method call). The preferred way to notify the user is to send a message via the `android.app.NotificationManager` class. The message appears on the status bar and the user can view the message at the user's convenience.

- **Use threads for lengthy activities**: Components that perform lengthy computations or are involved with other time-consuming activities should move this work to another thread. Doing so prevents the *Application Not Responding* dialog box from appearing and reduces the chance of the user uninstalling your app from the device.
- **Don't overload a single activity screen**: Apps with complex user interfaces should present their user interfaces via multiple activities. That way, the user is not overwhelmed with many items appearing on the screen. Furthermore, your code becomes more maintainable and it also plays nicely with Android's activity stack model.
- **Extend system themes:** When it comes to the look-and-feel of a user interface, it's important to blend in nicely. Users are jarred by apps that contrast with the user interface they've come to expect. When designing your UIs, avoid straying from standards as much as possible. Instead, use a theme – see `http://developer.android.com/guide/topics/ui/themes.html` . You can override or extend those parts of the theme that you require, but at least you're starting from the same UI base as the other apps.
- **Design your user interfaces to support multiple screen resolutions**: Different Android devices often support different screen resolutions. Some devices can even change screen resolutions on the fly, such as switching to landscape mode. It's therefore important to make sure your layouts and drawables have the flexibility to display themselves properly on various device screens. This task can be accomplished by providing different versions of your artwork (if you use any) for key screen resolutions, and then designing your layout to accommodate various dimensions. (For example, avoid using hard-coded positions and instead use relative layouts.) Do this much and the system handles other tasks; the result is an app that looks great on any device.

- **Assume a slow network**: Android devices come with a variety of network-connectivity options, and some devices are faster than others. However, the lowest common denominator is GPRS (the non-3G data service for GSM networks). Even 3G-capable devices spend lots of time on non3G networks so slow networks will remain a reality for a long time to come. For this reason, always code your apps to minimize network accesses and bandwidth. Don't assume that the network is fast, so plan for it to be slow. If your users happen to be on faster networks, their experience only improves.
- **Don't assume a touchscreen or a keyboard**: Android supports various kinds of input devices: some Android devices have full "QWERTY" keyboards, whereas other devices have 40-key, 12-key, or other key configurations. Similarly, some devices have touchscreens, but many won't. Keep these differences in mind when designing your apps. Don't assume specific keyboard layouts unless you want to restrict your app for use only on certain devices.
- **Conserve the device's battery**: Mobile devices are battery powered, and it's important to minimize battery drain. Two of the biggest battery power consumers are the processor and the radio, which is why it's important to write apps that use as few processor cycles, and as little network activity, as possible. Minimizing the amount of processor time occupied by an app comes down to writing efficient code. Minimizing the power drain from using the radio comes down to handling error conditions gracefully and fetching only the data that's needed. For example, don't constantly retry a network operation when one attempt fails. If it failed once, another immediate attempt is likely to fail because the user has no reception; all you'll accomplish is to waste battery power. Keep in mind that users will notice a power-hungry app and most likely uninstall the app.

Designing Secure Apps

Problem

You want to familiarize yourself with Android security best practices to make sure your apps take advantage of Android's security capabilities, and also to reduce the likelihood of inadvertently introducing security issues that can affect your apps.

Solution

Google's "Designing for Security" document (`http://developer.android.com/guide/practices/security.html`) identifies various security features that can help developers build secure apps. For example, Android offers an encrypted filesystem that you can enable to protect data on lost or stolen devices.

This document largely presents best practices that address various security implications for your app and its users. For example, although you can use Linux network sockets or shared files to perform interprocess communication (IPC), you should use Android's IPC mechanisms (intents, binders, services, and receivers), which let you verify the identity of apps to which you are connecting and to set IPC mechanism security policies.

Appendix D

Univerter Architecture

Chapter 1 introduced Univerter, an app for performing unit conversions. Although lack of space in that chapter prevented a detailed exploration of this app's architecture, Appendix D compensates by exploring Univerter's source code, resource files, and its manifest.

Exploring the Source Code

Univerter's source code is spread across four files: Category.java, Conversion.java, Converter.java, and Univerter.java. Each file begins with a package statement, which indicates that the file's class is a member of the ca.tutortutor.univerter package. Every reference type that is part of an app must belong to a package.

> **NOTE:** All reference types except for those being reused from another app must belong to the same package. The other app's reference types would be located in another package.

Exploring the Converter Interface

Listing D-1 presents the contents of Converter.java.

Listing D-1. *The* `Converter` *Interface Describing a Method for Performing Conversions*

```
package ca.tutortutor.univerter;

import android.content.Context;

interface Converter
{
   double convert(Context ctx, double value);
}
```

Listing D-1 declares the `Converter` interface, which declares a `double convert(Context ctx, double value)` method header for performing a conversion. The argument passed to `ctx` allows this method to access error message-oriented string resources when necessary. The argument passed to `value` is the value to be converted. This method returns the conversion result.

> **NOTE:** The `android.content.Context` class declares a `String getString(int resId)` method that is handy for accessing string resources.

Depending on the conversion, the passed argument may be invalid. For example, when converting from Celsius to Fahrenheit, an argument of -1000 is invalid because it is less than absolute zero (-273.15 degrees Celsius). In this case, `convert(Context, double)` should throw `java.lang.IllegalArgumentException`, which would be handled by the method's caller.

Exploring the Conversion Class

Listing D-2 presents the contents of `Conversion.java`.

Listing D-2. *The* `Conversion` *Class Describing a Single Conversion*

```
package ca.tutortutor.univerter;

import android.content.Context;

class Conversion
{
   private int nameID;
   private Converter converter;
   private boolean canBeNegative;
```

```
   Conversion(int nameID, final double multiplier)
   {
      this(nameID,
           new Converter()
           {
              @Override
              public double convert(Context ctx, double value)
              {
                 return value*multiplier;
              }
           },
           false);
   }

   Conversion(int nameID, Converter converter, boolean canBeNegative)
   {
      this.nameID = nameID;
      this.converter = converter;
      this.canBeNegative = canBeNegative;
   }

   boolean canBeNegative()
   {
      return canBeNegative;
   }

   Converter getConverter()
   {
      return converter;
   }

   String getName(Context ctx)
   {
      return ctx.getString(nameID);
   }
}
```

Listing D-2 declares the `Conversion` class, which describes a conversion as a combination of a name, a converter, and a flag that indicates whether or not the value passed to `convert(Context, double)` can be negative. (A negative Celsius temperature makes sense, but what does a negative number of hectares mean?) `Univerter` uses this flag to enable/disable the +/- button.

`Conversion` declares a pair of constructors:

- `Conversion(int nameID, double multiplier)`
- `Conversion(int nameID, Converter converter, boolean canBeNegative)`

Each constructor declares a `nameID` parameter that is passed the integer-based ID of a string resource that names the conversion.

The first constructor also declares a `multiplier` parameter that receives the multiplier for conversions of the form `value*multiplier`. It implements `Converter` to handle this kind of conversion, and it passes this instance to the second constructor. It also passes `false` to the second constructor's `canBeNegative` parameter.

> **NOTE:** The first constructor passes `false` to `canBeNegative` because nontemperature conversions (created by the first constructor) make no sense with negative input values.

The second constructor also declares a `converter` parameter for specifying a nondefault `Converter` implementation that handles more complex conversions, such as converting from Celsius to Fahrenheit. Also, it declares a `canBeNegative` parameter for specifying whether or not the conversion can handle negative input values.

Finally, `Conversion` declares `String getName(Context)`, `Converter getConverter()`, and `boolean canBeNegative()` methods that return the supplied name, converter, and flag indicating whether or not the value to be converted can be negative. The `getName(Context)` method is called with a `Context` argument so that it can retrieve the string resource specified by `nameID` (via `getString(int)`) and return this string.

Exploring the Category Class

Listing D-3 presents the contents of `Category.java`.

Listing D-3. *The `Category` Class Describing an Array of Conversions*

```
package ca.tutortutor.univerter;

import android.content.Context;

class Category
{
   private int nameID;
   private Conversion[] conversions;
   private String[] conversionNames;
```

```
    Category(int nameID, Conversion[] conversions)
    {
       this.nameID = nameID;
       this.conversions = conversions;
    }

    Conversion getConversion(int index)
    {
       return conversions[index];
    }

    String[] getConversionNames(Context ctx)
    {
       if (conversionNames == null)
       {
          conversionNames = new String[conversions.length];
          for (int i = 0; i < conversionNames.length; i++)
             conversionNames[i] = conversions[i].getName(ctx);
       }
       return conversionNames;
    }

    String getName(Context ctx)
    {
       return ctx.getString(nameID);
    }
}
```

Listing D-3 declares the Category class, which describes a conversion category as a combination of a name and an array of Conversion instances. Its Category(int nameID, Conversion[] conversions) constructor initializes a Category instance to an integer-based string resource name ID and an array of Conversion instances. Both arguments are stored in same-named fields.

Category also declares String getName(Context) and Conversion getConversion(int index) methods that return the supplied name and Conversion instance at array position index. The getConversion(int) method doesn't validate its argument because Univerter doesn't pass an invalid index. (If an invalid index was passed, java.lang.ArrayIndexOutOfBoundsException would be thrown.)

Finally, Category declares a String[] getConversionNames(Context) method that Univerter calls to obtain an array of conversion names for the current category (for display in a dialog box). This method is optimized to avoid unnecessary object creation by creating and caching the array only the first time it is called (and not also on subsequent calls).

Exploring the Univerter Class

Listing D-4 presents the skeletonized contents of Univerter.java.

Listing D-4. *The Univerter Class Describing the App's Solitary Activity*

```
package ca.tutortutor.univerter;

import android.app.Activity;
import android.app.AlertDialog;

import android.content.Context;
import android.content.DialogInterface;

import android.graphics.Color;
import android.graphics.PorterDuff.Mode;

import android.os.Bundle;

import android.text.Html;

import android.text.method.LinkMovementMethod;

import android.view.Gravity;
import android.view.LayoutInflater;
import android.view.Menu;
import android.view.MenuInflater;
import android.view.MenuItem;
import android.view.View;
import android.view.ViewGroup;
import android.view.Window;

import android.webkit.WebView;

import android.widget.ArrayAdapter;
import android.widget.Button;
import android.widget.EditText;
import android.widget.ImageView;
import android.widget.ListAdapter;
import android.widget.TextView;
import android.widget.Toast;

public class Univerter extends Activity
{
   // field and method declarations here
}
```

Listing D-4 declares the Univerter class, which extends android.app.Activity to make Univerter an activity. Univerter declares various fields and methods.

Exploring Univerter's Fields

Univerter first declares a categories array field followed by a static initializer that initializes this field to an array of Category instances.

```
private static Category[] categories;
static
{
   categories = new Category[]
                {
                   new Category
                       (R.string.cat_angle,
                        new Conversion[]
                        {
                           new Conversion
                               (R.string.cat_angle_circles_to_deg,
                                360),
                           // ...
                           new Conversion
                               (R.string.cat_angle_rad_to_grad,
                                63.661977237)
                        }),
                   // ...
                   new Category
                       (R.string.cat_temp,
                        new Conversion[]
                        {
                           new Conversion
                               (R.string.cat_temp_celsius_to_fahrenheit,
                                new Converter()
                                {
                                   @Override
                                   public double convert(Context ctx,
                                                         double value)
                                   {
                                      if (value < -273.15)
                                      {
                                         String s;
                                         s = ctx.
                                             getString(R.string.
                                                       error_less_than_abs0);
                                         throw
                                           new IllegalArgumentException(s);
                                      }
                                      return value*9.0/5.0+32;
                                   }
                                },
                                true),
                           // ...
                           new Conversion
```

```
                          (R.string.cat_temp_kelvin_to_celsius,
                           new Converter()
                           {
                              @Override
                              public double convert(Context ctx,
                                                    double value)
                              {
                                 return value-273.15;
                              }
                           },
                           false)
                 }),
            // ...
            new Category
                (R.string.cat_weightmass,
                 new Conversion[]
                 {
                    new Conversion
                        (R.string.cat_weightmass_ct_to_lb,
                         0.000440925),
                    // ...
                    new Conversion
                        (R.string.cat_weightmass_t_to_lb,
                         2204.622621849)
                 })
         };
}
```

Each Category entry consists of the category name string resource ID and an array of Conversion instances. Each Conversion instance consists of the conversion name string resource ID, and a multiplier or a Converter instance whose overriding convert(Context, double) method performs the conversion.

This initializer runs when Univerter's classfile is loaded into memory. A lot of objects are created, and it's more efficient to create them once at class-loading time rather than each time Univerter is instantiated, which would be the case if categories was a nonstatic field.

Additional field declarations follow the static initializer:

```
private String[] catNames;
private int curCat, curCon;

private StringBuilder buffer;
private int state;
private int nDigits;
private boolean isDecimal;
private boolean btnCvtClicked;
```

```
private Button btnPm;
private EditText etDisplay;
private DialogInterface.OnClickListener oclCat, oclCatClose;
private DialogInterface.OnClickListener oclCon, oclConClose;
private int choice;

private String helpText;
```

These fields have the following responsibilities:

- `catNames` references an array of category names, which are displayed to the user when `Univerter`'s CAT button is clicked.
- `curCat` provides the index of the current category.
- `curCon` provides the index of the current conversion for the current category.
- `buffer` stores a number as it is being input.
- `state` identifies the current state in a two-state state machine that controls numeric input.
- `nDigits` tracks the number of digits that have been input.
- `isDecimal` tracks whether or not the decimal point has been input.
- `btnCvtClicked` tracks whether or not the CVT button has been clicked.
- `btnPm` identifies the +/- button for the purpose of enabling/disabling.
- `etDisplay` identifies the display, which presents a number as it is being input or presents a conversion result.
- `oclCat` references the listener that responds to the CAT button being clicked. A dialog box that lists all category names is displayed.
- `oclCatClose` references the listener that responds to the Close button on the category names dialog box being clicked.
- `oclCon` references the listener that responds to the CON button being clicked. A dialog box that lists all conversion names for the current category is displayed.
- `oclConClose` references the listener that responds to the Close button on the conversion names dialog box being clicked.

- choice records the index of the most recently selected item on the category names or conversion names dialog box.
- helpText stores the HTML text that appears on the help dialog box.

Exploring Univerter's Methods

Univerter declares 15 methods in three categories: click listeners, callbacks, and helpers.

Exploring Univerter's Click Listener Methods

Following Univerter's field declarations are seven "do"-prefixed click listener methods. These methods respond to button-click events and are associated with their respective buttons via the onClick attributes of Button XML elements in the main.xml layout file, as discussed in Chapter 1.

The following void doCatClicked(View view) method responds to CAT button clicks:

```
public void doCatClicked(View view)
{
   choice = curCat;
   if (oclCat == null)
      oclCat = new DialogInterface.OnClickListener()
               {
                  @Override
                  public void onClick(DialogInterface dialog, int which)
                  {
                     choice = which;
                  }
               };
   if (oclCatClose == null)
      oclCatClose = new DialogInterface.OnClickListener()
                    {
                       @Override
                       public void onClick(DialogInterface dialog, int which)
                       {
                          curCat = choice;
                          curCon = 0;
                          updateConversionTitle();
                          reset();
                          btnPm.setEnabled(categories[curCat].
                                getConversion(curCon).
                                canBeNegative());
                       }
```

```
                  };
   new AlertDialog.Builder(Univerter.this).
       setSingleChoiceItems(catNames, curCat, oclCat).
       setTitle(R.string.categories).
       setNeutralButton(R.string.btnClose, oclCatClose).
       show();
}
```

doCatClicked(View) first initializes choice with curCat's value because choice tracks the currently selected category and because curCat is assigned choice's value when the category names dialog box is closed.

> **NOTE:** The android.view.View instance passed to this method identifies the button that was clicked.

Next, the oclCat and oclCatClose listeners are instantiated, but only when not instantiated previously to avoid unnecessary object creation. The former listener tracks category name selections; the latter listener responds to the dialog box being closed.

As selections are made, the former listener's void onClick(DialogInterface dialog, int which) method is invoked, with a reference to the dialog box passed to dialog and the index of the selected item passed to which. The listener assigns which to choice so that the currently desired category can be tracked.

When the dialog box is closed, the latter listener's onClick(DialogInterface, int) method is called. After assigning choice to curCat and resetting curCon to 0 (to reflect the first conversion in the new category), the listener presents the new conversion via updateConversionTitle(), resets the display to "0.", and enables or disables the +/- button.

doCatClicked(View) lastly creates and displays the category names dialog box. It uses the android.app.AlertDialog class and its nested Builder type for this purpose, and it takes advantage of the following Builder methods:

- AlertDialog.Builder setSingleChoiceItems(CharSequence[] items, int checkedItem, DialogInterface.OnClickListener listener) displays a list of items (catNames) in the dialog box as the content along with radio button-style checkmarks to the right of these items, where the selected item's checkmark is checked. Furthermore it initially checks the item whose index is passed to checkedItem (curCat), and it registers a listener (oclCat) to be notified of selections.

- `AlertDialog.Builder setTitle(int titleId)` sets the dialog box's title to the string identified by the string resource ID passed to `titleId` (`R.string.categories`).
- `AlertDialog.Builder setNeutralButton(int textId, DialogInterface.OnClickListener listener)` installs the dialog box's neutral button (Close button). The button's text is identified by the string resource ID passed to `textId` (`R.string.btnClose`), and the listener that is invoked when this button is clicked is identified by `listener` (`oclClose`).
- `AlertDialog show()` causes `AlertDialog.Builder` to instantiate `AlertDialog` and to display the resulting dialog box.

The following `void doClrClicked(View view)` method responds to CLR button clicks:

```
public void doClrClicked(View view)
{
   reset();
}
```

`doClrClicked(View)` resets the display to "`0.`".

The following `void doConClicked(View view)` method responds to CON button clicks:

```
public void doConClicked(View view)
{
   choice = curCon;
   if (oclCon == null)
      oclCon = new DialogInterface.OnClickListener()
               {
                  @Override
                  public void onClick(DialogInterface dialog, int which)
                  {
                     choice = which;
                  }
               };
   if (oclConClose == null)
      oclConClose = new DialogInterface.OnClickListener()
                    {
                       @Override
                       public void onClick(DialogInterface dialog, int which)
                       {
                          curCon = choice;
                          updateConversionTitle();
                          reset();
                          btnPm.setEnabled(categories[curCat].
                                getConversion(curCon).
```

```
                                    canBeNegative());
                        }
                     };
   ListAdapter adapter;
   adapter = new ArrayAdapter<String>(Univerter.this,
                                      R.layout.list_row,
                                      categories[curCat].
                                      getConversionNames(Univerter.this));
   new AlertDialog.Builder(Univerter.this).
       setSingleChoiceItems(adapter, curCon, oclCon).
       setTitle(categories[curCat].getName(Univerter.this)).
       setNeutralButton(R.string.btnClose, oclConClose).
       show();
}
```

doConClicked(View) is very similar to doCatClicked(View) except that the focus is now on selecting a new current conversion. The interesting part of this method is the code that deals with android.widget.ListAdapter. This interface and its android.widget.ArrayAdapter<T> implementation class are used with AlertDialog.Builder's AlertDialog.Builder setSingleChoiceItems(ListAdapter adapter, int checkedItem, DialogInterface.OnClickListener listener) method to install a custom view (referenced by R.layout.list_row and stored in res/menu/univerter.xml) that presents conversion names in a smaller size, which looks nicer.

The ArrayAdapter(Context context, int textViewResourceId, T[] objects) constructor is called with the current context (represented by Univerter.this), the resource ID of a layout file that describes a single row in the list of conversion names (R.layout.list_row), and the array of conversion names to present (categories[curCat].getConversionNames(Univerter.this)). The resulting ListAdapter instance is passed to the setSingleChoiceItems(ListAdapter, int, DialogInterface.OnClickListener) method to connect the dialog box to the array of conversion names and the layout of these names.

The following void doCvtClicked(View view) method responds to CVT button clicks:

```
public void doCvtClicked(View view)
{
   try
   {
      double value = Double.parseDouble(buffer.length() == 0 ? "0" :
                                        buffer.toString());
      value = categories[curCat].getConversion(curCon).getConverter().
              convert(Univerter.this, value);
      if (Math.abs(value) > 1.0e+18)
         throw new NumberFormatException(getString(R.string.overflow));
```

```
      else
      if (value != 0.0 && Math.abs(value) < 1.0e-8)
         throw new NumberFormatException(getString(R.string.underflow));
      buffer.setLength(0);
      buffer.append(""+value);
      etDisplay.setText(String.format("%,.8f", value));
   }
   catch (IllegalArgumentException iae)
   {
      Toast t = Toast.makeText(Univerter.this, iae.getMessage(),
                               Toast.LENGTH_SHORT);
      t.setGravity(Gravity.CENTER_HORIZONTAL|
                   Gravity.CENTER_VERTICAL, 0, 0);
      t.show();
   }
   btnCvtClicked = true;
}
```

doCvtClicked(View) first parses the input value whose character representation is stored in buffer, obtains the appropriate converter for the current category and conversion within that category, and invokes the converter to perform the conversion.

If the conversion succeeds, doCvtClicked(View) tests the resulting value for overflow or underflow. The java.lang.NumberFormatException class is instantiated and thrown when overflow or underflow is detected. Assuming that all is well, buffer's content is replaced with a character representation of the value. This value is also formatted and presented on the display.

For temperature converters where the input temperature can be negative, an input value less than absolute zero will result in a thrown IllegalArgumentException instance. An exception handler addresses this possibility along with IllegalArgumentException's NumberFormatException subclass. With either exception, a toast describing the problem is created, centered over the activity screen, and shown for a brief duration.

Lastly, btnCvtClicked is set to true, which causes buffer to be emptied when the next digit button is clicked, so that the digit is not appended to buffer's current content.

The following void doDigitClicked(View view) method responds to digit button clicks:

```
public void doDigitClicked(View view)
{
   if (btnCvtClicked)
   {
      reset();
      btnCvtClicked = false;
```

```
   }
   buildNumber(((String) view.getTag()).charAt(0));
   if (buffer.length() == 0)
      etDisplay.setText("0.");
   else
      etDisplay.setText(buffer.toString()+
                        (buffer.indexOf(".")==-1?".":""));
}
```

doDigitClicked(View) first examines btnCvtClicked to learn whether or not the CVT button has previously been clicked. If so, reset() is called to empty buffer and clear the display.

The subsequent buildNumber(((String) view.getTag()).charAt(0)) call appends to buffer the clicked button's digit, which is identified via the view.getTag() method call, which returns the value of a Button element's tag attribute (presented later).

If the user initially clicks the 0 button, nothing is added to buffer because leading zeros are not supported. As a result, it is possible that buffer's length will be zero. In this case, the display is set to "0.". Otherwise, the display is set to buffer's contents.

A decimal point normally appears to the right of the number as it is being entered. However, when the number contains a decimal point, this decimal point to the right of the number should not be shown; hence, the test for a decimal point that is already in buffer.

The following void doDotClicked(View view) method responds to decimal point button clicks:

```
public void doDotClicked(View view)
{
   if (btnCvtClicked)
   {
      reset();
      btnCvtClicked = false;
   }
   buildNumber('.');
}
```

doDotClicked(View) is similar to doDigitClicked(View) in that it resets buffer when the CVT button was previously clicked. Regardless, the decimal point is appended to buffer's content, unless already present.

Finally, the following void doPmClicked(View view) method responds to +/- button clicks:

```
public void doPmClicked(View view)
{
   buildNumber('-');
   if (state == 1)
      etDisplay.setText(buffer.toString()+
                        (buffer.indexOf(".")==-1?".":""));
}
```

doPmClicked(View) adds a minus sign to or removes it from the front of buffer, and it then outputs buffer's contents, but only when state contains 1 because buffer is empty when state contains 0.

Exploring Univerter's Callback Methods

Following Univerter's click listener methods are four "on"-prefixed callback methods. These methods respond to activity life cycle or user interface events.

The following void onCreate(Bundle savedInstanceState) method is invoked when the activity is created, which happens whenever the app is started from the launcher or whenever the device orientation switches between portrait and landscape:

```
public void onCreate(Bundle savedInstanceState)
{
   super.onCreate(savedInstanceState);

   catNames = new String[categories.length];
   for (int i = 0; i < catNames.length; i++)
      catNames[i] = categories[i].getName(Univerter.this);

   if (savedInstanceState == null)
   {
      curCat = 0;
      curCon = 0;
      buffer = new StringBuilder();
      state = 0;
      nDigits = 0;
      isDecimal = false;
      btnCvtClicked = false;
   }
   else
   {
      curCat = savedInstanceState.getInt("curCat");
      curCon = savedInstanceState.getInt("curCon");
      buffer = new StringBuilder(savedInstanceState.getString("buffer"));
      state = savedInstanceState.getInt("state");
      nDigits = savedInstanceState.getInt("nDigits");
      isDecimal = savedInstanceState.getBoolean("isDecimal");
      btnCvtClicked = savedInstanceState.getBoolean("btnCvtClicked");
```

```
}

boolean isLeftIconSupported =
   requestWindowFeature(Window.FEATURE_LEFT_ICON);
setContentView(R.layout.main);
if (isLeftIconSupported)
   setFeatureDrawableResource(Window.FEATURE_LEFT_ICON,
                              R.drawable.ic_launcher);

updateConversionTitle();

etDisplay = (EditText) findViewById(R.id.display);

int[] btnDigitIds =
{
   R.id.btn7,
   R.id.btn8,
   R.id.btn9,
   R.id.btnClr,
   R.id.btn4,
   R.id.btn5,
   R.id.btn6,
   R.id.btnCat,
   R.id.btn1,
   R.id.btn2,
   R.id.btn3,
   R.id.btnCon,
   R.id.btn0,
   R.id.btnDot,
   R.id.btnPm,
   R.id.btnCvt
};
for (int i = 0; i < btnDigitIds.length; i++)
{
   Button btn = (Button) findViewById(btnDigitIds[i]);
   if (btnDigitIds[i] == R.id.btnPm)
   {
      btnPm = btn;
      btnPm.setEnabled(categories[curCat].getConversion(curCon).
                       canBeNegative());
   }
   btn.getBackground().
       setColorFilter(Color.GRAY, Mode.MULTIPLY);
}

helpText = getString(R.string.help);
int colorHelpHiliteText = getResources().
                          getColor(R.color.helpHiliteText)&0x00ffffff;
helpText = helpText.replaceAll("#helpHiliteText",
                               "#"+toHexString(colorHelpHiliteText, 6));
```

```
    int colorHelpText = getResources().getColor(R.color.helpText)&0x00ffffff;
    helpText = helpText.replaceAll("#helpText",
                                   "#"+toHexString(colorHelpText, 6));
    int colorLink = getResources().getColor(R.color.link)&0x00ffffff;
    helpText = helpText.replaceAll("#link",
                                   "#"+toHexString(colorLink, 6));
}
```

onCreate(Bundle) responds by invoking its superclass counterpart. It then creates an array of category names (catNames), which (as you previously discovered) is used by the doCatClicked(View) method when creating its dialog box of category names.

Next, onCreate(Bundle) tests its android.os.Bundle argument to determine whether this method was called because Univerter was started from the launcher, or because the device orientation changed. When started from the launcher, onCreate(Bundle) is passed a null argument and initializes certain fields to default values. However, when the orientation changes, this method is passed a nonnull Bundle object and initializes these fields from this object.

To make Univerter look more professional, an icon is added to this app's title bar on the left side, as follows:

1. Activity's boolean requestWindowFeature(int featureId) method is called to enable the extended window feature identified by the argument passed to featureId, which happens to be Window.FEATURE_LEFT_ICON. requestWindowFeature(int) returns true when this feature is supported and enabled.

2. After executing setContentView(R.layout.main) to inflate the activity's layout into its view hierarchy (this method must be executed at this point), onCreate(Bundle) conditionally executes (when requestWindowFeature(int) returns true) Activity's void setFeatureDrawableResource(int featureId, int resId) method with arguments Window.FEATURE_LEFT_ICON and R.drawable.ic_launcher (the resource ID of Univerter's app launcher icon) to install the icon.

The setContentView(R.layout.main) method call inflates the contents of the main.xml layout file for the current orientation, and it creates a view hierarchy that defines the activity's user interface from the resulting objects. The main.xml file stored in res/layout is chosen when the device has portrait orientation; the main.xml file stored in res/layout-land is chosen when the device has landscape orientation.

onCreate(Bundle) now invokes updateConversionTitle() to update either the view hierarchy (in portrait mode) or the title bar (in landscape mode) with the name of the conversion. It then inflates the <EditText> widget element (declared in the main.xml layout file) that defines the display so it can subsequently access this widget.

Moving on, onCreate(Bundle) inflates each button, saving a reference to the +/- button so that it can dynamically enable or disable this button as required, and it also shades the button a darker gray to improve contrast with the button's cyan-colored text.

To shade the button, onCreate(Bundle) first invokes Button's inherited (from View) Drawable getBackground() method to return an android.graphics.drawable.Drawable instance. It then invokes this instance's void setColorFilter(int color, PorterDuff.Mode mode) method with Color.GRAY and Mode.MULTIPLY arguments, to shade the button's background by multiplying the button's color by Color.GRAY.

Finally, onCreate(Bundle) obtains the HTML-based help text that will be displayed via its help dialog box, along with color resources for coloring highlighted text, regular text, and links. Because the text contains #helpHiliteText, #helpText, and #link placeholders for these colors, the java.lang.String class's String replaceAll(String regularExpression, String replacement) method, along with the private String toHexString(int i, int numNibbles) method (discussed later), are used to replace these placeholders with the values of these color resources.

The following boolean onCreateOptionsMenu(Menu menu) method is invoked when the user chooses to open the activity's options menu. (This occurs when the user selects the MENU button [when present] or the overflow icon [three vertical dots] on an Android 3.0 or higher device's action bar. The MENU button has been deprecated as of Android 3.0.)

```
public boolean onCreateOptionsMenu(Menu menu)
{
   MenuInflater inflater = getMenuInflater();
   inflater.inflate(R.menu.univerter, menu);
   return true;
}
```

onCreateOptionsMenu(Menu) responds by inflating the menu resource via the android.view.MenuInflater class's void inflate(int menuRes, Menu menu) method. The menu's resource ID (R.menu.univerter), and the android.view.Menu argument passed to onCreateOptionsMenu(Menu) (where inflated menu items are placed) are passed as arguments. onCreateOptionsMenu(Menu) returns true to show the menu.

The following boolean onOptionsItemSelected(MenuItem item) method is invoked when an item in the options menu is selected:

```
public boolean onOptionsItemSelected(MenuItem item)
{
   LayoutInflater inflater;

   switch (item.getItemId())
   {
      case R.id.menu_help:
           inflater = (LayoutInflater) this.
                      getSystemService(Context.LAYOUT_INFLATER_SERVICE);
           WebView wv = (WebView) inflater.inflate(R.layout.help, null);
           wv.setBackgroundColor(Color.TRANSPARENT);
           wv.loadData(helpText, "text/html", "utf-8");
           new AlertDialog.Builder(Univerter.this).
               setView(wv).
               setNeutralButton(R.string.btnClose, null).
               show();
           return true;

      case R.id.menu_info:
           inflater = (LayoutInflater) this.
                      getSystemService(Context.LAYOUT_INFLATER_SERVICE);
           View view = inflater.inflate(R.layout.info, null);
           TextView tv;
           tv = (TextView) ((ViewGroup) view).findViewById(R.id.text1);
           tv.setText(Html.fromHtml(getString(R.string.info1)));
           tv = (TextView) ((ViewGroup) view).findViewById(R.id.text2);
           tv.setText(R.string.info2);
           tv = (TextView) ((ViewGroup) view).findViewById(R.id.text3);
           tv.setText(Html.fromHtml(getString(R.string.info3)));
           tv.setMovementMethod(LinkMovementMethod.getInstance());
           tv = (TextView) ((ViewGroup) view).findViewById(R.id.text4);
           tv.setText(Html.fromHtml(getString(R.string.info4)));
           tv.setMovementMethod(LinkMovementMethod.getInstance());
           ImageView iv;
           iv = (ImageView) ((ViewGroup) view).findViewById(R.id.image);
           iv.setImageResource(R.drawable.ic_launcher);
           new AlertDialog.Builder(Univerter.this).
               setView(view).
               setNeutralButton(R.string.btnClose, null).
               show();
           return true;

      default:
           return super.onOptionsItemSelected(item);
   }
}
```

onOptionsItemSelected(MenuItem) responds by invoking its android.view.MenuItem argument's int getItemId() method to determine which menu item was selected. This method returns the menu item's resource ID (the menu items are declared in the res/menu/univerter.xml file): R.id.menu_help or R.id.menu_info. A switch statement takes this value and executes the appropriate case. A default case that passes the MenuItem argument to the superclass version of onOptionsItemSelected(MenuItem) is present for good form.

Each menu item is associated with a layout resource describing the contents of a dialog box. This resource is stored in the res/layout/help.xml file for the help menu item, and the res/layout/info.xml file for the info menu item. Before either layout resource can be used, it must be inflated.

Inflation is handled via Android's layout service, which inflates the XML to a hierarchy of views. The service is obtained by invoking Context's Object getSystemService(String name) method with a Context.LAYOUT_INFLATER_SERVICE argument. This method returns a generic java.lang.Object, which is cast to android.view.LayoutInflater.

LayoutInflater declares a View inflate(int resource, ViewGroup root) method for performing the inflation. The argument passed to resource is the resource ID of the XML to be inflated (R.layout.help or R.layout.info). The argument passed to root is an optional view that is the parent of the inflated view hierarchy. Passing null means that the root element of the inflated XML serves as the parent.

The parent view is returned from inflate(int, viewGroup). For the help menu, the returned view is an android.webkit.WebView instance that displays web pages.

WebView declares a void setBackgroundColor(int color) method that sets this view's background color to Color.TRANSPARENT. This constant is passed to ensure that the underlying dialog background color shows through.

WebView also declares a void loadData(String data, String mimeType, String encoding) method for loading the specified data (in helpText) with the specified mimeType (text/html) and encoding (UTF-8) into the web view. This method is called to load the HTML data previously stored in helpText by the onCreate(Bundle) method.

For the info menu, the returned view is an android.widget.RelativeLayout instance that lays out its contained views according to how they relate to each other positionally.

The RelativeLayout instance contains four TextView instances for presenting four lines of text, as well as an android.widget.ImageView instance for presenting an image. Each of the third and fourth TextView instances displays a link, which is specified in the string resource via an HTML anchor element.

The anchor element must be converted to a string for display. This conversion is provided by the android.text.Html class's Spanned fromHtml(String source) method, which returns displayable styled text as an android.text.Spanned instance. This instance is passed to TextView's void setText(CharSequence text) method (Spanned extends java.lang.CharSequence).

Although the link is displayed with an underline, it is not possible to click the link until a movement method that traverses links is attached. This method is provided by invoking TextView's void setMovementMethod(MovementMethod movement) method with an android.text.method.MovementMethod argument set to an instance of the android.text.method.LinkMovementMethod class (obtained by calling this class's MovementMethod getInstance() method).

The ImageView class declares a void setImageResource(int resId) method that is used to set this widget's content to the resource identified by resId. In this case, the resource is the icon that appears on the app launcher screen.

After initializing its layout, each of the help and info switch statement cases creates an alert dialog box builder, and it sets the dialog box content to the inflated and initialized view by calling AlertDialog.Builder's AlertDialog.Builder setView(View view) method. The dialog box is then created and shown with its content.

Finally, the following void onSaveInstanceState(Bundle outState) method is invoked before the activity is killed (which happens when the orientation changes) to save its state:

```
public void onSaveInstanceState(Bundle outState)
{
   super.onSaveInstanceState(outState);
   outState.putInt("curCat", curCat);
   outState.putInt("curCon", curCon);
   outState.putString("buffer", buffer.toString());
   outState.putInt("state", state);
   outState.putInt("nDigits", nDigits);
   outState.putBoolean("isDecimal", isDecimal);
   outState.putBoolean("btnCvtClicked", btnCvtClicked);
}
```

onSaveInstanceState(Bundle outState) responds by invoking its superclass counterpart to save widget state (such as the text that appears on the etDisplay-referenced edittext widget). It then invokes various Bundle methods to save Univerter's app state. This state is restored in onCreate(Bundle) when the activity is recreated.

Exploring Univerter's Helper Methods

Following Univerter's callback methods are four helper methods that support the other methods.

The following void buildNumber(char ch) method is invoked when a digit button, the decimal point button, or the +/- button is clicked:

```
private void buildNumber(char ch)
{
   switch (state)
   {
      case 0: if (ch >= '1' && ch <= '9')
              {
                 buffer.append(ch);
                 nDigits = 1;
                 state = 1;
              }
              else
              if (ch == '.')
              {
                 isDecimal = true;
                 buffer.append("0.");
                 nDigits = 1;
                 state = 1;
              }
              break;

      case 1: if (ch >= '0' && ch <= '9')
              {
                 if (nDigits != 10)
                 {
                    buffer.append(ch);
                    nDigits++;
                 }
              }
              else
              if (ch == '.')
              {
                 if (isDecimal)
                    break;
                 isDecimal = true;
                 buffer.append('.');
              }
              else
              if (categories[curCat].getConversion(curCon).canBeNegative() &&
```

```
                 ch == '-')
            {
               if (buffer.charAt(0) == '-')
                  buffer.deleteCharAt(0);
               else
                  buffer.insert(0, '-');
            }
   }
}
```

buildNumber(char) examines state and it proceeds based on this field's value (0 or 1).

State 0 is the initial state of this state machine. Only digit buttons 1 through 9 or the decimal point button are processed in this state, which is set to 1 following processing. A digit button click results in the digit (stored in parameter ch) being stored in buffer; a decimal point button click results in "0." being stored in buffer.

State 1 is the final state of this state machine. Digit buttons 0 through 9, the decimal point button, and the +/- button are processed in this state:

- Digit button clicks result in the digits being stored in buffer until the number of entered digits surpasses 10.
- A decimal point button click results in a period being stored in buffer unless a period has been stored already.
- A +/- button click results in a test for negative values being supported for the current conversion. When negative values are supported, the first character in buffer is set to a minus sign. However, when a minus sign is present, this character is removed.

The following void reset() method is invoked when numeric entry must be reset (the buffer is emptied) and the display set to "0.":

```
private void reset()
{
   buffer.setLength(0);
   state = 0;
   nDigits = 0;
   isDecimal = false;
   etDisplay.setText("0.");
}
```

The following String toHexString(int i, int numNibbles) method is invoked in onCreate(Bundle) when replacing placeholder IDs with hexadecimal-based six-digit values in the text assigned to helpText:

```
private String toHexString(int i, int numNibbles)
{
   StringBuilder sb = new StringBuilder(Integer.toHexString(i));
   if (sb.length() > numNibbles)
      return null; // cannot fit result into numNibbles columns

   int numLeadingZeros = numNibbles-sb.length();
   for (int j = 0; j < numLeadingZeros; j++)
      sb.insert(0, '0');
   return sb.toString();
}
```

`toString(int, int)` is called with the number to convert to a hexadecimal string and the number of *nibbles* (four-bit values, which are also known as hex digits) to be stored in the string.

It first calls the `java.lang.Integer` class's `static String toHexString(int i)` method to perform the actual conversion, and it stores the result in a `java.lang.StringBuilder` object to avoid the unnecessary creation of `String` objects.

Because `toHexString(int)` does not store leading zeros, the number of leading zeros is calculated and subsequently prepended to the string builder, but only after verifying that the number of nibbles stored in the string builder does not exceed the desired number of nibbles (which results in a `null` return value).

Lastly, the string builder's content is converted to a string, which is returned.

Finally, the following `void updateConversionTitle()` method is invoked when the conversion name needs to be updated, at startup or following a selection via a CAT or CON button click:

```
private void updateConversionTitle()
{
   TextView tv = (TextView) findViewById(R.id.conversion1);
   if (tv != null)
   {
      String s = categories[curCat].getConversion(curCon).
                 getName(Univerter.this);
      tv.setText(s.substring(0, s.indexOf(">")-1));
      tv = (TextView) findViewById(R.id.conversion2);
      tv.setText(s.substring(s.indexOf(">")+2));
   }
   else
      setTitle(getString(R.string.app_name)+": "+
               categories[curCat].getConversion(curCon).
               getName(Univerter.this));
}
```

updateConversionTitle() first determines whether it is being called in portrait mode or landscape mode. In portrait mode, main.xml contains <TextView> elements whose resource IDs are R.id.conversion1 and R.id.conversion2. These elements are populated with the source and destination of the conversion name.

In landscape mode, the <TextView> elements are not present in main.xml because there is not enough vertical room to show them; otherwise, content would be cut off. Instead, the conversion is presented with the app name on the Univerter activity title bar, via a call to Activity's void setTitle(CharSequence title) method.

Exploring the Resource Files

Univerter's resources are spread across 14 files:

res/drawable/gradientbg.xml

res/drawable-hdpi/ic_launcher.png

res/drawable-ldpi/ic_launcher.png

res/drawable-mdpi/ic_launcher.png

res/drawable-xhdpi/ic_launcher.png

res/layout/help.xml

res/layout/info.xml

res/layout/list_row.xml

res/layout/main.xml

res/layout-land/main.xml

res/menu/univerter.xml

res/values/colors.xml

res/values/strings.xml

res/values/styles.xml

Exploring the App Launcher Icon Drawable Resources

When the Univerter project is created, android places a default ic_launcher.png file (containing an image of a greenish robot) in the project's res/drawable-hdpi, res/drawable-ldpi, res/drawable-mdpi, and res/drawable-xhdpi directories. Each file presents the same image but at a different resolution:

- The file in drawable-hdpi presents a 72-pixel-by-72-pixel image for a high-density (240 dots-per-inch [dpi]) screen.
- The file in drawable-ldpi presents a 36-pixel-by-36-pixel image for a low-density (120 dpi) screen.
- The file in drawable-mdpi presents a 48-pixel-by-48-pixel image for a medium-density (160 dpi) screen.
- The file in drawable-xhdpi presents a 96-pixel-by-96-pixel image for an extra-high-density (320 dpi) screen.

Although the default launcher icon could have been kept, something more professional that shows off this app was desired. Instead of creating this icon via Android Asset Studio (http://android-ui-utils.googlecode.com/hg/asset-studio/dist/index.html), an appropriate icon was found elsewhere.

Univerter's icon was obtained from Icon Archive (www.iconarchive.com/show/or-icons-by-iconleak/justice-balance-icon.html), and is courtesy of Icon Leak (http://iconleak.com/). This icon presents a golden balance scale that is appropriate to unit conversion, and it is shown in Figure D-1.

Figure D-1. *Univerter's app launcher icon is presented in four sizes.*

To learn more about launcher and other icons, check out Google's "Launcher Icons" (http://developer.android.com/guide/practices/ui_guidelines/icon_design_launcher.html) and "Iconography" (http://developer.android.com/design/style/iconography.html) pages.

Exploring the Background Drawable Resource

Univerter presents a gradient-colored background (from a darker shade of blue at the top to a lighter shade of blue at the bottom) to make this activity look more interesting. It achieves this background by defining it as a *shape drawable resource*, which is a generic shape described in XML. Check out Listing D-5.

Listing D-5. *Presenting a Gradient-Colored Background for the* `Univerter` *Activity*

```
<?xml version="1.0" encoding="utf-8"?>
<shape xmlns:android="http://schemas.android.com/apk/res/android">
  <gradient android:angle="270"
            android:endColor="@color/bgEnd"
            android:startColor="@color/bgStart"/>
</shape>
```

Listing D-5 presents the contents of res/drawable/gradientbg.xml. Following the standard XML prolog is a <shape> element, which lets you specify a shape via this element's shape attribute. When shape is absent, this element defaults to a rectangle shape.

A <gradient> element is nested inside <shape> to describe the shape's color in terms of a gradient. The gradient is described via the values assigned to its startColor and endColor attributes (which happen to be references to bgStart and bgEnd color resources in the res/values/colors.xml file). The angle attribute specifies the direction that the gradient sweeps across the rectangle. When this attribute is absent, the angle defaults to 0 degrees.

Check out http://developer.android.com/guide/topics/resources/drawable-resource.html#Shape for more information on shape drawable resources.

Exploring the Main Layout Resource

Univerter's screen is described by a layout resource stored in the res/layout/main.xml (portrait orientation) file or the res/layout-land/main.xml (landscape orientation) file. Either file specifies the screen's widgets and their relationships to each other. Listing D-6 shows you the contents of res/layout/main.xml.

Listing D-6. *Presenting the Layout of the* `Univerter` *Activity in Portrait Orientation*

```
<?xml version="1.0" encoding="utf-8"?>
<LinearLayout xmlns:android="http://schemas.android.com/apk/res/android"
              android:background="@drawable/gradientbg"
              android:gravity="center"
              android:layout_height="match_parent"
              android:layout_width="match_parent"
              android:orientation="vertical"
              android:padding="10dp">
  <TextView android:id="@+id/conversion1"
            android:layout_height="wrap_content"
            android:layout_width="wrap_content"
            android:textColor="@color/conversionText"
```

```
          android:textSize="15sp"/>
<TextView android:layout_height="wrap_content"
          android:layout_width="wrap_content"
          android:text=">"
          android:textColor="@color/conversionText"
          android:textSize="15sp"/>
<TextView android:id="@+id/conversion2"
          android:layout_height="wrap_content"
          android:layout_width="wrap_content"
          android:paddingBottom="30dp"
          android:textColor="@color/conversionText"
          android:textSize="15sp"/>
<EditText android:id="@+id/display"
          android:focusable="false"
          android:gravity="right|center_vertical"
          android:layout_height="wrap_content"
          android:layout_width="match_parent"
          android:text="0."
          android:textColor="@color/displayText"
          android:textSize = "15sp"/>
<LinearLayout android:layout_height="wrap_content"
              android:layout_width="match_parent">
  <Button android:id="@+id/btn7"
          android:layout_height="wrap_content"
          android:layout_weight="1"
          android:layout_width="match_parent"
          android:onClick="doDigitClicked"
          android:tag="7"
          android:text="@string/btn7"
          android:textColor="@color/keyText"
          android:textSize = "15sp"/>
  <Button android:id="@+id/btn8"
          android:layout_height="wrap_content"
          android:layout_weight="1"
          android:layout_width="match_parent"
          android:onClick="doDigitClicked"
          android:tag="8"
          android:text="@string/btn8"
          android:textColor="@color/keyText"
          android:textSize = "15sp"/>
  <Button android:id="@+id/btn9"
          android:layout_height="wrap_content"
          android:layout_weight="1"
          android:layout_width="match_parent"
          android:onClick="doDigitClicked"
          android:tag="9"
          android:text="@string/btn9"
          android:textColor="@color/keyText"
          android:textSize = "15sp"/>
  <Button android:id="@+id/btnClr"
```

```
            android:layout_height="wrap_content"
            android:layout_weight="1"
            android:layout_width="match_parent"
            android:onClick="doClrClicked"
            android:text="@string/btnClr"
            android:textColor="@color/keyText"
            android:textSize = "15sp"/>
</LinearLayout>
<LinearLayout android:layout_height="wrap_content"
              android:layout_width="match_parent">
  <Button android:id="@+id/btn4"
            android:layout_height="wrap_content"
            android:layout_weight="1"
            android:layout_width="match_parent"
            android:onClick="doDigitClicked"
            android:tag="4"
            android:text="@string/btn4"
            android:textColor="@color/keyText"
            android:textSize = "15sp"/>
  <Button android:id="@+id/btn5"
            android:layout_height="wrap_content"
            android:layout_weight="1"
            android:layout_width="match_parent"
            android:onClick="doDigitClicked"
            android:tag="5"
            android:text="@string/btn5"
            android:textColor="@color/keyText"
            android:textSize = "15sp"/>
  <Button android:id="@+id/btn6"
            android:layout_height="wrap_content"
            android:layout_weight="1"
            android:layout_width="match_parent"
            android:onClick="doDigitClicked"
            android:tag="6"
            android:text="@string/btn6"
            android:textColor="@color/keyText"
            android:textSize = "15sp"/>
  <Button android:id="@+id/btnCat"
            android:layout_height="wrap_content"
            android:layout_weight="1"
            android:layout_width="match_parent"
            android:onClick="doCatClicked"
            android:text="@string/btnCat"
            android:textColor="@color/keyText"
            android:textSize = "15sp"/>
</LinearLayout>
<LinearLayout android:layout_height="wrap_content"
              android:layout_width="match_parent">
  <Button android:id="@+id/btn1"
            android:layout_height="wrap_content"
```

```
            android:layout_weight="1"
            android:layout_width="match_parent"
            android:onClick="doDigitClicked"
            android:tag="1"
            android:text="@string/btn1"
            android:textColor="@color/keyText"
            android:textSize = "15sp"/>
    <Button android:id="@+id/btn2"
            android:layout_height="wrap_content"
            android:layout_weight="1"
            android:layout_width="match_parent"
            android:onClick="doDigitClicked"
            android:tag="2"
            android:text="@string/btn2"
            android:textColor="@color/keyText"
            android:textSize = "15sp"/>
    <Button android:id="@+id/btn3"
            android:layout_height="wrap_content"
            android:layout_weight="1"
            android:layout_width="match_parent"
            android:onClick="doDigitClicked"
            android:tag="3"
            android:text="@string/btn3"
            android:textColor="@color/keyText"
            android:textSize = "15sp"/>
    <Button android:id="@+id/btnCon"
            android:layout_height="wrap_content"
            android:layout_weight="1"
            android:layout_width="match_parent"
            android:onClick="doConClicked"
            android:text="@string/btnCon"
            android:textColor="@color/keyText"
            android:textSize = "15sp"/>
</LinearLayout>
<LinearLayout android:layout_height="wrap_content"
              android:layout_width="match_parent">
    <Button android:id="@+id/btn0"
            android:layout_height="wrap_content"
            android:layout_weight="1"
            android:layout_width="match_parent"
            android:onClick="doDigitClicked"
            android:tag="0"
            android:text="@string/btn0"
            android:textColor="@color/keyText"
            android:textSize = "15sp"/>
    <Button android:id="@+id/btnDot"
            android:layout_height="wrap_content"
            android:layout_weight="1"
            android:layout_width="match_parent"
            android:onClick="doDotClicked"
```

```
            android:text="@string/btnDot"
            android:textColor="@color/keyText"
            android:textSize = "15sp"/>
    <Button android:id="@+id/btnPm"
            android:layout_height="wrap_content"
            android:layout_weight="1"
            android:layout_width="match_parent"
            android:onClick="doPmClicked"
            android:text="@string/btnPm"
            android:textColor="@color/keyText"
            android:textSize = "15sp"/>
    <Button android:id="@+id/btnCvt"
            android:layout_height="wrap_content"
            android:layout_weight="1"
            android:layout_width="match_parent"
            android:onClick="doCvtClicked"
            android:text="@string/btnCvt"
            android:textColor="@color/keyText"
            android:textSize = "15sp"/>
  </LinearLayout>
</LinearLayout>
```

Listing D-6 follows the XML prolog with a `<LinearLayout>` element that specifies the activity's layout. This element controls the layout via the following attributes:

- `android:background="@drawable/gradientbg"` specifies the linear layout's background to be the rectangular gradient defined in `gradientbg.xml`.
- `android:gravity="center"` indicates that the linear layout's children are to be centered horizontally and vertically.
- `android:layout_height="match_parent"` indicates that the linear layout should match the width of its parent container (the activity).
- `android:layout_width="match_parent"` indicates that the linear layout should match the height of its parent container, which happens to be the activity screen window.
- `android:orientation="vertical"` indicates that the linear layout's children should be arranged in a vertical column. The default orientation is horizontal.
- `android:padding="10dp"` specifies a border area around the linear layout's children of 10 device-independent pixels.

Nested with `<LinearLayout>` are three `<TextView>` elements, followed by an `<EditText>` element, followed by four `<LinearLayout>` elements.

The <TextView> elements present the source of a conversion (such as Celsius), the > sign that is shorthand for "becomes", and the destination of the conversion (such as Fahrenheit). The first and third of these elements are identified via the values of their `android:id` attributes: `"@+id/conversion1"` (referenced in code as `R.id.conversion1`) and `"@+id/conversion2"` (referenced in code as `R.id.conversion2`).

Each of these elements also specifies the following attributes:

- `android:layout_height="wrap_content"` indicates that the <TextView> element should occupy only enough vertical space to present its content. If set to `fill_parent` or `match_parent`, the element would occupy all remaining vertical space.
- `android:layout_width="wrap_content"` indicates that the <TextView> element should occupy only enough horizontal space to present its content. If set to `fill_parent` or `match_parent`, the element would occupy all horizontal space and could not be centered horizontally.
- `android:textColor="@color/conversionText"` identifies the `conversionText` color resource in the `res/values/colors.xml` file as specifying the color of this widget's text.
- `android:textSize="15sp"` specifies the text size as 15 scale-independent pixels. Refer to Chapter 1 for a definition of this term.

The <EditText> element presents the widget for displaying input and conversion results. It is identified via its `android:id="@+id/display"` attribute (referenced in code as `R.id.display`). Furthermore, it presents the following attributes in addition to attributes that are similar to their <TextView> counterparts:

- `android:focusable="false"` indicates that this widget cannot receive focus. If it could receive focus, the user would be able to enter arbitrary characters into the widget, which would not be desirable. A related attribute that could be specified is `android:editable="false"` to prevent entry. However, this attribute is not needed when the widget is not focusable.
- `android:gravity="right|center_vertical"` indicates that this widget's text should appear on the right and be centered vertically. If not specified, the widget's text would appear on the left and be slightly off center vertically.

- android:layout_width="match_parent" indicates that this widget should match its linear layout parent in terms of width (less padding). If set to "wrap_content", this widget would shrink to wrap its text and not look like a calculator display.
- android:text="0." specifies this widget's initial text. You might want to replace the value with a string resource reference (such as android:text="@string/zerodisplay"). However, doing so is probably unnecessary.

Following <EditText> are four <LinearLayout> elements. Each <LinearLayout> element presents its content in a horizontal row and declares android:layout_height="wrap_content" and android:layout_width="match_parent" attributes. The former attribute indicates that the contained content should occupy only enough vertical space to present its content and not occupy all remaining vertical space. The latter attribute indicates that contained content should occupy all horizontal space (less padding).

Nested within each <LinearLayout> element are four <Button> elements. Each <Button> element specifies attributes that are similar to those previously shown, except for the following three attributes:

- android:layout_weight="1" indicates that the button wants to occupy as much of the remaining horizontal space as it can. Because all four buttons in a linear layout specify this attribute, each button has the same horizontal width.
- android:onClick="doDigitClicked" identifies the click handler method that will be called when the button is clicked. In this case, doDigitClicked(View) is clicked.
- android:tag="7" identifies the button by name in a locale-independent fashion. This value is independent of whatever text is assigned to the button, and the value is returned by calling the getTag() method on the View instance passed to doDigitClicked(View), as demonstrated earlier.

Except for the absence of the three <TextView> elements, the main.xml file located in res/layout-land is identical to Listing D-6.

Exploring the List Row Layout Resource

Figures 1-19 and 1-20 in Chapter 1 show the category names and conversion names dialog boxes. They have a similar appearance except for the conversion name text having a smaller size, which arguably looks better when dealing with lengthy conversion names. Listing D-7 shows the layout that achieves this smaller text.

Listing D-7. *Presenting the Layout of a Single Row in the Conversion Names Dialog Box*

```
<?xml version="1.0" encoding="utf-8"?>
<CheckedTextView xmlns:android="http://schemas.android.com/apk/res/android"
    android:checkMark="@android:drawable/btn_radio"
    android:gravity="center_vertical"
    android:layout_height="wrap_content"
    android:layout_width="match_parent"
    android:minHeight="?android:attr/listPreferredItemHeight"
    android:paddingLeft="12dp"
    android:paddingRight="7dp"
    android:textAppearance="?android:attr/textAppearanceSmall"
    android:textColor="?android:attr/textColorPrimaryInverseDisableOnly"/>
```

Listing D-7 presents the contents of `res/layout/list_row.xml`, which was previously mentioned in the context of the `doConClicked(View)` method. These contents are based on the `<CheckedTextView>` element, which is derived from the `<TextView>` element and which displays checkmarks along with text.

The `android:checkMark="@android:drawable/btn_radio"` attribute specifies the style of the checkmark that appears to the right of the text. This style is provided by the radio button platform resource (see Chapter 1), which is an Android resource that can be accessed in code as `android.R.drawable.btn_radio`.

The `android:gravity="center_vertical"` attribute vertically centers the text and radio button-style checkmark.

The `android:minHeight="?android:attr/listPreferredItemHeight"` attribute specifies a list row's minimum height. It references the value of the `android.R.attr.listPreferredItemHeight`-identified resource for the current theme.

> **NOTE:** Unlike the @ symbol, which references a resource value defined in another project resource file (such as `res/values/strings.xml`) or a platform resource (such as `android.R.drawable.btn_radio`), the ? symbol references a resource value in the current *theme* (a style applied to an entire app or activity rather than an individual view).

The `android:paddingLeft="12dp"` and `android:paddingRight="7dp"` attributes specify the padding to the left of the text (12 device-independent pixels) and to the right of the round checkmark (7 device-independent pixels), respectively.

The android:textAppearance="?android:attr/textAppearanceSmall" attribute specifies the text appearance in terms of size. It references the value of the android.R.attr.textAppearanceSmall-identified resource for the current theme.

Finally, the android:textColor="?android:attr/textColorPrimaryInverseDisableOnly" attribute specifies the color of the text. It references the value of the android.R.attr.textColorPrimaryInverseDisableOnly resource for the current theme.

> **NOTE:** Referencing theme resources lets the conversion names list maintain a consistent appearance with the category names list whenever Univerter's theme is changed.

Exploring the Options Menu Resource

Univerter presents an options menu consisting of help and info menu items. The organization of this menu is described in Listing D-8.

Listing D-8. *Presenting the Organization of the Options Menu*

```
<?xml version="1.0" encoding="utf-8"?>
<menu xmlns:android="http://schemas.android.com/apk/res/android">
  <item android:id="@+id/menu_help"
        android:icon="@android:drawable/ic_menu_help"
        android:title="@string/menu_help"/>
  <item android:id="@+id/menu_info"
        android:icon="@android:drawable/ic_menu_info_details"
        android:title="@string/menu_info"/>
</menu>
```

Listing D-8 presents the contents of res/menu/univerter.xml, which describes a menu resource. Nested within the <menu> element is a pair of <item> elements that describe the help and info menu items.

Each <item> element identifies itself via android:id so that it can be accessed from Univerter.java (via R.id.menu_help or R.id.menu_info). Furthermore, it references a platform icon resource via android:icon (see android.R.drawable.ic_menu_help and android.R.drawable.ic_menu_info_details) and a suitable title via android:title.

Exploring the Help Dialog Box Layout Resource

Clicking the help menu item results in a dialog box whose contents consist of the view hierarchy described by Listing D-9.

Listing D-9. *Presenting the Layout of the Help Dialog Box*

```
<?xml version="1.0" encoding="utf-8"?>
<WebView xmlns:android="http://schemas.android.com/apk/res/android"
         android:id="@+id/helpText"
         android:layout_height="match_parent"
         android:layout_width="match_parent"/>
```

Listing D-9 presents the contents of `res/layout/help.xml`, which describe a `<WebView>` element that fills out its dialog box parent. (The same effect could be achieved by assigning `"wrap_content"` to `layout_height` and `layout_width`.)

Exploring the Info Dialog Box Layout Resource

Clicking the info menu item results in a dialog box whose contents consist of the view hierarchy described by Listing D-10.

Listing D-10. *Presenting the Layout of the Info Dialog Box*

```
<?xml version="1.0" encoding="utf-8"?>
<RelativeLayout xmlns:android="http://schemas.android.com/apk/res/android"
                android:gravity="center_horizontal"
                android:layout_height="match_parent"
                android:layout_width="match_parent"
                android:padding="10dp">
  <ImageView android:id="@+id/image"
             android:layout_centerVertical="true"
             android:layout_height="wrap_content"
             android:layout_marginRight="10dp"
             android:layout_width="wrap_content"/>
  <LinearLayout android:layout_height="wrap_content"
                android:layout_width="wrap_content"
                android:layout_toRightOf="@+id/image"
                android:orientation="vertical">
    <TextView android:id="@+id/text1"
              android:gravity="center"
              android:layout_height="wrap_content"
              android:layout_width="match_parent"
              android:textColor="@color/infoText"/>
    <TextView android:id="@+id/text2"
              android:gravity="center"
              android:layout_height="wrap_content"
```

```
              android:layout_width="match_parent"
              android:textColor="@color/infoText"/>
    <TextView android:id="@+id/text3"
              android:gravity="center"
              android:layout_height="wrap_content"
              android:layout_width="match_parent"
              android:textColor="@color/infoText"
              android:textColorLink="@color/link"/>
    <TextView android:id="@+id/text4"
              android:gravity="center"
              android:layout_height="wrap_content"
              android:layout_width="match_parent"
              android:textColor="@color/infoText"
              android:textColorLink="@color/link"/>
  </LinearLayout>
</RelativeLayout>
```

Listing D-10 presents the contents of `res/layout/info.xml`. Unlike `main.xml`, which nests its contents in a `<LinearLayout>` element, `info.xml` nests its contents in a `<RelativeLayout>` element.

`<RelativeLayout>` lets you organize child views in relative positions. The position of each view can be specified as being relative to sibling elements (such as to the left of or below another view) or in positions relative to the parent `<RelativeLayout>` area (such as aligned to the bottom, left of center).

`<RelativeLayout>` specifies an `android:gravity="center_horizontal"` attribute to ensure that its content is centered horizontally. It specifies an `android:padding="10dp"` attribute to create an empty border of 10 device-independent pixels around the content.

The content is described by an `<ImageView>` element and a `<LinearLayout>` element that nests four `<TextView>` elements.

The `<ImageView>` element describes an image that is specified in code, specifies an `android:layout_centerVertical="true"` element to vertically center the image, and specifies an `android:layout_marginRight="10dp"` attribute to leave a margin of 10 device-independent pixels to the right of the image (to separate the image from the text).

The `<LinearLayout>` element specifies an `android:layout_toRightOf="@+id/image"` attribute to ensure that the nested `<TextView>` elements appear to the right of the image.

Each `<TextView>` element specifies an `android:gravity="center"` attribute to center the text within the element's space (provided by the parent `<LinearLayout>` element).

Exploring the Color Resources

Univerter.java and various resource files reference color resources declared in res/values/colors.xml. Listing D-11 presents these color resources.

Listing D-11. *Presenting Univerter's Colors*

```
<?xml version="1.0" encoding="utf-8"?>
<resources>
  <color name="bgEnd">#168fc7</color>
  <color name="bgStart">#000080</color>
  <color name="conversionText">#00ffff</color>
  <color name="displayText">#000000</color>
  <color name="helpHiliteText">#eeee00</color>
  <color name="helpText">#ffffff</color>
  <color name="infoText">#ffffff</color>
  <color name="keyText">#00ffff</color>
  <color name="link">#00ffff</color>
</resources>
```

Color resources are described by <color> elements nested within a <resources> element. Each <color> tag identifies a resource via its name attribute. Sandwiched between the <color> and </color> tags is the color value.

Exploring the String Resources

Univerter.java and various resource files reference string resources declared in res/values/strings.xml. Listing D-12 presents some of these string resources.

Listing D-12. *Presenting Univerter's Strings*

```
<?xml version="1.0" encoding="utf-8"?>
<resources>
  <string name="app_name">Univerter</string>

  <string name="btn0">0</string>
  <string name="btn1">1</string>
  <string name="btn2">2</string>
  <string name="btn3">3</string>
  <string name="btn4">4</string>
  <string name="btn5">5</string>
  <string name="btn6">6</string>
  <string name="btn7">7</string>
  <string name="btn8">8</string>
  <string name="btn9">9</string>
  <string name="btnCat">CAT</string>
  <string name="btnClose">Close</string>
```

```
  <string name="btnClr">CLR</string>
  <string name="btnCon">CON</string>
  <string name="btnCvt">CVT</string>
  <string name="btnDot">.</string>
  <string name="btnPm">+/-</string>

  <string name="cat_angle">ANGLE</string>
  <string name="cat_angle_circles_to_deg">CIRCLES > DEGREES</string>
...
  <string name="menu_help">Help</string>
  <string name="menu_info">Info</string>
  <string name="overflow">Overflow</string>
  <string name="underflow">Underflow</string>
</resources>
```

String resources are described by <string> elements nested within a <resources> element. Each <string> tag identifies a resource via its name attribute. Sandwiched between the <string> and </string> tags is the color value.

Some of these resources embed HTML text. Embedding is accomplished by sandwiching this text between the standard XML ![CDATA[prefix and corresponding]]> suffix, as demonstrated below (split across two lines for readability):

```
<string name="info1"><![CDATA[<html><strong>Univerter (Units Converter)
                     1.0</strong></html>]]></string>
```

Exploring the Style Resources

Previously in this appendix, you learned that Univerter displays a conversion name on the title bar when this activity has landscape orientation. Because some conversion names are long enough that they would be cut off on the right side, the size of the text on the title bar has been reduced by using a theme. Listing D-13 presents this theme.

Listing D-13. *Presenting Univerter's Theme*

```
<?xml version="1.0" encoding="utf-8"?>
<resources>
  <style name="CustomTheme" parent="android:Theme.Black">
    <item name="android:windowTitleStyle">@style/CustomWindowTitle</item>
  </style>

  <style name="CustomWindowTitle">
    <item name="android:shadowColor">#BB000000</item>
    <item name="android:shadowRadius">2.75</item>
    <item name="android:singleLine">true</item>
```

```
    <item name="android:textAppearance">@style/CustomTAWindowTitle</item>
  </style>

  <style name="CustomTAWindowTitle" parent="android:TextAppearance.WindowTitle">
    <item name="android:textSize">10sp</item>
  </style>
</resources>
```

Listing D-13 presents the content of `res/values/styles.xml`. This resource file has a similar structure to `colors.xml` and `strings.xml` in that a sequence of resources is nested between `<resources>` and `</resources>` tags. However, each resource is described by a `<style>` element.

The first `<style>` element introduces a style named `CustomTheme`. This style inherits style properties from the standard `android:Theme.Black` theme (which is a sequence of styles applied to an activity or an app), and it overrides this theme's `android:windowTitleStyle` property (via the nested `<item>` element) to refer to `CustomWindowTitle`.

> **NOTE:** Properties are inherited from `android:Theme.Black` instead of `android:Theme` to ensure that the background of a dialog box is black. This has to do with the HTML content to be displayed on the help dialog box having a transparent background style and white text. (It is undesirable to have a situation where white text is displayed on a white background.)

`CustomWindowTitle` is a `<style>` element that presents `android:shadowColor`, `android:shadowRadius`, `android:singleLine`, and `android:textAppearance` properties via `<item>` elements. The first three properties contain the same values as found in `android:Theme.Black`. The final property references `CustomTAWindowTitle`.

`CustomTAWindowTitle` is a `<style>` element that inherits style properties from its `android:TextAppearance.WindowTitle` parent style, and it presents an `<item>` element that overrides this style's `android:textSize` property to reduce the size of the text on the title bar to 10 scale-independent pixels.

If you're curious about this `<style>` element structure's origins, check out the contents of Android's `themes.xml` and `styles.xml` files via the following links:

- https://github.com/android/platform_frameworks_base/blob/master/core/res/res/values/themes.xml
- https://github.com/android/platform_frameworks_base/blob/master/core/res/res/values/styles.xml

After examining these files, you might be wondering why parent="android:WindowTitle" was not specified in the second <style> element, and therefore the android:shadowColor, android:shadowRadius, and android:singleLine properties were duplicated. The reason has to do with the Android API.

The android package contains a class named R with a nested style class. This class declares public constants for android:Theme.Black (android.R.style.Theme_Black) and android:TextAppearance.WindowTitle (android.R.style.TextAppearance_WindowTitle). However, there is no public constant for android:WindowTitle.

Exploring the Manifest

Univerter is described by the AndroidManifest.xml file shown in Listing D-13.

Listing D-13. *The Manifest File That Describes the* Univerter *App*

```
<?xml version="1.0" encoding="utf-8"?>
<manifest xmlns:android="http://schemas.android.com/apk/res/android"
          package="ca.tutortutor.univerter"
          android:versionCode="1"
          android:versionName="1.0">
  <uses-sdk android:minSdkVersion="10"/>
  <application android:label="@string/app_name"
               android:icon="@drawable/ic_launcher"
               android:theme="@style/CustomTheme">
    <activity android:name="Univerter"
              android:label="@string/app_name">
      <intent-filter>
        <action android:name="android.intent.action.MAIN"/>
        <category android:name="android.intent.category.LAUNCHER"/>
      </intent-filter>
    </activity>
  </application>
</manifest>
```

This file is similar to that shown in Chapter 1, but there are two main differences to note:

- A <uses-sdk android:minSdkVersion="10"/> element appears between the <manifest> and <application> tags. This element prevents Univerter from running on any Android version less than API Level 10 (Gingerbread 2.3.3).

- The `<application>` tag includes an `android:theme="@style/CustomTheme"` attribute. This attribute assigns the previously described `CustomTheme` to the app so that the title bar shows smaller text. (Because this app contains only a single activity, this attribute could have been assigned to the `<activity>` tag instead.)

Index

A

B

C

D

E

F

G

H

M

N

O

P

Q

R

T

V, W

X, Y, Z

CPSIA information can be obtained at www.ICGtesting.com
Printed in the USA
LVOW021525071212

310620LV00004B/5/P